1967

THE SATIRES OF HORACE

THE SATIRES OF HORACE

A STUDY BY

NIALL RUDD

Associate Professor of Classics at
University College, Toronto

CAMBRIDGE
AT THE UNIVERSITY PRESS
1966

PUBLISHED BY
THE SYNDICS OF THE CAMBRIDGE UNIVERSITY PRESS

Bentley House, 200 Euston Road, London, N.W. 1
American Branch: 32 East 57th Street, New York, N.Y. 10022
West African Office: P.M.B. 5181, Ibadan, Nigeria

©

CAMBRIDGE UNIVERSITY PRESS

1966

Printed in Great Britain at the University Printing House, Cambridge
(Brooke Crutchley, University Printer)

LIBRARY OF CONGRESS CATALOGUE
CARD NUMBER: 66-11031

To my wife Nancy

CONTENTS

PREFACE

In spite of their intrinsic quality and their immense influence on eighteenth-century literature, there has never been a full-length study of the *Satires* in English. Such neglect might seem to indicate a prejudice against Horatian satire, until one recalls that there was no comprehensive book on Ovid before 1945 or on Juvenal before 1954 or on Livy before 1961, and that there is still no such work on Propertius, Persius, Petronius, Lucan or Pliny. There are many reasons for this—not all of them discreditable. But to discuss them fully would be too complex a task and anyhow this would be no place to attempt it. Instead it will perhaps be enough to state the facts as above, bringing them to the attention of those who assume that Roman literature is 'worked out'.

The present book is intended mainly for university students and for teachers of Latin who are not Horatian specialists. But I hope it may also be of interest to non-Latinists and may help in some small way to bridge the alarming gap which has opened in the last fifty years between ancient and modern literary studies. As most people will probably wish to read the book without having to refer to a text, I have made fairly extensive use of translation and paraphrase. I have also tried to bring out the main lines of interpretation by consigning certain types of argument and comment to the notes. It is hoped that as a result it may be possible to read each chapter through without distraction and, in general, to use the book as a book instead of as a work of reference.

My thanks are due to the editors of the *Classical Quarterly*, *Hermathena*, *Phoenix* and the *University of Toronto Quarterly* for allowing me to reproduce in a revised form material which had previously appeared in those journals, and also to the Dial Press, New York, for permission to quote a stanza from a poem by Morris Bishop printed in *A Bowl of Bishop* (Dial Press Inc. 1954).

Grants from the President's Travel Fund enabled me to work in Oxford and Tübingen during two vacations, and a subvention from the Humanities Research Council of Canada helped to reduce the cost of printing. My colleagues in University College, Toronto—especially Professors Bagnani, Goold, Rist and Sumner—all gave help on points of detail. Mr R. G. M. Nisbet read certain chapters in draft form; Professor A. Dalzell read the whole work in typescript; and both scholars made perceptive criticisms. I would also thank those who, at different stages, read the book for the Cambridge University Press. Their vigilance has removed many errors. My chief debt, however, is to those who have worked on the *Satires* in the past. The commentaries of Palmer, Lejay and Heinze—'men whom one cannot hope to emulate'—have been on my desk for over ten years. I have often consulted the translations of Wickham and Fairclough; and one must not forget the small, but compact and independent edition of James Gow. Like so many scholars in other branches of classical philology I owe a great deal to the work of Professor Eduard Fraenkel. The chapters on the *Satires* in his *Horace* represent a major contribution to the subject, and where I have taken a different line I have done so with hesitation.

In writing a book of general interpretation it was necessary to touch on a number of matters about which I had little first-hand knowledge. What these matters are will be apparent soon enough, and I can only hope that the various experts will not be too grossly affronted. As the manuscript was finished at the end of 1964 I was unable to take account of anything which appeared after that date. Various other kinds of apology and justification come crowding in, but the moment has arrived when instead of prolonging his excuses the writer must finally grit his teeth and say *i, libelle!*

N.R.

University College, Toronto
January 1966

ABBREVIATIONS

AJP	*American Journal of Philology.*
Aristippus M.	*Aristippi et Cyrenaicorum Fragmenta,* ed. E. Mannebach (Leiden, 1961).
Cichorius	C. Cichorius, *Untersuchungen zu Lucilius* (Berlin, 1908).
CJ	*Classical Journal.*
CP	*Classical Philology.*
CQ	*Classical Quarterly.*
CR	*Classical Review.*
CW	*Classical World.*
Democritus D.	Diels' numeration of Democritus' fragments as found in Kathleen Freeman, *Ancilla to the Pre-Socratic Philosophers* (Oxford, 1956).
D.L.	Diogenes Laertius.
Edmonds	J. M. Edmonds, *The Fragments of Attic Comedy* (Leiden, 1961).
Fiske	G. C. Fiske, *Lucilius and Horace* (Madison, 1920).
Fraenkel	Eduard Fraenkel, *Horace* (Oxford, 1957).
JRS	*Journal of Roman Studies.*
Lucilius W.	*Remains of Old Latin,* III, Lucilius, edited and translated by E. H. Warmington (Loeb Classical Library, 1957).
Menander K.	Kock's numeration of Menander's fragments as found in the Loeb translation of Menander by F. G. Allinson.
Mnem.	*Mnemosyne.*
Phil.	*Philologus.*
P–W	Pauly–Wissowa–Kroll, *Real-Encyclopädie der Classischen Altertumswissenschaft.*
Rh. Mus.	*Rheinisches Museum.*
TAPA	*Transactions of the American Philological Association.*
Teles	*Teletis Reliquiae,* ed. O. Hense (Tübingen, 1909).
Varro B.	*Varronis Menippearum Reliquiae,* ed. Bücheler–Heraeus, reprinted with F. Bücheler's edition of Petronius (Berlin, 1958).
Wien. Stud.	*Wiener Studien.*

Note

The notes are to be found on pp. 274–307.

CHAPTER I

THE DIATRIBES OF BOOK 1

I.I, I.2, I.3

In the mid-twentieth century sermons are out of fashion. We submit with varying degrees of apathy to being told what to eat, how to dress, and where to spend our holidays, but if anyone presumes to lecture us on our moral character we regard it as the height of impertinence. This might seem to tell against any effort to revive interest in Horace's *Satires*, for although the collection contains several entertainment-pieces and some literary criticism its reputation must stand or fall by the diatribes, and the diatribes are essentially sermons.

They are sermons, however, of a rather special kind. They do not call for allegiance to any divine power or any sacred writings, nor do they urge us to repent and seek salvation. Their only appeal is to common sense. What is it, they ask, that makes man unhappy? Horace's age, like our own, was one of exceptional strain and anxiety. Under the threat of war men wore themselves out in competitive money-making, in romantic attachments which had no future, and in the endless struggle for power and prestige. Was all this striving really necessary? Why not, in our own phrase, withdraw from the rat-race and live quietly with one's friends? The suggestion was not meant, of course, to convert the Roman intelligentsia into a society of non-attached saints. Horace was no Gandhi. But he did see that a great many people who were, by his own standards, sufficiently well off never quite managed to enjoy what they had. And he made bold to point this out in poems which for good humour, lightness of touch, and absence of priggishness have never been surpassed.

The first three diatribes are broadly similar in structure. I shall begin with the third, because it is the most straightforward and also the most neglected. Here is a translation based mainly on the Oxford text:

Singers are all the same. When asked to perform for their friends they never will; when *not* asked they never stop. Tigellius, that typical Sardinian, had the same kink. If Caesar (who could have ordered a recital) had requested one on the strength of Tigellius' friendship with his father and himself, he would have wasted his time. Yet when he felt in the mood the fellow would keep breaking into 'Ho, ye Bacchanals!' throughout an entire meal, one moment singing in a high tenor and the next in a deep bass in tune with the lowest note of the 8 tetrachord.

The fellow was a bundle of inconsistencies; often he would dash along as if someone were after his blood, more often you would think he was carrying the sacred vessels of Juno. Sometimes he would keep a couple of hundred servants, sometimes only a dozen. One day he would talk in a high and mighty way about kings and princes he had known, the next he'd say 'I ask for nothing but a three-legged table, a shell of pure salt, and a cloak, no matter how coarse, to keep out the cold'. If you'd given a thousand pounds to that model of thrift and simplicity it would have burnt a hole in his pocket in less than a week. He never went to bed until dawn, and then spent the whole day snoring. He was 19 the most contradictory creature that ever lived.

Now someone may say to me 'What about yourself? Have *you* no faults?' Indeed I have, but they are different and perhaps less serious. Once when Maenius was pulling Novius to pieces behind his back, somebody said 'Just a minute. Are you blind to your own character, or do you think you can blind us?' 'Oh, where *I'm* concerned I just turn a blind eye', said Maenius. That kind 24 of egotism is stupid and brazen, and ought to be roundly condemned.

How is it that before you examine your own faults you smear your sore eyes with ointment, but when it comes to the failings of your friends your sight is as sharp as an eagle's or an Epidaurian snake's? The result is, however, that they in their turn also scrutinize *your* failings. So-and-so's a bit hot-tempered and not quite up to the fastidious standards of modern society; he may cause amusement by his countrified haircut, the sloppy fit of his toga, and by shoes a size too large which only just stay on his feet. Nevertheless, he's a good man— none better, *and* he's your friend, *and* there's a prodigious talent lurking behind that uncouth exterior. So just give yourself a thorough shaking in case the seeds of wickedness have already been planted in you, whether by nature her- self or through some bad habit. For if you once neglect a field, bracken appears 37 and eventually has to be burnt out.

Let's consider instead how a young man blindly in love fails to notice his sweetheart's unsightly blemishes, or is even charmed by them as Balbinus was by Hagna's wen. I only wish we made the same sort of mistake when judging our friends and that this delusion had an honourable name in the language of decent people. At any rate if a friend happens to have some defect we shouldn't view it with disgust, but should follow the example of a father with his son. If the boy has a squint his father calls him 'Boss-eye', if he is miserably undersized as the dwarfish Sisyphus used to be he is called 'Chick', if his knees knock together he is called 'Hen-toe', if he is so bandy that he can hardly stand then his father's pet name for him is 'Splay-foot'. So if one of our friends is rather close-fisted let's say he is thrifty; if another is inclined to be tactless and loud-mouthed, well, he wants his friends to think him sociable; or suppose he's rather ill-mannered, and outspoken to the point of rudeness, then let's call him forthright and fearless. Is he something of a hot-head? Then put him down as a keen type. In my view this habit both joins and cements friendships.   54

But in practice we turn the *good* qualities upside down, and we love to sling mud at a white fence. If one of our acquaintances is a decent, genuinely un-assuming fellow, we nickname him 'Slowcoach' or 'Fathead'. Another escapes every trap and never leaves himself open to malicious attack, for we are engaged in a life where envy is sharp and slander active. Instead of saying he's a wise fellow and no fool, we call him insincere and crafty. If a man has rather an open manner (and is the sort of fellow that I would often be glad to have you think me, Maecenas) so that he breaks in with some chatty remarks when his friend is perhaps reading or in silent thought, we say 'What a nuisance! He's got absolutely no *savoir faire*'.

How thoughtless of us to endorse a law which works against ourselves! For no one on earth is free from faults. The best is he who has to cope with the smallest. My kindly friend should, as is only fair, weigh my virtues against my failings, and if he wants my affection he should come down on the side of my virtues as being more numerous (provided of course they *are* more numerous!). On that principle he will be weighed in the same scales. If you expect your friend not to be put off by your boils, you will overlook his warts. It is fair that anyone who asks indulgence for *his* faults should grant the same in return.   75

Since, then, anger and the other failings which are ingrained in foolish mortals cannot be wholly cut out, why does Reason not use weights and measures of her own and suppress each type of offence with appropriate punish-ments? Suppose a servant who has been told to clear away a dish takes a lick at the half-eaten fish and the lukewarm sauce; if his master had him crucified, sane people would swear he was more insane than Labeo. How much madder and more serious a fault is this: a friend is guilty of some trivial offence which it would be churlish not to forgive, yet you hate him bitterly and avoid his company like some poor devil who owes Ruso money and just *has* to scrape up the interest or principal from somewhere before the grim first of the month or else put up his hands like a prisoner of war and listen to Ruso's histories with teeth on edge. What if a friend in a tipsy moment wets the couch or knocks off the table an old bowl worn down by the fingers of Evander? Or say he is

3   I-2

feeling hungry and snatches up a pullet which has been served in my side of the dish, shall I like him any the less for that? What would I do if he stole something or betrayed a trust or broke his word of honour? Those who hold that all sins are much the same are in a quandary when faced with actual situations. Common sense and tradition say no, and so does Expediency herself who is 98 virtually the mother of what is right and fair.

When living things crawled forth from the earth, which was still young, they were inarticulate, brutish creatures. They fought over their acorns and lairs with nails and fists, then with clubs, and so on, step by step, with the weapons shaped by experience. Eventually they discovered verbs and nouns which enabled them to give meaning to their cries and feelings. From that point they began to give up war, to build towns, and to pass laws against theft, brigandage and adultery. For Helen was not the first bitch to cause a war by her foul behaviour; but men in those days died in obscurity, making love hurriedly and promiscuously like animals and being done to death in the act by someone physically stronger, as in a herd one bull is destroyed by his rival. If you turn the pages of world history you will have to admit that justice arose from the fear of injustice. Nature cannot distinguish right from wrong as she distinguishes desirable from undesirable and the beneficial from its opposite. Nor will Reason ever prove that the man who breaks off a juicy cabbage in someone else's garden and the man who makes off at night with the holy emblems of the gods are committing one and the same offence. Let's have a scale to fix fair penalties for offences, otherwise you may flay with the terrible cat something which deserves no more than the strap. You might, of course, give a caning for some crime which deserved the lash, but that's not what I'm afraid of when you say larceny is on a par with armed robbery and threaten to use the same hook for pruning all crimes great and small if you were given the 124 crown.

But if the wise man alone is rich and handsome and a good cobbler and a king, why ask for something you already have? 'You don't understand', he says, 'what our father Chrysippus means. The wise man has never made himself shoes or sandals; nevertheless the wise man is a cobbler.' How's that? 'Well, even when he's silent Hermogenes is still a first-rate singer and musician; that clever fellow Alfenus even after throwing away all the tools of his trade and shutting up shop was still a cobbler; so too the wise man is the sole master of every craft, hence he is a king.'

Cheeky youngsters tug at your beard, and if you don't keep them at bay with your stick they swarm round and hem you in, while you, poor devil, roar till you burst your lungs—O highest of Royal Highnesses! In short, as you tread your kingly way to a sixpenny bath, with no one in attendance except that ass Crispinus, my friends will be kind enough to forgive me if I, a mere fool, do something wrong; I in turn will gladly forget their lapses, and (though only a commoner) I shall live a happier life than Your Majesty.

4

On studying the poem we find that the argument is presented in the following sequence:

Opening passage (*1–19*). The perversity of singers in general is illustrated by the case of Tigellius, but it soon becomes clear that Tigellius' vocal habits were but one example of his unbalanced behaviour—*nil aequale homini fuit illi* (9). Other examples follow, which are then rounded off by *nil fuit umquam | sic impar sibi* (18–19). Three cases (his spasmodic singing, his unpredictable gait, and the varying number of his slaves) have to do with inconsistent behaviour. The fourth is rather different: one day he would brag about kings and princes, the next affirm his devotion to the simple life. This points to inconsistent talk. We then hear that these professions of frugality were completely bogus—'If you'd given a thousand pounds to that model of thrift and simplicity it would have burnt a hole in his pocket in less than a week.' So here the inconsistency is between words and deeds. Finally, in staying up until dawn and then spending the day snoring Tigellius was not so much inconsistent as abnormal. This method of establishing and then varying a pattern is typically Horatian.

Transitional passage (*19–24*). A listener now intervenes, saying 'What about you? Have you no faults?' 'Why yes,' says Horace, 'but they are different and perhaps less serious.' A man like Maenius who backbites his friends is often blind or indifferent to his own defects. Such complacency is reprehensible: *stultus et improbus hic amor est dignusque notari*. This leads us into the first main section of the poem, which is a plea for tolerance amongst friends.

But if that is Horace's real concern, what is the function of the opening passage? We can see that the epigram on singers and the comic description of Tigellius are meant to provide an arresting introduction which, by leading casually to the main topic, will prevent the treatment from appearing too formal and precise. The poem, after all, is a conversation-piece, not a dissertation. We still wonder, however, whether there is any connexion of theme. Fraenkel says there is none.[1] Others believe that by his own

5

ridicule of Tigellius Horace has given a specimen of the behaviour which he is about to attack. This idea contains a germ of truth, in that both passages have to do with personal criticism. But Horace does not really fall under his own censure. Tigellius was now dead, and there is no suggestion that Horace was ever his friend. Also, unlike the scoffers mentioned in the main section, the poet was well aware of his own shortcomings. I believe, however, that the two parts are connected, and I hope the nature of the connexion will become clear in what follows.

First main section (25–75). If you are harsh in judging your friends, they will be harsh towards you. If a man is a little too hot-tempered (*iracundior*) or if he is a bit slovenly in appearance (*rusticius*) we should remember that he has other, admirable, qualities and that we ourselves are not perfect. Lovers are blind to each other's blemishes. 'I wish we made the same sort of mistake when judging our friends and that this delusion had an honourable name in the language of decent people' (38–42). Fathers give charitable names to their children's physical defects. (Notice how the idea of naming acts as a link between the two thoughts.) The same kindliness should be extended to our friends. If, for instance, a man is inclined to be boorish and too outspoken (*truculentior atque / plus aequo liber*), we should regard him as open and forthright. But in fact we do the very opposite (55). If a man is a bit too open in his manner (*simplicior*) we say 'He has absolutely no *savoir faire*'. Then, reverting to the idea with which the section opened, Horace observes how quick we are to pass an unfair law (*legem iniquam*) against ourselves. For no one is faultless. A kindly friend will, as is only fair (*aequum*), weigh one's virtues against one's shortcomings. In such matters it is fair (*aequum*) to give and take.

The comparatives, some of which are quoted above, indicate the sort of excess that constitutes a moral fault. In the case of a friend, however, we should minimize such faults by interpreting them in the kindliest possible way. This indulgence is not strict justice, but it is humane (*aequum*). Yet in another sense the *aequitas* required is quite objective and forbids any feelings of moral superiority; for we are also told to weigh the man's virtues against his faults. (Since the man is our friend it is assumed that the good will preponderate.) And finally we are to weigh his faults against our own. The first main section, therefore, is about *aequitas* or fairness. It will now be recalled that the opening passage dealt with the related concept of *aequabilitas* or consistency. Here the connexion lies in the fact that men like Maenius (21–3) and the person described in vv. 25–7—men who pounce on other people's faults while ignoring their own—are not only inconsistent but also unfair.

Second main section (76–118). *Denique* ('moreover') points forward, but instead of a sharp break we get a recapitulation. The progress of thought has been 'Everyone has his faults, so let us be fair in our judgements'. Moving from friendship to society as a whole, Horace now says 'Everyone is prone to do wrong, so let us be fair in our punishments'. He has been talking of *vitia* (68 and 70); therefore instead of saying *ira* he says *vitium irae* (76). He has just mentioned boils and warts (73–4); with these still half in mind he says 'Since the vice of anger cannot be wholly *cut out*'. He has spoken of weighing virtues against defects (70–2), so he now calls on Reason to use her own *weights and measures* (78) in determining punishments. The new element, namely crime and punishment, is left to the very end of the sentence, and thus the transition is accomplished. There follow in vv. 80–95 various examples of cruel retribution, which correspond to the examples of harsh judgement in the previous section. Then, at v. 96, the target comes into full view. It is the orthodox Stoic, who believes that all sins are equal (*paria esse...peccata*). As Horace has already indicated, such a belief is simply inapplicable to the realities of social life. He now goes on to show that it is also mistaken in principle, for it affronts Self-Interest or Expediency (*Utilitas*), which is 'virtually the mother of justice and fairness' (98).

The word *Utilitas*, especially when combined with *sensus* and *mores*, has strong Epicurean associations which prepare us for the

7

account of man's social evolution. A similar function is performed by the phrase *iusti prope mater et aequi*. Though apparently no more than a flourish to round off the paragraph, it introduces the idea of maternity, which is taken up by the image of mother earth in v. 99. More important, it points to the birth of laws. Like other features of civilization, laws are the product of need. They were worked out by man for his own protection, and since they are in essence social agreements rather than scientific discoveries they do not allow categorical judgements. Nature, as Horace says, cannot distinguish just from unjust (*iusto secernere iniquum*) as she distinguishes the beneficial from its opposite. That is, nature tells us it is wrong to eat deadly nightshade, but she says nothing about stealing a cabbage. This brings us back to the Stoics and their attempt to turn moral judgements into mathematical equations. For them stealing a cabbage would be no less serious than robbing a temple. *Peccet* (115) looks back to *peccata* (96), and the cases of theft in vv. 116–17 recall the theft in v. 94. The section is then summed up in the plea *adsit / regula, peccatis quae poenas irroget aequas* (117–18)—'Let us have a scale to fix fair penalties for offences'.There is nothing less equitable than the equality of sins.

Transitional passage (119–24). This opens, as often, with a subordinate clause tacked on to the end of the previous section—'lest you flay with the terrible cat something which calls for the strap'. This is taken up in v. 120: 'As for the chance of your giving too *light* a punishment, that's not what I'm afraid of when I hear you assert that larceny is on a par with armed robbery (*pares res*) and that you would use the same hook (*falce simili*) to prune all crimes great and small, if you were given charge of the kingdom.' Up to the last conditional clause we are still in touch with the equality of sins. But the mention of kingship leads into the final section, which is concerned with another Stoic tenet, namely that the true sage is a king. The whole sequence might be condensed as follows: Stoic social theory is impossible, since it flouts expediency, and social relations *function* by expediency; so do political relations, hence Stoic political theory is also impossible.

8

Final section (*124–42*). By calling the sage a king the Stoics meant that in virtue of his control over passion, his indifference to circumstances, and his willing acceptance of divine fate, he was superior to other men and hence was the only person fitted for kingship.[2] Horace understood this reasoning perfectly well, but the pretentiousness of the whole attitude annoyed him, and so he first reduces it to absurdity by making his Stoic adversary compare the potential king to a silent singer and a one-time cobbler; then he presents the sage as he really is—an object of derision.

So ends the most humane of all the diatribes. The picture of the royal sage forms a companion piece to the opening picture of Tigellius. At the same time it recalls the theme of forbearance by showing how the Stoic's harsh perfectionism has cut him off from the friendship of ordinary men. To the Stoic such ordinary men are fools (cf. the ironical *stultis* in v. 77 and *stultus* in v. 140); but to Horace the really foolish (*stultus* v. 24) are those who are so devoid of self-awareness that they condemn others while congratulating themselves.

The second satire begins with a brief obituary of Tigellius, observing how sadly his extravagance will be missed by all his raffish friends. Fufidius, however, is so afraid of extravagance that he never spends money; he only lends it—at ruinous interest. These and other unbalanced characters illustrate the text *nil medium est* (28)—'there is no middle course'. This theme continues for another eight lines, but from v. 28 all the examples of imbalance have been sexual. One man persists in adultery with society ladies, another confines his attention to the stews. After v. 36 the rest of the poem (four-fifths of the whole) is concerned with the folly of adultery and is therefore omitted from our English editions.

The game, it seems, is not worth the candle. One poor fellow when trapped throws himself off a roof, another is flogged, another raped by the husband's kitchen-boys, and another castrated (37–46). It is much wiser to choose freedwomen, for they represent a happy medium between married ladies and the lowest type of whore. But even here common sense is required; some fools have become so infatuated with these freedwomen that they've thrown away their money and reputation. Reverting to the hazards of adultery, Horace proceeds to give some sound tap-room advice: look here, the thing's simply an urge which has to be satisfied; why insist on social status? Anyhow, these high-class women are greatly over-rated; often you don't know what you're getting with those long dresses. And just think of the crowd they always have hanging round them. Now take my type of girl—she's lively and pretty, and everything's in the open without any nonsense. To go chasing after the other sort is sheer idiocy (47–110). Then (moving into the lounge): why not ascertain your minimum needs and distinguish what matters from what doesn't? When your throat's parched do you insist on a silver tankard? It's the same with women; that's why I go for the sort that's easy to get.

The closing lines recall some of the livelier scenes from *Tom Jones*:

When she slips her left side under my right she is Lady Ilia and the Countess Egeria—I call her what name I like. And when I'm hard at it I'm not afraid that her husband will come rushing back from the country, the hall door crash open, the dog bark, and the whole house reverberate with a terrible din; that the woman, deathly white, will jump out of bed, her maid (who is in the secret) will shriek and yell, and we'll all be in an agony of fear—the maid for her legs, the guilty mistress for her dowry, and I for myself. I have to flee barefoot with my clothes in disarray, otherwise it's all up with my cash or my backside or at least my good name. It's a grim business to be caught—I could prove that in court even before Fabius.[3]

The bawdy theme and treatment, the plentiful and aggressive use of names, and the absence of any reference to Maecenas all point to an early date. So does the rather uncertain structure. Up to v. 36, as we saw, the theme is *nil medium est*. The rest of the poem deals with the disadvantages of adultery compared with casual affairs. Now this would be quite consistent if Horace had kept a firm Aristotelian framework, rejecting the extremes of high and low society and recommending relations with an intermediate class. It would also be clear, though less consistent, if he had abandoned the idea of the mean and developed a simple two-term argument on the advantages of the 'call-girl' over married ladies. Unfortunately he appears to do now one, now the other, and the result is confusing.

A hint of the difficulty already occurs in vv. 31–6. Seeing a young man emerging from a brothel Cato congratulates him for sparing other men's wives. Cupiennius the adulterer comments 'I shouldn't care for such praise'. Probably Horace meant to censure both Cato and Cupiennius; for the foulness of *olenti in fornice* (30) carries over into *fornice* (31), and the lofty phrase *sententia dia Catonis* (32) is clearly ironical.[4] Nevertheless, the weight of Horace's attack falls so heavily on the adulterer that the brothel, which is represented as an *escape* from adultery, seems to be half condoned.

After expounding the tribulations of adulterers (37–46) Horace now recommends freedwomen as a happy medium between society wives and the lowest prostitutes. But he immediately adds that even this type of woman can ruin you if you fail to keep your head; there is no use in pleading that you've avoided adultery; your money and reputation are gone; what difference whether the cause is a *matrona* or an *ancilla togata* (63)? The position of the freedwoman as a desirable mean is therefore obscured, and Fraenkel goes so far as to say that 'dealings with an *ancilla togata* seem to be just as harmful as those with a *matrona*'.[5] Yet that is not quite the case, for it seems that a *matrona* invariably involves risk, whereas the other does not.

In vv. 64–79 Horace reverts to the hazards of adultery, and by now one may be wondering why he has let the other extreme (that is, the foul brothel) drop out of sight. Possibly it was because the only 'disadvantage' of the lowest whore as compared with the freedwoman was aesthetic, and this did not seem worth elaborating in a discussion whose primary aim was to distinguish amours which involved fear, trouble, deception and expense from those which did not. At any rate after v. 63 the *togata* no longer appears as an intermediate figure. When she returns in vv. 82 ff. she is treated as the simple antithesis of the *matrona*, and thus she comes to stand in a general way for cheap, available satisfaction 'with no strings attached'. The irrelevance of her intermediate position as a freedwoman is further underlined by the fact that in v. 117 her place is momentarily taken by two household servants, a girl and a boy.

While the structural uncertainties of 1. 2 are plain enough, there is much disagreement over 1. 1.[6] The extent of its unity may perhaps be seen if we set out the argument as follows. Men are discontented with their lot and envy those in other occupations. Why? *Answer*: because they want a change. But that can't *really* be the reason, for if offered a change they would not take it (1–22). If they don't like what they're doing, then why not give up? *Answer*: they want to save enough for a secure retirement. But that can't *really* be the reason, for even when they've saved enough they still go on making more (23–40). By now discontent is seen to proceed in some way from greed. Why, then, should a man be perpetually hoarding wealth? *Answer A*: because once you start to spend, the whole lot disappears. But use is money's only *raison d'être*. *Answer B*: it's *nice* to have a big pile. But enough is all you need. *Answer C*: money brings prestige. But this kind of prestige is purchased at the price of happiness. *Answer D*: money ensures attention when you're ill. In fact it does nothing of the kind. Such attention springs from love (41–91). After some further argument the opening topic is re-introduced in a modified form (108–9) and then developed in the next few lines. As a result of such envious greed, says Horace, few people can say they've had a happy life.

This summary, however, makes the poem appear more systematic than it is. Like 1. 3, it opens with an arresting generalization:

> qui fit, Maecenas, ut nemo, quam sibi sortem
> seu ratio dederit seu fors obiecerit, illa
> contentus vivat, laudet diversa sequentis?

How is it, Maecenas, that no one is content with his own way of life
—whether he has chosen it deliberately or taken it up by chance—
but envies those in other occupations?

Two pairs of examples follow: the soldier envies the merchant,
and the merchant envies the soldier; the lawyer envies the farmer,
but now the pattern varies, for the farmer envies not the lawyer
in particular but those who live in the city (12). Yet a connexion
with law is retained by bringing the farmer up to town for a
court case (*datis vadibus*). These types all grumble about their
jobs, and such grumbling, as we know, is often unrealistic. The
lawyer, for example, who complains about early clients, seems to
think that if he had been a farmer he could have lain in bed.
This lack of real seriousness is exposed by Horace, who points
out that if a god offered the grumblers a change of job they would
refuse. The chief point to note, however, is that this restless discontent, which the Greeks called μεμψιμοιρία, is here based on a
desire for easier work, not more money. When the types reappear
in vv. 28 ff., however, their yearning is said to be inspired by greed
(φιλαργυρία), a vice which occupies the central section of the
poem. We also note that the lawyer has been replaced by a crooked
innkeeper, presumably because the latter was thought to be a more
suitable example of avarice. The satire, therefore, is presented in
such a way as to suggest that the fundamental role of φιλαργυρία
only occurred to Horace in the course of writing. That is part of
the poem's informal aspect.

We are faced with a rather similar situation at the end:

> illuc unde abii redeo: nemon, ut avarus,   108
> se probet ac potius laudet diversa sequentis?
> quodque aliena capella gerat distentius uber
> tabescat? neque se maiori pauperiorum
> turbae comparet? hunc atque hunc superare laboret?[7]

I return to my starting-point: is no one, because of his greed, to be
content with his own situation, and is every man to envy, instead,
those pursuing other ways of life? Because his neighbour's goat

13

carries a more bulging udder is he to be consumed with jealousy, instead of comparing himself with the thousands who are worse off? Is he to struggle to surpass first this man, then the other?

Horace clearly intends to conclude the poem by relating his main theme of φιλαργυρία to his opening remarks on μεμψιμοιρία. We can see that most of v. 108 and all of v. 109 refer back to the start, while the central theme is recalled by *ut avarus* (108) and by vv. 110–12, in so far as they describe greed. In combining the two subjects Horace alleges, as he has already done in vv. 28 ff., that the discontent of the grumblers is ultimately based on greed, and that they envy people in other occupations because the latter make more money. Secondly, he now suggests that the greedy man is eager to surpass all competitors. This is something of a new development, because, except for a strong hint in v. 40, such hostile emulation has played no part in the picture of the *avarus*. As a result of these modifications μεμψιμοιρία and φιλαργυρία both converge towards the larger concept of πλεονεξία. This vice had two complementary aims—more money for oneself and more money than other people.[8] And so within this idea, for which there is no Latin word, *avaritia* and *invidia* are as inseparable as concave and convex.

Structurally, then, these poems are alike in having an opening theme of about twenty verses introduced by some striking hyperbole or comic effect, and then illustrated in a series of antithetical pairs. A second, related theme then emerges and receives a much more extended treatment, though here too Horace avoids the appearance of a systematic arrangement by gliding casually from one topic to another.[9] In two cases there is a short final section recalling earlier motifs, and in all three the end is enlivened by a gibe at the expense of a living person. This subtle control can hardly be ascribed to Lucilius or to any other satirist before Horace. It is a personal achievement of a very high order, and it is one of the factors which caused Roman *satura*, in spite of its modest pretensions, to be reckoned as a serious poetic form.

Certain features of this poetry are already clear. First of all, it

14

is concerned entirely with the behaviour of the individual in society. Institutions, whether political, religious or professional, are ignored, and when reference is made to a group of friends or relatives what matters is not the group as such but the private relations of its members. Moreover, this concern with the individual is largely a moral concern. Eccentricities of fashion, social *faux-pas*, odd habits of speech and dress, failures of taste, all the vanities and blunders which so enrich the eighteenth-century scene—these have but a small place in the Horatian diatribe. Instead the reader is laughed and argued out of his subjection to money (1. 1), sex (1. 2), and power (1. 6)—the three most magnetic forces in his life and the most dangerous to his peace of mind. The rejection of malice and cruelty in social relations (1. 3) is scarcely less fundamental. These wide issues are handled in a suitably general way. The figures who come under attack (one cannot call them characters in the full sense) are etched with a few quick strokes—just enough to provide a neat illustration; then they vanish in the wake of the argument. One does not, of course, look for rounded characters in satire, but two-dimensional figures (like MacFlecknoe, for example) can be presented in such detail as to dominate a satiric poem. This never happens in Horace. Even Tigellius, the most elaborate of his cartoons, is confined to a couple of introductory passages and has no part in the major themes.

The modern reader, who expects to have his moral judgements evoked by more devious means, may find this straightforward preaching rather naïve. Without assuming that such a response is entirely to our credit, we *can* maintain that Horace often argues his case at a very superficial level. If, for instance, a man has taken a job because it happened to be available (1. 1. 2), must he resign himself to it for the rest of his life? It may not suit his talents; it may cut him off from his friends; it may not pay even a decent minimum wage. Such criticisms, however, are really beside the point. Horace is not writing a philosophical disquisition. His argument is not intended to be comprehensive and unassailable.

It is quite enough if what he says is *often* true; and one does not need great insight to recognize that now, as in his day, a great deal of discontent *is* painful and unnecessary. As for Horace's phrasing, he does admittedly start off with a sweeping generalization, but anyone who holds that categorical *nemo* against him should give up reading satire altogether.

Finally, in its attitude to social conformity, the Horatian diatribe stands in contrast to two modern types of popular satire. One type, represented by magazines like *Punch* and the *New Yorker*, laughs at familiar forms of bourgeois behaviour. But the humour is usually so bland that it nourishes what it pretends to attack (like firing a water-pistol at a vegetable marrow). The victims, if they recognize themselves at all, are not in the least offended. They may be secretly grateful to the satirist for giving them some kind of identity in a featureless world. The other type, though purveyed in recent years on the professional stage, is essentially undergraduate in spirit. Its trademark is an exuberant mockery of everyone who forms or perpetuates an influential pattern; it is not concerned to establish any positive position of its own. This anarchic laughter can, of course, be highly entertaining, but we have to remember that it is only feasible in certain historical conditions. At other periods, like the eighteenth century and the end of the Roman Republic, satire will be seen as a social corrective. Its targets will be those who *deviate* from an acceptable norm, and it will use its traditional weapons in defence of balance and restraint.

Horace's satire is of this conservative kind, and to understand why, we must consider the intellectual climate in which he was writing. As so often, we have to start by going back to Athens. One of the most impressive features of the Athenian *polis* was its extraordinary integration. Religion and drama, art and sport were all associated with public worship, and the young were educated for a life in which they might become admirals, financial officials, and cabinet ministers, all within a few years. Such an organization gave the citizen an unusual *esprit de corps*, and with it a very high degree of participation and control. After the *polis* lost its independence in the latter half of the fourth century the authority of the Olympians, who had formerly guaranteed its safety, began to fade, and other strands which had held the unit in dynamic tension gradually went slack. The change can be seen most clearly in the New Comedy of Menander, which for all its charm lacks the political courage, the exuberant imagination, and the sheer rude energy of Aristophanes. So too, the post-Aristotelian philosophies reflect a world in which man has somehow lost the initiative in his struggle with life. Stoicism, Epicureanism, and Cynicism all teach that happiness can only be achieved by rendering oneself immune to shock. This immunity demands a careful discipline of the passions and a constant awareness that wealth, power, and sensual delight have no bearing on true contentment.

How, it may be asked, did these withdrawn, inward-looking systems exert such an influence on the Roman mind? First of all there is the simple fact that in the period after 200 B.C., when Rome's conquests brought her into close touch with Greek culture, these were the systems she encountered. Moreover, some of the extreme positions which had been adopted by the founders were modified in the course of time. This happened quite early in the case of Cynicism. The respect which people paid Diogenes for his independence and singlemindedness had always been tinged with horror at his rude unsociability. Crates of Thebes, however (who lived till about 290 B.C.), was an altogether more civilized figure. He spent less time denouncing his fellow-citizens and more in giving practical help. We are told that he would visit people's houses, reconciling enemies and cheering those in misfortune. He also took the very un-Cynical step of getting married, though admittedly our sources give the impression that Hipparchia made all the running and that Crates only said yes for the sake of peace.[10] Cynicism was further modified by Bion, the son of a fishmonger from the Black Sea port of Borysthenes.[11] After an unsuccessful attempt at tax evasion the father, with his whole family, was sold into slavery. Bion was lucky enough to be bought by a rhetorician who gave him an education and eventually left him enough money to move to Athens. Arriving there about 315 B.C. he seems to have spent some time in the Academy. Later he studied under Theodorus (an atheistic hedonist) and finally under Theophrastus the Peripatetic. Whereas Diogenes had practised an austere and often ill-tempered asceticism, Bion (influenced, no doubt, by Theodorus and Aristippus) said a man should enjoy any pleasure that came his way but should preserve a certain detachment so as to be ready for a change of fortune. Bion's other contribution lay in the field of homiletics (and here we can discern the influence of Theophrastus). Many of the techniques found in the Horatian diatribes, such as the fictitious adversary, character sketches, animal similes, allegorical personification, and verbal wit, had already been employed by Bion, and it is no wonder that in *Epist.* 2. 2. 60 Horace should have referred to his own poems as *Bionei sermones.*

Greek culture flowed into Rome through many channels. Officers who had campaigned in Greece brought back works of art to their Italian villas and then sent their sons to study in Athens. Greek poets and teachers (many of them prisoners of war) were employed as tutors in the houses of the Roman aristocracy. The most important focus of Hellenism was the circle of Scipio Aemilianus, in which men like Polybius and Panaetius were invited to expound their ideas.[12] Nor was the influence all in one direction. Polybius' Roman history was a monument to the new Mediterranean power; and if we consider the teaching of Panaetius, who rejected orthodox beliefs in survival, divination, and world cycles, and who concentrated less on theoretical perfection than on man's practical duties in society, we can see how the Stoic system became adapted to the pragmatic Roman mind.[13] Fifty years later the same kind of process was taking place in the Academy. Philo of Larissa, who came to Rome in 88 B.C., became dissatisfied with the rigid scepticism of Carneades regarding the possibility of knowledge, and this desire for surer foundations was reflected in the thought of his onetime pupil,

Antiochus of Ascalon.[14] Asserting that truth must be attainable, Antiochus developed a loose eclectic philosophy with a strong Stoic colouring, and these unsystematic ideas were disseminated in Rome by Cicero, who had studied under Antiochus in Athens. Even Epicureanism, the most conservative of all the schools, showed signs of development in the last century B.C. Arguments from sources later than Epicurus were used against post-Epicurean opponents, as when Velleius and Lucretius borrowed arguments from the New Academy to attack the Stoic belief in a benevolent Providence.[15] Moreover, instead of remaining a quasi-esoteric system, Epicureanism was now made known in popular writings like the *De Rerum Natura* of Lucretius and, more especially, the tracts of Philodemus. The latter, who may have been personally known to Horace, also wrote a work of literary theory in which he rejected the rhetoricians' distinction between style and content, and asserted that 'the moral effect of poetry, if it had one, was not an essential outcome of its aesthetic nature'.[16] Philodemus showed further evidence of his heretical interest in culture by shaping sophisticated epigrams, some of which are preserved in the *Greek Anthology*. Finally, in the last years of Caesar's dictatorship many Epicureans (Cassius among them) became so indignant at his acceptance of divine honours and at the general suppression of free speech that they felt justified in supporting violent political action.[17]

These few remarks will be enough to indicate that by the time when Horace was writing his *Satires*, i.e. from about 39 B.C. on, the distinctions between the main philosophical schools had become blurred at a number of points. There was also disagreement within particular schools—Posidonius, for example, reimported into Stoicism much of the nonsense which Panaetius had discarded. Such an atmosphere of freedom suited Horace well, for he was the least doctrinaire of men. This does not mean that his philosophical equipment was a mere rag-bag of multi-coloured scraps, but it does mean that he would never commit himself to any orthodoxy, whether Cynic or Academic, Epicurean or Stoic. The famous

19

phrase in *Epist.* I. I. 14 *nullius addictus iurare in verba magistri*
—a phrase from which the Royal Society takes its motto—was
valid for the whole of his career. So within the *Satires* themselves
there is no hope of tracing any development in the poet's philosophy. The final quip of I. I shows that this poem, like 2. 3,
contained much that would have been acceptable to the Stoics;
I. 2 has a Cynic flavour—so has 2. 5; Epicureans would have
endorsed most of I. 3, and the same is true of 2. 6. But it is time to
look more closely at the detail.

We shall start with passages illustrating the kind of material
which lay behind the opening of the first satire. Maximus of
Tyre, a sophist of the second century A.D., speaks about discontent as follows (I give a short paraphrase of the text, which can
be consulted in Heinze's note on *Sat.* I. I. 16): 'You could see
the farmer envying the townsman, and public figures complaining of their own situation and envying the peasant. You could
hear the civilian expressing his envy of the soldier and vice versa.
And if a god, as in a play, made each actor exchange roles with
his fellow, the very same people would yearn for their former
ways of life. So hard a creature to please is man.'[18] Differences of
scope and detail make it unlikely that Maximus copied Horace,
and it is generally agreed that both writers were drawing on a
common fund of Hellenistic material. Another reflexion on
discontent, also later than Horace, is found in one of the pseudo-
Hippocratic letters: 'Men continually seek things which they
dislike. After refusing to sail, they put to sea; after refusing to
farm, they farm; they divorce their wives and then take others;
they hope for old age and then complain when it is upon them.
Leaders and kings envy private citizens, and vice versa. Statesmen
and artisans envy one another.'[19] A third passage, which goes
back at least as far as the first century B.C., occurs in the pseudo-
Platonic *Axiochus*:'Is there anyone who, after choosing an occupation, does not find fault with it and complain about present
circumstances?'[20] Various illustrations then follow. Similar sentiments are found in Varro and Cicero,[21] and also in Lucretius:

nunc plerumque videmus
quid sibi quisque velit nescire et quaerere semper
commutare locum quasi onus deponere possit

. . . . . .

sed dum abest quod avemus, id exsuperare videtur
cetera; post aliud, cum contigit illud, avemus.[22]

As it is, we usually see people failing to realize what they want and
continually seeking a change of scene, as if that would relieve them of
their burden...But as long as we lack what we crave, that seems to
overshadow everything else; then, when we've got it, we crave for
something further.

Finally we have the remarks of Bion as preserved in Teles' essay
On Self-Sufficiency (περὶ αὐταρκείας): 'When old do not yearn
for youth...when poor do not seek riches.' Later Teles speaks of
one who 'as a little boy wants to be a youth, as a youth wants to
be a man, as a man is eager to reach old age...Then, when old,
he desires to be young once more...As a slave he wants to be free,
and when free he wants to be a slave.'[23] Discontent was therefore
one of the commonplaces of popular philosophy.

The same sources indicate that discontent was often closely
associated with greed. The pseudo-Hippocrates, after describing
various forms of discontent, says: 'And the cause of all these things
is φιλαργυρίη—love of money.'[24] Bion says the same: 'But we
are unable to remain satisfied with what we have, since we spend
a lot on luxuries.'[25] And he makes the same point more fully
later on, when he depicts the discontented man as insatiable.[26]
Finally, Maximus' sermon on discontent begins as follows: 'The
wholly adequate life is hard to find, as is the wholly adequate
man. Everyone feels within himself a certain lack in regard to
perfection, and one person strives to outdo (πλεονεκτεῖ) the
other whose deficiencies are fewer.'

Another reason for citing these passages is to stress the variety
of their provenance. For the tendency to label all such material
as Cynic can only be justified if the term is given an extremely
broad sense. Behind the words of Lucretius lies the thought

21

expressed by Epicurus in *Sent. Vat.* 35: 'We shouldn't spoil what we have by desiring what we lack; we should rather remember that what we have was also something desirable.' The speaker in the *Axiochus* is Socrates, and he attributes the ideas in question to Prodicus, the fifth-century sophist.[27] The words quoted from the pseudo-Hippocratic letter are there assigned to Democritus.[28] Horace himself reverts to the same theme in his first ode:

> luctantem Icariis fluctibus Africum
> mercator metuens otium et oppidi
> laudat rura sui; mox reficit ratis
> quassas, indocilis pauperiem pati.   (15–18)

The merchant in his dread of the African wind as it struggles with the waves of the Icarian sea longs for ease and the farms of his home town. In due course he repairs his battered craft, for he cannot learn to endure poverty.

This, in turn, recalls Euripides, *Philoctetes* (Frag. 793 Nauck):

> 'μακάριος ὅστις εὐτυχῶν οἴκοι μένει.'
> ἐν γῆ δ' ὁ φόρτος· καὶ πάλιν ναυτίλλεται.

(At sea the merchant says) 'Happy the man who in his prosperity remains at home.' But no sooner is his cargo ashore than he puts to sea again.[29]

As another example of Horace's easy eclecticism we shall take 1. 1. 92–107. In v. 92, towards the end of his lecture to the miser, Horace says *denique sit finis quaerendi*, 'so set a limit to your money-making'. Then in vv. 106–7 the idea of limit is brought in again to round off the section:

> est modus in rebus, sunt certi denique fines,
> quos ultra citraque nequit consistere rectum.

There is a certain proportion in everything. There are, in short, definite limits, and if you step outside them on this side or on that you cannot possibly be right.

Within this framework we hear the tale of Ummidius (the Roman counterpart of the Athenian miser in v. 64), who only attained a knowledge of the middle way when he was split down the centre by a freedwoman's axe. The opposite extreme is represented by two spendthrifts, and then the mean is affirmed once again in v. 105:

> est inter Tanain quiddam socerumque Viselli.

There is a state between Tanais and the father-in-law of Visellius.

Tanais, according to the scholiast, was a eunuch; the other extreme was typified by Visellius' father-in-law. The line has a gnomic sound and is supposed to have been adapted from the Greek proverb ἢ σπάδων ἢ κηλήτης, which is the equivalent of our more decorous 'feast or famine'.

Behind these seemingly frivolous lines, with their dialogue, anecdote, and vulgar humour, lie two sets of serious ideas. The first is the division of desires or pleasures into those which are both natural and necessary, those which are natural but unnecessary, and those which are neither natural nor necessary. This scheme was taken over from Plato[30] and Aristotle[31] by Epicurus, who sets it out in his *Letter to Menoeceus* 127 ff. It is also implied in other passages of Epicurus of which the most apposite is perhaps no. 21 of the Κύριαι Δόξαι:

The man who knows the limits of life realizes that what removes the pain due to want and renders the whole of life complete is easy to obtain; so there is no need for actions which involve competition.[32]

Within these natural limits Horace locates the happy medium—his second main idea. The fullest and most sophisticated treatment of the happy medium is found, of course, in Aristotle's *Nicomachean Ethics*,[33] but it goes back through Plato[34] to Pythagorean and Sicilian researches into music and medicine.[35] And even this is being over-precise, for the ideal of moderation was deeply embedded in the religion of early Greece. The precept 'Nothing too much' (μηδὲν ἄγαν) was inscribed above the portals of Apollo's temple at Delphi, where its primacy as a rule of moral wisdom was disputed only by 'Know thyself' and 'Give a guarantee at thy peril!'

23

In 1. 2. 111–13 the idea of nature's limit is applied to sexual gratification:

> nonne cupidinibus statuat natura modum quem,
> quid latura sibi, quid sit dolitura negatum,
> quaerere plus prodest et inane abscindere soldo?[36]

Is it not more useful to ask what limit nature sets to one's desires, what gain she will derive and what she will sorely miss if it is denied her, and so to mark off the solid from the void?

In his physics Epicurus postulated only two basic features, namely solid atoms and void; so in his ethics he used to speak of solid and empty desires. In *KD* 29, for instance, he states that desires which are neither natural nor necessary are due to κενὴ δόξα—'empty fancy'. Cicero, describing the system, says *inanium autem cupiditatum nec modus ullus nec finis inveniri potest* (*De Fin.* 1. 45)—'in the case of empty desires no limit or boundary can be discovered'. So Horace here contends that the desire for an affair with a Roman matron is *inane*—'empty'. Up to this point he has been working within a strictly Epicurean framework, but the questions which follow reflect a much more general outlook:

When your throat is parched with thirst do you insist on drinking from a silver tankard? When hungry do you wave away everything but peacock and turbot? When you are tense with passion and when a maid-servant or a slave-boy is at hand to gratify it, would you sooner be racked with desire? Not me. I like the sort of girl that's easy to get.

On the desirability of *Venus parabilis* there seems to have been some uncertainty in the teaching of Epicurus himself. In *Sent. Vat.* 51, which is written in answer to the queries of an over-ardent young man, Epicurus says:

Provided you don't break the laws or good customs and do not cause annoyance to any of your neighbours or do yourself physical harm or waste your money, you may indulge yourself as you please. But you are bound to encounter one of these obstacles, for sexual pleasure never did a man any good, and he is lucky if it doesn't do him harm.

On the other hand we have the doctrine reported by Diogenes Laertius (10. 118) that 'the wise man will not have intercourse with any woman with whom the law forbids it',[37] which implies that relations with *meretrices* were permissible. This is put more positively by Lucretius, who says that one way of avoiding the emotional disturbance of love is by having casual intercourse (*DRN* 4. 1065, 1071, 1073). And the same sentiment occurs in the epigram of Philodemus referred to by Horace in 1. 2. 120 ff. Casual liaisons of this kind were also advocated by the Cynics, as may be seen from a papyrus fragment of Cercidas which bears a notable resemblance to 1. 2. 125–7:

> ἁ δ' ἐξ ἀγορᾶς 'Αφροδίτα...
> οὐ φόβος οὐ ταραχά.
> ταύταν ὀβολῷ κατακλίνας
> Τυνδαρέοιο δόκει
> γαμβρός...[38]

As for Aphrodite of the market-place...there is no fear, no disturbance. Lay her for a shilling and fancy yourself son-in-law to Tyndareus. [That is, imagine she is Helen of Troy.]

The theme occurred in comedies by Philemon and Eubulus,[39] and it also played some part in one of Lucilius' satires.[40] It is sometimes suggested that in defending this widely held attitude Horace was asserting his opposition to the Stoics who maintained that fornication, though less injurious than adultery, was just as great a sin.[41] I should think, however, that if Horace had wished to draw our attention to the Stoics he would have mentioned them quite explicitly.

It is now time to show how Horace often gives an individual twist to the commonplaces of popular philosophy. In 1. 3 a large section is devoted to the misuse of complimentary and pejorative terms (38–66). The connexion between linguistic and moral behaviour was observed at least as early as the fifth century. Thucydides has a famous description of how in a period of civil strife ethical standards become perverted and words lose their proper meaning.[42] Plato (*Rep.* 560 DE) shows the same corrupting process at work within the soul of a democratic man. And

Aristotle, in a rather different vein, treats the misuse of terms as a conscious rhetorical technique (*Rhet.* 1367 A, 28 ff.). It is Lucretius, however, who provides the most illuminating parallel with Horace. In *DRN* 4. 1160 ff. he describes the lover's blindness as follows:

> nigra melichrus est, immunda et fetida acosmos,
> caesia Palladium, nervosa et lignea dorcas,
> parvula, pumilio, chariton mia, tota merum sal,
> magna atque immanis cataplexis plenaque honoris.

The black-skinned is *café au lait*, the dirty and stale is *savamment désordonnée*, the cat-eyed is the image of Athena, the wiry and desiccated is *une gazelle*, the puny mite is *une des trois Graces*—just the cutest thing—the large and ungainly is *une merveille* and every inch a lady.

In Horace (44–8) we have:

>   strabonem
> appellat paetum pater, et pullum, male parvus
> si cui filius est, ut abortivus fuit olim
> Sisyphus; hunc varum distortis cruribus, illum
> balbutit scaurum pravis fultum male talis.

If the boy has a squint the father calls him 'Boss-eye'; if he is miserably undersized as the dwarfish Sisyphus used to be, he is called 'Chick'; if his knees knock together he is called 'Hen-toe'; if he is so bandy that he can hardly stand, his father's pet name for him is 'Splay-foot'.

The first thing we notice is that, in the interests of pure Latinity, Horace has got rid of the Greek, which was the language of love.[43] In substituting parents for lovers he comes closer to his theme of friendship, and at the same time achieves a totally new effect, which cannot be translated; for all those names—Paetus, Pullus, Varus, and Scaurus—belonged to aristocratic families and were borne by some of the poet's most distinguished contemporaries. Finally, whereas Lucretius says 'Lovers are deluded, and what fools they are!', Horace says 'Lovers and parents are deluded—yes, and it's a pity there aren't more like them!' Thus by a deft surprise the scorn of the great Epicurean evangelist is transformed into Horatian benevolence.[44]

The second and third satires (and to a lesser extent the first) open with passages on inconsistency. This again was a commonplace, and was recognized as such by Plato, who quotes the saying 'Bad men are never the same and never consistent' (*Lysis* 214 c). The proverb suited the philosopher's teaching, for an inconsistent man lacked that steady, rational control which unified the personality and fitted it for the good life. This ideal of steadiness, passing down through Aristotle[45] and the Stoics,[46] gave men a centre of gravity; it told them not to be unsettled by adversity or prosperity, to show themselves reliable in dealing with others, and to preserve a decent restraint in their social habits. Such principles were not, of course, adopted by the Roman aristocracy merely as an exotic import. They were already firmly rooted in the Italian tradition. The *imperium Romanum*, after all, was not the work of bohemians.

Perhaps the easiest way to see how Horace handles this idea is to compare his method with Cicero's. In *De Off.* 1. 130, which is based on Panaetius, Cicero says:

adhibenda praeterea munditia est non odiosa neque exquisita nimis, tantum quae fugiat agrestem et inhumanam neglegentiam. eadem ratio est habenda vestitus, in quo, sicut in plerisque rebus, mediocritas optima est.

> In the matter of personal appearance one ought not to put people off by being over-fastidious. It should be enough to avoid a boorish and uncivilized carelessness. The same principle applies to dress, where, as in most things, the middle course is best.

In *Sat.* 1. 2. 28 Horace shows his familiarity with the philosophical tradition of *mediocritas* by the sentence *nil medium est*, but instead of theorizing he gives a personal illustration taken from the streets of Rome:

Maltinus tunicis demissis ambulat; est qui
inguen ad obscenum subductis usque, facetus
pastillos Rufillus olet, Gargonius hircum.[47]

> Maltinus walks with his tunic trailing, another with his hoisted up to the point of indecency. The exquisite Rufillus smells of tablets, Gargonius stinks like a goat.

(Notice the liquids and gutturals in that last verse.) In *De Off.*
1. 131 Cicero has

cavendum autem est ne aut tarditatibus utamur in ingressu mol-
lioribus, ut pomparum ferculis similes esse videamur, aut in
festinationibus suscipiamus nimias celeritates.

> Care must be taken to avoid an unmanly slowness of walk which
> would make us look like figures carried in a procession; nor must
> we use excessive haste in hurrying.

In *Sat.* 1. 3. 9–11 Horace, specific as ever, attributes both these
habits to Tigellius, and by eliminating the long abstract nouns he
gains a lighter effect:
saepe velut qui
currebat fugiens hostem, persaepe velut qui
Iunonis sacra ferret.

> Often he would dash along as if someone were after his blood; more
> often he would move like an attendant bearing the sacred vessels of
> Juno.

But again the description is given a philosophical framework by
the comments *nil aequale homini fuit illi* (9) and *nil fuit umquam |
sic impar sibi* (18–19)—the man lacked *aequabilitas*; he had no
steadiness or consistency.

Horace shows the same individual flair in his handling of other,
less philosophical, material. In 1. 1. 23-6 he compares his method
of mixing serious and gay to the practice of giving children
cakes as a reward for learning their ABC. Most scholars quote
Lucretius 1. 936, where the poet compares himself to a doctor
who smears the rim of a medicine-cup with honey. One or two
go on to point out that the medical analogy is also attributed to
Diogenes by Antonius Melissa.[48] And with all this *Wissenschaft*
it is easy to overlook the fact that Horace's simile is without
parallel.

Or suppose we take the comparison of busy men to ants. In
vv. 28 ff. Horace says:

That fellow who turns the heavy soil with his hard plough, this crooked barman, the soldier and the sailors who dash so bravely across the seven seas, claim

that their only purpose in enduring this toil is to enjoy a secure retirement in old age, when they have made their pile; just as the tiny ant (for he is their model) with immense toil hauls along in his mouth whatever he can and adds it to the heap he is building, thus making conscious and careful provision for the future.

The ant is an ambiguous creature. It may represent mere acquisitiveness, as in Crates, Aeschrion, and Theocritus.[49] But here Horace gives a kinder picture—one suggestive of thrift rather than greed. As a result he seems to accept the busy men's account of their motives, and we tend to forget the irony that plays over those early lines with their heavy toil, crooked barman and so on. In this unsuspecting mood we move on to v. 36:

[The ant] who (quae), as soon as the year wheels round into dismal Aquarius, never sets foot outside and very sensibly makes use of what he has laid in,

Then suddenly the trap closes:

whereas in your case neither scorching heat nor the cold of winter can interrupt your money-grubbing. Hail, rain, or snow—nothing can stop you; no one must ever be richer than you!

So the innocent quae in v. 36 has actually the force of at ea. It represents the very thin end of the wedge which Horace is about to drive between the ant and the greedy man. This, like the mock-epic description of winter in the same line, is a characteristically Horatian touch. It is not to be found in Lucilius, though he probably used the same simile (W. 586–7).

The image of life as a stage is, again, entirely conventional.[50] Even the special form employed by Horace in I. I. 15–22 (i.e. a deus ex machina who offers a change of roles) had numerous antecedents—in Plato, Herodotus, Heraclitus, and ultimately in the world of fairy tales.[51] Yet we shall appreciate what Horace has done if we recall the bare outline of the idea as sketched by Cicero (De Sen. 83), si quis deus mihi largiatur ut ex hac aetate repuerascam et in cunis vagiam, valde recusem—'if at this time of life a god gave me the opportunity of becoming a child again and screaming in my cradle, I should certainly refuse'. So too, Crato in Menander's Θεοφορουμένη or The Woman Possessed (K. 223) says:

If one of the gods came up and said to me 'Crato, when you die, you shall live all over again. And you shall be whatever you wish—a dog, a sheep, a goat, a man, or a horse; for you have to live twice. This is decreed by fate. Choose what you want', I think I should immediately say 'Make me anything rather than a human being'.

Here even Menander is less dramatic than Horace, whose god uses a mixture of interjections and brisk, peremptory commands:

If some god said 'Behold! Here am I, ready to grant your wishes. You who a moment ago were a soldier shall be a merchant; and you who were a lawyer shall become a farmer. Right! Exchange parts and away you go...Well? Why are you standing there?', they would refuse; and yet they could have their heart's desire.

It will be noted that the last few examples have all been drawn from the first satire. That is because the poem owes much of its character to the age-old similes of life as a stage, life as a race-course,[52] and life as a banquet.[53] The antiquity of these similes, along with the conventional nature of the characters and the scarcity of Italian names, prevents the satire from having any firm roots in Roman life. In its matter it is essentially a Hellenistic poem, though no one but Horace could have written it.

The distinctive character of 1. 2 is derived partly from its names, which will be discussed in chapter v, and partly from its use of literary material. In concluding his description of the miserly Fufidius, Horace says:

ita ut pater ille, Terenti
fabula quem miserum gnato vixisse fugato
inducit, non se peius cruciaverit atque hic.   (20–2)

So that the father who is represented in Terence's play as living in misery as a result of banishing his son never tortured himself worse than he.

The play referred to is, of course, the *Heauton Timorumenos* or *The Man Who Punished Himself*. But if the reader happened to be a little forgetful, or even downright ignorant, he did not suffer for it, because Horace provided him with a translation of the title (*se cruciaverit*) and a summary of the opening scene; verbal quotation plays no part in the effect.[54]

In vv. 31–5 we have an allusion of a different kind, namely a free rendering in verse of a saying ascribed to Cato. On seeing a young man come out of a brothel Cato exclaimed 'Good for you! Better to appease your lust here than with other men's wives.' The original form of the anecdote or *chria* is lost, so we cannot tell how much, if any, of the quotation is authentic, but we do know of a sequel which Horace has passed over. For, according to the pseudo-Acron, after meeting the man several times in the same place Cato said 'I commended you, young man, for paying an occasional visit, not for becoming an *habitué*'. Clearly the weight of the story falls on the second half, yet Horace did not hesitate to suppress it, presumably because adultery was his chief concern and it did not suit his argument to have the brothel associated with a virtuous moderation.

Like many satirists of note, Horace was an accomplished literary mimic. And he uses this gift to introduce the main theme of the poem. Thus the noble lines of Ennius:

> audire est operae pretium procedere recte
> qui rem Romanam Latiumque augescere voltis[55]

> It is worth your while to give ear, you who wish all success to the Roman state and increase to Latium

reappear in vv. 37–8 as:

> audire est operae pretium procedere recte
> qui moechis non voltis.

> It is worth your while to give ear, you who wish ill success to adulterers.

There are two allusions to the epigrams of Philodemus. In one case (120 ff.) Philodemus is mentioned by name and his poem is summarized in a masterpiece of vivid compression, in which syntax is almost squeezed out:

> illam 'post paulo', 'sed pluris', 'si exierit vir',
> Gallis, hanc Philodemus ait sibi, quae neque magno
> stet pretio neque cunctetur cum est iussa venire.

The 'later on'—'yes, but more money'—'if my man goes out' sort of woman is, according to Philodemus, for the Galli; his own choice is the one who doesn't cost much and comes at once when called.

The pun on *Galli*, 'Gauls', and *Galli*, 'eunuch priests of Cybele', must have been in the original, which unfortunately is lost. The attempt to identify the epigram with no. 126 in the fifth book of the *Greek Anthology* is no more than a bad guess.[56]

The other allusion to Philodemus comes at v. 92. Lovers, we are told, are often so infatuated with one or two features of the beloved that they fail to notice all the concomitant defects:

> o crus! o bracchia! verum
> depugis, nasuta, brevi latere ac pede longo est.

O legs! O arms! But she has too small a bottom, too big a nose, a short waist and huge feet.

In this case the poem in question is extant:

> ὢ ποδός, ὢ κνήμης, ὢ τῶν ἀπόλωλα δικαίως
> μηρῶν, ὢ γλουτῶν, ὢ κτενός, ὢ λαγόνων,
> ὢ ὤμοιν, ὢ μαστῶν, ὢ τοῦ ῥαδινοῖο τραχήλου,
> ὢ χειρῶν, ὢ τῶν μαίνομαι ὀμματίων,
> ὢ κατατεχνοτάτου κινήματος, ὢ περιάλλων
> γλωττισμῶν, ὢ τῶν θῦ' ἐμὲ φωναρίων.
> εἰ δ' Ὀπικὴ καὶ Φλῶρα καὶ οὐκ ἄδουσα τὰ Σαπφοῦς,
> καὶ Περσεὺς Ἰνδῆς ἠράσατ' Ἀνδρομέδης.[57]

O feet! O legs! O thighs for which I died (and with good reason)! O buttocks, O fringe, O flanks, O shoulders, O breasts, O slender neck, O arms, O eyes that fill me with madness, O clever movement, O superlative kisses, O little cries of 'love me!' If she's Italian and her name is Flora and she does not sing Sappho—well, Perseus loved the Indian Andromeda.

Here again Horace has been rather less than fair; for, whatever shortcomings Philodemus' poem may have, the vision of his lover is nothing if not comprehensive.

The fullest rendering is of an epigram by Callimachus, which runs as follows:

The huntsman, [Epicydes, on the hills] tracks [every] hare [and the trail of every hind] through the [frost and] snow. [And if anyone says 'Look, here is an animal] lying [wounded'] he does not take it. My love is [also] like this. It [constantly] pursues that which flies, but flies past what is ready to hand.[58]

As well as reducing the poem from six to three and a half lines by the omissions indicated, Horace moves from indirect to direct speech and reverses the final sequence so as to give a neat chiasmus. He also leaves out the author's name—perhaps as a tactful gesture, since he quotes the poem only to reject its sentiment.

These few examples show that even at this early stage Horace commanded various techniques of literary allusion and that he used them with an independence sometimes amounting to ruthlessness.

The third satire, unlike the first, has none of the universal similes of popular philosophy, nor, except for the Lucretian section in vv. 99 ff.,[59] does it make any use of literary material. It proves, however, to be richer in metaphor than either of the other pieces. I do not mean that we are startled by novel perceptions or daring feats of language; such effects are rare even in Horace's lyrics, and he seems to have felt that brilliance of that kind was inappropriate to his conception of satire. (And no doubt if satire is thought of as moral discourse delivered in an unpretentious, conversational style, this is a perfectly defensible opinion.) Nevertheless, I. 3 does contain several quietly successful metaphors, which are not restricted to one expression but are elaborated over a number of lines. A straightforward example occurs in vv. 58–61:

hic fugit omnis
insidias nullique malo latus obdit apertum
cum genus hoc inter vitae versemur ubi acris
invidia atque vigent ubi crimina.

This fellow escapes every trap and never leaves his flank open to malicious attack; for we are engaged in a life in which envy is sharp and slander active.

Sometimes we can watch the metaphor develop from a single word:

> amicus dulcis ut aequum est
> cum mea compenset vitiis bona, pluribus hisce,
> si modo plura mihi bona sunt, inclinet, amari
> si volet: hac lege in trutina ponetur eadem. (69–72)

My kindly friend should, as is only fair, weigh my virtues against my
faults, and if he wants me to like him he should come down on the
side of my virtues as being more numerous—provided they *are* more
numerous. On that principle he will be weighed in the same scales.

Here the idea implicit in *compenset* and *inclinet* emerges finally in
trutina. At the same time the form of the image is constantly
shifting. The friend first holds the balance, then appears to be
identified with the balance, and finally ends up *in* the balance.
The same kind of movement is encountered in vv. 34–7:

> denique te ipsum
> concute, num qua tibi vitiorum inseverit olim
> natura aut etiam consuetudo mala; namque
> neglectis urenda filix innascitur agris.

So give yourself a good shaking in case the seeds of evil have already
been sown in you, whether by nature or through some bad habit. For
if you once neglect a field, bracken springs up which eventually has
to be burnt out.

The personality begins as a garment in which the seeds of evil
have lodged, and it ends as an overgrown field.

This last example shows how Horace often combines a metaphor with a piece of proverbial wisdom. So too in vv. 55–6 we
have:

> at nos virtutes ipsas invertimus atque
> sincerum cupimus vas incrustare.

But we turn virtues themselves upside down and do all we can to dirty
a clean jar.

Finally, after the figure of the balance quoted above, Horace adds:

> qui ne tuberibus propriis offendat amicum
> postulat, ignoscat verrucis illius.

The man who expects a friend to overlook his boils will forget the
other's warts.[60]

34

Boils and warts—a typically Roman version of beams and motes.

In spite of their stylistic variety, which includes a free use of dialogue and reported speech, these satires are all straightforward diatribes in the sense that the poet speaks directly to his audience and takes responsibility for what he says. But while his manner is direct and unequivocal, his material is so general that we learn practically nothing about himself. That is the main point of contrast between these satires and 1.6—a remarkable poem, in which the diatribe has been made the medium of a personal declaration.

CHAPTER II

POET AND PATRON (1)[1]

I. 6

It is hard for an Englishman, with his long history of civic order, to imagine the almost continuous violence which Rome endured in the last sixty years of the Republic. Sulla, who played a large part in crushing the Italian rebels in 88 B.C., had only just left to take command in the east when Marius and Cinna seized power in Rome. The slaughter of their opponents went on for five days. Sulla's return brought a new outbreak of fighting which culminated at the Colline Gate in 82 B.C. Thousands fell in battle, thousands were killed after surrendering, and thousands more died in the proscriptions which followed. Savagery, even on this scale, failed to bring peace, and within four years the army of Lepidus was marching on Rome. After Lepidus' defeat many of his soldiers fled to Sertorius, the Marian general, who had been conducting successful operations in Spain. These operations, which included victories over Pompey, were brought to an end when Sertorius was assassinated in 72 B.C. Pompey returned to Italy in time to help Crassus stamp out the revolt of Spartacus. Six thousand slaves were crucified along the Appian Way. In less than ten years another revolt had broken out, this time under Catiline, and the senatorial armies were on the march again. Under the first triumvirate there was an uneasy peace (interrupted by gang warfare in Rome), until Caesar crossed the Rubicon in 49 B.C. The battles which ensued at Pharsalus, Thapsus and Munda took a terrible toll of Roman life. After Caesar's murder war flared up again. In 43 B.C. Antony was twice defeated at Mutina, but he found reinforcements in Gaul and returned to Italy, where along with Octavian and Lepidus he set up the second triumvirate. More proscriptions followed. Appian puts the number of those murdered as high as two thousand knights and three hundred senators. After the carnage at Philippi Octavian came back to Italy and within a year had to suppress a rebellion led by Antony's brother. And even now there was no peace. For Pompey's son, Sextus, was still carrying on a naval war from Sicily and Sardinia. He inflicted more than one defeat on Octavian before he was overcome in 36 B.C. When, after Actium, Octavian finally turned to the task of rebuilding the Roman state, the wonder is that there was anything left to rebuild.

Of all these calamities there is scarcely a trace in the *Satires*. The few political references are mostly confined to the later poems of Book 2, by which time the struggle was over. In fact it may be said that Horatian satire as a whole implies a conscious rejection of public life. Nevertheless, the violent social changes which took place in these years are reflected in the career of the poet, who was a freedman's son, a knight,[2] a military tribune, a treasury official, a friend of republican nobles, and an *amicus* of Octavian's first minister. The stresses imposed by this career are most apparent in 1. 6, and the way they are handled makes this a poem of unusual interest.

7–18: You say, Maecenas, that a man's parentage doesn't matter provided he is *ingenuus*. In taking this view you recognize that before the régime of Tullius and his far-from-noble kingship many men of no pedigree often lived good lives and were honoured with high offices, whereas Laevinus, a descendant of that Valerius who drove Tarquin the Proud from his throne into exile, was never rated higher than a brass farthing, even in the opinion of the people (that judge whom you know so well), who foolishly give positions of distinction to the undeserving, who are stupidly enthralled by family fame, and who gape in fascination at inscriptions and busts. *quid oportet | nos facere a vulgo longe longeque remotos?*

In view of the preceding clause (*quali sit quisque parente | natus*) the word *ingenuus* is naturally taken to mean 'freeborn', and in spite of his comparatively liberal outlook Maecenas may well have believed that no one of servile birth should be admitted to political office. We note, however, that Horace goes on to endorse

37

Maecenas' opinion by citing the case of Servius Tullius, who was *not* freeborn. He was *patre nullo, matre serva* (Livy 4. 3); and there were many good men before him, says Horace, who rose high without having a pedigree. Now this may be simply an oversight, but the effect of these lines, whether intentional or not, is to cast doubt on Maecenas' reservation and to remind us of the broader sense of *ingenuus*, which is 'noble in nature'.

Maecenas' main principle, though based on morality, is presented in political terms in such a way as to suggest that low birth should not be an obstacle to high office and that high birth should not be a guarantee of high office. We cannot say how deeply Maecenas believed in this principle, but it would be unrealistic to expect a man of Horace's status and temperament to make it the nucleus of a diatribe. Lucilius, Persius and Juvenal are all equally conservative in this respect, and indeed Roman satire is no place in which to look for a reformer's manifesto. So we are not wholly surprised when, after this opening passage, a new theme emerges in vv. 23–44. This is just what happened in the first three diatribes. The trouble here, however, is that the new theme runs counter to what has already been said: Commoners, no less than nobles, are the slaves of ambition. This is foolish, because when a man thrusts himself into prominence he at once arouses malicious curiosity. 'Who *is* this fellow? What was his father?' A man like the effeminate Barrus annoys the girls by his exhibitionism. They dislike the competition and make jealous inquiries about him. So a commoner who has become tribune provokes hostility, and such hostility is bound to cause unhappiness.

Now since these two ideas (the irrelevance of birth and the folly of ambition) pull in different directions—the first towards a dynamic society with a *carrière ouverte aux talents*, the second towards political quietism—there is a danger that between them they may dislocate the structure of the poem. The strain falls most heavily on vv. 19–22, and one must admit that the joint is perilously weak. To examine it we must return to the question in vv. 17–18, *quid oportet / nos facere a vulgo longe longeque*

38

remotos? From ancient times this has been interpreted in two different ways. Some commentators think it means 'How much more should we, who stand apart from the mob, assess a man at his true worth?'3 This makes excellent sense and provides a logical conclusion to the opening passage. But it does not lead smoothly to what follows. In vv. 19 ff. we have this: 'For, granted, the people would have preferred to give office to a Laevinus rather than to an unknown Decius, and Appius the censor would have struck me off the roll for not being the son of a freeborn father.' We now expect something like 'But men of our kind take a different view'. Instead, Horace says '—and it would have served me right for not resting contentedly in my own skin. Yet [i.e. in spite of prejudice from above and below] Glory drags behind her dazzling car the obscure no less than the noble.'

The other interpretation of vv. 17–18 is somewhat as follows: 'What am I to do, who am so far removed from the public's gaze?'4 The implied answer, i.e. 'stay out of politics altogether', leads directly to the next section. Unfortunately the link with the opening passage is now very much weaker, for one has to assume that the question has no connexion with Maecenas' liberal principle and arises solely from the behaviour of the people, as described in vv. 15-17. Whichever solution one adopts (I myself favour the first), it is clear that Horace's usual dexterity has deserted him. He might, after all, have taken the line that although birth *ought* not to matter, in fact it did, and therefore anyone who tried to force his way to the top should reckon with the consequences. Or he might have argued on a purely personal level by introducing a hypothetical opponent saying 'What? Do you mean that you, with your tastes and outlook, are eager to enter on the *cursus honorum*?' Horace could then have disclaimed any such ambitions in his own characteristic way. However, even if the transition is poorly managed, it does not follow that the two themes cancel each other out. We shall find presently that when one is subtracted from the other we are left with a highly significant remainder. In the meantime, lest we become too engrossed in general ideas, we should remember that the satire was written as a protest against something distressingly personal, namely the resentment which people felt at the poet's good fortune.

1–6: Though you, Maecenas, are noble (*nemo generosior*) and have distinguished generals amongst your ancestors, you don't despise me, as most people do, because I'm a freedman's son. This introduction is deliberately recalled in vv. 45–8. Thus

> nunc ad me redeo libertino patre natum,
> quem rodunt omnes libertino patre natum

> Now I revert to myself, a freedman's son, carped at by everyone because I'm a freedman's son

recalls *libertino patre natum* (6). Also *nunc quia...Maecenas* (47) echoes *non quia, Maecenas* (1), and *quod mihi pareret legio Romana tribuno* (48) harks back to *qui magnis legionibus imperitarent* (4). Therefore a new structural unit begins at v. 45. In this new section Horace points out that he is disliked not, strictly speaking, because he is a freedman's son, but because he has achieved fame in spite of being a freedman's son. Now in view of what has just been said about the hazards of ambition, surely this dislike was only to be expected. Why should Horace complain when he has broken his own rules? In answer the poet distinguishes between the two types of eminence he has known. The first, his commission in the republican army, was a position of military and potentially political power. As such it was perhaps bound to excite envy. But all that is over. His new distinction, i.e. his friendship with Maecenas, is something quite different. Being non-political it gives him no power over his fellow-citizens, and therefore it ought not to cause resentment.

Horace's aversion to politics, however, is not developed until the last section of the poem. In the meantime he deals with the social aspect of his position. This posed a more delicate problem. His prestige as a friend of Maecenas was undeniable, and he could not pretend it was unwelcome. What he could do was to ignore his position as a celebrity, thus implying that the relationship was a purely private affair. He could also contend that his privilege had been fairly won. With this in view he gives an account of his first interview with Maecenas:

The excellent Virgil previously told you what I was; then Varius did the same. When I came before you I gulped out a few words—for shyness struck me dumb and prevented me from saying more. I didn't make out that I had a distinguished father or that I rode round my estates on a Tarentine nag. I told you the facts about myself. Your reply was characteristically brief, and I left. Nine months later you sent for me again and invited me to join your circle of friends.

(54–62)

The meeting, then, was no haphazard affair (*non...casu, nulla... fors*, 52–4)—an important point to make, for as we learn from 2. 6. 49 there were many who called Horace *Fortunae filius*, 'Luck's pet'. Lady Luck in the Elder Pliny's words (*NH* 2. 22) was 'blind, fickle, inconstant, unreliable, shifting, and a patroness of the unworthy (*indignorumque fautrix*)'. Maecenas, however, was not a patron of the unworthy. Immediately before the passage just quoted he is said to be *cautum dignos adsumere, prava / ambitione procul*, 'careful to admit only the worthy, above all sordid ambition'.[5] And immediately after the same passage Horace says:

magnum hoc ego duco
quod placui tibi, qui turpi secernis honestum,
non patre praeclaro sed vita et pectore puro.

I consider it a great thing to have pleased you, who distinguish the honourable from the base, not by my father's glory but by my blameless life and heart.[6]

By focusing attention on Maecenas Horace has reminded his enemies that in criticizing him they were also criticizing his friend and patron. We notice, however, that he says nothing at all about the decisive factor in the whole business, namely his poetry. (Maecenas, after all, did not keep open house for every upright citizen.) No doubt Horace knew very well that, although he might possibly reduce people's resentment a little by protesting his decency, he would only inflame it if he mentioned his talent.

If we abstracted the argument in Hegelian terms we should find

41

that it had now reached a final synthesis: humble birth ought not to be an obstacle to success, at least when the success is of a non-political kind and when the man in question deserves the honour. That is the degree to which the opening themes have been reconciled.

Although there is a pause at v. 64, it is a mistake to think of the poem as falling into two halves. Lines 65–88 are linked much more closely with what goes before than with 89–131. The satire in fact consists of three groups of pairs. The first group (1–22 and 23–44) presents opposite aspects of glory, the second is concerned with merit (45–64 and 65–88), and the third with freedom (89–111 and 111–31). From now on this division will form the basis of our discussion.

In vv. 65–71 tone and structure are again complementary. By resuming the topic of merit these verses connect the two parts of the second group; at the same time they diminish our uneasiness at the poet's self-praise:

If my faults are not too serious or too many; and if my nature, apart from these blemishes, is otherwise sound—just as on a handsome body you might find a mole here and there; if no one can justly accuse me of greed or meanness or licentiousness; if (to indulge in a little self-esteem) my life is clean and above reproach; and if my friends are fond of me; the credit is due to my father.

Now comes the famous account of how Horace's father took him to school in Rome, accompanying him to and fro each day, providing him with the proper clothes and equipment, and watching over his moral welfare. It was an unusual step to take, but apart from recognizing his son's promise the father may well have decided that the local school was an undesirable place. It is likely that as a penalty for its defection in the Italian war (90–88 B.C.) Venusia had to relinquish some of its land to Sulla's veterans. If so, the centurions and their families must have formed an unpopular 'ascendancy' in the district.[7] This is supported by Horace's satirical phrase *magni . . . pueri magnis e centurionibus orti*, 'great sons descended from great sergeant-majors'. We can imagine these children jeering at the freedman's son as they swaggered to school with satchel and tablet swinging from the left arm (74).

The father's concern for the boy's purity (81–4) may seem rather exaggerated until we recall what other writers say about Roman education. 'Insist', says Juvenal, 'that the teacher himself be a father to the class, in case they play dirty games' (7. 239 f.). To encounter the same warning in Quintilian is rather like hearing the ghoulish fantasies of Ronald Searle confirmed by the headmistress of a public school. Yet that is what happens. 'I do not approve of young boys sitting beside adolescents', writes Quintilian. Then in words strikingly similar to Horace's he adds 'Not only should the charge of indecency be avoided, but also the very suspicion of it'.[8] The famous rhetorician also agrees with Horace in the stress he lays on purity. 'If anyone chooses a teacher for his son without taking care to avoid the most obvious kind of immorality, he may be sure that all the other precepts which I am trying to compile for young people's good are utterly useless...'[9] The same kind of sentiment is also found in Cicero and Pliny.[10] Now we may be sure that Orbilius, that stern old knight, saw to it that his school had a healthy atmosphere, but Orbilius was not Horace's only teacher and anyway he was an exception. Many teachers were slaves, all of them were wretchedly paid (even Orbilius was a poor man), and as a group they were treated with condescension or indifference. Nothing illustrates better the dilemma of the Roman social system. Fathers were anxious for their sons to be trained by reliable and dignified teachers; at the same time they were determined to retain the privilege of despising the profession.

What bearing does all this have on Horace's argument? He is contending that people should not grudge him his position, because he deserves it. And why does he deserve it? The first argument is *a posteriori*: 'Maecenas invited me to join his circle, and he chooses only those who are worthy of the honour.' The second is *a priori*: 'I am worthy of the honour because of the moral discipline I received from my father.' Such is the connexion of the two parts, but their power is not derived from their logical cogency so much as from the fact that they have been placed side by side at the very centre of the poem, to pay a debt of gratitude and affection to the two chief influences on the poet's life— Maecenas who recognized and accepted him for what he was, and his father who made him what he was.

The theme of merit ends, properly speaking, at v. 88, but the transition to the final section has already begun with the idea expressed in vv. 85 ff., 'I should have been quite content to follow my father's footsteps'. The notion of contentment is carried over into the following passage by *nil me paeniteat sanum patris huius*, 'never in my right mind would I be dissatisfied with such a father'. But the continuity is only apparent, because the story of Horace's education and the part played in it by his father is over. In its new context the poet's contentment with his parents is contrasted with the embarrassment of those who feel handi-capped by their low birth. Such embarrassment, says Horace, is useless and misconceived. If he had the choice he would pick the same parents again. Then seemingly as an afterthought he adds:

<blockquote>
demens

iudicio vulgi, sanus fortasse tuo quod
nollem onus haud umquam solitus portare molestum.

(97–9)
</blockquote>

Mad in the opinion of the mob, but sane perhaps in yours for re-fusing to shoulder a tiresome and unaccustomed burden.

But this is no afterthought. It is the beginning of the final theme. In this last section Horace returns to the folly of ambition,[11] emphasizing now not the unpopularity of a public career but rather its burdens. Making money, greeting callers, acquiring more servants and horses and wagons—these are the duties from which the poet is free. In the middle of the list we catch a glimpse of his *positive* freedom:

If I like I can go right to Tarentum on a gelded mule whose flanks are chafed by the weight of the saddle-bag and whose withers are chafed by the rider

44

—a vivid Lucilian cameo.[12] Passing through vv. 110–11, where *hoc* refers back and *milibus atque aliis* points forward, we find ourselves in the second part of the final section, which describes a typical, lazy day in the poet's life. The description starts in the afternoon, as Horace strolls through the markets comparing the prices of vegetables; later he explores the stalls round the Circus Maximus, an area which had all the seedy excitement of old Soho. Back in his house dinner is served, and as Horace looks at the table the various objects form themselves into an exquisite still life:[13]

> lapis albus
> pocula cum cyatho duo sustinet; adstat echinus
> vilis, cum patera gutus, Campana supellex.

> On a slab of white marble stand two cups and a ladle, beside them a cheap jug, an oil flask and saucer—all of Campanian ware.

We join the poet again next morning about ten o'clock and remain in his company until the afternoon. The whole description reflects his positive freedom—*quacumque libido est | incedo solus* (111–12), 'I go wherever I like on my own'. But again he gives variety, this time by inserting a negative expression in the middle—he is not worried about having to rise early (119–20).

This final section on freedom is an integral part of the poem, for it presupposes everything that has gone before. Without the father's moral training such a life would not have seemed worthwhile; without the generosity of Maecenas it would have been impossible. It is a life free from ambition, and it reminds us that the things most worth having do not depend on birth. The last two links are carefully provided in the closing lines:

> haec est
> vita solutorum misera ambitione gravique;
> his me consolor victurum suavius ac si
> quaestor avus pater atque meus patruusque fuissent.

> Such is the life of those who are free from the cruel pressure of ambition. I comfort myself with the thought that I shall enjoy life more fully in this way than if my grandfather, father and uncle had all been quaestors.

Horace himself could probably have had a quaestorship if he had wanted it, but there is no need to assume that Maecenas was pressing him to take the job. To understand the defensive tone it is enough to remember the picture which Horace presented to his enemies. In their eyes he was nothing but a small-town upstart with privileges beyond his deserts. His father, an absurdly ambitious man for one of servile birth, had pushed him into a respectable Roman school, and not content with that had sent him to study at Athens in the company of his social superiors. After Philippi, instead of being grateful for his pardon and working quietly in the civil service, the fellow had taken advantage of a slender poetic talent to ingratiate himself with Maecenas. Perhaps he had his eye on higher things. Had he not already shown a taste for power by acquiring a commission in Brutus' army? Many better men had changed sides after defeat and were now embarked on successful careers. Horace, with his extraordinary mixture of impudence and good luck, might well do the same.

Looking more closely at the poem we detect certain features of a conventional kind. The themes of high birth, foolish ambition and the quiet life need no illustration, but it is worth recalling that the autobiographical material (parentage, education, friends, habits) can easily be paralleled from ancient lives.[14] Another parallel can be found in ancient invectives, which were often a kind of 'anti-biography'. One started with the victim's parents, who came from some outlandish area and who, if not actually slaves, were invariably soiled by some menial occupation. From there one proceeded to his squalid upbringing, his schooldays which were already tainted with vice, his comic and bestial appearance, his grotesque dress and so on.[15] The prevalence of indecent abuse in lampoons of this kind may also help to explain the emphasis with which Horace asserts his purity.

Precedents can also be found for Horace's boasting. In Roman eyes self-praise was always justified in self-defence. Cicero, for instance, says:

dicendum igitur est id quod non dicerem nisi coactus—nihil enim umquam de me dixi sublatius adsciscendae laudis causa potius quam criminis depellendi.[16]

> I must therefore say what I would not say except under compulsion—for if I have ever sounded a little conceited it has always been for the purpose of rebutting a charge, not for eliciting praise.

Another excuse for boasting was the danger that one's proudest achievements might be put down to luck. Cicero took some trouble to prevent such a vulgar error:

ego committam ut ea quae pro salute omnium gessi casu magis et felicitate a me quam virtute et consilio gesta esse videantur?[17]

> Shall I allow all that I did for the safety of the state to be ascribed to chance and good luck instead of to my character and policy?

When massaging the ego in this way it was prudent, however, to keep in touch with one's listeners. Plutarch, writing a century after Horace's death, advises the speaker to congratulate his audience as well as himself, and to put them in a receptive mood by admitting some minor foibles.[18] As we have seen, both precautions are taken by Horace in the present satire.

Such techniques, of course, were conventional only because they had proved reliable in practice, and therefore the question here is not whether they are new but whether they are effectively employed. This question brings out the satire's true freshness. I am not thinking so much of the smaller touches—how envy is caught in a snatch of conversation at the theatre, how ambition is illuminated by Gloria in her triumphal chariot and by Tillius travelling east, complete with portable lavatory. I am thinking rather of the way in which the themes of glory, merit, and freedom are built into a unique artistic structure. This brings us back to the poet's ambiguous position in society. His dilemma was in many ways similar to those faced in 1.4 and 1.10. In 1.4 he had to maintain that wicked people deserved to be attacked while at the same time indicating his reluctance to attack them. In 1.10 the problem was to justify his divergence from Lucilius without repudiating the satiric genre. As he wrote 1. 6 Horace was well aware that high birth did not automatically confer the qualities of statesmanship. No doubt he felt equal in ability to many of the young aristocrats whom he had known at school and university. Therefore his pride demanded the *right* to attain eminence, and he was stung to indignation by taunts against his humble background. Yet he knew he was temperamentally unsuited to public life, and when he observed the type of person who *was* gaining power as a result of the civil wars he turned away in disgust:

> quid attinet tot ora navium gravi
> rostrata duci pondere
> contra latrones atque servilem manum
> hoc, hoc tribuno militum?   (*Epod.* 4. 17–20)

What is the point of sending so many ships with heavy beaks against a gang of pirates and slaves when he, yes he, is a military tribune?

'I have a perfect right to stand for office.' 'The whole thing is so sordid that I wouldn't dream of standing for office.' These two attitudes pull against each other, particularly in the first section of the poem. And even at the very end, after describing the joys of the quiet life, Horace cannot refrain from that sarcastic *consolor*— a word which betrays that his wounds were still smarting.

The relation of poet to patron was also a delicate affair. Horace realized that he owed some respect to Maecenas in virtue of his superior position, and that in winning his patronage he had contracted certain obligations in return. On the other hand he was not the sort of man to accept charity. Until the debacle at Philippi his career had been highly successful, and even now he had no intention of sacrificing his independence in order to become an official lackey. The result was a series of mutually qualifying assertions:

My father was a freedman, but I ought not to be penalized for that. That doesn't mean I have any political aims; such aims are foolish since they cause resentment. But my friendship with Maecenas should not cause resentment, for it was he who offered it; but he only offered because I deserved it; but I only deserved it because of my father. Anyhow the friendship involves no official duties; which suits me well, since I value my independence.

The poem however, like 1.4, is more than just a personal defence. This can best be appreciated by asking whether there is any concept which will include and unify the themes of glory, merit, and freedom. I believe there is such a concept and that it is developed in a series of antitheses which are sometimes so sharp as to seem paradoxical. Let us start with the *ignobile regnum* of Tullius (9). His reign was *ignobile* because of his low birth, but in comparison with the noble Tarquin who was *regno pulsus*, or with the worthless aristocrat Laevinus, he was clearly a distinguished ruler. In Horace's time, to be 'somebody' one had to point to freeborn ancestors; yet in former days many a good man who was by nature *ingenuus* had no ancestors at all (10). Of the *generosi* and *ignoti* who follow Gloria (24) the former are noble by birth and the latter hope to become so by their own efforts (27–8). Such efforts are hazardous, for even at the level of the tribunate people inquire whether a man is *honestus* or *inhonestus* (36), meaning 'Is he well-born or low-born?' Now to Horace's mind there was something wrong about applying the words 'noble' and 'honourable' to a tyrant or a reprobate or a man obsessed by ambition, while reserving 'disgraceful' and 'disreputable' for those whose parents happened to have been slaves. It was part of Maecenas' excellence that in spite of his high birth and his familiarity with power he distinguished the base from the honourable by purely moral criteria. So far Horace has isolated himself from his parents. Like Bion before him he has said in effect σκόπει με ἐξ ἐμαυτοῦ—'judge me on my own merits'.[19] But at v. 71 it now appears that when the right standards are applied his father was honourable too, though not made honourable by the appurtenances of office (97). And it was because he was a gentleman by nature that he was able to teach his son *virtus*. So Horace can be proud of his father after all.

Closely related to parentage was the question of *dignitas*. Cicero tells us that status had once been the prize of excellence (*Mur.* 17) and that after the expulsion of the kings it was agreed that access to the highest rank should be available to men of diligence and character (*Sest.* 137). Sallust says that in the old days one's status was based on noble deeds (*Cat.* 7); in fact nobility itself was once achieved by valour (*Jug.* 85. 17). According to Horace this was true even before the expulsion of Tarquin (9–11). But as the government passed into the control of a self-perpetuating oligarchy *dignitas* began to change its meaning. It was still attainable through public offices (*honores*), but since such offices were monopolized by an aristocratic clique the word acquired a class connotation, and status itself became something which could be claimed as an inheritance. As Marius fiercely declared, *nobilitas ...omnis honores non ex merito sed quasi debitos a vobis repetit* (*Jug.* 85. 37), 'the nobility command you to give them every high office not on their merits but as their due'. Hence a candidate of non-senatorial rank was almost bound to fail (however virtuous and diligent) on account of being *indignus*. If he succeeded, his enemies still regarded him as unworthy. Catiline says he was driven to revolution because he saw unworthy men elevated to high office—*quod non dignos homines honore honestatos videbam* (*Cat.* 35. 3)—the most unworthy of all being, of course, Cicero. This is the perversion of values that Horace is attacking. It is a perversion compounded by the stupidity of the people, who have often given office to the undeserving—*honores* / *saepe dat indignis* (15–16). And even now, when the old senatorial patronage is in decay, the men gaining power are no better; they are certainly no more popular. The only place where merit is still given its due is in certain areas of private life, such as the circle of Maecenas. The great patron was careful to accept only those who were worthy (*dignos* in v. 51), and with him worth was a question of character.

Our final concept is that of freedom. A manumitted slave ceased to be another man's property and acquired rights guaranteed by Roman law. But as a *libertinus* he could not record the name of his tribe or father; he was identifiable by his servile cognomen, and on certain formal occasions he wore the freedman's conical hat.[20] Again, though accepted by plebeians and often by knights as well, he could never hope to win political distinction.

Nor, unless he was a man of learning like some of the Greek professors,[21] was he admitted to aristocratic society. The stigma of slavery became fainter in the second generation, but although a freedman's son might occasionally reach the senate his position was always precarious. P. Popilius was ejected from the house in 70 B.C. (Cic. *Cluent.* 132). Others were expelled by Appius Claudius twenty years later (Dio 40. 63). More reappeared under Caesar (47–45 B.C.)[22] and more again under the Triumvirs in 39 B.C. (Dio 48. 34), but their presence was fiercely resented.[23] Furthermore, in senses other than the strictly legal one, *liber* and its cognates could indicate distinctions within the citizen body. What was *libertas* for the well-born was *licentia* for the lower orders.[24]

As a freedman's son, therefore, Horace knew what discrimination was like. But was *libertas*, he wondered, simply a question of birth? Were not the free men who competed in the scramble for office really the slaves of Gloria? And when they had climbed to one stage of the *cursus honorum* would they not have to acquire even more influence and more clients in order to reach the next? It was obvious that to win and maintain *gloria*, *dignitas* and *clientelae*,[25] which were the prerequisites of power, a man had to organize his day on a rigid plan, attending all kinds of tiresome functions and 'cultivating' people who in themselves were boring and disagreeable. That was not the kind of freedom which appealed to Horace. He preferred to live a quiet, relaxed life, enjoying his friends and realizing his creative talents. Such freedom was possible only for those who were *ambitione soluti* (129), and this detachment required moral discipline. It therefore turns out that Horace is more free than those who despise him, thanks to the guidance of a man who was once a slave.

It is clear, then, that this satire implies a thoroughgoing critique of the aristocratic-republican system. According to Horace the concepts of *nobilitas*, *dignitas*, and *libertas* have been perverted and misunderstood. They have lost their moral significance and have become identified with *gloria*, *honores*, *clientelae* and all the other prizes of ambitious self-interest. As a man with strong Epicurean sympathies Horace attempts to uphold the true meaning of these ideas, using all the resources of his satiric art. Some of these resources have already been noted, but two features are especially striking and both contribute to the same rhetorical effect. The first is the unusual number of comparative expressions: *non...ut plerique* (1–5), *contra* (12), *non...pluris licuisse* (14), *quid oportet / nos facere*, etc. (17–18), *mallet...quam* (19–20), *non minus* (24), *minor* (26), *dissimile* (49), *non ut honorem...ita te* (49–50), *maior* (88), *longe discrepat* (92), *demens...sanus* (97–8), *maior* (100), *plures* (101), *plures* (103), *nemo sordes mihi quas tibi* (107), *commodius quam tu* (110), *suavius* (130). The function of these expressions is to endorse some kind of choice—'this rather than that'. And the choice in its most general aspect is that between wisdom and folly. The second feature, already perceived by Hendrickson,[26] is the figure known as ἀναίρεσις, which takes the form 'not this (nor this) but that'. Thus, indicating the positive element with a capital letter, we have *non quia...nec quod...Referre negas* (1–7), *non hoc...nulla fors...Vergilius...Varius dixere* (52–5), *non ego me claro...non ego circum...Sed quod eram narro* (58–60), *non patre praeclaro Sed vita et pectore puro* (64), *neque avaritiam, neque sordis nec mala lustra...Purus et insons* (68–9), *noluit...Sed est ausus* (72–6), *nec timuit...neque essem questus...At hoc* (85–7), *non ut magna...pars...sic me defendam...Nam nollem* (90–7), *non avide, Quantum interpellet* (127). The figure can have various functions, but here it clearly represents an attempt to re-educate the moral judgement.

As well as defending himself against malicious detractors Horace is therefore trying to put across a persuasive definition, that is 'one which gives a new conceptual meaning to a familiar word without substantially changing its emotive meaning, and which is used with the conscious or unconscious purpose of changing, by this means, the direction of people's interests'.[27] Juvenal had a similar purpose in mind when he said *nobilitas sola est atque unica virtus* (8. 20), 'the one and only nobility is virtue', and indeed if titles were appropriate this satire might well be headed 'Of True Nobility'.

One last qualification is necessary. I have cited familiar passages from Livy, Sallust, and Cicero to illustrate the discontent which at one time or another was felt towards the ruling class. But it would be quite wrong to imagine that Horace was echoing the sentiments of Canuleius, Marius, or Cicero. Those men and others like them were passionately involved in political life, and their primary concern was to broaden the base of the governing class by securing the admission of new magistrates and senators. But Horace had seen too many new magistrates and senators. He knew what they were like and he saw the contempt in which they were held. To him, and to many thinking men, the whole constitutional system seemed to have gone rotten; honours and offices were no longer worth having. Disillusion with all kinds of political endeavour was reflected in a widespread longing for peace and security. And when it became clear that only one man could provide such blessings, the days of the Republic were over.

CHAPTER III

ENTERTAINMENTS

I. 5

In the spring of 38 B.C. Antony agreed to meet Octavian in Brundisium to discuss the threat presented by Sextus Pompeius. Octavian, who was in Etruria at the time (Dio 48. 46), failed to keep the appointment, but by sending ships, men and equipment he gave the impression that he intended to come, and he remonstrated with Antony for not waiting (Appian 5. 80). In due course, against Antony's advice Octavian attacked Sextus on his own, with such disastrous results that he was forced to send Maecenas to Athens, where Antony had his headquarters, asking for another conference in Italy the following spring. Since Antony was prepared to let Octavian have ships in exchange for infantry and was anxious to settle affairs in Italy before starting on his eastern campaigns, he agreed, and eventually in 37 B.C. a meeting took place at Tarentum which postponed the final clash for another six years.

The present satire, usually known as The Journey to Brundisium, relates what happened to Maecenas' party on the way to one of these conferences. We do not know for certain which,[1] but that does not oblige us to accept the view held by Musurillo and others that 'the poem itself is *a poetic fiction*, a composite picture perhaps of journeys made at different times and bound together as a *jeu d'esprit* in imitation of Lucilius'.[2]

About eighty years earlier Lucilius had travelled south to visit his estates in southern Italy and Sicily[3] and had sent an account of his experiences to a friend who was due to follow later. The forty-odd fragments (W. 94–148) suggest that it was a lively, intimate piece of work, typically Roman in character. It appealed to Horace in both conception and tone, and without it his own poem would have been very different, if indeed it had been written at all.[4] Yet I do not believe that Horace invented any episode in 1.5 either to provide a literary allusion or to invite stylistic comparisons. Since this is an unfashionable view at the moment, I had better say a few words in its defence. In 1.5. 82–5 we are told that at Trivicum, after waiting till midnight for a girl who never turned up, Horace went to sleep and had an erotic dream. Now there is an unplaced fragment of Lucilius (W. 1183) which has been convincingly emended so as to read *perminxi lectum, imposui pede pellibus labes* ('I wet the bed and with my member made a mess on the skins').[5] This is often taken as the 'model' of the Horatian passage, and is therefore assigned to Lucilius' Sicilian Journey. Then, since it is rather unlikely that both poets should have had the same experience on their respective travels, the next step is to allege that Horace is writing fiction. But this is bad methodology, for there is no evidence at all that W. 1183 does come from the *Iter Siculum*. Lucilius, after all, wrote quite extensively about his erotic escapades. To treat an isolated fragment in this way is like finding an unidentified anecdote of Boswell's about some olive-skinned girl and assigning it at once to his Corsican diary—a work which is in fact devoid of gallantry.[6]

If we rule out W. 1183, we can also rule out W. 136–7— verses which are supposed to describe Lucilius' sexual frustration:

> Tantalus qui poenas ob facta nefantia poenas
> pendit.[7]

Tantalus who pays a penalty, yea a penalty, for his unspeakable deeds.

If we must seek a clue in Horace I should prefer to quote 1.5.7–9:

> hic ego propter aquam, quod erat deterrima, ventri
> indico bellum, cenantis haud animo aequo
> exspectans comites.

Here, on account of the water (for it was appalling), I declared war on my stomach and waited impatiently for my friends as they had their dinner.

Horace was not the first or the last traveller to have trouble with his stomach. Suppose Lucilius had the same complaint and was forced to watch his companions dealing with a well-cooked meal, might he not have suffered the torments of Tantalus?[8] To sum up: while Lucilian influence may well account for the *mention* of the erotic episode we have no right to infer that the episode itself is fictitious.

Another fragment which Horace is said to have copied is W. 109–10, where the speaker says of his opponent *dente adverso eminulo hic est | rinoceros*—'this fellow with his tooth sticking out in front is a rhinoceros'. In Horace's poem (56 f.) an altercation begins when one buffoon says to another 'I declare you're the image of a wild horse' (*equi te | esse feri similem dico*). He then calls attention to a scar on the other man's forehead, suggesting that he once had a horn. More will be said about these lines later; here it is enough to point out that if Lucilius speaks of a tooth and a rhinoceros and Horace of a scarred forehead and a wild horse that is no proof that Horace borrowed the whole incident from his predecessor. Animal similes, after all, are one of the most basic elements in peasant abuse.

Finally, Horace has some descriptive touches of a general kind where it is merely silly to insist on literary dependence. As Tenney Frank has said, 'Critics point out that... there are muddy roads and a boat trip in Horace as in Lucilius—as though Horace ought to have trudged the wagon route and left the barge for originality's sake, or sent a commission to pave the road so as to avoid Lucilian mud'.[9] Unlike love elegy, the journey poem had not developed a set of conventions which allowed fact and fiction to exist side by side. Maecenas, Virgil and other members of Horace's audience were actually involved in the incidents described—indeed the poem was written largely for their sake. At least two possible dates can be found for the journey itself, and there is nothing in Lucilius to show that Horace was drawing on literature rather than life. And so we need not hesitate to join those readers who for two thousand years have accepted the poem as a piece of authentic narrative.

We now turn to the poem itself. Gibbon thought little of it. 'The maxim that every thing in great men is interesting applies only to their minds and ought not to be extended to their bodies.'[10] Clearly what bored Gibbon was the trivial nature of the episodes. In order to excuse Horace he felt obliged to suggest that the satire was written 'to convince his enemies that his thoughts and occupations on the road were far from being of a serious or political nature'. Other readers have not given up so easily. We are told that when Horace puts ointment on his sore eyes (30) it indicates his scepticism about the forthcoming conference;[11] that the slanging match in Cocceius' villa is a symbol of the diplomatic exchanges at Tarentum;[12] and that when Sarmentus compares Cicirrus to the Cyclops he is really poking fun at Sextus Pompeius.[13] What these critics overlook is that without the aid of fantasy the satire in question is an extremely neat and skilful poem. Anyone who doubts this should start from the article by H. Düntzer in *Phil.* LV (1896), where he will find the whole journey recounted stage by stage in about four and a half thousand words. Horace took six hundred.

His powers of compression are evident in the opening lines:

> egressum magna me accepit Aricia Roma
> hospitio modico.

On leaving mighty Rome I was received by Aricia in a modest inn.

The departure is contained in *egressum*, the arrival in *accepit*, and Aricia, as well as being contrasted with mighty Rome, is defined by the type and quality of its accommodation. All in eight words.

A more elaborate example occurs in vv. 77–80:

> incipit ex illo montis Apulia notos
> ostentare mihi, quos torret Atabulus et quos
> numquam erepsemus, nisi nos vicina Trivici
> villa recepisset.

From that point Apulia began to show me her familiar hills, which are scorched by the Altino, and over which we should never have crawled had not a villa near Trivicum taken us in.

As the hills of Apulia come into view we are told three quite different things about them. The first is a matter of sentiment—they hold memories of the poet's boyhood; the second is descriptive—they are parched by the Sirocco (here called by its local name) and are therefore exhausting to the traveller; the third is both descriptive and structural, for as well as indicating the long steep climb the subjunctive *erepsemus* points forward to the villa at Trivicum with its smoky dining-room and deceitful maid. Lightness and speed are achieved by ellipse, asyndeton, historic infinitives, and especially by clever variations in the use of the participle, e.g.

> milia tum pransi tria repimus atque subimus
> impositum saxis late candentibus Anxur.
> huc venturus erat Maecenas optimus atque
> Cocceius, missi magnis de rebus uterque
> legati, aversos soliti componere amicos.　　　(25–9)

> After breakfast we crawl three miles uphill to Anxur, standing on its white rocks which can be seen from far and wide. The admirable Maecenas was due to come here with Cocceius; both of them were envoys on an important mission, with experience in settling differences between friends.

These lines will show how useful the participle was for the terse, casual, and yet disciplined style of the poet's notebook.

The most obvious danger in writing a diary of this kind is that it may become a mere list of places visited. 'We started from *A*, then we went to *B*, and finally reached *C*.' A few examples will show how Horace deals with the problem. At v. 9 he begins the account of his embarkation at Forum Appii. But instead of saying 'We went aboard the barge', he lets the voices of the servants and bargees come drifting out of the dusk. 'Bring her in here!' 'You're packing them in like sardines!'[14] 'Hey there, that's enough!' Arrivals and departures are sometimes passed over altogether, and notice how rarely we meet a colourless travel-word like *pervenimus* (94). Instead we are shown pictures of the group 'crawling up' the Apulian hills (*erepsemus*) and 'bowling down' to the plain in their wagons (*rapimur raedis*), until the arrival at Brundisium, which is itself made part of a neat zeugma:

Brundisium longae finis chartaeque viaeque est.

Brundisium is the end of a long tale and journey.

The same ease and variety are discernible in his handling of time, which may be indicated by the sun (20), by the hour (23), by a meal (70), or by the weather (96). And it is worth remarking how careful Horace is to avoid concluding every entry at the end of a line. In nearly a quarter of the cases a new entry begins within the verse—and not always after the caesura either. All this gives the narrative a continuous flow, and so while it is possible to make a fair attempt at reconstructing the travellers' route and speed, the satire never reads like a log-book.

The details selected for comment throw an interesting light on the poet's sensibility. Forum Appii, where the Decennovium canal begins, is 'crammed with boatmen and stingy landlords', Canusium earns mention by its gritty bread, Gnatia by its local superstition. In other words the interest of a place lies in the comfort or entertainment which it affords the travellers. Horace is not concerned with natural beauty. Thus while 'fishy Barium' is a phrase worthy of Dylan Thomas, including as it does the site of the town, its occupation, its market, and to a modern reader perhaps even its smell, it does not present a precise visual image. Commenting on the journey through the Pomptine Marshes, Fraenkel says 'Horace has caught the true character of that melancholy stretch of marshland'.[15] Perhaps, but he has caught it by enduring it, not by painting it. For he is so distracted by croaking frogs, biting mosquitoes, and singing boatmen that he never looks beyond the towpath. To this general observation there is one striking exception:

impositum saxis late candentibus Anxur.

Anxur, standing on its white rocks which can be seen from far and wide.

But that is the only picture of its kind in the book. Moreover, in view of Lucilius W. 498:

Carpathium Rhodus in pelagus se inclinat apertum,

Rhodes slopes down into the open Carpathian sea,

and Catullus 67. 32–3:

Brixia Cycneae supposita speculae,
flavus quam molli praecurrit flumine Mella,

Brixia set under the Cycnean height, with the gentle stream of the yellow Mella running by,

it is hazardous to suggest, as Fraenkel does,[16] that landscape photography was invented by the generation of Horace and Virgil.

Early in this century Dr Dorsch was following Horace's route when he chanced to meet a peasant above Terracina (Horace's Anxur). After listening to Dorsch rhapsodizing about the beauty of the mountain view, the peasant turned towards the plain, and pointing to the carefully cultivated land below exclaimed, not without some guile, 'Che bel panorama!'[17] Our romantic heritage makes it hard for us to grasp that Horace is no more interested in natural beauty than in the progress of agriculture or the details of local government. 'Wir ergötzen uns', says Fritzsche, 'an der jugendlichen wahren Reiselust, welche sich durch das Ganze ergiesst.'[18] Here we catch a glimpse of Horace the happy wanderer, striding over the mountains with knapsack and *Lederhosen*. Yet if Fritzsche had read the sections where the travellers are *en route* he would have found not a word to prove that the poet's foot ever touched the ground.

We may be fairly sure, then, that the pleasure Horace felt at receiving Maecenas' invitation was mainly due to the prospect of spending a fortnight with his friends in rather novel surroundings. This in turn explains the nature of the poem; for it is not a private reverie, but rather an evening with slides. The selection is drawn from scenes in which the audience has taken part—an almost infallible formula—and on inspection they fall into two alternating types. One is the happy scene—Horace and Heliodorus wash in the spring at Feronia's temple; Maecenas joins the party from Octavian's headquarters; the arrival of Virgil, Varius, and Tucca; Cocceius entertains the travellers in his villa at Caudium. The other type ought to be the miserable scene, but it isn't. Why it isn't is something of a mystery. When someone back from the continent tells how he has been sea-sick in the Channel, fleeced in a French restaurant, and despoiled of his girl-friend by some smooth Italian, we laugh unreservedly—for is not comedy the tragedy which happens to other people? But the strange thing is that the victim himself enjoys reliving his woes. In the same way, as Horace's fellow-sufferers recall that sleepless night in the middle of a swamp, the foul drinking-water, the gritty bread, and the roads reduced to a quagmire by torrential rain, the whole experience begins to seem quite gay. Horace himself had a particularly bad time. He had a bout of diarrhoea at Forum Appii; after that his eyes became inflamed by the marsh gases—a condition which the smoke-filled room at Trivicum did little to relieve; and then there was that girl—all of which gave Horace a special claim on the others' amused sympathy.

Rueful memories of this kind demand two qualities which Horace possessed and Juvenal clearly did not. The first is detachment—the author must be able to see his own situation with the eyes of a spectator. And the second is assurance—the assurance which comes from feeling at ease with one's audience. The last point will be developed in connexion with 1.9; here it need only be observed that the Journey to Brundisium both reflected and consolidated Horace's position within Maecenas' circle.

There is also another aspect of the satire's spirit, and that is its delightful combination of Roman *urbanitas* with the humour of rustic Italy.

iam nox inducere terris
umbras et caelo diffundere signa parabat.   (9–10)

Night is coming on, 'the night of cloudless climes and starry skies'. It is a perfect setting for high romance. But the air is filled, not with music, but with raucous backchat. This is followed by a popular song—antiphonal, affectionate, and very drunken. Then the boatman moors his barge and settles on his back, and soon his snores are punctuating the frogs' chorus. Next morning a choleric eye peers out of the barge; it registers no progress. In a second its owner is on the bank with a branch of willow in his hand, walloping the boatman, who no doubt kept 'God's time'. Singing, snoring, walloping—it is all pure Plautus, or rather pure Italy, for these were elements in popular entertainment long before New Comedy was ever thought of. At Beneventum

> sedulus hospes
> paene macros arsit dum turdos versat in igni.   (71–2)

> The fussy host nearly burnt his house down while turning some skinny thrushes over the fire.

Pure farce. But it is developed in two lines which in spite of the *vetus culina* foreshadow Virgil's burning of Troy:

> nam vaga per veterem dilapso flamma culinam
> Volcano summum properabat lambere tectum.

> For as Vulcan slipped out through the old stove the darting flame quickly rose to lick the ceiling.

The alliteration of v's (often a violent sound), the stately metonymy of Vulcan for *ignis*, and the serpentine fire-imagery all anticipate Book 2 of the *Aeneid*. Then the action reverts to farce as the guests scramble frantically to save their dinner.

At Gnatia, amid a lot of banter, some locals try to convince the party that frankincense will melt if placed on the temple steps. Horace enjoys the fun but at the same time waves their superstition aside with a fine parody of Lucretius:

> namque deos didici securum agere aevum,
> nec, si quid miri faciat natura, deos id
> tristis ex alto caeli demittere tecto.   (101–3)

For I have learned that the gods live a carefree life, and that, if nature does anything abnormal, it is not the gods who send it down in anger from their high home in the sky.

This blend of simplicity and sophistication is also evident in the exchange of abuse which takes place in the centre of the poem and provides a diversion from the travelogue:

> nunc mihi paucis
> Sarmenti scurrae pugnam Messique Cicirri,
> Musa velim memores.   (51-3)

Now O Muse recount in brief, I pray thee, the fight between Sarmentus the clown and Messius Cicirrus.

This solemn formula would be recited in a deep resonant tone. But the names have already destroyed any hope of grandeur. Sarmentus suggests *sarmentum* 'a faggot' and obviously suits its owner's physique, while Cicirrus recalls the 'cock-man' who was a standard figure in local farces. Nevertheless, the poet continues as though he were singing of Aeneas and Turnus: 'And tell from what lineage each entered the fray of words. Messius comes from glorious stock—Oscans.' (Oscans were proverbially oafish and, according to some, supplied the origin of the word 'obscene'.) 'Sarmentus' mistress is still alive. Such was their ancestry as they joined battle.' In other words, Sarmentus was of servile birth and had no ancestors at all.

Sarmentus strikes first. 'I declare you're the image of a wild horse!' 'Right!' says Messius amid laughter, and tosses his head. 'Hey! If you can threaten us like that when your horn's been cut off, what would you do if it was still on your head?' (The left side of his hairy brow was in fact disfigured by an ugly scar.) After a string of jokes about the other's face and his Campanian disease he begged him to do the dance of the shepherd Cyclops—he would need neither mask nor tragic buskins.[19]

Cicirrus was not lost for a reply. Had Sarmentus dedicated, as promised, his chain to the household gods? The fact that he was a civil servant in no way diminished his mistress's claim upon him. And why had he ever run away when one pound of meal would have been ample for such a tiny puny fellow?

This immemorial peasant humour with its quick repartee and earthy similes is the germ of all popular drama. It is true that

Livy (7. 2) sees the first phase of Roman drama in the stately movements of some Etruscan dancers who visited Rome in 364 B.C. But the young men who parodied their dance and exchanged scurrilous abuse among themselves had enjoyed the same kind of fun long before that date; and when official performances became tainted with professionalism and art, they reverted to their old practice. Livy expressly connects this badinage with the Oscan farces, and Cicirrus, we recall, was an Oscan. Nor was such humour confined to the proletariat. Here is an example from Cicero (*De Orat.* 2. 266). The speaker is Julius Caesar Strabo:

'Caricatures are also exceedingly funny. They are usually directed at ugliness or some physical defect and involve a comparison with something rather discreditable—like my joke at the expense of Helvius Mancia. "Now I'll show what sort of a man you are." "Go on, then", he said. So I pointed at a Gaul portrayed on Marius' Cimbrian shield, which was hanging on one of the New Shops. His body was twisted, his cheeks were baggy, and his tongue was hanging out. There was loud laughter, for it was the very image of Mancia.'

So too Horace and his friends were amused—*ridemus* (57), *prorsus iucunde* (70). Clearly this boisterous humour appealed to something very deep in the Roman character, something which the imperial *gravitas* overlaid but never wholly effaced.

I. 7

A rather similar altercation comprises the seventh satire of Book I. The situation, in brief, is this: on being proscribed by the Triumvirs in 43 B.C., Rupilius Rex, a man of pungent wit, took refuge in Asia. There he became involved in a lawsuit with a tough businessman from Clazomenae called Persius. The case, which came before Brutus, soon developed into an exchange of invective, culminating in a sally by Persius. Turning to Brutus, whose ancestor had expelled King Tarquin from Rome and who himself had killed that uncrowned monarch Julius Caesar, he cried 'In heaven's name, Brutus! You are used to getting rid of kings. Why don't you cut this King's throat? Believe me, this is just the job for you!'

In itself the pun is not too bad. Cicero (*Att.* 1. 16. 10) tells how he used it in reply to Clodius. 'Quousque,' inquit, 'hunc regem feremus?' 'Regem appellas', inquam, 'cum Rex tui mentionem nullam fecit?'—'How long are we going to stand for this king?' he said. 'Do you speak of King,' said I, 'when King made no mention of you?' (Clodius had hoped for a legacy from Rex, who was his brother-in-law.) A few weeks before his death Caesar had evaded the title *rex* by shouting to the crowd that he was not Rex but Caesar—a remark which was subtly analysed by Francis Bacon.[20] Modern instances would not be hard to find. The late Mackenzie King, prime minister of Canada, used to be called Rex as an undergraduate. Today British journalists sometimes comment on the regal power of Mr Cecil King. Such considerations, however, would not have impressed Dryden. 'I am sorry to say it for the sake of Horace, but certain it is, he has no fine palate who can feed so heartily on garbage.'[21] Even if we grant that the joke falls short of the uproarious, Dryden's disgust is still out of place; for it is not really Horace's garbage. Here, as in 1. 5, he is playing a double game. He is amused by the characters and their repartee, but he also finds them rather crude and silly. So he introduces the contest in elaborate mock-heroic language:

inter

Hectora Priamiden animosum atque inter Achillem
ira fuit capitalis ut ultima divideret mors.   (11–13)

Between Hector, son of Priam, and the valiant Achilles the wrath was
so murderous that in the end only death could part them.

The gigantic shadows of Hector and Achilles are thus projected behind the squabbling litigants. Perhaps we may go further and suggest that it is Achilles' shadow which looms over the halfbreed Greekling Persius, while Hector's falls on his Roman descendant Rex. In any case the function of the irony is unmistakable. It dissociates Horace from the buffoonery which follows. And so in its full perspective the poet's position is that of a man at a party who stands on the fringe of a rather boisterous and drunken group. He stays close enough to enjoy what is being said, but for the benefit of the other guests he wears a satirical smile.

The poem's dramatic date is 43 or 42 B.C. When it was written is another question. The third line, which implies that the story is well known in Rome, points to a date after Horace's return from Philippi. Some critics have tried to fix a *terminus ante quem* on the assumption that the references to Caesar's murder and the subsequent proscriptions would have been unthinkable after the poet's introduction to Maecenas in 39 B.C. But then why was the poem ever published? Again, Heinze remarked that a short piece of this kind would have been preceded by a few longer works in the manner of Lucilius. Perhaps, but this doesn't help, because there may have been two or three other poems like 1. 2 which were not preserved in the collection. We are therefore left with a date some time between 40 and 35 B.C. I doubt if any greater precision is either possible or necessary.

What does matter is our estimate of the poem. I myself think it is a failure, and since Fraenkel (p. 118) admires 'its perfect neatness and easy poise' I had better give my reasons. First of all it is tiresome merely to be told that X is a brilliant raconteur and Y an incomparable wit. We must have evidence. Here we are offered only two specimens of Persius' talent and none at all of Rex's. It may be answered that the satire is simply a *chria* (or clever retort) inflated into a mock-heroic incident, and that therefore everything must be subordinated to the one climactic joke. This only proves that the basic idea was unworkable. By way of contrast consider Ovid's lament for Corinna's parrot (*Am.* 2. 6). The germ of this poem is provided by the dirge for Lesbia's sparrow (Catullus 3), but Ovid expands the idea into a successful burlesque 'by following the set form of a funeral elegy: the bidding to mourners (1–16); the regrets "Ah, what avails—" (17–24); the outburst against the powers responsible—σχετλιασμός— with a list of those who could have been better spared (25–42); the deathbed scene (43–8); the hopes of a suitable future life

(49–58); the committal (59–62)'.²² But whereas the death of a
bird has many aspects and lends itself to comic decoration, a
retort can only be simple and momentary. The difficulty is
reflected in the satire's structure. After an effective opening,
which prepares us for the clash of wits, Horace goes on to describe Persius and his rough tongue. Then comes a deliberately
ponderous transition *ad Regem redeo*. And what do we hear of
Rex? Nothing at all. Instead we have a lengthy and highly
wrought parenthesis designed to build up atmosphere. At v. 18
the construction is resumed without any sign of the story getting
under way, and in fact the poem is three-fifths over before the
first blow is struck. After all the fanfare and skirmishing the
knock-out punch comes as an anticlimax, and having paid for a
ringside seat we feel like demanding our money back.

I. 8

Though it resembles 1. 7 in being a tale of comic revenge, 1. 8
is a much superior work. One reason for this can be inferred from
the position of the revenge motif. Whereas in 1. 7 it is presented
in the second line, thus creating expectations which are never
properly fulfilled, in 1. 8 it does not appear until v. 44 (*non...
inultus*), where it heralds a surprising climax. The first part of 1. 8
is therefore more than prefatory material; the incidents and
observations exist in their own right. The opening is beautifully
concise:

> olim truncus eram ficulnus, inutile lignum,
> cum faber, incertus scamnum faceretne Priapum,
> maluit esse deum. deus inde ego...

> Once I was the trunk of a fig-tree—a useless lump of wood. Then the
> carpenter, in two minds whether to make me into a stool or a
> Priapus, decided that I should be a god; so a god I am.

After recounting his rather fortuitous birth Priapus goes on to
describe his distinguishing characteristic (a large vermilion member), his regalia (the sickle in his right hand and the split reed on

his head), his function (to frighten away thieves and birds) and his precinct (the gardens of Maecenas). This is the kind of information that might be given in a comic prologue—one thinks of Arcturus in Plautus' *Rudens*. And in fact Macrobius tells us (*Sat.* 6. 5. 6) that Priapus spoke the prologue in one of Afranius' comedies.

The opening lines also owe something to epigram. The *Greek Anthology* has several pieces in which an artifact speaks of its former mode of existence. Thus a bow remembers when it was a pair of horns (6. 113), a boat was once a pine-tree (9. 131), and a pen was once a reed (9. 162). Other relevant epigrams belong to the so-called *Priapea*.[23] This was originally a Hellenistic genre, but surviving specimens date from the beginning of the imperial age. Written mainly in elegiacs or hendecasyllables, they deal with various aspects of Priapus' worship, and they contain numerous references to his appearance and to his task, which was something between that of a head gardener and a scarecrow. Naturally enough, the personality which emerges is many-sided. Sometimes the god sounds like Catullus in splenetic mood; sometimes, like an elegant rake—perhaps one of Ovid's more disreputable friends; sometimes, as in no. 86, he becomes a kindly pastoral figure telling of the offerings he receives. But most often he is a clown who brags continually of the obscene outrage which he will visit upon thieves. The habit is most succinctly illustrated by no. 22, which is very much in the style of Martial:

femina si furtum faciet mihi virve puerve,
     haec cunnum, caput hic praebeat, ille nates,

which may be timidly paraphrased as 'If a woman or man or boy commits a theft, I shall punish each in the appropriate way'. From time to time, like all clowns, he is humiliated, and then his bluster subsides into querulous impotence, as in no. 55 where his sickle has been stolen and he is apprehensive of more serious losses.

But Priapus had not always been a buffoon. In Lampsacus, his place of origin, he was worshipped as the son of Dionysus and Aphrodite; he received the sacrifice of asses; his image appeared on the city's coins; and according to Pausanias (9. 31. 2) he was honoured above all other gods. From there his cult spread through the coastal towns of Asia Minor, where as well as promoting the fertility of crops and herds he also watched over fishing and navigation. In Greece Priapus blended with aspects of Hermes and Pan, and his adaptability is further proved by his admission to certain Orphic rites in which he was regarded as a symbol of regeneration. Perhaps the oddest episode in his history was the attempt of the gnostic Justinus to have him recognized as the first person of the Trinity. 'But the Good One is Priapus, who created before anything existed; whence he is called Priapus, because he first made all things.'[24] In spite of its absurd etymology the passage does bear witness to the resourcefulness of the old phallic god. For the most part, however, Priapus and his Italic forerunner Mutinus (Titinus) received a more primitive kind of respect. Their images were carried through the streets at public festivals; and Lactantius, Arnobius, and Augustine all speak of the custom whereby married women sat astride the god's member in the hope of joyful issue.[25]

After the official adoption of Christianity constant attempts were made to eradicate the older religion, but it continued to reappear with all the vigour and persistence of a weed. An eighth-century tract *Judicia Sacerdotalia De Criminibus* ordained bread and water for 'anyone who has chanted prayers to the phallus', and from then until the Synod of Tours in the fourteenth century the practice was regularly proscribed in ecclesiastical edicts. In certain areas the Church quietly compromised, and then history saw the emergence of that odd phenomenon, the phallic saint. The best known of several examples is Saint Foutin, whose name is apparently a corruption of Photinus, first bishop of Lyons. When the Protestants entered the church at Embrun in 1585 they found an object, alleged to be the saint's phallus, which had received numerous libations from women in need of help. His worship in the early seventeenth century is described by Pierre de L'Estoile as follows: 'Témoin Saint Foutin de Varailles en Provence, auquel sont dédiées les parties honteuses de l'un et de l'autre sexe, formées en cire: le plancher de la chapelle en est fort garni, et, quand le vent les fait entrebattre, cela débauche un peu les dévotions à l'honneur de ce Saint.' An even more recent priapic survival was the festival of Saint Cosmo and Saint Damian, described by Sir William Hamilton in a letter dated 30 December 1781. At this ceremony, which was held at Isernia in the Abruzzi, a brisk trade was done in votive offerings of the kind just described, and the healing oil of St Cosmo was either sold for private use or else applied by the priest. 'No less than 1400 flasks of that oil were either expended at the altar in unctions or charitably distributed... and as it is usual for everyone who either makes use of the oil at the altar, or carries off a flask of it, to leave an alms for St Cosmo, the ceremony of the oil becomes likewise a very lucrative one to the canons of the church.' On 26 July 1805 Isernia was destroyed by an earthquake.[26]

To revert to Horace's poem, Priapus tells us he is made of fig-wood—not unnaturally, since the fig was an emblem of fecundity, and the wood was cheap and easy to work.[27] His business is to protect the gardens which Maecenas is constructing outside the *agger* of Servius Tullius on the Esquiline Hill. As a result of the new landscaping 'the Esquiline is now a healthy place to live in, and one can stroll along the sunny Rampart'. Priapus' garden had not always been such a lovesome thing. Not long ago it had been the site of a paupers' cemetery, where corpses were carried out in cheap coffins and dumped into communal graves. Even now, when the transformation is almost complete, at night the macabre past takes over, and the place becomes a haunt of thieves, witches, and scavenging animals. Though worried at his inability to deal with the situation Priapus comforts himself with the memory of one glorious occasion on which he put the witches to rout and asserted his ancient power over sorcerers.[28]

The moon has just risen, when suddenly the air is filled with shrieking, a sound which exerts a magic control over the spirits of the dead.[29] Soon Canidia enters, along with her companion Sagana. Since one who binds another must not be bound,[30] she wears no shoes, and her hair is undone. Taking a lamb (black in colour, because destined for the powers of darkness) they tear it apart with their teeth and let the blood drip into a trench which they have scraped with their fingernails.[31] Their purpose in summoning the dead becomes more apparent at v. 30 with the mention of two dolls. The larger represents Canidia herself. It is made of wool (a powerful apotropaic material)[32] and is in the act of punishing a smaller figure of wax, which stands for the errant lover.[33] Sympathetic magic of this kind, where the victim's image is bound, pierced, and burnt, is familiar from all periods, but the best-known example in classical literature is the mime of Theocritus (*Id.* 2), where Simaetha's incantations are quoted at length, e.g.

ὡς τοῦτον τὸν κηρὸν ἐγὼ σὺν δαίμονι τάκω,
ὡς τάκοιθ' ὑπ' ἔρωτος ὁ Μύνδιος αὐτίκα Δέλφις.

As with the goddess's aid I melt this wax, so may Delphis the Mindian melt at once with love.[34]

The aim of Simaetha's spell is not to destroy Delphis, but to cause him unbearable anguish until he returns her love. Only if all else fails will she consign him to Hades. No doubt Canidia's purpose is much the same. Like Simaetha she invokes the aid of Hecate, while Sagana calls on the avenging Fury Tisiphone. The approach of these divinities is revealed by hell-hounds and serpents—a sight so dreadful that the moon hides her face behind the gravestones. All this is vouched for by Priapus in a suitably ordurous oath (37–9).

And now the ritual is reaching its climax. A wolf's beard and the tooth of a spotted snake are buried as a precaution against counter-spells, and finally the wax image is plunged into the fire. But at the very moment when the flame leaps up, Priapus is overcome with terror and breaks wind with a deafening explosion. The effect is immediate and shattering. The witches drop everything, and as they flee back to town in wild panic, herbs, love-knots, a chignon, and false teeth lie strewn in their wake.

Their discomfiture represents a dramatic reversal of roles. Instead of two fearsome witches with all hell at their command they are suddenly revealed as a pair of silly old hags. And as they scurry away they leave the god serenely in control, no longer a terrified spectator. It is in keeping, however, with Priapus' character that the catastrophe should be due not to any majestic assertion of *numen* but simply to muscular weakness. And this in turn may give us a clue to the origin of the poem; for when he was walking in Maecenas' gardens Horace may possibly have seen a wooden Priapus with an oddly warped posterior.[35] If so, the satire, as well as owing something to epigram and mime, will be in conception an aetiological poem.

Where official ceremonies were concerned, the Roman authorities were quite prepared to encourage a belief in magic. But they were less indulgent to witchcraft and astrology, which had an undesirable effect on the popular mind. Disapproval, however, was one thing, suppression another. In 33 B.C. magicians and astrologers were expelled from Rome on the orders of Agrippa (Dio 49. 43. 5). In A.D. 16 they had to be ejected once again.[36]

Among the upper classes many people professedly sceptical retained private superstitions. Julius Caesar, though 'never deterred or delayed from any enterprise by fear of the supernatural' (Suet. *Jul.* 59), used to repeat a certain charm three times after climbing into his carriage (Pliny, *NH* 28. 21). A deeper inconsistency is apparent in the work of the Elder Pliny, who can inveigh against *magicas vanitates* (*NH* 30. 1) and yet talk quite seriously about the marvellous virtue of Pyrrhus' big toe (*NH* 7. 20). However, it is safe to say that even if some of Horace's readers, like Maecenas himself, were not wholly free from superstition none of them would have had anything but contempt for a creature like Canidia. So too, in a more sceptical age, it is possible for a man who has read the evidence for psychic phenomena collected by G. N. M. Tyrell to feel that 'there may well be something in it', and yet to smile sarcastically at the gipsy palmist in the local fair.

On his evening stroll Horace himself would sometimes listen with amusement to the fortune-tellers outside the Circus (1. 6. 113–14). And on a later occasion he used the language of astrology in an effort to lift Maecenas from a bout of depression (*Carm.* 2. 17). But this does not mean that he ever paid serious attention to any kind of magic. I put it deliberately in this way, because (as with most of us) Horace's outlook is more a matter of pre-occupation than of doctrine. Instead of denying dogmatically that diseases could be cured by spells or that the future could be foretold, he preferred to convey his view of such beliefs by ignoring them. This healthy aversion to superstition was shared, as we might expect, by all the ancient satirists from Lucilius to Lucian. But in case we take such an attitude too much for granted we might consider the following extract, written by one of the most civilized men of the eighteenth century:

Three young ladies of our Town were on Saturday last indicted for Witchcraft. The witnesses against the First deposed upon Oath before Justice Bindover that she kept Spirits locked up in Vessels, which sometimes appeared in flames of blue Fire; that she used Magical Herbs, with some of which she drew in Hundreds of Men daily to her, who went out of her presence all inflamed, their mouths parched, and a hot Steam issuing from them, attended with a grievous Stench; that many of the said men were by force of that Herb metamorphos'd into Swine...It was proved against the second that she cut off by Night the Limbs from dead Bodies that were hang'd, and was seen to dig Holes in the Ground, to mutter some conjuring Words, and bury Pieces of the Flesh, after the usual Manner of Witches. The Third was accus'd for a notorious Piece of Sorcery...of moulding up Pieces of Dough into the Shapes of Men, Women, and Children; then heating them at a gentle Fire, which had a sympathetic Power to torment the Bowels of those in the Neighbourhood...But the Parson of our Parish, a strange refractory Man, will believe none of this...He goes about very oddly to solve the Matter. He supposes that, the First of these Ladies keeping a Brandy and Tobacco Shop, the Fellows went out smoaking, and got drunk towards Evening, and made themselves Beasts. He says the Second is a Butcher's Daughter, and sometimes brings a Quarter of Mutton from the Slaughter-house over Night against a Market-Day, and once buried a Bit of Beef in the Ground as a known Receipt to cure Warts on her hands.

The Parson affirms that the Third sells Gingerbread, which to please the Children she is forced to stamp with Images before 'tis baked, and if it burns their Guts, 'tis because they eat too much, or do not drink after it.

(*The Tatler*, 1, no. 21, 1709.)

A gay conceit; but Horace would not have asked his readers' indulgence for that bit of beef.

1. 9

This is an amusing account of how Horace, on his morning walk, fell into the clutches of one who has been variously described as 'an impertinent fellow', 'a forward coxcomb', and (more recently) 'a bore'. There is in fact no word which will include the garrulity, the conceit, the persistence, and the crass insensitivity of this social climber. Since, however, in the poem he is of equal importance with Horace himself, it is convenient to have some name for him; and so I shall call him 'the pest'.

Unlike Jonson's Crispinus, who with his red beard, little legs, and feathered cap was obviously Marston,[37] the pest has no individual features. His behaviour recalls certain characters of Theophrastus, such as The Chatterbox (ὁ ἀδολέσχης) and The Windbag (ὁ λάλος),[38] and also other Horatian figures like the *captator* of 2. 5. 32–7 who says:

Publius (susceptible gentlemen like the sound of their own first names), I admire your character and wish to be your friend. I know the ins and outs of the law and am a capable defence counsel. I'd lose a leg before I'd see you insulted or robbed of a nut-shell. I'll take care that no one swindles or makes a fool of you.

The pest, therefore, cannot be identified with any real person—least of all with Propertius, who was only in his teens at the time and whose mother was still alive.[39] Nevertheless, the poem was not simply the product of Horace's imagination. We know that he was envied for his intimacy with Maecenas and that he was sometimes accosted on the street by people in search of inside information. No doubt there were many who would have been glad to share his success, and it may well be that a genuine incident, in which the humorous Aristius Fuscus was involved,[40] provided the germ of the present poem. But having undertaken the work Horace immediately thought of the general type of person he was going to portray, and this led him to literature as well as life. His mind drew naturally from both sources and in the final product the ingredients cannot be distinguished.

The action of the piece may be described as a miniature drama. In each of the first three scenes Horace's attempts to escape end in frustration and despair. Early on he quickens his pace, stops, talks to his servant, and then starts off again. He even speaks of visiting a sick friend who lives two miles away on the other side of the river. But it is no good. The pest is a man of relentless energy and is prepared to go the whole way with him. Scene 1 ends with Horace's resistance broken (20). Scene 2 at once reveals that the pest is not really interested in exercise and casual conversation. He has a more sinister purpose in mind, namely friendship. Apart from one rather feeble interruption in vv. 26–7[41] Horace can only brood on the awfulness of this discovery. Hope flickers for a moment at the mention of a lawsuit which was due to be heard that morning,[42] but the pest decides to let the case go by default, and the pair walk on (43). So ends scene 2. As Heinze points out, the motif of the lawsuit which eventually leads to Horace's escape is introduced exactly half way through the poem; but here it only makes his plight seem worse, because it shows that the pest is willing to make serious sacrifices in order to achieve his purpose. The ultimate nature of this purpose, when revealed in scene 3, represents a further humiliation for the poet. Up to this he could console himself with the illusion that he himself was the coveted prize. It now becomes clear that he is merely a pawn and that Maecenas is the fellow's real objective. Thus after first intruding on Horace's privacy the man has now wounded his *amour propre*. Nor does the new discovery in any way improve Horace's position. The final objective may lie farther back, but he himself is still in the front line. It is therefore with immense relief that he sights reinforcements in the person of his friend Aristius Fuscus. But Fuscus turns traitor. Horace's hopes are again dashed, and the scene closes leaving him a helpless and deserted victim (74). But if the poet is beyond all human aid he has not been forsaken by his patron deity. From the beginning Apollo has watched the encounter, and he now intervenes by bringing the pest face to face with his accuser. The drama which began with one act of seizure (*arrepta manu*) ends with another (*rapit in ius*). Deliverance has come.

The satire's variety of incident is reflected in its means of communication. On the most simple level we have Horace himself relating the event to his friends. This narrative mode is of course implied throughout the poem, but it never exists for long by itself. Half way through the fourth line it becomes overlaid with dialogue. I say overlaid rather than supplanted, because although *suaviter, ut nunc est* in v. 5 is spoken to the pest, it is overheard by Horace's audience. A further degree of complexity is introduced in vv. 11 and 12. The words *o te, Bolane, cerebri | felicem!* are provoked by the pest, but they are not spoken to him. They are a private exclamation of the poet's; and yet they are not entirely private, for in a sense they are addressed to Bolanus. At v. 28 we find the same situation. *Felices! nunc ego resto. | confice* is a silent prayer occasioned by the pest's reply in the previous line. But again it cannot be called wholly private, since in form it is a command directed to the pest. Then, still further within this inner context, we have the words of the fortune-teller (31–4). And so the old gipsy is inside a private thought of Horace's which was caused by the pest and was intended ultimately for the poet's audience. When we add to these complexities the power of Apollo who can impose his will without words at all, we realize how many modes of discourse are included in the poem.

These modes are related to another aspect of the satire's variety, namely its variety of language. We know from Lucilius that *ibam forte*—'I happened to be going'—was quite a normal way of introducing a story. He has *ibat forte aries* (W. 559) and *ibat*

76

forte domum (W. 258). The phrase strikes the right casual note, and here it is continued by *nescioquid nugarum*—'some trifle or other'. So the reader is prepared for a piece of light-hearted narrative. If it is to be light it must also be rapid, an effect achieved by asyndeton and ellipse, and by using the historic infinitive and the historic present. Rhythm also plays its part. In v. 9 we can hear Horace accelerating in the dactyls *ire modo ocius*, slowing down in the molossus *interdum*, and coming to a halt with *consistere*. The language is enlivened by colloquialisms like *misere* (8)—'desperately'—a usage common in Plautus and Terence,[43] *cerebri* (11) which has the sense of 'temper' only in Plautus and Petronius,[44] and *garrio* (13)—'I chatter'—which, apart from half a dozen passages of comedy, is mostly limited to Cicero's letters. Still confining ourselves to the narrative, let us look at *ventum erat* in v. 35. Now there is nothing peculiar in this form being preferred to *venimus*,[45] but can it be pure chance that the actual encounter is never once described in the first person plural? Does it not look as if the poet is avoiding even a grammatical association with his adversary? True, the satire does contain two cases of the first person plural, but notice where they come. In v. 48 Horace says *non isto vivimus illic/quo tu rere modo*; here *vivimus* refers to Maecenas and his friends and *tu* only confirms the pest's exclusion. In v. 62 we find *consistimus*, but, as the subsequent dialogue shows, this means Fuscus and Horace. There is still no *rapport* between the poet and his tormentor.

Instead of analysing the dialogue in the same way I would simply point to certain colloquial expressions which can be readily paralleled from the comic writers and Cicero's letters: v. 5—*suaviter* (nicely), *ut nunc est* (at the moment), *cupio omnia quae vis* (all the best); v. 6—*numquid vis?* (nothing else, is there?); v. 38—*interenim* (confound me); v. 41—*sodes* (please); v. 53—*sic habet* (that's the way it is). These phrases are all spoken by Horace. The pest's language is on the same stylistic level, but its familiarity is more abrasive in view of his position: v. 4—*quid agis dulcissime rerum?* (how are things, my dear fellow?); v. 38—*si me amas*

77

(be a pal); v. 43—*quomodo tecum?* (how do you find him?); v. 47—*hunc hominem* (yours truly), *dispeream* (damn me); v. 52—*magnum narras* (a tall story). Such phrases delineate character like the strokes of a cartoonist's pencil. Rhythm also has its contribution to make, as when in v. 42 we are told that the pest walked on in front—*et praecedere coepit.* This hexameter ending, coming as it does in the first half of the line, has an air of finality and marks the second phase of the pest's victory. Or again, consider the two rhyming molossi in the middle of vv. 57 and 58—*corrumpam* and *desistam.* Here we have a statement of the pest's determination—a statement reiterated by the following *quaeram, occurram, deducam,* and completed by the old maxim 'if at first you don't succeed, try, try again'.

The *sermo cotidianus* represents one element in the poem's stylistic structure. But this only attains full significance when set beside another element which exists, as it were, on a higher emotional plane. In v. 26 Horace asks whether the pest has any next of kin. 'Not one,' he answers, 'I have buried them all.' *Felices! nunc ego resto,* cries Horace. 'Happy for them! Now I remain.' With the word *felices* we are at once transported to the realm of epic suffering. In *Odyssey* 5. 306 the storm-tossed hero exclaims:

τρισμάκαρες Δαναοὶ καὶ τετράκις οἳ τότ' ὄλοντο.

Thrice blessed, yea four times blessed are the Danaans who perished at that time.

And Aeneas has a similar cry (*Aen.* 1. 94). From the epic we pass easily to the oracular. Horace's doom is closing in, a doom predicted by an old fortune-teller many years before. The lines have a stately ring and should not be reduced to Christmas-card doggerel:

hunc neque dira venena nec hosticus auferet ensis,
nec laterum dolor aut tussis, nec tarda podagra;
garrulus hunc quando consumet cumque: loquaces,
si sapiat, vitet, simul atque adoleverit aetas.   (31–4)

Not deadly poison, no, nor foeman's hand,
nor pleurisy nor cough nor slow-foot gout
shall slay him; at some moment heaven has planned
a chatterbox will surely wear him out.
On reaching manhood let him keep this rule:
never to wait and hear a babbling fool.

Dirus perhaps never lost that aura of dread which made it such a natural epithet for Hannibal. *Hosticus* is an archaic word used by Plautus in a passage of urgent entreaty,[46] and by the tragedian Accius.[47] Varro (*LL* 5. 33) says that the phrase *hosticus ager* belonged to the official language of augurs. The one other Horatian instance occurs in *Carm.* 3. 2. 6—a passage of decidedly epic tone. Of *ensis* it is enough to say that Virgil uses it sixty times more often than *gladius*, whereas Livy uses *gladius* ninety times more often than *ensis*. We are struck by the semi-active sense of *tarda* and by its application to *podagra*. The phrase may derive comic overtones from a disreputable passage of Catullus (71. 2). The unusual use of *consumo* in the active with a personal subject seems to imply that the pest is a kind of wasting disease. 'Sooner or later' is not the normal sense of *quando cumque*, and Fraenkel calls attention to 'the archaizing tmesis' and 'the oracular mystery of the date'.[48] The same scholar has also illustrated the ominous significance of *vitet.*

In v. 54 the style rises again with the aid of a military metaphor. 'Such is your valour', says Horace with heavy sarcasm, 'that you will take Maecenas by storm. He is open to conquest; that is why he makes the outer approaches so difficult.' It is not the first time that the metaphor has appeared. It previously emerged in vv. 42–3, and before that it was implicit in such words as *occupo* (6), *consistere* (9), and *persequar* (16). Moreover, it does not fade out at v. 56; it continues in words like *eriperet* (65) and *fugit* (73), and it winds up the whole piece in v. 78, for *sic me servavit Apollo* ('thus did Apollo save me') is an imitation of Homer's τὸν δ᾽ ἐξήρπαξεν Ἀπόλλων, which describes how Apollo rescued Hector from the onslaught of Achilles (*Il.* 20. 443). Thus

79

the entire action may be seen as a running fight between Horace and his assailant.[49]

Between the worlds of conversation and heroic action lies a third which has affinities with both—I mean the world of civil law. Immediately after the gipsy's warning (35) the scene changes to the temple of Vesta and the law-courts, where proceedings have already been in progress for an hour. The pest must answer bail (*respondere vadato*) or else lose his case (*perdere litem*); he asks Horace to accompany him (*ades*), but Horace is unqualified to appear as a party (*stare*) and is ignorant of civil law (*civilia iura*). So the pest fails to present himself at the hearing (*relinquere rem*). Later in the poem, again after a moment of crisis (74), the law appears and takes charge of proceedings. The *adversarius* calls Horace as a witness (*licet antestari?*). Horace allows his ear to be touched as a sign of consent, and the pest is hustled off to court (*rapit in ius*). Civil law, as we all know, is a very mundane affair. Its material is depressingly human, its methods patient, prosaic, and exasperatingly tedious. But it has also another aspect, one which is attested by its formal ritual and its solemn, archaic language. I mean law as the preserver of civilized traditions and the guarantee of moral principles; law as Dike daughter of Zeus. This dual aspect of civil law becomes plain in the satire's conclusion. For although the *adversarius* is acting in his own interests, he is also the agent of a higher power. If he comes on the scene *casu* (74), it is the sort of chance that brought Oedipus to the cross-roads. But this time Apollo is bent on salvation, not on ruin; and so the drama turns out to be a comedy after all.

This poem, with its amusing tension between the appalling and the trivial, will always be a general favourite. As a condemnation of sycophancy and bad manners it also implies a moral judgement of universal validity. But to the Roman reader it must have given an additional pleasure, moving as it does among the familiar streets and buildings of the capital. The Sacra Via, Vesta's temple, Caesar's Gardens, and the Trastevere all receive special mention. Other sites are included by implication in *vicos* (13). Very little is known of the Sacra Via's topography at this period, but if the satire belongs to the year 36 or 35 B.C. then on coming through the Fornix Fabianus the two men could have seen the restored Regia with its white marble gleaming in the morning sunshine.[50] They might also have seen work in progress on the Basilica Aemilia,[51] and since the pest extended his praise so as to include the whole city we may imagine him becoming enthusiastic about other buildings under construction at the time, such as the temple of Apollo Palatinus, and possibly the Villa Publica.[52]

After noting the poem's universal appeal and the particular charm which it held for the Roman reader, we must take one step closer and discuss what it meant to Horace's friends, for in a sense this poem, like I. 5, is the document of a coterie. We do not have to review the whole course of Horace's friendship with Maecenas, but it is important to remember that in its early years at least it was by no means a simple spontaneous relationship. As their temperamental sympathy asserted itself the tension caused by class consciousness relaxed, and instead of being merely a member of his patron's retinue Horace gradually became an *amicus* in the fullest sense of the word. But it was not an easy process; it required tact on both sides, and it put Horace in a delicate position not only as a man but also as a writer. How was he to address his patron and his other distinguished friends without sounding either rude or obsequious? One answer was to tackle the problem boldly as in I. 6. That poem, with its series of qualified statements, is a skilful piece of balancing, and like all good balancing it looks effortless from a distance. But the feat was difficult to sustain, and it could not easily be varied or repeated.

There was, however, a more oblique method, which allowed many variations and was well suited to Horace's genius. As an illustration we may take I. 9. 48–50, where the circle of Maecenas is said to be free from internal rivalries:

> non isto vivimus illic
> quo tu rere modo; domus hac nec purior ulla est
> nec magis his aliena malis.

We do not live there in the fashion which you have in mind. No
household is cleaner than his and more free from such low intrigues.

This compliment is not addressed to Maecenas, and we are made
to feel that it might never have been uttered had it not been for
the vulgar insinuations of the pest (45–8). One is reminded of the
close of 1. 10, where by naming his opponents and revealing
their malicious attitude Horace is enabled to affirm his respect for
Maecenas, Messalla, Pollio, and the rest.

Or consider vv. 22–3:

> si bene me novi, non Viscum pluris amicum,
> non Varium facies.

If I'm any judge, you will not think more highly of Viscus or of
Varius as a friend.

This shows the very high place held by Viscus and Varius in the
poet's affections, and it must have given pleasure to the men concerned; the words, however, are spoken not by Horace but by
the pest, and so their testimony is strengthened by appearing to
come from an outside witness.

Again, the affirmation may be masked by ironic banter, as in
the episode of Aristius Fuscus (60–74). 'Ah,' says Horace, 'here
comes dear old Fuscus (carus). He'll help me to get rid of this
nuisance.' But Fuscus does nothing of the sort. With a mad-
dening smile he turns a deaf ear to Horace's appeals, and runs
away leaving the poet at the point of death. *Fugit improbus*—the
'dear friend' has suddenly become a scoundrel. Fuscus would
have taken this abuse very happily, because it confirmed the
effectiveness of his joke. In fact I should imagine that with the
possible exception of Maecenas no one enjoyed the poem more
than Fuscus. It may seem rather naïve that a man should take
pleasure in being mentioned in a *sermo* of this kind, but we should
remember that later on the emperor himself was not too proud to
ask for a similar favour.[53]

Maecenas and his friends knew very well that this was their
poem. Not only were they the object of the pest's endeavours,
but without them the whole episode would have been incon-

ceivable. As they listened to Horace's account of the fellow's efforts to ingratiate himself their amusement must have been spiced with a dash of self-congratulation. Secure in their own eminence they could smile on the antics of the social climber and enjoy that 'sudden glory' which Hobbes saw as the very essence of laughter. No one is pained by flattery when it is offered with such tact, and it may be assumed that Horace's friends liked him all the more for inviting them to admire themselves.

A lack of self-knowledge produces comic as well as tragic figures. Part of the fun in this satire comes from the pest's failure to recognize his own absurdity. An especially neat touch occurs in vv. 23–5, where he boasts of his facility in versification and of his prowess as a singer and dancer—arts which his listener happened to despise. Notice too the way in which Horace turns the pest's mistakes to his own advantage. It was impudent of the fellow to imagine that by accosting Horace in the street and forcing his company on him he could obtain even a casual acquaintance. So much is made clear in the first twenty lines. It follows that for such a man to covet the esteem enjoyed by Viscus and Varius was nothing short of grotesque. By implication, therefore, Horace arrays himself alongside his friends, and in doing so affirms the solidarity and exclusiveness of the group. It is clear throughout that the pest's attentions are inspired not by a genuine liking and respect, but by *invidia*.[54] Such *invidia*, however, is an index of Horace's success. The point is still plainer if we think in terms of *ambitio*. In vv. 56–60 the pest shows his mettle:

> haud mihi dero:
> muneribus servos corrumpam; non, hodie si
> exclusus fuero, desistam; tempora quaeram;
> occurram in triviis; deducam. nil sine magno
> vita labore dedit mortalibus.

I shan't be found wanting. I'll bribe his servants; and if the door is shut in my face to-day I shan't give up. I'll bide my time, contrive meetings in the streets, escort him home. If at first you don't succeed, try, try again.

Such an attitude sharpens the contrast between the two men; for Horace did not approach Maecenas directly, and when he was introduced he gave a simple account of his background, leaving it to others to praise his abilities.

The satire, therefore, contains a note of pride, which Horace would have cheerfully acknowledged. We can call it complacency if we like, but then we have to ask why no one finds it offensive. The answer, it seems to me, lies in the oblique, ironic approach which we have been studying. As David Daiches has observed: 'Irony and paradox are important because they are devices for including or at least taking account of all attitudes which threaten the one assumed by the poet in the poem.'[55] Horace's pride in his social success is threatened by the accusation of pretentiousness. He counters this by laughing at himself, appearing in turn as the harassed soldier, the dejected prisoner, and the helpless victim. Though proud and content in being a member of Maecenas' circle, he does not claim a position of absolute equality:

> nil mi officit, inquam,
> ditior hic aut est quia doctior; est locus uni
> cuique suus. (50-2)

It does me no harm, I assure you, that this man is richer or more learned than I; each has his own place.

So too in the final episode, although we are reminded of the poet's special status as the favourite of Apollo, we cannot grudge him his release, for by now he is a broken man. After v. 71 he no longer tries to control the course of events, and he appears to be just as surprised as we are at his miraculous escape.

This ironical technique clearly allows a greater tightness and economy. Whereas in 1. 6 Horace's ambiguous position had to be defined by carefully worded assertions and denials, in 1. 9 the qualifications are, as it were, built into the statement, and so a multiple effect is obtained. In the end, however, it is wrong to speak wholly in terms of 'devices' and 'techniques', for while there was no doubt an element of calculation in the writing of the poem, such an effort would have been quite futile had not the tact and wit been spontaneous projections of the poet's nature. So when we have finished our scrutiny, we should in fairness to Horace remove the poem from under the microscope and read it straight through from beginning to end. That, after all, was how Maecenas heard it.

CHAPTER IV

HORACE AND LUCILIUS

1. 4, 1. 10, 2. 1

In the hands of Ennius, its first known exponent, literary *satura* was an informal medley in which the author moralized in various metres on various aspects of life and society. The tradition was carried on by Ennius' nephew Pacuvius, and was then taken over and transformed by Gaius Lucilius, a wealthy knight from Suessa Aurunca on the borders of Campania and Latium. Lucilius began his satires about 133 B.C. after returning from the Spanish wars, and he continued to write until his death in Naples in 102. He started off like Ennius by using iambic and trochaic metres as well as the dactylic hexameter, but after a few years' experimentation he settled on the hexameter as being the most suitable vehicle for his purpose. This was an important decision for the future of the form.

But if he narrowed the metrical range of Ennius' miscellany Lucilius enlarged its scope in keeping with his personality. Meagre as they are, the thirteen hundred fragments bear witness to his multifarious experience and insatiable curiosity. Sailing and horsemanship, phonetics and orthography, medicine, cookery, politics, and sex—everything came within his province. Artistically he was often careless, but he compensated for this fault by an immense gusto of the kind which a modern reader associates with Rabelais. This wide-ranging energy, however, was very much an individual trait. Lucilius' main contribution to the development of *satura* lay in a more specialized area, namely that of censure and ridicule. Taking advantage of his position as a friend of Scipio Aemilianus he gave free rein to his pugnacious temperament, attacking Scipio's political enemies, his own literary opponents, and anyone he happened to dislike. We cannot tell how large a proportion of his writing was devoted to polemic; it is certain that later authors like Persius and Juvenal give a false picture by concentrating exclusively on this aspect of his work. Nevertheless, the vigorous criticism which he employed was regarded by his successors as an essential feature of the genre. In this personal sense it was Lucilius who made *satura* satirical.

After his death interest in Lucilius continued. His two friends Laelius Archelaus and Vettius Philocomus lectured on his satires, and their pupils included men like Pompeius Lenaeus and Valerius Cato.[1] Lenaeus, as his first name shows, was a freedman of Pompey, and when Pompey was attacked by Sallust after his death Lenaeus hit back in defence of his patron, calling Sallust 'a lecher, a glutton, a wastrel, and a boozer'.[2] Cato also put his Lucilian studies to good use in a short pamphlet entitled *Indignatio*, which affirmed the freedom of his birth and gave a spirited reply to his detractors.[3] The more academic side of Cato's work is attested by the eight lines prefixed to Horace's tenth satire, in which Cato is said to be preparing an edition of Lucilius' poems. Other work on Lucilius was done by Curtius Nicias, who like Lenaeus was a client of Pompey;[4] and it seems that one commentator specialized in Lucilius' fishes—traces of his monograph appear in Varro's *De Lingua Latina*.[5] Varro also speaks of Lucius Abuccius, a highly educated man whose books were written 'in the Lucilian style' (*Luciliano charactere*).[6] We do not know how closely Varro himself followed Lucilius in his four books of *Satires*, but Lucilian influence was certainly apparent in the lampoon written by Cicero's friend Trebonius against Mark Antony (*Fam.* 12. 16. 3) and presumably also in the poems by Varro of Atax mentioned by Horace in 1. 10. 46.

To Horace, who may well have read him at school, Lucilius ranked as the *inventor* of satire (1. 10. 48). It is hard to say how fair this was to Ennius. If we had more material the differences between the two poets indicated above might stand out more strongly; or possibly Horace saw the differences as greater than they really were. In any case the fact remains that Horace never mentions Ennius as a satirist. He also ignores Varro, who in addition to his four books of *Satires* had written 150 books of *Menippean Satires*—a form which contained a mixture of prose and verse. As far as we can judge from his fragments, Varro had only a very minor influence on Horace's work.

By taking up the Lucilian tradition Horace put himself in an awkward situation. In 39 B.C. as a pardoned Republican and a man of no social consequence he could not afford to give indiscriminate offence, and even if he toned down the inventor's polemic there would always be people who disapproved of satire on principle. In spite of this he wrote the diatribe on adultery (1. 2)—a work of courage as well as craftsmanship. It was read by people for whom it was not primarily intended and, predictably, complaints were made.[7] Horace therefore resolved to write another poem, justifying his activity as a satirist and setting out the main features of the genre as he saw it. This involved a further hazard, for any modification of satire whether in style or content would necessitate some criticism of Lucilius, and there were men in Rome (some of them quite influential in the world of letters) who would not relish criticism of this kind. Horace knew who they were and was undeterred by the prospect of their displeasure. The satire in question (1. 4) opens with these words:

The poets Eupolis, Cratinus, and Aristophanes, and the other men who constitute the Old Comedy, used to brand with great freedom anyone who deserved to be portrayed as a blackguard and a thief, a lecher or a cut-throat, or as notorious in any other way. Lucilius derives entirely from them, having followed them in every respect except rhythm and metre. He was witty and keen-scented, but harsh in his versification. This was where his fault lay. As a *tour de force* he would often dictate two hundred lines an hour standing on his head. He was a muddy river from which you would wish certain things removed. A man of many words, he was reluctant to take the trouble of writing —writing properly, that is; as for quantity, I care nothing for that.

Lucilius and Aristophanes are associated here in three general respects. First, and most important, both were quick to detect vice (*emunctae naris*—'keen-scented'—in v. 8 corresponds to the critical vigour of Old Comedy); secondly, both were amusing

88

(*facetus*—'witty'—in v. 7 recalls *comoedia* in v. 2); thirdly, both wrote poetry (*versus* in v. 8 harks back to *poetae* in v. 1). Within the last category we have a contrast, for Lucilius abandoned the metres of Old Comedy and he was also harsher in his composition. But in spite of his inferior craftsmanship and polish we are still meant to think of Lucilius as a poet.[8] So far as general influence is concerned, we may be pretty sure that, although there is nothing in the fragments to prove it, Lucilius had read the old comic poets.[9] In that case he must have admired their courage and wit. The dramatic techniques which he himself employed in the *Council of the Gods* (W. 5 ff.) may well have owed something to Old Comedy, and would not the *Frogs* have fascinated the man who, as Pliny says (*NH* Praef. 7), was the first Roman with a nose for style?

The problem here is not that Lucilius is compared to Aristophanes and the rest, or even that some general influence is discerned, but rather that he is said to 'derive entirely from' Old Comedy (*omnis pendet...mutatis tantum pedibus numerisque*). This, of course, is an absurd over-simplification, ignoring as it does not only the various Hellenistic influences on Lucilius' work but also its characteristically Roman flavour. To account for this some scholars have suggested that Horace did not know the facts—an incredible idea.[10] Others, like Leo, have thought he was paying a discreet compliment to Varro,[11] who is supposed (with some reason) to have held theories of this kind.[12] But even if Leo's view were correct it would not explain the function of the passage within the satire as a whole. The only satisfactory answer is to regard the lines as a piece of special pleading in which Horace exaggerates the dependence of Lucilius on Old Comedy in order to claim that Aristophanes, Lucilius, and himself are all links in the same illustrious tradition. This should warn us against taking the rest of the poem as a dispassionate, carefully balanced essay in literary theory.

In justifying his satire against the charge of malice Horace makes the following points: Old Comedy and Lucilius branded criminals (1–7); unlike Crispinus I write very little (17–18); unlike Fannius

I do not seek publicity (21-3); the innocent have nothing to fear (67-8); I do not intend my poems to be sold, nor do I give public recitations (71-4); real malice is something quite different—it means backbiting one's friends and spreading scandal (81-103); I was taught to notice wicked behaviour by my father; he used individuals simply as examples of different vices (103-31); I am really quite a good-humoured fellow (91-2, 103-4); my observations are for my own improvement (137-8); and my writings are just an amusing pastime (138-9). He then concludes the piece with a disarming smile (140-3).

It is clear from this summary that Horace at no time denies that his poems may have an aggressive tone; nor does he give any guarantee for the future. His evasive tactics can be seen in the opening passage quoted above. After hearing of Lucilius' wit and his keen nose, we expect Horace to clarify his own position in regard to personal attack. Instead he swerves aside to discuss the question of style. The same thing happens later on (33 ff.). Because people in general are prone to wickedness 'they dread verses and detest poets' (*metuunt versus, odere poetas*). To them the poet is a savage creature. 'Whatever he has smeared on his pages he will be eager to tell to all the people as they come home from the bakehouse and water-tank—servants and old women alike.' 'Well now,' says Horace, 'listen to a few words in reply. First of all, I shall exclude myself from those whom I would count as poets.' (In other words 'you may hate poets, but you shouldn't hate me; for I'm no poet'.) He then goes on to contrast the plain style of satire with the 'true poetry' of epic, thus evading the charge of malice by a quibble. The question is raised again in vv. 64-5: 'Are you right to regard this genre with suspicion?' In answer Horace says that the innocent are quite safe from the attacks of the soap-box orators Caprius and Sulcius. He then quickly adds 'Even if you are like the highwaymen Caelius and Birrius, I would not be like Caprius and Sulcius'. And where is the difference? 'No shop or stall would ever have my books exposed to the sweaty hands of Hermogenes Tigellius and the rest of the mob.' But what happens if some of the poems find their way outside Horace's own circle? We are not told. Nor does Horace give any firm undertaking that he will abstain from forthright censure. Rather the reverse. 'If I am a little outspoken in the future...remember that I got the habit from my father' (103–5). That may be an excuse; it is certainly not a promise.

Another point often overlooked is that 1. 4 carries no condemnation of Lucilius' spirit. In the opening lines we are told that the types of criminal portrayed by Old Comedy (and Lucilius) *deserved* to be shown up. There is no suggestion of disapproval until *durus componere versus* (8). This is made clear by the *nam* in v. 9, which explains the abrupt transition from praise to blame, and also by the emphatic *hoc*—'it was here that his fault lay'. Finally there is the statement in 1. 10. 3–4 that Lucilius had been *praised* in this earlier passage 'for scouring the city with plenty of wit'. It is sometimes maintained that in the reference to Caprius and Sulcius (65 ff.) Horace is criticizing Lucilius.[13] But there is no need to bring Lucilius into that passage at all. Caprius and Sulcius represent the most vulgar type of pamphleteer; and in any case even they cause no anxiety to the innocent. In vv. 86–90 Horace complains that the sort of person who calls him malicious is often prepared to traduce his own friends and to laugh at the jokes of the drunken parasite. Here too some scholars think that in the parasite, who makes insulting remarks about the guests and even about the host himself, we are intended to see a picture of Lucilius.[14] This I am unwilling to believe. In v. 90, immediately after the description of the parasite, we read:

hic tibi comis et urbanus liberque videtur.

That's the kind of man *you* regard as genial, witty, and frank.

Since 'you' refers to Horace's opponent, it follows that in Horace's opinion the parasite is *not* witty and frank; but according to the opening lines Lucilius *is*. If Horace has already justified himself by appealing to the example of Lucilius, he would hardly allude to him in the same poem as a malicious buffoon.

91

Why, then, is Horace not more explicit? It seems that he wanted to leave himself free to develop various lines of defence. If he identified himself too warmly with the censorious ridicule of Old Comedy and Lucilius he could not pose as a timid spirit anxious to avoid offence (17–18), and the influence of his father (103–29) would become a factor of minor importance. On the other hand he could not simply disavow the Lucilian spirit, partly because 1. 2 (and perhaps other pieces) had shown its influence, partly because he wanted to reserve the right to make personal attacks if he saw fit, and above all because he was writing satire—and satire without ridicule was like comedy without humour. For these reasons he declined to elaborate the distinctions which really did exist between Lucilius' outlook and his own.[15]

The problem of style was more straightforward. Although in certain quarters Lucilius was still regarded as the prince of satirists, Horace could see no reason why the genre should be associated with slapdash writing, and so in vindicating his own approach he says quite frankly that Lucilius was harsh and careless in his composition and that he wrote too much (8–13). Later on (39 ff.) he indicates the place which satire should occupy in the hierarchy of poetic kinds. If you claim, he says, that my satire is not great poetry I quite agree with you. The same is true of Lucilius. His verses, like mine, are more in the nature of metrical prose. In this respect, as well as in its subject-matter, satire has affinities with comedy. Even in its angry scenes the diction of comedy (and here we are to think of New Comedy) stays close to everyday speech, it does not rise to the heights of true poetry, whereas the sonorous and elevated language of Ennius would remain poetic even if his metre were destroyed.

As Horace no doubt foresaw, these remarks annoyed the champions of Lucilius. Rallying to the defence of their favourite, they stressed the colour and vigour of his style and affirmed that he had a genial and sophisticated wit. Since Lucilius had now been brought to the forefront of the controversy, Horace felt obliged to amplify and, where necessary, modify his earlier statements.

And so he composed the second of the 'literary' satires, namely
1. 10. The poem begins as follows:

> nempe incomposito dixi pede currere versus
> Lucili. quis tam Lucili fautor inepte est
> ut non hoc fateatur? at idem, quod sale multo
> urbem defricuit, charta laudatur eadem.
> nec tamen hoc tribuens dederim quoque cetera: nam sic
> et Laberi mimos ut pulchra poemata mirer.
> ergo non satis est risu diducere rictum
> auditoris: et est quaedam tamen hic quoque virtus:
> est brevitate opus, ut currat sententia, neu se
> 10 impediat verbis lassas onerantibus auris;
> et sermone opus est modo tristi, saepe iocoso,
> defendente vicem modo rhetoris atque poetae,
> interdum urbani, parcentis viribus atque
> extenuantis eas consulto. ridiculum acri
> fortius et melius magnas plerumque secat res.
> illi scripta quibus comoedia prisca viris est
> hoc stabant, hoc sunt imitandi: quos neque pulcher
> Hermogenes umquam legit, neque simius iste
> nil praeter Calvum et doctus cantare Catullum.

True enough, I did say that Lucilius' verses lurched awkwardly
along. Who is so perverse an admirer of Lucilius as not to admit
this? But he is also praised on the very same page for scouring the
city with plenty of caustic wit. While allowing him this quality,
however, I would not grant him the others as well; for then I should
have to admire the mimes of Laberius as beautiful poems. So it is not
enough to make your listener bare his teeth in a grin—though there
is some virtue even in that. You need terseness, so that the thought
may run freely on and not become tangled in a mass of verbiage which
will weigh heavily on the listener's ear. You also need a style which is
sometimes severe, sometimes gay, taking the role now of an orator
and poet, now of a clever talker who keeps his strength in reserve and
carefully rations it out. Great issues are usually resolved more forcefully and more effectively by wit than by castigation. This was the
mainstay of the men who wrote Old Comedy; this is what makes
them worth imitating—men who have never been read by the pretty
Hermogenes or by that ape whose only artistic accomplishment is to
croon Calvus and Catullus.

Horace therefore stands by his criticisms of Lucilius' style, but modifies what he said about his tone. While granting that Lucilius was witty, he now maintains that his wit was too often harsh and vulgar. This is a less favourable estimate than that given in 1. 4, where Lucilius was called frank and witty. But as we can see from the usage of Cicero the terms *liber* and *facetus* had considerable flexibility;[16] and so Horace could argue that his two judgements were quite consistent. 'I said Aristophanes and Lucilius both used *libertas*. So they did. But the *libertas* of Lucilius was apt to degenerate into abuse. I also said Aristophanes and Lucilius were both *faceti*. So they were. But the *facetiae* of Lucilius tended too often to be crude and hurtful. Admittedly Aristophanes and the others were not wholly free from these defects, but their lapses were less frequent and should certainly not be imitated.' The tenth satire, which contains the fullest exposition of Horace's literary theory so far, shows that he no longer needs the protection of Lucilius. He can stand on his own feet.

The rest of the poem is about style. In v. 20 an opponent commends Lucilius for producing an agreeable blend of Latin and Greek. That, replies Horace, was no great achievement; Pitholeon of Rhodes did as much. When men use language for a serious purpose, as in the law-courts, they invariably speak pure Latin. The same should apply to satire:

> scilicet oblitus patriaeque patrisque Latini,
> cum Pedius causas exsudet Publicola atque
> Corvinus, patriis intermiscere petita
> verba foris malis, Canusini more bilinguis? (27–30)

Whereas Pedius Publicola and Messalla Corvinus sweat out their cases, you I suppose would forget about your fatherland and father Latinus and would sooner interlard your fathers' speech with foreign importations like a two-tongued Canusian?

Horace himself had once tried his hand at Greek verses, but had been deterred by Romulus, who (he says) appeared in a dream and warned him of his folly. Now he writes only Latin. Unlike

94

the swollen Alpman (*turgidus Alpinus*) he prefers a modest style, and his pieces are not intended for recitation in any public contest (36–9).

When Horace began his career as a poet the main genres were capably represented: Virgil was writing pastoral, Fundanius comedy, and so on. Satire appeared to be the only area in which development was possible. This did not mean that Horace ranked himself above Lucilius. As a pioneer the latter had a place of special distinction, but stylistically he left much to be desired, whether because of his nature or his material.[17] Certainly, whatever his merits, he would have written more carefully had he been born a hundred years later:

> fuerit Lucilius, inquam,
> comis et urbanus, fuerit limatior idem
> quam rudis et Graecis intacti carminis auctor,
> quamque poetarum seniorum turba: sed ille,
> si foret hoc nostrum fato dilatus in aevum,
> detereret sibi multa, recideret omne quod ultra
> perfectum traheretur, et in versu faciendo
> saepe caput scaberet, vivos et roderet unguis.   (64–71)

Suppose, I say, Lucilius was genial and witty, suppose too that he was more polished than the author of a rough verse untouched by the Greeks[18] and than the crowd of older poets; nevertheless if destiny had postponed his birth until our own day he would now file his work down drastically, he would cut back everything that rambled beyond the limits of true art, and in composing his verses he would often tear his hair and bite his nails to the quick.

After expressing his contempt for those who aim at a large audience and whose works are used as school texts, Horace goes on to name some of his detractors—Hermogenes, Demetrius, and Fannius. By their vindictive gossip these men are trying to belittle his achievement; well, let them do their worst; if he can please patrons like Maecenas, Pollio, and Messalla, and poets like Virgil and Varius, he will be more than content. With one last gibe at Demetrius and Hermogenes ('Go and sing to your female students!') Horace rounds off the poem and the book.

To trace the genesis and growth of these literary theories would be far too complicated a task and would in any case have only an indirect bearing on our subject.[19] Part of the background, however, can be sketched in by summarizing two passages of Cicero. Describing the so-called Attic style of oratory Cicero says it is plain and unpretentious with a deceptive appearance of simplicity; the structure is loose but not rambling; the language scrupulously correct. The Attic orator is restrained in his use of metaphors, archaisms, and new words; his wit is revealed in the elegance of his narrative and in his use of ridicule. Buffoonery, obscenity and cruelty are all to be avoided (*Orat.* 75–90). The same concern for propriety is seen in the description of *sermo* in *De Officiis* I. 134–7. This conversational style, in which the Socratic writers excelled, should be lively but at the same time relaxed and free from dogmatism. It will be grave or gay according to the subject in hand; and except when reproof is called for it will avoid any display of anger. In remonstrating with a friend the speaker may be stern but never insulting.

Clearly Cicero had a strong and direct influence on Horace's view of satire. But Cicero was an eclectic with few claims to originality. The Attic style, which he regarded as only a part of the complete orator's equipment, was studied and practised by several of his contemporaries, who modelled themselves on Lysias, the fourth-century Greek. In the passage of the *De Officiis*, which was based on Panaetius' περὶ τοῦ καθήκοντος, we are told that the best exponents of *sermo* are the Socratics, i.e. writers like Plato and Xenophon. And the concept of refined wit had already been formulated by Aristotle.[20] Horace, moreover, drew on many sources besides Cicero. His preference for a minor genre, which would express his personal views in a careful and polished manner, doubtless owed something to Callimachus, and his reading of Philodemus must have contributed to his choice of a straightforward style which would suit the middle-brow reader.[21] So, too, when Horace calls for an easy alternation between severity and humour (*modo tristi, saepe iocoso*), he is affirming a widely acknowledged tradition. In Aristophanes' *Frogs* (391–2) the Chorus hopes to speak 'many funny *and* many serious things'— πολλὰ μὲν γέλοιά μ' εἰπεῖν, πολλὰ δὲ σπουδαῖα. The Cynic Diogenes would sometimes wag his tail and sometimes bite (D.L. 6. 60), and the Stoic Panaetius, as represented in *De Officiis* 1. 134, varied his mood according to his topic. Other writers used both manners simultaneously. Monimus, the pupil of Diogenes, wrote 'amusements blended with disguised earnestness', παίγνια σπουδῇ λεληθυίᾳ μεμιγμένα (D.L. 6. 83); Menippus, as described by Lucian (*Bis Accusatus* 33), 'used to bite as he grinned', γελῶν ἅμα ἔδακνεν, and the Epicureans were told by the master to 'laugh and philosophize at the same time', γελᾶν ἅμα δεῖ καὶ φιλοσοφεῖν (*Sent. Vat.* 41). All these passages imply a mixture of earnestness and gaiety, though of course the content of the earnestness and the type of gaiety varied enormously.

To see more clearly how these theories affected the development of satire we shall now examine Horace's criticisms of Lucilius in the light of the fragments themselves.

(1) Lucilius was too coarse and abusive (1. 10. 5–8, 14–17). This charge is not hard to substantiate. One satire apparently took a brothel for its title and subject (*Fornix* after W. 909); others portrayed scenes of violent farce, e.g. in W. 937–47 some characters attempt to smash in a door, while another threatens to throw a pot down on their heads. The same level of humour is found in fragments which refer to men feeding (W. 70), belching (W. 130), scratching (W. 356) and bellowing with laughter (W. 131); sometimes people are jeered at for their physical appearance (W. 37, 354–5), and often this effect is enhanced by some animal simile in the manner of Chaucer; thus one fellow has a jaw and tooth like a rhinoceros (W. 109–10), another resembles a huge butcher's dog (W. 1175), and another has one eye and two feet like half a pig's carcass (W. 112–13). It is also clear from a glance at the fragments that a good deal of Lucilius' humour is based on the bed-rock of sex and excretion. This element, which was recognized in Lucilius' work by Porphyrion,[22]

appears much more rarely in Horace. Apart from the early poem on adultery (1. 2), it is found only in scattered lines and words; a late example is the passage on fornication spoken by the slave Davus in 2. 7. 47–52.

Coarse humour was only one weapon in Lucilius' armoury. Direct abuse was another. Unfortunately a full appreciation of his invective is impossible, because we often cannot tell who the victims were and whether or not the insults were uttered by Lucilius himself. Who, for example, was the 'witless old sophist' (*senium atque insulse sophista*) in W. 1210, or the 'jailbird hardly good enough for the cage' (*carcer vix carcere dignus*) in W. 1176? And who was the speaker in W. 1181?

> vicimus o socii et magnam pugnavimus pugnam!
>
> Allies, we have prevailed and fought a good fight!

According to Donatus' note on Terence, *Eun.* 899, this refers to an act of debauchery, and the line may well be a parody of Ennius. Whether it is comedy or satire depends wholly on the context.

Nevertheless, the fragments which do preserve the victim's name are still numerous enough to bear out what Horace says. Other writers also refer to Lucilius' pugnacity. Persius (1. 114) says 'he lashed the city' (*secuit Lucilius urbem*), and Juvenal (1. 165) describes him as 'raging with drawn sword' (*ense velut stricto*). There were protests against Lucilius in his own day, if we can judge from certain fragments in Book 30, especially W. 1075:

> nunc, Gai, quoniam incilans nos laedis, vicissim...
>
> Now, Gaius, since you castigate us with your censure, in return...

We also know from *Auct. ad Herennium* 2. 19 that on one occasion an actor was bold enough to criticize him from the stage. Lucilius thought this such an outrage that he took the man to court. The case was dismissed.

(2) Lucilius was muddy and prolix (1. 4. 9–12; 1. 10. 50–1, 67–71). This can be illustrated by the longest fragment extant:

virtus, Albine, est pretium persolvere verum
quis in versamur, quis vivimus rebus potesse,
virtus est homini scire id quod quaeque habeat res,
virtus scire homini rectum, utile quid sit, honestum,
5   quae bona, quae mala item, quid inutile, turpe, inhonestum;
virtus quaerendae finem re scire modumque,
virtus divitiis pretium persolvere posse,
virtus id dare quod re ipsa debetur honori;
hostem esse atque inimicum hominum morumque malorum,
10 contra defensorem hominum morumque bonorum,
hos magni facere, his bene velle, his vivere amicum;
commoda praeterea patriai prima putare,
deinde parentum, tertia iam postremaque nostra.

(W. 1196–1208)

Virtue, Albinus, is the ability to pay what is actually due in our
business dealings and in our social life. Virtue is the knowledge of what
each issue involves for a man. Virtue is the knowledge of what is
right, advantageous, and honourable for a man, what is good and
likewise what is bad, what is disadvantageous, wrong, and dis-
honourable. Virtue is knowing the boundary and limit for acquiring
riches. Virtue is the ability to pay wealth its due. Virtue is giving
what is in fact owed to honour, being an enemy and an opponent of
bad men and habits, a champion on the other hand of good men and
habits, prizing the latter highly, wishing them well, and living on
friendly terms with them; it means, furthermore, putting the interests of one's country first, then one's parents', then, thirdly and
lastly, one's own.

Here we have Lucilius in his Sunday best. The language is pure
Latin, the arrangement of the various triads and antitheses shows
deliberate artifice, and the moral content is admirable, in its
hard-headed Roman way. One can almost see the poem hanging
on a boy's bedroom wall like some ancient precursor of Kipling's
If. And yet how un-Horatian it is. The Augustan would never
have dealt those hammer-blows of *virtus...virtus...virtus*; he
would have branded the fifth and tenth lines as otiose; and he
would have barred all those monotonous effects of rhyme and
alliteration from a piece which claimed to be serious poetry.

Describing an early stage in his journey to Sicily Lucilius writes:

> verum haec ludus ibi, susque omnia deque fuerunt,
> susque haec deque fuere inquam omnia ludus iocusque;
> illud opus durum, ut Setinum accessimus finem,
> αἰγίλιπες montes, Aetnae omnes, asperi Athones.

(W. 102–5)

But at that point all this was child's play and everything was free and easy; this was all, I say, free and easy and mere child's play and fun. But when we reached the outskirts of Setia, that was a tough haul—goat-forsaken mountains, each one an Etna and a rugged Athos.

This lively passage has several features which Horace would have avoided. Here we shall note simply that the second line is a good example of the older poet's *garrulitas*, and that in Horace 1. 5. 79 Lucilius' painful exertions have dwindled to the single word *erepsemus*; so too the passage on *virtus* has just the faintest echo in *Epist.* 1. 1. 41 *virtus est vitium fugere*—'Virtue is the avoidance of vice'.

An opportunity for a more direct comparison is supplied by some verses from the legend of the fox and the lion. Lucilius has:

> quid sibi vult, qua re fit ut introvorsus et ad te
> spectent atque ferant vestigia se omnia prorsus?

(W. 1119–20)

What does it mean, how does it come about that the tracks face inwards and towards you and all move forwards?

In *Epist.* 1. 1. 74–5 Horace writes:

> quia me vestigia terrent
> omnia te adversum spectantia, nulla retrorsum.

Because those tracks frighten me; they all face towards you, none the other way.

In Horace's shorter version the duplication of *quid sibi vult* and *qua re fit* has disappeared; and the thrice repeated notion of *introvorsus...ad te...prorsus* with its clumsy rhyme has been replaced by a new design which puts *vestigia* first and then observes the tracks from two aspects. The last two words of Horace show that a gain in neatness does not invariably entail a loss of strength.

It is rather surprising, however, when we come to Lucilius with Horace's criticisms in mind, to discover occasional fragments like these, which are admirably swift and concise:

> adsequitur nec opinantem, in caput insilit, ipsum
> conmanducatur totum conplexa comestque. (W. 157–8)
>
> She takes him by surprise from behind, jumps on his head, envelops him, and then chews him all up and devours him.

> aurum vis hominemne? habeas. 'hominem? quid ad aurum?'
> (W. 588)
>
> Do you want the money or the man? Take your pick. 'The man? What's he in comparison with the money?'

One recalls that Cicero often praised Lucilius for his elegance. Quintilian in a later age took Horace to task for calling him muddy (10. 1. 94), and Lactantius seems to have regarded the *virtus* passage as a miracle of compression (*Inst.* 6. 5. 2). Such contradictions will become familiar in the next few pages, and presently an attempt will be made to reconcile them. Meanwhile the following example might be of interest: Lucilius uses certain traditional devices for keeping his readers' attention—'to make a long story short', 'here's what I'm getting at' and so on. At one point he says:

> summatim tamen experiar rescribere paucis.
> (W. 1063)
>
> Nevertheless I shall try to write a short reply in a few words.

So even his promise of brevity contains a pleonasm. In a roughly similar situation Horace writes *pauca accipe contra* (1. 4. 38)— 'Hear a few words in reply'.

(3) Lucilius was eager for publicity. This criticism seems to arise from the remarks on Lucilius' style; for no direct accusation is made. In 1. 4 the charge is laid against Fannius, Caprius and Sulcius; in 1. 10 against those who wrote for the theatre and competition hall. One has the impression that Horace was mainly

concerned to justify his own position as a poet of the *élite*. How-ever, the innuendo against Lucilius cannot be ignored and it seems to gain support from fragments like:

gaudes cum de me ista foris sermonibus differs.

(W. 1085)

You enjoy spreading abroad those bad reports about me in your satires.

et sua perciperet retro rellicta iacere.   (W. 1090)

And saw that his own poems were being left behind in neglect.

et sola ex multis nunc nostra poemata ferri.

(W. 1091)

And that out of many poems only mine were now in circulation.

The first records a complaint about the publication of scandalous material; in the other two cases Lucilius seems to be boasting of his own popularity. But before we think of Lucilius' satires as a kind of *News of the Ancient World*, we should take account of the information preserved by Cicero (*De Orat.* 2. 25):

C. Lucilius...used to say that he wished to be read neither by the very ignorant nor by the very learned, since the former understood nothing and the latter perhaps more than himself. In this connexion he also wrote 'I don't want Persius to read me' (*Persium non curo legere*)—Persius, as we know, was about the most learned of our countrymen—'I do want Laelius Decumus to do so' (*Laelium Decumum volo*). The latter was a worthy man and by no means un-educated, but he was nothing compared to Persius.

Another piece of evidence is contained in *De Fin.* 1. 7 where Lucilius is quoted as saying that he feared the opinion of Scipio and Rutilius and was writing for the people of Tarentum, Con-sentia, and Sicily. This was clearly ironical. The places in question spoke very little Latin, as Lucilius who had estates in those areas knew quite well. The quotation does show, however, that Lucilius was sometimes wryly aware of his failure to meet Scipio's standards. As for the total size of Lucilius' work, we can-not form any reliable opinion about it. The average satire may have been longer than its Horatian counterpart, but an output of thirty books in thirty years need not have been excessive.

(4) Lucilius was rough in his language and versification.

Language. No special complaint is made on this score, but since diction played such a large part in the notion of correct writing (*scribendi recte*, 1.4.13) a few comments are in order. Purity of diction was based on *Latinitas*—a concept which had more than one aspect. Politically it meant restrictions on foreign words, socially the avoidance of provincialisms and vulgarisms (whether in vocabulary, grammar, idiom, or pronunciation), and historically it implied fairly close limitations on the use of archaisms and new words. In short, it represented the more formal type of urban upper-class speech. In what ways, then, could Lucilius have infringed these rules in the eyes of a critic like Horace writing in 35 B.C.? First of all his satires contained a large number of imported words. The great majority were Greek and will be discussed separately, but others came from Gaul, e.g. *bulga*, 'bag', *bracae*, 'trousers'; others were Oscan like *pipas*, 'you cheep', *sollo*, 'whole'; others Syrian (*mamphula*, 'loaf'); Etruscan (*mantisa*, 'makeweight'); Umbrian (*gumiae* 'gluttons'); and possibly Sardinian (*musimo* 'wild sheep'). These licences were not due to ignorance. Lucilius was quite alive to the effect of provincialisms, as may be seen from Quintilian 1.5.56, where he is said to have censured a certain Vettius for using Tuscan, Sabine, and Praenestine words, and from W.232 where Caecilius is mocked for his rural manner of speech. Other fragments testify to the satirist's interest in grammar, etymology, and euphony. So it looks as if he claimed certain priviliges for his *sermones* which he denied to other forms of speech and writing.

The same expansive view of the genre is reflected in Lucilius' coinages, of which Marx notes some thirty examples.[23] Here are a few specimens:

> depoclassere aliqua sperans me ac deargentassere
> decalauticare, eburno speculo despeculassere.
>
> (W. 640–1)

A woman hoping to decup, deplate and destole me and to demirror me of an ivory mirror.

huncin ego umquam Hyancintho hominem cortinipotentis
deliciis contendi?   (W. 311–12)

Did I ever compare this fellow to Hyacinthus, the darling of the Lord
of the three-legged cooking-pot [i.e. Apollo]?

viginti an triginta domi vel centum cibicidas alas
(W. 760)

(I do not care) whether in your house you feed twenty, thirty, or
a hundred food-murderers.

This is Lucilius the heir of Plautus. They did not talk like that in
the Scipionic circle.

The fragments contain a number of words which had become
obsolete by Horace's day, e.g. *incilo, peniculamentum, petilus*. A
few, like *pigror* and *zonatim*, are found only in Lucilius. Other
words are used in senses later abandoned, e.g. *prodo*, 'I defer',
delico, 'I make clear'. But the largest number of cases are simply
forms which were no longer current in 35 B.C. Thus Lucilius did
not object to using, say, *viai* for *viae, mani* as an ablative from *mane*,
and *fluvium* as a genitive plural; we find *guttur* and *collus* in the
masculine, *gladium* in the neuter, and *gracila* as a first declension
adjective. Occasionally *simitu* is used for *simul, indu* and *endo* for
in, noenu for *non*. Verbs may be ante-classical in form (*siem* and
potissem for *sim* and *possem*), in the case they govern (*fungor* with
the accusative), or in voice (*manducor* deponent, *partio* active). Not
all these usages were serious. *Endo*, for example, occurs only in
W. 1024:

omnia tum endo muco videas fervente micare

Then you could see everything shimmering within the seething
depths of the house

—a line which was almost certainly mock-heroic. Therefore, in a
sense Lucilius does not take direct responsibility for the word.
More will be said about this type of case in section (5) below. As
for the rest, Horace did not find fault with such features simply
because they were out of date. A man as sensitive as he was to

organic changes in language would never have made such a vulgar error. What did annoy him was the prejudice of those who either overlooked such features altogether or else used them as a means of extolling the dead at the expense of the living.

The situation is less clear-cut in regard to what might be called comic vulgarisms. If we take nouns of abuse, we find that Horace does not by any means exclude them—he has *agaso, popino, furcifer, vappa*, and others; but Lucilius has nearly three times as many. Again, Lucilius uses nearly twenty words metaphorically in connexion with the human body and its functions, e.g. *rostrum* ('snout') for face, *bulga* ('bag') for womb. Horace has about half a dozen instances—mostly confined to 1. 2. Another feature of popular speech was a frequent use of diminutives. Lucilius has more than twice as many as Horace, and it must be remembered that we are comparing twelve hundred lines of Lucilius, half of which are incomplete, with two thousand lines of Horace. Apart from categories of this kind, a reading of the fragments gives an impression of racy colloquial speech which is not easily reduced to statistics. I have in mind expressions like *nummos inuncat*, 'he gets his hooks on the cash', *me exenterat*, 'he's tearing my guts out', *depilati omnes sumus*, 'we've all been fleeced', *decumana ova*, 'king-size eggs'. Such effects do occur in Horace, but much less often.[24]

Versification. Here Horace's complaints are frequent and direct (1. 4. 8 ff., 10. 1–2, 9–10, 56–73). Unfortunately in this area above all others comparison is hindered by the state of Lucilius' text; so we shall have to confine ourselves to the general features which Horace had in mind. One of these, no doubt, was the treatment of final -s. In Lucilius' day a final -s after a short vowel was weakly pronounced and had no prosodic function, e.g. W. 4 ends *plānĭŭs dīcīt*. This practice was continued by Lucretius, but it sounded 'rather countrified' (*subrusticum*) to Cicero (*Orat.* 161) and was abandoned by Catullus and the Neoterics.

Since Horace calls Lucilius *durus*, it might be thought that Lucilius had a noticeably higher proportion of spondees; yet this does not seem to be the case. According to the calculations of D. Bo,[25] Horace's favourite combination in the first four feet consists of a dactyl followed by three spondees (DSSS); after that comes SDSS; the sequence SSSS is three times as common as DDDD. As for the fifth foot, it is true that whereas Horace never allows a spondee in this position Lucilius does so on three occasions. But two of these cases involve proper names, the third is defensible as a special effect, and anyhow the figure is too small to have much significance. Rather more important, perhaps, is the fact that Lucilius was much freer in his use of pentasyllabic endings. I have counted twenty instances in four hundred lines, i.e. 1 in 20; in Horace's first book there is 1 in 74, and in his second 1 in 217.

Horace's main complaint, however, was directed at the frequency of Lucilius' elisions. Horace occasionally permitted himself three in a line (there are eleven such lines in Book 1) and very exceptionally four (1. 3. 20; 2. 3. 86), whereas in four hundred fragments of Lucilius I counted twenty-three lines with three elisions, nine with four, and two with five. The overall frequency, according to Siedow, is 84·8 in a hundred lines of Lucilius as opposed to 40·1 in the case of Horace.[26] Of the vowels elided by Lucilius 27 per cent are long; for Horace's first book the figure is 18 per cent.[27] Apart from this there does not appear to be any notable difference in the kinds of elision practised or in the places where they occur.[28] The offensive feature about Lucilius' elisions was their sheer number. It was this that gave the impression that his only concern was 'to jam something into six feet' (1. 10. 59–60).

It would be wrong to conclude, however, that Horace's versification was in every way stricter than that of Lucilius. In certain respects he felt (at least when he was writing the first book) that his forerunner had been unnecessarily rigid. In the use of monosyllabic endings, for example, Horace allowed himself much greater freedom. In his first four satires, which contain 540 verses, there are 79 final monosyllables, omitting cases of elision; that gives a proportion of about one in seven.[29] The figure for four hundred hexameter-endings in Lucilius is twenty-six, i.e. less than one in fifteen. Horace also obtained greater smoothness by letting the sense flow on from one line to the next. Of his final monosyllables only a third mark the end of a clause; the figure for Lucilius is apparently nearer to a half. Closely related to this is the fact that Horace was willing to make a strong pause in sense within the last two feet, e.g. *relinquendis. age, quaeso* (1. 10. 51), *turba: sed ille* (1. 10. 67), *concurritur: horae* (1. 1. 7) and even *levius valeat: nam* (2. 7. 78). Such effects are scarcely ever found in Lucilius' fragments, though this is no doubt partly due to the circumstances of their preservation. In some respects, then, Lucilius took too many liberties; in others he did not take enough. It was all a question of relating the movement of the verse to the rhythms of educated conversation; and in deciding this question Horace could appeal to only one authority—the authority of his own ear.

(5) Lucilius was too rhetorical and poetic. This is implied in 1. 10. 12, where Horace states that the satirist should *occasionally* rise to the level of the orator and poet—*modo rhetoris atque poetae.* Lucilius' tendency to abandon the conversational manner is also mirrored by Crispinus (1. 4. 19–21), who resembles the bellows in a blast-furnace, and by Cassius (1. 10. 61–4), who is like a boiling torrent.

This contention can only be valid within a rather limited field. Horace maintains elsewhere (1. 4. 41, 56–62) that Lucilius was essentially an exponent of the plain style, and Varro (see note 6) chose him as an example of slenderness (*gracilitas*). The names which Lucilius used for his verse, such as *sermo* (causerie), *schedium* (impromptu), and *ludus* (amusement), indicate the modesty of his pretensions. There are, moreover, a few fragments which suggest that when Lucilius had the opportunity to write epic he declined to do so. In W. 713 and 714 we have:

hunc laborem sumas, laudem qui tibi ac fructum ferat.
percrepa pugnam Popili, facta Corneli cane.

You should undertake this task which will bring you distinction and profit; tell of Popilius' battle, sing of the deeds of Cornelius.

These lines look very much like the promptings of Trebatius in Horace 2. 1. 10–12:

> aude
> Caesaris invicti res dicere, multa laborum
> praemia laturus.

Dare to tell of invincible Caesar's exploits; you will win many rewards for your pains.

And the words:

ego si qui sum et quo folliculo nunc sum indutus, non queo...
(W. 691)

If I, because of who I am and the little frame in which I am now enclosed, cannot...

may well reflect a refusal like that of Horace in 2. 1. 12–13:

> cupidum, pater optime, vires
> deficiunt.

I am eager, sir, but my powers are insufficient.

(It is noticeable that both the metaphor and the diminutive are missing in Horace.)[30]

Finally, the ridicule which Lucilius directed at writers of epic and tragedy makes it impossible to believe that he himself aspired to the grand style. Homer seems to have come off more lightly than the others. He could be faulted on points of detail—'a line, a word, a thought, or a passage' (W. 410), and some of his fantasies, like the monster Polyphemus with his walking stick the size of a ship's mast (W. 522–3), appeared rather naïve to a sophisticated rationalist, but his greatness was unchallenged and the allusions to his work are made in a spirit of good-humoured parody. Ennius, though still respected, was treated less gently. According to Horace (1. 10. 54) Lucilius made fun of certain lines which he thought undignified. One such line was:

> sparsis hastis longis campus splendet et horret.

Dotted with long spears the plain gleams and shivers.

Horret was too much for Lucilius. Hinting that the line was *frigidus*, i.e. flat or tasteless, he said that Ennius should have written *horret et alget*—'shivers and freezes' (W.413).[31] Another line of Ennius, this time from his tragedy *Thyestes*, ran as follows (Thyestes is cursing his brother Atreus):

latere pendens saxa spargens tabo sanie et sanguine atro.
(W. 885)

May he hang by his flank, spattering the rocks with putrid gore and black blood.

We do not know how Lucilius used the line, but in view of the violent imagery it can hardly have been quoted with approval. Cicero, who preserves the fragment, points out that, since Thyestes has already prayed for Atreus to be drowned, the victim would never feel these agonies and so the line was mere empty bombast.[32]

Pacuvius fared no better. Apart from a reference to his involved prologues (W. 879), several fragments survive from parodies of the *Antiopa* (W. 727–30), the *Chryses* (W. 665–9, 880), and the *Armorum Iudicium* (W. 731–4). There is less evidence in the case of Accius, but Horace (1. 10. 53) says that Lucilius found fault with a number of individual passages; and this criticism is attested by both Gellius[33] and Porphyrion.[34]

If Lucilius was so suspicious of great writing, what substance can there have been in Horace's charge? First of all, though Lucilius attacked the epic and tragic writers for their fantastic subjects and high-flown style, both of which were remote from the realities of life, he could not suppress his admiration for their grandeur and power. As with Aristophanes, this admiration revealed itself in frequent and expert parody. When Lucilius called Apollo *cortinipotens* 'Lord of the three-legged cooking-pot' (i.e. of the Delphic tripod) he was glancing at compounds like *bellipotens* and *armipotens* which occurred in Ennius and Accius. When he talked of *pecus Nerei rostrique repandum* (W. 235), 'the herd of Nereus with upturned snout', he was mocking the Pacuvian description of dolphins as *Nerei repandirostrum incurvicervicum pecus* (W. 352), 'the upturnedsnouted neckin-curved herd of Nereus'. But however effective this may have been as parody it did involve a departure from the plain style. One cannot travesty a very tall man without using stilts.

Even when he was not satirizing tragedy, Lucilius' energy would carry him beyond the range of cultured conversation. This is obvious in the comic passages, which abound in colourful metaphors and verbal high jinks; it can also be seen in effects which are not so much funny as lively—in, for example, the alliteration of *porro procedere porcent* (W. 260), the accumulated rhymes of *surgamus, eamus, agamus* (W. 1007), and in the self-conscious cleverness of the lines on insatiability (W. 208–9):

> nam si quod satis est homini id satis esse potisset
> hoc sat erat.

> For if what is enough for a man could be enough, that would be enough.

It was probably in his invective, however, that Lucilius came closest to the style of the orator and poet. Rhetoricians of all periods gave an important place to the censure of vice (*vituperatio*), and it was recognized that this function called for a highly emotional style which would rouse the listener's indignation and carry him along with the speaker. In describing this type of orator Cicero (*Orat.* 99) calls him 'weighty, vehement, and fiery'—*gravis, acer, ardens*. Two of these terms are significant for us, because Lucilius is called an *acer et violentus poeta* by Macrobius (3. 16. 17) and he is called *ardens* by Juvenal (1. 165). The force and sweep of the grand style are described by Cicero (*Orat.* 97) in terms appropriate to a mighty river; the analogy with invective can be seen in Horace 1. 7. 26–7 where Persius in his abuse of Rex 'rushed on like a wintry river in a place where the axe seldom falls'. So too Juvenal's picture of 'the great son of Aurunca driving his team across the plain' (1. 20) may be compared to Cicero's description of the grand style in *Orator* 128–9, where he seems to have in mind a charging steed.

In making this last point, however, we must again beware of over-simplifying the picture. In W. 269 there is a fair specimen of the orotund style:

nequitia occupat hos petulantia prodigitasque.

They fall into the grip of wantonness, wastefulness, and irresponsibility.

We have good reason to believe that these words were delivered by a demagogue for whom Lucilius had nothing but contempt.[35]

(6) Lucilius was too fond of Greek importations (1. 10. 20–30). In his index to Lucilius Marx lists over 180 Greek words, ignoring those like *oleum* and *poena* which had become naturalized by the poet's day. This figure, which gives an average of one case in eight lines, remains remarkable even when one bears in mind that many of the fragments owe their survival to some linguistic oddity.

Greek words entered Latin at various levels. Starting at the bottom we find in Lucilius some half-dozen words of common abuse, like *mastigias* and *cinaedus*, which also occur in Plautus; other words were introduced by Lucilius for purposes of insult (*androgyni, moechocinaedi*) or fantasy (*cercopithecos, elephantocamellos*). All such words were avoided by Horace, not just because they were Greek but because he considered them vulgar or silly. At a rather higher level come nautical terms, like *carchesia* and *catapirates*, and military terms, like *ballista* and *catapulta*. The absence of such words from Horace is again due to his narrower social range rather than to his national outlook. On the few occasions when Horace does employ plebeian Hellenisms he usually has a satirical purpose; for example, *hybrida*, 'mongrel', describes Persius (1. 7. 2), and *pharmacopolae*, 'druggists', are among the mourners at Tigellius' funeral (1. 2. 1).[36] This effect is, of course, also found in Lucilius, as when he speaks of a *propola*, 'a huckster', and a *pistrix empleuros*, 'a massive bakeress'. Of the seven words used by Lucilius in connexion with sports and games[37] Horace has only *trigon*—the ball game mentioned in 1. 6. 126—but one should perhaps add *phimus*, the dice-box of the gambler Volanerius in

2. 7. 17. So too, whereas Lucilius uses *diallaxon, psolocopumai* and *eugium* in erotic contexts, Horace has only the hybrid *depugis,* and that in his earliest satire.

At the highest cultural level three types of usage can be distinguished. First, in keeping with his broad interests, Lucilius had no hesitation in using the vocabulary of rhetoric and philosophy in quite a straightforward way, simply to express his meaning. Of the two dozen rhetorical terms half are of this kind, and of these only two *(poema* and *epistula)* are found in Horace. As with *rhetor* itself (1. 5. 2), both these terms had lost their foreign character. An example will illustrate the divergence in the poets' practice. In W. 253 Lucilius speaks of a slaves' holiday 'which you obviously can't name in a hexameter line' *(hexametro versu).*[38] In the Journey to Brundisium (87) Horace refers to a town 'which can't be named in verse' *(quod versu dicere non est)*; later, in 1. 10. 59, he speaks of hexameter verse as 'closing up something in six feet' *(pedibus senis).* In each case Horace has avoided the Hellenism.

At a symposium (W. 815 ff.) Lucilius mentions the images and atoms of Epicurus—*eidola atque atomus*; he also uses the word *scole,* softening the alien effect by an explanatory *quam vocant.* Half-a-dozen other philosophical terms are used with varying shades of irony and therefore fall outside this category. Horace, however, does not employ such terms for any purpose, serious or ironic; instead he uses a Latin translation, as with the Epicurean *inane* and *soldum* (1. 2. 113), a fact which reminds us once again that Horace is separated from Lucilius by Lucretius and Cicero.[39]

Secondly, Lucilius often uses Greek to achieve an effect of stylishness, e.g. W. 491–2:

non paucis malle ac sapientibus esse probatum
ἢ πᾶσιν νεκύεσσι καταφθιμένοισιν ἀνάσσειν.

Not to prefer the esteem of the few and the wise rather than to reign over all the spirits of the dead.

Flourishes of this kind must have been as familiar in the conversation of the Scipionic circle as they are in Cicero's letters. When produced at the right moment they gave that feeling of being at once witty, exclusive, and highly civilized which comes to the elderly public school man who has hit on an appropriate Latin tag.[40]

The use of Greek as a status symbol shades off into our third category, which is that of parody and satire. Here there is considerable variation, depending on the nature of the attack. Take, for example, τὸν δ᾽ ἐξήρπαξεν Ἀπόλλων (W. 267)—'but Apollo snatched him away'. As we saw on p. 79, the original is Homer, *Iliad* 20. 443. If Lucilius used the phrase in connexion with some lucky escape, then obviously it represents a mild form of parody. Horace used the same idea (1.9.78), but in keeping with his principles he rendered it into Latin as *sic me servavit Apollo*, thus diluting both sense and wit.

A more trenchant example from Lucilius is the passage deriding the ideal of perfect womanhood:

num censes calliplocamon callisphyron ullam
non licitum esse uterum atque etiam inguina tangere mammis,
conpernem aut varam fuisse Amphitryonis acoetin
Alcmenam atque alias, Helenam ipsam denique—nolo
dicere; tute vide atque disyllabon elige quodvis—
κούρην eupatereiam, aliquam rem insignem habuisse,
verrucam naevum punctum dentem eminulum unum?

(W. 567–73)

Surely you don't think it impossible that any woman with 'lovely tresses' and 'lovely ankles' could have touched her womb and even her crotch with her breasts, that Alcmena 'the wife of Amphitryon's bosom' could have been knock-kneed or bandy, and that others too, even Helen herself, that—(I won't say—think of it yourself and pick any two-syllable word you like)—that 'daughter of a noble sire', could have had some obvious blemish, a wart, a mole, a pock-mark, or one buck tooth?[41]

Here Homer is both a victim and an instrument of satire, but as far as one can tell the ridicule has no serious moral content. For this we must go to the fragments which attack high living. In his recent monograph Mariotti attempts to distinguish between the cheaper and the more expensive fish mentioned by Lucilius.[42] It is perhaps significant that three of the cheaper sort (*muraena, ostrea, peloris*) are found in Horace, but none of the more exotic (*amia, acarna, helops, sargus*). As for drink, χρυσίζον (golden) and Χῖός τε δυνάστης (Chian lord) both refer to high-quality wine, though we cannot be sure how far they represent an attack on the consumers. There is less doubt in the case of the coverings mentioned in W. 13:

> psilae atque amphitapoe villis ingentibus molles.

> Soft coverlets with deep pile on one or both sides.

These are condemned as decadent. The following are also mentioned with disapproval (W. 60):

> chirodyti aurati, ricae, toracia, mitrae.

> Long-sleeved tunics interwoven with gold, veils, bodices, and hairbands.

According to Cichorius (p. 240), whose theory has been accepted by subsequent commentators, Scaevola was accused by Albucius of stealing these items for his mistress.

Finally, we have cases where Lucilius uses Greek as a weapon against itself. In the council of the gods we hear of someone who was so phil-Hellenic that he called a water-jug a *pot à eau*—'*arutaenae'que, inquit, 'aquales'* (W. 14); it had become fashionable to call the legs of a couch *pieds de lit* and lamps *chandeliers* (W. 15–16).[43] The craze was typfied by Albucius, whom Scaevola ridiculed by exclaiming *quam lepide lexis compostae* (W. 84)—'How exquisitely are his *mots* fitted together!' Scaevola took the joke further by greeting Albucius in Athens with the Greek word *chaere!* and instructing his attendants to chime in (W. 92–3). These last examples are important, for they show that Lucilius did set some limits to the use of Greek, though in this as in other respects he was far less strict than Horace.

On this rather hurried survey a few general comments suggest themselves. First, in defence of his coarseness Lucilius could point out that he was a quasi-dramatic author writing in a genre akin to comedy; he therefore had to make his characters convincing. 'If common people use vulgar language, that's not my fault.' Horace would have answered that there was a place for broad humour (*est quaedam hic quoque virtus*), but some restraint was necessary, otherwise the more important functions of satire would be obscured. The satirist himself was a man of society with certain standards of decency to maintain; he should not give too much prominence to scenes from low life.

In defending his invective Lucilius could, and apparently did, contend that evil ought to be exposed and that the innocent had nothing to fear from an honest watchdog like himself.[44] Horace granted that the argument had some force; in fact he used it himself. But he knew that it provided so wide an umbrella that the libeller and pornographer could take shelter along with the genuine reformer. And so he insisted that Lucilius' moral purpose could be served just as effectively, and indeed more so, by less drastic means (*ridiculum acri | fortius et melius magnas plerumque secat res*).

But perhaps when viewed in a wider perspective Horace's criticisms were misconceived; perhaps the humour and polemic of Lucilius, though distasteful to a purist of the late Republic, were quite appropriate in an earlier and more robust generation. Horace was aware of this viewpoint, but one has the impression that although he did not actually contradict it he was reluctant to agree. What he does is to concede the point provisionally, for the sake of argument: 'Suppose Lucilius *was* genial and witty (*comis et urbanus*), suppose too that he *was* relatively polished (*limatior*), nevertheless if he were alive today he would have to write more carefully.' And writing more carefully would imply less coarseness and abuse, for the social and artistic aspects of decorum were complementary. Horace, therefore, cannot be accused of lacking historical sense. It is true that as a contemporary of Virgil he believed that the standards of his own age were superior to those of a century before, and in making this confident assumption he may well have overlooked the merits of some earlier writers— his remark on Plautus, for example, in *Epist.* 2. 1. 175–6 is notably unfair. Nevertheless, Horace had a case, and it would be unwise for us with our vague catholicity of taste and our confusion about aesthetic values to patronize a man who believed that in art as in life the civilized virtues were the best.

When weighing the apparently conflicting evidence about Lucilius' quest for publicity one has to keep in mind the great variety of his work. Some pieces, like the letter in W. 186–93, were meant primarily for the recipient; others, like the essay on orthography in Book 9, would have interested only the intelligentsia. No doubt Lucilius hoped that most of what he wrote would win the approval of his friends, but he must have known quite well that much of it had sensational qualities which would appeal to a far wider audience. The ridicule of Scipio's enemies was certainly not intended as coterie verse, and we may be sure that the more farcical and erotic satires were enjoyed by large sections of the general public.

It has already been suggested that the difference between Lucilius and Horace was in part a difference of theory. Lucilius saw no harm in using a grandiose rhetoric to attack the faults of the epic and tragic style. Fantastic themes, far-fetched images, phrases which boomed because of their emptiness—these were to him failings not only of taste but of character, for they sprang from pretentiousness and insincerity and fostered the same vices in the reader. Horace, however, held that rhetoric was still rhetoric even when used against itself; this kind of effect should therefore be used sparingly in a genre which was close to conversation.

The same point can be made in connexion with Greek words. As we saw, these were often used by Lucilius in a sarcastic way to attack the more corrupting effects of Hellenic influence, one of which was the adulteration of Latin. While Lucilius was much more tolerant than Horace towards the use of conversational

Greek, he did recognize some limits. When a man's speech became so affected that he was unable to describe ordinary objects in his own tongue, and when every other sentence was decorated with a flourish of Greek, then Lucilius reached for his pen and struck. The impact must have been considerable, but the form of his attack was Greek, and to the purist this was like using Satan to cast out Satan. Horace's own practice is expounded in the *Ars Poetica* (48-53): if the poet wishes to use ideas for which there is no Latin name, he may go to the Greek, but this licence must be used with discretion (*dabiturque licentia sumpta pudenter*). Moreover, the foreign word should be taken into the language and given a proper Latin form. Here, as so often, it is hard to tell where nationalism ends and imperialism begins.

Even if Lucilius and Horace had shared the same theories their temperaments would have led to different results. When Lucilius saw the chance to exploit a comic situation his Rabelaisian spirit took control; and when his anger was roused he would hunt down his victims with volleys of invective, forgetting about Panaetius and his rules of taste. It must also be said that he had a far more scholarly mind than Horace. His disquisitions on orthography, etymology, euphony, and other branches of language were probably quite beyond the range of his successor, and the same is true of his interest in the technical details of various skills and trades. In dealing with these matters his chief concern was to convey information or to argue a case; the artistic shape of the verse was of secondary importance. This was never true of Horace, who felt that if a subject could not be subdued to an elegant form it was better handled in prose.

In comparing the two poets it must be agreed that Horace was the superior artist, just as Virgil was superior to Ennius. But while reading the fragments one is aware at times that in the attainment of this greater perfection some qualities were lost— qualities of freshness, spontaneity and rough vigour. And this is enough to cause regret at the decision of the ancients to let Lucilius fall into obscurity. He was a man of letters who participated heartily in life and wrote direct from his experience. In the substantial remains of Roman literature he is a type all too poorly represented.

In discussing the relation of Horace to Lucilius we have considered only two points of a triangular controversy. The third point was occupied by Horace's critics. Who were these people and what did they represent? At the beginning of 2. 1 Horace divided them into two classes:

> sunt quibus in satura videar nimis acer et ultra
> legem tendere opus; sine nervis altera quidquid
> composui pars esse putat, similisque meorum
> mille die versus deduci posse.

> Some people think I am too harsh in my satire and push the genre beyond legitimate limits; others maintain that my compositions have no muscle and that a thousand verses like mine could be turned out in a day.

Nothing can be said about the first group. They probably had little in common except the conviction that brawling in public was vulgar and undignified. In the second group we must include the pro-Lucilian critics who had been in opposition to Horace ever since the appearance of 1. 4 and perhaps earlier.

At first glance it might seem that the best label for the Lucilians would be 'archaists', but it soon becomes clear that some at least were archaists of a rather special kind. From the eight lines preceding 1. 10 (which although probably spurious may be held to contain genuine information) we learn that one of Lucilius' champions was the scholar Valerius Cato.[45] As well as being a scholar Cato was also a poet in the Neoteric manner; that is, he drew his inspiration from Callimachus and the Alexandrians. Hermogenes and 'the ape', who had taken Lucilius' side against Horace, also had Neoteric leanings, for Horace says that the ape's only artistic accomplishment is 'singing Calvus and Catullus'— *nil praeter Calvum et doctus cantare Catullum* (1. 10. 19). The musical interests of Hermogenes and his friends (1. 10. 90–1), along with the adjectives *pulcher*—'pretty', and *doctus*—'artistic' or perhaps 'intellectual', are in keeping with aesthetic tastes of an Alexandrian kind. A similar hint may perhaps be found in 1. 10. 23–4, where a defender of Lucilius says that a style which mingles Greek and Latin is *suavior* 'smoother', as when a Falernian wine is blended with Chian. This reminds us that we are dealing with a controversy rather than straight literary theory; for it is unlikely that Lucilius would have given *suavitas* as a reason for using Greek, whereas a Neoteric might well have done so.[46]

Why, we wonder, should a Neoteric poet like Valerius Cato have been interested enough in Lucilius to edit his work? One suggestion, made by R. P. Robinson, is that Cato's Lucilian studies were 'for professional purposes, to supply material for the instruction of his students'.[47] Perhaps so, but this is not enough to explain why he is called a *defensor* or 'advocate' of the satirist (v. 2 of the disputed lines); and a cold utilitarian attitude of this sort would not account for his part in the quarrel. A more personal theory is advanced by Bardon, who thinks that Cato's editorial work was due to the influence of his old master Vettius Philocomus, who had been a friend of Lucilius. Again, there is some truth in this, but Bardon adds 'je doute fort qu'il ait apprécié le style de Lucilius', and later 'le style en semblait vicieux'.[48] But if Cato was one of those who took exception to Horace's remarks in 1. 4, he must have found *something* to admire in Lucilius' style.

A much wider historical approach was taken by Tenney Frank, who maintained that the Neoterics shared a common hatred of Julius Caesar and therefore the survivors of the school formed a group which was politically antagonistic to Horace and the Augustan establishment:

Some of them, notably Catullus, Calvus, and Memmius, were silenced by Caesar before the civil war, but their published works still contained the bitter lampoons which the Augustan circle found so difficult to forgive. Horace's fling at the *collegium poetarum* and its chief critic Tarpa in *Sat.* 10. 38 should be connected with the fact that Pompey had chosen Tarpa to select and stage official plays during his consulship. Apparently Pompey had been a patron of the *collegium* which Horace scorns. We also remember that Cornificius...died in defence of the Republican cause, and that Cinna, perhaps not wholly by mistake as Plutarch thought, was killed by the mob at Caesar's bier. Of the men criticized in *Sat.* 10 Pitholaus the Rhodian had written a eulogy of Pompey and lampooned Caesar; Fannius had sent his portrait to the poets' club; Furius Bibaculus had ridiculed Augustus as well as Caesar; Valerius Cato...seems to have had a high position in the *collegium poetarum*, and Lucilius...was of course a favorite of Pompey's circle because of his kinship. [Pompey was a descendant of Lucilius on his mother's side.]49

The Neoterics, however, were less homogeneous than Frank implies. Some, like Memmius, Calvus, Catullus, and Cinna, had been reconciled to Caesar by the mid fifties. Cinna was in fact a Tribune of the People at the time of Caesar's death, and there is nothing to suggest that he had any sympathy with the conspirators. Others had supported Caesar from the beginning. Cornificius, for instance, gave excellent service in Illyricum and the East. He later sided with the senate against Antony, and died while resisting the take-over of his province; but that does not make him an enemy of Caesar.50 If his poems reflected any political feeling, which is unlikely, it was certainly not enthusiasm for Pompey. The writings of Varro of Atax, Gallus, and the young Virgil also disturb the tidiness of Frank's thesis.

As for the others mentioned in *Sat.* 1. 10, Frank is right about Tarpa, probably right about Pitholaus—if we accept the usual identification of Pitholeon (22) with Pitholaus,51 and just possibly right about Fannius and the poets' club (1. 4. 21–2). Except for Fannius, however, who is associated with Hermogenes in 1. 10. 80, we do not know how far these men were interested in Neoteric poetry, if at all.

The case of Furius Bibaculus is not relevant to our present point; for if he is identical with the Alpman of 1. 10. 36 and the Furius of 2. 5. 40 he is not attacked as a Neoteric.52 We are therefore left with Valerius Cato. His political affiliations are uncertain. Marx believed that, like the other Lucilian scholars mentioned earlier, Cato was a follower of Pompey. This view was favoured by Frank, and has recently been presented with as much detail as the evidence allows by W. S. Anderson.[53] If it is true (and it well may be), we now have professional, personal, and political reasons for Cato's interest in Lucilius. I still prefer to think, however, that literary reasons were the most important. One observes that in the case of Hermogenes and the ape (who, unlike Cato, are actually mentioned in the poem) we have no political evidence at all. We know only that they were teachers of music and poetry who supported Lucilius while at the same time admiring Calvus and Catullus.

What elements, then, can be found in Lucilius which would appeal to a devotee of Calvus and Catullus and not to Horace? This last restriction is important if we are to understand the controversy. It means that Lucilius' habit of self-portrayal, his avoidance of the major genres, and the more refined aspects of his wit must all be left out of account.[54] First, a Neoteric might well have admired Lucilius' metrical versatility—not just in the dramatic metres of Books 26–30 but in the elegies of Books 22–5, which dealt with members of his household. One couplet (W. 624–5) shows that the fierce lampooner had a tenderer side:

> servus nec infidus domino neque inutilis quaquam
> Lucili columella hic situs Metrophanes.

> Here lies a servant who was faithful to his master and a help in every way, Lucilius' little pillar Metrophanes.

We have already noted Lucilius' readiness to use a spondee in the fifth foot of a hexameter. In the ending *pedicis mens inretita est* (W. 1107)—'His mind was entangled by chains'—*inretita* foreshadows a favourite effect of the Neoterics; though Catullus would have used a pyrrhic (∪ ∪) rather than the long monosyllable *mens*.

Secondly, the satires included love-poems on at least two different girls. Commenting on Horace, *Carm.* 1. 22. 10, Porphyrion says that one of Lucilius' books was entitled *Collyra* because it was written about a mistress of that name—*quod de Collyra amica scriptus sit.* A second mistress is mentioned by Varro (*LL* 6. 69): 'Lucilius writes about Cretaea that when she came to sleep with him she was persuaded of her own free will to remove her tunic and the rest.' Another girl, Hymnis, occurs in five of the fragments, and it may be that she too was a mistress of the poet, though there is not enough evidence to prove it. One other fragment deserves mention because, apart from its tantalizing content, it preserves two of the names which Lucilius applied to his satires (W. 1039–40):

cuius vultu ac facie ludo ac sermonibus nostris
virginis hoc pretium atque hunc reddebamus honorem.

With my light conversation-pieces I gave the girl this recognition and reward for her pretty face and looks.

Although there is nothing in any of these pieces to suggest the passionate intensity of the Lesbia poems, and although the tone was probably more hearty than that adopted by the Neoterics, it is still a fair guess that his frank subjective treatment of *amor* was one of the features which commended Lucilius to followers of Calvus and Catullus.[55]

Another was his aggressiveness. Coming to Lucilius from the *nugae* of Catullus one finds the same ebullience, the same trenchant wit, the same dislike of subterfuge and evasion. In moments of anger neither would pause to ask whether their victim was a public figure or whether he might be dangerous to offend; their only concern was to brand him with ridicule.[56] This independent spirit was probably engendered by social as well as temperamental factors, for Calvus and Catullus, like Lucilius, were well off and moved in fashionable circles. In any case it gave rise to various similarities of style. In Catullus we meet the same easy unselfconscious use of everyday language, which included provincialisms, Greek importations, and numerous diminutives, and which sometimes sank to the grossest vulgarity. Occasionally he burlesqued the diction of Ennius or invented a comic compound for himself, and he loved devices like alliteration, assonance, rhymes, and puns. It is true, of course, that even within the *nugae* these features often produced quite un-Lucilian effects; Catullus, for example, was cleverer in his obscenity, and more subtle and versatile in his use of diminutives. In the longer poems it is mainly the contrasts that impress us. When Lucilius borrows the Ennian compound *caelicolae* ('Heaven-dwellers') in W. 21, the setting is a parody of a divine council; whereas in Catullus 64. 386 the word is used in a spirit of wistful reverence. So too, *anceps ferrum* ('double-headed iron'), which sounds like a noble Ennian periphrasis for 'axe', is used by a blustering clown in W. 942; in Catullus 64. 369 it is part of the song of the Fates. Nor is there anything comic or sarcastic in Catullan coinages like *erifuga*, *falsiparens*, and *silvicultrix*. As for the admission of Greek words, it is hard to imagine Lucilius using Greek for pretty, sentimental, or melodious effects, and he never shared Catullus' enthusiasm for romantic proper names. Nevertheless, Lucilius and Catullus were at one in their attempt to win new territory for poetic language. Horace, though lively and vigorous in his own way, was more concerned with entrenchment and organization. And that is why his verse might well have seemed 'lacking in muscle' to survivors of the other tradition.[57]

To sum up. The literary basis of the feud between Horace and his critics was the fact that they each admired Lucilius for different reasons. Hermogenes and Demetrius valued his metrical variety; Horace was glad that he eventually fixed on the hexameter. They saw his amatory verse as in some way clearing the ground for elegy; Horace, who was always reticent about his love-life, could find no room for such writing in his conception of satire. They relished the exuberance of Lucilius' language; Horace felt that it needed pruning. Above all, while they enjoyed the sharply personal element in Lucilius' invective, Horace was more interested in its moral content. To him Lucilius was essentially the good-humoured raconteur, the forceful preacher who in his exposure of vice had shown how the diatribe might be developed as an artistic verse-form.

These differences of theory were exacerbated by other factors. Hermogenes and Demetrius were professionals who made their living by teaching and study. No doubt they resented Horace's subsidized leisure and the kudos he enjoyed as a friend of Messalla, Pollio, and Maecenas. If, moreover, they were politically hostile to Octavian, it must have been galling to see a turn-coat received and acclaimed at enemy headquarters. Their resentment was answered from the other side by contempt. Horace openly scorned the type of criticism practised in the schools and the sort of poetry which it fostered:

> an tua demens
> vilibus in ludis dictari carmina malis?
> non ego. (1. 10. 74–6)

> Would you be mad enough to prefer your poems to be dictated in cheap schools? Not me.

A similar disdain appears in a letter of Messalla's (Suet. *De Gramm.* 4), which says that 'he has nothing to do with Furius Bibaculus or even with Ticidas or Cato the elementary school teacher' (*litteratore*). It was acrimony of this kind which sharpened Horace's critique of Lucilius. No doubt objective truth suffered in the process, and a sober assessment was made more difficult. However, it was not all loss; sober assessments can be so very dull.

2. 1

This is a deceptive poem. Though intended as a prologue to Book 2, it has certain links with the earlier collection which give it a transitional character. In time, moreover, it is the latest of all the satires and so (to risk an Irish bull) it looks forward to what is already written. The relevance of this fact will become apparent as we study the rather strange sequence of argument. In form the satire is a consultation. Horace, who affects to be troubled at the reception given to his previous book, asks the advice of C. Trebatius Testa, the most famous jurist of the day and a man twenty years his senior.[58] The dialogue opens with a passage which may be paraphrased as follows:

Some people think my satire goes beyond legitimate limits (*ultra legem*); others find it insipid. Tell me what to do, Trebatius.
Take a rest (*quiescas*).
Stop writing verses altogether, you mean?
Yes.
Well, no doubt that would be the best thing. But I can't sleep.
Those in need of sound sleep shall swim the Tiber three times (*ter...
transnanto*) and before retiring have their system well soaked with wine.
Or, if you have this compulsion to write, try recounting the exploits of
Caesar.
I would gladly do so, Sir, but my powers are unequal to the task.
Well, at least you could write in praise of Caesar's character, as Lucilius did
with Scipio.
I shan't be found wanting when the time is right. Only at a suitable moment
will Floppy's words (*Flacci verba*) enter Caesar's pricked-up ear (*attentam
aurem*). Rub him the wrong way and he'll lash out with his hooves in all
directions.
A eulogy of that kind would be far wiser than writing savage lines about
Pantolabus the parasite and the wastrel Nomentanus; invective only causes
fear and resentment.
I'm sorry; I can't help it. Milonius dances, when wine brings heat to his head
and plurality to the lights; Castor rejoices in steeds; the issue of the same egg
rejoices in fists. Everyone follows his own pursuit.

The implication surely is 'Similarly I have to vent my indignation
by writing satire'. And that is the inference drawn by many
commentators. They compare Persius 1. 12, 'I'm sorry; I can't
help it...I have to guffaw'. L. R. Shero says 'The poet makes it
perfectly clear that his temperament forces him not merely to
write, but to write satire in the manner of Lucilius'.[59] That is
certainly what we expect—especially in view of the gibe at
Milonius. But it is not what we get. Instead Horace says 'I have
to put words into metrical form' (28). So apparently what keeps
him awake is not hatred or anger, but simply problems of scansion.
Juvenal's Roman had better reasons for his insomnia.[60]

But what of the phrase *Lucili ritu* which follows? Since this
means 'in Lucilius' manner', perhaps Horace has in mind his
censorious spirit as well as his metrical form. But no. The phrase
leads on to something quite different, namely Lucilius' *confessional*
manner:

ille velut fidis arcana sodalibus olim
credebat libris, neque si male cesserat usquam
decurrens alio neque si bene; quo fit ut omnis
votiva pateat veluti descripta tabella
vita senis.

In days gone by he used to confide his secrets to his books as if they
were trusted friends. He never turned to any other quarter in failure
or success; as a result the old fellow's entire life lies before us as if
painted on a votive tablet.

Horace now continues with *sequor hunc* (34). Perhaps now we
shall hear something of the Lucilian spirit. Not yet. 'It is uncertain', he says, 'whether I'm a Lucanian or an Apulian; for
Venusia, my birthplace, is adjacent to both.' So that's it. Horace
comes from a long line of fighting men; there's pugnacity in his
blood.[61] But at once a qualification appears: 'This steely point
(*stilus*) will not attack any living person and it will protect me like
a sword in a scabbard' (39–40). Does this mean that after all his
fine talk Horace has formally renounced the idea of personal
attack and that, like Juvenal, he will assail only the dead? Not
quite. We have forgotten the little word *ultro*. 'I shall not attack
anyone *unless provoked*.' It is safe to say that since the time of
Romulus no Roman ever confessed to an act of unprovoked
aggression.

There follows a fervent prayer. 'O Jupiter, Father and King,
let my sheathed weapon decay with rust' (42–3). The effect, however, is rather spoilt by the next line, 'And let no man offend me,
desirous as I am of peace!' People had better treat this peaceable
man with caution. 'Anyone who annoys me ("Better keep
away!" I cry) will be sorry, and his name will become a byword
throughout the city.' The sword is now rattling noisily.

The next section opens on the same minatory note:

Cervius threatens his enemies with litigation; Canidia is dreaded for her poison;
Turius for his savage sentences. Everyone uses the weapon which suits him
best. It's the same in the world of nature. The wolf has his fangs, the bull his
horns; each acts from an inner instinct. Give the wastrel Scaeva ('Lefthand')

charge of his aged mother, and his filial right hand (*dextera*) will commit no crime. Of course not! A wolf doesn't kick or a bull bite. The old girl will be got rid of by a dose of hemlock. (47–56)

We now expect something like 'As for me, I fight with my pen'. And that is what Orelli supplies (*opprobriis dignos libere insectabor*).[62] But after this flamboyant approach Horace shies away into something wholly non-committal: 'Whether a quiet old age awaits me or death hovers round with sable wing, rich or poor, in Rome or, if chance so decree, in exile—whatever the complexion of my life, I shall continue to write' (57–60).

Trebatius, however, behaves as if Horace had threatened to write lampoons. 'I'm afraid, my boy, you won't last long; one of your influential friends will cut you dead.' To which Horace replies (and again I am paraphrasing):

What? Have you forgotten Lucilius the great pioneer of satire? He stripped off everyone's disguise. He wounded Metellus, buried Lupus in a shower of invective, and castigated the people tribe by tribe. So far from being offended by his wit Laelius and Scipio were his closest friends. They used to let their hair down (*discincti*) and romp around with him while the vegetables were cooking. (62–74)

We infer that Horace can be as censorious as he wishes without losing the friendship of Maecenas and Octavian. Orelli's comment is *tales autem nebulones ubi perstrinxero nunquam profecto timebo ne potentes amicos a me abalienem* (introduction to 2.1). But again, that is not what Horace says:

Whatever I am, although inferior to Lucilius in wealth and ability, Envy will have to admit that I have lived with the great, and if she thinks I am brittle she will find me a tough nut to crack. But perhaps, my learned friend, you hold a dissenting view? (74–9)

This is so discreet as to be almost meaningless. The implication seems to be that if Horace is attacked he can rely on the support of Maecenas. There is certainly no statement about any satirical attacks of his own.

Yet Trebatius replies as if Horace had expressed his determination to write abusive verse:

Well, I can't break the force of your argument (*diffindere*), but I must warn you in case your ignorance of the majesty of the law gets you into trouble. If a party compose foul verses against another party a hearing and a trial ensue. (79–83)

Horace once again steps neatly aside:

That is true in the case of *foul* verses, but what if a party compose *fine* verses and in Caesar's judgement win commendation?...
The charge will be laughed out of court and you will get off scot free. (83–6)

So ends the most brilliant piece of shadow-boxing in Roman literature. What are we to make of it? Perhaps, as hinted above, the position of the poem may give us a clue. The links with Book I are obvious. The very first line recalls the criticisms which had greeted the previous collection. Lucilius occupies the foreground as if he were still regarded as the model for satiric writing. In the use of proper names Horace continues his earlier practice, and there are numerous echoes of the former literary controversy.[63] And yet things are not quite the same. Horace is now eight years older than when he wrote the fourth satire, and therefore eight years steadier and more responsible (or eight years duller and more complacent, depending on one's point of view). His position in the social and literary world is well established; his enemies realize that any attempt to dislodge him will only injure themselves, and so they accept him, however grudgingly, as a celebrity.

Some scholars would maintain that there was also a risk of legal proceedings.[64] As far as we know there had been no alteration in the law of libel within the previous decade, though it is possible that with the return of order after Actium the existing law (presumably Sulla's *Lex Cornelia de iniuriis*) might be more strictly enforced. It is doubtful, however, if 2. 1 reflects any real anxiety. Horace, after all, had the other seven poems before him and he knew quite well that they contained little in the way of defamatory material. Why this was so is another question, which will be touched on in the next chapter. But so far as the present poem is concerned it seems best to attribute the threat of prosecution, like the other legal elements, to the poet's wit rather than to the hazards of contemporary life.

128

As Horace wrote 2. 1 he was about to publish a collection of hexameter verses which ridiculed the follies and vices of his fellow-citizens. To this extent the poems could claim to be a refined version of Lucilian satire, but they lacked the personal abuse which had come to be regarded as a distinguishing feature of the genre. In Horace's first book this had already been greatly modified, but there were several remarks which could have given offence and also touches of coarseness which suggested Lucilius' influence. In the new collection this element had been further diminished; and so in introducing the book Horace could not promise his readers a rich feast of scandal and gossip. Indeed as he looked through the poems he must have realized how far his satire had moved away from the scathing denunciations of his predecessor. Yet he did not wish to disparage the old tradition, even though he was now on the point of abandoning it. There were many aspects of it which he valued, and his admiration for the *inventor* remained unaltered.

The result of these stresses was the poem which we have been discussing. The links with Book 1 give the appearance of continuity. Horace's pose is the one he had previously adopted in his more bellicose moods. He has taken guard once again in the ring where Lucilius had battered so many opponents. But there is one big difference. Behind the pugilist's gloves we can detect a mischievous grin, and it gradually becomes apparent that in spite of the threatening stance and the elaborate feinting and ducking Horace does not really intend to come to blows. To use a word from an early article of Fraenkel's, it is all *Scheinpolemik*. He has disposed of his problem by a joke.

In this poem we are struck again and again by a playfulness almost amounting to farce. We catch glimpses of Milonius glassy-eyed and unsteady, poor Lupus smothered in a shower of Lucilian invective, Scipio and Laelius freed from the trammels of *gravitas* enjoying a bit of horseplay while the greens are cooking. The satire's vividness is matched by its verbal dexterity. One recalls the play on *stilus* (pen and dagger), the juxtaposition of Scaeva and *dextera*, and that amazing metaphor which begins with a pun on Horace's name (Flaccus) and ends with a comparison of the emperor to a nervous horse. In the resounding line *Panto-labum scurram Nomentanumque nepotem* everything is impressive except the content. And what of that superb periphrasis in v. 26 *ovo prognatus eodem* ('born from the same egg')? Pollux is at once exalted by *prognatus* and diminished by *ovo*, and the final *eodem* reaches back along the line to disturb the dignity of Castor. The myth of Leda was never touched more lightly. At the end of the satire the principles of aesthetics are cleverly confused with the law of libel, and this brings us back to the opening phrase *ultra legem* ('beyond legitimate limits'), which refers to the definition of satire as well as to illegal pasquinades.

The fiction of a consultation is maintained partly by Horace's respectful attitude (*pater optime, docte*), partly by his quasi-technical words (*praescribe, dissentis*), but mainly by the language of Treba-tius, who preserves not only the sententious brevity of a jurist (*quiescas, aio*) but also a correctly legal turn of phrase. The solemnity of this phrasing, however, is always compromised. I doubt if the verb *transnanto*, though impeccable in form, ever appeared in a Roman statute. The technical precision of *diffindere* is marred by the fact that it echoes *fragili quaerens illidere dentem* and therefore evokes a picture of the great lawyer trying to crack a nut with his teeth.[65] The libel law is cited in language reminiscent of the Twelve Tables, only to be turned upside down. Even the tablets of the indictment are dissolved in laughter.

As a piece of drama the satire is much more fully realized than the introductory poems of Persius and Juvenal, both of which are descended from it.[66] As we have seen, Horace keeps the professional setting before our minds, and in Trebatius he gives us a real person who is quite unlike the lay figures of Persius and Juvenal. The older man is anxious to restrain Horace from rashness and at the same time to enhance his material prospects (*multa laborum / praemia laturus*). He is not portrayed as a fool—far from it; but in his advice he recommends two pastimes which we know from Cicero to have been especially congenial to him, namely swimming and drinking.[67] His recipe for sound sleep can in fact be summed up in Heinze's comment: 'Nass äusserlich und innerlich appliziert.' Horace knew he would enjoy the joke, and indeed this whole poem is a confirmation of the very attractive picture which emerges from the correspondence of Cicero.[68]

Such, then, is the last of Horace's satires. It is designed as a bridge leading from the cultivated but open ground of Book 1 to the walled garden of Book 2. From a distance the structure appears strong enough, but at close quarters it is seen to be largely ornamental and incapable of bearing much weight.

CHAPTER V

THE NAMES

There is, perhaps, a natural tendency to assume that the best information about Horace's characters is to be found in the ancient commentators. Though Porphyrion's notes date from about the third century and the pseudo-Acron's may be as late as the fifth, both men had access to a lot of earlier material which has since been lost, including monographs on Horatian prosopography.[1] As a result they occasionally preserve fragments of a genuine tradition. But if we ask them for reliable detailed information they will let us down. Sometimes their notes conflict, as in the Fannius passage (1. 4. 21–2): *beatus Fannius ultro | delatis capsis et imagine*—'Fannius is happy after the presentation of a case of books and a bust of himself as an unsolicited gift'. Here we are told that Fannius presented book-cases to the senate, that the senate presented book-cases to him, that his heirs presented his books to public libraries, and (splendidly) that at the hour of death Fannius begged to be cremated on a pile of his own books.[2] Sometimes the scholiasts misinterpreted what was in front of them. At 1. 2. 64, for example, some of them missed the irony of *Villius...Sullae gener*—'Villius the "husband" of Sulla's daughter'—and stated that Villius (who was not, in fact, the husband) was a metrical substitute for Annius (who was). Often, as in the case of Trebatius the famous jurist, they tell us much less than we can learn from other sources. And often they are simply guessing. Recently I asked a group of students to comment on the name Mucius in Juvenal's line *quid refert dictis ignoscat Mucius an non?* (1. 154). The inventions of those who didn't know the answer sounded remarkably like the pseudo-Acron. On the whole, then, the scholiasts are not of much assistance, except where they provide corroborative evidence. In their treatment

132

of Horace's names they usually assumed that they were dealing with real individuals. As we shall see, this, like other simple theories, is far from adequate.

For the sake of convenience I have classified the material as (*a*) the names of living people, (*b*) the names of dead people, (*c*) the names of Lucilian characters, (*d*) significant names, (*e*) the names of other type characters, and (*f*) pseudonyms. Not all the categories are self-contained—(*b*) and (*c*), for example, obviously overlap. And there are several figures who cannot be assigned with confidence to any one group. In such cases the most we can do is to assess probabilities. We shall not be dealing with all the names mentioned. Only *satirical* references need be considered. And even here there is room for selection, for some of the figures are so obscure that nothing useful can be said about them.[3]

(*a*) *Living people*. The first ones we meet are the hot gospellers Crispinus and Fabius.[4] The bearded, 'bleary-eyed' Crispinus was an obvious target. Like Stertinius, who appears in a later satire, he denounced many habits which Horace himself found objectionable, but his doctrinaire idealism ('all sins are equally culpable'), his lack of social graces, and his eccentric pose disqualified him from serious consideration. Also, from an aesthetic standpoint his sermons were deplorable, being long-winded, over-heated affairs with as little art as his own doggerel verses. The 'gas-bag' Fabius represents the same type. He was one of those speakers who hit the nail on the head with such relentless persistency that the wood eventually splits. As well as being a pedantic bore he has also been put down as an adulterer, but that is unfair. In 1. 2. 134, after listing the dangers of adultery, Horace concludes *deprendi miserum est; Fabio vel iudice vincam*, 'To be caught is a horrid experience—I could prove that even before Fabius'. This has been taken to imply that Fabius had once paid the penalty himself, but a more natural interpretation is that even a Stoic like Fabius would find the consequences painful. So we may take it that Fabius was not an adulterer, but simply a man who had argued himself into believing that the true philosopher was immune to pain, or (to use the old paradox) that the good man could be happy on the rack. Horace would certainly have applauded the student who remarked that it would have to be a very good man and a very bad rack. On the trip to Brundisium (1. 5) three more characters make their appearance. One is Aufidius Luscus the mayor of Fundi, who receives the travellers with such amusing ceremony; the others are Sarmentus (a satellite of Maecenas)[5] and a local stalwart called Messius Cicirrus, both of whom kept the company amused by their bucolic repartee. Back in the city we come across the unfortunate Nasica (2. 5. 57), who married his daughter to a rich old fogey in the hope of a legacy and then discovered too late that his aged son-in-law had outwitted him. Two money-lenders also catch our attention. One is the younger Novius (1. 6. 121) who has his table beneath Marsyas' statue and whose face, we are told, accounts for the statue's gesture of abhorrence. The other is Ruso (1. 3. 86), an amateur historian whose readings are always well attended—debtors find his invitations so hard to refuse. A third member of the profession is the 'mongrel' Persius (1. 7. 2), but we do not meet him in Rome since the scene of his operations is Asia Minor. Finally, mention should be made of Turbo, the fierce but diminutive gladiator in 2. 3. 310. So far, then, we have two cranks, a petty official, a legacy-hunter, three money-lenders, a gladiator, and a couple of buffoons. Not an impressive collection. They may all be dismissed as harmless nonentities, provided we remember that a nonentity may be guilty of a very unpleasant vice and that nonentities also have feelings.

A more worthy target was presented by Tillius, a stingy and unpopular magistrate who had risen from lowly origins. At some time Tillius had lost the senatorial stripe but had regained it and become a tribune (1. 6. 24 f.). In 1. 6. 108 he is even referred to as a praetor. We do not know who this man was. It has been suggested that he was a brother of Tillius Cimber the conspirator, whose origins are also obscure. It seems unlikely that a brother of one of the conspirators would have been acceptable to the

Triumvirs. Yet it is not impossible. Casca, who was himself a conspirator, held the tribunate in 43 B.C. Tillius might have done the same. And he could even have been one of the sixty-seven praetors who were appointed in 38 B.C. (Dio 48. 43). At any rate, in view of his official position Horace's Tillius was clearly in a different category from the people already mentioned.

In I. 2. 48 a certain Sallustius is said to be just as mad on freed-women as an adulterer is on married ladies. Since the name is not common and the man concerned must have been fairly well known, it is usually supposed that Horace is referring either to the historian or to his adoptive son. If it was the son he must have made his reputation at an early age, for the satire was written about 39 or 38 B.C. and he did not die until A.D. 20. Moreover, since the younger man was in fact Sallust's grand-nephew, he can hardly have been born much before 55 B.C., for Sallust himself was born in 86. It is also quite possible, as Syme has pointed out,[6] that the heir did not acquire the name Sallust until the historian's death in 35 B.C. If this is so, then Horace would seem to be speaking of the older man. The trouble here is that while Sallust certainly had a reputation for sexual adventure it was adventure of the wrong kind. Varro, as reported by Gellius (17. 18), and Asconius, as reported by the pseudo-Acron on *Sat.* I. 2. 41, record the story that Sallust was caught in adultery with Fausta, Sulla's daughter, and was given a sound thrashing. But Horace's Sallust prides himself on his *avoidance* of married ladies—*matronam nullam ego tango* (54). One solution is to reject the allegation of adultery. Varro, as a Pompeian, was biased against Sallust, and Asconius may simply have taken the story from Varro without necessarily believing it. This on the whole is the answer favoured by Syme. Another answer, suggested by the pseudo-Acron in his note on I. 2. 49, is that Sallust was charged with adultery in the senate and defended himself by saying that he pursued freedwomen, not married ladies. This, however, looks like a forlorn attempt to reconcile Varro with Horace. Whatever the truth may be, it does seem that Horace was glancing at a man who, if not politically influential, was at least prominent in society. It may be pointed out quite rightly that none of these people *inspired* Horace's satires; they did not interest him enough to arouse his anger; and their main function was to provide his essays with coloured illustrations. But the victims might not have been mollified by such a delicate distinction.

From these rather detached and incidental allusions we turn to a few expressions of genuine dislike. They are to be found for the most part in 1. 10, where they centre on characters like Hermogenes, Demetrius, Pantilius, and Fannius. Of these gentlemen one, we are told, is a pansy, another is an ape, a third is a louse, a fourth a fool, and they are all a crowd of malicious backbiters. As we have already seen, the names belong not to any monsters of crime or vice but to men whose taste in poetry happened to differ from Horace's own. The only victim of this kind in Book 2 is Furius the writer of epic poetry. Horace first of all 'places' Furius by telling us that he is 'bloated with greasy tripe', *pingui tentus omaso* (2. 5. 40); a sample of the tripe is then displayed in the following line, which (except for the substitution of Furius for Jupiter) is taken from Furius himself:

Furius hibernas cana nive conspuet Alpis.

Furius bespews the wintry Alps with hoary snow.

Quite different in spirit from any of these passages is the treatment of Trebatius in 2. 1. As we have seen, the tone throughout is one of light-hearted banter, and this is one of the factors which give the poem a unique place in Horace's *Satires*.

Up to now we have been discussing people who were certainly or most probably living when the *Satires* were written. More doubt exists in the case of Fausta (1. 2. 64), Alfenus (1. 3. 130), the son of Albius (1. 4. 109), Damasippus (2. 3. 16), Labeo (1. 3. 82), the son of Aesopus (2. 3. 239), and the sons of Arrius (2. 3. 243). Fausta, that lady of high birth and low morals, was born in 86 B.C. She was certainly living in 51 B.C.,[7] and when the second satire was written she could not have been more than forty-seven years old. Her lovers Villius and Longarenus could also have been alive. Alfenus, if identical with Alfenus Varus the celebrated jurist,[8] was definitely alive; if not, there is no firm evidence either way. He was a man who had risen in the social scale, and it was naughty of Horace to recall his associations with trade. (See the translation in chapter 1.) To judge from the context, the son of Albius was a young spendthrift at the time of Horace's boyhood.[9] If we allow a difference of ten to twenty years in age, the former could easily have been alive in 35 B.C. when the satire was published. But we know no more about him than we know about Baius, Scetanus and Trebonius—the other examples of wickedness mentioned in 1. 4. 110–14. Damasippus the wealthy art dealer is shown by Cicero's correspondence to have been alive in 45 B.C.[10] In Horace he appears as a man driven out of his wits by financial losses and only saved from suicide by the timely intervention of Stertinius, who persuades him that he is really no madder than anyone else. The other names all belong to men who had achieved fame through some act of conspicuous lunacy. Labeo cannot be identified with certainty and should perhaps be put in another category,[11] but the son of Aesopus is mentioned by Cicero (*Att.* 11. 15. 3). He was a young man in 47 B.C.—about fourteen years before the poem in question was written. His mistress Caecilia Metella (2. 3. 239) may quite well have been alive too. Her divorce from Lentulus Spinther in 45 B.C. is the last we hear of her (*Att.* 13. 7. 1). Arrius, who is also mentioned by Cicero, must have died about 50 B.C.[12] His sons could well have survived to see the publication of Book 2 in 30 B.C. If they did, they must have been disconcerted to find themselves described as 'a famous pair of brothers, twins in depravity and silliness and in their love of evil'.

Certain other figures are mentioned as though they were contemporary, but it is often hard to tell whether they are real or fictitious. Those who appear to be fictitious will be discussed presently. In the case of the others one can point out that Cerinthus the pretty boy (1. 2. 81) is directly addressed in the most personal of all Horace's satires, that the reference to Rufillus and Gargonius and their contrasting odours (1. 2. 27) is repeated in 1. 4. 92 in such a way as to imply that it had given offence, that 'dirty Natta' (1. 6. 124) does not sound like a type name, and that the phase *fragilis Pediatia*—'dainty Miss Pediatius'—in 1. 8. 39 seems too carefully pointed to be without a target. But none of these arguments would impress a tough-minded sceptic.

(*b*) *Dead people*. A number of Horace's gibes, though perhaps not quite so many as one often assumes, are aimed at persons whom we know to have been dead. Some of these characters may be classified by their attitude to money. Thus while Staberius and Ummidius worshipped it with the devotion of true misers, Aristippus was senselessly indifferent to it; so was Marsaeus who ruined himself for the sake of an actress.[13] Fufidius the miser (1. 2. 12) may also belong to this group. One thinks first of the Quintus Fufidius mentioned by Cicero in *Pis.* 86, *QF* 3. 1. 3, *Att.* 11. 13. 3, 14. 3, 15. 2 (P–W, no. 1). If this is the man in question he must represent a type, because although dead he is spoken of in the present tense. Alternatively Horace might have had in mind a living person. We know of a Fufidius who was alive in 46 B.C.,[14] but there is no evidence that he was a miser.

Passing quickly over Sisyphus (Antony's dwarf, 1. 3. 47), the blustering poet Cassius Etruscus (1. 10. 61 f.), the black sheep Laevinus (1. 6. 12), and Volanerius the obsessive gambler (2. 7. 15), we come to Priscus (2. 7. 9) the senator whose life was a jumble of absurd contradictions. On reading Horace's description of him one is reminded of the French diplomat's comment on one of his English counterparts: 'Quel homme étrange! Son centre n'est pas au milieu.' Or perhaps we should say that Priscus had no centre at all. The problem of consistency, which in morals involves the integration of the personality and in art the achievement of unity amid variety, held a special interest for Horace. So it is no accident that whereas most Horatian characters are presented with a few strokes here and a touch of colour there, Priscus should be honoured with a seven-line verbal cameo. But even Priscus is eclipsed by another of his kind—I refer to that splendid bohemian Tigellius, who occupies the opening section of 1. 3. Tigellius was a musician from Sardinia who had been quite a well-known figure in Roman society a few years before. He was on familiar terms with Julius Caesar and Octavian; he knew Cicero well enough to quarrel with him; and he had the distinction of being lampooned by Calvus.[15] In 1. 2, written shortly after his death, he is depicted as one who spent money freely in rather raffish company. And the description in 1. 3 suggests a man who lived not according to this or that philosophy but simply for dramatic effect. Had someone reminded him of the old Delphic maxim 'Know thyself' he would have answered with a sigh 'Ah, but which one?' Flamboyant and unstable, amusing and insincere, Tigellius represented the antithesis of the ideal Roman type. The empire called for sound purposeful men with a strong sense of duty and not too much imagination; and Stoicism, when suitably adapted, provided the necessary intellectual framework—rather like public school Christianity. So in commending the man who is 'all of a piece' Horace is affirming a national ethical tradition. Yet the amount of time spent in deriding Tigellius reminds us that Horace himself was not always a model of *aequabilitas*. We all tend to be harsh towards our own vices, when they occur in other people.

Before leaving this group one should say a word about Cervius the informer, Turius the crooked judge, and Scaeva the poisoner, who all appear in 2. 1. 47–56. The charges against them are grave ones, but they are made in a poem which, because of its late date, is unlikely to contain any real aggressiveness; moreover, they come immediately after Horace's promise that he will not attack any live person unless provoked. Therefore it is best to assume that the characters in question were not living. This leaves two possibilities; they may be fictions, in which case we can hardly hope to guess why these particular names should have been chosen,[16] or they may be real people whose sinister reputation was still fresh. The second suggestion, which is that adopted by the scholiasts, would be well in line with the satire's jocular tone, for we all know how a criminal who has captured the popular imagination becomes on his death a kind of mythological hero-villain. Rasputin periodically makes his appearance in the Sunday newspapers, and Dr Crippen is still with us, enshrined by an affectionate public within the chamber of horrors.

(c) *Lucilian characters*. The most straightforward case is that of Gallonius (2. 2. 46–8):

> haud ita pridem
> Galloni praeconis erat acipensere mensa
> infamis.

Not so long ago the table of Gallonius the auctioneer became notorious on account of a sturgeon.

This is a clear reference to the gluttonous auctioneer attacked by Lucilius (W. 203):

> 'o Publi, o gurges Galloni, es homo miser' inquit.

'O Publius, O Gallonius of the maw, you are a wretched fellow', he says.

We can also feel fairly confident about Maenius. His extravagance is mentioned in *Epist.* 1. 15. 26–41, and also by Porphyrion on *Sat.* 1. 3. 21, who tells us that when Maenius was forced to sell his house in the Forum he reserved one column to enable him to watch the gladiatorial shows—a column which Lucilius referred to in the fragment *Maenius columnam dum peteret*.[17] So the Horatian and the Lucilian Maenius are probably the same person. There is an equal degree of probability in the case of Pacideianus, who according to Lucilius was 'far and away the best gladiator the world has ever seen' (W. 174–5). A Pacideianus also appears in *Sat.* 2. 7. 97 and it is most likely that the two men are identical, though Heinze thinks that the name had been adopted by a fighter of Horace's own day—a practice which was not unknown.[18] The Albucius of Horace 2. 1. 48, who succumbed to Canidia's poisons, has no apparent connexion with his Lucilian namesake. But the situation is rather different in the case of the other Albucius, who, we are told, was unnecessarily harsh in assigning work to his slaves (2. 2. 66–8). Now although we do not hear of any cruelty on the part of Lucilius' Albucius, we know from W. 87–93 that he was devoted to the Greek style of life. Cicero (*Brut.* 131) calls him 'a complete Epicurean' (*perfectus Epicureus*), but his Epicureanism seems to have been of a non-ascetic kind, if we may judge from Varro (B. 127), who speaks of 'matrices from Albucius' sows' (*volvae de Albuci subus*). If, then, Albucius was something of a gourmet, this would provide a link with Horace's character, for the latter shows his harshness in the context of a dinner-party.[19]

From now on more serious problems arise. Take the rich skin-flint Opimius (2. 3. 142 ff.). There is also an Opimius in the Lucilian fragments, in fact there are two. One is Quintus Opimius, consul in 154 B.C., who as a boy had a reputation for sexual depravity; the other is his son Lucius Opimius who held the consulship in 121 B.C. and was later exiled for accepting bribes from Jugurtha.[20] Obviously neither has anything to do with the Horatian figure, who owes his name to the oxymoron *pauper Opimius*—'Poor Mr Richly'. In *Sat.* 1. 4. 69 Caelius is a brigand. What was the Caelius in fragment 1008 of Lucilius? Wickham, very conveniently, thinks he was a brigand. Others have seen in him a poet, a historian, a judge, a ball-player, and a friend of the satirist's. The most likely guess is that of Lucian Müller, namely that he was an officer celebrated by Ennius for his deeds in the Istrian war.[21]

> quid mi igitur suades? ut vivam Naevius aut sic
> ut Nomentanus?
>
> Well, what do you want me to do? Live like Naevius or Nomen-
> tanus?

These exasperated words come from the miser in 1. 1. 101. Porphyrion comments: *Naevius autem fuit in tantum parcus ut sordidus merito haberetur Lucilio auctore.*[22] So Naevius appeared as a miser in Lucilius. That is very interesting, if true. But he is not a miser in Horace; in fact he is the very opposite. Porphyrion must have misread the lines. A further complication is introduced by 2. 2. 68–9 where Naevius is a careless host who gives his guests greasy water to wash in. This is certainly not the action of a spend-thrift, nor does it quite suggest a miser. It is rather a sign of slackness. The *simplex* Naevius carries informality too far.

Last of all there is Nomentanus.[23] He is so widely accepted as a Lucilian character that one is apt to forget that he owes his place in the fragments to the good offices of Scaliger and Stephanus. At W. 80–1 Scaliger proposed *Nomentani quae* for the MSS. *nomen iamque*. This conjecture is endorsed by Müller, Cichorius and Warmington,[24] and it is called 'uncertain, but neat and plausible' by Housman;[25] it is rejected by Baehrens, Marx and Terzaghi. The admission of Nomentanus to W. 82 is likewise disputed. Donatus on Terence, *Phormio* 1. 2. 73 gives *qui te montane malum*. By his correction *Momentane* Stephanus opened the way for *Nomentane*. In his text of Donatus Wessner prints *Nomentane*, but in the Appendix he apparently accepts *qui di te, montane, malum* with Marx.[26] Suppose, however, that Nomentanus should be restored in both passages, then the Lucilian character would appear to have been L. Atilius Nomentanus, an associate of Scaevola's. This suggestion is advanced by Cichorius (pp. 244 ff.), and notice what he adds: 'Eine Beziehung freilich auf den bei Horaz mehrfach vorkommenden Verschwender Nomentanus, der nach Porphyrio zu Horaz *Sat.* 1. 1. 102 L. Cassius Nomentanus hiess, muss ganz ausser dem Spiele bleiben.' This statement may be a little over-confident, because Porphyrion could have been wrong. It is also fallacious to argue, as Cartault does,[27] that since Nomentanus was present at Nasidienus' dinner-party he cannot have been the man mentioned by Lucilius. But at least we *can* say that no certain connexion has been established between the Horatian and the Lucilian Nomentanus.[28]

Under this heading, therefore, we have found three characters (Gallonius, Maenius, and Pacideianus) and perhaps a fourth

(Albucius) who may be said with confidence to have been drawn from Lucilian satire. There may be others, but we cannot be sure.[29]

(d) *Significant names.* Let us start with names which were certainly or probably chosen solely on account of their derivations. Opimius (2. 3. 142) has already been mentioned. Apart from the oxymoron involving his name, the context is that of a fable which could well have begun with 'once upon a time'. Then we have Maltinus (1. 2. 25). According to Nonius 37. 6 *malta* meant an effeminate fop,[30] and that is just what Maltinus was. The coincidence is too great and the name too uncommon to permit the possibility of a personal reference. Moreover the opposite extreme, namely that of virile exhibitionism, is represented by the colourless *est qui* (25). Cupiennius the adulterer (1. 2. 36) is a similar case. Again the aptness of name to context is too good to be true, and again the antithesis is supplied by an anonymous phrase *quidam notus homo* (31). Porcius (Hog) also belongs to this group. He is projected by his situation and we see him just long enough to catch his party piece, which was to polish off a whole cake in a single mouthful (2. 8. 24). He is linked with Nomentanus, who, whatever his origins, had now become a type figure. The same goes for Nomentanus' other comrade, the *scurra* Pantolabus (1. 8. 11 and 2. 1. 22).

If the five names just quoted are clear cases, another five can be cited which do not allow the same degree of confidence. In 2. 6. 72 the dancer Lepos no doubt epitomizes the subjects of fashionable gossip, but Lepos is also just the kind of name which a real dancer might have had. Heinze reminds us of an actor called Favor (he omits the reference, which is Suet. *Vesp.* 19), and Stein in P–W, 6. 2078 assures us that this was not an isolated instance. The mean Avidienus (2. 2. 55) looks like a type figure until we find that he possesses a nickname—*Canis* 'The Dog' (56). This is inconclusive, since *Canis* may recall simply the general notion of Cynic asceticism, but the pun in v. 64—*hac urget lupus hac canis*—is slightly improved if one assumes that Horace had not invented the nickname. Or consider Ofellus

(2. 2. 2). At first sight it seems a suspiciously neat paradox that the virtues of frugality should be expounded by a man called Mr Titbit (*ofella*), but when Horace steps forward in v. 112 with the words:

> puer hunc ego parvus Ofellum
> integris opibus novi non latius usum
> quam nunc accisis

When I was a small boy I remember this Ofellus living at the same level when his property was intact as he does now when it has been reduced,

and when we hear that Ofellus' farm has now been assigned to a veteran with the very specific name of Umbrenus, we begin to believe that we are dealing with a real person after all. There is also something more than word-play behind 'that louse Pantilius' (πᾶν τίλλειν = 'to nip everything') in 1. 10. 78. The name is found in *C.I.L.* x. 5925 (Dess. 6260), and it occurs here in a context full of personalities. The least we should assume is that Pantilius was a nickname for some carping critic of the day. Finally, let us take an instance where the balance appears evenly poised. In 1. 6. 40 the upstart Novius seems a perfect example of a significant name. What then are we to say of the younger Novius in 121 who, as we argued above, is almost certainly an individual? Perhaps the least difficult solution here is to break the balance in half and to say that the two figures are unrelated.[31]

A significant name, though in theory quite general, may be limited in some way by its context. Thus while Porcius on his own would represent The Glutton, his frame of reference is narrowed by his appearing at table in the company of Fundanius, Viscus, Varius and Maecenas. So that readers would tend to see him not just as The Glutton but rather as the sort of glutton that Horace knew.

This leads on to a further point. In English literature we are all familiar with My Lord Plausible, Sir John Brute, Lady Fanciful, and the other types which bow and sidle through the drawing-rooms of Restoration Comedy. Now in spite of the dramatist's assurance that no personal references were intended the audience would persist in using its imagination. This practice can be illustrated by the epilogue to *The Way of the World*:

> Others there are whose malice we'd prevent
> Such as watch plays with scurrilous intent
> To mark out who by characters are meant.
> And though no perfect likeness they can trace
> Yet each pretends to know the copied face.
> These with false glosses feed their own ill nature
> And turn to libel what was meant a satire.

Something of the same kind must have happened to Horace. Granted his readers were as a whole less idle, less sophisticated, and less malicious than the patrons of the London playhouses; on the other hand his names, unlike those of the Restoration Comedy, were in actual use at the time. The truth is that the Roman system of *cognomina* made it difficult to employ significant names *without* appearing personal. One need only recall the dramatic role played in republican politics by gentlemen called Pea, Bald, Dull and Soak—names which an Englishman would not expect to encounter outside a Shakespearian romance. Or think of that occasion in 59 B.C. when the actor Diphilus raised a storm of applause by declaiming the innocuous line *nostra miseria tu es magnus*—all because of Pompey's *cognomen*.[32] In much the same way when Horace's *Satires* first appeared they caused a certain amount of enjoyable if misguided speculation. Several of the names clearly belonged to individuals; as for the rest, a little stretching here, a little padding there, and the cap could usually be made to fit someone. Cupiennius, for instance, was linked by one tradition with C. Cupiennius Libo of Cumae, an acquaintance of Augustus, and some scholars still find this credible.

Apart altogether from readers' fantasies, there are several places where a definite person is named, and where the derivation, however apposite, can be of only secondary importance, e.g. Stertinius (*stertere*), Furius (*furere*), and Philodemus (φιλεῖν + δῆμος).[33] The last is of special interest, for Palmer (p. xvi) took Philodemus as a type name symbolizing 'the man of low tastes'. When Philodemus of Gadara joked about his name suiting his nature:

αὐταί που Μοῖραί με κατωνόμασαν Φιλόδημον
ὡς ἀεὶ Δημοῦς θερμὸς ἔχει με πόθος³⁴

It must have been the Fates themselves who named me Philodemus, for I am always an ardent Demophile [i.e. a lover of Demo],

he little thought that a similar coincidence would some day be used to argue him out of his place in a Roman diatribe. One other case may be mentioned here, since it is usually passed over. In 1. 2. 64–5 we have:

Villius in Fausta Sullae gener, hoc miser uno nomine deceptus.

Villius, who in connexion with Fausta was Sulla's son-in-law, was deceived to his sorrow solely by this name.

A Roman reader would have known that Sulla was Sulla the Happy (Felix) and that his daughter was called Joy. So language conspires with love to deceive the wretched Villius.

Etymology therefore, if used with restraint, does help us to appreciate the *Satires*. But when we are asked to note the significance of Luscus ('One-Eye'), Nasidienus ('The Nose'), and Arellius ('Dry Old Croesus'), and when we are urged to alter Gargonius to Gorgonius and Scetanus to Sectanus, then it is time to call a halt.³⁵

(e) *Names of Other Type Characters*. Under this miscellaneous heading we may include mythological figures such as Tantalus, Sisyphus, Agave, Orestes, Atrides, Ulysses, Ajax, Tiresias, Penelope and Helen;³⁶ the slave types Dama and Davus;³⁷ and also probably Apella the superstitious Jew.³⁸ Apella was a common name among freedmen, and most of the Jewish community in Rome belonged to that class. This would not rule out the further possibility that Horace was punning on the custom of circumcision. Such was the view of the scholiasts (the pseudo-Acron, for example, comments *finxit nomen quasi sine pelle*), and this would link up with the phrase *curtis Iudaeis*—'the circumcised Jews'—in 1. 9. 70.

Lastly, we should include the figures mentioned in 2. 3. 69 ff. Nerius suggests a man of wisdom and prophetic insight. Cicuta ('Hemlock') is the keen financier. In spite of their astuteness, we learn that both can be tricked by Proteus, that archetype of slippery customers. Since in the context Proteus cannot be a nickname, it is unlikely that Nerius and Cicuta are nicknames either. Moreover, in v. 175 Cicuta is associated with the type figure of Nomentanus. Therefore it is best to take Nerius and Cicuta as standing for 'Something in the City'. This leaves us with Perellius in v. 75. As it is not taken from legend and as it is neither a significant name nor a nickname, one concludes that it belonged either to the man who had been foolish enough to lend Damasippus money or else to one who had become well enough known to represent a type.

(*f*) *Pseudonyms*. It is well known how love poets like Catullus and Propertius used to conceal their girl-friends' identity under false names. Perhaps 'conceal' is hardly the right word, for since the pseudonyms were metrically equivalent to the real names (Lesbia = Clodia, Cynthia = Hostia), and since tongues wagged as busily in the Forum as they do in Mayfair or Park Avenue, the disguise tended to be about as effective as Coan silk. What we should like to know is whether Horace used the same device in the *Satires*. Certainly the scholiasts thought he did, and there is no *a priori* reason why he should not have done so. Nevertheless, not one case has been proved, and the guesses vary greatly in plausibility. The most widely accepted case is that of the poet Alpinus (Alpman) in 1. 10. 36 whose real name was Furius. The nickname may be due to his place of origin, his subject matter, or his notorious metaphor about the Alpine snows. Another probable case is Pitholeon (1. 10. 22) whom Bentley identified with the Pitholaus mentioned in Suetonius, *Jul.* 75. Tenney Frank may also be right in his theory that Heliodorus (1. 5. 2) is the scholar Apollodorus.[39] But these last two instances are somewhat exceptional in that the alteration would have been made for metrical reasons, not for the sake of concealment. One of the ancient rumours which have come down to us alleges that Maltinus (1. 2. 25) is a mask for Maecenas. The latter certainly dressed in an effeminate style,[40] and the satire in question was written before Horace met him. But if this was a genuine allusion it is hard to explain how Horace could have published the poem unchanged after enjoying Maecenas' patronage for over three years. As for other proposals, while it is interesting to toy with the idea that Catius (2. 4. 1) is a skit on the gourmet C. Matius or that Nasidienus Rufus (2. 8. 1) is based on memories of Salvidienus Rufus,[41] one may pass quickly over attempts to link Baius (1. 4. 110) with Bavius and the son of Aesopus (2. 3. 239) with Ticidas.[42]

The most tantalizing name is, of course, Canidia. In addition to other brief appearances she plays a major role in *Sat.* 1. 8 and *Epodes* 5 and 17. Porphyrion on *Epod.* 3. 8 says her real name was Gratidia and that she was a cosmetician from Naples. The first detail may be an invention, and the second a combination of Neapolis (*Epod.* 5. 43) with *nardo perunctum* (*Epod.* 5. 59). On the other hand, it must be conceded that no other fictitious character crops up so persistently, and a detail like *cum Sagana maiore* (*Sat.* 1. 8. 25) makes one pause before saying anything too dogmatic. The problem is largely a matter of degree. No one believes that Canidia is either a personified idea or a recognizable portrait, but between these limits there is room for argument. Three intermediate types of creation may be distinguished: (1) a figure constructed imaginatively on the basis of a group, (2) a figure constructed imaginatively on the basis of a group but with overtones hinting at a real individual, (3) a figure constructed imaginatively on the basis of an individual. If Canidia belongs to type (1) we can say that Horace created her from his knowledge of contemporary witchcraft, intending her, perhaps, to serve as a fictitious substitute for Archilochus' Neobule. If we are dealing with a case of the second type then the individual, whoever she may have been, will remain a shadow in the background and can never be identified. If Canidia falls under the third heading the witches will cease to have much importance, and Canidia herself will emerge as a travesty of one of Horace's acquaintances. Some supporters of the last view have even been bold enough to hazard an identification.[43] My own feeling is that the second possibility is the most likely. On points like this Roman opinion was probably as divided as our own. Not everyone would have accepted Canidia and the rest as composite figures, and Horace's lack of precision may well have increased rather than checked the flow of rumour and conjecture. Martial gives us an example of this ageless curiosity in 9. 95 b:

> nomen Athenagorae quaeris, Callistrate, verum.
> si scio, dispeream, qui sit Athenagoras.

You want to know Athenagoras' real name, Callistratus. Blow me if I know who Athenagoras is.

An earlier instance occurs in 2. 23:

> non dicam, licet usque me rogetis,
> qui sit Postumus in meo libello.

Though you ask me again and again, I will not tell you who is the Postumus in my little book.

The foregoing analysis shows that Horace's use of names was far from uniform. Such a conclusion is neither new nor surprising, but this variety has to be constantly reaffirmed if we are to avoid the generalizations which so often appear in editions and literary histories. Clearly the scholiasts and modern critics of similar leanings such as Cartault and Courbaud[44] cannot be right in maintaining that Horace usually had real people in mind. But there is an opposite way of thinking which can also mislead and which is more frequently encountered. Put crudely it goes like this: Lucilius, a man of high social standing protected by the powerful Scipio family, could afford to attack contemporary statesmen (so far so good); 'the conditions under which Horace wrote were altogether different', 'the political situation between 42 and 31 B.C. would not have borne rough handling and the softening of manners had put a check on personalities'. 'Personality is the essence of satire and Horace dared not be personal.' He had to beware of infringing the law of libel—'there is a touch of serious anxiety beneath the jest upon the *mala* and the *bona carmina* with which *Sat.* 2. 1 closes'. Horace's *Satires* are therefore 'free from vehemence', 'they are directed against types rather than individuals'. 'Horace is the dragon-fly of satire, ornamental but stingless', and one can hardly doubt that 'he was acting wisely...in avoiding personal attacks on living men'. In brief Horace 'stood to Lucilius in much the same relation as Menander to Aristophanes'.[45]

There is much truth in these statements, but they are so oversimplified as to be misleading. It is, of course, a fact, and a significant fact, that Horace did not attack men of real importance—least of all prominent politicians. Something more will be said about this below; here I would simply point out that the political and the personal are not coextensive. The absence of Marcus Antonius does not make Crispinus fictitious. Moreover, even where no living individual is involved it is hardly enough to say 'so-and-so is a type figure', for, as we have seen, type figures can be of several kinds.

In drawing attention to the diversity of Horace's names I have also tried to bear in mind the effect which the *Satires* were likely to produce when they first appeared. This point should not be overstressed, and I have only given it this much prominence because it is usually ignored altogether. It would be absurd to suggest that the first book of *Satires* caused anything in the nature of a public outcry or even widespread resentment; but it does seem that in certain quarters Horace was regarded with suspicion. True, the names were mostly employed as a means to some ethical or aesthetic end. (An indication of this is the fact that with Horace, as opposed to many of the eighteenth-century satirists, our ignorance concerning a name rarely if ever makes a passage unintelligible.) But people do not like being used to point a moral or adorn a tale, especially when the tale is one of vice and stupidity.

As for the dead, they were beyond taking offence, but their relatives were not, and in the Roman family relatives mattered. We may therefore assume that 2. 1. 23:

cum sibi quisque timet, quamquam est intactus, et odit

When everyone is afraid on his own behalf and hates you, though untouched,

for all its ironic exaggeration, contains a core of truth, and that the opening words of Book 2 *sunt quibus in satura videar nimis acer* ('Some people think I am too sharp in my satire') do reflect an authentic situation. The critics were naïve in their judgement and too remote from the poet to appreciate his real intentions, yet occasionally they were right, and sometimes their mistakes were excusable.

So much for Book 1 and its reception. In Book 2, which is over fifty lines longer, the total number of names drops by 20 per cent. Much more significant is the fact that in 1083 verses there are scarcely ten satirical references to living people. One notices, on the other hand, that most of the type characters in group (*e*) above are drawn from the second book. We can guess at some of the factors behind the change. For one thing, unlike its predecessor, Book 2 must have been written with the prospect of publication in mind, and so it is possible that by cutting down the number of personal references Horace wished to forestall the kind of half-informed criticism mentioned above. Moreover, the poet now enjoyed a position of esteem and security such as he had never known before, and as the gliding years carried him into his middle thirties he began to take a more detached view of his material. I do not mean that he became less sensitive to moral evil, but rather that he saw it in less personal terms. This tendency towards greater detachment can also be seen in the form of the poems; for instead of being delivered by Horace himself the sermons are in most cases put into the mouths of intermediate characters like Ofellus and Stertinius. The increase in dialogue is part of the same process.

It may be asked how far the change was due to political developments. The chief development in the years 34–31 B.C. was the
widening of the rift between Octavian and Antony. While this
was taking place, the friendship between Horace and Maecenas
was growing steadily stronger, as is shown by the gift of the Sabine
farm. It is therefore true, no doubt, that Horace would have
found it very difficult to deride any important member of the
pro-Octavian faction. On the other hand, if he had really wanted
to attack public figures, he could surely have chosen some Anto-
nian sympathizers as examples of vice and folly. Antony himself
was a favourite target for lampoons at this period. As we have
seen, however, Horace *reduced* the personal element in his second
book, and when his security was finally guaranteed by Octavian's
victory at Actium he abandoned satire altogether. So it looks as if
fear was not a significant factor in Horace's change of policy.

To conclude this survey I should like to consider a more general
question of interpretation which is closely connected with
Horace's use of names. I have in mind what might be called the
evolutionary approach to the *Satires*. This approach, which
regards Horatian satire as a kind of living organism passing through
the phases of growth, maturity, and decay, is associated in particular with the distinguished name of Eduard Fraenkel, who
presents it in some detail in 'Das Reifen der horazischen Satire',[46]
and again, more briefly, in his *Horace*.[47] The facts underlying
this analysis are as follows. In 1. 2, which is by common consent
one of the earliest of the *Satires*, numerous people are mentioned
by name and the poet himself remains out of sight; in 1. 6 the
names occur in the first half only, and the rest is autobiographical;
names play a much smaller part in Book 2 as a whole, and in
2. 6, one of the latest pieces, they have almost disappeared, leaving
the entire stage to Horace himself; finally the *Epistles* may be said
to abandon personal censure still more completely in favour of a
genial moral discourse centred on the poet and his friends.

Abstracted in this way the scheme is certainly impressive, but
we have to see how the pattern is affected when all the other

satires are included. The biological analogy when applied to art has two aspects, both of which cause trouble in the present case. The first aspect is chronological. If 1. 3 comes immediately after 1. 2 we can argue, as Fraenkel does, that it shows signs of growth, since names are fewer and vv. 63–5 (which allude to the poet's friendship with Maecenas) give the first hint of self-portraiture. But it may well be that 1. 4, which lacks any reference to Maecenas, is earlier than 1. 3. If so, then 1. 3 marks a retrogression, for its autobiographical content cannot be compared with the account of Horace's upbringing in 1. 4. 105 ff. Again, 1. 1 is probably later than both these pieces, yet it contains no self-portraiture at all. If, however, it is earlier, why are there so few names? Finally, why should 1. 10, the latest poem in the book, be so sharply personal in tone?

The problem is not confined to Book 1. A poem like 2. 3 proves on these grounds to be a less developed specimen of Horatian satire than 1. 6; yet it can hardly represent a decline, since it was written two years before his crowning achievement (2. 6). Fraenkel does point out that 'the evolution of the style of a poet... does not, as a rule, proceed in an unbroken straight line'.[48] But once this is admitted the comparison with nature is weakened, since no fruit or vegetable periodically recedes in the course of its growth.

The other aspect of the analogy is evaluative, as may be seen from terms like 'ripeness' and 'maturity'. This means that Fraenkel's approach involves some rather severe judgements. The first part of 1. 6, for instance, is a 'parade of dreary characters' and both writer and reader are relieved 'to get out of the Lucilian masquerade'.[49] This implies that using names was a rather regrettable mannerism which Horace had to grow out of.[50] To Fraenkel 2. 6 represents the acme of Horace's career as a satirist—the poet is the centre of interest and there is an absence of personal ridicule. Accepting this for the moment we ask how the rest of the book fares when measured by the same standards. All the poems, it appears, except one are found wanting. The third 'looks like a prolonged *tour de force*', the fifth is 'full of vigour and brilliant wit, but acid and cynical throughout', and when Tiresias returns to Hades 'we are not sorry to see him go'. All six indicate that 'the stage of over-ripeness has now arrived', and in some of them Horace has 'betrayed his noble ideal of *satura*'.[51]

These verdicts prompt us to ask whether the criteria adopted are really satisfactory. If maturity in Horatian satire is marked by self-portraiture and an absence of names, then a poem like 2. 5, which on other grounds would be considered excellent (and which is just as late as 2. 6), must be classed as inferior. Also is it not strange that the *Satires* should reach their highest point of perfection in a poem which, to quote Courbaud, 'est déjà une véritable épître'?[52] One cannot help feeling that the *Satires* are being assessed as so many imperfect attempts at writing epistles, and that the τέλος of the form has been placed outside the form itself.

Against these criticisms it may be urged that since the *Satires* and *Epistles* both belong to the same genus the latter must represent a more mature conception of what the genus should be like. The biological method might then be justified in this larger perspective. There is something to be said for this objection and it demands careful consideration.

Ancient writers, including Horace himself, had no uniform method of referring to the hexameters. If we let A stand for the *Satires* and B for the *Epistles* we get the following scheme:

(1) Horace: A   *satura* (generic) (*Sat.* 2. 1. 1)
             saturae (*Sat.* 2. 6. 17)
             sermones (*Epist.* 1. 4. 1 and *Epist.* 2. 2. 60?)

    A⎫
      ⎬ *sermones* (*Epist.* 2. 1. 250)
    B⎭

In *Epist.* 2. 2. 60 Horace speaks of his *Bioneis sermonibus et sale nigro*—'Bionean talks and their caustic wit'. The great majority of modern commentators take this as referring only to the *Satires*, on the ground that the *Epistles* are not characterized by caustic wit. Hendrickson, however, argues that Horace has the

Epistles in mind too, and that *sal niger* is merely a conventional phrase.[53] No certain conclusion is possible. What we can say is that Horace himself never uses *satura* in reference to the *Epistles*.

(2) Persius (1. 114–19) justifies his satire by appealing to the precedent of Lucilius and Horace:

> secuit Lucilius urbem,
> te Lupe, te Muci, et genuinum fregit in illis.
> omne vafer vitium ridenti Flaccus amico
> tangit et admissus circum praecordia ludit,
> callidus excusso populum suspendere naso.
> me muttire nefas?

> Lucilius cut the city to pieces—you Lupus, and you Mucius—and smashed his tooth on them. Horace cunningly puts his finger on all the faults of his laughing friend, and after gaining access plays about his heart, clever as he is at hanging the public on the end of his critical nose. May I not even mutter?

Our analysis of the names has shown that friendly, personal banter is not a feature of the *Satires*. Trebatius is the only instance, unless we include the hot-headed Bolanus of 1. 9. 11. Some scholars, therefore, like Conington and Némethy, maintain that Persius is referring more particularly to the *Epistles*. Perhaps so, though I can find no more than half a dozen instances of such banter even in the *Epistles*. In that case Persius has attempted to combine the *Epistles*, as described in vv. 116–17, with the *Satires*, as described in v. 118, and the effect is clumsy to say the least. I prefer to think, however, that it is *through* his satirical criticism of the public in general that Horace twits his friends. They laugh at his wit, and at the same time (or perhaps a little later) they realize that their own faults are being discussed.[54] 'Change the name,' says Horace in 1. 1. 69–70, 'and the story is about you'—*mutato nomine de te / fabula narratur*. If this is correct, Persius is referring primarily to the *Satires*, though one cannot prove that the *Epistles* are excluded. It should be noted, however, that in general Persius draws quite freely on Horace's *Epistles* and actually includes an epistle among his own *Satires* (viz. no. 6). Lucilius had done the same (W. 186 ff.).

(3) Quintilian: A ⎱ *satura* (generic)
　　　　　　　B? ⎰

In discussing the tradition of *satura* represented by Lucilius, Persius, and Horace, Quintilian (10. 1. 93–4) praises Lucilius for his learning, his frankness, his pungency, and his wit. Horace is commended for his terseness and the purity of his style. Persius is said, quite generally, to have won distinction. Did Quintilian consciously include Horace's *Epistles* or was he thinking only of the *Satires*? Again, certainty is impossible.

(4) Statius: A　*satura* (singular for plural)
　　　　　　 B　*epistula* (singular for plural)

With Horace's *œuvre* in mind Statius writes in *Silvae* 1. 3. 102–4 to his friend:

　　　　　　　　　　　　　　　　　　sive
　　　liventem satiram nigra rubigine turbes,
　　　seu tua non alia splendescat epistula cura.

> Whether you stir up (?) dark satires with black blight or whether your letters sparkle with just the same polish.[55]

Statius therefore regarded the *Satires* and *Epistles* as similar in style but distinguishable in spirit and in name.

(5) Suetonius: A ⎱ *saturae*
　　　　　　　 B? ⎰

In his *Life of Horace* Suetonius says 'He was short (*brevis*) and fat (*obesus*) as described by himself in the satires (*in saturis*) and by Augustus in a letter'. Now there is quite a long passage about Horace's shortness in *Sat.* 2. 3. 308 ff. and a brief reference (*corporis exigui*) in the self-portrait at the end of *Epist.* 1. 20. His fatness is mentioned in *Epist.* 1. 4. 15–16—*pinguem* and *Epicuri de grege porcum*. If, then, Suetonius was being precise, he must have regarded the *Epistles* as *saturae*. It could be argued that he was referring only to the *Satires* and that he thought of Horace's obesity as being included in *Sat.* 2. 3. 308 ff. This is not impossible, for in that passage Horace is compared to a frog which inflates itself in a vain attempt to rival a calf. Or he might have thought in a moment of error that the phrase *Epicuri de grege porcum* occurred in the *Satires*. Or perhaps he was just being vague. The weight of probability, however, favours the view that Suetonius classified the *Epistles* as *saturae*.

(6) Horace, according to the scholiasts:

A *sermones*⎫
B *epistulae*⎭ *satura* (generic)

In the introduction to Book 1 the scholiasts say:

quamvis igitur hoc opus satyram esse Horatius ipse profiteatur cum ait 'sunt quibus in satyra videar nimis acer...' tamen proprios titulos voluit ei accommodare, hos priores duos libros Sermonum, posteriores Epistularum inscribens.

> So although Horace himself asserts that this work is *satura* when he says 'Some people think I am too sharp in my satire', nevertheless he wished to give specific titles to it; so he inscribed these first two books as *Sermones* (Talks) and the later ones as *Epistulae* (Letters).

This shows that the scholiasts thought of the *Epistles* as *satura*; but their reason for doing so is unsound. For they have taken the word *satura* from *Sat.* 2. 1. 1 and extended it to the *Epistles*.

(7) Sidonius: A *sermones*
B *epistulae—saturae*

With direct reference to Horace's works Sidonius (9. 221-2) speaks of the *saturas epistularum sermonumque sales*—'The medleys of the *Epistles* and the wit of the *Sermones*' (i.e. the *Satires*). He therefore believed that the *Epistles* could be termed *saturae*, though he used *satura* in the early sense of medley rather than in the sense given to it by Diomedes, i.e. 'an abusive poem written to attack men's vices in the manner of Old Comedy'.

The picture, therefore, is not as clear as one could wish. 1 and 4 indicate that *satura* should be confined to the *Satires*; 7, probably 5, and (on false reasoning) 6 suggest that it can include the *Epistles*, and this is supported by Persius, *Sat.* 6; 2 and 3 are inconclusive. If we forget labels for the moment and consider only the facts, we find that the *Satires* and *Epistles* are broadly similar in metre, in stylistic level, and in subject-matter (that is, both are concerned with the behaviour of men in society). But they present important differences in form and manner. In the *Epistles* dialogue gives way to letter, and the lively direct speech which was such a prominent feature of the *Satires* is greatly reduced. A recent writer has described the change by saying that 'the conversationalist...absorbs the dramatist'.[56] This is a good way of putting it, though one should perhaps substitute 'talker' for 'conversationalist'. More important is the change of manner. The emphasis moves from censure to affirmation. Moral defects are still observed, but instead of exposing them to ridicule the poet is more concerned to reform them by exhortation and advice. Adapting the remark quoted above, we might say that 'the moralist absorbs the satirist'. Names occur less frequently than in *Sat.* 2, and the old practice of ὀνομαστὶ κωμῳδεῖν (ridicule by name) is abandoned. It is significant that *Epist.* 1. 19, which is an angry poem, does not name a single adversary—a remarkable contrast with *Sat.* 1. 10. In short, Lucilius has been left behind.

In the present book I have indicated these differences by using the separate titles of *Satires* and *Epistles*, reserving the term *sermones* for the hexameter poems in general. This is a very common procedure, and in adopting it I can appeal to the authority of Professor Fraenkel himself, who says of Horace's later work 'He returned to the writing of *sermones*...but not as satires' (p. 153) and 'The potentialities of the Horatian *satira* were exhausted, the potentialities of the Horatian *sermo* were not' (p. 309). If one prefers to call the *Epistles* satires too (and in view of the evidence presented above this may well be correct), it is still fair to uphold the distinction between the Lucilian, or quasi-Lucilian, satire of the first two books and the non-Lucilian satire of the rest. And within this framework the evolutionary approach would break down again.

Reverting to the *Satires*, one feels that these poems are not a very suitable field for the biological method, partly because they were all written within the space of eight or nine years and therefore belong to the same period of the poet's career, partly because within that period so few of the pieces can be dated with certainty, but mainly because, being *saturae*, they show a considerable variety of subject and treatment. Is 2. 8 more 'evolved' than 1. 1? Or is 2. 2 more 'developed' than 1. 6? Such questions are hardly to the point.

The discussion may be summed up by saying that while there are fewer names in Book 2 than in Book 1 the decrease is not a regular process, nor does it either enhance or diminish the satires' literary merit. As for self-portraiture, this forms an element in several of the finest pieces, but it appears as often in Book 1 as in Book 2, and as we shall see in the next chapter it is probably more straightforward in the first collection. Moreover, self-portraiture is not the only element, nor even the most essential. Throughout Horace's *Satires* it is ridicule and criticism (however impersonal and however mild) that remain predominant. When these activities cease to be Horace's main concern he abandons satire and turns to other forms of poetic creation.

CHAPTER VI

THE DIATRIBES OF BOOK 2

2. 2, 2. 3, 2. 7

Before moving on to the poems of Book 2 it may be well to say something about the arrangement of the *Satires* as a whole. Like Virgil's *Eclogues*, Book 1 contains ten pieces.[1] Of these the first three go closely together in form and subject, and the same is true of the literary satires—numbers 4 and 10. Apart from this, however, there is scarcely any discernible pattern. It is true that 6 recalls 1 by its theme of contentment as well as by its opening address to Maecenas, and this might lead the reader to expect some kind of balance between numbers 1–5 and 6–10. In fact there is none. Some scholars would arrange the satires in three groups of three, taking 1, 2 and 3 as diatribes, 4, 5 and 6 as poems about Horace himself, and 7, 8 and 9 as short anecdotes. They then leave 10 aside as a concluding piece.[2] But 10 is also about Horace himself and it is closely related to 4, whereas 5 and 6 are not. Nor does 9 bear any significant resemblance to 7 or 8. If, however, we bracket 4 with 10 and 5 with 9 (the latter pair being concerned with Horace's relation to Maecenas' circle), we are then left with the ill-assorted 6 and 8 enclosing the trivial 7.

With Book 2 the situation is rather different. There is a clear thematic connexion between 4 and 8, which are both concerned with the follies of gastronomy. Numbers 3 and 7 have a Saturnalian setting and each contains a sermon on one of the Stoic paradoxes. F. Boll, who pointed out these correspondences over fifty years ago,[3] went on to connect 2 with 6 on the grounds that both satires were written in praise of rural simplicity. He then balanced the consultation of Trebatius in 1 with the consultation of Tiresias in 5. The parallels, of course, are by no means exact. Numbers 1 and 5 have no similarity of content; 4 and 8

are quite different in form, as are 2 and 6. Yet the correspondences are close enough to establish that this was Horace's
principle of arrangement. And when we contrast such symmetry,
limited though it is, with the rather miscellaneous character of
Book 1, it is hard not to believe that one or two of the poems
were written to fit the scheme. Nevertheless, any precise and
detailed theory is threatened by the fact that 1 and 5, which are
probably the latest pair, have less in common than any of the
other pieces. No doubt we shall never know how the book
came into being, but at least we can say that the present sequence
gives the maximum amount of variety within a fairly regular
plan. The plan itself, however, has no symbolic significance;
it confers no extra meaning on any individual poem; and as far
as I can discover it involves no mathematical secrets.

2. 2

'Dis-moi ce que tu manges, je te dirai ce que tu es'—such was the
boast of M. Brillat-Savarin, that dedicated gourmet who worshipped Gastéréa as the tenth muse. If he ever thought of the
ordinary Roman, as distinct from kindred spirits like Lucullus,
the great savant must have shaken his head, for the plebeian diet
had little to excite him. In order to visualize its content we have
to set aside even such common items of our own experience as
potatoes, butter, sugar, tomatoes, oranges, bananas, chocolate,
coffee, tea and beer. Fresh meat was a rarity available only at
religious celebrations. Cattle, bred for draught purposes, provided tough and inferior beef; sheep were reared for wool rather
than mutton, and goats were kept for milk. The commonest
meat was pork, which could be dried, smoked or salted for winter
consumption. But even pork was beyond the means of the very
poor. Salt fish was more familiar, but the fresh variety cost
nearly five times as much and was therefore a luxury. The staple
food consisted of the cereal grains—often in the form of porridge
rather than bread—and a few vegetables like beans, peas, lentils,

turnips, and cabbage. To this might be added chestnuts, occasionally eggs, and fruit such as figs, dates, apples and grapes. The usual drink would be cheap local wine from the Alban hills.[4]

In the early centuries such a diet was almost universal, and throughout Rome's history most of the population never knew anything better. But as her armies marched over Greece and Asia Minor they encountered a new world of luxury and refinement. Clothes, furniture and jewellery, food and wine, statues, paintings and books—never had they seen such magnificence, and they at once resolved to seize as much as could be transported. No doubt the bulk of this plunder found its way into the villas of the aristocracy, but once the demand for such goods had been created the new mercantile class made sure that the supply was maintained and in so doing enriched itself.

Describing the effect of the new affluence Livy (39. 6) says:

Female lute-players and harpists and other kinds of festive entertainment became a feature of banquets; and from now on greater care and expense were bestowed on the banquets themselves. The cook, who in earlier times was regarded and treated as the cheapest kind of slave, began to be valued more highly, and what had once been a menial occupation came to be viewed as an art.

The excesses which resulted from this concentration of wealth led historians to connect Rome's moral decline with the rise of her imperial power. In the passage from which I have just quoted Livy attributes the beginning of corruption to the army's return from Asia in 187 B.C. For Polybius the significant date was 168 B.C.—the year of Pydna; Piso the annalist chose 154. But after Sallust the turning point was usually placed in 146 B.C., when Carthage and Corinth were overthrown.[5] As Pliny the Elder said: 'The year that saw the birth of luxury also witnessed the downfall of Carthage; and so by a fateful coincidence the desire and the opportunity for embracing vice occurred simultaneously' (NH 33. 150). Whatever its date of origin, this complex process continued through the first century, assisted by the victories of Sulla and Pompey. And Tacitus shows that it did not stop at Actium (Ann. 3. 55).

Concern was expressed in many ways. The commonest, and not necessarily the shallowest, reaction was to say: 'Our parents did not bring us up to admire luxury. Rome's greatness was won by toughness, discipline and hard work. And apart altogether from our training and history we have always believed that laziness and self-indulgence are, quite simply, wicked.' Some, more politically-minded, would say: 'Extravagance calls attention to the gulf between rich and poor. It encourages the disruptive emotions of envy and contempt and so endangers the stability of the state.'[6] Others, arguing on an individualistic basis, would contend that the spendthrift was ruining his health and reputation as well as his fortune. And a few might add that by purchasing vast quantities of foreign goods he was leading indirectly to the impoverishment of Italy.[7]

As a result of such feelings repeated efforts were made to curb extravagance, especially in the matter of food.[8] In 181 B.C. the *Lex Orchia* placed a limit on the number of guests allowed at dinner. Twenty years later the *Lex Fannia* decreed that on ordinary days a dinner should cost no more than ten asses. On ten days of every month the host could spend thirty asses, and on special occasions like the *Ludi Romani* and the *Saturnalia* a hundred.[9] Towards the end of the century the *Lex Licinia* raised the ordinary daily figure to thirty asses. It placed no limit on the amount of bread, wine, fruit and vegetables, but fixed a certain weight per day for dried meat and salted fish. In Sulla's time the terms of the law had to be revised again. The maximum cost on ordinary days was now fixed at thirty sesterces. Later we find Augustus trying to hold the line at two hundred. Admittedly these figures are less dramatic than they look, for allowance has to be made for rises in price and alterations in currency. But I am assured by Professor F. M. Heichelheim that when these factors have been taken into account the sums mentioned still indicate an impressive change in the standard of living.

They also indicate the futility of sumptuary legislation. The trouble was, of course, that those who supported the laws did so in the belief that such measures would be highly salutary for other people. Senators agreed that the ostentation of businessmen really ought to be curtailed, but insisted that they themselves had to maintain a style appropriate to their rank; and such feelings were, in fact, recognized by Julius Caesar.[10] Again, it was admitted that office-holders might be open to certain temptations, and accordingly Antius Restio had a law passed about 70 B.C. forbidding magistrates and candidates to dine out, except with certain specified people. But if you were, shall we say, an aedile, and you knew that a contractor or a merchant or a fellow-politician was relying on you to do him a favour—in the public interest of course—it would surely have seemed rather churlish to refuse the man's hospitality.

We are not surprised, therefore, to find that in practice these well-intentioned laws were defied or evaded. In response to the *Lex Fannia* men like Tubero, Rutilius and Mucius bought game and fish from their servants well below market price. Athenaeus, who gives this information, adds approvingly that they did not make such arrangements only for themselves; they gave presents to others as well—especially to their friends, 'for they adhered to the teachings of the Stoa'.[11] A character in Lucilius speaks contemptuously of 'Fannius' miserable little hundred'[12]—a hundred asses being the *maximum* allowed for any occasion. Outside the city the Fannian law was apparently disregarded, for eighteen years later Didius had it extended to the whole of Italy. We are told by Macrobius (*Sat.* 3. 17. 13) that after the enactment of the *Lex Antia* poor Antius dined at home for the rest of his life because he couldn't bear to see his own law flouted. Julius Caesar's regulations were also unpopular. And no wonder, for under his régime not only did inspectors snoop around the markets in search of illegal delicatessen, but according to Suetonius (*Jul.* 43) policemen would suddenly descend on a man's dining room like harpies in uniform and carry off any titbits which had escaped the inspector's eye. One scarcely needs the words of Cicero (*Att.* 13. 7) to establish that even Caesar's laws were ignored when the great man was away.

luxury could only have been quelled by a
...at which followed Cannae, or else by a much
...and efficient dictatorship than Rome ever possessed.
...ost that could be done (and this was little enough) was to
...fluence the attitude of the wealthy classes in a general way.
According to Tacitus (*Ann.* 3. 54), the disenchanted Tiberius
once said *reliquis intra animum medendum est: nos pudor, pauperes
necessitas, divites satias in melius mutet*—'The other ills must be
healed within the heart. Let us all learn to behave better—the
senators through self-respect, the poor through necessity, and the
rich through surfeit'. It was one of Horace's aims to arouse men's
self-respect, but he was not so cynical as to believe that *pudor* was
a prerogative of the senatorial order. In fact the diatribe which we
are about to discuss is based on the conversation of a peasant. Its
thought may be paraphrased as follows:

Introduction (1–7). Here are the virtues of simple living. (This talk is not my
own but represents the teachings of the peasant Ofellus, a sage unattached to any
school, a man of sturdy common sense.) Consider the matter now, before
lunch—not amid the splendour of a banquet when the eye is dazzled by senseless glitter and the mind inclines in favour of the sham, rejecting what is better.
Section 1A (8–22). A corrupt judge does not weigh the truth properly. Do
some hard riding or hunting, or (if you prefer the softer exercises of the Greeks)
play a game of ball or throw a discus. Then, when the exertion has knocked the
finickiness out of you, see if you can resist plain food. The butler is out, the
stormy sea protects the fish—well, bread and salt will appease your yelping
stomach. How so? Because the chief pleasure does not reside in the rich
savoury smell but in yourself. Get your sauce by sweat. The man who is pale
and bloated from excess will not enjoy oysters, trout, or grouse.

After establishing his principle Horace turns to those who reject
it in practice, and the satirical tone now emerges more strongly.

1B *(23–38).* In spite of this fact you can hardly be prevented from choosing a
peacock in preference to a pullet. You are led astray by empty appearances;
for the peacock costs gold and its coloured tail is a pretty sight. But do you eat
the tail? Does it look so magnificent when cooked? Although there is no
difference in the meat, you try to obtain this bird rather than that, deceived as
you are by their difference in looks. Well, suppose you *can* distinguish their
flavours, how do you tell whether this bass was caught in the Tiber or in the

sea, between the bridges or at the river mouth? You praise a three-po
mullet, you silly fool, though you have to cut it into separate helpings. You ề
attracted solely by its appearance. Why then dislike long bass? Presumably
because the bass is large by nature and the mullet small. It's not often that a
hungry stomach spurns everyday food.

1 C (39–52). 'I'd like to see something huge stretched out on a huge dish', says
a gullet which in its voracity would do credit to the Harpies. Oh ye warm
south winds, come and 'cook' the delicacies of these fellows! And yet their
fresh boar and turbot are *already* rotten, because their stomachs are sick of
gorging and prefer radishes and pickles.

This folly is relatively recent. The poor man's food has not yet been wholly
banished from the tables of the rich—eggs and black olives still have a place. It
is not so long since Gallonius won notoriety by serving a sturgeon.[13] Why is
that? Did the sea feed fewer turbots in those days? The turbot was safe and the
stork safe in its nest until the authority of a praetor taught you the new fashion.
Nowadays if someone issued an edict proclaiming the deliciousness of roast
seagull the youth of Rome would obey him, amenable as they are to everything
perverse.

Before concluding the first half, Horace now redresses the balance,
as in 1. 1. 101 ff., by asserting that the opposite extreme is just as
vicious.

1 D (53–69). According to Ofellus a simple style of living is quite different
from stingy squalor. The latter is no less a vice than extravagance. Avidienus
eats olives five years old and cornels from the forest. He hates to open his wine
till it's sour; and the smell of his oil is unbearable. On festive occasions he does
make an effort. He dons a white toga and pours out the oil drop by drop with
his own hand. He is lavish with his vinegary wine.[14] That's *his* idea of a celebration. The wise man will avoid both extremes. He will not be over-particular,
like Albucius, in superintending dinner, nor will he be so slack as to tolerate
dirtiness, like Naevius.

So far, then, the main themes have been: hunger is the best
sauce; the craving for exotic food has really nothing to do with
flavour but is simply a matter of appearances based on fashion;
the right kind of diet represents a mean between extravagance
and stinginess.

The thread connecting 1 A, 1 B, and 1 C is provided by the
idea of corruption—a corruption which cannot distinguish the
genuine from the fake. Thus in the introduction the mind is said
to be misled by the glitter of a banquet (*stupet acies...acclinis*

falsis animus). This notion of a judgement unbalanced by corruption is taken up in 1 A, *male verum examinat omnis / corruptus iudex* (8–9), and it reappears at the end of the paragraph in connexion with the man whose enjoyment has been ruined by excess. In 1 B the gourmet is said to be corrupted or led astray by irrelevancies (*corruptus vanis rerum*), deceived by appearances (*formis deceptum*), and attracted solely by looks (*ducit te species*). And in this search for the unusual there is more than a touch of the perverse. This last observation leads into 1 C, which opens with the cravings of an unnatural appetite. In the end, says Horace, such morbid desire is self-defeating, for when the huge meal comes the jaded stomach is unable to accept it.

In v. 44 Horace turns rather abruptly to the vagaries of fashion. Every new vogue must have a leader. Of the two examples given Gallonius the rich auctioneer was a contemporary of Lucilius, but there is less certainty about the unnamed praetor who introduced a craze for storks.[15] Porphyrion says he was called Rufus and quotes an epigram to the effect that he suffered an ignominious defeat at the polls—a defeat which was supposed to represent the people's vengeance for the death of the storks. At any rate the fame of such men implied the existence of a public waiting to be pampered and exploited. This leads Horace back to the theme of corruption—the youth of Rome will follow any leader, provided he is blatantly frivolous.

All this does not mean, of course, that Horace had no palate. He enjoyed good food as much as anyone and he respected the character of an old Falernian. He did sincerely feel, however, that the gluttony which flourished around him was wasteful and foolish and that a great deal of his contemporaries' connoisseurship was no more than snobbish affectation.

Section 2A (70–93). These are the benefits of simple living. First, good health. Remember how fit you were when you ate plain food. A mixture of delicacies will cause the stomach to revolt. The body, sluggish from yesterday's excesses, weighs down the soul and nails to the earth a particle of the divine spirit. The man who eats sparingly falls asleep at once and rises fresh to his daily business.

And yet he can enjoy a treat from time to time—when a holiday comes along, when he's run down, or when he's getting old. The glutton, however, has no pleasure to fall back on. How different from the men of old, who instead of devouring all their meat when it was fresh, would keep it in case of a guest's arrival, even though in the end it might be rather high. What giants they were in those days!

2B (94–111). Secondly, restraint earns a good reputation. Huge turbots and dishes bring notoriety and ruin. And when you are destitute you won't be able to afford a rope to hang yourself. 'You can talk like that to Trausius,' says the listener, 'but my fortune is large enough to support this kind of luxury.' Well, is there nothing better to spend it on? Why should any good man starve when you are rich? Why are the temples in decay? Why not give some of your vast wealth to the country of your birth? I suppose you of all mankind are bound to stay rich for ever. What glee there will be at your fall! Who, then, is better trained to meet misfortune—the man accustomed to every kind of excess or the man content with little?

2C (112–36). Ofellus lived his philosophy. Before his eviction, in the days when he owned his property, his life was just as simple as it is now. You can see him today, working with his cattle and sons on the farm which now belongs to someone else. This is what he has to say: 'On a working day I usually ate no more than a shank of smoked ham and greens. But when I had a visitor I celebrated with a pullet or a kid, and for dessert we had nuts, raisins and figs. Then we would enjoy a pleasant evening's drinking. Whatever troubles lie ahead, this style of living cannot be greatly reduced, and indeed it has remained much the same even though a new occupant is now in residence.

'I say "occupant", for actual ownership of the land is not granted to him or me or anyone else. He turned us out, and he will be turned out by his own worthlessness or his ignorance of the tricks of the law, or finally by the heir who outlives him. This land is now in the name of Umbrenus; once it was called Ofellus'. No one will ever own it, but the use of it will pass now to me now to someone else. So be brave and confront adversity with brave hearts.'

In 2A we have a fresh beginning which corresponds closely with the opening lines. Compare *quae quantaque* with *quae et quanta*, *victus tenuis* with *vivere parvo*, and *accipe* with *discite*. Also the contrast between good and bad health has much in common with Section 1A, the main difference being that the benefits of a simple diet which were implied in the earlier passage are now made explicit. Half way through 2A (at v. 82) a second argument appears, namely that a simple diet leaves room for an occasional treat. This is not a new theme; it occurred previously in connexion with the miserly Avidienus (59–62). But the effect is one of ironic contrast rather than repetition, for Avidienus' idea of a celebration was painfully restricted—in spite of his white toga. A further contrast comes in vv. 89 ff. The men of old, who preferred to eat their pork high so that they could share it with a guest, are the very reverse of the jaded sensualists in 1 C to whom even a fresh boar tasted unpleasant.

Except for the big turbots and the big dishes (95), which recall v. 39 and vv. 49 ff., 2B is unconnected with anything in Section 1. To the medical and aesthetic arguments which have gone before it adds considerations of ethics, finance, and common prudence. The ethical argument appeals to the regard which a man has for the opinions of society (*fama*), of his neighbours (*vicinos*), and of his family (*patruum*); but it rests ultimately on his own self-respect (*te tibi iniquum*). The financial argument cannot be divorced from this, though of course it also includes the element of material self-interest. The concluding argument, on the precariousness of fortune, is drawn from the deepest wells of ancient thought and religion. Such an awareness provides material for every kind of utterance from the most elaborate and sophisticated odes of Greek tragedy to the tritest clichés of popular wisdom. At an intermediate level the idea received its most memorable form in the words:

> sperat infestis metuit secundis
> alteram sortem bene praeparatum
> pectus. (*Carm.* 2. 10. 13–15)

The heart which is well prepared hopes for a change of fortune in adversity, is on guard against it in prosperity.

The mutability of fortune leads smoothly into the last section (2C), which describes the altered circumstances of Ofellus and his reaction to them. In Horace's boyhood Ofellus owned a small farm near Venusia. Like many another, he was evicted after Philippi (42 B.C.) to make room for one of Octavian's ex-servicemen (Appian, *BC* 4. 3). The new owner, however, allowed Ofellus to work the farm, in return, presumably, for a regular payment in kind. In his closing speech Ofellus begins by dealing with his experience wholly in terms of food and drink, and so continues the satire's main theme. In particular, the idea of a special celebration looks back to Avidienus (59–62) and to the healthy man (82–8). But towards the end we are taken on to quite a different level, from which the glutton and all his concerns fade into insignificance. In Lucretius' famous words, *vitaque mancipio nulli datur, omnibus usu* (*DRN* 3. 971)—'And life is granted to none on freehold, to all on lease'—a line which, like many in Shakespeare's sonnets, transmutes the dry terminology of law into memorable poetry.

A closer look at the opening verses will reveal some of the sophisticated art which makes the poem what it is. In *boni* (1)—'Gentlemen'—Horace has chosen a mode of address directly parallel to the Greek ὠγαθοί—a trivial point until we read *nec meus hic sermo est* (2). As the editors say, this is an echo of Plato's οὐ γὰρ ἐμὸς ὁ μῦθος—'The tale is not mine'. It may be just a happy accident that the quotation comes from the *Symposium* (177A) and is spoken there by the doctor Eryximachus; but it is a kind of accident to which Horace is markedly prone. The lines on Greek games, introduced by the slightly pejorative *graecari* (11), contain three Greek importations (*austerum, aera, disco*). The gnomic injunction *tu pulmentaria quaere | sudando* ('Get your sauce by sweat') goes back to a remark of Socrates who, when asked why he was walking so long, replied ὄψον συνάγω πρὸς τὸ δεῖπνον—'I'm getting my sauce for dinner'.[16] Finally, the reader who knew his Homer by heart would remember on seeing *latrantem stomachum* (18)—'yelping stomach'—that Odysseus had said οὐ γάρ τι στυγερῇ ἐπὶ γαστέρι κύντερον ἄλλο (*Od.* 7. 216)—'There is nothing more cur-like than the belly in its hateful persistence'.

With this allusiveness go a continual variation of long and short sentences and a lively mixture of statement, question, and command. There is even one notorious passage where the speaker loses for a moment the thread of his construction and has to pick it up again in the next line.[17] The flow of spontaneous discourse is also assisted by the metre. If we except the anacoluthon just mentioned, there is not a single end-stopped line between vv. 8 and 22. When we add to all this the kind of thematic development already described, it is clear that the passage represents a very subtle and very unusual type of verse. Anyone who tends to believe that the *Satires* are *really* little more than metrical prose would do well to read Cicero's treatment of the same subject in *Tusc. Disp.* 5. 97 ff.

In one general respect, however, 2. 2 is less satisfying than other satires in the book. There is a lack of clarity in the setting which reflects a larger uncertainty about the relationship of Horace to Ofellus. In v. 7 the speaker says 'Discuss the matter here (*hic*) with me before lunch'. Palmer is convinced that *hic* refers to 'some spot on Ofellus' farm'. This involves the view that *quae* (2) means 'the words which' and hence that 'Ofellus is reported *verbatim*'. Now it is true that the last twenty lines or so do purport to be Ofellus' actual words; and there is nothing in the ideas to prevent us from accepting the fiction. But for the greater part of the poem such acceptance is impossible. Even granting that Ofellus owned the farm before his eviction, it is hard to imagine a Venusian peasant being so familiar with the high life of the capital. He knows about the best mead and the choicest fish and game; he has heard of connoisseurs who can tell whether a bass has fed in the estuary or in the city centre; and he is concerned about the state of Rome's temples. Odder still, he is conversant not only with jokes from Plautus and Terence but with topics from Lucilius.[18] Even this is not too much for Lejay, who tells us (p. 313) that Ofellus could have had some rolls of Lucilius in his house. Presumably he also had works of Stoic or Pythagorean philosophy, for in v. 79 he speaks of bodily indulgence as nailing the soul to the earth.[19]

If, however, one believes (as I do) that the setting is Rome and that Horace is transmitting the teachings but not the words of Ofellus, then the old farmer becomes rather a feeble device. Clearly he is supposed to have some kind of independent existence which will prevent the reader from ascribing all the sentiments in the poem to Horace himself. But for the most part Ofellus is too vague and shadowy a figure to perform this function, and so dramatically 2. 2 is weaker than several of the other pieces.

Editors like Morris may well be right in interpreting this technical uncertainty as a sign of early composition. But even if the satire was written in 34 B.C. it still contains two passages which provide interesting hints cf Horace's later career as a lyric poet. In v. 100 the glutton claims that he can well afford his extravagance: 'I have a large income and a fortune big enough for three kings.' Horace answers 'Well, is there nothing better for you to spend your money on? Why does any good man stand in need when you are rich? How is it that the ancient temples of the gods are in decay? You worthless wretch! Why don't you give a portion of that great pile to the country of your birth?' This passage is unique in the *Satires*. In several other places we hear that the happy life consists in living on good terms with one's family, friends, and neighbours, and this implies a certain degree of kindliness and hospitality. (The miser in 1. 1 is an example of one who has failed to reach this standard.) But there is nothing else-where to suggest that a man has any responsibility to the state. Temples and public works did not come within the field of private morality, and that is what the *Satires* are about.

In addition to civic virtue there is another element missing from the *Satires'* ethical scheme. That is, the relation of an individual to the universe as a whole. A genre whose laws were developed to deal with the follies and vices of social behaviour was not equipped to move in the vaster areas of human experience. The age of the earth, the transience of human life, and the absolute dominion of death—these are not satiric themes, and so the reflexions of Ofellus in vv. 129 f. have a rather unusual sombreness:

> nam propriae telluris erum natura neque illum
> nec me nec quemquam statuit.

> For nature has appointed neither him nor me nor anyone else as master and owner of the land.

A similar mood appeared for a moment at the end of 1. 1 and was hastily laughed off; it recurs in 2. 6 in the philosophy of the city mouse, but thanks to the atmosphere of the fable and the character of the mouse himself it is easily contained within the limits of satire. Here there is no irony to diminish the effect, and as a result the satire looks as if it is going to end on a note of solemnity far removed from its main subject. Horace realized this himself, but there was no going back, and so he took one step further, *exaggerating* a little so as to lighten the air of gravity and to finish, as it were, in a major key:

> quocirca vivite fortes,
> fortiaque adversis opponite pectora rebus.

So take your stand bravely and confront adversity with brave hearts.

2.3

In this, by far the longest of the *Satires*, time and setting are cleverly supplied in the first few lines, which, amusingly enough, are part of a severe scolding administered to Horace by Damasippus. In paraphrase, the introduction begins as follows:

1–16. 'You write so little that you scarcely finish four poems a year; instead you unravel everything you've written. You are angry with yourself because in spite of generous amounts of wine and sleep you produce nothing worth talking of. You say you've taken refuge out here during the Saturnalia. Very well, if you're so abstemious, give voice to something worthy of your promises. Go on, begin...There is nothing forthcoming. It's no use blaming your pen or cursing and beating at the wall. Yet you had a purposeful air which promised great things as soon as you had time and could get away to your warm country house. What point was there in packing Plato, Archilochus, and the comic poets? Do you think you can reduce your unpopularity by deserting the cause of virtue? You will win only contempt, you poor creature. You must either keep away from that brazen Siren Sloth or else bid farewell to whatever you've achieved in better days.'

We are to imagine, I take it, that Damasippus is visiting Horace at the Sabine farm during the Saturnalia (17–19 December), and has seized the opportunity to give the poet a good lecture. Horace replies equably:

16–38. 'In return for your sound advice, Damasippus, may heaven reward you—with a barber! But how do you know me so well?'

'I've been minding other people's business ever since my own crashed on the Stock Exchange. Once I enjoyed asking what bronze basin Sisyphus had washed his feet in; I valued such and such a statue expertly at five thousand pounds; no one else got such bargains in real estate. And so the crowds at the auctions used to call me "The Man of Mercury".'

'Yes, I know, and I'm amazed that you've been relieved of that ailment. Yet the amazing thing is that a new ailment has driven out the old, as happens with physical complaints when, say, a headache passes into the stomach or when a torpid patient suddenly becomes a boxer and attacks the doctor. Provided nothing like that happens, have it your own way.'[20]

'My dear fellow, don't deceive yourself. You are just as mad, and so are all fools, if there is anything in Stertinius' spiel. It was he who taught me this lesson. After consoling me he urged me to cultivate the beard of wisdom and to go home from the Fabrician bridge leaving my sadness behind. For when my business collapsed I intended to cover my head and jump in the river. But providentially he appeared beside me and said...'

The subsequent speech, which comprises the main part of the satire (38–299), expounds the Stoic paradox that all fools are mad. This introductory section is characteristically gay. 'That brazen Siren Sloth' comes well from a proselytizing Stoic. Such men could see no value in the *Odyssey* until they had turned it into a moral allegory. Sisyphus' footbath is also a nice touch. Corinthian bronzes fetched high prices, and as Sisyphus was the founder of Corinth a very early piece like his footbath would have caused quite a stir at the Roman Sotheby's. It was, in fact, a famous antique even in the fifth century. In a fragment of Aeschylus' *Sisyphus*, which was one of his satyr plays, the king calls imperiously for water:

καὶ νίπτρα δὴ χρὴ θεοφόρων ποδῶν φέρειν·
λεοντοβάμων ποῦ σκάφη χαλκήλατος;[21]

Water must be brought for the feet that bear a god. Where is the bronze
bowl with the lion base?

And yet there are one or two disappointing features. The first concerns Damasippus as a character. His opening tirade, his beard, his salvation by the Stoic Stertinius, his habit of quoting Chrysippus—all these suggest the zealous convert, earnest and confident in his new-found faith. Such a character would make an excellent foil for the ironical Horace. But unfortunately the picture becomes blurred at a number of points. Damasippus' remark about minding other people's business after wrecking his own (*aliena negotia curo, | excussus propriis*) might be just inadvertence, but he ought not to use the disrespectful 'spiel' (*crepat*) in connexion with his teacher's sermon,[22] and he ought not to refer so flippantly to his own beard, which was the symbol of his belief.[23] All these are Horace's jokes and should not be put in Damasippus' mouth. Moreover, Damasippus remains oddly ambiguous about his present condition. Is he insane or not? Clearly we are meant to suppose that after his conversion he is in some sense wiser than before. Yet when Horace begs him not to become violent his only reply is 'You too are insane' (32). Later, after recounting Stertinius' teaching he says 'These were the weapons which Stertinius gave me, so that I could hit back if anyone called me names. Whoever says I am mad will be told as much in reply' (296–8). This seems to imply a lack of certainty in Damasippus' own mind and it weakens the effect of the final gibe in which he is addressed as *insane* (326). In this respect Catius in 2. 4 is a more convincing figure, for he never doubts his wisdom for a moment.

The other difficulty is one which we have met before, especially in 1. 6. It is the absence of any firm link between the introduction and the main theme. Damasippus upbraids Horace for his idleness; the poet, it seems, has been so lazy that when he does try to write he is unable to do so. This, however, has really nothing to do with the gospel which Damasippus learned from Stertinius, namely that all fools are mad. Horace is apparently aware of this, for in v. 301, when the sermon is over, he asks what particular form of madness he is suffering from. He is told that by building extensions to his farm he is attempting to emulate Maecenas—a ridiculous ambition. Then, warming to his theme, Damasippus says:

> adde poemata nunc, hoc est, oleum adde camino,
> quae si quis sanus fecit, sanus facis et tu.

> Now throw in your poems, that is, throw oil on the furnace; if any sane man ever wrote poetry then you are sane too.

175

All this fooling, amusing as it is, cannot alter the fact that the very activity which Damasippus enjoined at the beginning now turns out to be a form of madness.

More will be said about the overall structure of the poem when we go on to consider the homily of Stertinius. Before this, however, we should note a few points in the closing dialogue between Damasippus and Horace. After citing Horace's poetry as a proof of his insanity Damasippus continues with a time-honoured trick of rhetoric: *non dico horrendam rabiem*—'I say nothing of your appalling temper'.[24] At the mention of his temper Horace, who has been admirably cool so far, gives himself away. 'Now that's enough!' he cries. Damasippus ploughs on 'Your living beyond your means'. 'Mind your own business, Damasippus!' shouts the poet. But, as we know, that is the one thing Damasippus cannot do. 'Your infatuation with thousands of girls and boys.' In desperation Horace cries out 'O have mercy, please! You are indeed my superior—in madness'—*o maior tandem parcas, insane, minori!*

The largest element in the concluding dialogue is the fable of the calf and the frog:

absentis ranae pullis vituli pede pressis
unus ubi effugit, matri denarrat, ut ingens
belua cognatos eliserit. illa rogare
quantane, num tantum, sufflans se, magna fuisset.
'maior dimidio.' 'num tantum?' cum magis atque
se magis inflaret, 'non, si te ruperis' inquit,
'par eris.'

When a mother frog was away her young were crushed under the hoof of a calf. One escaped and told his mother how a huge beast had trampled on his brothers. She asked how big it had been—had it been this big?[25]—puffing herself out. 'Half as big again.' 'This big?'[26] As she inflated herself more and more, he said 'Not if you burst yourself will you equal it'.

In the Greek version of Babrius (28) an ox who was drinking trampled on a young toad. When the mother returned she asked the toad's brothers where he was. They said:

τέθνηκε, μῆτερ· ἄρτι γάρ, πρὸ τῆς ὥρης,
ἦλθεν πάχιστον τετράπουν, ὑφ' οὗ κεῖται
χηλῇ μαλαχθέν.

He is dead, mother. For just an hour ago there came a huge four-
footed creature and he was crushed to pulp under its hoof.

This little scene is more poignant than Horace's in its detail,
and the 'huge four-footed creature' gives a more convincing
toad's-eye view of the accident. Horace's account, however,
is more economical. With his compressed hypotactic style he
takes only two and a half lines to reach this point as compared
with Babrius' five and a half. Moreover, whereas Babrius set
out to make a well-rounded story, Horace was primarily concerned with the second part, and here he is much superior.
Babrius gives no increase in tension. The toad only inflates herself once, and the final warning is less forceful.

In Phaedrus' version (1. 24), which is followed by La Fontaine
(1. 3), the frog sees the ox in a field and in envy of its size blows
herself up until she bursts. This is a rather cruder treatment, not
only because the tragedy of the young frogs is abandoned but
because the mother, instead of being amusingly absurd, is made
into a complete fool. In Horace's account she doesn't know
what she is competing with; her performance is designed for the
benefit of her son, but the little fellow knows the truth and remains
unimpressed. In Phaedrus, however, she is motivated solely by
envy; and the violent conclusion is also less subtle.

Analysing the history of the Graeco-Roman fable, Perry distinguishes three stages of development.[27] Down to the end of the
fourth century the fable was used incidentally to illustrate some
point in a larger context; in the Alexandrian age fables were
gathered into collections for the use of writers and speakers;
about the time of Phaedrus (i.e. the first century A.D.) the com-
piler turned his collection into verse and presented it as literature
in its own right. The third period saw the emergence of the
epimythium, that is, the appended moral which gave the fable a
general application. It is clear, therefore, that Horace's version

represents the fable in its earliest form. By this I mean that he uses it as a literary tool with a specific purpose; the moral refers directly to the situation described:

haec a te non multum abludit imago.   (320)

This picture fits you pretty well.

La Fontaine's version, representing the third stage, adds a general moral, which begins as follows:

Le monde est plein de gens qui ne sont pas plus sages:
Tout bourgeois veut bâtir comme les grands seigneurs.

We know where he found the bourgeois builder.

We turn now to the main body of the poem, in which Stertinius preaches to Damasippus on the Stoic text 'All fools are mad'. The reasoning may be summarized as follows:

You, with your misplaced sense of guilt, are afraid that people will think you mad; but these people are mad themselves. I shall begin by asking what madness is. According to Chrysippus and his flock a madman is one impelled by folly and ignorance. That accounts for everyone except the sage. Now I want to tell you why those who call you mad are just as mad themselves. They think that because you've gone astray in one respect they are perfectly sound, failing to realize that they've gone off the rails in other ways. One type of fool is absurdly timid, another is incurably rash. Damasippus is mad on collecting old statues; but what of the man who lends him money? If the fellow asks no security he is virtually giving the money away; if he asks for a whole series of written guarantees he is equally foolish, for the guarantees of a rascal are worthless.

This part is almost the same length as the introduction (38 lines). The next is much longer. Making a fresh beginning at v. 77, and no longer confining his remarks to Damasippus, Stertinius undertakes to prove that everyone who suffers from greed, ambition, self-indulgence, or superstition is mad. The section on greed (82–157) is much the longest, being equal in length to the introduction and the first part put together— i.e. 76 verses. It begins with the tale of Staberius:

Staberius' one purpose in life was to save money. When he came to write his will he was so proud of his thrift that he ordered the sum of his estates to be inscribed on his tombstone. Now a non-musician who kept buying harps or a non-cobbler who collected knives and lasts or a non-sailor who amassed quantities of sail-cloth would be considered mad. So why not Staberius? Take the sort of man who lies awake with a club in his hand, watching over a huge supply of grain, and yet refuses to eat anything except bitter leaves; one who drinks vinegar though he owns a well-stocked cellar and who lies on straw when he has a chest full of soft coverlets. No doubt few would judge him mad, because most men suffer from the same disease. Yet he must be out of his mind, for his behaviour is utterly senseless.

If you threw stones at people in the street or at slaves who had cost you money, all the boys and girls would mock you as a lunatic. Strangle your wife and poison your mother—and you are perfectly sane! How is that? Presumably because you do not perform this deed at Argos, nor do you kill your mother with a sword like the mad Orestes. Or perhaps you think that Orestes was only mad *after* killing his mother? That is not true. He was driven mad before the murder; afterwards he did nothing unusual.

The attitude attacked by Stertinius in this last paragraph was something like this: 'Throwing stones at people is a recognized sign of madness[28]—especially if you injure a slave who has cost you money. But my wife and mother didn't cost me anything, so there's nothing absurd about killing them. Moreover, Argos is the place where men butcher their mothers in a fit of madness. This is Rome; here we do it quite sensibly and unobtrusively with poison or a length of rope.' Stertinius' own attitude is: 'You are thought mad if you throw stones at strangers or slaves; how much madder must you be to kill your mother, who is so much more precious?'

After speaking of another miser, Opimius (whose story will be translated below), Horace reminds us that avarice is not the only form of madness. Extravagance is just as senseless, especially when combined with ambition. Then, concentrating on the lust for power and glory, Horace presents a scene in which Agamemnon is cross-examined by a Stoic in the guise of a Greek soldier (187 ff.). The subject is Ajax who, after attempting to kill the Greek leaders in a fit of madness, had committed suicide on recovering his wits. He now lies unburied on the orders of Agamemnon. In opposing this decision the Stoic tries to get Agamemnon to admit that he himself was guilty of a far madder act in murdering his daughter Iphigenia. Ajax in his frenzy had only killed some sheep; Agamemnon had slaughtered his own kith and kin. If anyone treated a lamb as his daughter he would be judged insane by law. For the sake of his own glory Agamemnon treated his daughter as a sacrificial lamb; how is he any saner?

Self-indulgence (*luxuria*) is handled under the headings of extravagance and infatuation (224–80). First we have a short dramatic sketch in which a young rake who has just inherited a fortune summons all the ministers of his pleasure—fishmonger, fruit-merchant, perfumer, etc. A pander speaks on their behalf, promising that the young man's orders will receive prompt attention. But instead of placing orders the prodigal cries 'You deserve the money far more than I do!' and immediately gives it all away. The section ends with a couple of short anecdotes— one about the son of Aesopus who swallowed a pearl dissolved in vinegar,[29] the other about the sons of Arrius who lunched on nightingales.

If, continues Stertinius, a man built dolls' houses and rode on a rocking horse, he would obviously be mad. The behaviour of a lover, with his stockings and scarves and garlands, is no more sensible. Like a perverse child who refuses an apple when you offer it and clamours for one when you don't, the lover cannot decide what he really wants. He moans when he is shut out, but refuses to return when invited. He plays little games with apple pips in the hope of a good omen and goes in for silly baby-talk. More seriously, the lover may be driven to an act of violence —as in the case of Marius, who killed his beloved Hellas and then jumped to his death.

The sermon ends with a short passage on superstition (281–95). A certain freedman would fast and wash and then implore the gods to grant him immortality. A mother prays for the life of her son who is in a high fever; if the gods spare him she will make him stand naked in the Tiber as a sign of gratitude. The boy recovers 'thanks to luck or to the doctor', and thereupon the mother kills him by plunging him in the cold river.

Most of the forms of lunacy already mentioned are referred to again in the epilogue. Horace, says Damasippus, is ambitious in his building programme; he has a terrible temper (the word used is *rabiem*); he lives recklessly beyond his means; and he is wildly promiscuous. One is given the impression that, if Horace had not interrupted, Damasippus would have completed the list with superstition. But superstition, like greed, was so out of character that Horace could not allow himself to be accused of it, even as a joke.

Roman lawyers never discussed the question of what constitutes insanity.[30] When in a specific case a man was adjudged insane (*furiosus*), the *praetor urbanus* deprived him by an *interdictum* of the control of his property and handed him over to the care of his *agnati*, i.e. those who were related to him through the male line.[31] If there were no *agnati* the duty devolved upon his *gentiles* or clansmen. In a passage of the *Tusculan Disputations* (3. 11) Cicero distinguishes *furor*, which involved an incapacitating frenzy or delusion (and which might be only temporary), from the much vaguer *insania*, which meant a general lack of sense. But he did not always observe his own distinction,[32] and Horace uses the two terms interchangeably.

Such imprecision did not matter in ordinary discourse, but a reading of Celsus—a prominent physician of the first century A.D.—shows that even within the medical profession the classification of mental illnesses was rudimentary. The treatment was correspondingly haphazard. Some of the methods were sensible enough —the patient was soothed with sleeping-draughts or rocking or massage, or cheered up with stories or games; but raving madmen were restrained by starvation, fetters, and beatings. Blood-letting was a common procedure, and so was the administration of emetics and purges.[33]

The best-known of these was hellebore, of which there were two

types—one black and one white. Both were used in the treatment of insanity and were regarded with considerable awe.
Pliny (NH 25. 56) says the white variety was much more terrible
than the black. But the black must have been quite bad enough,
for according to a modern authority 'in overdose it produces
inflammation of the gastric and intestinal mucous membrane,
with violent vomiting, hypercatharsis, vertigo, cramp, and con-
vulsions which sometimes end in death'.[34] All these treatments
were derived from the Greek theory that one's health depended
on a correct mixture of the four humours—blood (αἷμα), phlegm
(φλέγμα), yellow bile (χολὴ ξανθή), and black bile (χολὴ μέλαινα).
Disease was a sign that one of the humours had become excessive.
It was the doctor's task to reduce it and restore a proper harmony.
In the case of madness the harmful humour was usually thought
to be black bile.[35]

Horace takes it for granted that the reader of 2. 3 will be as
familiar with these legal and medical affairs as he is with the pranks
and pastimes of children. And this sense of actuality is further
enhanced by stories of peasant life, society gossip, and several
references to banking, marketing, real estate, politics and the
theatre. The literary background is equally broad and miscellaneous. One short scene (259–71) is transferred almost literally
from the opening of Terence's Eunuchus, another (187–213) is
based on Roman tragedy,[36] and the description of madness probably owes something to Lucilius, who according to Porphyrion
demonstrated what madness is (after W. 1247). No doubt
Horace had also read Varro's Eumenides. In this work a man sets
off to find a cure for his madness. After approaching various
religions and philosophies without success he concludes that
'no invalid could dream anything so unspeakable that some
philosopher would not affirm it'. He then meets white Truth
(cana Veritas) who presents a catalogue of human follies and so
convinces him that he is no madder than anybody else.[37] The
resemblance to Horace, however, does not go very deep. Apart
from obvious differences of language and metre Horace is much

simpler in the structure of his narrative. He discards Varro's vision of the Furies harassing mankind, he assigns no part in the action to allegorical figures like *Veritas* and *Existimatio*, and he is not interested in the vagaries of rival schools.

Through Varro, Terence, and Roman tragedy Horace is, of course, indebted to Greek literature, but he also draws on it more directly in proverb, fable and myth,[38] as well as in stories from popular philosophy. Furthermore, although the satire as a whole centres on a Stoic paradox, several of the arguments are based on the commonplaces of Hellenistic morality. Thus in the long section on avarice Horace insists on the folly of not enjoying what you have—*nescius uti / compositis* (109–10), *numquam utare paratis* (167). The idea is found, as usual, in Plato and Aristotle,[39] but was especially important to the Epicureans. 'We regard self-sufficiency as a great good,' says the Master (*Menoec.* 130), 'not that we may always enjoy just a few things, but rather that if we do not possess many things we may enjoy the few we have....' A character in Menander voices the same sentiment: 'I have never envied a very rich man who gets no good out of what he has' (ἀπολαύοντα μηδὲν ὧν ἔχει).[40] The failure of such a man, says Teles (37), is a sign that his possessions are κτήματα rather than χρήματα, for the latter term implies use. Senseless hoarding is also attacked by Phoenix of Colophon, and the theme recurs in such diverse writers as Lucilius, Cato, Plutarch, and Epictetus.[41]

The organization of all this material called for considerable skill. In the main part of Stertinius' sermon (77–295) monotony is avoided by a clever variation in the placement of key words.[42] Sometimes the word occurs in the first line of its section, as in *danda est ellebori multo pars maxima avaris* (82)—'Much the biggest dose of hellebore should be given to misers'—and in *nunc age, luxuriam et Nomentanum arripe mecum* (224)—'Come now and arraign with me self-indulgence and Nomentanus'. In vv. 247–80, however, the key word *amare* is withheld until the fourth line, and so we are kept guessing about the type of folly in question. In the closing section (281–95), although we know what the folly

is, we are not given its proper name until the very last line—
timore deorum ('superstition').

Ambition is named more than once, e.g. *gloria* (179), *vitrea
fama* (222), but the topic is introduced in a somewhat loose and
uncertain way. In the course of a rather obvious demonstration
that not all fools are misers (158–63), Horace says in effect 'Although a man may not be given to lying and meanness he may
be ambitious and rash'. Lying has previously been associated
with avarice (127) and rashness may conceivably look forward to
the action of Agamemnon, but here they have no immediate
function in the argument. What we do expect, in view of the promise in vv. 78–9, is some comment on ambition. Rather surprisingly, however, Horace continues by saying 'For what difference
does it make whether you consign all you have to a pit or never
use your savings?' With these words ambition seems to disappear,
and we are back with the old antithesis of prodigality and avarice.
Now comes the story of Servius Oppidius who had two sons, one
a spendthrift and the other a miser. On his death-bed he forbade
the former to reduce and the latter to increase the fortune he left
him. At this point, when we have almost forgotten about ambition, Oppidius goes on to say 'Moreover, to protect you from
the itch for glory I shall make you both swear that whoever
becomes aedile or praetor shall be an accursed outcast'. This does
get us back to the theme of ambition, but it is clumsily managed,
for the miserly son will not in fact be open to that temptation—
public life is far too expensive, as Horace shows in the following
lines. And so one is left with the impression that instead of being
set cleanly side by side or welded smoothly together the vices of
greed and ambition have been rather awkwardly interlocked.

A much firmer control is evident in the section on infatuation
(247 ff.). This begins by mentioning a number of children's
games, such as building toy houses and riding on reeds. The
lover's behaviour is then woven into these pastimes (*amare...
trimus...amore*) and so put in a ridiculous light.[43] After the reference to Polemon (253 ff.) Horace reverts to the child analogy,

comparing the lover's games and baby-talk to the child with his toy house (272–5).

The first part of the section on avarice ends with the words *metuensque velut contingere sacrum* (110). This reminded Horace of *tamquam parcere sacris*—a phrase he had used in 1. 1. 71 in connexion with a miser lying on a heap of money-bags. And so he now goes on to describe a miser lying beside a heap of corn (111 ff.). In most of Horace's discussions about greed there is no clear distinction between the acquisitive and the hoarding instincts.[44] It is assumed that the greedy man will indulge both. Thus the frantic pursuit of gain in 1. 1. 38–40 is followed at once by the burial of the proceeds. Here, after the squalor of the miser's life (111–26), we get a glimpse of the way he makes his money—it is by lying, stealing, and plunder. This goes some way towards preparing us for the violence of the next paragraph in which we are told that even murder is condoned when it involves no waste of money. The sardonic, almost Juvenalian wit of this passage is followed immediately by the comic tale of Opimius which pushes the argument to its final absurdity: some people are so stingy that they'd sooner die than pay for medicine.

The folly of avarice, then, can lead to death. As the sermon proceeds we learn that the same is true of ambition, for Agamemnon slew his daughter; the same is true of infatuation, for Marius killed Hellas and then took his own life; and the same is true of superstition, for a mother killed her son in fulfilling an idiotic vow.

One of the minor techniques of style is the introduction of an anonymous listener. I say 'listener' rather than adversary, for in 2. 3, unlike 1. 1, the figure does not answer back. The most he does is to ask Stertinius for further information (97, 160). Yet at times he acquires an identity, becoming a mean old man (123), or a besotted lover (252, 273); and once he joins a group of fellow-invalids (81). Another device is to adopt the style of a Stoic disquisition. This comes in with rather implausible suddenness in v. 41, where Stertinius, after restraining Damasippus from suicide, launches forth with 'First of all I shall inquire what madness is'.

Then, with a dutiful reference to Chrysippus, he goes on to define a madman as 'anyone who is driven blindly on by accursed folly and by ignorance of the truth'. After this definition or *formula* he says 'Now I shall proceed to tell you how it is that those who call you mad are just as mad themselves'. As further examples of Stoic methodology Lejay (pp. 357 ff.) would add the enumeration of cases, the frequent appeals to common opinion, and the habit of putting the point in the form of a question. But one doubts whether in Horace's day these were thought of as primarily Stoic techniques. They belonged rather to the general tradition of the diatribe.

More could be said about the brilliance of individual passages and the deftness of the poet's joinery, but it is time to give some estimate of the satire as a whole, and one has to admit that it is not among Horace's best. This is due in some degree to the lack of proportion in its parts. One does not ask for symmetry, but by writing seventy-six lines on avarice and only fifteen on superstition Horace has produced a disturbingly lop-sided effect. Lejay remarks (p. 357) 'Le prédicateur populaire n'a ni prévu son discours ni calculé son effort. Il s'essouffle en parlant et finit court.' No doubt this is true, but we cannot exonerate Horace from his failures by attributing them to Damasippus or Stertinius. If Horace intended to parody the faults of a Stoic sermon it was his business to do so without reproducing the same faults himself. Furthermore, by choosing to deal with a number of different vices Horace ruled out any possibility of a continuous development. All he could do was to strike out in one direction after another, always returning to his central theme of insanity. Given his virtuosity even this might have come off—it has been noted, for example, that he uses nearly thirty different expressions for madness. But unfortunately the paradox itself has no real profundity, and so the axle on which the poem revolves is not strong enough to support it.

The germ of the paradox is found in Xenophon's *Memorabilia* (3. 9. 6) where Socrates is said to have maintained that madness (μανία) was the opposite of wisdom (σοφία). Socrates went on to assert, however, that a man was usually considered mad only if he went wrong on matters which most people knew about. He did not contend, as the Stoics did, that the majority were themselves mad. In the pseudo-Platonic *Alcibiades 2* (139 c) it looks at first as if the writer is arguing that all people without sense (ἄφρονες) are mad. But this is recognized to be a mistake; for, as wise men are few, the majority would then be mad and the rest would be subjected to knocks and blows and similar violence. The conclusion therefore is that not all unwise men are mad (140 c). Some of them are, namely those who are *most* lacking in sense. Others are called 'simple-minded', 'stupid' and so on. This is perfectly straightforward, because madness is used in its regular sense and the speaker recognizes degrees of imbecility. Neither of these rules was observed by the Stoics.

The paradox is perhaps most clearly presented by Cicero. In the *Tusculan Disputations* (3. 7 ff.) the leader of the discussion says that perturbations or commotions, such as fear, lust and anger, are signs of an unsound *animus* or *mens*, and the name for unsoundness of mind is *insania*. What worries us about this is not so much the failure to distinguish mental from moral (a distinction which has become blurred in our own time), as the absence of any sense of proportion. Fear, suspicion, anger and lust are not signs of insanity unless they are experienced with abnormal frequency, in abnormal circumstances, and in an abnormal degree. Admittedly the Stoics did not insist that fools always behaved insanely; but the tendency, they said, was there and would be revealed in certain conditions. Mud does not always give off a nasty smell, but stir it and you will find it stinks. Stir up an irascible man and you will see him raging (*Tusc. Disp.* 4. 54). But this does not remove the difficulty; for non-Stoics, then as now, did not count an angry man mad unless he constantly became enraged at things which would leave a normal person unmoved. Another interpretation of the paradox is recorded by Athenaeus (11. 464 D), who says that according to Chrysippus

187

μανία (madness) is commonly applied to very many things, e.g. to men who are 'woman-mad', 'fame-mad' and so on. But this reduces the paradox to the status of a vulgar idiom.

It has to be admitted, then, that the satire's central idea is rather weak—at least in the form presented by Stertinius. Yet architectural unity is not the only virtue. When the impression of the poem as a whole has faded, we may still recall stories like this (142-57):

Mr Richly, a poor man in spite of all the silver and gold which he had stored away, used to drink cheap Veientine wine from a cheap Campanian mug. That was on holidays; on working days he drank fermented must. Once he was sunk in so deep a coma that his heir was already running round the chests and keys in triumphant joy. The doctor, who was a loyal fellow with really quick reactions, roused him by this method: he had a table brought; then he ordered some bags of coins to be poured out and several people to step forward and count them. After bringing the patient to in this way he added 'If you don't watch your money, your greedy heir will make off with it at any moment'. 'Over my dead body!' 'All right then, wake up and stay alive. Here.' 'What's this?' 'Your pulse is dangerously low. Your system is running down. It needs food and a really strong tonic. What are you waiting for? Come on, take a sip of this rice gruel.' 'How much was it?' 'Oh, not much.' 'Well *how* much then?' 'A bob.' 'Ah dear me! What difference does it make whether I die from illness or from theft and pillage?'

2. 7

Here, as in 2. 3, the scene is set by the opening speaker. This time it is Davus, one of Horace's slaves. He has been listening at the door, eager but afraid to address his master. Horace calls him in and, because it is the Saturnalia, invites him to speak his mind. Davus at once launches into a diatribe, which I paraphrase throughout:

Some men are loyal to their vices, but most are not. They vacillate weakly between good and evil. Priscus, for instance, would change his clothes and insignia every hour; he would emerge from a mansion to go slumming; and after living the life of an adulterer in Rome he would depart to the scholarly seclusion of Athens. Volanerius was quite different. Gambling was so important to him that when he became crippled by arthritis he employed a man to replace the dice in the box. Because of this single-mindedness Volanerius was the happier man.   (6-20)

Here we have a neat symmetrical introduction: steadiness (*constanter*) and vacillation (*modo...interdum*), vacillation (Priscus) and steadiness (Volanerius), steadiness (*constantior*) and vacillation (*iam...iam*). As in the diatribes of Book 1, there follows a line in which the listener demands to know where all this drivel is pointing—*non dices hodie quorsum haec tam putida tendant, | furcifer?* Davus replies 'At you'. And he then proceeds to lecture Horace on his inconsistencies (22–43):

> You praise the habits and conditions of the good old days, but if a god suddenly offered to take you back you'd refuse to go—either because you're a hypocrite or because you're weak-willed. At Rome you long for the country, in the country you praise city life. When no one has asked you to dinner you say 'Thank God!'—as if dining out were a form of servitude. Then comes a late invitation from Maecenas, and you shout and bellow in your impatience to be off. The hangers-on who came to dine with you are turned away cursing. You can imagine Mulvius, one of their number, saying 'Granted I'm easily led by food and drink. But as you're no better how can you have the face to preach at me and to wrap up your own vices in euphemisms?' Why, you may even be a bigger fool than I, whom you bought so cheaply.

We think first, perhaps, of 1.1 with its theme of μεμψιμοιρία and the god who offers to grant wishes. But the earlier poem was concerned only with occupations, not with time or locality. Moreover, the third example of Horace's inconstancy mentioned here—i.e. his dining habits—is not a case of μεμψιμοιρία at all. Rather the reverse, for Horace claims he *enjoys* eating at home. The connexion with 1.3 is somewhat closer. Horace (foreshadowed by Priscus) takes the place of Tigellius, and the treatment of *aequabilitas* is much the same. In 1.3 we found that the introductory passage on inconstancy was related to the main theme of fairness through the common idea of balance. Here there is also a connexion, for the lack of steadiness described in the long introduction leads naturally enough to the lack of control which is the satire's main topic. The control in question, however, is that which ought to be exercised by the reason over irrational desires. When such control is wanting, the unruly desires gain the upper hand and the true self becomes enslaved. This, says Davus, is what has happened to Horace. Therefore, except for his legal status, the master is in no way superior to the slave. The Stoics contended that as the slave was free if he was a wise man, so the free man was a slave if he was a fool. This belief was expressed in the paradoxes μόνος ὁ σοφὸς ἐλεύθερος ('Only the sage is free') and πᾶς ἄφρων δοῦλος ('Every fool is a slave').[45]

Apart from the underlying notion of firmness, the relation of the opening passage to the main theme of slavery is indicated in two ways. The first is by introducing the antithesis of freedom and servitude at various points in vv. 1–43. Thus Davus, a slave, takes advantage of the freedom provided by the Saturnalia (4); Priscus' behaviour was sometimes hardly worthy of a freedman (12); the inconsistent man struggles with the rope which is now tight, now loose (20); Horace, though he sees the good, is unable to drag his foot from the mire (27); he pretends that dining out is a dreadful 'bind' (31); but he is away like a shot when summoned by Maecenas (32 ff.); Mulvius, the *scurra* or hanger-on, is led by his stomach (38). The second way is by contriving a smooth transition between the two parts. This begins with Mulvius, who confesses that he is *levis* ('easily swayed'). The same has been said of the inconstant man in v. 19 (*levius*) and of Horace himself in v. 29 (*levis*). But Mulvius' *levitas* is restricted to the area of food and drink—a sign that the general idea of inconstancy is being abandoned. The rest of Mulvius' words show that in the matter of gluttony Horace is no better than his own *scurra*, that he is, in fact, a *scurra* himself. The final step is for Davus to assert that Horace is no better than his own slave. The notion of *inconstantia* has now receded; for whether Davus is inconsistent or not is irrelevant. And the idea of slavery has come to the fore.

As this part of the lecture ends Horace glares at the speaker and raises his fist. But Davus restrains him and proceeds to his main theme, which he has picked up from another eavesdropper, viz. the janitor of Crispinus (46–115):

You are captivated by another man's wife, Davus by a tart. Which of us commits the worse sin? When I sleep with a girl, everything's straightforward and above board. I incur no social disgrace and I don't care if a richer or more handsome rival enjoys the same favours.[46] You remove all the badges of your rank and throw a cloak over your perfumed head, disguising yourself as a slave. But isn't that just what you are? You are let in, torn between lust and terror. When you leave you may be handed over to be whipped or cut to pieces; or you may be smuggled out in a chest with your head stuffed between your knees. In either case you've made yourself a slave. The husband of the lady who sins has the right to punish both, more particularly the seducer. She, however (unlike the seducer), does not change her clothes or her station, nor does she *inflict* the sin. When the woman is reluctant and suspicious will you deliberately humiliate yourself like a slave and put your whole estate and life and reputation at the mercy of a raging master? (46–67)

In tone and subject this takes us back to 1. 2, in which adultery, with all its dangers and indignities, is contrasted with a casual liaison. The writing here is just as vivid, and a greater unity is obtained through the technique of theme and variations. The theme, of course, is servitude, and the first variation is found in *capit* (46), which denotes sexual captivity. Then, in v. 47, Davus asks 'Who sins more deservingly of the cross (*cruce dignius*)?'— the cross being a punishment inflicted on slaves. The adulterer in disguise is on the same level as Dama, a typical slave. When detected he may be *auctoratus*, i.e. be 'delivered up' like a gladiator to be beaten and killed; or, to escape capture, he may be enclosed in a chest—another form of confinement. The adulterer falls into the husband's power (*potestas*). He puts himself under the fork (*furca*)—another servile punishment, in which the wrists were bound to a beam resting on the neck; and he surrenders everything to his *dominus*.[47] One other point deserves mention. The frankness of Davus' transaction is symbolized by the bright lamp (*lucerna*) in v. 48; the furtive guilt of the adulterer by the concealing cloak (*lacerna*) in v. 55. So the all-important difference depends on a single vowel. The effect may be unintentional, but who can say it was an accident?

Davus goes on to speak of the compulsive nature of the adulterer's vice (68–82):

You've escaped. I suppose you'll be careful in future. Not a bit of it. You'll seek another opportunity for terror and ruin—slave that you are. What animal

191

after escaping gives itself up again to its chains? 'I'm not an adulterer', you say. No! Nor am I a thief when I carefully leave the silver untouched. But take away the danger! Then, when the snaffle is removed, nature will leap forward. Are you my master—you who are under the control of so many things and people, and who, though manumitted again and again, are still the slave of fear? Better call me your under-slave or fellow-slave; for you are not a master. You serve someone else and have no more independence than a wooden puppet.

Here Davus continues to ring the changes on slavery, but at v. 72 the argument takes a new turn. So far the case against adultery has rested entirely on prudence—the adulterer is a fool to take such risks. But in v. 72 Horace is supposed to say *non sum moechus* ('I'm not an adulterer'), a simple statement which deprives Davus of a target and ought to leave him speechless. But after shooting wide, Davus, like an ancient Dr Johnson, proceeds to knock his adversary down with the bow. 'Take away the danger!' he cries, as if the danger had not been the foundation of his case, 'And then your nature will be seen in its true colours.' However clumsily made, this point takes the argument to another, more purely Stoic, level. For while the Cynics and Epicureans condemned adultery because of its risks, the Stoics concentrated on the unhealthy state of the offender's soul. Even if there were no risks, they said, the virtuous man would abstain because of his inner discipline. This helps to prepare us for the noble description of the truly free man (83–8):

Who, then, is free? The wise man, who is master of himself, who is undaunted by poverty, death, or bonds, who bravely defies his passions and despises positions of power, who is complete in himself, smooth and round, so that no foreign element can adhere to his polished surface, and who always causes Fortune to lame herself when she attacks him.

Davus now mentions four respects in which Horace fails miserably when measured by this standard (88–115):

A woman asks you for a couple of thousand, bullies you, shuts you out and drenches you with cold water. Then she invites you back. Shake the yoke off your neck! Say you are free! You can't. For a harsh master turns you round and goads you back against your will.

You stand entranced by one of Pausias' pictures. Am I any worse when with my legs rooted to the spot I admire a charcoal poster of a gladiatorial fight? Yet I am a good-for-nothing dawdler while you are called a fine and expert critic.

If I follow the whiff of a cake I'm a worthless wretch. But can you say no to a rich dinner? Why does it do more harm for *me* to be the servant of my belly? Because, you say, I am beaten as a punishment. But you suffer just as much when you go in quest of expensive food. Your endless banquets turn sour, and your legs can no longer support your bloated body. A slave steals a scraper and sells it for a bunch of grapes. But is there nothing servile about one who sells whole estates at the behest of his gullet?

Moreover, you can't stand your own company or manage your leisure properly. Like a runaway slave you try to escape from yourself and to beguile your *Angst*—all to no purpose, for that black companion follows hard on your heels.

After failing to uncover any illicit relationship between Horace and a married woman Davus here accuses him of subservience to a *meretrix*—a sequence which can be paralleled from 1. 2. 57–9. The treatment, however, is in the style of comedy. One thinks immediately of the Terentian scene in 2. 3. 259–64, but the absurdly high price and the bucket of cold water are more in the Plautine manner. The peculiarly Horatian contribution lies in the blending of this comic situation with a strong didactic tone. The picture of lust as a charioteer is in the grand style.

As McGann has pointed out,[48] there is a clever connexion between the passage on art and that which goes before, in that Pausias (a fourth-century painter of the Sicyonian school) was distinguished not only for his subtle technique but also for the gay wantonness of his subjects. There is one other point here which has not, I believe, been properly understood. Davus says he gazes at a drawing of two gladiators *contento poplite* (97). From the time of the scholiasts this phrase has been taken either with *miror* or with the gladiators. I believe it goes with the colourless *miror*, thus balancing the vivid *torpes* of v. 95. Yet neither 'on tip-toe' nor 'with legs straddled' gives the proper sense. Surely, as *torpes* implies physical immobility, so *contento poplite* means that Davus is rooted to the spot. He cannot tear himself away, and *that* is why he is a dawdler (*cessator*). This means that the theme of constraint or servitude is present here as well as in the preceding and following lines, and so Heinze's note on v. 95 should be modified.[49]

The verses on gluttony, along with vv. 29–42, bracket the passages on sex. They also recall the diatribe of Ofellus (2. 2) in both language and subject. Finally, the ending of the poem, with its allusion to the crazy poet, is very similar to that of 2. 3. As Davus takes a breath Horace suddenly breaks in:

'Someone give me a stone!' 'What for?' 'Or arrows!' 'The man's raving or else composing verses.' 'If you don't get out of here mighty quick you'll make drudge number nine on my Sabine farm!'

From what has been said above it is clear that 2. 7 is the most inclusive of all the diatribes. It contains the discontent of 1. 1, the adultery of 1. 2, the inconstancy of 1. 3, the subservience of 1. 6, and the gluttony of 2. 2. The most important comparison, however, is offered by 2. 3. Both poems have a Saturnalian setting. They open with a dialogue in which the poet is in a good humour, proceed to a central section in which a Stoic paradox is expounded at second or third hand, and end with an exchange in which Horace shouts the speaker down. The weaknesses which we noticed in 2. 3, however, have now been remedied. The sprawling length has been cut to a third, and the masses of argumentation have been better distributed. Thus, allowing for some blurring at transitions, we have a prologue (5 verses) followed by four large units (15, 25, 22, 15). Then, after the picture of the free man (6 verses), we have four shorter units (6, 7, 10, 4) followed by the concluding dialogue (3). Moreover, the gap which we noted in 2. 3 between introduction and main theme has here been closed; for a lack of constancy is closely akin to a lack of rational control.

As well as being more appropriate to the Saturnalian scene Davus is a clearer character than Damasippus. He stays before us more constantly through the poem; he knows himself better; and he is more independent in adapting his borrowed material.

By using the second person throughout Davus keeps a single target in view. Thus whereas Damasippus drew his specimens of madness from every quarter, Davus employs just the one figure—that of Horace or 'the master'—to illustrate the various types of servitude. And this brings a gain in tightness.

Last of all, the paradox 'all fools are slaves' appears to be more substantial than 'all fools are mad'. I am not sure why this is so, for both formulae rest on the same principle, namely that irrational desires are not a part of the true self. Perhaps the first suggests something of more positive significance whereas the second looks rather like the proposition 'all grays are black'. Or perhaps it is because freedom, with its social, political and religious implications, has a wider interest than sanity, which seems largely a matter of the individual's psychology. At any rate the idea of freedom contained in 'all fools are slaves' and in its corollary 'only the sage is free' has played an immense role in the history of religion and philosophy, and in one form or another it is still a force in modern thought.

Among the features which we noted as common to the diatribes of Book 1 was the fact that the poet spoke *in propria persona* and took direct responsibility for what he said. In the diatribes of Book 2 this is no longer the case. The critique of table luxury in 2.2 is supposed to be based on the teachings of Ofellus; the substance of 2.3 is ascribed to Stertinius and communicated by Damasippus; and in 2.7 the source of wisdom is even more remote, for Davus heard the sermon from a janitor who heard it from Crispinus. Accordingly the nature of the impact is different. The first method is undoubtedly more incisive, but it is the method of one who, if not an outsider, is still not a member of the establishment. By 33 B.C., however, Horace was a more familiar figure in society and had numerous friends among the rich and powerful. As a result he seems to have felt unable to preach with his former directness. Perhaps we find this regrettable, and it may well be that in the end Horace's career as a satirist was destroyed by social success. But the later and subtler method should not be dismissed too quickly. Horace may have had reason to believe that he could get his message across *more* effectively in this way. It is as if he were saying:

Now I don't presume to lay down the law to an audience like this. Of course not. Old Ofellus may praise the virtues of peasant life, but I'm not Ofellus, gentlemen, and neither are any of you. Damasippus and Stertinius are rather absurd; Crispinus, as we all know, is a figure of fun; and certainly I'm not so doctrinaire as to take those Stoic paradoxes literally. So you won't imagine, will you, that I'm *lecturing* you on your moral failings? But as you leave, you might consider whether there's anything in what these odd people have been saying. Truth, after all, is found in some unlikely quarters.

So instead of a sermon the preacher has presented a sort of comic morality-play. But the message is still there.

By now a general picture of Horace's thought should have emerged, but perhaps a few comments may be added on those aspects which are less congenial to us. In regard to 1. 2 there is no point in pretending that the discussion is conducted on a decent moral level. The arguments against adultery are almost entirely selfish, and the recommendation of the 'call-girl' takes it for granted that she will be used simply as an instrument of gratification. But before applying the censor's mark too gleefully we should remember that to a young man in his twenties, who was watching his country tearing itself to pieces and who scarcely dared to think of the future, independence seemed essential for survival. Friends were safe enough; but it was folly to think of a wife and children; and even a romantic affair might bring dangerous emotional entanglements. Sex therefore was to be treated as a recurrent need which might be satisfied with zest and gaiety so long as it involved no commitment to another person or to society at large. If this outlook seems unduly cynical it is worth recalling that in our own time, when sexual mores are in a state of ferment, many competent observers have maintained that *some* of the trouble arises from over-romantic and over-sentimental notions of what sex is about. Such notions have not always been current. On 11 December 1762 Boswell records the observations of Mr Macpherson:

He told me that he was very susceptible of tormenting love. But that London was the best place in the world to cure it. 'In the country,' said he, 'we see a beautiful woman; we conceive an idea that it would be heaven to be in her arms. We think that impossible almost for us to attain. We sigh. We are dejected. Whereas here we behold as fine women as ever were created. Are we fond of one of them? For a guinea we get full enjoyment of her, and when that is over we find that it is not so amazing a matter as we fancied. Indeed, after a moderate share of the pleasures of London, a man has a much better chance to make a rational unprejudiced marriage.'

Mr Macpherson's sentiments would have sounded quite normal to Horace, though as it turned out the poet was never to make a marriage—even of a rational unprejudiced kind.

If 1. 2 strikes us as cynical, 1. 1 may seem reactionary. It is certainly conservative in tone—that was almost ensured by the combination of Roman temperament, Hellenistic philosophy, and the state of the country at the time. But we should be clear on what the poet does and does not say. First, he is concerned with certain misguided attitudes to money rather than with the amount of money a man should have. He never says that poverty is a virtue and wealth a vice, nor does he decry the ordinary business of earning a living. What he does say (amongst other things) is that if you spend all your time and energy *making* money, you'll never enjoy it, and that resentment is not a good recipe for happiness. Later, in 2. 2, he adds that if you have a large fortune there are more useful and satisfying ways of spending it than on food and drink. To see how inoffensive Horace really is in his treatment of μεμψιμοιρία one may compare 1. 1 with Swift's sermon *On The Poor Man's Contentment*. There Swift sets out to show that the poor have many temporal blessings not enjoyed by the rich and the rich have many temporal evils not enjoyed by the poor. As a preliminary he excludes beggars, drunkards, and debtors, for they mostly deserve their condition, and also the *honest* destitute, for they are few in number. Taking 'the honest industrious artificer, the meaner sort of tradesman, and the labouring man', Swift goes on to assert that such men are healthier, sleep better, and are more assisted by their children; they incur no general hatred or envy, are untroubled by ambition, and are unworried by party squabbles. Whereas the rich are plagued by gout, dropsy, stone and cholic; they have no appetite; they cannot sleep because of their fear and vexation; and worst of all, their idleness exposes them to sin. As they stood in St Patrick's listening to the great man preach, the Dublin poor must surely have marvelled at their own good fortune.

The idea of freedom as expounded in 2. 7 also calls for comment. Epictetus, who holds the same theory, begins his essay on the subject (4. 1) with the deceptive words ἐλεύθερός ἐστιν ὁ ζῶν ὡς βούλεται[50]—'He is free who lives as he wishes'. In spite of having the air of a truism this masks a serious confusion between wishes and constraints. Suppose you have the opportunity of going on a world tour (i.e. you are not prevented by lack of money, leisure, or the necessary documents), yet you do not wish to take advantage of it, then you are *free* to go, although to you the freedom will be of little importance. If you have neither the opportunity nor the wish, you will *not* be free to go, though you will not feel any distress in consequence. In the last type of case the Stoics argued as if they had removed the constraint by removing the wish. Thus if a man was debarred from a political career on the orders of a dictator, he might in their view still be free if he eliminated his ambition.

In answer to this criticism a Stoic might say that the freedom to tour the world or campaign for office was not a *real* freedom. If you pointed out that in his ordinary speech he still *called* it a freedom, he might then assert that it was an *unimportant* freedom. This would be quite defensible, one supposes, on an individual basis. Such freedoms would not matter to one who had voluntarily restricted his wishes in those respects. But they might well matter to others, and it is here, in the broader social and political field, that the dangers of the view become apparent. Anyone who insists that certain freedoms, which other people value, are insignificant or unworthy is encouraging their suppression. And when they have been suppressed the same kind of talk will hinder their revival. From holding that freedom of the reason is the *only* freedom it is all too easy a step to say that people must be *made* free by having their undesirable impulses restrained. And so the rational freedom of the philosopher passes into the tyranny of a party, institution, or church.[51]

Yet one would still wish to maintain that rational or moral freedom was one of the most important freedoms. And that is probably all that Horace, as distinct from Crispinus, would have cared to say. He would certainly not have denied the importance of those freedoms which were guaranteed by law, and however much he may have valued character above birth he would never have claimed that the social distinctions between slave and free were trivial or unreal.

If we concede that, in spite of the more objective and dramatic form employed in Book 2, Horace's opinions are still discoverable, and that the poet is not, like Joyce's perfect artist, 'invisible, refined out of existence, indifferent, paring his fingernails', we are then faced with the question of his consistency. Luckily the problem is not too complex in our area of concern. If we were studying Horace's work as a whole we should have to ask how the inspired *vates* of the Augustan renaissance was related to the cultivated wit who shunned politics and wrote bitter-sweet lyrics on wine, friendship, and death. But in the *Satires* it will be sufficient to consider, very briefly, two or three main points.

First, Horace had a genuine respect for men of homogeneous character. He recognized their potential heroism, and could formulate the ideal in memorable terms. Thus the description of the truly free man in 2.7 anticipates the *iustum et tenacem propositi virum* of *Carm.* 3.3 and the famous portrait of Regulus in *Carm.* 3.5. But he evinces no affection for such men, and it is clear that he himself was made of quite different stuff. He was a man of changing moods, sensitive to the feelings and behaviour of others, and responding quickly to the events of his world. The equilibrium which he attained came not so much from a placid temperament as from wisdom and experience, and even in his later years that equilibrium was not always stable.

As an example we may take 2. 6, a poem in which Horace thanks Maecenas for the Sabine farm, and celebrates the joys of the country by contrasting them with city life: Rome is a place of sickness and noise and frenetic bustle; there is no rest, no privacy, and one lives amid the hum of malicious gossip. The poem concludes with the story of a country mouse who was lured to Rome by his city friend and was frightened out of his life when he got there. All this suggests that Horace will never willingly set foot in the capital again. In fact, of course, he will return quite regularly; for Rome is more than smoke and corruption. As queen of cities it represents some of man's greatest achievements, and to the poet it offers fame, fellowship, and gaiety. And so one motif in Horace's life is the fruitful alternation between town and country. Sometimes, to be sure, the spiritual gyroscope breaks down, and then he becomes restless and depressed as in *Epist.* 1. 8. 12:

Romae Tibur amem ventosus, Tibure Romam.

Changeable as the wind I long for Tibur when in Rome and for Rome when in Tibur.

But abnormal phases of this kind reveal the regular pattern all the more clearly.

Finally there is the matter of diet. Here we find the same kind of alternation. Its limits can be inferred from the habits of Ofellus in 2. 2 and of Catius the epicure in 2. 4, and I say 'inferred' because Horace's own habits cannot be equated with either. More will be said about Catius in the next chapter. Here I would only suggest that the satire on his 'foodmanship' reveals a lively interest and appreciation on the part of the poet. There is nothing surprising in this; for Maecenas, with whom Horace must have dined fairly often, was not renowned for his frugality. And there are several indications elsewhere that the poet could do justice to a well-cooked meal. Nevertheless, Horace's interest in food stopped well short of the obsession revealed by Catius, and, whatever he may have eaten at Maecenas' table, his normal fare, both in Rome and in the country, was of a much plainer kind.[52] We need not imagine, however, that it was quite so Spartan as the diet of Ofellus. The function of the old peasant is to show that even at that degree of simplicity it is possible to live not only a healthy life but also in some measure a pleasant one. For Ofellus is not an ascetic. He enjoys his food and is glad to allow himself extra when entertaining a guest. In these respects he is contrasted with Avidienus, who represents the extreme of joyless parsimony.

The essence of Horace's life, as of his style, will therefore be found in the idea of controlled variety. Because the limits are relatively narrow and the movement normally *is* controlled, the poet is in a position to mock the wild oscillations of Priscus and Tigellius. But he does not pretend that the control is infallible. He admits that, sometimes at least, there is a gap between his principles and his performance. And it is this faculty of wry self-criticism that makes him the most likeable of Roman moralists.

CHAPTER VII

FOOD AND DRINK

2. 4

Prometheus has always been a hero of mankind, and for a very good reason. Without his gift of fire cookery would never have been discovered, and this, after all, is what raises us above the beasts. The role of cooking in the ascent of man was well understood by the Greeks, as may be seen from the chef's remarks to his assistant in the *Samothracians* of Athenion:

C.   Do you not realise that piety
         owes most of what it is to cookery?
A.   Really?
C.   Of course, you poor barbarian!
         It turned a lawless animal into man,
         brought order, stopped our cannibalistic strife,
         and dressed us in our present mode of life.

Like all great inventions, cooking was something of a happy accident. But if we are to believe the dramatist, the first barbecue was not quite so fortuitous a discovery as Lamb's roast pig:

When man ate man and human life was cheap,
a clever lad once sacrificed a sheep
and cooked the flesh; men found it more delicious
than human chops, and ceased to relish dishes
consisting of their kin. Liking the treat
they henceforth roasted sacrificial meat,
and pressing onward from that simple start
enlarged the realm of culinary art.

As one researcher discovered sausages, and another stew, and another mincemeat, the old life began to lose its attractions:

Because of such delights men grew soft hearted
and disinclined to eat the dear departed.
They said 'Let's live together!' Crowds collected
and, thanks to cooking, cities were erected.[1]

In addition to its historic importance in effecting a gourmet's
social contract, cookery had also a high place on the epistemo-
logical scale. According to Sosipater and Nicomachus it entailed
a knowledge of astronomy (for how else could one tell when a
dish was in season?), architecture (for kitchens had to be scientifi-
cally designed), medicine (for obvious reasons), and even strategy.[2]
The strategic side of cookery brings out the connexion between
culinary and verbal art. As Cicero's orator marshals his material
and advances his arguments, so the chef knows exactly how the
various dishes should be arranged and brought in. As Horace's
dramatic poet can see the right style for a character to employ at a
critical moment so the chef will size up the morale and capabilities
of each guest and serve him accordingly. The same Horatian
decorum is also an asset to the diner. In Hoffman's words: 'Avant
de vous faire initier aux mystères de la gueule, consultez bien vos
forces et vos dispositions naturelles, examinez sans présomption
quid valeat stomachus, quid ferre recuset.'[3]

The technical virtuosity of these comic chefs has a sound
scholarly foundation. They are acquainted with the work of
their predecessors and are proudly aware of their own contributions to the great tradition. Thus a young cook in Anaxippus says:

> The chief Ionian authority
> is Sophon; he, you know Sir, tutored me.
> I am an expert too; my highest aim
> is that a standard work shall bear my name.[4]

So, too, a cook in Alexis gives a detailed recipe for one of his
original creations.[5] And Euphron has a professional chef who
boasts about his pupils in the accepted common-room style.[6]

This interest in gastronomy, which at times amounted to an obsession and for which I have never seen a satisfactory explanation,
was not continued to anything like the same extent by Plautus
and Terence. So in this case Horace's affinities to the New Comedy
are largely confined to the Greek originals. As usual, however,
there is no single source for his work. In trying to define the

203

tradition behind 2. 4 we must also take account of Archestratus and his Roman imitators. About 330 B.C. Archestratus, a Sicilian from Gela, wrote a poem called *Hedypatheia* or 'Gracious Living', which described and criticized the various dishes he encountered on a gastronomic voyage of discovery. Although it lacks the conventional invocation, it is, as Athenaeus realized,[7] essentially a didactic poem in the manner of Hesiod and Theognis. Early on, the writer announces his topic and the name of the recipient:

πρῶτα μὲν οὖν δώρων μεμνήσομαι ἠυκόμοιο
Δήμητρος, φίλε Μόσχε· σὺ δ'ἐν φρεσὶ βάλλεο σῇσιν.[8]

> First then, dear Moschus, will I tell the gifts
> of lovely-haired Demeter; listen carefully.

In the 350-odd lines preserved by Athenaeus we meet the various types of recommendation and assertion that are characteristic of the genre. Yet this is a didactic poem with a difference; for in spite of his extensive researches the author does not take himself too seriously. He parodies his more earnest predecessors and gives his subject a comic elevation by frequent Homeric allusions, e.g.

> At Rhodes demand the fox-shark (that's the one
> the Syracusans call 'fat dog'), and if
> they will not sell, then seize it for yourself.
> This may mean death—who cares? Enjoy the fish,
> then brave whatever Fate may hold in store.[9]

> If you are in Ambracia's happy land
> and see a boar-fish, buy it; never fail,
> e'en though it cost its weight in gold; for else
> the terrible wrath of heaven may strike you down.[10]

Determined to put eating on a scientific basis Archestratus makes no concessions to individual taste. His manner throughout is one of magisterial authority. It is true that at one point, after condemning the cod of Anthedon for its unpleasant sponginess, he adds:

> And yet it holds a place of high esteem
> with some—for one likes this, another that.[11]

But we suspect that if anyone had dared to challenge him on the principle of *de gustibus* he would have retorted in the style of Morris Bishop's friend:

> 'Twas long ago in Boston, Mass., I knew a wise old person.
> (He was an advertising man named Edward K. McPherson.)
> Esthetic problems he'd resolve in words I've not forgotten.
> 'It's all a question of taste,' he'd say, 'and your taste
> is rotten.'[12]

In Archestratus, then, we have a cheerful sensualist with an extremely erudite palate. The one thing we do not expect from him is moral criticism; after all, tirades against the cult of the belly do not come well from Michelin inspectors. But when this genre was taken over by the Romans it was inevitable that sooner or later the note of censure would be heard. We cannot be sure about Ennius' *Hedyphagetica* ('Delicatessen'), which was a translation, or imitation, of Archestratus; for Apuleius, who implies that it was a work of pure science, is not concerned to give a full account of it.[13] But when we come to Varro's περὶ ἐδεσμάτων ('On Eatables') the testimony is very much clearer. According to Aulus Gellius it contained a clever description in senarii of the eatables 'which those gormandizers (*helluones isti*) procure from land and sea'.[14] Later Gellius speaks of the foods 'which insatiable greed (*profunda ingluvies*) has tracked down and which Varro has described with disapproval (*opprobrans exsecutus est*)'. The passage ends with a few lines of the work quoted from memory.[15] The only other fragment of the περὶ ἐδεσμάτων is in prose:

si quantum operae sumpsisti ut tuus pistor bonum faceret panem, eius duodecimam philosophiae dedisses, ipse bonus iam pridem esses factus. nunc illum qui norunt, volunt emere milibus centum, te qui novit, nemo centussis.

> If you had spent on philosophy a twelfth of the trouble which you have taken to ensure that your baker makes good bread, you yourself would long ago have become a good man. But now those who know your baker would gladly buy him for 100,000, while no one who knows you would give sixpence for you.[16]

This shows that Varro's work contained a dialogue between a gourmet and a moralist, and it may well be that the former, like a Roman Archestratus, recited a long list of exotic foods while the latter arraigned him in the manner of a Cynic or Stoic preacher.[17]

The Ofellus satire has already shown what Horace could do in this line. The present poem, however, is a very much subtler piece of work. The preacher gives way to the ironist, and the merits of rustic simplicity are left behind. The disquisition on eating and drinking, which is delivered second-hand by Catius, follows the order of a Roman *cena*. So one might perhaps have expected the speaker to begin by recommending a good aperitif. According to the Elder Pliny, however, this outlandish habit did not develop until the time of Tiberius; its introduction was, like many other evils, 'due to foreign ways and to the doctors' policy of continually advertising themselves by some new-fangled idea' (*NH* 14. 143). And so Catius begins with the *hors-d'œuvres* (*gustum* or *gustatio*), consisting of eggs, cabbage, various kinds of shellfish, mushrooms, and a fowl. He then unexpectedly shifts to lunch, saying that it is advisable to round off the midday meal with black mulberries, a fruit which Celsus mentions as a laxative (2. 29. 11). The digression may be due to the fact that the items just named in the *hors-d'œuvres* often figured on the luncheon menu as well. At any rate Catius immediately returns to the *gustatio*, or rather to the drink which followed it. This consisted of dry wine, or sometimes must, mixed with honey. It was called *mulsum*; hence the term *promulsis*, which was yet a third name for this part of the meal.

As possibilities for the *mensae primae*, or main course, Catius mentions boar, venison, hare and fowl. Then, giving a few tips on the preparation of Massic and Surrentine wine, he proceeds to the *mensae secundae*, which includes prawns, snails, sausages and other savouries intended for the flagging drinker. Two recipes, one simple, the other more complicated, are suggested for sauces to accompany the prawns and snails. Then the section ends with a brief discussion of apples and grapes. At this point (73) Catius mentions a couple of minor innovations for which his teacher is responsible. One is the practice of serving a certain type of raisin along with the apples; the other is the provision of *faex* and *allec* on small dishes. *Faex* is wine-lees which have been dried, roasted, and ground to powder. *Allec* can best be described in conjunction with *garum*—a delicacy which added zest to the banquet of Nasidienus (2. 8. 46). According to one recipe *garum* was made as follows: take the entrails of a tunny, along with its gills, juice and blood. Add sufficient salt. Leave it in a jar for two months at the most. Then knock a hole in the jar. What trickles out is the type of *garum* called 'blood-garum'.[18] What is left behind is *allec*.

If this recipe makes the reader uneasy, let me assure him that this was the very best *garum*. Many other grades were available, and there was even a recognized technique for freshening up stale *garum*. In any case it seems rather parochial to entertain doubts over other men's meat. The two ladies who a few years ago edited and translated Apicius' cookery book actually made some *garum*, and they insisted that 'even considerable quantities could be used without leaving an unpleasant taste'.[19] So too Pierre Grimal tells us that *garum* is still manufactured in Turkey, that it is virtually identical with the Indo-Chinese delicacy known as *nuoc-mam*, and that when you get used to it it smells no worse than Camembert.[20] In view of its popularity in Indo-China, one may predict that *nuoc-mam* or *garum* will eventually reach America, where they will probably spread it on a strawberry sundae.

After going through the dinner *ab ovo ad mala* Catius finishes with a few remarks on service. The ware should be of ample size and scrupulously clean. 'It really turns the stomach if the waiter has been handling the cup with fingers which are greasy from nibbling at stolen pickings.' And how little it costs to keep a dining-room decently tidy!

This is all straightforward enough. The critic's problem is to decide about the satire's tone. How are we supposed to take this gastronomical lecture, and what are we to think of Catius and his anonymous professor? The obvious place to start our investigation is the prologue. Horace's opening words *unde et quo Catius?* are a conventional greeting and in themselves have no special significance. But when Catius answers that he has just come from a lecture which beat anything by Pythagoras, Socrates, or Plato, then Horace's audience would almost certainly have caught the allusion to Plato's dialogues, several of which begin with a similar encounter.[21] The academic background is also conveyed by the fact that Catius is about to write notes on what the professor has been saying. Thus, as Fiske points out,[22] what follows can be classified both as ὑπομνήματα (notes to aid a student's memory) and as ἀπομνημονεύματα (recollections of what a notable personality has said). But if all this is meant to prepare us for a piece of heavenly wisdom, something has gone badly wrong; for Catius' haste (*non est mihi tempus*, etc.) is more in keeping with the comic stage than the philosophical school, and his ecstatic claims for the teacher's *praecepta* warn us of irony ahead. So we are not wholly surprised when, in response to Horace's elaborately polite request, Catius reveals this as the first of his doctrines:

> longa quibus facies ovis erit, illa memento,
> ut suci melioris et ut magis alba rotundis,
> ponere; namque marem cohibent callosa vitellum.
>
> (12–14)

Remember to serve eggs which are long in shape, for they are superior in flavour to the round, and their whites are whiter—the reason being that their shells are harder and contain a male yolk.

In the epilogue Horace resumes his tone of ironic deference, addressing Catius as *doctus* and complimenting him once again on his amazing memory. But however admirable a spokesman Catius may be, Horace is eager to hear the master in person:

> at mihi cura
> non mediocris inest, fontis ut adire remotos
> atque haurire queam vitae praecepta beatae. (93–5)

I long for the chance to approach those secluded springs and to draw therefrom the rules for a life of blessedness.

The Lucretian parody is more complicated than in 1. 5. 101–3. First of all Horace has altered the context. In Lucretius 1. 927 ff. the *integri fontes* and the *novi flores* symbolize a new poetic theme; to render Epicureanism into poetry is a formidable task, but well worth undertaking; success will be a sign of the Muses' favour. In Horace, however, it is Catius' teacher who is the *fons*, and what issues from him is not poetry but wisdom. In other words Lucretius' poetic springs and his philosophical teacher (Epicurus) have been combined into a single metaphor. Secondly, the irony is subtler than in 1. 5, because instead of using Lucretius directly to attack a wrong-headed attitude he makes his point by pretending that Catius, Lucretius and himself are all fellow-converts.

By now it is obvious that Catius is a figure of fun. Engrossed in his new learning he seems to be quite unaware of what is happening to him. In this respect he is closer to the pest than to Trebatius; for the old lawyer has his wits about him, and in the verbal fencing of 2.1 he gives as good as he gets. But if Catius is ridiculous it does not follow that his instructions are absurd in principle or that where they are amusing they are all amusing in the same way. In particular we must beware of assuming that because a proposal sounds silly to us it must have sounded silly to a Roman. Our own certainties are irrelevant, even when true. So although we may be inclined to dismiss as nonsense what Catius says about the sex of eggs, we should bear in mind that this was a matter of genuine controversy amongst the ancients. Aristotle believed that round eggs were male and long eggs female. In this he was opposed by Antigonus of Carystus and (after Horace) by Columella and Pliny.[23] What, then, is Horace's point? Is it not that the attempt to discriminate between the male and female flavours is carrying connoisseurship a little too far, and that to enunciate this distinction as a gastronomic principle is mere pompous foolery? Again, it is quite common to kill a fowl by stifling it or wringing its neck. To drown it in wine, as Catius prescribes, is a little recondite. I am told that in modern Normandy ducks are drowned in wine and subsequently appear on the tables of certain Parisian restaurants as *le canard au sang*. But even today the refinement is not widely known.

In his *Natural History* Pliny says with a notable lack of dogmatism 'It seems that the best way of treating the finest Campanian wines is to place them in the open air and to let sun, moon, rain and wind beat upon them' (14. 136). Catius is much more precise: 'To remove the coarseness from Massic wine you should put it out of doors *in the night air, when the weather is clear*' (51–2). This practice, he says, will also get rid of the aroma, which is bad for the sinews. Pliny often mentions the effect of wine on the sinews, but he never goes so far as to suggest that the aroma by itself is deleterious.[24] Furthermore, is it not rather odd of Catius to distrust the wine's aroma, when in the next sentence he deplores the common process of straining on the grounds that it weakens the natural flavour?

The section ends with a hint for clearing a Surrentine which has been fortified with Falernian lees. There is nothing abnormal in the idea itself. Surrentine was by all accounts a thinnish, rather dry wine, suitable for convalescents. Tiberius and Caligula both had to take it as medicine. The former called it *generosum acetum*, 'high-quality vinegar', and the latter *nobilis vappa* (*vappa* was wine which had gone flat).[25] Galen, as reported by Athenaeus, calls it ἀλιπής and ψαφαρός—words usually interpreted as 'thin' and 'dry'.[26] Warner Allen takes ψαφαρός in the sense of 'powdery' and infers that it threw a heavy sediment. He then has to believe that Catius would make Surrentine 'even thicker with a blend of Falernian lees'. But this seems unlikely, and even Allen admits that 'a very old Surrentine...might seem rather flat and thin compared to the full-bodied Falernian'.[27] In any case the satiric point lies not in the practice of clearing but in the method which Catius lays down. The sediment, he says, should be collected by means of pigeons' eggs; 'for the yolk will sink to the bottom carrying the foreign matter with it'. Most people realized that the sediment actually clung to the white. The originality of Catius' teacher lay in stressing the role of the yolk (which was important only for its weight) and in specifying pigeons' eggs. Finally, the man who treats Surrentine in this way is said to be *vafer* (55)— a word which, like *sapiens* in v. 44, implies the knowing wink of a connoisseur. Many of Catius' rules reflect a pedantic fussiness which fastens on some minor detail as if it were crucial. After recommending a laxative of shellfish and sorrel, he adds that it must be taken with white Coan wine (29); in making a sauce one must use only the brine which comes from Byzantium (66). In fact Catius' head is so full of brand-names that he often sounds like a second-rate ad-man—or perhaps the hero of Mr Fleming's thrillers.

In other cases the advice seems quite balanced and straight-forward. 'Aufidius used to mix honey with strong Falernian— mistakenly, for when the veins are empty nothing which is not mild should be introduced into them.' It was a common belief that wine passed directly into the veins, and Falernian was thought to have a particularly violent effect—*nullo aeque venae excitantur*, says Pliny.[28] What we are supposed to note is how the teacher enhances his prestige by bluntly contradicting a rival authority. Again, Catius is quite sensible in his remarks about mushrooms— more sensible than Pliny.[29] But the gnomic brevity of his advice and his quasi-technical language give an impression of pedantry and conceit. This impression is strengthened by didactic clichés like *doctus eris*, *decet* and *nec satis est*, which sometimes assume a more ceremonious note, as in *memento* ('forget not') and *est operae pretium* ('' tis worth one's while'). The same effect is produced by the teacher's confident assertions about local speciali-ties (32–43,[30] 70–2), by claims which he makes for his art (it demands a mastery of detail, a wide general view, and a har-monious blend of intellect and taste), and finally by his unabashed boasting, e.g. 'The right age and the natural properties of fish and fowl were never disclosed to any researcher's palate before mine' (45–6). In this last passage it would be wrong to imagine that Horace had lost sight of the distinction between Catius and his teacher. The truth is that Catius has memorized his master's words so thoroughly that he does not think of changing the pronouns. He has ceased to exist as a separate person. The acolyte has surrendered his identity.

What we have been saying about Catius and his teacher runs counter to Lejay's interpretation at several important points. The French scholar sees no parody in any of Catius' remarks. To him Catius is an Italian countryman like Ofellus, with no interest in foreign delicacies; he is opposed to wealth and extravagance, unimpressed by novelties, and genuinely concerned for people's health. 'Malgré ses prétentions, Catius reste l'homme simple et sans pédantisme imaginé par Horace.'[31] I have already indicated what I regard as parody and pedantry. As for foreign foods, they are not, admittedly, given much prominence, and the satire is in a large measure *un éloge de l'Italie* (p. 451); but one cannot simply brush aside Catius' insistence on Coan wine (29), African snails (58), Byzantine brine (66) and Corycian saffron (68). To say that Catius is unimpressed by novelties is to overlook his original discoveries. And while Catius may not be addressing millionaires, he does take for granted a comfortable prosperity. Let us consider the passages cited by Lejay. It is not enough, says Catius, to buy expensive fish if you cannot prepare a decent sauce (37–9), nor should one spend a large sum on fish and then serve them in a dish that is too small (76–7). Brushes, napkins and sawdust are cheap; to forget them is a disgrace (81–2). It is inexcusable to sweep a mosaic (*lapides varios*) with a dirty broom and to put soiled covers on Tyrian cushions. These things require relatively little trouble and expense (83–6). This, surely, is not a plea for the simple life but for decent standards of tidiness. A man who urges his readers to keep clean covers on the upholstery of their Rovers and Pontiacs can hardly be called an apostle of austerity.

If our view of Catius and his teacher is sound, what then is the satirical point of vv. 76–87? Horace is certainly not indifferent to cleanliness—if proof is wanted we need only turn to *Epist.* I. 5. 21–4. What Catius says on this score is quite acceptable in principle. But surely there is something a little excessive in his language. A man who calls a small dish an *immane vitium* ('an atrocious offence') and a soiled cover a *flagitium ingens* ('an absolute scandal') will have no words left for things that really matter. *Adsit regula*—let's have a scale of values.

I would contend, therefore, that Catius is ridiculous because he is the mouthpiece of someone else's ideas and because the ideas themselves are those of a pompous and over-fastidious gourmet whose obsession with food and drink is from the moralist's viewpoint basically frivolous. I do not think we are justified in going further and arguing that by making fun of Catius in this way Horace is really attacking luxury. The points made about large (silver) plates and Tyrian cushions are not strong enough to assume this kind of prominence. And the various dishes are mentioned with the zest of one who appreciated a well-cooked dinner as much as the next man. Consequently, whereas the diatribe of Ofellus shows how far Horace would go towards the asceticism of Diogenes, this satire implies (perhaps unwittingly) a limit in the direction of Aristippus.

2. 8

About twelve years before this satire was written Cicero sent a letter to his friend Paetus urging him not to give up the habit of dining out.

There is nothing more appropriate to life, nothing more conducive to happy living. I am not thinking of the sensual pleasure involved but of the life and living in common and of the mental relaxation which comes above all from friendly talk. This kind of talk is at its most pleasant on convivial occasions. Here our countrymen have been wiser than the Greeks, for the Greeks call such occasions συμπόσια or σύνδειπνα, that is 'drinkings together' or 'dinings together', but we call them 'livings together' (*convivia*), because then we most truly share a common life.[32]

Since the dinner-party was virtually the sole method of private entertaining in the ancient world, it provided a background for many kinds of social activity. Guests might expect to hear singers and musicians, to watch exhibitions of dancing and acrobatics, and to enjoy the jokes of professional comedians. All these features, however, were secondary to the food and conversation. And so when, from the fourth century on, banquets became an independent literary topic, writers tended to fall into two categories—those who, like Plato and Xenophon, concentrated on what was said, and those who, like the poet Matron and the historians Hippolochus and Lynceus, concerned themselves primarily with the food and drink.[33] Although comparatively little is extant from the period before Christ, it is clear that a great deal of material existed. We know, for instance, that symposia were written by representatives of all the philosophical schools; and one later specimen by Heracleides of Tarentum was virtually a medical treatise in disguise.[34] Anyone wishing to follow the matter further may consult Hug's outline in Pauly-Wissowa, or if his stamina is equal to the task he can tackle Josef Martin's huge survey, *Symposion*.[35] The point to be made here is that none of the pre-Horatian material bears much resemblance to the dinner of Nasidienus, and certainly nothing should be regarded simply as its 'model'.

The ʼΑττικὸν δεῖπνον by Matron of Pitane begins thus:

δεῖπνά μοι ἔννεπε, Μοῦσα, πολύτροφα καὶ μάλα πολλά,
ἃ Ξενοκλῆς ῥήτωρ ἐν ʼΑθήναις δείπνισεν ἡμᾶς.[36]

Sing, O Muse, of the dinners sumptuous and right many, on which Xenocles the orator dined us in Athens.

The poem continues in the same vein for about 120 lines, describing how the guests encountered and dealt with a succession of dishes, which came before them like figures in a Homeric catalogue. As parody it is quite a clever piece of work, but it has no dialogue and no dramatic form; it has no satirical target, and, except for the parasite Chaerophon who is 'like a ravenous gull, empty, but well versed in dinners provided by others', it makes no attempt at characterization.

Menippus, the third-century satirist, is known to have written a *Symposium*. This fact has led to an argument which runs as follows: Lucian resembles Horace, Lucian could not have imitated Horace, Lucian is known to have imitated Menippus, therefore Horace must have imitated Menippus. If we consider only the first proposition and compare Lucian's *Symposium* (or *Lapiths*) with *Sat.* 2. 8, we shall find that Lucian's work describes a wedding-feast; the food, however, is scarcely mentioned, and the satire is directed not at the host, who behaves throughout like a gentleman, but at philosophers of various schools who squabble over places, exchange crude invective, and finally turn the whole proceedings into a bloody brawl in which the groom has his head split open and a flute girl is nearly raped. The resemblance to Nasidienus' banquet is not obvious.

Only a few fragments of Lucilius' *cenae* need concern us here. We know from Cicero, *Brut.* 160, that at least one of the satires described a dinner-party given for Crassus by the auctioneer Granius in 107 B.C. It is practically certain that the description came in Book 20 and contained the line:

> purpureo tersit tunc latas gausape mensas

> Then he wiped the wide tables with a crimson towel

—a line which leads at once to a comparison with *Sat.* 2. 8. 11:

> gausape purpureo mensam pertersit.

> He wiped the table well with a crimson towel.

On the strength of this one parallel Fiske (p. 165) refers to Lucilius' poem as 'the original of Horace's *Sat.* 2. 8'. But even if other correspondences existed, we still could not speak of anything more than a superficial likeness, because while Nasidienus, like Catius, is portrayed as a humourless ass, such a treatment would have been impossible in the case of Granius, who was renowned for his agile wit.[37] Shero, who sees this point, goes on to suggest that 'in the *cena Nasidieni* we have a *contaminatio* (i.e. a conflation) of the picture of lavish entertainment at Granius' dinner-party with a picture of meanness and bad taste in connexion with a

215

dinner-party which occurred elsewhere in the satires of Lucilius, perhaps in Book 14'.[38] But the sordid meal described in Book 14, like that in Book 5, would only be relevant to *Sat.* 2. 8 if it could be proved that Nasidienus was guilty of meanness. This, in fact, is a widely held opinion,[39] and since the matter is of basic importance to our view of the poem we had better examine the evidence.

(*a*) Vv. 6–7. The boar, which was served cold as part of the *hors-d'œuvres*, was slightly high. This cannot have been due either to meanness or to bad cooking, for Nasidienus was *proud* of the fact and drew attention to it more than once. In his view the rather strong flavour was an added refinement, and such an idea did not seem unreasonable to Porphyrion. This does not mean, of course, that the meat was rotten. The animal was caught when a *gentle* South wind was blowing. A really strong Auster would have ruined the meat entirely—cf. *praesentes Austri, coquite horum obsonia* (2. 2. 41). Finally, boar's meat was not cheap. According to Diocletian's edict of prices it was the dearest kind of big game.[40]

(*b*) Vv. 10–11. The table was of maple-wood. 'Maple is named by Pliny, *NH* 16. 66, as an inferior material "*citro secundum*". It would seem that what is laughed at is the pretentious care of a second-rate table.' So Wickham, following an opinion which goes back to the commentator Cruquianus. But what Pliny says (in an account which deals with many types of wood and their uses) is *acer...operum elegantia ac subtilitate citro secundum*. That is, as a material for high-quality furniture maple was second *only* to citrus. One type, according to Pliny, was actually superior to citrus, but this was suitable only for small objects (16. 68).

(*c*) Vv. 14–15.
> procedit fuscus Hydaspes
> Caecuba vina ferens, Alcon Chium maris expers.

Dark Hydaspes entered with Caecuban wine, Alcon with Chian unmixed with sea-water.

Our attention centres on *maris expers*. Why was the Chian unmixed with sea-water?[41] Since Greek wines were frequently salted, some scholars have believed that Nasidienus intended to make his Chian less drinkable. But this would be strange behaviour in a man who served his Caecuban 'straight'—for Caecuban too was a wine of first-rate quality. Moreover it has been pointed out that according to Galen, who was writing in the second century A.D., some of the finest wines (including one from Chios) were left without salt.[42] In the first century A.D. Columella states that the best wines require no preservative (12. 19. 2). We may therefore picture Nasidienus as a member of a self-conscious *avantgarde* who preferred to drink their Chian unsalted. Warner Allen observes that the legitimacy of salting has also been debated in modern times.[43]

(*d*) Vv. 16–17. Nasidienus now turns to Maecenas and says 'If you like Alban or Falernian better than what is before you, we have both'. Since Pliny (*NH* 14. 62) rates Alban and Falernian below Caecuban, the host is probably implying something like this: 'I have served what I regard as the very best; but if you prefer Alban or Falernian, which are admittedly respectable, I can provide them also.' If Nasidienus had served all four wines (including Chian), he might have appeared less of a connoisseur; if he had served only two and left it at that, his resources and his knowledge might have seemed less comprehensive. The result was a clumsy compromise, but the chief point has been successfully made—namely that Nasidienus' cellar is equal to all demands. 'You name it, we got it.' Such behaviour is not mean, whatever else it may be.

(*e*) V. 18. Horace greets this account, which is given by his friend Fundanius, with the exclamation *divitias miseras!*—'Ah, the miseries of wealth!' There has been much dispute about this phrase, but it certainly need not imply stinginess on Nasidienus' part. Probably it is just a vague expression referring sarcastically to his foolish ostentation. If, however, we want to examine it more closely, we may start from the remark of Ofellus in 2. 2. 65–6:

> mundus erit qua non offendat sordibus, atque
> in neutram partem cultus miser

(The wise man) will be stylish enough to avoid giving offence through meanness, and in his way of living he will not be unhappy in either direction (i.e. towards meanness *or* extravagance).

When a man's conduct misses or exceeds the appropriate mean he fails to achieve happiness and becomes to that extent *miser*. He may be unaware of this himself; he may not *feel* unhappy. But the fact that others view him with dislike or contempt is an index of his true condition. 'So-and-so's a miserable character', we say. By a slight extension the adjective can then be applied to the cause of the man's condition, as in *misera ambitione* (1. 4. 26). In Nasidienus' case it is lavish ostentation which makes him an object of ridicule; hence riches are *miserae* 'unhappy'—a striking way to speak of something which is supposed to make a man *beatus*. And one remembers that in the first line Nasidienus *is* called *beatus*.

(*f*) Vv. 25 ff.

If anything happened to escape our notice, Nomentanus was there to point it out with his forefinger; for the uninitiated, that is we ourselves, were dining off fowl, shell-fish, and fish, which contained flavours quite unlike the usual ones. This became clear right at the beginning when Nomentanus passed me the inwards of a plaice and turbot which no one had previously tasted (*ingustata*).

By *ingustata* Fundanius means that during the meal no one had yet tasted this particular preparation; he was the first to discover its surprising flavour. That, at any rate, is how I take the word; the more common view that *ingustata* means 'which I had never tasted in my life' conflicts with the only natural interpretation of *dissimilem noto* (28). But whatever one's opinion on this point, the fact remains that the startling effect of all these creations was intentional. The chef had not bungled the job, as Palmer thinks; he had merely given proof of the talent which had earned him his post—namely his perverse ingenuity.

In reading this passage one thinks of the elaborate artifice encouraged by Trimalchio, but it would perhaps be a mistake to imagine that such tricks were confined to the tables of rich parvenus. Apicius has a recipe for Patina of Anchovy without Anchovy, consisting of minced fish, pepper, rue, liquamen, eggs, oil and jellyfish. 'Serve with ground pepper', he says, adding with a craftsman's pride *ad mensam nemo agnoscet quid manducet*— 'at table no one will recognize what he is eating'.[44] The various sauces had much the same effect. One is reminded of Henry Thrale's remark to Johnson in Paris in 1775: 'The cooking of the French was forced on them by necessity, for they could not eat their meat unless they added some taste to it.' Thackeray held a similar view:

> Dear Lucy, you know what my wish is—
> I hate all your Frenchified fuss:
> Your silly entrées and made dishes
> Were never intended for us.

It is, of course, a perennial British conviction that the French cuisine is a technique of meretricious concealment. That is why, when Horace pleads for some recognition of nature, he is hailed as a genuine beef-eating Englishman.

(*g*) In vv. 35 ff. one of the company, who is anxious to begin some serious drinking, calls for larger cups; whereupon Nasidienus turns pale—a sign which editors at once attribute to his stinginess, ignoring the fact that Fundanius himself gives two quite different explanations. Nasidienus, he says, foresaw an outbreak of ill-mannered abuse or else was apprehensive in case too much strong wine would dull the palate and so stultify his chef's art. Both fears were perfectly reasonable. Why invent others?

(*h*) Vv. 90 ff.

> tum pectore adusto
> vidimus et merulas poni et sine clune palumbes

> Then we saw blackbirds with crisped breasts laid before us and pigeons without their rumps.

According to Palmer the blackbirds were not crisped but burnt— a theory refuted by the very next line:

> suavis res, si non causas narraret eorum et
> naturas dominus.

> These were real delicacies, if only the host had not kept recounting their underlying causes and their natural properties.

219

As we have seen in the case of Tigellius, Priscus and others, Horace was very much alive to inconsistencies of character. If he had intended Nasidienus to appear both mean and extravagant he would surely have exhibited the contrast in bold colours.

It will be inferred from all this that in his attitude to food and drink Nasidienus stands very close to Catius. The lamprey served in the main course was pregnant when caught; after spawning, its flesh would have been inferior (44). The gourmet eats only the wings of a hare (cf. 2. 4. 44); the crane provided is a male bird, and the goose's liver comes from a female; the pigeons are served without the rump. The last three items all indicate refinements on the usual practice. Nasidienus is also a pedant. His lecture on fish sauce, which occupies the central position in the poem, has much in common with the recipes given by Catius. He is aware of other work done in the field (52) and has made contributions of his own. All these affectations are treated by Horace with grandiose irony. Asking Fundanius to describe the party he says:

> da, si grave non est,
> quae prima iratum ventrem placaverit esca.

Tell me, if it is not too much trouble, what dish first appeased your raging belly.

The appeasement of wrath is Homeric, the *da* parodies an epic invocation, and *prima* reflects the traditional desire to hear a tale from the start.[45] Later, when all his plans seem about to be wrecked by his guests' intemperance, Nasidienus turns pale in the time-honoured epic manner:
> vertere pallor
> tum parochi faciem.[46]

So too, the host's reappearance in v. 84 is hailed with a solemn apostrophe:
> Nasidiene redis, mutatae frontis

Nasidienus, thou dost return with altered countenance.

In all these points, as well as in its Platonic preamble, 2. 8 resembles 2. 4. But its dramatic form makes the *cena Nasidieni* a much more interesting poem. Whereas Catius is a mouthpiece and his teacher a disembodied voice, Nasidienus emerges from the background of the *cena* as a distinct personality. The fact that the dinner began at noon instead of at three o'clock already tells us something about him; so does the fact that his waiters were dressed like chorus-girls and were trained to move like priests in a procession. We are told that he assigned his own place to his client Nomentanus with instructions to keep Maecenas informed about what he was eating—perhaps a wise precaution, for instead of offering one or two special dishes Nasidienus was determined that every course should be a sensation. Unfortunately, in his anxiety to impress his distinguished guests he overlooked the fact that Maecenas and his friends had other conversational resources besides food and drink, and that they would not appreciate being reduced to what Lucilius had described as so many 'bellies'.[47]

Our picture of Nasidienus is further illuminated by the collapse of the awning. The episode is described with a fine epic simile:

> interea suspensa gravis aulaea ruinas
> in patinam fecere, trahentia pulveris atri
> quantum non Aquilo Campanis excitat agris.
>
> (54–6)

Meanwhile the awning spread above fell with a mighty crash upon the platter, dragging with it more black dust than the North wind raises on Campanian fields.

When the guests lifted their heads they found the feast in ruins and the host sobbing like a bereaved father.[48] The great god Bathos had taken his revenge. At this point Nasidienus' vanity and his utter lack of humour are cruelly exposed. 'What a shame!' cries Balatro. 'To think of all the trouble you took over the bread and the sauce and the waiters' uniforms! And then look what happens. The canopy goes and falls down. But after all, a host is like a general; adversity shows his mettle, success conceals it.' It is all the most patent ridicule, but Nasidienus is too stupid to see it. 'God bless you!' he exclaims. 'You're a fine fellow, and it's a pleasure to have you as a guest.' With that he calls for his shoes (another neat touch) and disappears into the kitchen.

Nasidienus is therefore wholly credible as a character. But he is more than a character. He stands for a type common enough in Horace's day, a type which always appears when wealth is acquired without either education or a social conscience. Hence as a piece of social criticism *Sat.* 2. 8 has a wide field of reference. It might be urged that with all his silliness Nasidienus deserves sympathy, and that, like his distant descendant Jay Gatsby, he is basically pathetic in his quest for recognition and esteem. I doubt, however, if Horace saw him that way. In this, as in most other matters, we are more sensitive than the Romans, and we must avoid reading our own preconceptions into an ancient text. At the end of this satire Fundanius, Maecenas and the others rush out of the house leaving the latter part of the meal untouched. Structurally it is the weakest ending in the book, and (however fictitious in content) it puts the guests in an exceedingly poor light—to our way of thinking. But this cannot have been Horace's intention, for the piece, like 1. 9, was written for the entertainment of these very people. He must have seen their departure as a dramatic gesture which paid the host back for his absurd and vulgar display.

If, after this, we wish to remind ourselves of the relative gentleness and good humour of 2. 8 we need only compare it with the fifth satire of Juvenal. In both poems the scene is recounted by a guest, but whereas the *cena Nasidieni* is described by a man whom the host was honoured to entertain, Virro's dinner-parties are seen through the eyes of a despised client. Granted, there are clients at Nasidienus' table too, but they are not humiliated as they are in Juvenal; in fact it is they who make a fool of the host. As for Nasidienus himself, in spite of his vanity and his naked ambition, he does try to please his guests and he treats them all, including Porcius and Nomentanus, with the same consideration. Consequently, when set beside the appalling Virro, he appears quite a tolerable human being. At every course Virro's clients receive inferior food, served by ugly and contemptuous waiters. Even the water is different. And always there is the threat of violence. These indignities are recounted with a bitter resentment and a hyperbolical wit quite alien to Horace's temper. One example must suffice. In 2. 8. 31–3 the apples reveal Nasidienus' astonishing expertise, for according to Nomentanus they owe their rich red glow to the fact that they were picked by the light of a waning moon. In Juvenal the apples illustrate Virro's calculating cruelty; for the host eats apples like those of Phaeacia or the Hesperides, while his clients are given the sort of rotten object that is gnawed by a performing monkey (149–55). The violence of Juvenal's contrast, with its sardonic use of legend and its squalid realism, is wholly characteristic. It is also fair to see a symbolic correspondence between the frightened, miserable monkey and the downtrodden client. Juvenal makes it clear that Virro's behaviour is due solely to malice. His object is to degrade his dependants while enjoying his own sense of power. And there is, says Juvenal, a certain grim justice in it all; for if you can endure such treatment then you don't *deserve* to be free.

CHAPTER VIII

A CONSULTATION

2. 5

Viewed as a social document this satire has something in common with 1. 6. As the earlier poem reflects the decline of the old caste system, 2. 5 arises from the disintegration of family life. The old custom had been that a girl should marry early (twelve was the minimum age), and that she should then devote her life to managing the household and bringing up her numerous children. Since marriage represented an alliance between two houses with the primary purpose of producing children who would perpetuate the name, prestige, and property of the family, no one thought of demanding that there should be a romantic affection between the two partners. In all likelihood the girl would be betrothed without her consent; and although consent was supposed to be necessary before the marriage took place, it is clear that in many cases this amounted to no more than a passive acceptance of the father's decision.[1]

One cannot easily account for the decay of this highly organized system; but it must have been partly due to factors which have been operating in our own society during the last hundred years. While their husbands were away, fighting wars from which many would never return, the womenfolk had to face greater responsibilities at home, and these responsibilities helped to engender a spirit of independence. At the same time the proceeds of empire brought larger and more luxurious houses, with a ready supply of cheap labour. While a suffragette movement would have been out of the question, there is evidence that by the first century B.C. women were wielding an unofficial, but by no means negligible, influence in political affairs.[2] The social effects of their growing independence were wider still. The old *manus* marriage, which brought the wife and her property under the husband's control, fell into disuse. Most women now contracted free marriages in which they retained ownership of their property and were not legally dependent on their husbands for financial support. Freedom within marriage resulted in a higher divorce rate, and at the same time the birth rate began to fall. The liberalization of divorce was almost certainly easier for the Romans than it has been for us. In our experience it has involved the extension of grounds, the simplification of procedure, and the reduction of costs. Time has also been required for people to modify their religious objections. For the Romans, on the other hand, divorce could be effected by a simple formula based on the wish of either party.

In view of the usual pious moralizing on Rome's falling birth rate, it is refreshing to find Fritz Schulz asserting that 'the true cause of the decline was not debauchery, not a general aversion to marriage, not a mysterious decline in the reproductive capacity of the Roman population, not race-mixture, and least of all the liberal law of marriage. The main cause was Roman *humanitas*. It led to drastic birth-control, i.e. to one- or two-child families, which, owing to the state of medicine and hygiene, was glaringly insufficient for the replacement of the population.'³ This emphasis on *humanitas*, by which Schulz means the acceptance of a woman as a person in her own right, is wholly welcome, though one wonders what this 'drastic birth-control' may have meant in terms of abortion and infanticide. It may be, however, that the violence and insecurity of these years had as much to do with the falling birth rate as anything else.

Aversion to marriage must also be reckoned as a contributory cause. Celibacy, after all, had many advantages. When combined with wealth, it offered not only the various freedoms which it offers today; it also brought a certain kind of social esteem. As he carried out the ceremonial duties of the day, receiving greetings, appearing in court, witnessing documents, attending recitations, and so on, the rich bachelor could be sure of company. He also knew that this company would become more numerous, more attentive, and more deferential as the years went by. It was generally recognized that personal services merited something in return, and even people whose motives were not wholly mercenary would expect some friendly acknowledgement in the rich man's will. Parting gestures of this kind became so normal that silence was tantamount to insult. And so the will itself came to be regarded both as a final judgement on the deceased's friends and as a mirror of his social life.[4]

In view of all this it might be assumed that the *captator*, or legacy-hunter, would confine his attentions to rich bachelors. But two passages in 2. 5 indicate that this was not always the case. In vv. 45–50 the *captator* is told that if the rich man has a delicate son he should contrive to be named second heir; then, if anything happens to the boy he can step into his place. In vv. 27–31 Tiresias says that in a legal action a childless rascal should always be supported against a man who has at home a son or a fertile wife—which suggests that children, not wives, were the *captator*'s chief enemy. It may now be asked why a rich, childless husband, if wooed by a legacy-hunter, could not exploit the odious creature for all he was worth and then cheat him in the end by leaving everything to his wife. It must be remembered that a wife was not legally part of her husband's family. Her property remained separate, except for her dowry, which could be used by the husband during the marriage but which reverted to her on his death. Now admittedly a man was not obliged to choose an heir from among his own immediate kin. He could appoint someone else, but if he belonged to the 'top income bracket' he was forbidden by the Lex Voconia of 169 B.C. to institute his wife *heres*.[5] By *heres* the Romans meant a person who would assume the rights and duties of the deceased, which included settling the dead man's debts and paying the *legata*, or bequests, decreed in the will. In former times this system was open to abuse, because the testator might assign so many *legata* to his friends that little or nothing remained for the heir. But in 40 B.C. (that is, ten years before the writing of 2. 5) the Lex Falcidia enacted that if legacies exceeded three-quarters of the total, they should be cut down *pro rata*. Thus the heir, after paying out his various dues, could be sure of at least a quarter of the estate. To the *captator* this meant that even if the wife received a substantial legacy he himself might still hope for a handsome profit.

The seriousness of this whole situation was recognized by Augustus, and eventually, about 18 B.C., he tried to cope with it by legislation.[6] Under the terms of the *Lex Iulia de maritandis ordinibus* (later modified in A.D. 9 by the *Lex Papia Poppaea*) the inheritance rights of *orbi*, that is childless men, were curtailed, and fatherhood was encouraged by certain privileges in public life. Marriage was made easier by limiting the parents' veto and by allowing men outside the senatorial class to marry freedwomen. At the same time, by the *Lex Iulia de adulteriis coercendis*, an effort was made to safeguard the purity of family life. Whatever success they may have had in other respects these laws did little to check the disease of legacy-hunting. In fact, to judge from numerous passages in Tacitus, Seneca, Petronius, Pliny and Martial, the practice actually increased in the century following Horace's satire.[7] The advantages of childlessness became so impressive that 'some men pretended to hate their sons, and disowned them, thus depriving themselves of parenthood'.[8] Other *orbi* avoided the official penalties as follows: 'When elections were drawing near or when provinces were to be assigned, they would acquire sons by fake adoptions; and then, as soon as they had received their praetorships and provinces by lot among the other fathers, they immediately emancipated those whom they had adopted.'[9] These and similar passages are cited in the social histories of Friedländer and Dill.[10]

Here, however, we are concerned with the problem as treated by Horace. The poem opens as follows:

> hoc quoque, Tiresia, praeter narrata petenti
> responde, quibus amissas reparare queam res
> artibus atque modis.

Answer me this question too, Tiresias, in addition to what you've told me. By what ways and means can I recover my lost wealth?

The reader has come unawares upon a private conversation and remains to eavesdrop. Before the voice stops speaking he knows he is present at a famous Homeric scene which has been familiar to civilized men for over two thousand years. What exactly has gone before? Ulysses, on Circe's instructions, has come to visit Tiresias in the land of the dead to obtain information about his voyage home. Tiresias has warned him that if he harms the cattle of the sun he will face disaster:

I foresee ruin for your ship and your companions; even if you yourself escape, you will return late, on board a foreign ship and in a miserable plight, having lost all your companions. And you will find trouble in your house, for arrogant men are consuming your resources and courting your noble wife with suitors' gifts. (*Od.* 11. 112–17)

After the prophet's speech, which predicts many other things, including Ulysses' death, the hero answers 'No doubt, Tiresias, the gods themselves have spun these threads; but come, tell me this as well, and tell me true...' (139–40). Here, I think, is the point at which Horace takes up the dialogue; for his opening line corresponds closely with this request, and he is not at all concerned with what follows, i.e. with the question of how the spirit of Ulysses' mother can be enabled to recognize her son.

So the scene is a heroic one. But already a disquieting note has entered, because in a Horatian context the acquisition of *res*— even of *res* which have been lost—is something irredeemably squalid. So, too, by even listening to such a request, Tiresias is in danger of compromising himself. At first he is sarcastically non-committal. 'Well well! Is it not enough for the man of many wiles to reach Ithaca and to see the gods of his ancestral hearth?' But soon he accepts his new role. 'Since, not to mince words, poverty is what you're afraid of, here's the way to get rich...' He then proceeds to instruct Ulysses in the art of legacy-hunting. This is what has become of the prophet whom Sophocles called 'the divine man in whom alone truth is implanted' (*OT* 298–9).

After advising Ulysses to concentrate on wheedling a legacy out of some rich old man, Tiresias continues:

228

qui quamvis periurus erit, sine gente, cruentus
sanguine fraterno, fugitivus, ne tamen illi
tu comes exterior si postulet ire recuses.   (15–17)

He may be a liar and a man of no family, a runaway slave, stained
with his brother's blood; nevertheless, if he asks you to accompany
him, be sure to walk politely on his outside.

Ulysses' reaction is instructive:

utne tegam spurco Damae latus? haud ita Troiae
me gessi certans semper melioribus.

What? Am I to give the position of honour to filthy Dama? I did not
comport myself thus at Troy, where I always strove with my peers.

In other words a liar and a murderer may pass, but to show respect
to a social inferior—that is a different matter. Such humiliations
were never dreamed of 'far on the ringing plains of windy Troy'.
Tiresias shrugs and makes to turn away. 'Very well, in that case
you'll be a pauper.' That is the one unbearable thought. With an
immense effort Ulysses conquers his repugnance. If dancing
attendance on a menial is the price of prosperity, well, then it
must be paid:

fortem hoc animum tolerare iubebo;
et quondam maiora tuli.[11]

I shall bid my heart to be brave and endure this. I have borne even
greater ills before today.

After removing this scruple Tiresias proceeds to develop his theme.
The rhythm of the poem is now clear. It consists of a satiric
interaction between the speaker's Homeric background and the
context in which the poet is writing. After a long passage on the
techniques of legacy-hunting, which is purely Roman in character,
the Homeric background is in danger of being forgotten; so at a
point half way through the poem Horace reaffirms the speaker's
identity in a piece of oracular bombast:

plerumque recoctus
scriba ex quinqueviro corvum deludet hiantem,
captatorque dabit risus Nasica Corano.   (55–7)

More than once will a raven with open beak be outwitted by a civil servant cooked up out of a police official. And Coranus will have the laugh over Nasica the fortune-hunter.

'Are you raving?' asks Ulysses, reasonably enough. 'Or are you deliberately teasing me?' 'Son of Laertes,' comes the answer, 'whatever I say will or will not come to pass, for mighty Apollo has granted me the gift of second sight.' Ulysses is in no mood to notice that this proud boast may easily be an absurd tautology. Instead he presses for information about Nasica and Coranus, and Tiresias' answer (62 ff.) takes us forward again to first-century Rome in the period immediately following Actium.

> tempore quo iuvenis Parthis horrendus, ab alto
> demissum genus Aenea, tellure marique
> magnus erit, forti nubet procera Corano
> filia Nasicae metuentis reddere soldum.

In the day when a young hero, the scourge of the Parthians, born of Aeneas' noble line, shall rule over land and sea, the gallant Coranus shall take in marriage the queenly daughter of Nasica who hates to pay his debts in full.

'In the day when...' This solemn formula, which is derived from the Delphic oracle,[12] puts us in mind of a later parallel:

> cum iam semianimum laceraret Flavius orbem
> ultimus et calvo serviret Roma Neroni.[13]

At the time when the last of the Flavians was tearing at a world already half dead, and Rome was in bondage to a bald Nero.

These two passages, the one humorous but basically respectful, the other acid and resentful, epitomize the contrast between Horace and Juvenal in their attitudes to their respective sovereigns.

But what of the story? Well, Nasica placed great hopes in the marriage of his daughter. His son-in-law Coranus was rich and encouragingly decrepit, while he himself had some very tiresome debts. When the wedding was over, Coranus offered to show him the will. After a few token refusals Nasica took it in his hands and read to his dismay that neither he nor his daughter had been

left a penny. That is the prophecy of Tiresias. As a glimpse of the
new age it provides an interesting contrast with another vision
of Rome from beyond the grave, which was soon to take shape in
the mind of the poet's friend.

After a few more verses of purely Roman material we are again
reminded of the Homeric setting:

> scortator erit: cave te roget; ultro
> Penelopam facilis potiori trade.   (75–6)

Suppose he is a lecher. Don't wait to be asked; Do the decent thing
and hand over Penelope voluntarily to your successful rival.

Ulysses is astounded at the very idea: putasne,

> perduci poterit tam frugi tamque pudica,
> quam nequiere proci recto depellere cursu?[14]

What? Do you think she can be seduced, a lady so proper and so
virtuous, whom the suitors have been unable to tempt from the
strait and narrow path?

Astounded rather than shocked. As Madame Dacier points out,
with feline acumen, 'Ulysse ne marque pas la moindre répugnance,
et toute son inquiétude est que sa femme ne se rende trop diffi-
cile'.[15] Tiresias disposes of his doubts: The suitors have failed
simply because their price was not right; in fact 'they were less
interested in sexual conquest than in the palace cooking. That's
why Penelope is virtuous.' We are moving towards that beautifully simple view of womanhood which Ovid summed up for all
time: *casta est quam nemo rogavit.*[16] It is a proposition which half
the male world would like to be true and the other half actually
believes.

In all these manœuvres, however, Tiresias has a nice sense of
proportion. He is, after all, a Horatian Tiresias. The *captator*, he
says, must not appear over-eager, or else all may be lost. That is
the point of his next story, which is set in his native Thebes:

In Thebes an outrageous old woman was buried as follows in accordance with
the terms of her will: her body was thoroughly soaked in oil; then it was

carried out on the bare shoulders of her heir. No doubt she hoped to slip out of his clutches after her death—presumably because he had pressed her too hard when she was alive.

Except for the mention of Ulysses' name in v. 100, that is the last Greek reference until the closing words:

> sed me
> imperiosa trahit Proserpina; vive valeque.
> But stern Persephone calls me back—*Lebe wohl!*

With these words Tiresias breaks off the interview and returns into the darkness to walk among the lowest of the dead.

The Greek background is, of course, no more than a witty pretence. The poem is firmly rooted in the social life of Rome. Thus Ulysses is returning to his *Penates* (4). To become rich, however, he must pay more respect to his quarry than to his *Lar* (14). He will undertake litigation in the *forum* (27), becoming the rich man's *cognitor* (38). The rich man himself may be called Quintus or Publius (32). The *captator's* persistence is conveyed by a parody of a Roman poet (41). And so on. The Roman sections have a design of their own. Up to v. 44 (i.e. for about the first half of the poem) the emphasis falls on the *captator's* persistence and audacity. After this Tiresias is more concerned with the need for subtlety and caution. The two sections are drawn together by the theme of flattery, which runs through the satire like a thread of gilt.[17]

The instruction in *captatio* contains some of the poet's most brilliant writing. Two features may suffice by way of illustration. The first is his use of the central metaphor, which is taken from hunting (whether it be fish, flesh, or fowl). 'If a thrush or some other delicacy is given to you for your own use, let it fly away to the glitter of a great household where the master is aged' (10–12). On its first appearance the metaphor has already been given an ironic twist, because the bird which the old man will receive is in fact only a lure. Such a ruse will suit the *dolosus Ulixes*; for is not *dolosus* connected with δέλεαρ, the Greek for bait?

In 23 ff. the metaphor changes to fishing. 'You must fish cunningly for old men's wills wherever possible. If one or two are clever enough to nibble the bait off the hook and so escape your clutches, don't give up hope, and don't abandon your craft because of an occasional disappointment.' In this, as in other fields, nothing succeeds like success. By being attentive to one or two the *captator* will attract the notice of others. 'More tunnies will come swimming up', and his fish-ponds will grow (44).

Then the metaphor alters again. 'If there is a danger of exposing yourself by paying open respect to a bachelor, find a man who is bringing up a delicate son in affluent circumstances, and then by your constant services creep slowly towards your goal.' The verb *adrepe* and the idea of cover suggest that Horace has in mind the stalking of game. Then in vv. 55–6 birds come to the fore again as Tiresias predicts that 'more than once a raven with open beak will be outwitted by a civil servant cooked up out of a police official'. This is sometimes supposed to refer to the fable of the raven who was flattered by the fox into dropping a piece of cheese. But the parallel is far from clear, and it is wiser with Heinze and others to regard the raven as simply a creature that feeds on carrion.[18] This represents another variation in the metaphor, because now the bird is itself the predator.

The second stylistic feature is the lively use of colloquial expressions. 'Breeding and character without assets are *vilior alga*— more worthless than seaweed.'[19] Tell me, says Ulysses, how I can rake together 'piles of cash'—*aeris acervos*. The *captator* will not allow his prey to be cheated of even a nut-shell, *cassa nuce*, and he advises him to go off home and 'look after his precious skin'— *pelliculam curare*. To have oneself named second heir is 'a gambit that rarely fails'—*perraro haec alea fallit*. Once Penelope gets a taste of cash there'll be no holding her; 'she'll be like a bitch which cannot be kept away from a greasy hide'—*ut canis a corio numquam absterrebitur uncto*.[20] The fawning *captator* is told to 'keep on blowing and inflate the old balloon with windy compliments', at which point the poor dupe has ceased to be even a sentient creature.

The satire's wit, however, defies all simple categories. What of the art whereby *honores* (13) anticipates *venerabilior* in the next line, and *sparge* (103) prepares us for *illacrimare*? What of the secondary meaning in *carum caput* (94)? (One is reminded of the fashionable physician in Cronin's *The Citadel*, who after sounding a rich old lady with his stethoscope turns to his friend and murmurs 'My dear fellow, that's an absolute treasure-chest!') And what of those expressions which resist translation because they embody the unique power of the Latin language, e.g. *ante Larem gustet venerabilior Lare dives* (14), or *laudes, lauderis ut absens* (72)? These are the marks of a master craftsman.

Finally, amid the parodies of Homer, Furius and the Delphic oracle, amid all the legal niceties and the technical rules, notice how a single theme is brought to its conclusion. In v. 18 a horrified Ulysses says 'What? Am I to walk politely on the outside of filthy Dama?' In v. 101 he is to sob 'Ah well well! So my old friend Dama is no more!' That is the lesson to be learned. And it does not end with Dama's death. 'If one of your co-heirs is getting on in years and has a churchyard cough, tell him that if he'd like to buy an estate or a town house which is part of your share, you'll let him have it for a song.' Fishing, after all, like cricket, is a way of life.

Scholars more interested in the history of ideas than in literary appreciation have sometimes suggested that this satire was written as a protest against the early Cynic and Stoic practice of idealizing Ulysses. Antisthenes, writing in the late fifth century, had commended the hero for his endurance, his self-sufficiency and his loyalty to a common cause.[21] A hundred years later the Stoic Zeno read the *Odyssey* as a record of the good man's triumphs over hardship and temptation. Traces of this moralizing approach, which sometimes developed into allegory, may be seen in Horace (*Epist.* I. 2), Plutarch, Seneca, Marcus Aurelius, and various Christian authors.[22] Now there is good evidence that some of the later Cynics reacted against this roseate conception of Ulysses' character. Crates pointed out that the figure so admired by

Antisthenes had no real existence in Homer's work. So far from being the tight-lipped man of adamant, Ulysses had in fact shown himself lazy, sensual, and inconsiderate; to represent him as the father of Cynicism was a grotesque perversion of the truth.[23]

But this philosophical controversy, though interesting in itself, has very little to do with the poem we are studying; because Horace was not seriously concerned with Homer's character at all. The Ulysses of 2. 5 is a comic abstraction, designed as an instrument of social satire. And the target of that satire is legacy-hunting. In the same way (and it is strange how often this is forgotten) the Ulysses who appears in *Epist.* 1. 2 as an example of *virtus* and *sapientia* is an abstraction designed to meet the purpose of a moral epistle. It is needless condescension on our part to imagine that Horace's real view of the Homeric Ulysses differed in any essential feature from our own. And indeed the two abstractions just mentioned, when set side by side, point to a lively awareness of that ambiguity in the hero's character which Stanford has so fruitfully explored.

There are other, more general, reasons against limiting the satire's scope. For centuries men had amused themselves by writing parodies of Homer. One early specimen was *The Battle of Frogs and Mice*, a skit on those bloody and over-numerous engagements in the *Iliad*.[24] Another, of which we have only fragmentary information, was the tale of Margites, a character 'who knew many things but knew them all badly'. One of the things he knew badly may be inferred from the fact that he was afraid to sleep with his wife for fear she would complain about him to her mother.[25]

Homer's characters were no more immune than his language. From early times his gods and heroes were guyed in both comedy and satyr drama, and Ulysses was a favourite target. After surveying the extensive though fragmentary evidence E. D. Phillips remarks 'His cleverness and cunning, his odd adventures, his familiarity with all kinds of people, his ready tongue and many disguises, and the strain of rascality in him which from time to time delights Athena in the *Odyssey*, all contribute to make him by far the most suitable for comedy of the great heroes of epic and legend'.[26] The same kind of irreverence, which is quite compatible with genuine respect, found expression in art. A well-known example, involving Ulysses, is the so-called Dolon crater. This Italian red-figure vase of the late fifth century, now in the British Museum, shows Ulysses and Diomedes about to pounce on Dolon as the spy tip-toes gingerly through the wood. As Pfuhl remarks, the exaggeration is slightly comic but not to the point of caricature.[27] A much coarser type of humour is represented by a Boeotian black-figure vase of the fourth century, now in Oxford. On one side it shows Ulysses being driven across the sea by the blasts of Boreas, and on the other threatening Circe with drawn sword as she proffers him the magic cup.[28]

In Roman literature aspects of the Ulysses theme had been handled long before Horace's time. Lucilius in his seventeenth book showed Penelope in conversation with a servant or a suitor. The latter says:

nupturum te nupta negas, quod vivere Ulixen speras.[29]

Married as you are, you insist that you will not get married because you hope that Ulysses is still alive.

The same poem contained some very plain speaking on the subject of Greek heroines; if the truth were known, all of them had some unfortunate blemish.[30] More recently Varro had written a piece called Sesculixes—'Ulysses and a half'—which, to judge from its title, treated the hero in an ironical vein. A certain amount of calculated silliness may be discerned in the longest fragment extant, in which Ulysses, speaking of the winds, says 'But if they continue any longer to stir up the sea, I am afraid that when I come back home from Troy no one will recognize me except my dog'.[31]

A favourite form of burlesque was a visit to Hades, based sometimes on the eleventh book of the *Odyssey*, sometimes on other descents such as those of Orpheus and Heracles.[32] The most famous example, of course, is the *Frogs* of Aristophanes, in which

Dionysus sets off to fetch Euripides from the underworld in the hope of reviving tragic drama. But while Horace had certainly read Aristophanes, there were other writers whose purpose was closer to his own. Timon of Phlius, a Sceptic writing in the third century, composed three books of *silloi* or lampoons directed against rival philosophers. 'Book one', says Diogenes Laertius, 'is written in the first person. Books two and three are in dialogue form. Timon represents himself as questioning Xenophanes of Colophon about each philosopher in turn, while Xenophanes answers him.'[33] So here we have an interview like *Sat.* 2. 5; an interview, moreover, which is conducted in the underworld and written in the style of a Homeric parody. With Menippus of Gadara (also writing in the third century) we come a step nearer still, for we know that he wrote a *Nekyia*, which probably included, like Timon's, an attack on contemporary philosophers.[34] Four hundred years later Lucian acknowledged his debt to Menippus by making him one of the chief speakers in his *Dialogues of the Dead*, and by using his name to designate two other works— *Icaromenippus*, in which Menippus flies up to consult Zeus, and *Menippus*, in which he descends to Hades to interview Tiresias.[35] Menippus' interest in supernatural fantasy may be further attested by Varro's περὶ ἐξαγωγῆς. This work, which was one of his *Menippeans*, seems to have described a conversation with certain spirits of the dead on the subject of suicide.[36] Varro, it should be remembered, was still alive when Horace published his second book of *Satires*. These few remarks will indicate how certain features of *Sat.* 2. 5 had already occurred in a wide range of comic and satirical writing—not all of it Cynic. Anyone who wishes to explore this area more fully can start from the references in Lejay's introduction to the poem.

In considering the satire's individuality we shall look first of all at a few fragments of Timon:

ὄγκον ἀναστήσας ὠφρυωμένος ἀφροσιβόμβαξ.[37]

An arrogant blusterer who has reared a great structure of bombast.

That was his verdict on Menedemus. Antisthenes he calls παντοφυῆ φλέδονα[38]—'a prolific babbler'. Of Zeno he writes:

καὶ Φοινίσσαν ἴδον λιχνόγραυν σκιερῷ ἐνὶ τύφῳ
πάντων ἱμείρουσαν· ὁ δ' ἔρρει γυργαθὸς αὐτῆς
σμικρὸς ἐών· νοῦν δ' εἶχεν ἐλάσσονα κινδαψοῖο.[39]

And I saw a Phoenician, a greedy old woman in a dark cloud of
arrogance, yearning for everything. But her little fishing-basket
was gone, and she had no more intelligence than a banjo.

That disposes of the founder of Stoicism. What we have, then, is
personal invective of a simple and rather obvious kind. At times
it must have been quite entertaining, but one suspects that in the
course of a long reading the Homeric parody would begin to
wear thin, and that the writer's energy would not be enough in
itself to sustain interest. The contrast with Horace needs no further
elaboration. Nor is anything to be gained by comparing the
satire with Menippus' *Nekyia*, a work which itself has to be
'reconstructed' from the *Menippus* of Lucian. In attempting to
make this comparison Fiske (p. 401) says '(1) the motive for the
visit to the lower world on the part of Menippus in Lucian, and of
Ulysses in Horace, is to question the seer Tiresias as to the best
means of improving their fortunes. (2) Hence both themes
appear to be sarcastic attacks on the teaching of Chrysippus and
the early Stoa that the sage is a χρηματιστικός [i.e. clever at
making money]...(3) Menippus is directed in Lucian to call
himself either Heracles, Odysseus, or Orpheus.' To take these
points in order: (1) Menippus in Lucian has actually quite a different motive. Bewildered by the contradictions and hypocrisy
of philosophers he comes to ask Tiresias 'What is the best life and
the right choice for a man of prudence?' (7). He eventually learns
that 'the life of the ordinary man is the best' (21). (2) Since
Fiske's first point is mistaken, his second cannot follow from it.
Moreover, in Lucian the greed of philosophers is confined to a
single paragraph of a very long essay; Horace, it is true, makes
Ulysses greedy, but there is no reference (as there is in *Sat.* 1. 3. 124
and *Epist.* 1. 1. 106) to the doctrine that the wise man is rich. Any

Stoic who complained that the satire was directed at his philosophy rather than at a contemporary social evil would only have revealed the distortion of his own critical perspective. (3) Lucian chose Heracles, Odysseus and Orpheus because they had all visited Hades in their lifetime. It is possible that Menippus in his own *Nekyia* had disguised himself as Odysseus, but that would simply provide another point of contrast with Horace. As for the works of Lucilius and Varro, the scanty fragments we possess indicate a treatment so different from Horace's that only the vaguest and most general kind of influence can be assumed.

If no one else had ever written anything quite like *Sat.* 2. 5, neither had Horace himself. And in fact the poem is generally recognized as the sharpest of all the satires. Analysis, however, usually ceases at this point, and one is left wondering what it is that produces such an effect. The subject may be partly responsible. For legacy-hunting, as depicted by Horace, seems to involve elements of almost every vice. On the part of the *captator* it is inspired by envy and avarice, and pursued with deceit; while in the quarry it engenders pride, sloth, gluttony and lust. This dual action suggests a further point, namely that whereas other vices often degrade only one person, *captatio* degrades hunter and hunted alike. Thus in Horace's poem the vain and gullible old man is only one degree less contemptible than Ulysses himself. The root of our distaste, however, is probably the fact that legacy-hunting, like no other vice, takes advantage of our defencelessness against death. We are accustomed, of course, to having our mortality exploited by organized business. Yet it has to be admitted that in the end the insurance man, from whatever motives, is interested in one's life (*vive valeque*), whereas the *captator* is not. Martial as usual has packed it all into a poisonous capsule:

> munera qui tibi dat locupleti, Gaure, senique,
> si sapis et sentis, hoc tibi ait 'morere!'[40]

You are rich and old, Gaurus. If you had any sense you'd realize that whoever gives you presents has a message for you—'Drop dead!'

As a result of the subject's nastiness Horace's attitude is exceptionally simple and direct. This may be seen in his portrayal of character. Unlike, say, Damasippus in 2. 3, who although he is turned into a figure of fun does offer some quite sensible advice, Ulysses is an unscrupulous rascal from start to finish. The same is true of Tiresias.

There are also certain features of style, or rather strategy, which, when taken together, distinguish the poem from Horace's other work. First there is the device whereby a tyro receives instruction from some expert authority. This derives its power from the vast difference in level between the two minds—a difference which ensures that the information given will fall with the maximum impact. At the same time the expertise of one character and the naïve ignorance of the other are exploited for ironic effect. Such a device is not, of course, confined to 2. 5; it is already familiar from other poems in the second book. But here it receives a new cogency from its setting. The setting has also its own special function in that the underworld, like the world of animals, provides a novel standpoint for observing human society—a standpoint shared by writers from the time of the first satiric *nekyia* to the hell scene in *Man and Superman*. Finally, except for 1. 8, where the social criticism is merely incidental, this is the only poem from which Horace has completely withdrawn. He is not even present as a listener. And so 2. 5 represents the culmination of those other pieces in which, after setting the scene, the poet stands back and allows his message to be dramatized rather than stated.

On account of its 'un-Horatian' quality 2. 5 is often regarded as an anticipation of Juvenalian satire. 'If Juvenal recognized any affinity between his own invective and the "*Venusina lucerna*," it must have been with the spirit of this satire, and perhaps the second of Book 1, that he found himself in sympathy.'[41] That is the judgement of W. Y. Sellar, and (except for the reference to 1. 2) Fraenkel (p. 145) pronounces it 'perfectly adequate'. What exactly does it mean? 'Spirit' is not something which exists by itself. It is the product of subject-matter, setting, form, language and other factors. Now the subject of legacy-hunting, perhaps surprisingly, does not bulk large in Juvenal. Apart from brief references, the longest passage devoted to it is 12. 93–130. So this does not bear out Sellar's case, which is that 2. 5 exhibits some feature which is *characteristic* of Juvenal and not of Horace. Nor does Juvenal provide any comparable setting, since he never wrote a *nekyia*. As for the form, Juvenal wrote only one complete satire in dialogue—the ninth, and even there he himself (or, if you like, his *persona*) remains continuously on the stage. At no time does he detach himself from his creation as Horace does in 2. 5. But perhaps Sellar was referring to the poem's irony? Granted, this type of irony is not very common in Horace; I mean the type (in which Swift excelled) where a manner of behaviour which both poet and reader agree to be disreputable is not only spared from explicit censure but actually commended. Now by itself 2. 5 represents rather less than one-twentieth of Horace's *Satires*; but it is fair to add the 95 lines of 2. 4, even though the attitude described is not so much disreputable as absurd. The proportion then rises to about one-tenth. What is the position with Juvenal? The only satire where this technique is applied throughout is the ninth, in which Juvenal commiserates with Naevolus, an unemployed male prostitute. The passage nearest in spirit to Horace 2. 5 begins at v. 125, where Naevolus asks Juvenal's advice:

'Well, what do you advise me to do, now that all my time has been wasted and all my hopes have proved dupes? Like a momentary flower our brief portion of oppressed and sorry life moves swiftly to its close. As we drink our wine, as we call for garlands, perfumes, and girls, old age steals up behind us unnoticed.'

'Courage! So long as these hills stand firm you will never be in need of an effeminate friend. Those who scratch their heads with one finger will come flocking in from all parts of the world in carriages and ships. Greater hopes lie ahead than the ones you have lost. Just crunch up plenty of aphrodisiacs [and the crowd of pansies which is growing all the time][42] will simply love you.'

The ninth, as we have said, is the only satire which employs this type of irony throughout. Elsewhere it is rather rare, the best example being the last fifteen verses of no. 7 which describe the absurd demands made on the average schoolmaster. A passage like 14. 189–224 does not really count, because it is followed by straightforward preaching in which the ironic mask is doffed. But even if such cases were included, the total fraction would still be small—certainly less than one-fifteenth of Juvenal's work. So it seems that Horace 2. 5 is not Juvenalian in its irony either. Last of all, it is certainly not Juvenalian in language, for the strategy which Horace adopts, with its matter-of-fact acceptance of wickedness, does not permit any violent denunciation.

In the end Sellar's dictum boils down to something like this: 'Sat. 2. 5 has a nasty subject; nasty subjects (though not this one) are commoner in Juvenal than in Horace. Sat. 2. 5 is unusually sarcastic in tone; sarcasm (though not this kind of sarcasm) is common in Juvenal. Hence 2. 5 is Juvenalian in spirit.' So there is perhaps some residue of significance, but not very much.

CHAPTER IX

POET AND PATRON (2)

2. 6

Hoc erat in votis. This is a poem about wishes. It begins with a day-dream—a piece of land, a vegetable garden, a spring, and a few trees. Such a dream, based, perhaps, on childhood memories, must have haunted the poet during those terrible days in 42 B.C. which he mentions with such reserve:

> dura sed emovere loco me tempora grato
> civilisque rudem belli tulit aestus in arma.

> But cruel times took me away from that happy place,[1] and the tide of civil war carried me, raw recruit as I was, into arms.

The storm passed and Horace returned to Italy, but in the meantime his father's estate had been confiscated, and so for nearly eight years he had no property in the country. Now at last his dream has come true, and the poet is full of delight and gratitude —though still a little incredulous. As he addresses Mercury the god of luck he says 'I ask no more, O son of Maia, except that thou shouldst make these gifts mine for ever'.[2] One is reminded of the old Irish belief that if you catch a leprechaun he will offer you gold, or a field full of cattle, in return for his freedom. But you must be careful to stipulate that the gift remain with you; otherwise it will disappear as soon as the little man is released.

As usual with Horace, happiness is related to limit. In itself a reverie often gives harmless pleasure, and if it is not fulfilled, well, that is no great loss. If it is, then we should rest content. To be continually pining for what is not ('if only I had that extra bit of ground'), to become obsessed with the vision of some unlikely stroke of luck ('if only I could find a pot of gold')—such yearnings are merely foolish, and unless they are kept in perspective they can poison a man's happiness.

The poet, then, is content. His one prayer is that what he has may thrive:

si quod adest gratum iuvat, hac prece te oro:
pingue pecus domino facias et cetera praeter
ingenium, utque soles, custos mihi maximus adsis.   (13-15)

If what I have satisfies and delights me, this is the blessing I ask of thee:
Make fat the flocks I own and all else, except my head; and as ever
be my chief protector.

The slight inconsistency in the prayer for wealth is muffled by the introductory *si quod adest gratum iuvat*, and is then blown away completely in the joke which follows.[3]

By returning to Horace's wishes these lines round off the opening section, but, as usual, the transition to what follows is contrived with the utmost art:

ergo ubi me in montis et in arcem ex urbe removi,
quid prius illustrem saturis Musaque pedestri?

Well, now that I have retreated from the city to my mountain citadel,
what should I rather celebrate in the satires of my pedestrian Muse?

The *montis* looks back to the rural happiness of vv. 1-15, while the *urbe* looks forward to the next passage, which begins at v. 20. Moreover, although we were not aware of it, the pun in vv.14-15 prepared us for the *saturis* of v. 17. Horace's *Satires* are a product of his *ingenium tenue*; that is why his wit must be kept slim. Finally there is the link between *custos* and *arcem*. Mercury's protection follows the poet imperceptibly into his mountain retreat, a lofty spot where we are surprised to encounter the *Musa pedestris*. And yet why not? The satiric Muse is concerned with the tedium of the megalopolis. What more natural than that on reaching his farm Horace should draw a deep breath and say 'My God, it's good to be out of Rome!'?

This thought is developed in two sections. The first (20-39) presents scenes from a morning in Rome, showing how social life conflicts at every point with the poet's private wishes. As he

fights his way through the crowds, a voice cries 'What do you
want?' This is followed by curses (*preces*) and sneers. On reaching
the Esquiline, where Maecenas lived, Horace is plagued by other
people's concerns, which take the form of unwelcome requests:
Roscius orabat...scribae orabant...cura. 'All right,' he says desperately, 'I'll try.' 'You can if you *want* to', comes the reply.
As this section develops, the strain of living in Rome becomes
more and more closely associated with the disadvantages of knowing Maecenas. In v. 40 this theme takes over, and the second of
the two Roman sections (40–59) has begun. 'Ever since Maecenas
befriended me, even though at first he was only prepared (*vellet*)
to exchange small talk in his carriage, I have been the object of
malicious gibes.' The malice is revealed in requests, this time for
information. 'What's happening about Dacia?' 'Whose land is to
be given to the ex-servicemen?' While the poet is being bombarded with questions his mind steals away to his farm in the hills,
non sine votis.

This echo of the opening words introduces the second half of
the poem, which consists of a rustic idyll (60–79) corresponding
to the initial prayer of thanks, and a double section on country
and city life (79–100, 100–17) which balances the double section
on Rome. The expression *non sine votis* also introduces a further
complication in the poet's reverie; for it means that Horace, who
is writing in the country, is thinking of himself in Rome thinking
of the country. Moreover, whereas the original dream showed
only the appearance of the farm, vv. 60–79 reveal the kind of life
it stands for—reading and dozing in the afternoon, dining, and
then talking into the night. The conversation does not turn on
properties and incomes or on the trivia of the entertainment
world, but rather on general ethical questions. 'Is it money or
goodness that makes men happy?' 'What is the purpose of friendship—self-interest or the good life?' 'What is the nature of goodness and what is its highest form?' Then, for a little frivolous
relaxation, Horace mentions the old wives' tales of Cervius
(*garrit* and *anilis* both convey gentle ridicule). Yet the tale we are

given is so serious that it sums up a great deal of the satire's message, and though told by a country neighbour it shows the poet at his most urbane.

The subject, again, is wishes. A country mouse is eager to please his city guest (*cupiens*, 86). He fails, and the other says ' Why do you want to live in the backwoods? (*iuvat*, 90). Would you not like to move into town? (*vis*, 92).' The country mouse agrees, and they make eagerly for the city (*aventes*, 99). For a short while, as they sit nibbling at the remains of a banquet, it looks as if luxury and peace of mind are after all compatible (*gaudet*... *laetum*, 110–11). But this illusion is suddenly destroyed by banging doors and barking dogs. After narrowly escaping with his life the rustic sets off home, a sadder and wiser mouse.

In form the fable is a *cena*, or rather two *cenae*, within a *cena*. Like Horace with his farm and his bit of woodland (*rus*, 60 and *silvae*, 3), the country mouse entertains in rough and ready surroundings (*silva cavusque*, 116 and *praerupti nemoris*, 91). The town mouse, however, lives in a mansion with a dining room of scarlet and ivory (102–3). The country mouse's simple dinner of peas, oats, bacon, and raisins is not unlike that of Horace, who has beans, green vegetables, and bacon. The town mouse, on the other hand, offers many courses, and provides a much more fashionable type of service (107–8). He even tastes each morsel beforehand to make sure it is acceptable.[4] Unfortunately for him Horatian satire is a genre in which no *repas gastronomique* is ever properly finished. The catastrophe, which is splendidly described, provides an ending even better than that of I. 2 (because it is part of a specific tale) and far superior to the anticlimax which concludes the *cena* of Nasidienus.

The foregoing is a mere sketch-map of the poem. If we wish to indicate a few contours we must start on high ground, for the opening lines, like certain arias of Mozart, radiate a benign tranquillity which can only be called religious, though it is wholly of this world. The point can be illustrated by a comparison with Swift's imitation:

I've often wished that I had clear
For life, six hundred pounds a year,
A handsome house to lodge a friend,
A river at my garden's end;
A terrace walk, and half a rood
Of land, set out to plant a wood.

This is neat and agreeable enough, but the short iambic lines with their rhyming couplets and rows of monosyllables cannot match the power of Horace's hexameters, and the note of joyful thanksgiving has been lost.

A strict agnostic is always slightly embarrassed by good fortune. He knows it is more than he deserves, but he doesn't quite know whom to thank. This is a dilemma which never troubled Horace. True, his sophistication had taken him beyond conventional piety; nor could he ever commit himself to the Stoic view of providence. Nevertheless, the agnostic position as we understand it today, with its scientific rigour and its imaginative poverty, would not have satisfied him either. He felt that in the gift of the Sabine farm certain human factors could be discerned which were neither mechanical nor fortuitous. Among these would be the sacrifices made by his father, Virgil's kindly assistance, and the generosity of Maecenas. Another such factor would be the conscious discipline which contributed to his own achievement as a poet. Therefore, in so far as the gift was explainable it was explainable in spiritual terms. Yet it was clear that a full explanation would be utterly beyond the compass of the human mind. The causes of his good fortune ramified into infinity. And the most important of them—namely his own poetic talent—was itself a perpetual mystery. The Greek imagination, however, had provided a vocabulary for dealing with these superhuman phenomena which so deeply affected the private life, and Horace had no hesitation in using it. He would express his feelings by offering thanks to Mercury. And, after all, what option did he have? Even Lucretius, that ardent foe of traditional belief, could not dispense with *alma Venus*.

This religious mood, for all its light-heartedness, is quite un-characteristic of the *Satires*, and so, while the poem as a whole recalls I. 6, the opening lines direct us forward to the *Odes*, where we find Mercury, along with Faunus, the Muses, Apollo, and other divine company, once again associated with Horace's deepest feelings on earthly happiness.

In v. 6 the satirist makes his first appearance, and the level begins to drop, but not so steeply as one might expect. For the series of 'if' clauses, which recalls I. 6. 65 ff., is a form of self-justification. And although the subject is criminal folly the verses remind us by their incantatory sound that they are still part of a prayer:

> si ne*que maiorem* feci ratio*ne mala rem,*
> nec sum facturus vitio culpa*ve minorem...*

> If I have not increased my wealth by dishonest means, and do not intend to decrease it by wickedness or bad behaviour...

Then, still within the prayer, we have a parody of another kind of petition: *o si angulus ille...o si urnam argenti.* Such is the prayer of the fool who is never satisfied. As for the play on *pingue* (14), it conveys that informal intimacy which in a Christian context the northern Protestant finds hard to understand but which the Catholic often shares with a friendly saint.

The ceremonious note is resumed in the soliloquy which follows, for *quid prius illustrem* is a formula associated with stately lyric,[5] but the effect is promptly diminished by *saturis Musaque pedestri.* So too the invocation of Janus has a distinguished Greek ancestry.[6] One notes the alternative forms of address:

> Matutine pater, seu 'Iane' libentius audis

> O Father of the morn, or Janus if thou dost prefer that name

and the appeal to the god to form the prelude of the song—*tu carminis esto / principium*; but respect is rudely dispelled by what Janus actually does—he pulls Horace out of bed and sends him off to pay his calls. The relentless demands of social duty overrule the elements:

248

sive Aquilo radit terras seu bruma nivalem
interiore diem gyro trahit, ire necesse est.   (25–6)

Whether the north wind is sweeping the earth, or winter draws the
snowy day into a smaller circle, go I must.

It is not the first time that Horace has used the phraseology of
epic as a counterpoint to his own rueful groans.

After all this impressive poetry we now descend to the language
of the streets. What follows is a brilliant performance, revealing
a technique which might well be envied by the radio journalist
with his tape-recorder and scissors. For the scraps of talk not only
indicate what the poet is subjected to, they also provide an audi-
tory cartoon of the speaker. Thus we have the surly resentment of
'What do you want, you idiot, and what do you think you're
doing?' Then comes the deferential functionary: 'Roscius would
like you to be with him at the Wall tomorrow before eight a.m.'
Another, working on the maxim *gaudent praenomine molles
auriculae*,[7] says 'Oh Quintus, the Secretaries would like you to be
sure to come back today. An important piece of civil service
business has just cropped up.' He is followed by a man who has
made his reputation by refusing to take 'no' for an answer: 'Get
Maecenas' signature on these papers.' 'I'll try', says Horace. 'Oh,
you can if you want to', he replies, and continues to badger him.
After this we hear a snatch of conversation from Maecenas'
carriage, recollected from the early days of the friendship. 'What
time do you make it?' 'Is the Thracian Chick a match for the
Arab?'[8] 'These mornings are quite nippy; you've got to be careful.' Then we are back in the streets again: 'Excuse me Sir, but
you must know (for you are so close to the all-powerful)—you
haven't by any chance heard some news about the Dacians?'
These, and the lines which follow, show that inquisitive impertinence was no less annoying then than it is today, though in
Horace's time it had not become a profession.

The second half of the poem opens with a passage of intense
longing: *o rus, quando ego te aspiciam? quandoque licebit. . .o quando?*

POET AND PATRON (2)

When, when, when? The love of his country estate, which is also reflected in the intimacy of *ego/te*, has been amply explained by the description of life in Rome, and that, in its turn, illuminates the prayer of thanksgiving with which the satire began. Writing about this passage Brower has justly remarked that 'no commentary or translation can quite catch the attitude of laughing reverence for the country, for sweet idleness, good food, good friends, and "heavenly philosophy"'.[9] But if we wish to say anything at all it is perhaps best to concentrate on the 'heavenly philosophy'. The topics discussed at Horace's table are the perennial problems of ancient ethics as propounded by Socrates, Aristotle and the Stoics;[10] and in this philosophical milieu even the beans are Pythagoreans. Nevertheless, the predominant spirit is undoubtedly that of Epicurus:

> ducere sollicitae iucunda oblivia vitae.
> To drink sweet forgetfulness of life's troubles.

This mild, lotus-eating existence has been made possible for Horace, periodically at least, by the gift of the Sabine farm. Its desirability is confirmed by the fable of the two mice, with its warning against troublesome wealth (*sollicitas opes*). In this fable it is well to remember that the town mouse is not a true Epicurean, though he may well typify some who used the name. His seductive speech concludes with the words:

> dum licet, in rebus iucundis vive beatus;
> vive memor, quam sis aevi brevis.
> Live while you may in the enjoyment of pleasant things; live in constant awareness of how short a time you have.

These exhortations proceed from that melancholy hedonism which occurs in Greek literature of all periods from Mimnermus on, and which represents, in fact, one of mankind's perennial moods. It is the mood of one who is conscious of the spectre moving up behind him and is determined to regale himself before he is beckoned away from the feast. A similar spirit is found, of course, in some of Horace's most famous odes, usually with qualifications which are too often ignored.[11] But that does not make it Epicurean; and indeed to keep the prospect of death before you and to counter it by an urgent sensuality was a practice wholly contrary to the master's teaching.

The country mouse is much closer to Epicurus' ideal. True, he is not an intellectual; neither is Ofellus (2. 2), whom he resembles in several ways. But he lives a wholesome, untroubled life, and enjoys the occasional celebration which Epicurus sanctioned.[12] It is easy to imagine him taking part in the festivities of Lucretius' peasants,[13] and we are told that when a guest arrived he would 'unfasten his tightly-buttoned spirit'. (One notes the collocation *artum/solveret*, an image perhaps unconsciously suggested by *attentus quaesitis*.) The mouse is well content with this 'hard primitivism'[14] until, in a moment of weakness, he is tempted away by the blandishments of the *bon vivant*. The palatial house which they enter has amenities which recall those mentioned by Lucretius (4. 1131–2):

> eximia veste et victu convivia, ludi,
> pocula crebra, unguenta, coronae, serta parantur.

> With splendid coverings and dishes banquets are served; games are provided along with constantly replenished cups, perfumes, wreaths and garlands.

But unlike Lucretius' lover, the country mouse does not learn of their futility through a nagging remorse. His enlightenment comes in a sudden moment of terror, described by Horace with graphic, Disney-like effects. Doors crash open, the house reverberates with deep barking, and the revellers are sent scuttling from their couches half dead with fright. That is enough for the mouse. After a brief and nervous farewell he hurries back to the safety of the woods, where he hopes to regain his peace of mind.

This brings us back to Horace, whose rural retreat is also *tutus ab insidiis*. How closely does the fable apply to what he has been saying? For three-quarters of the poem Horace has been contrasting the anxiety and physical strain of city life with the peaceful leisure of the country. Then, by passing from *sollicitae vitae* (62) to *divitiis* (74) and from there to the *sollicitas opes* of Arellius (79), he imperceptibly alters the contrast to one between luxury and austerity. Now although his life on the farm has been presented as simple, there has been no indication that his city life is luxurious; so it looks as if this new contrast has been introduced for the sake of the fable. Moreover, as the fable develops, it becomes clear that two other terms, leisure and exertion, have been switched. For the city mouse can hardly be said to wear himself out, and his friend in the country certainly does not pass his time 'in sleep and idle hours'. It might therefore be argued that this tale of mice and men is less firmly integrated into the structure of the poem than is sometimes assumed. Yet in the end the fable does endorse Horace's original point, for it shows that peace of mind (even when accompanied by hard work and austerity) is not to be exchanged for anxiety (even in the midst of leisure and luxury).

The picture of Horace's carefree life and simple diet recalls the earlier description in 1. 6. There are even some verbal links like *solabitur* (2. 6. 117) and *consolor* (1. 6. 130), *removi* (2. 6. 16) and *remotos* (1. 6. 19). But whereas in 1. 6 the sense of being apart is purely spiritual—for Horace had then no place in the country—in 2. 6 it is geographical too. The central idea in these two satires reappears in the story of Volteius Mena in *Epist.* 1. 7. Volteius, who made a modest living as an auctioneer's crier, was tempted into becoming a landowner by Philippus, a busy lawyer who envied him his contentment. In spite of much hard work Volteius' animals died and his crops failed. Finally he threw the whole venture up in disgust, returned to Rome, and urged Philippus to restore him to his former way of life. Here it is farming which involves the busy pursuit of profits; the city stands for modest contentment. Within the context of the epistle this constitutes a reversal of terms, for Horace is writing from the country to Maecenas, who has, it seems, been pressing him to return and take up his duties as a client. It is clear, then, that in these αἶνοι Horace allows himself considerable freedom in points of detail. The constant factor is the quest for tranquillity.

The other bond connecting these three poems is the relationship of poet to patron. Now the way Maecenas is treated in 2. 6 is, to say the least, somewhat ambiguous. Horace lets it appear, over a space of thirty lines, that from his point of view the friendship has some very tiresome drawbacks. The complaints, it is true, are presented in a tone of ironic suffering reminiscent of the Journey to Brundisium and the Encounter with the Pest. Nevertheless, if vv. 29–39, which describe the morning scene on the Esquiline, had survived by themselves, or if we had only the harassing questions reported in vv. 51–6, we might well think them ungracious—in spite of the brief admission in v. 32 (*hoc iuvat et melli est*). But of course they have not survived by themselves, and they are transformed by what comes before and after. For the strain of city life is far outweighed by the joy derived from the farm. As Maecenas heard that magnificent opening, in which a human name would have been quite out of place, and as his mind dwelt on the rustic idyll which has a corresponding position in the second half, he must have felt a glow of friendly satisfaction. And knowing Horace as he did, he probably realized that in the years ahead town and country life would each add zest to the other.

As a final comment on the spirit of the satire, and as an example of the profound influence which Horace exerted on the eighteenth century, I should like to recall Dr Johnson's famous letter to Lord Chesterfield, dated 7 February 1755, at the centre of which we find these words: 'Seven years, my Lord, have now passed, since I waited in your outward room, or was repulsed from your door; during which time I have been pushing on my work through difficulties, of which it is useless to complain, and have brought it at last to the verge of publication without one act of assistance, one word of encouragement, or one smile of favour. Such treatment I did not expect, for I never had a patron before.'

By itself that has weight enough, but when one hears underneath it (as the recipient surely would) the rhythms of:

> septimus octavo propior iam fugerit annus
> ex quo Maecenas me coepit habere suorum
> in numero...
> per totum hoc tempus...

> Seven years have now passed—indeed almost eight—since Maecenas began to count me as a friend...during all this time...

the effect is overwhelming.

The latest satires of Book 2 contain a few passages which signify the end of Horace's first poetic phase and point forward to his later achievement as a writer of national lyrics. As we saw, Horace's first engagement with politics ended at Philippi. For the next ten years he avoided any declaration of allegiance, and his only comments on national affairs were two impassioned protests of a purely general kind against the madness of civil war.[15] The first step towards recommitment came with his admission to Maecenas' circle, but that was an implication which Horace failed or refused to notice at the time. In fact the poem which records his gratitude most warmly—i.e. 1. 6—also contains his most emphatic rejection of public life. This somewhat anomalous position is reflected in 1. 5, which shows Horace travelling in Maecenas' entourage, but studiously avoids political comment and (except for the oblique *amicos* in v. 29) never mentions Octavian.

During the next six years Horace came to believe for one reason or another that the future welfare of Rome lay with Octavian rather than Antony. Yet in the first epode, written on the eve of the fleet's departure for Actium, Maecenas is still the dominant figure. In *Epod.* 9 Octavian is assuming a more important position, but he does not appear without Maecenas until *Carm.* 1. 37, and there he has to share the limelight with Cleopatra. In the *Satires*, a genre unsuited to encomia, politics are virtually ignored until after Actium, though the reference to Agrippa in 2. 3. 185 (dated 33 B.C.) may be seen as a straw in the wind. Following

Antony's defeat, when Octavian was still out of the country and
Maecenas was in charge at Rome (2. 6. 38), Horace speaks of the
anxiety which people felt about the emperor's plans for settling
ex-servicemen (2. 6. 55–6). But (leaving aside the question
whether this poem preceded 2. 5) the first *compliment* to Octavian
comes at 2. 5. 62–4:

> tempore quo iuvenis Parthis horrendus, ab alto
> demissum genus Aenea, tellure marique
> magnus erit. . .

In the day when a young hero, the scourge of the Parthians, born
of Aeneas' noble line, shall rule over land and sea. . .

Many Romans expected that after settling affairs in Egypt
Octavian would march against Parthia to avenge the defeats of
Crassus and Antony and to fulfil the plans of Julius Caesar—hence
Parthis horrendus. In fact he returned home, and the standards
taken from Crassus remained in Parthian hands until 20 B.C.,
when they were recovered by a diplomatic manœuvre. Yet in
Horace's national odes the Parthians figure more prominently
than any other people, perhaps because, apart from any threat
which they may have presented to Rome's frontiers, they stood
for a way of life which the poet found at once fascinating and
repellent.

The other phrase in our quotation (*ab alto / demissum genus
Aenea*) also has a patriotic ring. The connexion of Aeneas with
Latium can be traced back as far as Hellanicus, a Greek historian of
the fifth century B.C. The tradition was developed by other writers,
including the Sicilians Timaeus and Callias, before being adopted
in Rome by Naevius and Fabius Pictor. From them it passed to
Ennius, Cato, Varro, and eventually Virgil.[16] The story had a
special significance for the Julian *gens*, since they claimed descent
from Venus through Iulus the son of Aeneas. Whether or not
Perret is right in dating the origin of this claim to the period between 115 and 95 B.C., it is certain that Julius Caesar was appealing
to a well-established tradition when he asserted at his aunt Julia's

funeral that she was a descendant of Venus.[17] How this genealogy was then used as an instrument of political power and eventually became part of the imperial mystique makes a fascinating story, of which the best account in English is still Miss L. R. Taylor's *The Divinity of the Roman Emperor*.[18]

By referring to the military and religious prestige of the emperor these lines adumbrate some of Horace's greatest odes; yet in their context they are the prelude to a squalid anecdote; they parody the portentous style of an oracle and are uttered by a character who is morally discredited. In other words, they are part of a satire.

The same situation recurs in 2. 1, which contains the latest references to Octavian. In chapter IV we noticed the poem's light-hearted mood. Here we are concerned with its patriotic implications and with the new relationship which it indicates between Horace and the emperor.

> aude
> Caesaris invicti res dicere, multa laborum
> praemia laturus. (10-12)

> Have the courage to tell of invincible Caesar's exploits. You will be rewarded handsomely for your pains.

The suggestion is declined, for not everyone can portray the rout of Gauls and Parthians. 'But', persists Trebatius, 'if you will not sing of his achievements, you could at least describe his personal qualities—his justice and his valour—as Lucilius did with Scipio.' 'All in good time', says Horace. 'Not until the right moment will the words of Floppy penetrate the pricked-up ear of Caesar. Rub him the wrong way and he will lash out with his hooves, defending himself on all sides.' Later in the poem Trebatius warns Horace that foul verses may lead to a libel action. 'No doubt', he answers. 'But what if they are fine verses and win the praise of Caesar?'

Here, then, we have all the materials for a panegyric. Caesar is just and brave; his enemies have no chance against him. Such tribute goes beyond anything we have encountered in the *Satires*, and it foreshadows Horace's new concern for the fortunes of Rome and her leader. The ship of state which was once a *sollicitum taedium* is now becoming a *desiderium* and a *cura non levis*. Yet the tone is one of jocular banter, and the compliment comes not from Horace but from the slightly comic figure of Trebatius who is the formal counterpart of Tiresias.

As well as hinting at a new political loyalty the poem also points to a direct acquaintance between Horace and Octavian. The *praemia* of v. 12 may not mean much, but Horace would hardly have mentioned them had they been out of the question. So too the possibility of some kind of official encomium is here broached for the first time. As the patriotism is conveyed in an ironic *recusatio*, so the connexion between poet and emperor, which gave a splendid opportunity for snobbery and conceit, is treated with a perky independence almost amounting to cheek.

Nevertheless, the amusing style of the *sermo* cannot conceal the way things are moving. A hundred years of turmoil had come to an end, and in spite of terrible sufferings the fabric of the state had somehow survived. Hope and excitement were beginning to stir; and whether men thought of what was happening as revival or progress they were conscious of taking part in a great historic transition. This feeling had a profound effect on Horace's mind. We can, if we like, say that he was running short of satiric themes and settings, and point to the fact that Book 2 has only eight pieces instead of the usual ten.[19] But this was not a sign of exhaustion. On the contrary, Horace responded to new conditions by contriving new poetic forms. His resources extended beyond the ridicule of vice and folly, and as the Augustan régime took root he began a fresh phase of activity in a field which no Roman had ever entered.

DRYDEN ON HORACE
AND JUVENAL

A full discussion cannot be attempted here, but it does seem desirable by way of an epilogue to make a few general points about Horace's relation to his great successor. As a framework for our discussion we will use the observations made by Dryden in his *Discourse Concerning The Original And Progress Of Satire*[1]—an essay which has had an immense influence in the past and may still provide many students of English with their only information about the two major satirists of antiquity.

At the outset (p. 79) Dryden concedes that Horace was 'the better poet', but he bases this superiority on the *Epodes* and *Odes*, which he then excludes from his discussion of satire. He is of course right to exclude them, but his reasons for doing so are not satisfactory. 'Horace', he says, 'has written many of them satirically, against his private enemies... but (he) had purged himself of this choler before he entered on those discourses which are more properly called the Roman Satire. He has not now to do with a Lyce, a Canidia, a Cassius Severus, or a Menas; but is to correct the vices and the follies of his time.' First of all it is incorrect to suggest that the *Epodes* and *Odes* precede the *Satires*. The first book of satires was published about 35 B.C. and the second about 30. As for the *Odes*, the first collection, comprising Books 1–3, did not appear until 24 or 23 B.C., and there is no proof that any of these poems were written before 30.[2] So we cannot speak of Horace purging himself of his choler before undertaking the *Satires*.

Then there is the question of names. Cassius Severus, in spite of Dryden's statement (p. 90), is not mentioned in the *Epodes*, nor indeed anywhere else in Horace. His presence in the tradition is due to the imagination of some ancient scribe who prefixed his name to the anonymous sixth epode, forgetting that the poem did not suit his character and was in all probability written before he was born.[3] The same kind of speculation made Sextus Pompeius Menas the object of *Epode* 4. These are both historical persons, but the same cannot be said of Canidia, who is probably a composite character, based on someone known to Horace but heavily overlaid with fiction. Even if she is counted as a private enemy this will not help Dryden's case, for she also appears in three of the satires. And she is not without company. If Dryden had re-read the fourth and tenth satires of Book 1 he would have found that Pantilius, Demetrius, Fannius and Hermogenes all suffer for their criticisms of Horace and his poetry. The distinction which Dryden had in mind would therefore be more clearly stated by saying that whereas the *Epodes* contain five lampoons, the *Satires* have none. By 'lampoon' I here mean a poem addressed to a person named or unnamed with the sole object of abusing him. Thus Horace's meeting with the pest (*Sat.* 1. 9) and his account of Nasidienus' dinner-party (*Sat.* 2. 8) would not rank as lampoons. Nor would the fourth and tenth satires of Book 1, for there Horace is not really concerned to abuse his critics but rather to defend his work against the charges of malice and incompetence, and in doing so to present his conception of the genre.

Lampoons, says Dryden, may occasionally be justified as revenge 'when we have been affronted in the same nature, or have been any ways notoriously abused, and can make ourselves no other reparation' (p. 79). Personal attacks of a more general kind are defensible when the person is a public nuisance. 'All those, whom Horace in his Satires, and Persius and Juvenal have mentioned in theirs, with a brand of infamy, are wholly such. 'Tis an action of virtue to make examples of vicious men' (p. 80). By 'brand of infamy' Dryden means, I take it, charges of a serious nature. If, then, his point is that the Roman satirists only made serious charges against people who were a public nuisance, that may indeed be true; but it is not a great compliment to say so, for all it means is that the poets were not guilty of libellous invective. But Dryden has, I suspect, quite a different idea in mind, namely that the vicious characters attacked by the satirists were all living contemporaries. We have already seen how limited an application this has to Horatian satire; it does not apply to Persius at all. As for Juvenal, he himself says that his victims will be 'those whose ashes lie under the Flaminian and the Latin Road'. The vices he castigates are for the most part contemporary, but the names are usually the names of the dead. Using the dead as *exempla* is a very different thing from making examples of the living.[4]

From the victims of satire Dryden now turns to its general subjects, developing the view that 'folly was the proper quarry of Horace, and not vice' (p. 83). Folly, he says, was a more difficult target, for 'as there are but few notoriously wicked men, in comparison with a shoal of fools and fops, so 'tis a harder thing to make a man wise than to make him honest; for the will is only to be reclaimed in the one, but the understanding is to be informed in the other'. Instead of examining this rather questionable reasoning we shall concentrate on the proposition that Horace's chief concern was not vice but folly. It sounds attractive, offering as it does a neat contrast between the aims of the two satirists; for this reason, it has been accepted by generations of readers and is sometimes found in handbooks today.[5] Unfortunately it does not happen to be true. Let us glance quickly at the subjects of the relevant Horatian satires. First book: (1) greed and envy, (2) adultery, (3) cruelty and intolerance, (4) backbiting and malice, (6) snobbery and ambition, (8) witchcraft and superstition, (9) ill-mannered place-seeking. Second book: (2) gluttony and meanness, (3) avarice, meanness, murder, prodigality, megalomania, erotic obsession, superstition, (4) gluttony, (5) legacy-hunting, (7) the tyranny of lust and gluttony. One shudders to contemplate the moral system of a man to whom these are but 'follies'.

One of the factors behind this error may be that passage of Persius which we discussed above:[6]

secuit Lucilius urbem,
te Lupe, te Muci, et genuinum fregit in illis.
omne vafer vitium ridenti Flaccus amico
tangit et admissus circum praecordia ludit,
callidus excusso populum suspendere naso.

Dryden (p. 83) prints the third and fourth lines only, and then proceeds as follows: 'This was the commendation which Persius
gave [Horace]: where, by *vitium*, he means those little vices which
we call follies, and defects of human understanding, or, at most,
the peccadillos of life, rather than the tragical vices, to which men
are hurried by their unruly passions and exorbitant desires.' This,
as we have already argued, is a misreading of the lines, for
Horace practically never teases his friends about their foibles.

The main reason for this misconception, however, is undoubtedly the attitude and tone of the two satirists. Horace's
basic objection to greed, lust, ambition, and so on, is that they
make the man himself unhappy and bring consequences which
may ruin his life. To the Christian, who is aware that other people
also suffer from the man's vice, and who bears in mind the offence
against God and his commandments, this outlook is bound to
appear superficial. It is easy to feel that a writer who appeals to
our self-interest in this way can hardly be taken seriously as a
moralist. Moreover, since Horace's tone is one of sensible ridicule
('Don't be such a fool, man! Can't you see that you're making
yourself miserable?'), the Christian reader tends to forget that
most of the faults attacked by Horace really are vices. Take,
for example, these lines from the first satire (70–9):

You scrape your money-bags together from every side and fall asleep on top of
them with your mouth still gaping open. You have to keep them inviolate like
sacred objects and only enjoy them as you would a painted tablet. Don't you
know what money is for? What use it offers? You can buy bread, vegetables,
and half a litre of wine, and other things too which human nature cannot conveniently do without. Or perhaps you *enjoy* lying awake half dead with fright,
spending your days and nights in terror of wicked burglars or fires or slaves who
might clean you out and then disappear? I should always hope to be very
badly off in goods of that sort!

Here the miser is undoubtedly vicious by Roman and Christian standards alike, but Horace has presented him as a ludicrous, slightly pathetic, fool.

It should not be inferred from this that Horace's subjects were really the same as Juvenal's. There are a few very notable differences. First, in every period of his work Juvenal is concerned not only with folly and vice, but with crime. He constantly inveighs against forgery, robbery, perjury, adultery, fraud, murder and treason. In Horace such material is less prominent. Secondly, we do not find any Horatian satire devoted to such themes as homosexuality, male prostitution, or cannibalism. Horace drew his subjects from within the domain of nature, whereas Juvenal often used the perverted and the monstrous in his representations of vice. Finally, while Horace's conception of *nugae*, or trifles, can be inferred from pieces like the seventh and eighth satires of Book 1, the only trifle in Juvenal is an account of how a giant turbot was received at the court of Domitian. There is certainly humour here, but it is humour of a grim kind, and an atmosphere of dread hangs over the scene. Juvenal's own comment is this:

atque utinam his potius nugis tota illa dedisset
tempora saevitiae, claras quibus abstulit urbi
illustresque animas impune et vindice nullo. (4. 150–2)

Yes, and what a blessing it would have been if frivolities of this kind had filled all those cruel years in which he robbed the city of its noblest and most distinguished souls, with none to punish or avenge.

Nevertheless, in a number of cases the poets' subjects are broadly similar, and here it is the contrast in treatment which proves instructive. We have already seen the gulf which separates Nasidienus (Horace 2. 8) from Virro (Juvenal 5). Even *Sat.* 11, which is sometimes called the most Horatian of Juvenal's satires, contains several details which distinguish it from the sermon of Ofellus—a poem with which it has something in common. Thus Juvenal spends a dozen lines telling how a gluttonous wastrel can end up eating gladiators' hash (20), whereas Horace presents a similar situation in a short comic phrase—the poor fellow will long for death in vain because 'he won't have a penny for a rope'. In vv. 56–76 Juvenal describes the simple menu which he has planned for his guest, Persicus, and compares it with the diet of the men of old. But watch how he continues: I will not invite the sort of people who will sneer at my modest circumstances; the meat will not be carved by a graduate of Trypherus' school for chefs; there will be no pretty waiters; and you needn't expect to see a performance by Spanish belly-dancers. That is not Horace's voice. Concluding his invitation, Juvenal urges Persicus to forget his business troubles and to enjoy a day's holiday (183–5). Horace could easily have written that, but he would never have gone on to say: 'Don't let your wife cause you secret anger because she goes out at dawn and comes home at night with her fine-spun clothes damp and suspiciously creased, her hair rumpled, and her face and ears burning.'

Other poems offer similar contrasts. In 2. 6 Horace tells how glad he is to get out of Rome, because he enjoys a rest from the noisy merry-go-round of social life. Juvenal's Umbricius is leaving for ever (*Sat.* 3), because the old virtues have disappeared and Rome has passed into the hands of charlatans, pimps, and gangsters. In Juvenal's eyes an adulterous *matrona* typifies the avarice, dishonesty, and utter rottenness of Roman womanhood (*Sat.* 6); she is a monster, a creature of abhorrence. To Horace (1. 2) she is simply a hazard which can easily be avoided with a little common sense. In 1. 6 Horace delivers a sermon on ambition and in doing so gives a memorable account of his upbringing and his present way of life. In Juvenal (*Sat.* 8) the informal personal note is missing, and instead the theme of ambition develops into a long tirade against the aristocracy, who in the recent past have sunk so low as to make a spectacle of themselves in public.

The difference in treatment implies a different attitude on the part of the satirist. Like the Epicureans (and all sensible men) Horace recognized various degrees of folly. Stealing a cabbage is not the same as robbing a temple. Each case must be judged on its merits. Juvenal's attitude, however, is more like that of the doctrinaire Stoic who regards all sins as equally culpable. The suggestion of philosophical rigour is perhaps misleading, but it is true that in the main Juvenal does not invite us to make distinctions. In the third satire, as Umbricius leaves Rome for good he says 'Let those fellows stay behind who can turn black into white, who don't mind accepting contracts for temples, rivers or harbours, for cleaning drains or carrying corpses to the pyre' (30–2). Here our indignation at fraud and perjury spills over into the following lines, so that the men who make their living from those essential services appear not merely unattractive but actually criminal. Later in the same satire (58–112) we are asked to believe that the clothes, the complaisance, and the lechery of the immigrant Greek are all equally repulsive. Again, in his most elaborate poem—the invective against Roman women—we find the following sequence (6. 379 ff.): If your wife is musical she will plan adultery with professional singers; but let her be musical (with all it entails) rather than a chatterbox in male company; no less insufferable is the woman who gives her plebeian neighbour a brutal beating; worse still is the bluestocking who holds the floor on literature, history, and philosophy, and corrects her husband's grammar. In synopsis this sounds merely funny, but it must be emphasized that in the full version of the passage, which runs for nearly eighty lines, there is no suggestion of anticlimax.

In 8. 211 ff. Juvenal contrasts Nero with Orestes: both killed their mothers, but Orestes was avenging his father's death, and Orestes never murdered his sister or wife, never sang on the stage, never composed an epic on Troy. Juvenal knows we will naturally tend to take this as satiric bathos, so he immediately seeks to cancel this effect by insisting that Nero's artistic performances were as damnable as anything he ever did. In 3. 7–9 no attempt is made to reverse our normal reaction and we are left with an anticlimax: What could be worse, says Juvenal, than living in fear of fires, falling houses, and the thousand and one dangers of this savage city, and poets reciting in the month of August (*Augusto recitantes mense poetas*)? Like many famous quotations, however, this is quite untypical of the author; in fact it would be hard to find a parallel in the *Satires*. For although Juvenal often contrives an anticlimax in order to belittle the person he is speaking of—as in the lines on Hannibal (10. 166–7)—in this case he has undermined the force of his own words, for the reader begins to suspect that Umbricius is not so appalled by the other dangers as he pretends. Nevertheless, if we allow for this and perhaps one or two other exceptions, it still remains true that whereas Horace permits some discrimination, which is an exercise of the reason, Juvenal often overpowers the reason altogether.

This brings us back to Dryden's ill-judged remark about the informing of the understanding being harder than the reclaiming of the will. Ill-judged, because apart from its dubious validity it is largely irrelevant to Juvenal. As a rule Juvenal is not in the least concerned with reclaiming the will. His object is to provoke the same derision, indignation, and disgust as he feels himself. And his technique exactly suits his purpose, for instead of developing a consecutive argument as Horace usually does, he presents a series of lurid pictures accompanied by emotive noises which are designed to play upon our deepest fears, resentments, and tabus:

When a soft eunuch takes a wife, and Mevia goes in for pig-sticking in the amphitheatre with a spear poised beside her naked breast; when a fellow who made my stiff young beard grate under his razor takes on single-handed the entire aristocracy in the contest of wealth; when a guttersnipe of the Nile like Crispinus—a slave bred in Canopus—hitches a cloak of Tyrian purple on to his shoulder and waves a light gold ring on his sweaty finger (for in summer he can't bear the weight of a larger stone), then it is hard *not* to write satire.

(1. 22–30)

Sexual scorn, male arrogance, social snobbery, xenophobia, jealousy, and physical revulsion—one is piled on the other until the satirist explodes with a shout of fury and contempt. That is why the cause of Juvenal's satire is usually identified as an efficient cause: *facit indignatio versum*. Both he and the reader experience through their savage laughter a kind of emotional release, but

265

there is no constructive purpose, no thought of healing the disease of his time, because for a man who assumes this attitude the state of Roman life is irremediable.

This gloomy spirit is visible even in poems which are not prompted by indignation.7 The cynical quietism to which the tenth satire leads is a wisdom reserved for the few. The rest of Rome and the rest of mankind will continue their misguided dreams. Satire thirteen, though different from the tenth in tone and strategy, takes the same pessimistic view of human virtue:

> rari quippe boni: numera; vix sunt totidem quot
> Thebarum portae vel divitis ostia Nili.   (26–7)

Good men are scarce. Count them—they are hardly as many as the gates of Thebes or the mouths of the rich Nile.

Turning back to Horace, we recall that the cause of his satire is a final cause: *ridentem dicere verum*—'to tell the truth with a smile'. The smile is important, for as well as being enjoyable in itself it makes the truth more palatable and therefore more easy to ingest. In Horace's own words 'Great difficulties are usually cut away more forcefully and more effectively by laughter than by vituperation' (1. 10. 14–15). This must always be the motto of the reforming satirist. It is basically optimistic in outlook, for it implies that the major cause of human unhappiness is a defect of vision, and that once the satirist has made his diagnosis the remedy is in the patient's hands.

This brings us to the question of style. Dryden takes issue with Casaubon over the alleged vulgarity of Horace's style, maintaining quite rightly that it 'is constantly accommodated to his subject, either high or low' (p. 78). Later, however, he seems to modify this position, asserting that 'the low style of Horace is according to his subject, that is, generally grovelling' (p. 85). This remark suggests that Dryden has overlooked many of those subtle gradations which make Horatian satire such a delight. And when it is taken in conjunction with his praise of Juvenal, whose expressions are 'sonorous and more noble', whose verse is 'more numerous', and whose words are 'suitable to his thoughts, sublime and lofty', then it becomes clear that once again Dryden has distorted the picture in his endeavour to produce a striking contrast. For Juvenal's sonorous and vehement rhetoric is inseparable from another feature of his style, which Dryden has seen fit to ignore, namely his brilliant use of demeaning detail. Indeed Juvenal's most characteristic effects result from the tension set up by these two forces co-existing within the same phrase or sentence, or succeeding one another in violent alternation. Because of this ironic method it is not often that the total effect of any Juvenalian paragraph is one of simple nobility. An exception which comes to mind is that magnificent passage in the fifteenth satire beginning ' When nature gave tears to man she showed that she was giving him a tender heart' (131 ff.). But the extreme rarity of such cases refutes Dryden's point. Far more typical is an example like this, picked at random from the seventh satire:

> frange miser calamum vigilataque proelia dele,
> qui facis in parva sublimia carmina cella,
> ut dignus venias hederis et imagine macra.   (27–9)

(If you have your eye on any patron other than the emperor) break your pen, you poor fool, and destroy the battles which have kept you awake at night, you who fashion lofty verse in a tiny garret with the hope of earning a crown of ivy and a skinny bust.

For further evidence of this polarity in Juvenal's style one can hardly do better than read the tenth satire along with *The Vanity of Human Wishes*.[8] If, therefore, we have to generalize on the styles of the two poets, it would be safer to say that whereas Horace rises and falls between relatively narrow limits Juvenal shoots up and down at a speed which leaves us breathless, exhilarated, and sometimes slightly sick.

The next point is the matter of wit. Here again we are disconcerted by Dryden's vacillations. It will be recalled that at the outset he chose Horace for his instruction and Juvenal for his delight (pp. 81–2). Then, finding that Horace's instruction consisted of ridiculing men's follies, he asserted that 'the divine wit of

Horace left nothing untouched' (p. 83) and that 'Horace laughs to shame all follies, and insinuates virtue rather by familiar examples than by the severity of precepts' (p. 84). By now it looks as if Dryden has received as much delight as instruction. But no. He now states that the delight which Horace gives him is 'but languishing', that the poet's wit (which a page ago was 'divine') is 'faint' and his salt 'almost insipid'. Juvenal on the other hand 'is of a more vigorous and masculine wit'. 'He gives me', says Dryden, 'as much pleasure as I can bear; he fully satisfies my expectation; he treats his subject home; his spleen is raised, and he raises mine.' As far as it goes this is a fair assessment of Juvenal's wit. And since preferences in wit are highly subjective we are quite willing to let Dryden keep his opinion of Horace, an opinion which after some bewilderment we think we have finally grasped: Horace's wit is feeble and intermittent. But Dryden has not yet finished. On p. 92 he takes up Barten Holyday's silly remark that 'a perpetual grin like that of Horace rather angers than amends a man'. Rallying to Horace's defence he says 'Let the chastisement of Juvenal be never so necessary for his new kind of satire; let him declaim as wittily and sharply as he pleases; yet still the nicest and most delicate touches of satire consist in fine raillery'. There follows a delightful and justly famous account of what Dryden means by this 'fine raillery'. It is the ability 'to make a man appear a fool, a blockhead, or a knave, without using any of those opprobrious terms'; it is 'the fineness of a stroke that separates the head from the body and leaves it standing in its place'; or again it is a method which effects 'a pleasant cure with all the limbs preserved entire'. Has Horace, then, been once more reinstated? Alas no, because we are now told that fine raillery, as described by Dryden, represents only Horace's *intention*; his *performance* was sadly inferior (pp. 94–5). We shall not stop to ask whether Dryden thinks he has now answered Holyday's objection, or how he himself can ever have enjoyed the instruction of so feeble a wit. It is more important to inquire where his analysis has gone wrong. In the first place, Horace has been credited with a purpose which he never conceived; for Dryden's fine raillery not only involves an attack on living people but also, to judge from the character of Zimri in *Absalom*,[9] entails a great deal more than the passing thrust which was Horace's favourite technique. Secondly, the two pairs of characters chosen by Dryden as illustrations of Horace's incompetence can scarcely be called satiric at all. Sarmentus and Cicirrus in 1. 5 and Persius and Rex in 1. 7 are not censured as either vicious or foolish; they are merely meant to be funny. It has been contended in chapter III that the humour consists not so much in what they say as in the way they are presented. By overlooking the element of parody Dryden seems to have been misled into equating Horace's humour with that of his characters.

The last point which I wish to take up concerns the historical background of the two poets and its effect on their satire. After asserting that Juvenal was the greater satirist, Dryden goes on to say (pp. 86–7):

His spirit has more of the commonwealth genius; he treats tyranny, and all the vices attending it, as they deserve, with the utmost rigour: and consequently a noble soul is better pleased with a zealous vindicator of Roman liberty, than with a temporising poet, a well mannered court-slave, and a man who is often afraid of laughing in the right place; who is ever decent because he is naturally servile...There was more need of a Brutus in Domitian's days, to redeem or mend, than of a Horace, if he had then been living, to laugh at a flycatcher. This reflection at the same time excuses Horace, but exalts Juvenal.

In fact the reflexion does neither, because it is entirely misconceived. Horace wrote his *Satires* at the end of the republican era, when there was no court; and where there is no court there can be no court slaves. It is true, of course, that after Philippi no writer could snipe at Antony, Octavian, or even Sextus Pompeius from an independent position. Pollio, with all his prestige, declined to swop insults with Octavian—'it is not easy to write against a man who can write you off'.[10] But the question still remains whether Horace's reticence was solely, or even primarily, due to fear. If he had been sure of his personal safety, would he then have castigated his enemies with Lucilian abandon? The question cannot be answered for the first half of the decade, but at least we can watch how the poet behaved when conditions altered. As the thirties wore on and hopes of a permanent settlement between Antony and Octavian began to fade, the air became thick with propaganda and personal abuse. Credit for many of the most scurrilous pamphlets must go to the leaders themselves, but they did not insist on a monopoly of invective and were quite happy to enlist the help of friends. Here, surely, was Horace's opportunity. With the protection of Maecenas, and ultimately that of Octavian, the risks would have been minimal. Yet he never joined in.[11] In fact, as we have seen, the more security Horace acquired the milder and less personal his work became, until finally he abandoned satire altogether. It may be, of course, that when he became emperor Octavian discouraged such writing in the hope of promoting social unity. But I prefer to think that Horace had more positive reasons for turning to other forms. The matter may perhaps be summed up by saying that, although Horace was not free to attack all and sundry, such freedom would have made little difference.

It remains to inquire whether Dryden's history is any more accurate in the case of Juvenal. In recent years scholars have done their utmost to treat Domitian fairly. Most people now accept the view that he was moderately successful in war, shrewd in financial affairs, and notably fair in his administration of the provinces.[12] But as time passed he had to contend with a mounting hatred on the part of the senate. Various reasons have been suggested, e.g. his monopoly of certain republican *honores*, his increasing emphasis on his own divinity, his restraint of greedy governors, his lack of tact, his habit of choosing non-senatorial executives, and in general his tendency to by-pass the senate as an organ of government. Whatever the causes, this hatred led to conspiracies against the emperor's life and consequent charges of *maiestas*, or treason. According to a recent article by Waters,[13] we know of at least nine executions on this charge, two others probably on this charge, and six more 'for non-political reasons'. In addition to the executions several people were sent into exile. In view of these figures, which represent the minimum number of victims, I am not inclined to accept Waters' contention that the terror which is said to have prevailed in the last years of Domitian's reign is simply a myth. For many senatorial families it must have been all too real. A few men, who might be called 'zealous vindicators of Roman liberty', protested—and suffered accordingly, but Juvenal was not one of them. Very sensibly, he waited for the assassin to strike. Tacitus, the only contemporary writer of comparable power, chose the same course.

Nerva became emperor in A.D. 96 and was followed two years later by Trajan. 'Now at last our spirits are reviving', says Tacitus. 'Nerva has harmonized the old discord between the principate and liberty, and every day Trajan is increasing the happiness of our times' (*Agricola* 3). Later he speaks of 'the rare good fortune of this age in which we can feel what we like and say what we feel' (*Hist.* I. I). The new spirit is also attested by Dio (58. 6. 4), who stresses Trajan's indifference to slander, and by Pliny, who in his panegyric on the emperor (66. 4) says 'You are urging us to be free, and so we shall be; you are urging us to express our feelings openly, and so we shall'. Such liberty was, of course, a privilege rather than a right, and no doubt it fell far short of anything which we would regard as tolerable. Nevertheless, it did represent some easing of tension, and it meant that the régime of Domitian was no longer immune from criticism. Several years passed, however, before Juvenal published his first book of satires. The precise date cannot be fixed; recent estimates vary from A.D. IIO to II7. The second book came out about the time of Trajan's death (A.D. II7), and the rest appeared in the reign of Hadrian, the last complete satire belonging to about 130. As successive books were published it became clear that Juvenal meant what he said about avoiding Lucilian polemic. The evidence on this point has been weighed by Syme, who assures us that 'Juvenal does not attack any person or category that commands influence in his own time'.[14] This does not justify charges of cowardice or timidity; no such charges are made by Syme, and indeed it would be rather unfair if a poet were expected to commit suicide in order to satisfy a modern critic.[15] Anyhow, even in their present form, the *Satires* can hardly have pleased the emperor or any of his magistrates who felt responsible for the state of the nation. But Syme's point does mean that the *Satires* cannot have had the direct and immediate impact which Dryden imagined. And so in this area too we must reject the sharp antithesis which Dryden has presented between Juvenal and Horace.

Finally, in view of Dryden's remark about Juvenal having 'more of the commonwealth genius' we should perhaps recall that in spite of his invective against Nero and Domitian there is no evidence that Juvenal wanted the principate abolished. Still less did he envisage anything like our own form of democracy. As Highet points out, 'Juvenal does not say that the poor are exploited by the governing class or that the middle class is being crushed out of existence. He does not say that "the system" should be changed to put a different social class on top.'[16] What he does deplore is that as a result of Rome's imperial power the old social order has been upset; unscrupulous blackguards with no breeding (many of them Greeks or Syrians) have acquired money and prestige, while decent Romans like himself have been reduced to poverty and humiliation. Thus his angriest satires proceed from a vague sort of reactionary idealism enforced by feelings of personal injustice.

The type of analysis which we have been conducting is often unsympathetic, and it may be urged in defence of Dryden that he had few of the scholarly resources available to a modern critic. He could not walk into a library and inspect the serried ranks of Pauly–Wissowa; and seventeenth-century commentaries, admirable as they were, had not experienced that long process of scrutiny and sifting which lies behind the works of Heinze and Lejay. Moreover, Dryden was in no way eccentric in holding such views. They were shared not only by his contemporaries but also by his successors in the eighteenth century; and indeed some of them flourish today. But however important these considerations may be (and they are of prime importance for an understanding of Dryden's own approach to satire) they ought not to obscure the fact that, as far as Horace and Juvenal are concerned, Dryden's essay is wrong or misleading on almost every major point. And this is the more unfortunate in that its writer was a man of genius.

NOTES

1 Fraenkel, p. 86:'What does follow is something totally different.'
2 For the sage as king see H. von Arnim, *Stoicorum Veterum Fragmenta*, I. 53. 10; 3. 81. 31; 3. 150. 17; 3. 158. 35 ff.; 3. 159. 1.
3 For the punishments of adulterers see Mayor on Juvenal 10. 315–17 and Ellis on Catullus 15. 19. For the adultery mime see R. W. Reynolds in *CQ*, XL (1946), 77–84, and cf. *Sat*. 2. 7. 59–61.
4 Cf. Lucilius W. 1240; and Cichorius, p. 348.
5 Fraenkel, p. 78, n. 2.
6 A very full and learned guide to this debate is provided by H. Herter in *Rh. Mus*. XCIV (1951), 1 ff.
7 On the text and interpretation of v. 108 these, I think, are the chief points:
(1) *Ut avarus* cannot mean that the miser is an instance of contentment. Such an idea would conflict with the whole tenor of the poem. The miser who congratulates himself in vv. 66–7 is the victim of a delusion, as is clear from *iubeas miserum esse, libenter | quatenus id facit* (63–4).

(2) Nor can the miser be an instance of discontent; for in vv. 30–2 Horace has maintained that greed is the *basis* of discontent. It is against his purpose to suggest that there are any discontented people who are not greedy. Even if we take the *avarus* as referring only to the types presented in vv. 41–100, the theory still does not work. For if *ut avarus* is comparative the miser ought to be an instance of the proposition *nemo | se probet ac potius laudet diversa sequentis*. But at no time does the miser wish to change his occupation.

Therefore if *ut avarus* is a separate phrase, as I believe it is, it must mean 'inasmuch as he is greedy', which is virtually the equivalent of *ob avaritiam*.

(3) The objections to the *qui* of the oldest Blandinian MS., which is printed by most modern editors, are:

(a) That the formula *illuc unde abii redeo* cannot be continued by an indirect question. I am not sure that this objection is fatal. Such a formula is sometimes taken up by a phrase in agreement (*Sat*. I. 6. 45), sometimes by an accusative and infinitive (Cic. *Fam*. I. 7. 5; 4. 8. 2), and sometimes by a *quod* clause (*Sat*. I. 3. 38–9). On these points see E. L. Harrison, *Phoenix*, XV (1961), 43–4; C. Becker, *Gnomon*, XXXI (1959), 601; and W. Wimmel, *Zur Form der horazischen Diatribensatire* (Frankfurt, 1962), pp. 74–6.

(b) That if *ut avarus* equals *ob avaritiam* then Horace's question would contain its own answer. This also may be over-strict. For the sequence might be: why is it that no one, in his greed, is content with his own life and envies those in other occupations? The answer, indicated by the whole poem and especially by the closing lines, would be 'For *no* good reason'.

(c) Even allowing for the -*qui*- of *nequit* directly overhead, it is hard to account for the absence of *qui* from the MS. tradition, especially as it would derive some prominence from being a repetition of the opening word. It is more probable that, like many modern conjectures, *qui* was proposed as an easier reading by someone who had failed to make sense of what was before him.

(4) Reading *nemon ut avarus*, Fraenkel renders 'Can it be that no greedy person is content with his own situation?' But such a question would imply the answer 'no', and anyhow there is nothing astonishing in the discontent of greedy men. Mr S. A. Handford has pointed out to me that *nemon ut se probet* could also mean 'Is no one ever to be content?' But, as he observes, *ne ut* cannot go together here, because then *nemo* would have to be taken with *avarus*, and the question 'Is no greedy man ever to be content?' does not give satisfactory sense.

If the reading which I have given is correct, then Horace returns to his opening topic, not to repeat his original question (that has already been answered) but to ask another one in various forms. The repeated interrogatives *probet, laudet, tabescat*, etc., do not indicate the poet's indignation; they rather draw attention to the wearisome futility and the wasted energy of πλεονεξία. As for the subjunctives, they are similar to those mentioned by Handford in section 84 of *The Latin Subjunctive*. It should perhaps be added that although this position was reached independently I do not imagine it to be original. It was probably held by various scholars before the nineteenth century, and others may hold it today. The remarks of Professor G. B. A. Fletcher in the *Durham University Journal*, n.s. XXI (1959), 33, certainly point in the same direction.

8 Cf. Plato, *Rep.* I. 349 B–350 C.

9 A special study of this technique was made by U. Knoche in *Phil.* XC (1935), 372–90 and 469–82.

10 D.L. 6. 96. For a general account of Crates see D. R. Dudley, *A History of Cynicism* (London, 1937), pp. 42–53.

11 D.L. 4. 46–58. Dudley, *op. cit.* pp. 62–9. See also A. Oltramare, *Les Origines de la diatribe romaine* (Lausanne, 1926), pp. 36–9.

12 For the Scipionic circle see Fiske, ch. 2.

13 For Panaetius see M. van Straaten, *Panaetii Rhodii Fragmenta* (Leiden, 1952).

14 Cf. E. Zeller, *A History of Eclecticism in Greek Philosophy*, Eng. trans. (London, 1883), pp. 87–99.

15 Cf. P. H. DeLacy, *TAPA*, LXXIX (1948), 12–23. Velleius represents Epicureanism in Cic. *De Nat. Deorum*.

16 C. O. Brink, *Horace on Poetry* (Cambridge, 1963), p. 177 and reff.

17 Cf. A. Momigliano, *JRS*, XXXI (1941), 149–57.

18 Teubner text (Hobein) 15. 1.
19 Ed. E. Littré (Paris, 1861), IX, 368–70. Cf. Diogenes in D.L. 6. 29.
20 *Axiochus* 368 A.
21 Varro B. 78, Cic. *De Off.* 1. 120 (though Cicero allows for the possibility of a change). A later Stoic instance is Epictetus, Frag. 2.
22 Lucretius, *DRN* 3. 1057 ff. and 1082 ff.
23 Teles, pp. 10–11, 42–3.
24 For love of money as the root of all evil see H. Herter, *Rh. Mus.* XCIV (1951), 19. Varro wrote a treatise called περὶ φιλαργυρίας; cf. also Varro B. 126. The μεμψίμοιρος in Theophrastus' *Characters*, however, shows that discontent was not restricted to questions of money.
25 Teles, p. 11. This, like the last example, was noted by Fraenkel, pp. 92–3.
26 Teles, p. 43. Cf. the excerpt from a Byzantine collection cited by Heinze (Kiessling–Heinze, *Satires*, 6th ed. Berlin, 1957, p. 8) and Lejay (*Satires*, Paris, 1911, p. 8) after Wachsmuth: διὰ φιλαργυρίαν μετὰ πόνων γεωργεῖς etc.
27 J. Souilhé (*Platon* III, 3. 117–36) thinks the author of the *Axiochus* was a member of the Academy living in the first century B.C. and drawing without much insight on various schools.
28 Cf. Democritus D. 202. For Cynic interest in Democritus see Z. Stewart, *Harv. Stud. Class. Phil.* LXIII (1958), 179–91.
29 This seems to be the right interpretation, though the construction is certainly awkward.
30 E.g. *Rep.* 8. 558 D–559 C and 9. 571 ff.
31 E.g. *NE* 7. 1147 B–1150 A.
32 Cf. *KD* 29; Cic. *De Fin.* 1. 45 and *Tusc. Disp.* 5. 93. In view of the ascetic tone of many Epicurean sayings it is well to keep in mind a fragment like *Sent. Vat.* 63: 'Frugality also has its limit, and the man who disregards it is on a par with the man who errs through excess.' The notion of nature's limit also occurs in vv. 49–51, 54–6, and 59–60 of the present satire. Cf. also Democritus D. 102, 211, 233; Aristippus M. 71a; Lucilius W. 1201, *virtus quaerendae finem re scire modumque*; and Lucretius, *DRN* 5. 1432–3.
33 *NE* 2. 1106 AB and 4 *passim*.
34 E.g. *Rep.* 1. 349 E, 4. 443 D; *Phileb.* 31 C–32 B, 64 D–65 D.
35 For references and discussion see W. K. C. Guthrie, *A History of Greek Philosophy* (Cambridge, 1962), vol. 1, index under *medicine* and *music*.
36 Cf. vv. 74 and 124.
37 In *Menoec.* 130 Epicurus says that 'everything natural is easy to obtain'. He even declares that he cannot envisage the good if he rules out the pleasures of taste, sex, hearing, and sight (Frag. 10). But if a pleasure was good *per se*, it did not follow that it should be *chosen*, for the harm involved might be too serious. Some of the school's uncertainty is reflected in Cicero, *Tusc. Disp.* 5. 94.

38 A. D. Knox, *Herodes, Cercidas, and the Greek Choliambic Poets* (printed with the Loeb Theophrastus), p. 204. See also *Oxyrhynchus Papyri* 8. 1082. Horace's relation to Cercidas is discussed in three Italian articles: L. de Gubernatis, *Bollettino di Filologia classica*, XIX (1912), 52–6; Q. Cataudella, *La Parola del Passato*, V (1950), 18–31; M. Gigante, *Rivista di Filologia*, n.s. LXXXIII (1955), 286–93. Philodemus is a likely intermediary. Diogenes, extreme in this as in all else, is supposed to have thought even Aphrodite of the market-place too much trouble (Dio Chrys. 6. 17; ps.-Diog. *Epist.* 42 (Hercher, *Epist. Graec.* p. 256)). Bion, according to D.L. 4. 49, said that if Socrates desired Alcibiades and refrained he was a fool; if he did not, then his conduct was in no way remarkable. This observation refers to the incident mentioned in Plato, *Symp.* 218 c ff.

39 In *The Brothers* of Philemon (Edmonds, 3 A, Frag. 4) Solon is supposed to have safeguarded Athenian marriage by setting up brothels. The girls stand in full view; there is no deception, no prudery, no nonsense; take cheap and immediate satisfaction with whatever woman you choose, and then let her go hang—she's nothing to you, ἀλλοτρία 'στί σοι—a phrase which for its crass, self-deluding egotism rivals Aristippus' ἔχω καὶ οὐκ ἔχομαι—'I have and am not had' (M. 57). See also Eubulus, *Nannion* 67 and *Pannychis* 84 (Edmonds, II).

40 E.g. Lucilius W. 923–4 and 927–8.

41 It is interesting to find Epictetus later attempting, in the manner of some modern theologians, to narrow the gap between moral theory and moral practice:

In your sex-life remain chaste as far as you can before marriage, and if you indulge take only those liberties which are not forbidden by law. At the same time, you should not be objectionable or censorious to those who do indulge, and you should not keep harping on the fact that you yourself abstain.   (*Enchiridion* 33)

It is not surprising that the man who wrote these words should have provided the noblest reason for respecting marriage: ὁ ἄνθρωπος πρὸς πίστιν γέγονεν—'man is born to fidelity' (*Discourses* 2. 4). Anyone who undermines good faith is undermining the characteristic quality of man. Adultery destroys self-respect, loyalty, neighbourly feeling, friendship, and (ultimately) the state itself. All of which is a far cry from the cheerful squalors of the second satire.

42 Thuc. 3. 82; cf. Isoc. *Antid.* 284–5 and *Areop.* 20.

43 For a later period cf. Juvenal 6. 195; Martial 10. 68.

44 Plato, *Rep.* 474D, also speaks of lovers' euphemisms, but the topic is employed in a way quite different from that of Horace.

45 E.g. *NE* 1166–7.

46 E.g. Panaetius, as represented in Cic. *De Off.* 1. 90 and 111; Laelius as

represented in *De Amic.* 65 and 92. We shall be cautioned from thinking too much in terms of schools if we recall Democritus D. 102: 'In all things τὸ ἴσον (balance or equity) is fair, excess and deficiency are not.'

47 For the contrast in dress, cf. Varro B. 301–2.

48 Migne, *Bibl. Patr. Graec.* cxxxvi, 1083. Cf. Themistius as cited by Gildemeister and Bücheler in *Rh. Mus.* xxvii (1872), 440.

49 For Crates see Julian, *Or.* 6. 200 A and 7. 213 C; for Aeschrion see Knox, *op. cit.* p. 262; for Theocritus see Theoc. 17. 107.

50 E.g. D.L. 2. 66 (Aristippus), 7. 160 (Ariston); Teles, p. 5 (Bion); Menander K. 165; Cic. *De Off.* 1. 114; Epictetus, *Enchir.* 17.

51 Cf. L. Radermacher, *Wien. Stud.* xlvii (1929), 79–86.

52 *Sat.* 1. 1. 114–16. The simile grows out of *superare* (112). The tradition can be seen in Alexis (Edmonds, II, Frag. 235), Varro B. 288, and Cicero, *De Sen.* 83. Horace's language, like that of Virg. *Georg.* 1. 512 ff., recalls certain lines of Ennius' *Annals*, in particular W. 443–4. The failure to compare oneself with those who are worse off (111) goes back to Democritus D. 191.

53 Cf. Bion (Teles, p. 16), Lucretius, *DRN* 3. 938 and 960, Cic. *Tusc. Disp.* 5. 118, Plutarch, *Cons. ad Apoll.* 120 B, Epictetus, *Enchir.* 15.

54 It is possible, however, that Horace had at the back of his mind vv. 147–8, in which Menedemus says:

> decrevi me tantisper minus iniuriae,
> Chremes, meo gnato facere dum fiam miser.

> I have decided, Chremes, that I diminish the wrong done to my son in proportion as I make myself miserable.

The link between Fufidius and Menedemus is supplied by the combination of harshness and unhappiness. The phrase *patribus duris* (17) may have had some influence at the subconscious level.

55 Ennius, *Ann.* W. 471–2. Cf. Varro B. 542.

56 See F. A. Wright, *AJP*, xli (1921), 168–9.

57 *Greek Anth.* 5. 132. Cf. Ovid, *Amores* 1. 5. 19 ff.

58 A. W. Mair, Callimachus (Loeb), *Epig.* 33.

59 Cf. Lucretius, *DRN* 5. 925 ff.

60 The commonplace is represented by Democritus D. 60, Crates in D.L. 6. 89, Menander K. 710 and K. 631, Anon. 359 (Edmonds, III A). See also the commentators on Catullus 22. 21.

CHAPTER II

1 For 'Poet and Patron (2)', see ch. IX.

2 This is not certain but probable. See L. R. Taylor, *AJP*, xlvi (1925), 161–70.

3 This goes back to the notes of Porphyrion and ps.-Acron on vv. 17 and 18. For a modern discussion see F. Klingner, *Phil.* xc (1935), 461–3.

4 In essence the idea goes back to the first part of ps.-Acron's note on v. 17: *quanto nos, inquit, minus ad honores possumus pervenire, qui vulgo ignoti sumus?* For a modern discussion see K. Büchner, *Riv. di Cult. Class. e Med.* v (1963), 82 ff.

5 It is a fine point, but I prefer to take *prava ambitione procul* as backing up *cautum adsumere* rather than as an extension of *dignos.* In vv. 50–5 it is part of Horace's tact to imply his own worthiness by stressing the careful discernment of Maecenas, who stands aloof from people on the make.

6 Büchner's article cited above (n. 4) brought it home to me that in *Phoenix,* xv (1961), 196 ff., I had not properly considered the punctuation of vv. 63–4. It is better grammar to take *non patre praeclaro sed vita et pectore puro* with *placui* rather than with *secernis*; it is also rather better sense, for it makes the *vita* Horace's own life, which is then taken up in 65 ff., and the *pater* Horace's own father, who is brought in in 71 ff. Büchner takes *patre, vita* and *pectore* as ablatives of quality loosely connected with *ego* (62), but I do not find this convincing. As for *turpi* and *honestum* (63) I cannot see that it makes much difference to the sense whether these are masculine or neuter, but again I may perhaps have given too little weight to some of Büchner's arguments.

7 This is the suggestion of Niebuhr, recorded by Fraenkel, p. 2, n. 3.

8 Quint. 2. 2. 14; cf. 1. 2. 2 and 1. 2. 4.

9 Quint. 2. 2. 15; cf. 1. 3. 17; Juv. 10. 224; Plut. *De Lib. Educ.* 4AB; Petron. 85–6.

10 Cic. *Cael.* 6–11; Pliny, *Ep.* 3. 3; cf. 4. 13 and Juv. 10. 295–8.

11 Note how Tillius occurs in the middle of the first and third sections (24 and 107). The name Novius has a similar function (40 and 121).

12 The commentators cite Lucilius W. 101. No one seems to have associated this Lucilian reference to Tarentum with the similar reference in v. 59. For the gelded mule see W. D. Ashworth and M. Andrewes, *CR*, n.s. VII (1957), 107–8.

13 The phrase 'exquisite still life' and the point itself are due to Fraenkel, p. 104.

14 The most recent work on ancient biography is W. Steidl, 'Sueton und die antike Biographie', *Zetemata*, I (1951). G. L. Hendrickson, *AJP*, XXIII (1902), 389, quotes the rhetorical divisions of γένος, τροφή, ἀγωγή, φύσις ψυχῆς καὶ σώματος, ἐπιτηδεύματα, πράξεις.

15 A summary of the characteristics of Roman invective will be found in Appendix 6 of R. G. M. Nisbet's edition of the *In Pisonem* (Oxford, 1961). The exchange of insults between Antony and Octavian is chronicled by K. Scott in *Memoirs of the American Academy in Rome,* XI (1933), 7–49. The *Indignatio* of Valerius Cato (Suet. *De Gramm.* 11) must have been written in a situation not wholly unlike that of Horace.

16 Cic. *Dom.* 95; cf. *Har. Resp.* 17, and Quintilian 11. 1. 18.

17 Cic. *Sull.* 83; cf. *Fam.* 5. 2. 8, and *Att.* 1. 20. 3.

18 Plut. *De Se Ipsum Citra Invid. Laud.* 542–4. Cf. the present writer's article 'Humble Self-Esteem: A Mannerism of the Younger Pliny', *Classical News and Views*, VII (December 1962), 5–8.

19 D.L. 4. 47. A glance at Bion's letter will reveal how far removed it is from the sixth satire. Not only is Bion's tone ruder but his attitude to his father (whom he candidly admits to have cheated the revenue) is quite different. Here as elsewhere scholars in search of Horatian 'imitations' have often been misled.

20 See A. M. Duff, *Freedmen in the Early Roman Empire* (Oxford, 1928), pp. 52–5.

21 See, for example, Suet. *De Gramm.* 10, 12, 14, 15, and esp. 21—Gaius Melissus the friend of Maecenas and Augustus.

22 Dio 42. 51. 5 and 43. 47. 3. For Caesar's senate see R. Syme, *BSR Papers*, XIV (1938), 12–18.

23 Dio 52. 42. 1; Suet. *Aug.* 35. 1.

24 See, for example, Livy 23. 2. 1; Cic. *Flacc.* 16; and later Quint. 3. 8. 48; 11. 1. 37.

25 'Sallust', *Ad Caes. Epist.* 11. 3; cf. Sall. *Jug.* 85. 4.

26 *Op. cit.* (n. 14 above), p. 396.

27 C. L. Stevenson, *Mind*, XLVII (1938), 331.

CHAPTER III

1 Wesseling (*Observ. Var.* II. 15, quoted in Schütz's ed. (Berlin, 1889) p. 63) thought Maecenas was travelling south to prepare for the conference, which never took place, in the spring of 38 B.C., in which case 2. 6. 42–3 could refer to the journey. Schütz himself preferred to think that Maecenas was on his way to Athens in the autumn of 38 B.C. He and Palmer, arguing against the traditional date of spring 37 B.C., have asked why the party should have travelled to Tarentum via Brundisium. To answer this one has to rely on Plutarch (*Ant.* 35), who says that Antony first crossed to Brundisium and then, after failing to gain access, sailed on to Tarentum. Other objections to 37 B.C. are more trivial. Palmer, for instance, states that, since Octavian and Antony met in person, there were no ambassadors present at Tarentum. But he has forgotten Dio 48. 54, in which the leaders are said to have presented their grievances 'first of all through friends, and then personally'. Palmer is also wrong in saying that 'the annoying gnats and noisy frogs; the chilly evenings and the fire of branches with leaves on; the heavy rains: these suit Autumn better than early Spring'. If the time was April or early May the travellers would have heard the chorus of frogs in the Pomptine Marshes, just as Cicero had heard it sixteen years before

NOTES

(*Fam.* 7. 18. 3, written on 8 April). According to the naturalists consulted by Gow, such a chorus would not be expected after the beginning of May (*CR*, xv, 1901, 117). As for the chilly evenings and the fire, the party was then in hilly country and was being served with a cooked meal. Finally, in reply to Schütz, who uses the Sirocco (78) to support the autumn against the spring date, we can cite the *Encyclopedia Britannica* (1961) which says 'these winds... are most prominent in the Spring, when cyclonic winds are common and the sea is much cooler than the desert' (23. 652). The question, therefore, remains open, but that is not enough to dispose of the satire's historicity. (The references above are to A. Palmer's 5th ed., London, 1896).

2   *CW*, XLVIII (1955), 159–62.

3   This is made likely by W. 287–8, 655, and Cic. *De Fin.* 1. 3. 7 (quoted after W. 635). Too much stress, however, has been laid on W. 133–4, where a ploughman called Symmachus is said to be dying of pneumonia. It is surely improbable that a squire like Lucilius would have undertaken such a journey on account of a farmhand's illness.

4   Lucilius' poem was the first of its kind in Latin, and no Greek prototype exists. Horace, however, was doubtless familiar with Caesar's Journey to Spain (Suet. *Jul.* 56), and after Horace the tradition was carried on by Valgius (W. Morel, *Frag. Poet. Lat.* p. 106), Ovid (*Trist.* 1. 10) and Persius (if ὁδοιπορικῶν is the right reading in *Vita Persi* 45). At a much later period the form was still alive, as may be seen from the journey of Lactantius to Nicomedia (St Jerome, *De Viris Illust.* 80), the introduction to Ausonius' *Mosella*, and the *De Reditu Suo* of Rutilius Namatianus (see *Minor Latin Poets*, trans. by J. W. and A. M. Duff in the Loeb series). The texts have been collected by L. Illuminati in *La satura odeporica latina* (Biblioteca della 'Rassegna', 1938), and they are the subject of a dissertation by H. Grupp, *Studien zum antiken Reisegedicht* (Tübingen, 1953).

5   The significance of the fragment is established by Porphyrion (on 1. 6. 22), who connects it with a bed (not with a dining couch), and by the use of *pede*. A Hebrew parallel for this use is given by P. Haupt, *AJP*, XLII (1921), 166.

6   The purity of the Corsican diary is perhaps due to the Corsicans' timely warning. 'They told me that in their country I should be treated with the greatest hospitality; but if I attempted to debauch any of their women, I might expect instant death' (*The Journal of a Tour to Corsica*, ed. S. C. Roberts, Cambridge, 1923, p. 9).

7   For the second *poenas* Lafaye has suggested *pronus*, *Rev. Phil.* XXXV (1911), 27.

8   Cf. *egens benignae Tantalus semper dapis*, *Epod.* 17. 66. W. 136–7 may have been one of the passages in which Lucilius made fun of Accius—see Porph. on 1. 10. 53, and cf. Warmington, *Remains of Old Latin* II, 610–11, nos. 66–7.

9   T. Frank, *Catullus and Horace* (New York, 1928), pp. 178–9.

10 Gibbon, *Miscell. Works*, ed. John, Lord Sheffield (London, 1837), p. 567.
11 A. Noyes, *Portrait of Horace* (London, 1947), p. 75.
12 V. D'Antò, as reported by W. S. Anderson, *CW*, XLIX (1955), 57–9.
13 J. J. Savage, *TAPA*, XCIII (1962), 413–15.
14 This also offended Gibbon. 'The gross language of a boatman, and the ribaldry of two buffoons, surely belong to the lowest species of comedy. They might divert travellers in a mood to be pleased with everything; but how could a man of taste reflect on them the day after?' Well, well.
15 Fraenkel, p. 109.
16 *Ibid.* p. 110.
17 J. Dorsch, 'Mit Horaz von Rom nach Brindisi', *Jhb. des St Gym.* (Prag, 1904), p. 5. Norman Douglas has some characteristically lively remarks on Horace's view of nature in *Old Calabria* (London, 1923), p. 42.
18 Quoted by A. Bischoff, 'De Itinere Horatii Brundisino Commentatio', *Sollemnia Anniv. in Gym. Landavino* (Landavi Palatinorum, 1880), p. 1.
19 I cannot find any support in either Aelian 3. 41 or Pliny, *NH* 8. 76 for the notion that *equus ferus* meant a unicorn. There is plenty of evidence that it meant a wild horse, e.g. Varro, *RR* 2. 1. 5, Pliny, *NH* 28. 159 and 197; cf. also Apuleius, *Met.* 7. 16. The mention of a horn in v. 58 shows that Sarmentus has now changed to another animal. A bull seems the most likely; to introduce a unicorn even at this second stage is rather fanciful. The circular scar on Messius' forehead, which may have resulted from the removal of a large wart, reminded Sarmentus of the Cyclops' eye.
20 G. Norwood, *CR*, XXIII (1909), 240. All the relevant authorities are cited by Monroe Deutsch, *CP*, XXIII (1928), 394–8.
21 Dryden, *Essays*, ed. W. P. Ker (Oxford, 1926), II, 95.
22 L. P. Wilkinson, *Ovid Recalled* (Cambridge, 1955), p. 68.
23 For the Greek *Priapea* see *Greek Anth.* 16. 236–43, 260–1. The Latin *Priapea* are printed by F. Bücheler in his edition of Petronius (Berlin, 1882). His commentary is in *Rh. Mus.* XVIII (1863), 381 ff. The most recent work on the subject is the monograph by V. Buchheit, *Zetemata*, XXVIII (München, 1962), which argues strongly for unity of authorship. With the opening of Horace's satire compare no. 10. 4–5: *sed lignum rude vilicus dolavit, / et dixit mihi 'tu Priapus esto'*.
24 Hippolytus, *Philosophumena* 237 (Cruice).
25 Lactantius, *Div. Inst.* 1. 20; Arnobius, *Adv. Gentes* 4. 7; Augustine, *Civ. Dei* 7. 24.
26 This information is based partly on R. Payne Knight, *A Discourse on the Worship of Priapus* (London, 1865), and the anonymous essay printed with it, partly on F. Cumont's article in Daremberg–Saglio, IV, 1 partie, 645–7. The chief modern authority is H. Herter, De Priapo (*Religionsgeschichtliche Versuche und Vorarbeiten*, XXIII (1932)). Herter has also written the article on Priapus in P–W.

27 Priapus' connexion with the fig is illustrated by amulets in the Musée Secret at Naples, consisting of two arms joined at the elbow, one ending in a phallus, the other in a closed fist with the thumb tucked between the first and second fingers. 'The Italian called this gesture *fare la fica*...the Spaniard *dar una higa*...and the Frenchman...*faire la figue*' (Payne Knight, *op. cit.* p. 150). It has been widely used as a device for warding off the evil eye and for expressing contempt in general. Hence the English 'I don't care a fig'. Cf. the article on *fascinum* by G. Lafaye in Daremberg–Saglio, II, 2 partie, 983–7. For further demonstration of the fig's connexion with fertility, see H. J. Rose's remarks on the Nonae Caprotinae in *Religion in Greece and Rome* (New York, 1959), pp. 217–18.

28 Diodorus 4. 6. 4.

29 Shrieking derived this power from its resemblance to the cries of tormented souls, cf. Tib. 1. 2. 47 *iam tenet infernas magico stridore catervas*. Other examples are cited by K. F. Smith in his article on Graeco-Roman magic in *Hastings' Encyclopedia*, VIII, 280. He relates this sound to the screeching of the owl (*strix*) and to the wailing of the banshee. Another device to make contact with the dead was gathering their bones—a practice mentioned in v. 22 of Horace's satire. The principle here is that the part can be made to attract the whole.

30 See Frazer on Ovid, *Fast.* 5. 432.

31 No knives or spades were permitted, because iron, being a very late invention in the history of magic, was a dangerous novelty and therefore tabu. See Frazer on Ovid, *Fast.* 5. 441. The purpose of the ceremony is that the spirits should drink the blood and so regain the power of speech—a parody, of course, of the great scene in *Odyss.* 11.

32 See A. S. F. Gow on Theocritus 2. 2.

33 The latter stands in an attitude of supplication, like a slave about to be flogged or tortured to death. No doubt its hands are bound as in the figurines reproduced by Hubert in his article on magic in Daremberg–Saglio, III, 2 partie, 1518. A somewhat similar pair are described in the Great Paris Papyrus (C. Wessely, *Denkschrift Wien. Acad.* 36. 2. 44 ff.). For other spells see e.g. H. I. Bell *et al.*, *Proc. Brit. Acad.* XVII (1931), 237–87. Some modern instances of envoûtement are quoted in Maurice Bouisson, *Magic*, Eng. trans. (London, 1960), pp. 30 ff.

34 Cf. Virg. *Ecl.* 8. 80–1.

35 Wooden statues were apt to split in the hot sunshine, cf. 2. 5. 39–40.

36 Tac. *Ann.* 2. 32. For magical beliefs and ceremonies as they appear in Roman literature see E. Tavenner, 'Studies in Magic from Latin Literature', *Columbia Univ. Stud. Class. Phil.* (New York, 1916), S. Eitrem, *Symb. Osl.* XXI (1941), 56–79, and G. Luck, *Hexen und Zauberei in der römischen Dichtung* (Zürich, 1962).

37 The third act of Jonson's *Poetaster* begins with an adaptation of this satire.

Another interesting treatment will be found in the eighth satire of Régnier.

38 The ἀδολέσχης inflicts himself on strangers, skips from one topic to another, and refuses to leave his victim alone (cf. D.L. 4. 50). He differs from the λάλος in that (a) he is an empty-headed fool, whereas the λάλος may be genuinely well informed, (b) he does not demand one's attention, whereas the λάλος does, (c) with his grasshopper mind he is incapable of pursuing a topic, whereas the λάλος is unable to leave off. The λάλος complacently admits his defects (cf. vv. 14–15 of this satire, where the pest knows he is being a nuisance), he is tenacious, aggressive, and (unlike the pest) a 'know-all'. Earlier stages in this tradition of character-drawing are represented by Plato, Rep. 8. 554 and Aristotle, NE 1115 a ff. On the Latin side Horace's poem owes much to the cheerful self-revelation of Catullus (especially no. 10) and Lucilius. I am not convinced, however, that there was a 'pest satire' in Lucilius—see Phoenix, xv (1961), 90–6.

39 If Propertius was born in 50 B.C. and this satire was written in 36 B.C. we are left with a fourteen-year-old pest. Even if we stretch the termini to 54 and 34 B.C. we still have a young man of twenty, and one feels that if Horace had been cowed by someone ten years his junior he would probably have used this for comic effect. As for the pest's mother, we know from vv. 27–8 that she was dead.

40 Fuscus was the recipient of the light-hearted Carm. 1. 22 (Integer vitae) and Epist. 1. 10 (see R. G. M. Nisbet's note in CQ, n.s. IX, 1959, 74–5). Porph. on Epist. 1. 10 says he wrote comedies.

41 The words are est tibi mater, / cognati, quis te salvo est opus? Some take the query as a veiled threat, but this is inappropriate because Horace is on the defensive throughout; others take it as a hint that the fellow is mad or that so accomplished an artist could not hope to live long, but the question ought to be an attempt to get rid of the man. Nor, in view of non sum piger (19), can Horace be stressing the length of the walk. L. J. D. Richardson, who collected various ideas in Hermathena, LXVII (1946), 93–6, suggested that te salvo was an oblique form of the salutation salve or salvus sis. His transla-tion was '(Have you a mother or relatives) who are obliged to greet you?' It would be rather better if this could be emended to 'Have you a mother or relatives who are waiting to greet you?' But I am not sure if this can be extracted from the Latin. Palmer thought Horace was about to warn the pest against the danger of catching his friend's illness. This gives tolerable sense, but one does not expect to be referred back to v. 18. The most recent suggestion by R. Bogaert in Les Études classiques, XXXI (1963), 159–66, does not, I think, bring us any closer to a solution, though his collection of material is useful.

42 For the legal problems posed by the satire see H. J. Roby, Journ. Phil. XIII (1885), 233–41.

43 Cf. the use of pulchre in v. 62.

44 Plaut. *Poen.* 770, *Bacch.* 251; Petron. 75. Cf. Lucilius W. 519 and Horace, *Sat.* 1. 5. 21 *(cerebrosus)*; Petron. 45 and 58 *(caldicerebrius)*.

45 See A. A. Deckman, *A Study of the Impersonal Passive of the Ventum Est Type*, Diss. (Philadelphia, 1920).

46 Plaut. *Capt.* 246. Other possible instances are *Most.* 357 and *Mil.* 450.

47 W. 314.

48 Fraenkel, p. 117. Several of the foregoing points are noted by J. Marouzeau, *Introduction au Latin* (Paris, 1941), pp. 153–64.

49 See W. S. Anderson, *AJP*, LXXVII (1956), 148–66.

50 See Platner and Ashby, *Topog. Dict. Ancient Rome* (London, 1929), pp. 441–2.

51 *Ibid.* p. 72; cf. G. Lugli, *Roma Antica* (Rome, 1946), p. 172.

52 Work began on Apollo Palatinus in 36 B.C. (Platner and Ashby, *op. cit.* p. 16). The Villa Publica was probably restored in 34 B.C. *(ibid.* p. 581). Lejay's topographical notes on *Sat.* 1. 9. 13 and 1. 6. 42 are not reliable. E. T. Salmon in a paper in *Studies in Honour of Gilbert Norwood* (Toronto, 1952), pp. 184–93, sees the pair as walking down the Vicus Tuscus, through a Jewish area around the Forum Boarium, and finally being separated near the temple of Apollo Medicus. F. Castagnoli *(Bull. Comm. Arch. Com.* LXXIV, 1952, 53) objects, maintaining *(a)* that Horace would have crossed the Aemilian not the Fabrician Bridge to reach Caesar's Gardens, *(b)* that Salmon's theories about the Jewish area and about the temple of Apollo are far from certain, and *(c)* that the end of the episode took place near the tribunals of the Forum, for that was where the pest was seized by his adversary *(rapit in ius)*; also the crowds are the crowds of the Forum. Of these objections the third seems to me to be the strongest. I agree with Salmon, however, that the explanation of *sic me servavit Apollo* should be either literary or topographical. If we try to accommodate both, one weakens the other.

53 *Post sermones vero quosdam lectos nullam sui mentionem habitam ita sit questus: irasci me tibi scito quod non in plerisque eiusmodi scriptis mecum potissimum loquaris. an vereris ne apud posteros infame tibi sit quod videaris familiaris nobis esse?* Suet. *Vita Horati.*

54 The pest's *invidia* is obvious enough. One should not, however, attempt to illustrate it by quoting v. 45 *nemo dexterius fortuna est usus*; for those words probably refer to Maecenas, not to Horace. Both v. 44 and v. 45 should then be given to the pest. The main arguments for this are presented by Lejay in his textual note. Cf. also K. Büchner, *Horaz* (Wiesbaden, 1962), pp. 113–24. I must therefore withdraw the remarks I made in *Phoenix*, XV (1961), 89, n. 37.

55 D. Daiches, *Critical Approaches to Literature* (London, 1959), p. 161. Daiches is discussing the theories of Robert Penn Warren.

CHAPTER IV

1 Suet. *De Gramm.* 2.

2 *Ibid.* 15. From Suetonius' words Bücheler conjectured that the original line ran *lastaurus lurco nebulo turpisque popino*; see his ed. of Petronius (Berlin, 1882), p. 243, n. 1. Cf. E. Fraenkel, *Eranos,* LIII (1955), 78.

3 Suet. *De Gramm.* 11.

4 *Ibid.* 14.

5 See F. Marx, *C. Lucilii Carminum Reliquiae,* I, lii–liii.

6 Varro, *RR* 3. 2. 17. Although Varro's context implies social criticism we cannot tell how censorious Abuccius' *libelli* were. The word *character* suggests style, not just tone. When discussing the characters of style Varro chose Lucilius as the representative of *gracilitas* (Gellius 6. 14. 6).

7 In *AJP,* LXXVI (1955), 165–75, I argued that *Sat.* 1. 4 was prompted in part at least by charges of malice arising from 1. 2. I still think that such evidence as there is favours this view and that the burden of proof rests on those who believe with Hendrickson that 1. 4 is just 'a criticism of literary theory put concretely'. There must be more doubt, however, on the question whether at this stage Horace had also been criticized for reasons of style. In any case the important point is that the satire belongs to a real polemical context.

8 The opposite view, namely that Horace is contrasting the 'true poetry' of Old Comedy with the non-poetic satire of Lucilius, is advanced by G. L. Hendrickson in *AJP,* XXI (1900), 125–30. For a more detailed argument on this point see *CQ,* n.s. V (1955), 154–6.

9 See *Mnem.* s. 4, X (1957), 319–21.

10 See T. Frank, *Catullus and Horace* (New York, 1928), p. 161; A. Y. Campbell, *Horace. A New Interpretation* (London, 1924), pp. 65–6, 152; J. Wight Duff, *Lit. Hist. of Rome* (London, 1960), p. 174.

11 F. Leo, *Hermes,* XXIV (1889), 75 ff. Cf. Heinze's note on *omnis pendet.*

12 Cf. C. O. Brink in Fondation Hardt, *Entretiens,* IX (1962), 175–200.

13 So G. L. Hendrickson, *AJP,* XXI (1900), 131.

14 So T. Frank, *AJP,* XLVI (1925), 72–4.

15 The foregoing arguments are set out more fully in *CQ,* n.s. V (1955), 142–8. In that article, however, I went too far in saying that 'this poem must be studied primarily in terms of contemporary feuds' (148).

16 Cf. *Mnem.* s. 4, X (1957), 325–32.

17 In this context *res* refers more naturally to Lucilius' subject-matter than to the circumstances of his time. (In 1. 2. 76, the first passage cited by Heinze, there is no problem, for *res* cannot be anything *other* than circumstances. In Heinze's second passage, Quint. 10. 1. 97, *res* does not occur at all.) This view also gives a neater line of argument: 'Whether Lucilius' rough-

ness was due to his nature or to his subjects, he would have to write more smoothly if he were alive today.'

18   See *Phoenix*, XIV (1960), 36–44.

19   Useful material will be found in Fiske, chh. 2 and 3, and in Mary A. Grant's monograph on 'Ancient Rhetorical Theories of the Laughable' in *Univ. Wisconsin Stud. Lang. and Lit.* XXI (1924).

20   Aristotle, *NE* 4. 1128A.

21   For a survey of the theories of Philodemus see now G. M. A. Grube, *The Greek and Roman Critics* (London, 1965), ch. 12.

22   Porphyrion on *Epist.* 1. 19. 34.

23   See Marx's grammatical index under *compositio verborum*.

24   A useful and up-to-date investigation of Lucilius' language will be found in I. Mariotti, *Studi Luciliani* (Firenze, 1960); for a recent survey of the *sermo cotidianus* in Horace see D. Bo, Q. *Flacci Opera* (Paravia, 1960), III, 335–50. The older study by J. Bourciez, *Le Sermo cotidianus dans les satires d'Horace* (Paris, 1927), is still of value.

25   D. Bo, *op. cit.* pp. 58–62. Bo's calculations include the *Epistles* and *Ars Poetica*.

26   Siedow's figures are cited by N.-O. Nilsson, *Metrische Stildifferenzen in den Satiren des Horaz* (Uppsala, 1952), p. 8.

27   Sturtevant–Kent cited by Nilsson, *op. cit.* p. 12.

28   The elision of a long vowel before a short syllable accounts for 4·8 per cent of Lucilius' elisions, 2·9 per cent of Horace's in Book 1, 4·3 per cent in Book 2 (Nilsson, *op. cit.* p. 15). On five occasions Lucilius elides the last vowel of a cretic word before a short syllable, e.g. *asperi Athones* (W. 105); see Marx's metrical index under *elisio*. There is only one case in Horace's first book, namely *tantuli eget* (1. 1. 59); see Nilsson, *op. cit.* pp. 26–7. In *occupo at ille* (1. 9. 6) the -o was short. Lucilius elides an opening monosyllable six times in seven hundred hexameters (i.e. 1 in 117), Horace seven times in 1030 (i.e. 1 in 147). In Book 2 Horace's rate drops to 2 in 1083 (i.e. 1 in about 540). Lucilius used a few types of synizesis usually avoided by Horace, in particular *ui* as in *fuïsse* (5 times) and *ec* as in *ēodem* (3 times). For instances in Horace see Bo, *op. cit.* pp. 81–2. According to Braum's figures quoted by Nilsson (*op. cit.* pp. 86–7) Lucilius has a monosyllable just before the main caesura in the third foot three times more often than Horace in Book 1. There seems to be no significant difference in regard to hiatus or tmesis.

29   There is a slip at this point in Heinze's calculations (p. xlii of his edition). Heinze's is the best short survey of the metre of the *Satires*; I have omitted many of the features noted by him, because they did not seem to represent any significant contrast with the practice of Lucilius. Nilsson (*op. cit.* pp. 114–15) points out that final monosyllables in Horace drop from 119 cases in Book 1 to 83 in Book 2. I was unable to consult J. Hellegouarc'h, *Le Monosyllabe dans l'hexamètre latin* (Paris, 1964).

30 Traces of another *recusatio* have been found in W. 1008–15. See Cichorius, pp. 183–92.

31 L. A. Mackay, *CR*, n.s. XIII (1963), 264–5, maintains that the Ennian line is not a hexameter but an incomplete trochaic septenarius.

32 Cic. *Tusc. Disp.* 1. 107.

33 Gellius 17. 21. 49. Cf. *Vita Persi* 50–5.

34 Porphyrion's note on 1. 10. 53.

35 The demagogue is described in W. 273–4:

> haec, inquam, rudet ex rostris atque heiulitabit
> concursans veluti Ancarius[?] clareque quiritans.

> This, I say, he will keep yelling and roaring from the platform, rushing up and down like Ancarius and making loud appeals.

36 Other examples are *drachma* (2. 7. 43), *lasanum* and *oenophorum* (1. 6. 109).

37 *Naumachia, petaurum, trigon, stadium, gymnasium, schema* and (figuratively) *palaestra*.

38 Cf. Archestratus—ἰχθύος..., ὃν ἐν μέτρῳ οὐ θέμις εἰπεῖν—'a fish which cannot be named in metre'—quoted in Athenaeus 7. 284e.

39 In the sphere of medicine Horace has *cardiacus, cheragra, collyrium, helleborus, lethargus,* and *podagra.* Lucilius has *apepsia, arthriticus, gangrena herpestica, icterus, mictyris, panacea, podagrosus.* Half of Horace's terms come from the satire on madness (2. 3). Lucilius may well have had many more than those quoted above; it is also probably due to chance that while Horace has two musical terms (*chorda* and *cithara*) Lucilius has none.

40 'Entremêlé aux mots de la langue nationale, le mot étranger déroute les indiscrets, établit entre les interlocuteurs une sorte de complicité, d'intimité; il réveille les souvenirs de l'adolescence studieuse, des voyages faits autrefois aux terres d'une civilisation plus brillante' (J. Perret, *Information littéraire*, III, 1951, 185).

41 This is the interpretation of N. Terzaghi, *Lucilio* (Torino, 1934), pp. 365–6. The hypothetical disyllable is parallel to *acoetin* and has a social not a physical meaning; therefore it is a word like *moecham*, πόρνην, or (in the figurative sense) *cunnum.* But after inviting us to supply our own word Lucilius unexpectedly and ironically supplies κούρην *eupatereiam.* To introduce Tyro, as some editors do, in the sixth line ruins the climax formed by *Helenam ipsam denique.* Nor does it help to transpose the lines, for then the missing disyllable would have to be something physical (Munro, *Journ. Phil.* VII, 1877, 308, suggests *lippam* and *fuscam*); but after using so many physical terms already why should Lucilius balk at another? The aposiopesis must carry a moral imputation, as in Juv. 8. 275 and Prop. 3. 6. 22. Also the list of blemishes *verrucam, naevum,* etc. should not be moved forward; they should form a climax with *alias* and *Helenam.*

42 I. Mariotti, *op. cit.* pp. 55–7.

43 The precise interpretation of these fragments is very difficult. It is likely, as Cichorius (p. 227) maintained, that the speaker was reflecting the old-fashioned Roman hostility to all things Greek. Lucilius himself probably allowed Greek terms in everyday speech in connexion with items of luxury but ridiculed their application to more mundane objects. So Mariotti, *op. cit.* p. 54.

44 See W. 1067–9.

45 G. L. Hendrickson's articles on Horace and Valerius Cato in *CP*, XI and XII (1916 and 1917), are still essential reading, though they contain a good deal of controversial material. For articles on the eight lines prefixed to 1. 10, which Hendrickson wrongly (I think) regarded as genuine, see E. Burck's appendix to Heinze's edition, p. 411.

46 These points all tell against the view (most recently advanced by J. Perret in his book *Horace*, Paris, 1959, p. 59) that *cantare* in 1. 10. 19 means 'to mock'. In 2. 1. 46 the verb (with strong aid from the context) refers to the lampooning of a living person. It never means 'to parody', and there is no parallel for its use in connexion with the dead.

47 R. P. Robinson, *TAPA*, LIV (1923), 109.

48 H. Bardon, *La Littérature latine inconnue* (Paris, 1952), pp. 338–9.

49 T. Frank, *AJP*, XLVI (1925), 74, n. 6.

50 The biographical material on all these men is collected and discussed by C. L. Neudling in *A Prosopography to Catullus* (Oxford, 1955). The monograph is no. 12 of the series *Iowa Stud. in Class. Phil.*

51 I do not know what Frank's source was for Pitholaus' eulogy of Pompey.

52 On the old problem of whether Horace's Furius is the Neoteric poet Furius Bibaculus the following points may be made. (1) The epic on Gaul alluded to in 1. 10. 36–7 and 2. 5. 40–1 was surely a contemporary work. Otherwise Horace's phrasing (*dum...dumque...haec ego ludo*) would be very strange and the gibe exceedingly weak. (2) The scholiasts both identify the author as Bibaculus. (3) We know from Macrobius (W. Morel, *Frag. Poet. Lat.* pp. 81–3) that a certain Furius wrote *Annales*. A Virgilian scholiast (Schol. Veron. *Aen.* 9. 379) speaks of *Annales Belli Gallici* and this could be what ps.-Acron on 2. 5. 41 refers to as *Pragmatia Belli Gallici*—a work which he ascribes to Bibaculus. On the other hand (1) we should not expect a Neoteric to have written an epic of this type, (2) at least two of the lines quoted by Macrobius have a decidedly archaic flavour, viz. *pressatur pede pes, mucro mucrone, viro vir* and *quod genus hoc hominum, Saturno sancte create?* (3) Furius Bibaculus, who is known to have abused Caesar and Augustus (Tac. *Ann.* 4. 34), would hardly have written an epic in Caesar's praise. Of the last three points (1) and (2) are not weakened by the precedent of Varro of Atax, for Varro almost certainly wrote his epic on the *Bellum Sequanicum* before he assumed the Neoteric style—see Else Hofmann, *Wien. Stud.* XLVI (1928), 159–76. Nor

NOTES

is there any parallel in the career of Virgil. So one turns without much confidence to the view that Horace's Furius was contemporary with but distinct from Bibaculus.

53 W. S. Anderson, *Univ. California Publ. Class. Phil.* XIX (1963), 63 ff.

54 In certain respects, e.g. his small output and careful craftsmanship, Horace was closer than Lucilius to Callimachus. All the main points of resemblance are stated with force and economy by F. Wehrli in 'Horaz und Kallimachos', *Museum Helveticum*, I (1944), 69–76. Some interesting comparisons are suggested by M. Puelma Piwonka in his large book *Lucilius und Kallimachos* (Frankfurt, 1949). It has to be said, however, that the author is sometimes reckless in his use of the fragments.

55 Lucilius may also have written lines of a homosexual character about the boys Gentius and Macedo, though we cannot be sure of the context. See Apuleius, *Apol.* 10. The fragments containing their names (W. 308–10) are by no means clear. In W. 308–9 Cichorius (p. 288) is probably right in reading *nunc, praetor, tuus est: meus, si discesseris horno, | Gentius.* 'Now, Praetor, Gentius is yours; but he will be mine if you depart this year.' If this is correct, then Donatus, who preserves the fragment in his note on Terence, *And.* 976, presumably meant *nunc...tuus est...Gentius* as a parallel to Terence's *tuus est nunc Chremes.* Warmington, more naturally, sees the parallel in *nunc praetor tuus est.* But this, unfortunately, makes no sense of the fragment. (Two minor points: Warmington was mistaken in attributing *discesserit* to Cichorius; Cichorius himself accidentally omitted the important comma after *praetor* on p. 287.)

56 Diomedes (*Gram. Lat.* I. 485. 11) mentions Lucilius, Catullus, Horace and Bibaculus as the chief iambic writers. Horace, of course, is included for his *Epodes*, not for his *Satires*.

57 It might perhaps be argued that the scholarly element in Lucilius was a further attraction to men like Cato, Hermogenes and Demetrius. The type of scholarship, however, associated with Neoteric poetry (and in particular with the poetry of Cinna) was rather different from what we find in Lucilius. The satirist showed little interest in obscure myths, remote places, esoteric cults, and elaborate genealogies.

58 See P. Sonnet, P–W, under Trebatius 2252–3.

59 L. R. Shero, *Univ. Wisconsin Stud. Lang. and Lit.* XV (1922), 155.

60 Juv. I. 77–8:

> quem patitur dormire nurus corruptor avarae,
> quem sponsae turpes et praetextatus adulter?

Who can sleep when his son's greedy wife is being seduced, when brides have no morals, and adolescents practise adultery?

On the subject of Horace's insomnia it is perhaps worth remarking that when he says *at nequeo dormire* he still has Trebatius' *quiescas* in his mind.

61 Heinze points out that Horace's father was not descended from the Roman colonists of Venusia but from some Lucanian or Apulian prisoner of war. No doubt this is historically correct and I accepted it in *Hermathena*, xc (1957), 48, n. 4. But it is better to assume that for dramatic purposes Horace is representing himself as a Venusian colonist protecting Roman territory.

62 Cf. Lejay, introd. to 2. 1, p. 295; Fiske, p. 377; Shero, *op. cit.* p. 157.

63 These points are listed in *AJP*, LXXVI (1955), 174.

64 For the libel law at Rome see R. E. Smith, *CQ*, n.s. 1 (1951), 169–79.

65 The double meaning of *diffindere* is untranslatable. It means to 'break off' or adjourn a meeting as well as to 'break off' something from what has just been said, i.e. to diminish its truth. As for the nut-cracking, I am perhaps over-interpreting. But Horace cannot have meant grit in a piece of bread or a stone in a soft fruit. Envy bites the surface, expecting it to be brittle, but instead finds it hard. Horace may have had in mind the fable of the viper and the file (Phaed. 4. 8), but the file is able to bite back, which is more than *solido* implies. P. H. L. Eggermont, *Mnem.* s. 3, x (1942), 69–76, thinks there is an allusion to the proverb *e nuce nucleum qui esse vult, frangit nucem*—'If you want to eat the kernel crack the shell'.

66 These poems have been compared by L. R. Shero, *op. cit.*, and more recently by E. J. Kenney, *Proc. Camb. Phil. Soc.* n.s. VIII (1962), 34–8.

67 See Cic. *Fam.* 7. 10. 2; 7. 22.

68 See E. Fraenkel, *JRS*, XLVII (1957), 66–70.

CHAPTER V

1 Keller's findings on the scholiasts are summarized in E. C. Wickham's edition (Oxford, 1877), I, xxi–xxiii.

2 See *Hermathena*, LXXXVII (1956), 52–60.

3 Certain aspects of this whole subject have been treated by Fr. Vogel, *Berl. Phil. Woch.* XXXVIII (1918), 404–6; W. Becher, *ibid.* LII (1932), 955–8; N. Terzaghi, *Arcadia*, IX–X (1932), 159–72; J. Marouzeau, *L'Ant. class.* IV (1935), 365 ff. The last general treatment to be published was that of A. Cartault in his *Étude sur les Satires d'Horace* (Paris, 1899). This work is still useful, but in his chapter on the names Cartault was apt to look for real individuals where none existed.

4 Crispinus 1. 1. 120, 1. 3. 139, 1. 4. 14, 2. 7. 45; Fabius 1. 1. 14, 1. 2. 134.

5 What we know of Sarmentus comes mainly from the scholiast's comment on Juv. 5. 3. It is all set out in Palmer's note on Hor. *Sat.* 1. 5. 52.

6 R. Syme, *Sallust* (California, 1964), pp. 281–2.

7 Cic. *Att.* 5. 8. 2. Fausta's twin brother was killed after Thapsus in 46 B.C. Her lover Villius is usually equated with the Sextus Villius mentioned in *Fam.* 2. 6. 1 (53 B.C.). Longarenus is unknown. Another of Fausta's

paramours, Pompeius Macula (Macrobius 2. 2. 9), was probably the man referred to in *Fam.* 6. 19. 1 (45 B.C.).

8 This is the traditional view; see Klebs in P–W, I, 1472, and Frank in *CQ*, XIV (1920), 160–2. Such an eminent contemporary, however, seems rather out of place in this satire.

9 An Albius is also mentioned in 1. 4. 28 as having a compulsive interest in bronzes. If he is identical with the *filius* of v. 109, then we have to believe that a man who nearly beggared himself by extravagance in his youth acquired a fortune large enough to support an expensive hobby. We also have to believe that Horace is referring to two different phases in the man's career. All this seems very unlikely. If the Albius of v. 28 is the father in v. 109, then he was dead; for the son is described as wasting his inheritance.

10 Cic. *Att.* 12. 33. 1; *Fam.* 7. 23. 2 and 3.

11 M. Antistius Labeo, the lawyer, is possible temperamentally but not chronologically, having been born *c.* 50 B.C. His father, who died at Philippi, is of the right age, but there is no evidence of any *insania*. The tribune C. Atinius Labeo committed an act of *insania*, but this took place in 131 B.C. Fraenkel, p. 89, suggestst hat we overcome this chronological difficulty by assuming that the name occurred in Lucilius.

12 He was alive in 52 B.C. (*Pro Mil.* 46), but dead before the *Brutus* was composed—i.e. before 46 B.C. (P–W, II, 1253 (Klebs)).

13 Staberius 2. 3. 84; Ummidius 1. 1. 95; Aristippus 2. 3. 100; Marsaeus 1. 2. 55.

14 Cic. *Fam.* 13. 11. 1, 12. 1 (P–W, no. 7).

15 Cic. *Att.* 13. 49, 50, 51; *Fam.* 7. 24. The evidence is summarized by Wickham in his introduction to *Sat.* 1. 3. I have distinguished the Sardinian Tigellius of 1. 2. 3 and 1. 3. 4 from the Hermogenes (Tigellius) mentioned in 1. 3. 129, 1. 4. 72, 1. 9. 25, 1. 10. 17–18, 80, 90. The two men were regarded as identical by the scholiasts and this opinion has been held in recent times by Münzer (P–W, VI, A1, 943–6), Ullman (*CP*, X, 1915, 270–96) and Fairclough (Loeb, p. 54). But since Kirchner many scholars have recognized two different men. Argument has centred on personal characteristics, on the names employed, on the relationship with Calvus, and on the question whether Hermogenes was alive or dead. Nothing can be proved under the first two headings; the traits and names could belong to one person but need not do so. As regards Calvus, we know that he ridiculed the Sardinian (*Sardi Tigelli putidum caput venit*), but according to 1. 10. 17–19 he was *admired* by Hermogenes and his friend (*nil praeter Calvum et doctus cantare Catullum*). The natural interpretation of this point is in favour of the separatists. Realizing this, Ullman wanted to take *cantare* either ironically or else in the sense of 'satirize' (*op. cit.* pp. 295–6). But, as we argued above (p. 289), *cantare* cannot be given a pejorative sense here. Fairclough, who purports to follow Ullman, translates it by 'dron-

ing', but this does not bring out the opposition required by Ullman, namely Horace–Calvus–Catullus–Atticists versus Lucilius–Tigellius–Asianists. We know that the Sardinian was dead. What about Hermogenes? He certainly appears to be alive, because his actions occur in the present tense, except at I. 10. 18, and there the verb is always taken as perfect rather than preterite. Again the unitarians have to provide another explanation, and they do not offer the same one. Münzer says that Hermogenes had become a type figure and could therefore be referred to in the present tense. Ullman regards Hermogenes as a very specific individual and would explain the tense in terms of expressions such as 'Horace tells us to enjoy our youth'. Münzer's is the more plausible theory (Ullman's idioms are not strictly analogous), and it must be tested by an examination of each passage. Now in I. 3. 129, I. 4. 72, and I. 9. 25 it is possible to substitute some general phrase for Hermogenes, e.g. 'a Hermogenes', or 'someone like Hermogenes'. But in the other passages this cannot be done so easily. In I. 10. 18 Hermogenes is associated with a particular ape (iste); in 80 he is closely connected with Fannius, and almost as closely with Demetrius and Pantilius. And if they are all banished from reality, the following lines with their references to Maecenas, Virgil, and the rest are gravely weakened. Finally, in 90–1 a general substitution of this kind is virtually impossible.

16 Vogel, *op. cit.*, points to the antithesis *Scaeva/dextera*. I should think, however, that *dextera* was put in on account of *Scaeva* rather than vice versa.

17 W. 1136–7. In 180 B.C., when Cato was buying land for the Basilica Porcia, Maenius sold his house, reserving the right to build a balcony on one of the columns of the new Basilica. K. Lehmann-Hartleben in *AJP*, LIX (1938), 280–90, rejects the evidence for an earlier column in honour of C. Maenius.

18 See Friedländer, *Roman Life and Manners*, IV, pp. 257–63 of the Eng. trans. by A. B. Gough (London, 1913). The other two names in the passage do not help us. Fulvius is common enough. Rutuba may be a significant name. Varro used *rutuba* in the sense of *perturbatio* (Non. 167.9); hence Marouzeau, *op. cit.* p. 374, renders Rutuba by *Le Grabuge*. All this proves nothing about the figure's reality. No one who saw 'The Brown Bomber' in action would have mistaken him for an abstract type.

19 This is the theory of Terzaghi, *op. cit.* pp. 165–6. He quotes the following note from the ps.-Acron, claiming that it preserves a genuine tradition:

Albucius, cum convivaretur, servis suis officia distribuebat et antequam aliquis eorum peccaret caedebat eos, dicens vereri se ne, cum parassent [sic], caedere illi non vacaret.

NOTES

When Albucius was giving a dinner-party he used to assign
duties to his slaves, and before any of them did anything wrong
he used to beat them, saying he was afraid that when they had
made preparations he would have no time to beat them later.

I do not know what authority there is for *parassent*. Hauthal's *peccarent*
gives better sense—'when they did something wrong he would have no
time etc.'.

20 W. 450–3.
21 See Cichorius, pp. 187 ff.
22 *Lucilio auctore* is a conjecture of Marx (1212 in his edition).
23 1. 1. 102; 1. 8. 11; 2. 1. 22; 2. 3. 175, 224; 2. 8. 23, 25, 60.
24 In W.'s translation, however, 'questioning him' appears to be a slip.
25 Housman, *CQ*, 1 (1907), 59.
26 Donatus, vol. II, P. Wessner (Teubner), p. 536. *Montane* was defended in
    both places by F. Leo in *Gött. Gel. Anz.* XI (1906), 843–4.
27 A. Cartault, *op. cit.* p. 288.
28 The occurrence of Lucilius in the ps.-Acron's comment on 2. 1. 22 makes
    no sense and must be a slip.
29 Fraenkel has suggested that Labeo (1. 3. 82) and Barrus the effeminate fop
    (1. 6. 30) may have figured in Lucilius (*Horace*, p. 89, and *Festschrift
    Reitzenstein*, 1931, p. 130, n. 1). Lejay thinks that Galba (1. 2. 46) may be
    connected with the Galba mentioned by Cicero in *De Orat.* 1. 239–40, and
    that Horace may have found the name in Lucilius. Terzaghi, *op. cit.*
    pp. 166–8, thinks that the Albius of 1. 4. 28 is the slow-witted man who is
    referred to by Cicero in *De Orat.* 2. 281 and who probably appeared in
    Lucilius. But *stupet aere* does not necessarily imply slowness of wit, and
    the identification is unconvincing on chronological grounds.
30 See W. 744.
31 Caprius and Sulcius (1. 4. 65 f. and 70) also present a problem. Rader-
    macher (*Wien. Stud.* LIII, 1935, 80 ff.) thinks (*a*) that the names suggest
    figs called *caper* and *sulca*—an inference from *caprificus* and Columella
    5. 10. 11; (*b*) that this in turn suggests the Greek συκο-φάντης, an informer
    (cf. Porph.'s note: *hi acerrimi delatores et causidici fuisse traduntur*); (*c*) that
    the names also hint at *caper* and *sulcus* (=*cunnus*). (*c*) is scarcely apposite.
    (*b*) is ingenious but somewhat far-fetched. It also depends on (*a*) which is
    by no means certain. I have not seen *caper* alone in this sense, and the
    reading at Columella 5. 10. 11 is doubtful. On the whole it is probably
    best to take the names as referring to contemporary lampoonists (see
    Ullman, *TAPA*, XLVIII, 1917, 117–19). This would be still more likely if
    we followed Fraenkel's suggestion (*Horace*, p. 127, n. 3) and read *Sulgius*.
32 Cic. *Att.* 2. 19. 3. The Roman audience was always on the look-out for a
    line which could be given a contemporary application. Cf. *Sest.* 57, 120.

294

NOTES

33 Stertinius 2. 3. 33; Furius 2. 5. 41; Philodemus 1. 2. 121.
34 *Greek Anth.* 5. 115. Cf. *Epig. ascribed to Martial,* 20. 5–6 (Demophiles).
35 Luscus 1. 5. 34; Nasidienus 2. 8. 1; Arellius 2. 6. 78; Gargonius 1. 2. 27; Scetanus 1. 4. 112. These suggestions are to be found in Palmer, p. xvi, and Marouzeau, *op. cit.*
36 Tantalus 1. 1. 68; Sisyphus 2. 3. 21; Agave 2. 3. 303; Orestes 2. 3. 133; Atrides 2. 3. 187 ff.; Ulysses 2. 5. 100; Ajax 2. 3. 187; Tiresias 2. 5. 1; Penelope 2. 5. 76; Helen 1. 3. 107. Tyndaridae (1. 1. 100) should also be included.
37 Dama 1. 6. 38; 2. 5. 18, 101; 2. 7. 54; Davus 1. 10. 40; 2. 5. 91; 2. 7. 2.
38 Apella 1. 5. 100.
39 *CP,* xv (1920), 393.
40 See Seneca, *Epist.* 114. 4 ff., and Mayor on Juv. 1. 66 and 12. 39.
41 Palmer (*Satires,* 5th ed. London, 1896), pp. 314 and 368.
42 Frank, *Class. Stud. presented to Capps* (Princeton, 1936), pp. 159 ff.
43 *Ibid.*; E. A. Hahn, *TAPA,* lxx (1939), 213 ff.
44 E. Courbaud, *Horace. Sa vie et sa pensée à l'époque des Épîtres* (Paris, 1914), p. 5, n. 2.
45 The quotations are taken respectively from Palmer, p. xii; Morris, p. 15 of the introduction to his edition (New York, 1909); Palmer, p. xii; Fiske, p. 370; Page, in his edition (London, 1901) of the *Odes,* p. xv; Hadas, *Hist. of Lat. Lit.* (New York, 1952), p. 167; Highet on *Satura* in the *Oxford Classical Dictionary*; Wilkins, *Roman Lit.* (London, 1890), p. 95; Palmer, p. xiii.
46 *Fest. Reitz.* pp. 119 ff.
47 See, for example, pp. 87–8, 101, 144, 152.
48 *Ibid.* p. 101, n. 2.
49 *Ibid.* p. 103; cf. *Fest. Reitz.* p. 130.
50 It is a short step from this to the not uncommon idea that what Horace took from Lucilius was not 'his own', and that the early poems did not really indicate his true 'self'. The violence and grossness of certain epodes are often excused by reference to the Greek iambic tradition or the harsh circumstances of the poet's life at that period—circumstances which are supposed to have goaded him into writing poems essentially alien to his nature. The ultimate stage in this approach is reached by Courbaud, *op. cit.* p. 21, according to whom neither epode, nor satire, nor ode provided the natural vehicle for Horace's genius; the epistle, it appears, was the only genre for which 'il fût réellement né'. One can only feel thankful that the poet discovered his proper *métier* before it was too late.
51 The quotations are taken respectively from *Horace,* pp. 144, 145; *Fest. Reitz.* p. 135 (das Stadium der Überreife eingetreten ist); *Horace,* p. 129.
52 Courbaud, *op. cit.* p. 11. Cf. on the same page the remark that 'une telle œuvre...n'est plus du tout une satire'.

53 G. L. Hendrickson, *AJP*, xviii (1897), 323. It should perhaps be added that *Epist.* 2. 2. 22 is the one place where Horace uses the word *epistula*.

54 That is the way the scholiast understood the lines; see O. Jahn's ed. of Persius (Lipsiae, 1843) p. 275).

55 The *turbes* has been disputed. Certainly the metaphor is far from clear. I take it, however, that *splendescat* is contrasted with *nigra rubigine*. This seems to indicate a difference of spirit. *Non alia cura* would suggest that the same pains had been taken over the style of both.

56 R. A. Brower, *Alexander Pope. The Poetry of Allusion* (Oxford, 1959), p. 184.

CHAPTER VI

1   Other collections containing ten (or a multiple of ten) pieces include Horace, *Epist.* 1, *Carm.* 2 and 3; Tibullus 1; Ovid, *Am.* 2.

2   E.g. Heinze, p. xxii. K. Büchner, who accepts Heinze's division in *Horaz* (Wiesbaden, 1962), p. 123, speaks of a movement from the heavy to the cheerful. This is true to the extent that the second trio contains one piece (5) which is lighter than anything in the first, and the third trio contains two pieces (7 and 8) which are lighter than anything in the second.

3   F. Boll, *Hermes*, xlviii (1913), 143–5.

4   A useful work of reference is J. André, *L'Alimentation et la cuisine à Rome* (Paris, 1961). For the living conditions of the Roman *plebs* see Z. Yavetz, *Latomus*, xvii (1958), 500–17.

5   Polybius 31. 25. 3 ff.; Pliny, *NH* 17. 244; Sallust, *Cat.* 10. 1, *Jug.* 41. 2. Cf. Velleius 2. 1. 1–2. On this whole question see D. C. Earl, *The Political Thought of Sallust* (Cambridge, 1961), chh. 1 and 4.

6   This view is based on Aristotle, *Pol.* 4. 11. 6–7.

7   See Tacitus, *Ann.* 3. 53 with Furneaux's note, and Suet. *Jul.* 43.

8   See Aulus Gellius 2. 24; Macrobius, *Sat.* 3. 17.

9   For a few more details about the *Lex Fannia* see Athenaeus 6. 274 c.

10 Suetonius, *Jul.* 43. For the sentiment compare Livy 34. 4. 14 and Tacitus, *Ann.* 3. 54 (*splendidissimo cuique exitium*).

11 Athenaeus 6. 274 E.

12 W. 1241, cf. Pliny, *NH* 10. 140. For a similar attitude to the Licinian law, cf. Lucilius W. 599.

13 The sturgeon was valued highly in the time of Gallonius, who was a contemporary of Lucilius. Although there is a favourable reference in Cic. *Tusc.* 3. 43, the fish seems to have become less fashionable towards the end of the Republic, and in the middle of the first century A.D. it had, according to the Elder Pliny (*NH* 9. 60), no reputation. By Martial's time, however, it appears to have recovered its former distinction (13. 91). The fortunes of the sturgeon can be followed in Macrobius, *Sat.* 3. 16—a passage which recent commentators on Horace have tended to ignore. (It may be noted, incidentally, that Macrobius and his source have confused the two Plinys.)

14 Palmer is surely right to take *acetum* as wine—cf. *Sat.* 2. 3. 116–17 and Persius 4. 32. This gives the sequence: sour wine (58), oil (59), oil (62), sour wine (62).

15 The most likely possibility is that he was C. Sempronius Rufus, for whom see P–W, Sempronius no. 79. Palmer is probably right in suggesting that the defeat which he suffered was in the elections for the consulship, not, as Porphyrion says, for the praetorship. It would surely be a feeble witticism to refer to the man anonymously as *praetorius* and to expect that people would remember that ten years earlier he had *failed* to become praetor.

16 Athenaeus 4. 157E. Cf. Teles 7–8, Dio Chrys. 6. 12.

17 The syntax of vv. 9–13 is certainly loose, but the following summary, based on Wickham, seems adequate: 'After a day's hunting or riding (or, if you prefer ball or the discus, play with them), in any case when exertion has given you an appetite then see if you can despise plain food.' There is a contrast between *fatigat* and *studio fallente laborem*. The man who likes Greek games may find the sports of the Roman army wearisome, but when he plays ball he forgets about the exertion in his keenness. The phrase *pete cedentem aera disco* with its vivid metaphor and its Greek words is far too good to lose. Gow (Cambridge, 1896) who, followed by Palmer (p. lxi), deletes v. 13 cannot make sense of the contrast between Roman and Greek mentioned above; he puts a strain on the tense of *fatigat*; and, as he realized himself, he brings *laborem* (12) too close to *labor* (14).

18 With vv. 98–9 cf. Plautus, *Pseud.* 88; with v. 77 cf. Terence, *Phorm.* 342; with v. 47 cf. Lucilius W. 203, 211.

19 The closest verbal parallel seems to be Plato (*Phaedo* 83 D), who says that every pain and pleasure nails the soul to the body.

20 I have assigned these words to Horace, for it would be too gross an infringement of character if Damasippus spoke about the incompleteness of his cure or called his new missionary zeal an ailment. *Esto ut libet* (31) means in effect 'I shan't argue with you about your cure'. This gives the impression that Horace himself is perfectly healthy, and so Damasippus hastens to disabuse him.

21 A. Nauck, *Trag. Graec. Frag.* (Lipsiae, 1926), Aesch. 225; Loeb, II, no. 121.

22 Cf. the use of *grex* in v. 44.

23 For the importance of the Stoic's beard as a sign of sternness and masculinity see A. C. van Geytenbeek, *Musonius Rufus and the Greek Diatribe*, Eng. trans. by B. L. Hijmans (Utrecht, 1963), pp. 119 f.

24 This was called antiphrasis (see Lucilius W. 1174).

25 In printing v. 317 question marks are in order but surely quotes are not.

26 The reading in v. 318 must be *num tantum*, for we need a more urgent repetition of *num tantum* (*magna*) in the previous line. In connexion with this fable I have sometimes wondered whether Horace got the idea

(consciously or otherwise) from Maecenas' seal, which represented a frog (Pliny, *NH* 37. 10). The roles, of course, had to be reversed.

27 B. E. Perry, *Studium Generale*, XII (1959), 17 ff. Cf. the same author's previous article in *TAPA*, LXXI (1940), 391–419.

28 Cf. Menander, *Dysc.* 81 ff.; Plautus, *Capt.* 593, 600, 602; Plutarch, *Pomp.* 36; and perhaps Aristophanes, *Vesp.* 1491 (reading βαλλήσεις). The examples are taken from A. O'Brien-Moore, *Madness in Ancient Literature*, Diss. (Princeton, 1924), pp. 58–9.

29 According to B. L. Ullman in *CJ*, LII (1956), 197, it takes over three hours to dissolve a pearl in boiling acetic acid. If the pearl is pulverized, cold acid will dissolve it in ten minutes. Chemically the pearl would act as a rather expensive kind of Alka-Seltzer.

30 F. Schulz, *Classical Roman Law* (Oxford, 1951), p. 197.

31 This was laid down in the Twelve Tables, 5. 7 (Warmington, *Remains of Old Latin*, III, 450–3). For notes on the *cura furiosi* see F. De Zulueta, *The Institutes of Gaius* (Oxford, 1953), part 2, p. 52.

32 See, for example, *De Off.* 3. 95. For an account of *furiosus, insanus*, and other such words see the index of D. M. Paschall, 'The Vocabulary of Mental Aberration in Roman Comedy and Petronius', Supplement to *Language*, XV, no. 1 (1939) = Language Dissertation, no. 27.

33 Celsus 3. 18.

34 The U.S. Dispensatory, 25th ed. (1955), p. 1712.

35 See O'Brien-Moore, *op. cit.* pp. 20 ff.

36 In v. 197 Ajax imagines he is killing Ulysses. In Sophocles' version Ajax, believing that he has taken Ulysses prisoner, intends to flog him before killing him. There are extant two verses of a Roman tragedy:

> video video te. vive Ulixes, dum licet.
> oculis postremum lumen radiatum rape.

By suggesting that Ulysses' death is imminent these lines foreshadow Horace's reference and may, indeed, be its source. They are preserved by a combination of Cic. *Acad.* 2. 89 and *De Orat.* 3. 162, and in view of the contexts it seems almost certain that they belong to Ennius' *Ajax*. Yet they are not admitted by Vahlen, and they are attributed to an uncertain poet by Warmington (II, 610) and Klotz (*Scaen. Rom. Frag.* 1, 324). Varro, who says that Ajax thought he was killing Ulysses (*Eumenides* B. 125), is also un-Sophoclean, but unlike Horace he makes Ajax cut down trees and pigs instead of sheep.

37 This outline of the *Eumenides* is based on J. Vahlen, *In M. T. Varronis Sat. Menipp. Rel. Coniect.* (Lipsiae, 1858), pp. 168 ff. The fragments are found in B. 117–65.

38 Proverb v. 276 *ignem gladio scrutare*—'poke the fire with a sword'; fable v. 186—cunning fox imitates noble lion. Némethy (*Rh. Mus.* LXI, 1906,

139) refers to Halm, *Fabulae Aesopicae Collectae*, no. 41, but the resemblance is not very close. Myth vv. 71–3—Proteus.

39   Plato, *Euthydemus* 280 B; Aristotle, Frag. 56 (Rose), trans. by W. D. Ross, XII, 57.

40   Menander K. 624. Antiphanes 328 (Edmonds, II), Philemon 99 (Edmonds, III); Terence, *Heaut.* 196.

41   Phoenix, Knox Frag. 3. 7–8; Lucilius W. 583; Cato, ed. Jordan, p. 73; Plutarch, περὶ φιλοπλουτίας 525 (*Moralia*, vol. VII in the Loeb series); Epictetus, Frag. 2. Other references are given by Gerhard, *Phoenix von Kolophon*, pp. 113 ff. In his note on *Agamemnon*, v. 350, and in *Horace*, p. 138, n. 4, Fraenkel has collected a number of passages in which the enjoyment of one's present blessings forms part of a prayer.

42   I owe this and other points to M. J. McGann's B.Litt. Dissertation *Some Structural Devices in the Satires and Epistles of Horace* (Oxford, 1954).

43   One recalls that in the Peripatetic tradition a child did not count as a fully rational being.

44   Similarly no distinction is made between gluttony (γαστριμαργία) and gourmandise (ὀψοφαγία). Or, more precisely, the first includes the second.

45   See Cic. *Paradoxa Stoicorum* 5. This work is translated in the Loeb series after *De Oratore*, Book 3. For a comparison of Horace's treatment with that of Cicero see Lejay, pp. 541–2. In the Cynic–Stoic tradition the idea of the fool as a slave goes back to Diogenes (D.L. 6. 66) and Zeno (D.L. 7. 32–3). For other references see Lejay, pp. 539 ff.

46   One wonders whether the idea of crucifixion in v. 47 led to the metaphorical lashes (*verbera*) in v. 49, and whether the suggestion of driving (*acris...natura intendit*) had anything to do with the riding metaphor in v. 50.

47   The interpretation of vv. 64–7 is controversial. I would put a full stop after *superne* (64), for the *cum* clause is needed by vv. 66–7 if they are not to hang in the air. It is not needed by vv. 63–4, and indeed it is rather awkward to tack *mulier* (65) on to *illa* (63). The paraphrase indicates that I am inclined to follow Schütz in putting a query after *famam* (67), but this is not essential. As for the *furca* and the *dominus furens* in v. 66, I would agree with Lejay in giving them a figurative or psychological sense. For (1) Horace is primarily concerned with the psychological condition of the sinner. In vv. 56–61 the man is in a slavish condition *irrespective* of the mode of punishment or escape, and in v. 71, even though he has escaped, he is still a slave. (2) The same emphasis falls at the end of three other paragraphs, namely in 20, 82 and 94. (3) *Dominus furens* exactly suits lust as an irrational master; indeed we have *dominus* in this very sense in v. 93. The phrase is less suitable for the injured husband.

48   M. J. McGann, *CR*, VI (1956), 99.

49   Heinze on v. 95: 'Davus bleibt nicht im Schema der Argumentation', etc.

50 Cf. Cic. *Parad. Stoic.* 5. 34: *quid est enim libertas? potestas vivendi ut velis.*
51 For a lucid and readable discussion of freedom see M. Cranston, *Freedom. A New Analysis* (London, 1954). Interesting illustrations of the various theories of freedom and their perversions have been collected by Miss D. Fosdick, *What is Liberty?* (New York, 1939).
52 See, for example, *Sat.* 1. 6. 115–18; *Sat.* 2. 6. 63–4; *Carm.* 1. 20. 1–2; *Carm.* 1. 31. 15–16.

CHAPTER VII

1 Excerpts from Athenaeus 14. 660 E; Edmonds, III A, 252–5. My translation is based on Edmonds' at a few points.
2 Sosipater in Ath. 9. 378; Edmonds, III A, 280–5. Nicomachus in Ath. 7. 290 E–291 D; Edmonds, III A, 266–9. Cf. Anaxippus in Ath. 9. 404 C; Edmonds, III A, 158–61. So too, in a later age, Brillat-Savarin was to insist that gastronomy involved natural history, physics, chemistry, cookery, commerce, and political economy (*Physiologie du goût*, Paris, n.d., p. 45). Of the many descriptions of culinary skill perhaps the cleverest comes in a scene from *The Foster-Brothers* of Damoxenus, in which the chef directs his staff like the conductor of an orchestra, blending all his dishes into a delightful harmony. The passage shows a verbal ingenuity which is seldom conceded to New Comedy (see Ath. 3. 102–3; Edmonds, III A, 214–15). The most recent and substantial account of comic cooks is by H. Dohm in *Zetemata*, XXXII (1964).
3 Hoffman's foreword to Brillat-Savarin, p. 2.
4 Ath. 9. 404 B; Edmonds, III A, 158–9.
5 Ath. 12. 516 D; Edmonds, II, 456–9.
6 Ath. 9. 379 D; Edmonds, III A, 270–1.
7 Ath. 7. 310 A.
8 Ath. 3. 111 f.; P. Brandt, *Corpusculum Poesis Epicae Graecae Ludibundae* (Leipzig, 1888), p. 141, no. 4.
9 Ath. 7. 286 A; Brandt, *op. cit.* p. 149, no. 21.
10 Ath. 7. 305 E; Brandt, *op. cit.* p. 147, no. 15.
11 Ath. 7. 316 A; Brandt, *op. cit.* p. 146, no. 14.
12 Morris Bishop, *A Bowl of Bishop* (New York, 1954), p. 1.
13 Apuleius, *Apology,* 39; *Remains of Old Latin* (Loeb), I, 408–11.
14 A. Gellius 6. 16.
15 A. Gellius, *ibid.*
16 A. Gellius 15. 19. 2.
17 For examples of such homilies see O. Hense, *Rh. Mus.* LXI (1906), 1–18.
18 *Geoponica* 20. 46. (The *Geoponica* consist of twenty books of Greek writings on agriculture, dating from various periods. They were collected by Cassianus Bassus of Bithynia in the tenth century A.D.) Another recipe,

from Gargilius Martialis 62, is cited by J. André, *L'Alimentation et la cuisine à Rome* (Paris, 1961), p. 198.

19 B. Flower and E. Rosenbaum, *The Roman Cookery Book* (London, 1958), p. 23. A new Teubner text is being prepared by Miss Mary Milham. It would be hard to imagine a work in which the textual critic had graver responsibilities.

20 P. Grimal and Th. Monod, *Rev. ét. anc.* LIV (1952), 27–38. The chief authority in English on this subject is T. H. Corcoran. See his article in *CJ*, LVIII (1963), 204–10.

21 'At 2. 4. 1 it is not sufficient to compare *Unde et quo Catius?* with phrases used at the beginning of certain Platonic dialogues. The answer of Catius *non est mihi tempus* (1)......*Platona* (3) should make it clear that this whole passage is an elegant transformation of the beginning of the *Phaedrus*' (Fraenkel, p. 136). Anyone who looks up the relevant passage of the *Phaedrus*, which extends over nine sections and has only a few points of similarity with the satire, may feel that Fraenkel is asking rather a lot of Horace's readers. There are similar questions at the beginning of the *Lysis*, the *Ion*, the *Protagoras*, and the *Menexenus*; and in the *Menexenus* Plato, like Horace, uses the third person. Furthermore, in the *Protagoras* Socrates is asked about the man he has just met 'Is he a citizen or a foreigner?' (309 C)—cf. *Sat.* 2. 4. 10 *Romanus an hospes*. In the *Theaetetus* (143 A) Eucleides tells how he took notes (ὑπομνήματα) of Socrates' conversation with Theaetetus and added to them from memory (ἀναμιμνῃσκόμενος)— cf. *Sat.* 2. 4. 2, 6, 8, 11. I should therefore prefer to take the allusion to Plato as a general one.

22 Fiske, p. 158.

23 Aristotle, *Hist. Anim.* 6. 2. 2; Antigonus, *Mirab.* 96; Columella 8. 5. 11; Pliny, *NH* 10. 145. Anyone interested in modern superstitions might inquire why an English housewife prefers brown eggs, while her North American counterpart insists on white.

24 Pliny, *NH* 23. 37, 38, 39, 46. Lucretius (6. 804–5) may testify to a belief that the smell of wine had a violent effect on a man suffering from fever (see Bailey's note). But Catius says nothing about fever.

25 Pliny, *NH* 14. 64.

26 Ath. 1. 26 D.

27 H. Warner Allen, *A History of Wine* (London, 1961), pp. 112–13.

28 Pliny, *NH* 23. 35. To the parallels cited by Lejay and Heinze add Servius on *Georg.* 2. 93.

29 In *NH* 22. 92–9 Pliny has quite a lot to say about mushrooms. Realizing that certain types may be dangerous he is careful to prescribe antidotes: 'Fungi are less harmful when cooked with soda—at least if they are well cooked. They are safer when cooked with meat or pearstalks. Pears too are helpful if taken immediately after them. The nature of vinegar is also

opposed to them and combats their effects.' On this cautious and well-intentioned passage Jones (Loeb trans.) comments 'Nearly everything Pliny says about toadstools and poisonous fungi is false, and his advice would lead to fatal results if followed'.

30 W. Clausen in *Phil. cvi* (1962), 205–6, would delete v. 32 as an interpolation.
31 Lejay, p. 453.
32 Cic. *Fam.* 9. 24. 3.
33 For Hippolochus and Lynceus see Athenaeus 3. 126 E and 4. 128–30 D.
34 For Heracleides see Gulick's index to the Loeb Athenaeus, vol. VII.
35 Josef Martin, *Symposion* (Paderborn, 1931).
36 For Matron see Ath. 4. 134 D–137 C; Brandt, *op. cit.* pp. 53–95.
37 See Cic. *Brut.* 160, 172, *De Orat.* 2. 244, 253, 281 f., *Planc.* 33, *Att.* 6. 3. 7, *Fam.* 9. 15. 2.
38 L. R. Shero, *CP*, XVIII (1923), 129–30. Shero (p. 133, n. 2) rightly rejects the theory of Fiske (pp. 384 and 411) that Lucilius wrote a banquet satire about Gallonius.
39 It is held, for example, by Palmer, Wickham, and Lejay.
40 Edict of Prices 4. 43.
41 Housman (*CQ*, VII, 1913, 28) took *maris expers* in the sense of 'emasculated', maintaining that Hydaspes was a negro and Alcon a eunuch. The need for a second adjective to balance *fuscus* is not so great as he makes out; the phrase *maris expers* in this context would surely suggest the Greek ἀθάλατ-τος, and in Persius 6. 39 it probably means 'insipid'.
42 Galen 10. 833 (Kühn); cf. 12. 839. According to Pliny, *NH* 14. 73 and 75, little or no salt was required in wines from Clazomenae, Lesbos, and Ephesus.
43 Warner Allen, *op. cit.* pp. 70–1.
44 Apicius 4. 2. 12. Apicius sometimes shows an appealing simplicity: 'You can make bad honey good for selling as follows: mix one part of bad honey with two parts of good' (1. 11. 2).
45 Cf. *Il.* 1. 6, *Aen.* 1. 753.
46 Cf. *Od.* 11. 43, *Il.* 7. 479.
47 W. 70.
48 The commentators point out that he was *pater cenae*.

CHAPTER VIII

1 See P. E. Corbett, *The Roman Law of Marriage* (Oxford, 1930), pp. 2–5, 51–7, 239–40; H. J. Roby, *Roman Private Law* (Cambridge, 1902), vol. I, book 2, chh. 4 and 12; H. F. Jolowicz, *Historical Introduction to the Study of Roman Law* (Cambridge, 1939), chh. 8 and 14.
2 See *Cambridge Ancient History*, IX, 781 ff.; and now J. P. V. D. Balsdon, *Roman Women* (London, 1962), ch. 2.

3　F. Schulz, *Classical Roman Law* (Oxford, 1951), p. 1c7. On the meaning of *humanitas* see the same author's *Principles of Roman Law* (Oxford, 1936), ch. 10. In his discussion of the falling birth rate Schulz also quotes para. 100 of the *Report of the Royal Commission on Population* (1949): 'The number of children tended to be limited also...because the fewer the children in the family the more could be spent on each child, and the better start it might have in life.' This is partly what H. Last had in mind when he spoke of the standard of living rising faster than people's incomes (*Cambridge Ancient History*, X, 437). Such considerations no doubt affected the rising middle class, but their influence on the really wealthy is less clear.

4　See, for example, Cic. *Phil.* 2. 40–1, *Att.* 1. 16. 10; Pliny, *Epist.* 8. 18; Plut. *Sulla* 38 and *Pomp.* 15.

5　F. von Woess, *Das römische Erbrecht und die Erbanwärter* (Berlin, 1911), lists the sources of our knowledge of the *Lex Voconia*.

6　See N. Lewis and M. Reinhold, *Roman Civilisation* (New York, 1955), II, 48–52, and *Cambridge Ancient History*, X, 441–56.

7　Many references are given in the notes of J. E. B. Mayor on Juv. 3. 129, 4. 19, and 12. 123. (A casual reader should be warned not to overlook Mayor's *Addenda*, which are printed in his first volume.)

8　Seneca, *De Consolatione ad Marciam*, 19. 2.

9　Tac. *Ann.* 15. 19.

10　L. Friedländer, *Roman Life and Manners under the Early Empire*, Eng. trans. by L. A. Magnus, I, pp. 213–16; S. Dill, *Roman Society from Nero to Marcus Aurelius* (reprinted by Meridian Library, New York, 1957), see index s.v. *captation*. Cf. *Cambridge Ancient History*, X, 438 f. The fullest treatment of the phenomenon is in the dissertation of D. Schmid, *Der Erbschleicher in der antiken Satire* (Tübingen, 1951).

11　Cf. Hom. *Od.* 20. 18.

12　Cf. such passages as Herodotus 1. 55 and 6. 77.

13　Juv. 4. 37–8. It should, of course, be remembered that Domitian was dead at the time of writing.

14　The emotional power of this rhetorical figure may be seen in *Epod.* 16. 3–10 and Virg. *Aen.* 2. 197–8. Notice also the spluttering plosives.

15　Quoted by Lejay on v. 76.

16　Ovid, *Am.* 1. 8. 43.

17　Horace's *captator* has many points of contact with the flatterer and the parasite as portrayed in Theophrastus and Graeco-Roman comedy. A large amount of comparative material on the flatterer will be found in O. Ribbeck, 'Kolax', *Abh. der Königl. Sächs. Ges. d. Wiss.* (Philologisch-Historische Classe 9 (Leipzig, 1883). See also R. G. Ussher's commentary on the *Characters* of Theophrastus (London, 1960), pp. 43–50. Within Horace's work reference may be made to *Sat.* 1. 9 and to those rather uncomfortable epistles 1. 17 and 1. 18.

18 Cf. Petronius, *Sat.* 116. What exactly is the relevance of the Nasica/ Coranus anecdote? Most editors think that its purpose was to instil caution. But if Ulysses was to avoid the fate of Nasica he should have been told where Nasica went wrong. This is not at all clear. Perhaps he should have contrived to see the will before handing over his daughter; but there is no indication of that in the text. Certainly in his reluctance to read the will (67) Nasica complied with one of Tiresias' own maxims (51–2). Or did Tiresias mean to suggest that even the best rules did not always guarantee success? Again there is no hint of this in the text. I suspect that strictly speaking there is no relevance, and that the tale was included simply because it was too piquant and too topical to be omitted. The absence of logical rigour is concealed by the oracular darkness of vv. 55–60.

19 Cf. Virg. *Ecl.* 7. 42; Hor. *Carm.* 3. 17. 10.

20 The proverbial expression is discussed by G. W. Williams in *CR*, n.s. IX (1959), 97–100. Passages concerning the behaviour of the ancient bitch are also collected by M. M. Gillies in the *Annals of Archaeology and Anthropology*, XIV, 51–4.

21 See W. B. Stanford, *The Ulysses Theme* (Oxford, 1954), pp. 96–100, and his references.

22 *Ibid.* pp. 121–7. The distinction between the use of example and the use of allegory is emphasized by J. Tate in *Eranos*, LI (1953), 14–22.

23 R. Hercher, *Epistolographi Graeci* (Paris, 1873), pp. 211–12.

24 A translation by H. G. Evelyn-White is to be found in the Loeb series, printed after the same scholar's rendering of Hesiod and the Homeric Hymns.

25 *Ibid.* pp. 536–9.

26 E. D. Phillips, *Greece and Rome*, n.s. VI (1959), 66.

27 E. Pfuhl, *Malerei und Zeichnung der Griechen*, II, 598. Illustration in III, 358, no. 800; or in *Enciclopedia Dell'Arte Antica*, III, 163.

28 E. Pfuhl, *op. cit.* III, 249, nos. 615 and 616; Jongkees and Verdenius, *Platenatlas Bij Homerus* (Haarlem, 1955), nos. 42 and 43; M. Bieber, *Die Denkmäler zum Theaterwesen im Altertum* (Berlin and Leipzig, 1920), pp. 154–5. Other caricatures of heroes will be found on the Phlyakes vases, reproduced in Bieber, pls. 76–86. See also A. D. Trendall, *Paestan Pottery* (London, 1936), esp. pp. 28–9 and fig. 13.

29 W. 565–6.

30 W. 567–73. For a discussion of this fragment see p. 113 above, and the accompanying note.

31 B. 471.

32 See G. Ettig, 'Acheruntica', *Leipz. St. z. Class. Phil.* XIII (1890), 251–410.

33 D.L. 9. 111. Cf. C. Wachsmuth, *Sillogr. Graec. Rel.* (1885), II, 39–40.

34 D.L. 6. 101. The pitiful remnants of Menippus are printed by A. Riese in the appendix to his edition of Varro (Leipzig, 1865).

35 Some of the characteristics of Menippus are mentioned in Lucian, *The Double Indictment*, 33.

36 B. 405–10, esp. 407. This interpretation was mentioned as a possibility by Vahlen in his *Conjectanea* (Leipzig, 1858), and was accepted by Lejay, *op. cit.* p. 476.

37 D.L. 2. 126. The ὄγκον is a conjecture of Diels.

38 D.L. 6. 18. Wachsmuth thinks that παντοφυῆ means 'protean'.

39 D.L. 7. 15. The words σμικρὸς ἐών are a conjecture of Diels.

40 Martial 8. 27; cf. 11. 67 and 12. 40.

41 W. Y. Sellar, *Horace and the Elegiac Poets* (Oxford, 1924), p. 70.

42 I have translated Housman's supplement.

CHAPTER IX

1 *Epist.* 2. 2. 46–7. The happy place was Athens, where Horace was a student.

2 Permanence is the main idea here: cf. Virg. *Ecl.* 7. 31; *Aen.* 6. 871; Hor. *Carm.* 2. 2. 22, *Epist.* 2. 2. 171–4.

3 Cf. Callimachus, *Aetia* 1. 23–4; Virg. *Ecl.* 6. 4–5.

4 *Praelambens* is often taken as an extension of *verniliter* (108) in the sense of 'furtively licking beforehand'. I prefer to follow those who see it as a straightforward continuation of *ipsis fungitur officiis*. The mouse is both a gracious host and a polite servant. His dignity ought not to be diminished at this point, otherwise the catastrophe is weakened. Also the parallels usually adduced, e.g. 1. 3. 81, are inexact, for they refer to dishes which are being taken away.

5 Cf. Pindar, Frags. 9 and 80 (Bowra). These and other examples are cited by Fraenkel, pp. 140 and 292–3.

6 For parallels see Fraenkel on *Agamemnon*, v. 160.

7 *Sat.* 2. 5. 32–3.

8 The Thracian Chick and the Arab were two gladiators.

9 R. A. Brower, *Alexander Pope. The Poetry of Allusion* (Oxford, 1959), p. 172.

10 See W. S. Maguinness, *Hermathena*, LI (1938), 29–48, and LII (1938), 27–46.

11 The qualifications which I have in mind are (a) the conviviality to which Horace invites his friends is usually a temporary relaxation from routine business, and is often limited to a particular festive occasion. Cf., for example, *Carm.* 4. 12. 26–8 with the exhortation of the city mouse in *Sat.* 2. 6. 95–7. In spite of the verbal similarity the spirit is quite different, and *part* of the difference consists in the *brevem* and the *loco* of the former passage. Or again, an ode like 1. 20 (*vile potabis*) is not a recommendation

that Maecenas should retire from public life. (*b*) The fare which Horace offers is not luxurious. He could never put on his invitation card the motto of the city mouse *in rebus iucundis vive beatus*. Food and drink make a relatively minor contribution to his convivial spirit. (*c*) The awareness of death varies considerably in intensity between, say, *Carm*. 3. 21 and *Carm*. 4. 12. Where this awareness is most intense the *carpe diem* mood is least Epicurean.

12 See Bailey's note on Lucretius 2. 20–33, and the passages cited there.

13 Lucretius 2. 29–33; cf. 5. 1392–1404.

14 The term is taken from A. O. Lovejoy and G. Boas, *Primitivism and Related Ideas* (Baltimore, 1935).

15 *Epodes* 7 and 16.

16 The material is presented very fully by J. Perret in *Les Origines de la légende troyenne de Rome* (Paris, 1942), but Perret's extreme scepticism does not carry conviction. See the reviews by P. Boyancé in *Rev. ét. anc.* XLV (1943), 275–90, and A. Momigliano in *JRS*, XXXV (1945), 99–104.

17 Suet. *Jul.* 6.

18 Philological Monographs of the APA, I (1931).

19 See Fraenkel, p. 137.

1 Quotations are from W. P. Ker's edition of the Essays (Oxford, 1926), II.

2 The fourth book, which contains the attack on Lyce, was published over fifteen years after the *Satires*. The same historical error is repeated on p. 101, where Dryden associates himself with Holyday's view that 'there was never such a fall as from his *Odes* to his *Satires*'. No doubt the mistake is largely due to the editors' habit of printing the *Odes* before the *Satires*. Another point of the same kind crops up in connexion with Persius. On p. 70 Dryden says that Persius' words 'are not everywhere well chosen, the purity of Latin being more corrupted than in the time of Juvenal, and consequently of Horace, who writ when the language was in the height of its perfection'. This seems to imply that Persius came after Juvenal, which is an odd mistake seeing that Persius died in A.D. 62—a date very close to Juvenal's birth. Presumably it is just a slip, for on p. 103 we are told that in treating only one main subject in each satire 'Juvenal...has chosen to follow the same method of Persius'.

3 *Epod.* 6 is aimed at a cowardly libeller. Cassius fearlessly denounced men and women of high rank (Tac. *Ann.* 1. 72). He died about A.D. 34, over sixty years after the poem was written.

4 Cf. E. J. Kenney, *Proc. Camb. Phil. Soc.* n.s. VIII (1962), 38.

5 E.g. the article on Horace in the *Oxford Classical Dictionary* says 'Horace's humour...is directed against...foibles rather than vices'.

6 P. 155.

7 W. S. Anderson reminds us that not all of Juvenal's satires are prompted by indignation—*CP*, LVII (1962), 145–60. I have made no distinction in this chapter between Juvenal the declaimer (or actor) and Juvenal the man, not because I believe that the two are always identical but because the whole question of the relation between biography and criticism is too difficult and controversial to open here. My opinions, such as they are, will be found in 'The Style and the Man', *Phoenix*, XVIII (1964), 216–31. As for Juvenal's biography, it is a pity that Highet's interesting reconstruction, which was suggested as a hypothesis in *TAPA* (1937), should have hardened into assertion in the course of *Juvenal the Satirist* (1954) and appeared as undoubted fact in *Poets in a Landscape* (1957). It has been accepted as an authentic record by Miss Mary Lascelles in *New Light on Dr Johnson*, ed. F. W. Hillis (Yale, 1959).

8 Cf. H. Gifford, *Rev. Eng. Stud.* VI (1955), 157–65; D. Eichholz, *Greece and Rome*, n.s. III (1956), 61–9; J. Butt and M. Lascelles in their contributions to *New Light on Dr Johnson*, ed. F. W. Hillis (Yale, 1959); and esp. H. A. Mason, in *Critical Esays on Roman Literature. Satire*, ed. J. P. Sullivan (London, 1963), pp. 107–23.

9 Zimri is chosen by Dryden himself as an example of fine raillery.

10 Macrobius 2. 4. 21.

11 *Epod.* 9 and *Carm.* 1. 37, which celebrate the defeat of a foreign enemy, fall outside the domain of *satura*.

12 See H. W. Pleket, *Mnem.* s. 4, XIV (1961), 296–315.

13 K. H. Waters, *Phoenix*, XVIII (1964), 76.

14 R. Syme, *Tacitus* (Oxford, 1958), II, 778.

15 E. J. Kenney, *op. cit.*, has some realistic remarks on this. His quotation of Quintilian 9. 2. 68 is particularly apt.

16 G. Highet, *Juvenal the Satirist* (Oxford, 1954), p. 51.

BIBLIOGRAPHICAL NOTE

Surveys of modern Horatian scholarship will be found in

L'Année Philologique.

K. Büchner, *Bursians Jahresberichte*, CCLXVII, 1939.

E. Burck, Bibliographical appendix to Kiessling–Heinze's commentary (Berlin, 1957), 353–413.

W. S. Anderson, *CW*, L (1956), 33–40, and *CW*, LVII (1964), 293–301.

E. Thummer, *Anzeiger für die Alterturnswissenschaft*, XV (1962), 129–50.

Works which proved of immediate assistance in preparing this book have been cited in the notes. The authors are mentioned in Index 2.

INDEXES

I. HORATIAN PASSAGES QUOTED OR REFERRED TO

Figures in bold type indicate the pages on which the main treatment will be found

INDEXES

2. NAMES AND TOPICS

Bold figures indicate the pages on which the main treatment will be found. Hyphens do not necessarily indicate continuous discussion. Names which occur only in chapter v have been omitted.

312

This is a critical and historical study of the *Satires*. Strangely—for the poems are often read and have influenced much later literature—this is the first book in English to examine them in depth.

The critical aspect of the study by Professor Rudd involves an analysis of the structure, thought-sequence and style of the *Satires*, and an appreciation of their varied tone. The historical element includes Horace's relationship to his predecessors—especially Lucilius. Professor Rudd shows how far Horatian satire continues a tradition, and how far it departs from it. He also examines the relationship with Horace's own life, and sets the poems in their social and historical context. This involves some exploration of interesting by-ways in Roman life. Professor Rudd also notes the literary influence of the *Satires*; he refers in passing to the English satirical writers, and there is an appendix on Dryden's *Essay on Satire*.

In short, this is a comprehensive introduction to the work and its setting, providing an interpretation for the student of Latin and other literatures (especially neo-classical writing in France and England). Professor Rudd provides lively modern translations of his longer quotations.

To Jonathan and Sherry,
Thanks for sharing this
with me. I hope you
enjoy the book!

also by Thomas M. Doerflinger

A VIGOROUS SPIRIT OF ENTERPRISE:
MERCHANTS AND ECONOMIC DEVELOPMENT
IN REVOLUTIONARY PHILADELPHIA

Risk and Reward

RISK
and
REWARD

Venture Capital
and the Making of
America's Great Industries

THOMAS M. DOERFLINGER
JACK L. RIVKIN

Random House 🏠 New York

Grateful acknowledgment is made to Harvard University Press for permission to reprint a map drawing from *Boston Capitalists and Western Railroads: A Study in the Nineteenth Century Railroad Investment Process,* by Arthur Johnson and Barry Supple. Reprinted by permission of the publisher, Harvard University Press.

Library of Congress Cataloging-in-Publication Data

Doerflinger, Thomas M.
Risk and reward.

Bibliography: p.
Includes index.
1. Venture capital—United States—History.
2. Capitalists and financiers—United States—History.
I. Rivkin, Jack L., 1940– . II. Title.
HG4963.D66   1987   332.6'78   86-10107
ISBN 0-394-54929-5

Manufactured in the United States of America
24689753
First Edition

TO TOM'S WIFE, JANET,
AND TO JACK'S FAMILY:
JANE, SUSAN, AND MICHAEL

Acknowledgments

We owe a major intellectual debt to our colleagues in the PaineWebber Equity Research Department, whose insights contributed much to the later chapters of the book. A special thanks to Margo Alexander, Director of Research, who suggested this collaboration and accommodated it for two long years. We are grateful to Peter Osnos for his valuable editorial advice. We are also grateful to Frederick R. Adler of Adler and Company; Harold Bigler of Crossroads Capital; J. W. Birkenstock; Christopher Brody of M. Warburg, Pincus and Company; Alfred D. Chandler of the Harvard Business School; David Costine, Max Charlet, F. Duffield Meyercord of Venturtech Management, Inc.; Hugh A. D'Andrade of the Schering-Plough Corporation; Angus Duthie of F. H. Prince and Company; Robert Garnet of AT&T; Edward Glassmeyer of Oak Investment Partners; Stanley Golder of Golder, Thoma, and Cressey; Robert F. Johnston of Johnston Associates; Eugene Kleiner of Kleiner, Perkins, Caufield, and Byers; Stanley Pratt of Venture Economics; Merlin Schulze of PaineWebber Ventures; Robert Swanson of Genentech; Don Valentine of Sequoia Partners; and Jonathan Warner of the Albert Einstein School of Medicine. We are also indebted to the staffs of the Columbia University Library System; the Eleutherian Mills-Hagley Foundation Historical Library; the Manuscript Room of Harvard Business School's Baker Library; the AT&T archives; the Brooklyn Business Library; the New-York Historical Society; the New York Public Library; the Princeton University Library; and the Charles Babbage Institute for the History of Information Processing. And our thanks as well to Cathy Tomasulo, Regina Taylor, and Jody Spallone for their valuable secretarial assistance.

Contents

Preface

As a journalist licensed to explain things I don't understand, I consider myself a beachcomber on the shores of other people's knowledge. No discovery is more to be treasured in the search than an account well written of how the world works—especially a world where I am a stranger. Venture capital, for example. I know that wondrous and terrible things happen in this world: empires rise and fall, fortunes are made or lost, nations grow rich and powerful, whole communities prosper or languish and wither away. The consequences of transactions in this strange world can be intensely personal to those of us who do not understand them—the quality of the tools of my trade, the speed and cost of the messages I send, the price of the shoes on my feet, the interest my savings earn—and most important, the shape of my children's future. If business is the engine of our economy, venture capital is the lubricant of business; without it, there is a shudder and rattle and a grinding to a halt, and one vehicle is hauled away to junk while another, nicely oiled, speeds into the lead. Think of the questions this race resolves: Whose ideas live or die? Whose dreams come true? Whose society flourishes with innovation and growth?

It seems self-evident that what air, light, and water are to our natural world, risk and reward are to capital. Yet how little we understand— the journalist especially—of the forces that drive the process. As Jack Rivkin and Thomas Doerflinger point out in their book, money may make the world go round, but smart money makes it go in very particular directions and at varying rates of speed, determining the winners and losers among individuals and nations. It is more critical than ever that we understand why and how this is so. The United States is losing its primacy in the world economy. Let me say that again, acknowledging that the authors say it more eloquently: The United States is losing its primacy in the world economy. Where and how we invest our money in what they call "the Fourth Industrial Revolution" is no abstract exercise. Nor is this book an airy meditation. Rivkin and Doerflinger have looked at American history: How did this company make it and how did that one flounder? They have drawn from their own considerable experience on the Street. And they have fashioned a work that is a pleasure to read and informative, too. Their knowledge is impressive, their writing is lucid, and the implications for our time and our country's future are there for all to see, stranger or not.

—Bill Moyers

Risk and Reward

1

Risk and Reward

At the close of the nineteenth century blue-ribbon delegations of English steel manufacturers frequently traveled to Pittsburgh, toured the mills of the grimy but prosperous city, and asked the local entrepreneurs probing questions. How, they wanted to know, did the American steelmakers manage to produce steel so damn cheaply? Why were they able to undersell British manufacturers who had the benefit of cheaper labor, more abundant capital, and greater experience? The reply of Andrew Carnegie and his colleagues was straightforward enough: more aggressive investment. Americans kept their plants up-to-date by installing the most modern equipment, pushing it mercilessly for a few years, and then replacing it with still better machinery. It was a prodigiously expensive strategy, to be sure. Perfectly good equipment was often scrapped because more technologically advanced machines were available. But by following this approach, the ambitious entrepreneurs who built their businesses on the banks of the Monongahela became low-cost producers of the ubiquitous metal. And America rapidly became the leader in the burgeoning world steel market. By failing to invest aggressively, the British lost out. As Carnegie triumphantly observed, "That is what is the matter with the British steel trade. Most British equipment is in use twenty years after it should have been scrapped. It is because you keep this used-up machinery that the United States is making you a back number."

Carnegie's remarks have special poignancy for Americans today because now the roles have shifted. We are the British, and the Japanese have assumed the position of the hard-charging Americans of the nineteenth century. A crowded island nation that is nearly bereft of natural resources—a nation that was shattered and impoverished just four decades ago—has vanquished U.S. corporations in market after market. First it was textiles, and then radios, television sets, steel, shipbuilding, automobiles, and semiconductors in rapid succession. There are many factors behind Japan's extraordinary success, but none is more important than the one singled out by Andrew Carnegie and his colleagues more than a century ago. Instead of maximizing short-term profits, the Japanese "overinvest" in the latest capital equipment; consequently their workers are more productive and their products are cheaper. There are, for example, more than twice as many robots at work in Japan as in the United States, even though the U.S. economy is far larger. Heavy investment in plant and equipment is one reason why Japanese semiconductor makers have managed to seize market share from U.S. companies, contributing to the consistently large U.S. trade deficit with Japan. And Japan is far from being our only formidable Far Eastern competitor; Taiwan, Korea, Hong Kong, and soon mainland China are also on the list.

Intensifying Far Eastern competition highlights a sobering historical fact often cited by the former governor of California Edmund G. ("Jerry") Brown. Throughout history, Brown points out, the nation that has led the world economy at the beginning of a new century has fallen behind by the end of that century. Since the Renaissance, Italy, Spain, the Netherlands, and Great Britain have each in turn achieved primacy in the world economy, only to fall behind a more disciplined and determined rival. Today it is the United States that is slipping, making room for the dynamic economies of the Pacific basin.

Against this historical background the central economic issue of the 1980s seems clear: How can the United States continue to remain a leader of the world economy? The answer is no less obvious: by dominating the high-growth, knowledge-intensive industries of the future. Computers, telecommunications, biotechnology, advanced material engineering, underseas mining, space colonization—these will be the battlefields of industrial warfare in the decades ahead. Because these are knowledge-intensive and capital-intensive rather than labor-intensive economic sectors, they are fields in which U.S. companies should be able to excel.

If the United States is to do this, it must invest effectively in the leading-edge industries. This is not as easy as it might seem because much more is involved than mere money. Simply pouring capital into high technology will not make the United States a world leader in electronics or biotechnology, any more than heavy spending on social programs quickly eliminated ghettos or heavy spending on defense necessarily makes the United States more militarily secure. As in decades past, what is needed to maintain America's competitive edge is *not just money, but smart money—money provided by people who understand pathbreaking technologies and, just as important, know how to use them to dominate world markets.* How should the United States proceed in order to ensure that the money spent on industrial innovation is smart money? What paths should be followed, and what pitfalls avoided? What are the appropriate roles of Washington and Wall Street? And how can individuals participate in the transition of the United States from commodity-oriented basic industry to the new industries of the twenty-first century? These are the central issues addressed in *Risk and Reward.*

THE USES OF HISTORY

Since these questions involve trends of the future, it might seem that the last place one would look for answers is in the past. Yet that is precisely what we have done in this book. To understand the best ways to grow the industries of the twenty-first century, we have begun by examining the way the great growth industries of the nineteenth and early twentieth centuries were financed and managed. For it is our conviction that many of the tensions and patterns that conditioned the development of the railroad and steel industries in the nineteenth century, for example, will reappear under a different guise in the years ahead. Take the matter of junk bonds, the low-grade, high-yielding bonds that T. Boone Pickens, Carl Icahn, and other corporate raiders have sold (or, more often, threatened to sell) in profusion to finance their attacks on such major corporations as Gulf Oil, Revlon, and TWA. In a recent meeting of an investment banking firm's Investment Policy Committee a securities analyst from its Fixed Income Department suggested that the junk bond phenomenon, though potentially troublesome because it reduces the quality of outstanding debt in the U.S. economy, was very difficult to analyze because it was completely unprecedented. In fact, however, junk bonds are anything but new. During the nineteenth century they were used extensively to finance construction of a very large proportion of the U.S. railroad system. Junk bonds were a lot better than nothing because they did get the job done. But as we will see in the chapter on railroads, their extensive use by financial gunslingers such as Jay Gould, Jay Cooke, and Daniel Drew contributed to the regular occurrence of deep depressions during the nineteenth century.

Most professional investors recognize that a firm grasp of historical trends is really indispensable to succeeding in the stock market. In the late summer of 1985, for example, many on Wall Street were bearish because the U.S. economy was depressed by the strong dollar and the huge U.S. trade deficit, making for poor corporate profits. How can stock prices rise, the bearish logic ran, if corporate profits are so disappointing? But investors who knew their economic history looked back to the 1950s and remembered that then, too, corporate profits grew slowly and yet stock prices more than tripled because inflation remained low and price/earnings (P/E) ratios expanded dramatically. Applying this lesson from the past, bulls remained fully invested during the summer of 1985 and profited from the dramatic rise in stock prices.

Historical analogies can be similarly valuable in understanding how the United States can better finance new industries. Professional economists conventionally chart the history of the U.S. economy with the concept of the business cycle. From the colonial period straight up to 1986 the typical pattern has been for an economic boom to be followed by faltering economic growth and finally a recession, which in turn was followed by economic recovery and eventually another boom. As these cycles unfold, they receive close scrutiny from economists because to them are tied such sensitive variables as unemployment, inflation, and interest rates. But observers who focus on the business cycle are in danger of missing the big picture. A different and in some respects better way to conceptualize U.S. economic history is as a *succession of industrial revolutions.* As the great economist Joseph Schumpeter first pointed out in the 1930s, economic history is marked by waves of "creative destruction." Every so often the matrix of large and mature industries that constitutes the backbone of the U.S. economy collapses in a painful upheaval, making way for a cadre of dynamic new industries.

By our count there have been no less than three such industrial revolutions in the history of the U.S. economy. In the First Industrial Revolution of 1815 to 1845 northeastern industrialists mechanized the production of textiles, shoes, and other consumer goods, which had previously been imported from Europe or produced by the village artisan. These factory-made goods were distributed to a fast-growing national market via canals, steamboats, and coastal trading vessels. But before 1845 or so the United States was still predominantly agricultural, and wood, rather than steel, was the primary building material. The Second Industrial Revolution, lasting from about 1840 to 1900, was the age of steel and steam—of the railroad magnate Cornelius Vanderbilt and the great ironmaster Andrew Carnegie. As they criss-crossed the landscape in chaotic profusion, railroads swiftly rendered many gigantic canals obsolete just a couple of decades after they had been built. This was the era when the entire U.S. economy began to take on an urban and industrial character—the time when modern corporations made their initial appearance and Chicago, St. Louis, Detroit, and other big cities mushroomed in the Midwest. During the Second Industrial Revolution booms and busts in railroad construction set the pace for the entire U.S. economy.

Toward the end of the nineteenth century a cluster of new technologies centered on electricity, modern chemistry, and the internal-combustion engine gradually ushered in the Third Industrial Revolution. After 1910 the railroad waned in importance as automobiles proliferated, but production of steel and energy continued to be a mainstay of the American economy until the 1970s. And today we are once again witnessing an industrial revolution, as such heavy industries as automobiles, steel, petroleum, and chemicals stagnate or shrink (much as the railroads did after 1910) while computers, telecommunications, biotechnology, and eventually space technologies give rise to an economy based on manipulating information rather than materials.

Clearly, then, the industrial transformation that we are witnessing today is nothing new; it has happened three times already. The future success of the U.S. economy hinges on its ability to participate successfully in this Fourth Industrial Revolution. The decline of the British economy during the late nineteenth century, for example, stemmed from its failure to master the key industries of the Third Industrial Revolution, particularly automobiles, chemicals, and electrical machinery. The importance of these leading-edge high-technology industries lies *not* primarily in direct creation of new jobs but rather in raising the efficiency of the entire economy—in accelerating the pace and increasing the precision of economic activity. This point bears emphasis, for in his latest book, *Innovation and Entrepreneurship*, Peter Drucker argues that the importance of high-tech industries is usually exaggerated because they create relatively few jobs. While admitting that high tech is qualitatively important because it "provides the excitement and the headlines," he emphasizes that "quantitatively . . . high tech is quite small still." Drucker's caveat strikes us as true but beside the point; job creation simply is not the best measure of an industry's importance. If it were, one would have to conclude that the "most important" industry of the nineteenth and early twentieth centuries was not railroads, or steel, or telephones, or automobiles, or electric utilities (each of which profoundly transformed many aspects of American economic and social life) but rather farming, which employed more people than all the rest of these industries combined. But of course, agriculture was not the most important because it did not hold the keys to the future competitiveness of the U.S. economy.

THE CRITICAL TASK: SUPPLYING SMART MONEY TO AMERICA'S INDUSTRIAL REVOLUTIONARIES

No nation can remain the leader of the world economy unless it *does* develop the leading-edge industries, and to make this critical transition, *capital must be intelligently shifted out of mature, low-technology industries and into high-technology enterprises.* In the 1980s that means shifting capital out of petroleum, steel, autos, chemicals, and textiles into semiconductors, telecommunications, computers, and biotechnology. To gain insights into how this difficult and delicate task can best be accomplished, *Risk and Reward* shows how six revolutionary industries that have transformed the U.S. economy since 1830—railroads, steel, telephones, automobiles, computers, and biotechnology—were financed in their early phase of rapid growth and development. It is a fascinating story, full of remarkable accomplishments by commanding figures in the history of American enterprise. It is also a profoundly important story for Americans to understand—important to the corporate executive, the financier, the stock market investor, and anyone else who is interested in the future of the U.S. economy. Yet despite its great importance, this is a question, surprisingly enough, that has received virtually no systematic analysis from either academic or popular writers. While there are dozens of books describing how individual industries have been financed, not one to our knowledge has examined the financial origins of many different industries in order to develop general insights into the process.

Although the six core chapters of the book each deal with a different industry, they all focus on the same essential process: *the fusion of ideas and money to create a thriving business in a revolutionary industry.* It is a process of cooperation between entrepreneurs and venture capitalists. Entrepreneurs provide the ideas, while venture capitalists furnish the money (either their own money or that of their clients). Together they can generate extraordinary wealth in just a few years. It is a complex, delicate, highly charged relationship because if either party to the venture lacks the requisite guts, brains, patience, and integrity, the new business will fail in a hurry. A venture capitalist who is greedy, impatient, or timid can impede or ruin the plans of even the most inspired entrepreneur. Many solid railroads were wrecked in the nineteenth century, for example, by Wall Street speculators and financiers, and Henry Ford's backers vociferously opposed the development of a small and inexpensive car, the Model T, which seemed certain to lose money. One of Alexander Graham Bell's financial supporters considered his experiments with the telephone a waste of time, warning, "While you are flying from one thing to another you may accidentally accomplish something but you probably will never perfect anything."

A central conclusion of our book is that, surprisingly enough, industrialists who are already running a successful business often are not very effective at financing dynamic young enterprises. This is a major problem for the U.S. economy, particularly because the early tax reforms of the Reagan administration greatly increased the amount of capital that large corporations were able to invest in new industries. One obvious reason for the phenomenon is simply that established business leaders have a vested interest in maintaining the status quo; in 1910 not many railroad executives were keen on backing a fledgling automaker whose very success would help make the passenger railroad superfluous. But there is actually a more subtle and important reason for this pattern: *Entrepreneurs, like other revolutionaries, are committed to a new way of thinking and acting that is alien to members of the business and financial establishment.* Entrepreneurs have a fresh perspective and novel skills, and typically they are clustered in a certain locality which becomes the intellectual and operational base of the new industry. For steel it was Pittsburgh, for autos it was Detroit, for computers it was Silicon Valley and Route 128, and for robotics it will be Ohio and Michigan. Here one finds a group of brilliant people who truly understand the new technology, are excited by its great potential, and are committed to seeing that potential fully realized in the marketplace. They possess a clear vision of the future that well-entrenched business or government interests simply do not have.

A case in point is raised by Peter Drucker, who describes how both UNIVAC and IBM, the two leading computer makers in the early

1950s, thought of the machines strictly as tools for scientists. "But then," he writes, "businesses began to buy this 'scientific marvel' for the most mundane of purposes, such as payroll. UNIVAC, which had the most advanced computer and the one most suitable for business uses, did not really want to 'demean' its scientific miracle by supplying business. But IBM, though equally surprised by the business demand for computers, responded immediately." The business utility of computers may well have been a surprise to the executives of IBM and UNIVAC, who at the time had had limited exposure to them. But our research in the unpublished business records of Eckert-Mauchly, the world's first computer company (which in 1950 sold out to Remington Rand, where it became the UNIVAC division), shows that the computer's applicability to routine business purposes was anything but a surprise to the real technical leaders of the computer revolution.

J. Presper Eckert, Jr., and John Mauchly were young University of Pennsylvania scientists who played a major role in developing a computer for the War Department during World War II. After the war they founded the Eckert-Mauchly Corporation to perfect a computer known as UNIVAC, which they planned to sell to corporations and government agencies. Although (or, perhaps, because) they were scientists who had limited business backgrounds, Eckert and Mauchly clearly understood from the outset the capacity of the computer to streamline the paperwork of bureaucracies as well as to "crunch numbers" for scientists. In 1948, a full six years before IBM shipped its first computer designed for business administration, Eckert-Mauchly salesmen visited a diverse array of bureaucratic organizations that might want a computer for payroll, billing, and the like, including the Veterans Administration, A. C. Nielsen, Prudential Insurance, Metropolitan Life, Western Electric (which was reported to be "thoroughly disgusted with IBM"), and several big banks. Having developed computers from the ground up, Eckert and Mauchly fully understood the computer's potential from the outset. They were many steps ahead of the executives at IBM, who were caught napping by UNIVAC.

Here lies the great dilemma of the American entrepreneur. Like the guerrilla leader who must feed his army by living off the existing economy, *the entrepreneur must obtain funds to sustain his enterprise from members of the business establishment—both established corporations and Wall Street bankers—who do not fully understand and support the new industry.* Financial power confers managerial power; by obtaining the financial support of these outside venture capitalists, an entrepreneur gives up some control of his project. He risks the danger that his financial allies will interfere with the successful operation of his fragile young company. Once again the computer industry provides a splendid example. Eckert-Mauchly ran out of money shortly before it could finish development of its UNIVAC computer, and the little company had to sell out to Remington Rand. But Remington Rand salesmen were much more interested in peddling typewriters and adding machines than the exotic and expensive "electronic brain" that customers had never seen before. Therefore, the UNIVAC division was neglected by Remington Rand's top executives, fell far behind IBM, and did not become profitable for many years.

Similar sad stories are to be found in the history of most of America's great growth industries; he who pays the piper very frequently calls for the wrong tune. But as we will see, the specific pattern of interaction between entrepreneurs and venture capitalists varies widely from one industry to the next, depending upon its capital intensity, the character of U.S. financial markets at the time, the decisions of a few key individuals, and a host of other factors. In general, the more capital-intensive an industry is (hence the more dependent it is on capital from outside sources), the more likely it is to be damaged by interference from venture capitalists. The best example is the railroads, which, as noted, were repeatedly raped by Wall Street. Alexander Graham Bell's telephone company was likewise damaged by excessive interference from financiers who were more interested in milking the company for current income than in reinvesting profits to maximize the long-term success of the company. The steel industry, by contrast, developed relatively smoothly because it was not much hindered by outside capitalists—until J. P. Morgan bought out Andrew Carnegie in 1901 to create U.S. Steel, a huge but mediocre conglomerate that smothered the spirit of excellence that had inspired Carnegie Steel.

As for the automobile industry, it was so fabulously profitable that many of the best companies in the industry had almost nothing to do with Wall Street bankers. The industry was so dependent on the technical skill and marketing savvy of Detroit's automotive aces that very few auto companies that *were* backed by Wall Street managed to thrive. For their part, many bankers considered the auto an expensive fad the chief economic significance of which was to reduce the credit-worthiness of the people who owned them.

In the computer industry what stands out most clearly is a remarkable David and Goliath pattern: A number of rich and technically proficient corporations, including GE, RCA, Exxon, and Xerox, entered the business and failed miserably, even as solitary entrepreneurs who started in the proverbial garage managed to create such mighty computer companies as Digital Equipment, Data General, Wang, and Hewlett-Packard. Because it takes so long to generate a profit in biotechnology, there is a real danger that this industry will not have nearly so many successful independent start-up companies as the computer or semiconductor industries. Most of the potential winners in biotech will have to sell out to huge chemical and pharmaceutical firms, which may smother the entrepreneurial spirit of the acquired companies much as Remington Rand did to Eckert-Mauchly. Indeed, the history of both the computer and biotechnology industries points up a troublesome feature of U.S. business that is too often ignored: From the standpoint of financing new industries, the billions of dollars held by America's largest corporations is frequently "dumb money" that produces meager results.

Fortunately the U.S. capital markets have developed since World War II a source of "smart money" that at least partly offsets the low IQ of corporate cash. Consider this contrast. In the late 1940s Eckert-Mauchly, though run by two outstanding computer pioneers, had to sell out to Remington Rand because it ran short of cash shortly before it could put UNIVAC on the market. Yet three decades later dozens of small biotechnology companies received ample funding even though they could not hope to ship a product—let alone generate a significant profit—for several years. This remarkable change was primarily caused by a quiet financial revolution that has created America's secret weapon in its battle for industrial competitiveness: the venture capital firm. A venture capital firm is simply a small partnership of financiers who take the money of outside investors and invest it in start-up companies. They review hundreds of proposals drafted by hopeful entrepreneurs, back a few of these would-be industrialists, and then provide not only the financial but intellectual, managerial, and moral support that the entrepreneurs need to succeed. The significance of the venture firm is that for the first time ever Wall Street is *systematically* seeking out promising entrepreneurs and supplying them with smart money.

One way to distill the insights of our historical survey is to delineate five different character types that make their appearance in new industries:

Entrepreneurs are the industrial revolutionaries who understand the technology and are genuinely committed to commercializing it. Their role in creating new industries is gigantic—bigger, in our judgment, than is often realized. Far from all being temperamental visionaries who have a hard time running a large business (in the manner of Apple Computer's Steven Jobs), a great many entrepreneurs, including Andrew Carnegie, Theodore Vail, Cornelius Vanderbilt, Henry Ford, Kenneth Olsen of Digital Equipment, and (one can anticipate) Robert Swanson of Genentech, have been highly successful corporate managers.

Venture capitalists are the people who give entrepreneurs the capital they need to get their enterprises off the ground. They must have a gut feel for what makes high-technology companies tick, and they need the patience and discipline to work with an entrepreneur over a long period of time to help a company grow. Not surprisingly, the best venture capitalists in America today are professionals, but highly accomplished independent businessmen have been just as good.

Financiers who make a living by "doing deals"—whether equity issues, mergers and acquisitions, leveraged buyouts, or whatever—do not make good venture capitalists because their time horizon is too short. They focus on generating particular transactions rather than on helping a company grow over a long period of time.

Stock market investors also tend to be poor venture capitalists because their time horizon is too short, their financial instincts too conservative, and their knowledge of high-tech industries too superficial. Accustomed to investing in companies that generate steady earnings and dividends, they are seldom comfortable making long-term bets on technology start-ups. Even William C. ("Billy") Durant, a kingpin of the early auto industry who was in love with "his baby," General Motors, became too mesmerized by the gyrations of the stock market to serve his company well.

Executives of large companies have a surprisingly difficult time financing small companies in innovative high-technology industry. The corporate culture, energy level, financial ambitions, and reaction time of large corporations, though often appropriate to the markets they serve, are ill suited to dynamic small enterprises.

KEY RECOMMENDATIONS

So the bottom line is this: The task of financing new industries in the United States is best left to insiders who really care about the long-term health of their industries. Financiers, speculators, portfolio managers, and executives of large companies often do not make a positive contribution, despite their best intentions. The same may be said of government bureaucrats, who have little familiarity with the problems of high-tech companies.

What lessons do these historical patterns hold for the future management of the U.S. economy? We believe that the United States is *already successfully developing novel technologies and creating the small start-up companies to commercialize them*. Thanks to a very effective three-way partnership between universities, the federal government, and private firms, the U.S. economy is the world leader at developing promising technologies. And thanks to the entrepreneurial character of American society and the existence of the venture capital industry, these new technologies quickly give rise to good small companies. Since this system of creating new technologies and start-up companies is not broken, it should not be fixed. For example, direct government involvement in the allocation of venture capital would be dangerous; history suggests that entrepreneurs should be allowed to flourish independent of interference from the financial establishment. An "industrial policy" to encourage industrial innovation is not needed and would probably work no better than Washington's discredited efforts to solve the "energy crisis" and stabilize farm incomes.

Where the U.S. system of financing new industries *does* need to be improved is in *the second stage of turning small companies into giant world-class corporations;* all too often the United States breeds promising new industries that our foreign competitors snatch up and commercialize on a large scale. We have to make sure that industries that germinate in U.S. laboratories do not achieve a sturdy maturity in overseas factories. Our research suggests that the U.S. companies most likely successfully to make this transition from the laboratory to the factory are independent but well-financed new companies, such as Digital Equipment, Hewlett-Packard, Data General, and Genentech, that are firmly focused on the new technology and run by people who grew up with this technology. Such firms typically fare better than divisions of conglomerates run by executives whose expertise and commitments lie in a more traditional economic sphere. From this observation flow three recommendations:

1. Corporate restructuring that, among other things, breaks up conglomerates and returns capital to shareholders is a beneficial phenomenon.

2.   Large corporations that do choose to invest in dynamic new industries should make sure that the employees in these divisions have plenty of operational autonomy, strong financial incentives to excel, and the opportunity to develop a distinctive corporate culture.

3.   The federal government should simply strive to make the entire U.S. economy internationally competitive—a responsibility that has too often been neglected. Among other things we need a balanced federal budget, a tax system that encourages rather than discourages personal saving, an assertive international trade policy that supports high-tech industries, and strong support for basic research and education.

Individual investors can play an important and rewarding role in keeping the United States on top by themselves investing in high-quality growth industries. While *Risk and Reward* is not another stock market manual, it contains, we believe, dozens of insights that will help investors identify good growth companies to invest in. Knowledge and self-discipline are the keys to success, much as they are for professional venture capitalists. Identify industries that will grow faster than the U.S. economy for a number of years, find the truly superior companies that are firmly focused on these growth industries, and then buy the stocks of those companies when Wall Street is bored with or frightened by them and is offering them at a discount. Although this advice is so simple as to sound platitudinous, surprisingly few investors actually follow it because they place too much emphasis on short-term swings in stock prices and far too little on the underlying quality of the companies they own.

There may be other lessons to draw from the experiences of the entrepreneurs and capitalists described in this book. We urge readers to reach their own conclusions. Understanding more about how the United States has created and grown its major new industries in the past and how that process can be improved today will help ensure that the United States remains the leader of the world economy.

II

Smart Money:
The Role of the Venture Capitalist

Who is attempting to finance new industries in the United States today? Personal savings, borrowings from friends and relatives, and mortgages on homes are still the major source of seed money used by entrepreneurs to start business ventures. But money from such sources does not go far, and entrepreneurs are quickly forced to seek financial backing from outsiders. While wealthy families and large corporations provide some of this risk capital directly, most of it is channeled to start-up companies through venture capital firms, a relatively new financial institution that came into existence after World War II. Its role is to seek out talented engineers, scientists, and business executives who have an idea for a promising new business and give them not just money but "smart money"—money that is imbued with the entrepreneurial savvy, business contacts, executive talent, and patience of financiers with long experience in helping small companies succeed. It stands in contrast with the "dumb money" to be found in the treasuries of many large corporations (which have a poor record of financing new industries) and of many Wall Street speculators and deal makers (who have short attention spans and a superficial understanding of American industry).

Although the *institution* of venture capital firms is relatively new, the *function* they perform is very old. So long as the United States has been developing new industries, it has needed capitalists to finance them. As we will see, this was the contribution made by the New England merchants who built the textile industry; by the Boston Brahmin John Murray Forbes when he shifted his attention from the China trade to western railroads; and by Andrew Carnegie when he combined his financial skills, executive ability, and intimate knowledge of the railroad market to create the greatest steel company in the world.

Though no strangers to speculation, these men were builders at heart. They preferred to take the long view in order to develop a business over a number of years, instead of grabbing quick gains in the stock market or the commodity pits. Nor were they merely well-connected financiers, like investment bankers Jay Cooke and J. P. Morgan, who were virtuosos at fixing deals on Wall Street and Capitol Hill but seldom stepped foot in factories and laboratories where corporate profits are actually generated. Like their forerunners of the nineteenth century, good venture capitalists immerse themselves in the details of the business. They do not merely stand above the fray, pulling strings and collecting fees.

Since professional venture capitalists systematically apply themselves to the task of financing new companies, this vital economic function is today carried out far more effectively than ever before. Indeed, it is not too much to say that venture capitalists are America's secret weapon in the battle to remain internationally competitive. "The threat from Japan is aimed at commodity products," notes one practitioner, "and the counterbalance has to be new and innovative products from new companies." Copious spending by the federal government (particularly the Pentagon and National Institutes of Health), together with the high quality of American universities and the constant immigration of talented foreigners into the country, make the United States the technological leader of the world. Venture firms are the financial catalysts that take ideas developed in universities and large corporations and turn them into small, profitable companies. Some of these companies make modest but meaningful contributions to the U.S. economy, others grow into powerful giants, and still others prod existing giants into rapid innovation (IBM's response to Apple Computer being the outstanding example). Dollar for dollar, the smart money of the venture capitalists contributes much, much more to the long-term health of the U.S. economy than the dumb and lazy money of mediocre corporations and complacent government bureaucracies.

BETTING ON PEOPLE AND PRODUCTS: THE CRAFT OF THE VENTURE CAPITALIST

The first venture capital firms were the investment arms of such super-rich American families as the Rockefellers, Whitneys, and Phippses. Instead of locking up all their capital in real estate and municipal bonds, they backed small and risky enterprises that stood a chance of prospering almost as mightily as the founders of the family fortune. Since they had more than enough money to pay the rent and did not need to impress clients, these families could afford to be patient and wait five to ten years before getting a payoff. But by the early 1950s private capital fell far short of meeting America's need for farsighted risk capital because investors were demoralized by the Great Depression, the New Deal, and the inflation of the 1940s. Instead of confidently moving to commercialize the technological breakthroughs of World War II, investors in the late forties were getting ready for the next depression, which was expected to hit the country once military spending wound down. To fill the gap, General Georges Doriot, a professor at the Harvard Business School, together with a few prominent members of the Boston financial community, established a firm called American Research and Development which financed a wide array of high-technology start-ups. ARD was followed by a few other firms, located mainly in Boston, New York, and California, and the venture capital industry grew slowly during the 1950s and early 1960s before expanding rapidly in Wall Street's go-go years of the late 1960s.

On the surface a venture capitalist's task is simple. He obtains capital from a group of investors—usually wealthy individuals or institutional investors such as pension funds or endowment funds—and establishes a fund of $10 million to $150 million. Then he reviews business plans submitted by prospective entrepreneurs, invests in a handful of the most likely candidates, and waits seven to ten years for these portfolio companies to turn a profit and move into their phase of rapid growth. At this point they are sold off either in a public offering on Wall Street or a private placement to a large corporation. After closing out the fund and distributing the profits to the three interested parties—the entrepreneurs, the investors, and himself—the venture capitalist retires or starts a new fund. The profit shares of the three parties vary with market conditions and the quality of the deal. In general, the investors get a 65 to 85 percent ownership share, and the entrepreneur gets a 15 to 35 percent share; the venture capitalists receive 20 percent of the investors' share of the profits as well as annual management fees amounting to 2 to 3 percent of the capital originally invested in the fund. In essence, then, venture capitalists spend most of their time doing one of three things: persuading individuals and institutions to invest in a fund, selecting entrepreneurs to back, and making sure that the portfolio companies actually turn a profit. Since all these activities are time-consuming, venture capitalists are very busy people. Airports are their homes away from home. They are at once salesmen, bankers, consultants, and corporate troubleshooters. They have to woo investors, wade through piles of tedious new business proposals, interview entrepreneurs, and visit companies throughout the country. And when a business does not perform as expected, they may have to take over the helm of a troubled company while fighting or firing the entrepreneur and attempting to calm the fears of investors.

The crowded schedules of venture capitalists limit the size of individual venture capital firms and, indeed, of the entire industry. Max Charlet, senior partner of Venturtech, puts it this way: Since the partners of a venture firm must cooperate on deals, the overall efficiency of the firm tends to drop as it grows larger than four partners. Each of these partners can comfortably handle no more than five or six portfolio companies at any given time, and each company initially needs $500,000 to $1.5 million to get off the ground. That means an individual partner can manage only about $5 million, and an entire firm about $20 million—peanuts by the standard of Wall Street, where individual portfolio managers may "run" stock portfolios of $1 or $2 billion. This is the problem with the smart money of the venture capitalist: It is calendar-constrained. Because he spends so much time with portfolio companies, he cannot leverage his talent by managing a larger and larger fund. In the stock market, for example, a good mutual fund manager may start with a smallish fund of $20 million, generate annual returns of 30 percent, quickly attract fresh funds, and in a few years find himself running a portfolio of $200 million, $300 million, or, in the spectacular case of one fund, $3 billion. The portfolio's rate of return is likely to decline as it grows larger, but the talented mutual fund manager will still be able to outperform most competitors by a significant margin. But time constraints make it physically impossible for venture firms to expand their operations in this way. To manage more money, they have to hire green M.B.A.'s from Harvard and Stanford; these rookies tend to be ineffective at the start, and as the firm grows in size, its overall efficiency and its rate of return decline.

The limited supply of talent explains why the venture capital industry handles relatively small amounts of capital; only about $4.5 billion was raised in 1983, a record year, even though thousands of talented entrepreneurs are not getting funded. The total pool of venture capital at the end of 1985 was $18.9 billion, or as much as the total assets of one moderately large bank. Over the long term the size of the venture industry will expand to fill the need, but in the meantime the venture industry is in the odd position of operating on the fringes of Wall Street. The players are smart, the compensation is high, and the rates of return are sometimes spectacular; but the scale of operations is limited. The tens of billions of dollars invested by giant insurance companies, bank trust departments, and corporate pension funds loom over the venture industry the way greater Los Angeles overshadows Beverly Hills. Venture capital is a rich and glamorous but still small corner of the investment universe. Corporate pension funds, for example, move into venture investing from time to time (almost invariably the wrong time), but they cannot operate on a large enough scale to have a significant impact on the overall performance of the fund.

Though they do many things, venture capitalists are first and foremost investors; their abiding preoccupation is where to put their clients' money. Investment styles, like sexual habits, are shaped by personal passions and predilections, making generalization difficult, but the seasoned perspective of a Max Charlet is a good place to begin. Since investing in small start-up companies is potentially risky, he argues, one must strive to "substitute knowledge and ability for risk. It's a lot like walking on a tightrope between the World Trade Center towers. It would be risky for me and you but not for a tightrope walker." Three variables must be carefully checked to minimize the risk of slipping from the tightrope: the product, the market, and the people. As for the product, "You have to understand it and know for sure that it will do what it is supposed to do and is on the forefront of activity. We have never missed on this." Secondly, "You have to know that there is a market for it and that your company can get a certain percentage of it. Basically, since sales determine rate of return on invested capital, you have to know for certain that the percentage of the market that you are likely to get is compatible with the desired rate of return and that you will not have to get a hundred percent of the market to get the needed rate of return." Furthermore, says Charlet, the market must be large enough so that the company's stock, if it is taken public, will command a high price/earnings ratio because growth potential is high. He notes that it is easier to get into a market that does not exist than to penetrate an established market. Careful research, supported by the work of outside consultants, should answer these questions; one should not miss on the market. Finally, there are the people. "This is where the skill is. And it's a people game. You have to bring to bear every aspect of psychology, human relations, business judgment. It touches every base I know. You have to get involved in things you'd never think you would get involved in. . . . You find that the management and especially the chief executive officers of small companies are perhaps the loneliest people on earth. They've got nobody to talk to. They normally don't talk to their board of directors because they don't want them to really know what is going on." Here is where most of the risk comes in. "You never really know whether an entrepreneur is up to the job until after you sign the check."

Venture capitalists disagree about which is more important to the success of a small company: the people or the product. The obvious answer is management, for any company will fail unless its leaders possess technological talent, demonic energy, and an ability to handle the myriad of irritating details that plague entrepreneurs. Venture capitalist Arthur Rock claims that "Nearly every mistake I've made has been because I picked the wrong people, not the wrong idea." J. H. Whitney's Benno Schmidt agrees, noting that "The best idea in the world can't succeed in a start-up without good management." But the fact is that good people are no panacea. "People will tell you that all you need is good management," says Fred Adler, "but that isn't true. You need the right product, too. Without the right product, you aren't going to be successful." The product defines a company's franchise; if it is no good, the enterprise is doomed. Adler has built a large fortune and a reputation for toughness by buying into troubled but technologically sound deals on the cheap and turning them around by replacing ineffective managers. "The quality of the product idea is more vital than the quality of the managers," he asserts. "You can replace poor managers. In fact, we had one situation where we went through four managements before finding the one that could make the company work. Happily, this doesn't happen very often."

Although this approach certainly works for Adler, most venture capitalists attempt to cultivate a more cordial relationship with their entrepreneur, along the lines of a long-term partnership. Many entrepreneurs cannot be axed because they have effective control of the company—either outright financial control or intellectual control of the firm's technology. A partner of a major New York venture firm says, "There's legal control, and there's practical control. And you can own twenty to twenty-five percent of a company, if you have a relationship of trust and respect with the entrepreneur, and even though he owns more than you, you can often prevail just by powers of persuasion. On the other hand, you can own sixty percent of the company, and the entrepreneur can own ten percent, and if the company's major asset is its technology and it's all in the head of the entrepreneur, you can throw away your legal agreements." (This capitalist notes: "The closer to the point in time when he's going to run out of money, probably the more useful one's powers of persuasion are.")

Though they might appear to hold great leverage because they have the cash, venture capitalists are actually dependent on the entrepreneurs who send them business plans. "We can't push on a string," notes one financier. Fortunately the United States has an extraordinary number of capable entrepreneurs—far more than any other nation on the globe and far more than it had fifteen years ago. "We see maybe eight hundred to nine hundred proposals a year, almost twice as much as two or three years ago," boasted one capitalist in 1981, "and they're all pretty good." Despite the rising volume of venture capital financing, observers are unanimous in the opinion that the number of good deals far outstrips the available funding. Deep social trends underlie this upsurge in entrepreneurship. The women's movement has had a profound effect both because many women become entrepreneurs and because members of two-earner households can rely on their spouses to pay the routine household bills if they decide to strike out on their own. The disaffection with big mainstream institutions—corporations, universities, government, the military—that erupted in violence during the late 1960s has had a similar effect. By setting up a health food co-op or leading the fight to push the ROTC off campus, a brainy mathematician could develop self-confidence and leadership skills in the late sixties that would come in handy when he tried to run a software company two decades later. "The big corporation was nirvana for a whole postwar generation," notes one business school professor. "There was an implicit faith and trust in these huge corporations. But that love affair with bigness and big business institutions blew apart during Vietnam." A third spur to entrepreneurship, so obvious that it is easy to overlook, is that the real income of Americans generally declined during the 1970s unless they were fortunate enough to receive an inflation-adjusted pension from the federal government. When baby boomers came of age financially, they faced a future pockmarked by high inflation, oil shortages, one-term presidents, and overall "limits to growth." Entrepreneurship offered a way out.

America's entrepreneurial efflorescence is a pervasive phenomenon, embracing high tech, low tech, and no tech. But since venture capitalists prefer high-tech businesses, they deal heavily with engineers who are refugees from large corporations. Many of these engineers worked on a new product for an extended period but failed to get the backing of top management, not because the project was a technological failure but because its economic potential was too small to have a meaningful impact on the corporate bottom line or perhaps did not fit into the overall corporate strategy. Rather than toss the idea into the intellectual trash bin after many months of hard work, ambitious engineers are tempted to commercialize the product on their own. Of course, financial incentives are important, too. Engineers are the creative guts of most large industrial companies, and they can become tired of paltry pay envelopes padded with the Confederate money of the industrial psychologist—"engraved letters from God, thank-you letters, and plaques." Thus high-tech companies in fast-changing industries are like microorganisms that reproduce by splitting off a bit of protoplasm to form a new cell. Digital Equipment was founded by someone who had worked with IBM, Data General was founded by alumni of Digital Equipment, and Convex was set up by alumni of Data General. No fewer than twenty-six companies were set up by former employees of Fairchild Semiconductor, making it the unofficial business school of the semiconductor industry.

The best of these renegade engineers are Henry Ford figures manning the high frontiers of technology, far ahead and above the competition—and their own bosses. Refusing to be bound by corporate strategic plans that were shaped less by technological imperatives than by considerations of today's business, finance, marketing, office politics, and the stock market, they may take technology in unimagined directions. A case in point is the Xerox Corporation's Palo Alto Research Center. In the early 1970s it began to produce pioneering technology that would become the foundation of a then-nonexistent machine, the microcomputer; when Xerox failed to put this technology to work, much of it migrated to smaller competitors, such as Apple Computer, Grid Systems, Microsoft, and Convergent Technologies. Xerox ignored the microcomputer because corporate dogma held that the "office of the future" would be an "integrated system" using workstations linked to a central mainframe—a field that Xerox and IBM, given their mammoth financial, technical, and marketing prowess, were destined to dominate. The microcomputer blindsided them both.

The dividing line between quitting one's job to start a company and actually stealing the technology of a former employer is exceedingly thin; some executives indict venture capital as "vulture capital" that disrupts the continuity of major corporate research programs. But on balance this phenomenon is a positive force for the U.S. economy. It multiplies the number of paths into the technological future, preventing big corporations with a vested interest in the status quo from quashing technological innovations. Moreover, it is an economically efficient system because more products are ultimately squeezed from the massive overhead and research and development (R&D) expenditures of large corporations. And it is healthy for corporations to know that they will lose their brightest, most ambitious people unless they give them ample creative scope.

Of course, technical creativity is just the first prerequisite for an entrepreneur. When they evaluate deals, venture capitalists are looking for winners, people who have the ability to focus all their talent and energy on one problem for an extended period of time, making great sacrifices to achieve a far-off goal. Since they cannot achieve the goal single-handedly, they should have leadership skills and good judgment. They must be supremely self-confident but able to recognize and address problems before they get out of hand, independent but willing to surround themselves with other strong people who will make a real contribution to the company's bottom line. They may well be eccentric characters, hard-driving egotists whose formidable creative energies surge through a narrow channel. Many are afflicted with "founderitis —these guys have egos that are so big they are tripping over them." They may not make the best dinner party guests, but their intensity and tenacity are just what is needed to get a product out the door fast. One capitalist brags, "We have a guy as the chief operating head of one of our companies—a Hungarian who spent two years in a Communist concentration camp in the 1950s. He just goes straight ahead, and nothing can stop him. If I had a hundred of him, I could sell him and stop investing in risky companies. That's how valuable he is." If these virtues are alloyed with vaulting egotism and a certain quirkiness, so be it; venture capitalists ask only that entrepreneurs know what they don't know, so that they will take advice along with the money. A computer programmer may have a great feel for the software market, but advertising and finance are likely to be another matter. Most Nobel prizewinners in biophysics probably would not know a subordinated debenture from a comic strip—although these days it can often be hard to tell the difference. This is where the venture capitalist can "add value" to the entrepreneurial process. He has the technological knowledge and the business experience needed to make a start-up succeed. "It is not an analytical thing, like picking a winning stock," cautions one practitioner. "You don't pick a winning company; you develop it." If the people and the product are the key players, the venture capitalist is the indispensable coach.

Because they accept very high risks by supporting start-ups, venture capitalists demand high potential rewards from the companies they support. For every ten investments, four or five go bankrupt, three or four break even or score minor successes, and only one is a big hit. That big hit must be hugely profitable because its profits have to be large enough to deliver a high return on investment for the capital invested in the *entire* portfolio. And even an overall portfolio return that any stock market investor would be proud of—say, 18 to 20 percent—is not high enough for venture capitalists because venture capital has many disadvantages over the stock market, notably the large investment of management time and the extra risks that go with committing capital for seven to ten years. Consequently they seek a very high potential rate of return in the deals they back: "What everybody wants to do is back a Seagate or a Digital Switch and make twenty or thirty times your money." A 25 percent growth rate was not good enough for one manager, who explained, as he strode back and forth in his corner office overlooking the Hudson River and midtown Manhattan, why one of his companies might have to be shaken up:

"It is growing twenty-five percent per year. It is very solid financially, with debt to equity ratio of fifty percent, a million dollars in cash, twenty million in sales, fourteen percent pretax margins. But it's not a home run. It's not even a triple or a double. A twenty-five percent, grower in our industry is not a great investment. . . . Venture capitalists don't like it. We just had a board meeting. And we informed [the chief executive] who had turned this company around:

" 'Let's go. Let's do something. Buy technology. Do whatever you have to do. Grow twenty-five percent, make fourteen percent! That is not what we are here for.'

"The guy's standing there with tears in his eyes. The guy says, 'I have done a great job.'

"And I say, 'Right, let's do better!' Now he's got the message. He's got ninety days. Ninety days to come up with something or we have to make changes."

. . .

The products that can achieve the supergrowth demanded by venture capitalists are overwhelmingly concentrated in high technology for three reasons: high growth rates, strong business franchises, and financial sex appeal. Good high-tech companies tend to have the same financial characteristics that we will encounter in the early auto companies: Brainy engineers, beginning with a relatively small amount of capital, can develop and assemble a new product, sell it in large quantities, and quickly generate a large cash flow that will finance further product development and expansion of the physical plant. The payoff is quick, the earnings growth rapid, and the initial investment relatively modest. In September 1979, for example, Apple Computer had shareholder equity of $9.7 million, and in 1980 the company raised $90.4 million in the stock market, for a total of $100.1 million. But in the three years ending September 1982 the company generated total profits of $112.4 million. To get this supergrowth, companies must have a unique product that occupies a profitable and protected niche in a fluid, fast-growing market, be it minicomputers, microcomputers, software, computer peripherals, or artificial intelligence. At any given time the venture industry focuses on two or three hot areas where technological breakthroughs are flowing thick and fast and word is sweeping through corporate and academic laboratories about Dr. X who struck it rich by selling his brain to a banker. Of course, other types of companies—specialty retailers, fast-food chains, personal-service firms—can also deliver fast growth and high profitability, and venture capitalists *do* back a certain number of low-tech deals.

As for smokestack industries, venture capitalists are fearful that "the business is going to be so capital-intensive that the dilution based on growth [i.e., expansion of the capital base] will take some of the fun out of your return." Disclaiming any high-tech bias, one Park Avenue capitalist said, "We have invested in some pretty basic and boring and unglamorous businesses. That doesn't bother us a bit. What we are looking for are attractive risk reward ratios for our partnership. . . . We did a leveraged buyout of a secondary lead smelter based somewhere in the South. The cash flow was nice, though. It actually helped revitalize the company. Talk about an unglamorous business. Turned out to be a very good deal." But this is very much the exception. When venture capitalists are looking for fast earnings growth, they prefer high tech because the competition appears to be less intense: "Anybody can start a service business, and the market risk is accordingly very high. On the other hand, a winning bet on a technology risk can lock in an exclusive market—and even create an entirely new industry."

Once venture capitalists have found a smart, aggressive, committed entrepreneur who seems to have a winning product, they do all they can to make certain that the new enterprise is a success. This is where they really earn their money. "Money is less than forty percent a factor of success," says one capitalist. "It is the talent that you bring as a group to help that company." This talent factor has an important bearing on just which venture firms end up backing a given start-up firm. Normally three or four venture firms will put money into the first round of financing. This spreads the risk of the venture among many firms, just as several merchant firms in eighteenth-century America would invest in a particular sloop in trade with the West Indies. A second factor fostering cooperation is that venture capitalists want a diversity of talents involved with the deal. Individual venture capitalists or venture firms tend to develop a special competence, and that competence is respected by others in a particular aspect of the business. In a typical comment one capitalist said of a partner, "Dave works on the numbers and the financing structure. I am the negotiator. What you really try to do is to work off each other's strengths. David can do everything I can do. He's good at it. He just does other things better, that I don't do." This specialization extends beyond individual firms. A partner in one firm may have special expertise in software development, while a partner at another firm is a marketing whiz, and a partner at a third is a financial expert. If you are backing a software company, you want all three sorts of expertise represented in the financing syndicate. "We don't invite other firms into our deals generally just because we need their money," says Christopher Brody of M. Warburg, Pincus and Company. "We often include them because they have some talent that is relevant to the deal that we don't have or because we think they will show us good deals that they find." As this last comment suggests, venture capitalists, like lawyers, investment bankers, and other professionals, form mutually supportive cliques. Particularly powerful and illustrious firms that attract good deals will cut their friends into the deal and in turn be brought into the good deals that their allies turn up. This is how the old, rich, and well-established firms—Adler and Company, J. H. Whitney, Venrock Associates, T.A. Associates—manage to stay on top. The influence of these firms is such that according to one authority, "It's very important to get the right people in the first round. If a respected firm backs a deal, the other venture capitalists follow like sheep."

Because their time is precious, "The venture capitalists do not want to control the company. They don't want to have to run it. That is not their business." Rather their mission is to place a start-up firm on the path to success and make sure it stays there. This means, among other things, starting with enough capital; entrepreneurs frequently underestimate the amount of money that they will need to commercialize an idea because they do not realize how many hazards can arise to delay the process. Equally important is assuring that the new company is properly staffed. Here is where the capitalists can easily make a mammoth contribution. As specialists in the business of building companies they have an array of contacts among professionals and managers who can be invaluable assets to a fledgling concern. *Fortune* editor Gene Bylinsky, author of one of the first and best books on the venture capital movement, quotes Chicago venture capitalist E. F. ("Ned") Heizer:

> Our job is first of all to see that every company is organized and staffed properly. See to it that they have the right auditing firm—and not only the right auditing firm but the right guy from the right auditing firm; that they have the right commercial bank, the right lawyer. See to it that they have all the professionals that they should have. We can do it much better than they can do themselves. We have contacts and know-how. Most entrepreneurs don't have the foggiest notion how to get the best bank or the best auditor—but we do. We can go to the top of Arthur Andersen and say that we need a top-flight guy. The same is true of law firms and banks. . . . We can get good operating executives with our contacts—this is an invaluable resource.

One of the great advantages that a start-up has over a big corporation is that it can attract superior employees and spur them on to tremendous productivity with the lure of stock options. If their employer prospers, so will they. And not in a small way. One engineer who joined Daisy Systems in his mid-twenties was able to buy, for two-tenths of a cent per share, stock that was worth $24 per share in a few years. His investment increased in value by a factor of 12,000. Given this appreciation potential, entrepreneurs are strongly tempted to hog all the equity for themselves, but venture capitalists resist such gluttony: "We demand that ownership is spread through management. You can't have one guy sitting in the company with all the equity. That just doesn't work. You have got to have everybody involved in the results." Nothing is new or profound about this philosophy. Andrew Carnegie took this approach in creating Carnegie Steel in the 1870s.

Ideally, venture capitalists will help the entrepreneur hone his business plan, while he helps him assemble his management team, and then make certain that it is followed in a disciplined and consistent way. One venture capitalist says, "We try to set milestones for each year, break them down into monthly or quarterly segments, and then check every month or quarter to see if they're making them. And in our own firm once a year we try to involve another partner who's got nothing to do with the deal, or at least nothing to do with the deal on a day-to-day basis, to take a fresh look at the whole thing." A good measure of management performance is whether or not the company is staying within budget. But venture people caution that a successful, rapidly growing company often gobbles up more capital than is expected: "When a company needs more money than you thought, there might be good reasons and there might be bad reasons. A company can need more money because its product is selling faster than you thought, and you need more money for working capital. It really depends what the reason is. . . . But a lot of successful companies may very well have overspent budget for good conscious reasons—decided to get more aggressive about fronting their marketing infrastructure, because they thought they had a product that would be hot and they wanted to get the critical mass."

For precisely this reason, most companies need several rounds of financing before they go public. As the company makes progress on its business plan and moves closer and closer to profitability, the value of the investment should rise, and the stock of the company can be sold for a higher price. Accordingly, "You try to sequence financings based on significant events that will let you do the next financing at a higher price. Product development, preproduct launch, there are a lot of checkpoints. Sometimes you miss a checkpoint; it doesn't mean that you have a bad company." Not all financing is equity-based; banks, insurance companies, and other institutional investors are called mezzanine financers because they come to make secured loans or equity financings in the later stages of the deal, after the company is up and running but before it has gone public.

THE TRIBULATIONS OF FASTCOMP

Despite the best efforts of financiers to build a solid start-up, things can go wrong—very, very wrong. So among all their other talents venture capitalists have to be effective crisis managers. They must be willing to singe their fingers to pull chestnuts out of the fire, for there really is no choice when the chestnuts are worth $2 million or $3 million apiece. To appreciate how intimately involved in the operations of a company venture capitalists can become—and how much at the mercy of the entrepreneur they may be—it is valuable to examine a specific example. Names and certain identifying details have been changed, but the circumstances are real.

FastComp, a small southern Arizona computer company, was founded in 1969 by an entrepreneur named Hoyt Wexler. For a time its minicomputer was the fastest in the world—hence the name. Wexler ran the company for several years out of his home. Cables crisscrossed his living room, and hardware sat in various stages of assembly in the dining area. The employees of the company became part of an extended family, sleeping at the house and using the pool on short breaks from their living room workstations. There were some very tough times. As Wexler recalls, "Neither my wife nor I took any salary during our roughest year. We literally had no money. Ann would actually go to swap meets on weekends with things from the house to get a few bucks to buy food. We did not turn the heat on that whole winter. Don't let anyone tell you southern Arizona winters can't be cold! We never had to worry about the machines overheating."

But Wexler's company survived the financial droughts, and by the late 1970s FastComp looked like a venture capitalist's dream. It sold an excellent product to the booming minicomputer market, and unlike many potential deals, it was not merely a dream and a prototype but a functioning company. All it needed was more capital that would allow it to finance an acceleration of production and sales. FastComp's founder took a first major step in this direction in 1980 by bringing in Walter David, a State Street money manager with a background in engineering and operations research. A longtime friend of Wexler and a member of FastComp's board of directors, David invested money in the company in 1979, moved his family from suburban Massachusetts to southern Arizona, and in March 1980 joined the corporate staff as vice-president—finance. At the time FastComp had just twenty employees and $2 million in sales; but sales were doubling every year, and its future was bright. The company needed capital to expand, so David began to raise funds from the venture capital community—starting with $300,000 obtained from Sam Duffield, a former neighbor in Massachusetts, who was a partner in TechCapital. With more capital required for continued product development, FastComp received a second round of venture capital financing in 1981, when a syndicate of prominent venture firms invested $2.5 million for 16 percent of the company.

FastComp had a fiscal year ending in March; its fourth quarter coincided with the first quarter of the calendar year. During the first three quarters of fiscal 1981 revenues and expenses were on budget, but because the company was growing fast, a disproportionate share of the year's earnings was expected to accrue in the first three months of 1982. There was only one problem with this plan: The U.S. economy was in a depression. To kill off inflation, Federal Reserve Chairman Paul Volcker kept his foot on the monetary brakes throughout 1981, raising the prime rate to 21.5 percent and FastComp's bank rate to a murderous 26.5 percent. Worse still, FastComp's customers were in trouble, and revenues were collapsing. In December 1981 sales were $1.4 million but in January were just $0.5 million, while the break-even point for revenues was $1.2 million.

That was the good news. The bad news was that the man who controlled the company, entrepreneur Hoyt Wexler, refused to trim sails as the company entered a financial hurricane. The reason: Wexler believed the downturn was temporary and that he could still achieve the ambitious goals laid out by the venture capitalists as a condition of their funding. In addition, Wexler had continued to manage the company "family style," just as he had during the hard times when his home was also the business location. His wife was in charge of credit and collections, and her desk was in Wexler's office much as it had been in their home. Moreover, Wexler had encouraged nepotism. For example, two brothers from India married to two sisters from Germany all worked in the plant. "There was a period when the nepotism worked for us," Wexler recollects. "The family thing and the interracial thing created a certain loyalty. In addition, because we were growing, I had never had to fire anyone except for a case of dishonesty."

For six important months in late 1981 FastComp's senior managers insisted that the staff had to be cut, but Wexler refused, believing that the economy would recover and that capital could be raised if needed.

Finally, in late January and again in February 1982, Wexler accepted 5 percent staff cuts. But the break-even point for sales was still a third higher than current revenues, making a financial crisis inevitable. One Saturday in early March 1982 Walt David called Sam Duffield in Massachusetts with a brief message: "We've got a big problem." Duffield called the other venture capitalists, boarded a plane, and arrived at the FastComp offices that Sunday afternoon. Walt David, Chief Operating Officer Willem Kicinski, and the venture capitalists quickly developed a plan to save the company. Its linchpin was a $1 million capital injection by the venture firms.

Wexler was asked to respond to the venture capitalists' plan in three days. Instead, he took ten days. As if to alienate his backers all the more, Wexler "shopped" their offer with other possible investors, hoping to land a better deal. As FastComp's cash steadily dribbled away, David carefully measured the process. Each morning he ran an elaborate computer program, modeling FastComp's cash flow, that produced four pages of results. The program not only generated cash flow projections but showed which suppliers to pay first and how much. There were more than 300 of them, including such big names as Advanced Micro Devices (to which $100,000 were owed), Control Data ($500,000), and Texas Instruments ($175,000). Some suppliers were nasty, and some were nice; but David was on intimate terms with all of them: "I would spend my time on the phone with suppliers. The secretaries knew who the critical suppliers were, and if they called, I always talked to them." With the national economy continuing to slide, interest rates skyrocketing, FastComp's bank credit line exhausted, and the suppliers beginning to snarl, another $1 million injection of venture capital offered the only escape from bankruptcy. After ten days of procrastination Wexler, David, and the other inside board member sat down to consider the offer and plot their next move. Wexler led off the meeting with a bombshell: "I am not going to accept their [the venture capitalists'] offer. I will reject it."

David: "You can't do this. You've got to reconsider. Hoyt, look at this cash flow. We can't make it without the new money."

Wexler: "I think we can make it."

David: "Hoyt, this is an interactive cash flow model. You can change the variables. What assumptions would you like to change?"

Wexler: "Well, I don't believe your model."

Everyone was silent until David said, "Hoyt, please do not finalize this decision. We aren't going to get anyone else to come in."

After another hour of discussion Wexler finally said, "OK, we'll think about it a little bit longer."

It was then, David later recalled, that "I believed Hoyt Wexler had lost his ability to be rational, realistic, and to make good judgments. It was a total surprise. He was a nice guy. Very analytical, very bright. I went back to my office. I felt that Hoyt had gone crazy. I knew we were in deep trouble." Crazy or not, Hoyt Wexler controlled the company because he owned more than 50 percent of the stock. He was in the odd but common position of holding his backers by the throat even as he slid into bankruptcy. Their money was sunk into a company which he controlled. Indeed, that is one reason why Wexler rejected the venture capitalists' cash: According to the terms of their offer, he would be diluted down to 25 percent of the company instead of 56 percent, while the venture capitalists went from 16 to 55 percent. "The venture capitalists offered to put in their million dollars at an outrageous price," Wexler says. "It triggered a condition in the original venture capital agreement that repriced the earlier investment and produced tremendous dilution. I wanted to see if we couldn't find some alternative way of raising money. This infuriated the vc's."

The spurned venture capitalists withdrew their offer, and Wexler started to look frantically for alternative sources of funding. His main hunting ground was FastComp's overseas customer base—not the sort of thing that bolsters an original equipment manufacturer's (OEM) confidence in the longevity of its hardware supplier. With the company still losing money in late March 1982, Wexler stopped coming to the office on a daily basis. In April Kicinski and David unilaterally fired 35 percent of the staff. The two executives were effectively running Wexler's company, trying to keep it afloat, but it was a bitter trial. David recalls, "I had trouble sleeping. I stopped drinking coffee, and that helped a little bit. The trouble with not sleeping is that you are always tired. Every element of the problem required attention. The creditor problem. We had employees who sued us because they got fired. Legal problems. Employees would steal things. The lawyers were there daily." The senior managers probably could not have saved the company except that they received vital support from the venture capitalists whose funds were at risk. As is often the case in the venture world, it was a team effort. One capitalist recalls how "Synvest brought in one of their partners, Westport brought in one of their partners, and everybody went to work. We really got a lot done. Well, the Synvest partner is the technical guy. Really knows a lot about that stuff. I am more on the management, business, cash flow side."

In the spring of 1982 FastComp's future was dark but not quite desperate. Kicinski and David cut costs so much that it was profitable in April, and despite the recession, the long-term trend of revenues was still clearly up. Meanwhile, Hoyt Wexler's search for capital was apparently bearing fruit: A major Belgian conglomerate in Brussels was interested in buying FastComp computers on a large scale and also providing some financing. But the financial situation of the company was still untenable. The venture capitalists decided to force the issue of new venture capital financing by calling a board meeting. Wexler agreed to attend, provided both the Brussels deal and the venture capitalists' offer were considered. David recalled that "famous board meeting on April the nineteenth. We started at two o'clock. We didn't break for dinner. The meeting ended at ten o'clock at night. The venture capitalists presented their proposal, and we went through the cash flow model to show what it would mean. Then Hoyt brought his documentation, which consisted of just a telex [from Brussels]. It said, 'We will consider the possibility of buying up to five hundred thousand dollars' worth of equipment. We will pay you in thirty days, and delivery will be in six months.' And an outside director said, 'Hoyt, this is not a proposal. It is just a discussion of what this guy might do.' Then Hoyt called a recess. He went into his office for two hours to call the guy in Belgium, who was eventually reached in Spain. Hoyt got him at four in the morning."

Then Wexler talked to all the inside directors and asked them what they thought. They agreed that the thing to do was to take the venture capital deal. David recalls, "Then Hoyt said, 'I think I am going to take the Brussels deal.' The problem was that it was not a deal. It took us into Chapter Eleven in seventy-two hours. I said, 'All the equity that we have all built up will be wiped out!' " Other insiders spoke up. After strenuously insisting that the ".Brussels deal" was superior, Wexler finally reversed himself and said he *would* vote to accept the venture capitalists' offer. "All the documents came the next day. All he had to do was to sign it. But he did not sign it for six days. We found out he spent those days negotiating with bankruptcy lawyers again. When he finally came in to sign, he said, 'I have one price. I want to fire Walt David.' Then he signed the papers. I was mad as hell."

When the money came in, the suppliers were paid off. David admits that it was not enough money. "We had to string them out for another six months. But we were turning a profit. We should have brought in more than a million dollars. It was not enough." Meanwhile, the venture capitalists on the board, who now had control of FastComp, countermanded the order that David be fired. This was hardly surprising, for David and the venture capitalists had been close allies in the battle with Wexler to salvage the company and preserve the investment. Here was a case where a company's problems overwhelmed its people, who were too entrenched to be easily removed by the financiers. The doctors were not allowed to amputate until the patient had gangrene. The whole process, however, did make the doctors part of the problem. "In retrospect," Wexler says, "the venture capitalists demanded, and we promised to deliver, too much. There was no room for error. I didn't see how we could achieve the revenues we had promised if we began laying off people. I don't think any of us expected the economy to be so bad for so long. If we were ever going to raise any more money, we had to meet those targets."

Wexler, while remaining the largest single shareholder, left the company. He is still an entrepreneur, running his own consulting firm and working with several southwestern computer peripheral firms. As for FastComp, it recovered under a new chief executive officer (CEO), a savvy, no-nonsense senior executive with twenty-two years of problem-solving experience with Burroughs and other smaller companies. In early 1986, a $15 million cash offer for the company was rejected by the shareholders. With revenues of over $20 million growing at 20 percent annually and profits approaching $2 million, the company is now considering whether to go public. If the $15 million had been accepted, Hoyt Wexler and his family would have received $3 million for their holdings and the venture capitalists would have earned a solid 18 percent plus annual return on their money—not particularly good by venture capitalists' standards but a lot better than the financial wipeout that seemed imminent in the dark days of 1981.

But if the capitalists were disappointed by the financial return from FastComp, they still performed an invaluable function for the national economy. By doling out smart money to the enterprise in modest quantities and then investing massive amounts of time and energy at a critical juncture, they ensured the survival of a company that today employs several hundred people and enhances the productivity of its customers. No earlier financial institution in American economic history performed this function in such a *systematic* and *effective* way. Chapter VI will show that if the venture capital industry had existed in 1876, Alexander Graham Bell could have teamed up with hard-charging capitalists who would have retained Theodore Vail as president—instead of selling out to passive, coupon-clipping capitalists who milked the business rather than build it. If they had existed in 1903, Henry Ford would not have had to get funding from an erratic coal dealer who nearly ruined the Ford Motor Company in a power struggle. And if the venture capital system had been well developed in the 1940s, the Eckert-Mauchly Corporation, headed by two of the great technical pioneers of the computer industry, could have received solid funding and much-needed business advice instead of being forced to sell out to a mediocre corporation, Remington Rand, that mismanaged the company.

Prior to the 1960s, in short, the linkage between investors possessing risk capital and entrepreneurs in need of that capital was haphazard, indefinite. Sometimes the right connections were made, but often they were not. The rise of the venture capitalists has changed all that because they methodically accumulate risk capital, search for good investments with high-growth potential, and then do their damnedest to make sure that the investment is a success.

III

From Smart Money to Dumb: How Bull Markets Seduce Venture Capitalists

Though they are relatively patient and disciplined company builders, venture capitalists nevertheless move to the frenetic rhythms of Wall Street trading rooms. Not, perhaps, to the same degree as a pension fund manager under unremitting pressure to beat the market averages each quarter but, still, enough to corrupt the process of new company formation from time to time. In theory, as we have seen, venture capitalists ignore the current passions of Wall Street, back companies on their fundamental merits, develop them over a period of years, and eventually sell them off when conditions in the capital markets are propitious. When the bulls begin to run in lower Manhattan, venture capital practice at first *does* follow theory, and the capitalists take public the high-quality companies that they have been developing for a number of years. Unfortunately the new-issue action does not stop there. Once the good companies are sold off and perform well in the aftermarket, *the causation begins to work in reverse:* Instead of simply *using* the stock market as a source of liquidity for long-term investments, venture capitalists become the market's servant or, more accurately, its supplier. With the bull market surging upward and investors indiscriminately ingesting every new issue that can scrape past the Securities and Exchange Commission (SEC), venture capitalists and investment bankers rush to meet the demand by drastically lowering their investment standards. Smart money's IQ suddenly drops as once-savvy financiers stand in line to bankroll entrepreneurs they would not have touched twelve months earlier.

Such made-for-the-market start-ups turn in mediocre results for a variety of reasons. In the heat of a bull market the financiers have less time to evaluate deals, they cannot drive as hard a bargain with the entrepreneur, they tend to rush into "me too" deals that have a low chance of business success but a high chance of initial stock market acceptance, and finally, many clumsy neophytes clamber out of the business schools to become venture capitalists. (There is no better way to spot promising short sales than to identify the most popular starting jobs of Harvard M.B.A.'s—security analysts in 1968, real estate developers in 1972, energy specialists in 1980, venture capitalists in 1983.) Notwithstanding their mediocrity, some of these put-together high-tech companies are taken public at unrealistically high P/E multiples while others languish in the venture capitalists' portfolios. What makes this company fabrication process all the more damaging is that as in all market crazes, much more money is invested at the top of the market than at the bottom. Nor are the buyers merely average citizens who hear about the stock market after it has been going up for a couple of years. Multibillion-dollar pension funds that could not be bothered to toss a few pennies into start-ups when deals were reasonably priced suddenly become intrigued when high tech is once again fashionable and pricey. It's an old story, as we will see—a replay of the railroad booms of 1836, 1856, and 1873; the automobile boom of 1919; the stock market boom of 1929. Andrew Carnegie's withering denunciations of stock market gamblers apply no less to a go-go mutual fund manager of 1968 or 1983 than to a railroad promoter of the previous century. Certainly the mental dynamic is identical: Investors mistake *market* reality for *economic* reality by valuing companies in terms of what some other speculator will be willing to pay for a *stock* in a few weeks or a few months rather than how much real wealth the underlying *company* will be able to create over a period of years.

Over the last two decades new-issue madness has been clustered in two periods, 1967–72 and 1980–83, which rise like lofty, jagged peaks in the financial history of the United States. Plunging between them is the valley of death for the U.S. stock market, the years of the mid-1970s, when Sheikh Ahmed Zaki Yamani, Richard Nixon, Arthur Burns, Jimmy Carter, Ralph Nader, and the U.S. Congress conspired to raise inflation and interest rates. In so doing, these gentlemen destroyed stock prices and virtually killed off the new-issues market. Close scrutiny of this uneven financial terrain is instructive from two perspectives. For the individual investor it vividly demonstrates what nearly every investor knows and constantly forgets: that the safe is unsafe, that the investor who runs with the bulls in a new-issues craze is in the company of lemmings. And for the student of public policy this history shows that the process of new-company formation in the United States, linked as it is to the health of the stock market and thus to overall confidence in the American economy, is *extremely fragile*. A depressed stock market, combined with a few policy blunders by Washington bureaucrats, can swiftly derail the company creation process, to the great benefit of our foreign competitors.

Like the fog, the post-World War II bull market crept in on little cat feet, eluding the fretful gaze of overcautious investors for a number of years. In 1950 stocks were cheap. Even though real gross national product (GNP) grew at a near-normal 2.7 percent rate between 1929 and 1950, the Standard & Poor's (S&P) 500 was lower in 1950 than it had been in 1928. Stocks yielded considerably *more* than bonds on the theory that investors had to be compensated with high current income for the greater risk of holding equities. Many blue-chip stocks sported P/Es of just 4 or 5. Despite these bargain prices, most investors stood clear of stocks; they had just endured two decades of disappointment in the stock market and feared that a new depression would hit as soon as the Korean War ended. Noting that lower Manhattan was a depressingly placid place despite the surging national economy, *Fortune* concluded in 1954 that the stock market was "obsolete" as a gauge of corporate profits.

Fortune's conclusion was peculiar, to say the least, because in fact, stock prices surged upward 153 percent between 1950 and 1956. Still preoccupied by the trauma of 1929, investors viewed this bull move with trepidation. New York Stock Exchange (NYSE) trading volume merely matched that of the mid-1920s, when the U.S. economy was less than half as large. By the time that equities were finally perceived to be safe, in the late 1950s, a good part of the bull move was already completed. A speculative spike in 1961 brought the market P/E to 21 —three times the multiple of 1950—before falling back to the range of 16 to 18 for the balance of the 1960s. But strong, steady economic growth pushed corporate earnings and stock prices higher until 1968, when the S&P 500 averaged 98.7, 436 percent above its 1950 level. As investors' profits climbed, caution dissipated. Prudence seemed superfluous now that the U.S. economy had liberated itself from the grim constraints of the pre-Keynesian era. Typical of the times was a 1966 *Business Week* article on the U.S. economy entitled "Soaring—and Then Some" which disclosed some "important discoveries about U.S. capitalism." Among the magazine's findings were the "facts" that "the

U.S. economy is not perpetually chained to a business cycle," that "the U.S. is well able to exceed its historic growth rate" and—most important of all—that "rapid growth is not inevitably accompanied by inflation." On this score *Business Week* got no argument from *Fortune,* which in the fall of 1965 told its readers not to fret about financing the Vietnam War because the U.S. economy was "so immense that it can take almost any foreseeable defense increase in stride."

Fortified by this soothing wisdom and by a fifteen-year rise in stock prices, individual investors clambered into the market just as inflation was heating up and the overall fundamentals of the U.S. economy were beginning to deteriorate. Thus in the late sixties, as in the early fifties (or, for that matter, the disinflationary period 1981–85), investor perceptions of economic fundamentals lagged far behind a changing reality. By 1967 volume on the NYSE was so heavy that the back offices of Wall Street firms were unable to digest the flood of paper, so trading was cut back to four hours per day. But trading volume continued to climb, and with it a speculative fever that manifested itself in four different ways. First there were the conglomerates, using a form of leveraged buy-in to achieve fictitious earnings per share (EPS) gains by exchanging their high-P/E stock or other convertible securities for the low-P/E stocks of the companies they acquired. Secondly, speculative pools manipulated selected issues in the over-the-counter (OTC) market. "Everybody knows it's crap shooting," confided one broker, "but the clients can afford to lose, and they stand to make some very sizable gains if these so-called special situations work out. Usually their own buying power is enough to guarantee some kind of move. If the public follows them in, they've got it made." Closely related to this OTC speculation was the sale of much shiny junk in the new-issues market, which embraced such diverse fields as semiconductors, minicomputers, nursing homes, and fast-food restaurants. A major factor in the trading of all these speculative vehicles—conglomerates, new issues, "hot" OTC issues, and also well-established "glamour" stocks such as Xerox and Control Data—was a new Wall Street institution known as the performance mutual fund. A descendant of the speculative pools that had manipulated GM and RCA in the bull market of the 1920s, performance funds were frankly devoted to beating the market averages by speculating rather than investing. Speculation or investment—the public was not particular so long as stock prices went up. When star performance manager Gerald Tsai opened a new fund in 1965, he hoped to attract $25 million in subscriptions; instead, the public poured in nearly ten times as much.

One of the healthier ramifications of this speculative fervor was a blossoming of the venture capital business, in which brokerage firms became a significant factor. Since their aim was to create "product" for the new-issues market rather than profits for long-term investors, many brokers were not inordinately particular about the quality or the pricing of deals. One venture capitalist recently recalled how his firm "offered a half million for 40 percent of a company, with the proviso that the entrepreneur try to do only two things at once—not eight or ten. A brokerage firm down the street offered a million dollars for twenty-five percent of the company, and would impose no controls. They were willing to pay more than three times as much as we were." Like many other Wall Street houses, this overgenerous brokerage firm later went bankrupt. So did many of the companies that such firms brought to market. In 1969 *Forbes* made a list of forty-six companies that had recently gone public, including such intriguing issues as Broadway Joe's, Gamma Process, and Viatron Computer Systems, and twelve years later published a follow-up article that asked, in effect, "Where are they now?" The answer, for seventeen of the forty-six companies, was "ten feet underground." Thirty-three other companies were worth less in 1981 than in 1969, and only four were real winners. If one had invested $1,000 in each of the forty-six new issues in 1969, the $46,000 investment would have been worth $45,000 twelve years later, even though the stock market had climbed by 31 percent.

The wisdom of Wall Street was duplicated in Washington, where the twin wars on poverty and North Vietnam were financed not with taxes but with budget deficits and printing presses. The results were fairly predictable: a worldwide inflationary boom in 1973 that precipitated the OPEC oil embargo and, in 1974, the most severe recession since 1930. The unnerving combination of commodity shortages, soaring interest rates, and plunging corporate earnings caused stock prices to fall by nearly 44 percent between January 1973 and December 1974. This was no ordinary cyclical market correction; it was a financial revolution that cut P/E multiples in half even as inflation was raising the nominal value of tangible assets. Stocks had constituted 45 percent of individuals' financial assets in 1968 but just 23 percent in 1974.

THE VENTURE CAPITAL DROUGHT OF THE 1970S

The great bear market of the 1970s slammed shut the new-issues window and forced the venture capital industry to shrink dramatically. But instead of driving talented financiers out of the industry and reducing its quality, adversity had precisely the opposite effect, as it often does in the business world. The survivors became more patient and disciplined, less enamored of the stock market and more intent on building strong companies over the long term. As Stanley Pratt of Venture Economics told a congressional committee, "The recession of 1974 and 1975 weakened the industry, but paradoxically provided the disciplines that serve as the industry's principal strength today. When the public stock market for small company new issues virtually disappeared in 1974 and 1975, venture capitalists had to learn to work with their portfolio management teams over an extended period and found that this was the most successful way to develop new businesses and realize significant investment returns." The subdued but disciplined mood of the venture capital survivors was conveyed by an excellent *Institutional Investor* article published in 1975. The industry consensus was that the easy money of the previous decade was gone; venture capitalists would have to settle for lower returns and forsake access to the stock market. Avowed one financier: "We've been through such hellfire that we're now making investments on the basis that there will never again be a public market." Fred Adler asserted: "We're not concerned about the state of the public market. We're not looking to turn over our portfolio. We want to create large, new companies, to sit it out over the long term and let the value build." In a similar vein a manager noted: "Today there is the requirement that you be a hell of a lot more intrinsically interested in the companies than you were before, because you may be in them a hell of a lot longer. You will have to be satisfied with their growing intrinsic values until the market finally provides some liquidity."

Investment styles changed in other ways as well. With venture capital in short supply investors could afford to be choosy. Instead of taking equity positions in risky start-ups, they could lend money to established firms and also receive warrants convertible into the stock of the company at some point in the future. Many firms abandoned nonpublic start-ups altogether and hunted for bargains on the floor of the New York Stock Exchange. As one capitalist later explained, "The stock market was way down in the mid-seventies, and if you can buy small high-technology companies that are already public that are doing fifty million dollars a year at ten times earnings, what's your motivation to go out and start a whole bunch of new ones?" Though perfectly logical, this approach was uninspiring for businessmen who were trained to create companies, not just to buy their stock. All in all, the mid-seventies were a lonely time for venture capitalists, and a perilous one as well. One industry observer warned in 1975: "Most venture capital managers are in the same state of mind as the partners of Wall Street brokerage firms were three years ago. They don't see the writing on the wall, because it's not affecting them now, personally. But a lot of them could be obsolete five or seven years ahead."

As things turned out, most of these venture capitalists were not obsolete by 1980. They were rich. For as venture capital became less glamorous in the mid-seventies, it also became more lucrative for the very reason that the business was *less competitive*. Generally speaking, a choosy investor is a successful investor, and venture capitalists could afford to be choosy while risk capital was in short supply. And there were still plenty of talented entrepreneurs to choose from, for America's technological genius did not suddenly evaporate when the stock market collapsed. Equally important, venture capitalists were forced to consider projects on their merits—without an eye to what would sell on Wall Street—and to work with the entrepreneur in a disciplined way to build value over a number of years. *How much* value did not become evident until 1980 or so, when the most successful companies were sold off in the public market. Then it became clear that between 1973 and 1980 most venture capital portfolios earned compound returns of 30 to 40 percent, which means they appreciated between 716 and 1,375 percent. Some did even better.

In a sense, the venture capitalists' gain was the nation's loss because during the venture capital drought of the 1970s many talented entrepreneurs were deprived of funding. Some entrepreneurs had to go overseas to find capital; when Gene Amdahl, IBM's top computer designer, formed a rival mainframe computer company in 1972, he had to obtain funding from Fujitsu, Ltd., a Japanese company that was frankly intent on obtaining technical information to help it enter the computer business. Such cases did not faze Congress, which seemed to be oblivious of the linkage between risk capital, entrepreneurship, and economic vitality. Indeed, Congress exacerbated the venture capital drought by gradually raising the capital gains tax rate from 25 to 49 percent on the ground that it was an unfair "loophole." Moreover, the tax treatment of employee stock options was unfavorably altered, forcing employees to pay taxes on the paper appreciation of unexercised stock options. Not infrequently employees had to borrow to pay these taxes, much as a homeowner would if he were liable for taxes on the market appreciation of a house he was still living in. Although Washington ignored the problem of capital formation, the venture capital drought did alarm informed observers in the mid-1970s. One academic expert warned that high-technology growth companies were no longer being formed "in sufficient numbers to provide the jobs and technical products for export which will be needed in the decades ahead." Noting that rapidly growing private pension funds failed to provide risk capital, Peter Drucker asserted: "We are organizing a capital market totally unequipped to supply entrepreneurial capital needs." And *Business Week* conveyed the mood of the times when, in an article, "The Breakdown of U.S. Innovation," it singled out the "no-risk, supercautious management" of large companies as one of the "prime villains."

TAX REFORM AND A NEW BOOM

The response of the Carter administration to the developing capital crisis in high-tech America—a crisis that was exacerbated by high inflation and low defense spending—was to propose in 1978 that the tax on capital gains should be *raised* still higher. This was not really the blunder of one man. The president was merely reflecting the economic dogma of his fellow Democrats, who, in fact, frequently criticized him for being too conservative on economic issues. For example, such Democratic economists as Walter Heller frequently chastised Carter for exaggerating the danger of inflation in 1977—for being a virtual clone of Gerald Ford. One group that did attack the president's proposed tax hike was the American Electronics Association, which prepared a powerful study of its members that documented the contribution made by small firms to the U.S. economy. The study showed that $100 of venture capital invested in new electronic businesses formed between 1971 and 1976 was by 1976 already returning to the economy $15 annually in federal corporate income tax, $5 in federal taxes paid by new employees, $5 in state and local taxes, and $70 in new export sales. Furthermore, these companies were responsible for a disproportionate share of new job creation and research and development. Congress was impressed. Instead of raising the capital gains tax, as the president had proposed, it lowered it from 49 to 28 percent.

The results were dramatic. After averaging just $58 million annually between 1970 and 1977, new private capital committed to venture capital firms averaged $596 million between 1978 and 1980—despite high inflation and weakening economic growth. Stanley Pratt has pointed out, "[Venture] capital commitments from 1978 to 1984 totaled some $13.2 billion, more than 28 times the capital raised in the prior eight years combined, where there was no differential between the capital gains tax and the tax on ordinary income." And instead of reducing revenue, as the Treasury had feared, revenue from the capital gains tax *rose* after the tax rate had been cut. The reduction of the capital gains tax did to the venture capital industry what a strong blast of pure oxygen does to a blast furnace. Within a year the new-company formation process in the United States was back on track; though energy issues were the stars of the 1980 bull market, a large number of high-tech new issues, including Apple Computer and Genentech, also went public. As venture firms sold off the companies they had been developing since 1973, investors came to realize that the sector offered gains of 30 to 40 percent, and capital poured into the industry at an accelerating rate.

With this resurgence of venture investing came a revival of all the bull market vices of the late 1960s. Even in the economically depressed spring of 1981, long before the frothy run-up of stock prices in 1982 and 1983, the industry was beginning to move to the rhythms of the go-go years as risk capital became more abundant and the balance of power shifted from capitalist to entrepreneur. "There's so much money chasing these deals," complained one financier, "that venture capitalists are in competition with each other. They spend their energies marketing themselves instead of screening the deals. It's gotten silly." Investment decisions were made in a hurry. "We have less time to make up our minds. It used to be that you had two or three months. Now it's a matter of weeks or even days, because if we don't, somebody else will." It did not take the old pros long to see the historical parallels. One veteran warned, "They're paying too much. Low-quality companies that could be financed for $3 million to $5 million are rushing in at the $8 million to $10 million level. I never thought established venture capital firms would do this, but they are—they're reaching.

. . . We saw a lot of that in the late sixties too. I hope this isn't a precursor of collapse, but I think it may be."

This gloomy assessment was right on the trend but wrong on the timing. For another three years the Wall Street success stories proliferated—inspiring tales about obscure entrepreneurs and their financial backers taking their companies public and became instant multimillionaires. In May 1983 Alfred J. Stein's holdings of VLSI Technology were worth $19.4 million; venture capitalist Arthur Rock's Diasonics stock was worth $77.8 million, and so it went with John Poduska of Apollo Computer ($43 million), K. Philip Hwang of Televideo Systems ($794 million), Walter Gilbert of Biogen ($8.4 million), Allen Paulson of Gulfstream Aerospace ($546 million), Neil Hirsch of Telerate ($66.7 million). Fortified by such intoxicating success stories—and by the 30 to 40 percent return that venture funds had earned in the 1970s— venture capitalists found it possible to raise funds in quantities undreamed of a decade earlier. A large venture fund now ran $100 million, not $20 million. Money poured into the high-tech sector from many sources: from Europeans, who were understandably jealous of America's prowess in commercializing technology; from pension funds that committed capital to start-ups and later-stage financing; from institutional portfolio managers who flipped (bought and quickly sold) new issues in order to make a very fast 20 percent. Direct public participation in the new-issues game was more limited than in the late sixties, but many individuals unwisely invested in huge high-tech mutual funds that had access to the new issues.

Once capitalists had raised the money, they had a problem. They had to invest it. After all, that was their job; that was why the client was paying 2 percent of capital annually to the financiers. An investor did not have to pay that kind of money to put his money in treasury bills. And a capitalist certainly was not likely to squeeze an additional $10 million out of an investor until he had "put to work" the first $10 million. Then, too, a capitalist would have a credibility problem if he closed a deal with an investor on a Friday, amid much good cheer about the glittering future of high tech, and then phoned up on Monday morning to explain that every deal in Silicon Valley was absurdly overpriced. Not that very many capitalists ever gave that idea a thought; they were as enamored with paper profits as anyone else. A firm could pay $1 million for half the equity of a promising start-up and then, a year later—after the company had made some demonstrable progress in its business plan—sell off a half of its half to another venture firm for $5 million, making a cool 1,000 percent profit in the process.

Since the essence of investing is price, the mere fact that venture capitalists were plying an overheated market seriously prejudiced their high-tech investments of 1982 and 1983. But the price problem was compounded by related difficulties. Excessive haste was one, for it vitiated the creative relationship between capitalist and entrepreneur. Christopher Brody of Warburg, Pincus, explains: "If he has spent three to six months working with the entrepreneur, rewriting the business plan, reshaping the company's strategy, identifying the soft spots in the company going forward, maybe even trying to ameliorate or plug some of them before the closing, he's lived with the guy. He's developed some feel, or at least a better feel, as to what kind of relationship he's likely to have with the guy going forward. In a period like 1983, many entrepreneurs were trying to run an auction to pick a venture capitalist. The probabilities are high that in such a case the venture capitalist will not have had an opportunity to really get to know the entrepreneur well."

The industry also suffered the group think syndrome—difficult to avoid when you have dozens of venture capitalists in Boston and the Bay Area, eating lunch together regularly, cooperating on deals, incessantly exchanging the same stale investment ideas. Such an environment does not make for original investment decisions. "You have fifty-five companies that are all financed to shoot at the same peripheral memory market—they may call themselves different names, but there ain't room for fifty-five companies—and as time goes on, even a good stock market can't paper over the lack of fundamentals." The classic case of an overcrowded market was personal computers, which chewed up a long and lustrous list of firms, ranging from start-ups to corporate heavyweights, including Victor Technologies, Fortune Systems, the Gavillan Computer Corporation, Atari, Commodore, Osborne, ITT, Texas Instruments, and a gaggle of computer retailers. (There may have been only two unambiguous winners from the personal computer craze: IBM and Silicon Valley auctioneers. "I get lots of letters," said one auctioneer boastfully. "They always say, 'This isn't a distress sale, but could you get rid of the stuff by next week?'") Part of this silicon carnage was tied to the business cycle. Since the high-tech boom reached its apogee in the summer of 1983, new companies had only a year of strong growth before the economy was slowed markedly by the strong dollar, and only eighteen months before the high-technology sector experienced a severe slowdown in orders that forced extensive layoffs from Boston to Palo Alto.

Oddly enough, in a period when capital was cascading into the coffers of venture capitalists, the industry was setting itself up for a *capital shortage* in the future. Most small companies require more than one round of financing—often three or four rounds. By aggressively bankrolling start-ups in 1983, capitalists were locking themselves into future financial requirements that they expected to be met by institutional investors. But by the spring of 1985 high tech was decidedly out of fashion on Wall Street, institutional investors were not coming through with the second-tier financing, and venture capitalists were starting to fear that they would run out of money before their portfolio companies became self-financing. "They are concerned because they have a lot of companies in their portfolio that are burning money at the rate of a million or two million or three million dollars a month. You can run out of the money in a hurry if you have a burn rate like that."

Many financial events are utterly unpredictable, but the crash that has to follow a speculative craze is not. Many observers realized that the high-tech boom of 1983 was unsustainable. One entrepreneur candidly predicted: "We will see a fallout. I believe that the price at which we went public was insane. I don't know how to set value, but I know insanity when I see it." But it is extraordinarily difficult to let go of stocks that seem to go only up, and even levelheaded skeptics, after watching the prices climb month after month, can reluctantly come to the conclusion that the economy really has entered a "new era." For example, *Forbes* columnist and venture capitalist Thomas Murphy, though fully cognizant of the uncomfortable parallels between the eighties and the sixties, argued that the venture industry had indeed improved fundamentally, thanks to the ready availability of second-stage financing, more effective underwriters of new issues, better market research to focus companies' strategies, more and better entrepreneurs, and a superabundance of new technologies to commercialize.

Murphy's points were well taken but could not offset the investor's equivalent of the law of gravity: Hot markets offer no value. Bull markets have an internal logic, an inner dynamic, that no investor can afford to ignore. At any given time there is only so much good merchandise available in a given segment of the market. When that segment is unpopular, as high tech was in the mid-seventies, investors can be choosers and buy quality companies cheap. Precisely because start-up capital is scarce, these companies are likely to meet limited competition in their line of business and achieve a high return on invested capital. (Competition may be wonderful for consumers and much lauded by economists, but it is the enemy of profit-hungry investors.) Eventually investors will take note of these good returns (e.g., the 30 plus percent returns of venture capital in the 1970s), and the sector will suddenly be "discovered." By flashing the glittering earnings record to potential investors, Wall Street salesmen can lure billions of dollars of fresh capital into the industry, and as the capital pours in, investors will assign much higher P/E multiples to these rising earnings. Prescient investors who beat the crowd see the market price of their stocks skyrocket. This price appreciation will pull in still more investors, but while the *prices paid* for companies soar, the *actual value* of these companies will fall because return on capital will begin to fall as new competitors multiply like maggots.

The bull run is likely to last longer than anyone expects—remember that many venture capital veterans were beginning to frown by the spring of 1981—but when the craze is at its height, it is time to get out. While bells do not ring at the top of a bull market, clairvoyance is not a necessity. There are signs. One is the mutual fund test. Whether it is gold, energy, medical technologies, or high tech, when a market fad is sufficiently advanced to call into being a bevy of new mutual funds, it is time to run, not walk, to the nearest exit. The *Time* and TV test is equally valuable. When an investment phenomenon is making the news in a really big way—not just the business news but the cover of *Time* and the feature stories on the network news—it is time to become concerned. In general, the lone investor is the successful investor.

IV

The Railroads:
Wall Street's Mistress

One of the most striking recent developments in the business world is the rise of corporate raiders such as T. Boone Pickens, Carl Icahn, and Irwin Jacobs. Although sometimes lumped into the general trend of "merger mania," the raiders are really a distinct phenomenon. Instead of merely collecting large fees for arranging transactions between corporations, as investment bankers have done through most of the postwar period, the raiders act as independent financial operators who challenge corporate executives for control of their companies. Typically the raider buys a major stake in a company, creating an impression that he wants to take it over. Then he has three ways to make a killing: He can scare the frightened management into buying him out at a higher stock price than he paid for his stake in the company; he can induce the company to sell out—again at a higher price than the price he paid for his shares—to a friendly company that acts as a "white knight"; or finally, he can take over the company, break it apart into its major divisions, and sell off the individual pieces to other companies for an amount that exceeds in the aggregate what he paid for the company in the first place.

Because the raider phenomenon is relatively new, its implications are difficult to assess. Clearly raiders have played a valuable role in forcing ineffectual companies to take steps, such as share buy-backs and dividend boosts, that return capital to shareholders and raise stock prices —a theme discussed further in Chapter X. But the question arises: Would it be healthy for the independent financier's role to be expanded—for him to have, for example, greater power in the financing of new industries? An excellent way to gain insight into this issue is to review the history of nineteenth-century railroad finance, in which independent financial operators played a central role. Unfortunately the verdict of this analysis is resoundingly negative: Financiers hindered the progress of U.S. railroads almost as frequently as they helped. Even though ethical and regulatory standards have risen substantially since the nineteenth century, we doubt that things would be much different today. For it is not merely a matter of integrity. The truth is that despite the great analytical ability, entrepreneurial drive, and financial expertise that Wall Street operators possess, their understanding of pioneering industries is necessarily somewhat superficial. They are not well qualified to make the basic strategic decisions that will shape an infant industry. As we will see again and again in this book, these are best left to industry insiders rather than opportunistic deal-oriented financiers.

DOES JAY COOKE HAVE A DEAL FOR YOU!

A case in point is Jay Cooke, one of the foremost financiers of the Gilded Age. Cooke was the quintessential stockbroker. A superb salesman and prodigious letter writer who seemed to know everybody, he took great pleasure in doing well and living well in the bustle of big commercial cities such as Philadelphia and New York. In the spring of 1869 Cooke was mulling over the future of his firm. Jay Cooke and Company had a luminous reputation and attractive long-term prospects, but it needed new sources of business right away. Cooke had become instantly famous during the Civil War by using a revolutionary financing technique to raise millions of dollars for the Union. Eschewing the traditional method of selling government bonds to tightfisted banks and brokerage firms, Cooke had employed a massive publicity campaign to sell bonds directly to the general public. Not only had he secured badly needed funds for the government in a time of crisis, but by playing on the patriotism of northerners, he was also able to raise the money at a much lower interest rate than bankers would have charged. But now the war was over, and with it Cooke's lucrative government financing business. If the firm's branches in Washington, Philadelphia, and New York were to keep their doors open, they would need new business. One option, favored by Cooke's cosmopolitan partner in New York, was to open a London office that could finance foreign trade and deal in currencies.

Cooke himself leaned toward the booming field of railroad finance for future profits. He was pondering the scheme of a group of New

England promoters to create the Northern Pacific Railroad, a 2,000-mile road running parallel to the Canadian border that would link Lake Superior with the Pacific Ocean. Led by a Vermont railroad executive named James Smith, the Northern Pacific syndicate had obtained a massive land grant of 44 million acres from the U.S. Congress. To lend prestige to the venture, Smith had persuaded several leading railroad capitalists to sit on the Northern Pacific's board. But because Congress refused to provide direct financial assistance, the company had no funds with which to begin actual construction. That was where Cooke could help. He had proved himself a virtuoso at distributing huge quantities of bonds to the American public; if he could do it again, to the tune of $100 million, James Smith and his cohorts could build the Northern Pacific and make a fortune in the bargain.

Cooke would be a catalyst in a chain reaction involving Wall Street bankers, western pioneers, and professional railroad engineers. The company's land would serve as collateral for the bonds sold by Cooke to American and European investors, and funds from this source would initially finance construction of the railroad. Meanwhile, a massive sales campaign in Europe and America would attract pioneers to the Northern Pacific's wilderness in the Dakotas and Minnesota. These settlers would help finance construction both by purchasing lands from the company and by using the road to ship their crops to market. It was a daring scheme, to say the least, but not without precedent; during the 1850s the Illinois Central had parlayed a federal land grant into investment capital that financed construction of one of the finest railroads in the Midwest. And the potential rewards of the deal seemed commensurate with the risk. If it succeeded, Jay Cooke and Company would earn millions of dollars in commissions from the sale of Northern Pacific bonds and the purchase of equipment and rails for the road. Moreover, the firm would have use of the railroad's funds until they were spent. In short, if the Northern Pacific prospered, Jay Cooke and Company would prosper.

To size up the proposition more carefully, Cooke dispatched representatives to the West to examine the Northern Pacific's only real asset, its land. The reports home were ecstatic. After viewing the splendid forests near the Puget Sound, one scout wrote: "Oh!! what timber. On the Atlantic slope, where it was my misfortune to be born . . . there are no woods. East of the Rocky Mountains, trees are brush. . . . Puget Sound, anywhere and everywhere, will give you for the cutting, if you are equal to such a crime with an axe, trees that will lie straight on the ground, and cover two hundred and fifty feet of length and measure twenty-five feet around." Far less enthusiastic were the letters that Cooke received from his partner William Moorhead, who had gone to Europe to find out whether the Rothschilds or some other leading financial house would be willing to help sell Northern Pacific bonds. Baron de Rothschild did not like the smell of the thing. "The old gentleman said they never engaged in anything that required risk, or trouble, in the management. This he regarded involved both. The amount [of bonds] too he said was very large. And there was no road built—no considerable amount of cash capital paid in—he said it would be impossible to sell the bonds." Moorhead concluded that the Northern Pacific promoters had to be viewed in "the light of speculators—men who have nothing to lose but everything to gain, in getting the road built, with the money of others."

Despite these mixed reports, Cooke decided to go ahead with the project. The nation was in the midst of a massive railroad building boom, after all, and for Wall Street firms "railroads are the big plum right now." Many houses had grown rich by hitching their fortunes to a major railroad: Henry Clews was aligned with the Rock Island; John Cisco and Son with the Union Pacific; Fisk and Hatch with the Central Pacific. Moreover, the promoters of the Northern Pacific had sweetened the deal by giving Cooke the opportunity to own more than half the railroad's stock, although he would not be allowed to control its management.

As matters stood, the Northern Pacific was entitled to mortgage only its railroad and telegraph lines. Since the company possessed neither, the first step in the bond sale was to push through Congress an act permitting the Northern Pacific to mortgage its lands. To secure this favor, the company had to fend off the criticisms of competing railroads and a skeptical public, which was beginning to attack the profusion of subsidies lavished on the railroads. As the *Philadelphia Ledger* observed, "Public attention all over the country, is being aroused to the huge robberies of the public domain. . . . There is scarcely a doubt that the next financial crisis in this country will come through the wild and extravagant expenditures of money on railroads, many of which projects are not only in advance of any existing business from which they can derive the least traffic, but it is openly confessed that the roads are expected to make the business on which they hope to live." To counter such criticism and win the right to mortgage its lands, the Northern Pacific lobbyists went beyond plausible counterarguments to a more nakedly direct method of persuasion: They simply bought off several leading newspapermen and congressmen. These were accepted tactics in the game of railroad financiering as it was played in the nineteenth century. Major journalists and politicians would have been dangerously offended if they had not been "taken care of."

With the legislative formalities out of the way Jay Cooke set about unloading a mass of bonds on the investing public. For more than two years he bombarded Europe and the United States with a barrage of pamphlets, articles, speeches, and advertisements. At its height no fewer than 1,371 newspapers and 1,500 salesmen were enlisted in the campaign. Cooke knew his trade too well to focus on the bonds themselves or even on the great corporation that supposedly stood behind them. The average investor, he calculated, would be far more interested in the wild, romantic, and little-known corner of America through which the railroad was to run. So Cooke's publicists painted an alluring picture of the Northwest's "Fertile Belt"—a bountiful wonderland of moderate temperatures, fertile soil, splendid timberland, and unparalleled mineral wealth. Historically such territory had supported "the most enlightened, creative, conquering, and progressive populations." Before long, Cooke promised, no fewer than 30 million industrious souls would be living in the region, and every one of them would be dependent on the Northern Pacific to get their crops to market. For the benefit of the financially minded, Cooke offered reassuring details on the bonds themselves. They paid a very generous interest rate of 7.3 percent, payable in gold, and both principal and interest were secured by a mortgage on "Over Two Thousand Miles of Road, with rolling stock, buildings, and all other equipments" as well as "Over Twenty-two Thousand Acres of Land to every mile of finished road."

Unfortunately for Cooke, the fish did not bite. Investors recognized that Northern Pacific bonds were not backed by meaningful amounts of liquid capital, and wilderness land—no matter what its ultimate value might be—could not be depended upon to pay interest for many years. Clearly this was a highly speculative scheme, and bondholders were being asked to shoulder almost all the risk. If it failed, they would lose everything, but if it succeeded, their rewards would be modest— a return on their bonds amounting to perhaps 1.5 percent more than they could earn on much safer securities.

Tepid investor response pushed Jay Cooke ever deeper into financial quicksand in 1871, 1872, and 1873. While he struggled to sell the bonds, the Northern Pacific promoters were hard at work on the railroad, financing construction with copious drafts on Cooke. Since these drafts greatly exceeded the proceeds from bond sales, they had to be paid out of Cooke's own pocket. By honoring them, the banker placed himself in an intolerable position, for he was betting his company on a project he did not control. Unfortunately his only alternative course of action—to have stopped paying the drafts—was no more acceptable; it would have halted construction on the road, frozen bond sales completely, led to default on the bonds already sold, and shattered Cooke's reputation. So the banker carried on, committing more and more of his resources to the Northern Pacific. The noose tightened at first gradually, then more violently as America's third railroad boom came to a close. When a series of minor bankruptcies convulsed the financial markets in September 1873, the firm had few liquid assets with which to pay its creditors, so on September 18 Jay Cooke and Company, "the foremost American banking-house," closed its doors, plunging Wall Street into panic and the nation into a long depression.

VIRTUES AND VICES OF JUNK BONDS

Jay Cooke's fatal foray into railroad financiering captures the essence of that Byzantine art as it was practiced in nineteenth-century America. Cooke had not taken on the Northern Pacific project because it made economic sense and was likely to produce a good return for the investors who purchased its securities; his main concern was simply to provide business for his investment firm—to do a deal, in the parlance of the 1980s. So it was with many of the railroads built in nineteenth-century America. The railroad promoter's aim was to build a road that would make him large profits *even if it filled no real economic need and did not earn a good return for investors.*

Railroads were the behemoths of the nineteenth-century economy. As they lumbered westward across the American landscape, the ground shook, the mountains moved, the rivers parted, and the economic terrain was changed forever. The businessman lucky enough to control his own railroad could partially shape his economic environment and seize a variety of lucrative opportunities for self-dealing. He could sell the railroad's bonds, as Cooke attempted to do. He could supply the road with rails, equipment, and construction services. He could speculate in lands made suddenly valuable by the arrival of his railroad. He could reap trading gains on Wall Street by manipulating the company's operating performance and financial policies. Or he could merge it with competing roads and reward himself with large helpings of the securities of the new company. If by some miracle the road was not financially crippled by these assorted tortures, so much the better for the promoter who controlled its stock. But if the road was indeed destroyed, it did not much matter; so long as the promoter had already made a fortune by using other people's money to build the road, the project was a success. Little wonder that the *Times* of London once remarked that the American railroad ran "from nowhere in particular to nowhere at all."

The prudent promoter strenuously avoided putting his own capital at risk when organizing a road—that was where Jay Cooke had gone wrong—but instead employed assets supplied by governments and private investors. Public officials were an easy mark. They eagerly encouraged the building of railroads that rendered remote and worthless acres suddenly valuable by providing a means of getting crops to market. Editors and orators spared no superlative in describing the transformation that railroads would bring. It was claimed that the Illinois Central would "be of greater importance to the State, the government, and the whole Union, than any similar work yet projected. It will open the most speedy and direct communication at once from the navigable waters of the Ohio and Mississippi, from Pittsburgh and New Orleans, to the farthest frontier settlement in the northwest, AT ALL SEASONS OF THE YEAR—. . . Those who may have travelled in Illinois in the winter season will attest to the almost impracticability of passing through that fertile State, except on horseback." For individual localities the importance of a railroad was, if possible, even greater. It was no exaggeration to say that "A railway or no railway in many instances is but a new version of to be or not to be." Savvy promoters were expert at manipulating this mentality to wring subsidies from public authorities. Massive federal land grants are the best-known form of railroad subsidies, but state and local governments also held out a host of inducements, including equity capital, free labor, and guarantees of bond issues.

While government support often got railroads started, private capital was usually needed to bring them to fruition. Private capital constituted roughly 75 percent of total investment in railroads before 1861 and about 87 percent between 1861 and 1890. The typical railroad investor was yield-oriented and purchased American railway issues because they provided higher current income than the alternatives. Unlike, say, the stock of an auto company in 1910 or a computer company in 1968, railroad shares were not bought by investors who hoped to make a killing as the company's earnings per share exploded. Railroads required far too much capital to encourage such dreams. It took so much money to build a mile of road that expansion could not normally be financed out of profits; instead, additional securities—stocks or bonds—had to be issued. This meant that the value of the assets and profits *behind each share of stock* did not dramatically increase, even if the road was prosperous. In the parlance of the modern security analyst, railroads were highly capital-intensive and consequently needed external financing (sales of new securities) to expand, instead of relying on internal financing (reinvestment of profits).

The conscientious investor searched for a railroad that would faithfully pay interest on its bonds and ample dividends on its stock. Such a road would possess a strong balance sheet showing a substantial cash surplus even after interest payments had been made, dividends on the common and preferred stock had been paid, maturing bonds had been redeemed, and expenditures for maintaining and upgrading equipment had been made. Companies of this quality were exceedingly rare, but this fact was lost on several generations of American and European investors, who seem to have been mesmerized by the apparent safety of American railroads as investments. Perhaps the greatest irony of nineteenth-century railroad finance is that investors whose aims were fundamentally conservative—to increase their incomes by one or two percentage points—frequently ended up buying dubious securities that swallowed large shares of their principals. Yet in the overgrown jungle of railroad finance, this was an easy mistake to make. To the unsuspecting observer railroad securities had the look of solid obligations that were almost as safe as government bonds. A major railroad provided an indispensable service to a clearly defined market, after all, and therefore seemed to have an assured source of profits with which to pay interest and dividends. Moreover, the real estate and equipment that secured railroad bonds greatly comforted many investors, particularly land-conscious Europeans.

Unfortunately these apparent safety factors were often more than offset by several serious risks that made them, in actuality, junk bonds. The greatest danger by far was dishonest insiders—*vampire capitalists* is not too strong a term—who sucked the financial lifeblood out of a railroad and left investors with a carcass. The hard fact was that much of the railroad paper that brokers and bankers bandied about Wall

Street was nearly worthless from the moment it rolled off the printing press. And even legitimate railroads were in real danger of becoming unprofitable investments once they faced competition. Unlike modern utilities, which are also owned by yield-oriented investors, most railroads had no assured monopoly of the traffic of a certain region. To fend off rivals and maintain their position in the nation's rapidly evolving transportation network, railroads frequently entered into ambitious expansion programs that stretched their finances. Eastern trunk roads added feeder lines designed to attract local traffic. Western roads expanded ahead of the line of settlement in order to link up with the next transportation hub expected to arise on the frontier, whether it was Cincinnati, Chicago, St. Louis, or Kansas City. These aggressive expansion programs involved spending millions of dollars on roads that did not generate substantial cash flow for several years, and only the strongest roads could do this without endangering their dividends. Even if an investor selected a railroad that was well financed and soundly managed, he ran the risk, when he entered the market to buy the stock, of being cheated by professional speculators who manipulated the stock market with impunity by such mechanisms as wash sales that temporarily inflated its trading volume and price.

The buccaneer style of the railroad financiers was not without its advantages, for by getting the roads built in a hurry, they expeditiously unlocked the riches of a continent. The wizards of Wall Street were masters at turning a financially inert asset—frontier land donated by the federal government—into liquid capital that could be used to build a road that would make the land productive. But the excesses of railroad finance were so outlandish that its social and economic costs were prodigious. Redundant railroads, squandered capital, widespread bankruptcy, frequent mismanagement, and dissatisfied customers riddled the industry. These ubiquitous maladies inspired an endless stream of exposés by nineteenth-century writers, ranging from the lurid tracts of muckrakers to the learned treatises of college professors and the unreadable tomes of securities analysts. Even Wall Street financiers excoriated the railroads. After surveying "the discredit, the embarrassments, the bankruptcies and the robberies of our railroad system," the banker Henry Clews estimated that fully 60 percent of the system had gone through corporate reorganization. In analyzing the origins of the panic of 1873, the Boston financier John Murray Forbes highlighted the "extreme activity in Railroad Construction, stimulated by returning prosperity and by the inflation of the currency going on unchecked when no longer needed for war purposes. . . . Contractor business was also at its height. It may be called Shoddy or Mushroom period of Railroad building, accompanied by much swindling."

The classic fraud of railroad finance, which took root in the 1850s but did not blossom in all its noxious glory until the 1860s and 1870s, was the inside construction company. It was a sort of big-time confidence game that operated as follows: A ring of promoters obtained a charter to build a road and issued stock worth, let us say, $5 million. The promoters immediately *subscribed* for all this stock but *paid in* only 10 percent in cash, perhaps using a bank loan to finance even this limited investment. Then the corporation issued first-mortgage bonds with a face value of $15 million (which might be guaranteed by a state or municipality) and sold them to investors at a 20 percent discount to their par value, thereby netting $12 million. For this feat of stockjobbing the promoters might promptly pay themselves a commission of 5 percent on the par value of the bonds, or $750,000—more than enough to pay off the $500,000 loan that had financed the initial stock purchase. Having thereby covered their own expenses in the venture, the promoters proceeded to make some really significant money by raiding the corporate treasury of the funds obtained in the recent bond issue. After setting up a separate construction company, the promoters (acting as the railroad's management) made an exceedingly generous construction contract with themselves (acting as the construction company's management). As compensation for building the road they agreed to pay themselves $12 million in cash, perhaps tossing in, as a sort of warmhearted afterthought, a couple of million dollars in second-mortgage bonds and newly minted stock. If all went according to plan, they earned a large profit on the construction contract *and still controlled the railroad's stock.*

The coup de grace of most deals was sale of the railroad's shares at a good price. This maneuver required deft management and good luck, for the road's bonded debt exceeded its real value—hence its earning power—by such a large margin that it might have difficulty meeting the interest on its bonds, to say nothing of paying dividends on its stock. Much depended on the tone of the financial markets. In buoyant times short-term bank loans could be used to pay the road's bonded debt even while its stock was puffed on Wall Street as a blue-chip issue that would pay an excellent dividend for generations to come. If profits threatened to lag embarrassingly as the shares came to market, it was a simple matter for management to cook the books. A common method was to charge operating costs to the construction account. A reduction in operating costs produced an equivalent gain in operating profits, while the capitalized expenses increased the amount of assets on the road's balance sheet. By the time these machinations became apparent the shares would be "absorbed" by the investing public, and ringleaders long since departed for parts unknown.

Since the total capitalization of these "mushroom railroads" usually exceeded the actual cost of construction by more than 50 percent, few of them managed to pay interest and dividends for long. Once credit had tightened and traffic had declined in the next economic downturn, the road would have to be reorganized. Bonded debt would be scaled back, and the stockholders called upon to supply more equity capital. Unfortunately such financial engineering might not be enough to make the road a useful part of the American transportation network. Having been built for quick promotional gain rather than bona fide investment, many of them were badly constructed and functionally redundant, able to do little more than depress freight rates and pinch the profits of legitimate roads. Some were bought out by competitors; others were abandoned and allowed simply to rust in the desert, bizarre monuments to the handiwork of dishonest entrepreneurs and undisciplined investors.

THE FINANCIAL ROLLER COASTER

Depending as it did upon the fickle passions of Wall Street, the process of railroad expansion was extraordinarily cyclical. A graph of nineteenth-century railroad construction resembles a profile of the Sierra Nevada, and the earliest decades call to mind a cross-sectional view of the Grand Canyon. The American railroad network grew rapidly during the frothy prosperity of the mid-1830s, but the panic of 1837 and the ensuing depression slashed the industry growth rate to an anemic 5 percent for several years in the early forties. However, the gradual economic recovery of the late forties, which was accelerated by the discovery of gold in California, eventually gave rise to a new period of expansion that saw the nation's rail network grow about 19 percent per year between 1849 and 1856. The booms of the 1830s and 1850s were financed very differently, however, and the classic pattern of nineteenth-century railroad finance did not emerge until 1853 or so.

Many of the earliest railroads were hasty responses to that brilliantly conceived ditch the Erie Canal. By linking the port of New York with the Midwest via the Great Lakes, the canal threatened to give New York an even tighter grip on the trade with America's heartland than it already had. If they intended to remain viable ports, Boston, Philadelphia, and Baltimore would have to pierce the Appalachian chain with transportation networks of their own. As often as not, this meant building railroads. It was not excessively difficult for promoters to finance the early eastern railroads because they were generously supported by both state legislatures and the commercial nabobs of the major ports. Whether financed with private or government funds, these railroads were viewed as public works. As one executive later said of two of them, "A profitable investment for Capital was not the moving cause for the construction of either. . . . They were constructed for the promotion of the interests of their respective states and the Cities where they terminate." Though infused with public spirit, private capital was not called upon to make inordinate sacrifices; most of the early railroads of the eastern seaboard were highly profitable because they provided passenger service between major cities that was faster and more reliable than canals, steamboats, or stagecoaches. The combination of private capital, public subsidies, and healthy profits meant that these projects could be financed conservatively, using relatively little debt.

Not so the Midwest, which caught the fever for "internal improvements" even before the major eastern transportation projects had penetrated the Appalachian chain. Dependent on wretched roads and erratic steamboat service, the inhabitants of Ohio, Michigan, Indiana, and Illinois convinced themselves that railroads and canals would be so beneficial as to be virtually self-financing. One booster claimed that "it is estimated that exceeding twenty million acres of public lands will be sold in ONE FOURTH THE TIME than it otherwise would, without the construction of some such highway through the States. As a pecuniary consideration alone, this would justify the construction of a railroad through the public domain, AT THE EXPENSE OF THE GOVERNMENT." It is hardly surprising that this early version of supply-side economics made sense to residents of isolated frontier settlements. What is far more remarkable is that it won over the financiers of Great Britain as well. There were several reasons—in addition to generous yields—why British financiers stuffed their portfolios with the bonds of western states during the 1830s. Having recently burned their fingers with unwise loans in Latin America, they were impressed that the

United States managed to pay off its entire national debt in 1834. Moreover, Jacksonian America was waxing rich off cotton and slaves, and in the mid-thirties the United States entered upon a full-fledged boom that saw the general price level rise by 25 percent between 1830 and 1836. Feverish speculation in the cotton lands of Arkansas, Texas, and Louisiana spread to the financial markets, and enormous quantities of state bonds were sold to British investors. Between 1830 and 1838 the debt of the various states expanded from $26 million to $172 million.

This bout of railroad fever was unceremoniously cured by the panic of 1837 and the ensuing depression, which eventually caused no fewer than nine states to default on bonds issued to finance "internal improvements." The speculative bubble in the U.S. economy finally burst in part because Andrew Jackson, in the aftermath of his war on the Bank of the United States, mandated that all public lands could be bought only with gold and silver—not with paper money. Horrified European investors fled the American capital markets, not to return for more than a decade. Many states wrote into their constitutions prohibitions on the floating of securities to finance transportation projects. Such building as took place was concentrated in the East, giving the United States an ever more lopsided transportation system. By 1850 most of the major northeastern cities were linked by railroads, but only 600 miles of road were in operation west of the Appalachians. For the contrarian investor who sailed against the prevailing winds on Wall Street, this imbalance argued in favor of investing in western railroads. As one investment banker later recalled, "During the twelve years that had elapsed since the great calamity of 1837, the West had increased rapidly in population and wealth, and the necessity for improved highways was felt to be more imperative than ever. The acquisition of California, and the discovery of immense deposits of gold within it, gave to the whole nation an impulse never before felt." The first investors to inject capital into midwestern states "strewn with the wrecks of State Railroads" were shrewd New England merchants, who knew a bargain when they saw it, and their efforts received strong support from local boosters, such as the Ohio newspaper editor who exulted: "The steam is rising. The people of Columbus, who have been sleeping so profoundly, while the enterprize [sic] of their neighbors has been actively employed, are now beginning to arouse themselves, to shake off their lethargy. But they seem to awaken from their Van Winkle repose."

The interest of foreign investors in western railroads likewise revived in the late forties and early fifties. Drawn by the California gold rush and repelled from the European continent by the revolutions of 1848, a second wave of European capital washed across the Midwest between 1848 and 1857 and turned the visions of promoters into steel and steam. A new breed of financier appeared in lower Manhattan to channel this powerful financial flood; indeed, it was during the 1850s that Wall Street began to assume its modern character. The process of financing western roads involved a joint effort by western farmers, Wall Street middlemen, and British investors. As the chief beneficiaries of the new roads, local farmers willingly contributed enough land, labor, and cash to clear the ground, construct the roadbeds, and build the bridges. Then the bonds of the railroad—or of a municipality acting on behalf of the railroad—were sold in New York in order to purchase rails and rolling stock for the line. At first these small western roads were at the mercy of sharp Wall Street brokers, who formed manipulative rings to depress the prices of the securities they purchased, but soon a more efficient and equitable system for negotiating securities took shape. Dozens of brokers, merchants, and private bankers shifted to the field of investment banking and became specialists in selling corporate securities to investors in Europe and America. These bankers also served as the financial advisers of the roads that they represented, providing in this capacity a wide range of services. Because they had a long-term relationship with the roads and had professional reputations to uphold, these investment bankers were more honest and expert than the brokers they superseded. The best of them eventually acquired reputations for guaranteeing the integrity of the railroads they represented.

In contrast with their predecessors of the 1830s, many of the western roads that were built in the 1850s were sensible, if unspectacular, investments. Construction costs were moderate because the land was flat and cheap, and unlike eastern roads, they faced limited competition from canals and turnpikes. Moreover, these roads, owing to the hiatus of construction during the 1840s, were not built ahead of demand. Most of them served prosperous agricultural communities that actually existed in the here and now, rather than in the fertile imaginations of promoters like Jay Cooke. Not a few generated substantial operating revenue even before they were completed. Though solidly profitable, such roads were hardly bonanzas for their shareholders. They typically earned between 5 and 7 percent on invested capital—hardly an impressive showing when compared with such later fast-growing, highly profitable companies as Ford Motor or Carnegie Steel. Nevertheless, this was enough to please many British investors, who could earn only 3.2 percent from government bonds. And as many as half the bonds sent to Britain may have been held by iron manufacturers, who acquired them not as investments but rather as payment for the massive quantities of rails that they sold to American railroads. Like the junk bonds issued today, these bonds carried unusually high yields, but also unusually high risk because payment of interest and principal depended on the success of the project financed.

The risk of these railroad junk bonds was greatly compounded by the malfeasance of the people who issued them. As these issues reestablished their credibility and the speculative sap began to rise on Wall Street during the 1850s, financial abuses soon appeared. The root of the problem was that investors exerted little meaningful oversight of a railroad's managers and directors. One leading commentator on railroad finance observed, "Directors of railroads may not only be incompetent, but they may be corrupt with impunity. They are seldom called to account till they show themselves incapable of longer carrying on their road. The only penalty then paid is dismissal. There are numberless ways in which, if so disposed, they can defraud the company. They can be interested in contracts for construction, or for furnishing materials; they can charge extravagant commissions for making loans; or for endorsements; or for services of one kind or another. All these things can easily be kept from the knowledge of the stockholders or from brother directors till the mischief is past remedy, and the road sapped of its life-blood." The ignorance of shareholders was so great that they might not even know that a road was carrying a heavy load of short-term floating debt, over and above its bonded debt. More than one investor learned about such significant financial details the hard way—by watching his property go bankrupt in the panic of 1857. The financial analyst Henry Varnum Poor estimated that about a quarter of the bonded debt of American railroads was not paying interest in 1858, and a "considerable portion" of this debt was permanently lost. And so the railroad roller coaster continued to soar and plunge until the end of the nineteenth century, with construction slowing seriously during the Civil War and the major depressions of the 1870s and 1890s.

JOHN MURRAY FORBES, CONTRARIAN INVESTOR

To be sure, not all railroad financiers were crooks. The leading investors of Massachusetts, imbued with the Puritan tradition of integrity, industry, and thrift, took a constructive and even enlightened approach to railroad development that was not much in evidence west of the Hudson River. By the 1840s Massachusetts businessmen were well positioned to invest in western railroads effectively. Between 1790 and 1840 the state had prospered in a far-flung foreign commerce that encompassed whaling, the China trade, the pepper trade with the East Indies, and the cotton trade centered on Liverpool and New Orleans. Moreover, Bay State businessmen had proved themselves adept at rechanneling maritime profits into building up the local economy. Shortly after the end of the War of 1812 Boston merchants had built fabulously successful cotton spinning mills in Waltham, Lowell, and Lawrence, and foreign trade also furnished much of the capital for the extensive railroad network built in Massachusetts in the 1830s. With profits from foreign trade beginning to stagnate by the 1840s, the rich and resourceful businessmen of the Bay State shifted to the railroads of the Midwest for future profits.

The leader of this effort was a versatile capitalist named John Murray Forbes. Reared in a good family of limited means, Forbes was educated at an excellent boarding school and then entered the mercantile firm of his uncle, one of Boston's leading China merchants, at the age of eighteen. After working as a clerk for just sixteen months, he was sent to China to replace his older brother, who had been drowned in a shipwreck. It did not take Forbes long to make a fortune in Canton. He assumed his brother's role as commercial agent to a superrich Chinese merchant known as Houqua, who was said to be worth $15 million to $20 million, and he earned large commissions for planning and executing extensive commercial ventures on Houqua's behalf. In addition to making him rich by the age of thirty, this business gave Forbes experience that was to be valuable in railroad promotion. He earned the confidence of some of Europe's leading financiers and learned how to conceptualize and carry out projects that spanned great distances and required extensive delegation of authority.

When he returned to Boston in 1837, Forbes took up the life of the cultured gentleman of substantial means but moderate tastes. He read widely, cultivated such intellectuals as Nathaniel Hawthorne and

Ralph Waldo Emerson (who became his son-in-law), and avidly supported the abolitionist cause and the Republican party. There was a sensible balance to his life that is rare among the highly successful. Emerson said of Forbes, "How little this man suspects, with his sympathy for men and his respect for lettered and scientific people, that he is not likely, in any company, to meet a man superior to himself. I think this is a good country that can bear such a creature as he is." Forbes preferred "farming, shooting, and other gentlemanlike occupations" on his suburban estate to the glitter of urban living. Luxury positively frightened him. In the instructions written for the guardians who would care for his children in the event of his death Forbes stipulated: "I would like to have their circle formed among families of moderate means where children are being brought up to labor, and not among the rich alone." Their fortune, he emphasized, was "not theirs to enable them to roll in luxury and self-indulgence but rather a trust to be judiciously used to assist others in doing good." He added: "Fashionable watering-places, and resorts" were to be avoided, as were "fine dinners and entertainments and shows, fashionable balls and parties."

Still Forbes thought of money, for he had plenty to invest—not only his own funds but also the assets of Houqua and of various family members and business associates. It was a distinctive feature of Forbes's business career that his reputation for rectitude and good management made his financial clout larger than his own pocketbook. When he found a really promising opportunity, Forbes could raise funds in the rich and tight-knit fraternity of Boston China traders, as well as from the great whaling fortunes of New Bedford and leading financiers in Europe. Partly because he was exercising fiduciary control over the assets of others, Forbes's investments were unusually hardheaded and systematic. While most railroad men were promoters or speculators who looked for the big deal and the quick killing, Forbes was a true investor who strove to obtain a superior long-term return on capital. And by 1846 he was not at all satisfied with the results he had obtained over the past eight years. "My trade operations, . . . since I returned from China in 1837, have not averaged over six per cent interest on the amount invested, if you TAKE OUT the first lucky hit of the [ship] Acbar by being out during the China war, and the very nice tea speculation that was made for me at the same time."

These disappointing investment results put Forbes in a mood to listen carefully when two New Englanders came to him in 1846 with a proposal to take over the Michigan Central. This railroad was not a

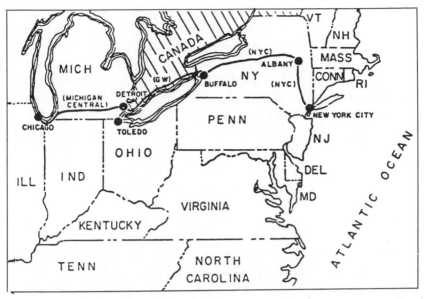

THE MICHIGAN CENTRAL AS PART OF A THROUGH ROUTE
FROM CHICAGO TO NEW YORK CITY, 1856.

company but a corpse—the remains of Michigan's abortive effort to
build a transportation network in the boom of 1837. Like other American railroads, it is most easily understood by glancing at a map. As
Figure 1 shows, the Central ran along Michigan's southern border,
from Detroit to Kalamazoo, and connected the western end of Lake
Erie with the southern end of Lake Michigan. It cut the length of a
trip from Buffalo to Chicago from four to six days to only thirty-six
hours because a traveler could take the direct overland route from
Detroit to Chicago instead of taking a steamboat all the way up Lake
Huron and down Lake Michigan. It was a well-conceived route, but not
much more than that, because when capital dried up after the panic
of 1836, the railroad was never finished. The completed segment was
left to rot in the wilderness, and a decade later it was "in a deplorable
condition, the iron broken up often into pieces not a foot long, and
sometimes we could not see any iron for some feet, only wood." By
1846 the financially hard-pressed state of Michigan was understandably
eager to turn this "railroad" into cash by selling it to capitalists who
would finish it and begin to provide the state with railroad service.

The purchase price was $2 million, a quarter to be paid immediately
and the balance within two years. Since western railroads were anath-

ema to eastern capitalists, John Murray Forbes had to take the lead in assembling the capital. In addition to digging deep into his own pocket, he contacted businessmen in Boston, New Bedford, and New York, and to win over investors, Forbes agreed to become president of the new enterprise, even though he had no expertise in railroading. Although he was actually beginning a new career, the Boston financier initially viewed the Michigan Central as a speculation that would not consume much time and would furnish an attractive managerial position for his older brother. "Little did I dream of the load I was taking on when I agreed to be president," he later recalled. He quickly discovered that a railroad deal was infinitely more complex than any venture in the China trade. The number of people was too great, the distances too vast, the amounts of money too large for a capitalist to make a swift profit and get out. To begin with, the purchase of the road had to be guided through a recalcitrant Michigan legislature. (One skeptical lawmaker suggested that the act be called "a bill to transfer the sovereignty of the State of Michigan to a company of Yankee speculators.") Managerial responsibility had to be divided between the investors in the East and the railroad managers in Michigan. There was friction between the New York investors and the Bostonians, who insisted on keeping control of the enterprise. And as was so often the case in railroad projects, the cost of construction greatly exceeded the investors' expectations. But once these hurdles had been cleared, it became evident that Forbes and his associates had made a shrewd and profitable purchase. The Midwest was rapidly filling up with settlers and the railroad was so well situated that it had an easy time stealing passenger traffic from the steamship lines that ran on the Great Lakes. By 1847 Forbes was chortling that "before the summer is out I shall show you some results that beat the China trade." A year later he informed his fellow shareholders, "The business of the road has been more profitable than we had any right to expect from it in its unfinished state."

But if the Michigan Central was profitable, it was also vulnerable. Soon after it had been completed, a group of New York investors bought up another defunct state railroad, the Michigan Southern, which ran parallel to the Central and also linked Lake Erie with Lake Michigan. In addition to providing head-to-head competition for the Central, the Southern threatened to outflank its rival by establishing a route around the southern tip of Lake Michigan to the town of Chicago. Having little firsthand knowledge of the West, Forbes did not at first appreciate the severity of this danger; he even passed up an opportunity to acquire cheaply a line running toward Chicago. But he soon realized that his entire investment was in jeopardy if he did not push through to the Windy City. "We are bound to use every exertion," he wrote, "to make our road a link in the great chain of communication between the East and the West." Since one had to pass through Indiana and Illinois to get to Chicago from Michigan, the Central had to grant substantial financial aid to railroads in those two states in order to obtain a right-of-way. This costly expansion was just the first of many extensions of the Forbes system between 1850 and 1880 that were motivated by strategic imperatives. In order to funnel local traffic into the system's east-west trunk line, the New Englanders built an extensive network of feeder routes during the 1850s that branched out from Chicago into the fertile Illinois plains. Eventually the network stretched out across the Mississippi River into Missouri and Kansas and reached all the way to Wyoming and Colorado.

Though he busied his life with many other affairs, John Murray Forbes was deeply involved in this expanding railroad network. He was not a megalomaniacal empire builder, in the mold of Cornelius Vanderbilt or E. H. Harriman, but rather a shrewd, active investor whose hard-nosed approach to purchasing corporate properties is still instructive today. Unlike so many investors of his time, he recognized that railroads, like other corporations, were no better than their managements. "While there are a hundred good projects, you will find it hard to choose ten men to manage them," he once wrote. Forbes would not even buy the bonds of a railroad if he did not think highly of the men who ran it: "I have no personal knowledge of the Marietta Road & my experience with R. Roads is such that I should not touch *any* Bonds whether *first* or tenth mortgage without having considerable positive information about the Road and its managers." In comparison with management quality, landholdings were of minor importance to Forbes when he evaluated a railroad. He was not comfortable with the Illinois Central, which owned millions of fertile acres, because he did not feel that he thoroughly understood the corporation: "If I had had any discretion given me I should have tried to keep you *out* of Illinois Central shares. . . . It is one of these big things hard to fathom & depending much on skill & honesty combined. *If it had both* I don't know enough about it to feel sure of it." Occasionally Forbes's emphasis on operating efficiency and disdain for western acreage led him astray. On an early tour of the Michigan Central he turned down an offer to buy land in Chicago at the rate of $1.25 an acre; by simply investing a sum equal to his hotel bill, he ruefully calculated, he could have purchased land that was later worth $8 million to $12 million.

The reason why Forbes feared any railroad investment—even a bond investment—unless he had "confidence enough to own some of the Stock & use influence as to management" was simply that so many railroad managers were corrupt. Forbes and other Boston Brahmins drew a sharp distinction between their own aboveboard approach to business and the frequently underhanded "ways in New York." When New Englanders collaborated on a project with such New York railroad men as the Albany merchant Erastus Corning, they kept a sharp eye on the books and frequently complained about the New Yorkers' self-dealing in land and equipment. In a typical comment (but to a westerner rather than a New Yorker) Forbes snapped, "I found to my *utter* surprise that you and all the other active directors upon whose judgment I had relied were interested in contracts for building the roads . . . that you were practically sellers of the bonds to us outside the ring, and that they and all the assets of the company had belonged to you as contractors—on such terms that with ordinary care (in *my* judgment) you ought to have made among you over a million of dollars by the bargain." No less troublesome were the "gamblers" on Wall Street; in order to keep the stock of their roads out of brokers' hands and thus safe from raids and speculations, the Bostonians encouraged ownership by small investors and the trustees of estates.

Like most great investors, Forbes was preoccupied with finding good value; an investment did not excite him unless he could buy it cheaply. Because he did not speculate with borrowed funds and owned railroads of the highest quality, Forbes was not seriously endangered by economic depressions and could afford to view financial panics with equanimity rather than alarm. To him they were opportunities to buy rather than occasions to sell. During one brief panic in the 1850s he characteristically observed, "I dont [sic] believe the world is coming to an end & consider this check up good for all good THINGS as it reduces labor [costs] and shuts off competition." Therefore, he grew increasingly excited as security prices plummeted: "I think we could make 50% clear in two years CERTAINLY IN 3 YEARS by taking of things WE KNOW and which will by that time have developed so that they cannot fail to be profitable." This value orientation motivated Forbes to make an excellent purchase in the Michigan Central, which was of no interest to investors in the mid-1840s, and he repeated this coup by picking up properties at distress prices in the panics of 1857 and 1873.

In sum, John Murray Forbes had four traits that made him a superior investor, and all of them can be valuable to an investor today. First, he was a contrarian—an independent thinker who bought intrinsically valuable property that was currently being ignored by investors. Secondly, he was a countercyclical investor who bought when the markets were depressed and sold when the markets were hot. This may sound simple but is actually very difficult. Not only is the countercyclical investor deprived of the psychological support of running with the crowd, but he or she has to buy investments the prices of which are depressed and currently "going nowhere" and to sell investments that have performed very well and are, in many cases, still rising in price. Thirdly, Forbes refused to purchase an investment unless he had good personal knowledge about it; he was not satisfied by rumor and inference. Finally, Forbes realized that the key to any investment is the people—not the property—that stand behind it. A railroad could have huge quantities of land, but that land was worth little unless it was intelligently managed and developed. So it is with most growth companies; since they operate in fast-changing, highly competitive markets, success hinges on the talent of individuals.

BULLS, BEARS, AND RAILROADS

As New York became the center of railroad finance in the 1850s and 1860s, the honest and disciplined investment style of such Bostonians as John Murray Forbes seemed increasingly anomalous, even quaint. A giant chasm of thought and feeling separated the austere counting-houses of State Street from the handsome halls of the New York Stock Exchange. Wall Street in the Gilded Age was a vortex of speculation and peculation, of gladiatorial contests between bulls and bears that resembled nothing so much as a popular pastime of the day, rat fighting, in which a vicious terrier was thrown into a pit of rats while spectators took bets on whether or not the dog could snap the rodents' necks, one by one, and come out alive. Like rats and terrier, the bulls and bears of Wall Street fought ferociously, for the stakes were very high. Not infrequently one contestant landed in a Fifth Avenue mansion, his vanquished adversary in the poorhouse.

The violent ways of Wall Street were not out of place in Boss Tweed's New York. The city of 1870 bore a definite resemblance to the New York of today, for it was dirty, dangerous, and overpriced. Then, as now, it was a polyglot city, full of Germans, Irish, and other European immigrants who had streamed into New York in the decades after 1830 and raised its population to nearly a million by 1872. Housing was in short supply. The poor lived in crowded tenements if they were lucky and deadly dank cellars if they were not. The alleys and side streets of the slums were notoriously filthy, strewn with offal, manure, and garbage; they would have been impassable if troops of pigs had not scavenged faithfully. In the more fashionable districts beggars were everywhere. A popular guidebook lamented that "they hang onto you with the utmost determination, exposing the most disgusting sights to your gaze, and annoying you so much that you give them money in order to get rid of them." Of still greater concern to wealthy citizens was the persistent crime problem, which extended far beyond the pickpockets, prostitutes, and confidence men who were much in evidence. In 1871, 171 people were "found drowned" in New York Harbor, presumably the victims of foul play. Not a few of these killings were the work of organized gangs of "roughs" who hung out at the waterfront and bore such picturesque names as the Dead Rabbits and Plug Uglies. Loosely connected with the larcenous Tammany Hall machine, the gangs figured largely in the New York draft riot of 1863. Actually a civil war within a civil war, this "riot" saw a huge mob ravage the city for three terrible days, burning buildings, lynching blacks, and battling the police. All told, including blacks and whites, civilians and policemen, more than 2,000 people were killed.

Poignant in itself, the squalor of New York was powerfully magnified by the splendors of the city—the mansions on Broadway and Fifth Avenue, the lavish banquets at Delmonico's and the Hotel Astor, the enormous carriages rushing through the streets. Yet informed observers of the New York scene did not simply emphasize the stark contrast between the rich and poor; rather, they saw them as inseparable parts of the same frenetic social system. In contrast with Boston or Virginia, money was everything in New York society. "Society here is organized upon a pecuniary basis," one writer claimed, "and stands not as it should upon the personal merits of those who compose it, but upon a pile of bank-books." In the expansive but chaotic economy of the Civil War years, shrewd and unscrupulous parvenus could scale the social ladder in a few years—and descend it just as rapidly. Consequently the line between rich and poor was not so wide as it seemed. "Watch the carriages as they whirl through Fifth Avenue, going and returning from the park," wrote one commentator. "They are as elegant and sumptuous as wealth can make them. The owners, lying back amongst the soft cushions, are clad in the height of fashion. By their dresses they might be princesses. This much is due to art. Now mark the coarse, rough features, the ill-bred stare, the haughty rudeness which they endeavor to palm off for dignity. Do you see any difference between them and the footman in livery on the carriage-box?"

There were many ways for a New Yorker to make the proverbial transition from footman to "gentleman," but none was more important than securities speculation. To moralists, Wall Street was one of the darkest corners of the American economy, "a gambling-den—a cage of unclean birds, an abomination where men drive a horrible trade, fattening and battening on the substance of their friends and neighbors." For better or worse, nineteenth-century securities markets were quite unlike those of today. The outstanding difference was that far fewer issues were available to trade in quantity. A handful of important railroads, including the Erie, Reading, Harlem, Hudson, and West Shore, were the chief trading vehicles on the Street, and the essence of speculation consisted of betting on the future price of one of these stocks. But speculators did not make their bet and then, in the manner of the modern options trader, sit back and see if it would pay off. They did everything possible to *make sure* the bet paid off by manipulating the market—making purchases for future delivery in order to force the stock price up (a "bull raid") or short sales to force it down (a "bear raid"). In major bull markets, when the general public was drawn into the market by the lure of easy profits, professional speculators fleeced small investors who did not understand the nature of the game. But more commonly the speculators battled each other, and they spared no weapon to win. They bought off judges and legislators to change the fortunes of railroads, they damaged a road's prospects by threatening to build parallel lines, they made bogus securities trades to confuse the opposition, they expanded the capitalization of a road (issued additional shares) in order to impede speculation, and they manipulated earnings and dividends.

Frequently the ultimate purpose of these tactics was to corner the foe. For example, Speculator A (a bear) was cornered if he had sold short the shares of a security and then discovered that he could not cover his position—that is, deliver the stock that he had sold short—

because his rival, Speculator B, (a bull) had purchased all the floating stock of the road. Unable to fulfill his contract to deliver the shares, the cornered bear was at the mercy of his victorious foe and would have to settle privately or go to court. Conversely, a bull was cornered when he contracted to buy a stock at some point in the future at a specified price—$90, let us say—and, when the time for purchase arrived, discovered that the stock was then selling at $50 and there were no more floating shares available for purchase.

This was no game for gentlemen. The great "operators" of Wall Street were typically petty capitalists of obscure rural origins—upstate New York was an especially fertile breeding ground—who had accumulated some capital by flitting from one commercial opportunity to another. Perhaps because inland railroads were their favorite prey, relatively few were immigrants, and not many had been highly successful businessmen before coming to Wall Street. By making it big in the markets, they became instant celebrities, on a par with illustrious prizefighters, and like prizefighters, they tended to have spectacular and short careers. Wall Street operators were said to have "a prematurely old look, and . . . they died at a comparatively early age. This is not strange. They live too fast. Their bodies and brains are taxed too severely to last long." So it was with the German speculator Charles F. Woerishoffer, who, after making a fortune by developing and manipulating the Denver and Rio Grande Railroad, got into trouble by being short stocks and long wheat in 1885—precisely the wrong market strategy. Woerishoffer died the following year "because of the great strain of mind growing out of his business transactions." Then there was Sam Hallet, by turns a schoolteacher, lumberman, bookkeeper, and banker. He became a broker at age thirty-one, attempted to manipulate the shares of the Kansas branch of the Union Pacific Railroad, and was assassinated at age thirty-seven by an irate civil engineer who worked for the road. Still more colorful was the career of James Fisk, Jr. After a stint of service with a traveling menagerie, the flamboyant operator became first a Yankee peddler and later a dry goods merchant associated with the firm of Jordan & Marsh. After the Civil War he met up with the devious genius Jay Gould, becoming one of Gould's chief henchmen in the violent and protracted battle with Cornelius Vanderbilt for control of the Erie. As a business partner Gould was no more dependable than a cobra, but it was a liaison of a different sort that led to Fisk's demise. His buxom mistress Josie Mansfield deserted him for another man and then proceeded to blackmail

Fisk mercilessly, threatening to disclose to the public the assorted crimes committed during the Erie war. When Fisk finally stopped paying the hush money, Mansfield decided to enforce her rights in court, but the widely publicized trial ended abruptly when Fisk was gunned down by her new lover.

One of the preeminent operators of the 1850s and 1860s was a former drover, tanner, and steamboat operator named Daniel Drew. "Uncle Daniel," as he was generally known, was unlettered, uncouth, and unscrupulous, but also very pious. Among his many philanthropic deeds was the creation of a seminary in Madison, New Jersey, that became a university and still bears his name. A personal acquaintance penned this deft portrait: "In personal appearance Drew was tall, strong, and sinewy, and in his later days his face was seamed with deep lines, indicating intense thought and worry. He had restless twinkling eyes, with a steady cat-like tread in his gait. His general demeanor was bland, good-natured and insinuating, with affected but well dissembled humility, which was highly calculated to disarm any resentment, and enable him to move smoothly in society among all shades and conditions of men." A story that penetrates Uncle Daniel's sunny exterior tells of a young man known as California Parker (he had made a fortune in the gold rush) who began to buy Erie stock aggressively and raised its price 20 percent. He then asked Drew to lend him money so that he could raise the stock still higher and later sell out at that elevated price. Drew, of course, would share in the gains. After agreeing to join this scheme, Drew proceeded to double-cross his new ally. He waited for Parker to push the price of Erie stock still higher and then informed the Californian that unfortunately he would not be able to supply the requisite funds after all. Since Parker had no more money with which to manipulate the stock, the bubble in Erie shares quickly collapsed. Having already sold Erie short, Drew made a killing on the fall.

Although Drew made his mark in several different fields, it was from the Erie Railroad that he squeezed most of his fortune, which reportedly amounted to $13 million by the end of the Civil War. This mammoth railroad, which ran from the Hudson River to Lake Erie through the southern tier of New York counties, was started in 1833 but not completed until 1851, after surviving a shattering series of trials and crises. The road was financially weak in the fifties, in part because of vicious rate wars with the New York Central. Drew gained power over the Erie both by lending it funds in times of financial stringency and by controlling a small but strategically situated railroad in western

New York. After the panic of 1857 he assumed the position of treasurer. As a major creditor, director, and treasurer of the troubled road Drew was able to manipulate its fortunes almost at will, while reaping large profits by trading its widely fluctuating stock. So well known were Uncle Daniel's tactics that he earned the title of the "speculative director."

Able though he was, Daniel Drew was not in the same league with the crafty genius Jay Gould. Gould's commanding strength was corporate finance, rather than stock market operations or railroad management. He was unsurpassed in the subtle art of bending securities laws to secure his own ends, and what Gould could not do legally he accomplished with bribes. His "management" of the Union Pacific during the 1870s shows the art of railroad financiering at its most refined. When Gould acquired a controlling interest in the Union Pacific, the nation's first transcontinental line, it faced stiff competition from a parallel road, the Kansas Pacific. After a bitter struggle with other financiers Gould took control of the financially strapped Kansas Pacific and also purchased at bargain rates controlling interests in three other feeble but strategically placed roads: the Denver Pacific, Missouri Pacific, and Central Pacific. Only a few short links were needed to give Gould a railroad system running clear through to the Pacific. A ruinous rate war staring them in the face, the directors of the Union Pacific were more than willing to discuss a merger when Gould came to them in December 1879. His terms were stiff. He demanded and won a stock-for-stock exchange between the solid, dividend-paying securities of the Union Pacific and the shares of two of his ramshackle roads. Gould reportedly made $10 million on the deal. This was simply a variety of greenmail, for he threatened to make life miserable for Union Pacific management unless he was bought out.

CORNELIUS VANDERBILT: THE BUCCANEER AS BUILDER

Whereas Drew and Gould were corporate predators who pounced on vulnerable railroads and mauled them savagely, Cornelius Vanderbilt was a builder. The son of a common Dutch farmer who lived on Staten Island, he began his career in 1810 as a fearless and tireless ferryboat operator, plying the route between his hometown and the Battery on Manhattan Island. After the War of 1812 Vanderbilt branched out into the coastal trade and soon was involved in the booming field of steamboating, initially serving as the point man in a desperate attempt to break the official monopoly in steamboating in New York Harbor. From these small beginnings "Commodore" Vanderbilt prospered in steamboating in the next three decades, becoming the largest operator in the country. The quintessential parvenu, he was a big, strapping, plainspoken man with muttonchop sideburns and a minimum of social graces. He was not inclined to beat around the bush. When some New York businessmen challenged his interests while he was traveling in Europe in 1853, he sent this simple missive:

Gentlemen:
  You have undertaken to cheat me. I won't sue you, for the law is too slow. I'll ruin you.

Yours Truly,
Cornelius Vanderbilt

The Commodore's vessels plied the Hudson River and dominated the traffic on Long Island Sound, and to cash in on the California gold rush, he established a transit line running from New York to San Francisco via Nicaragua. In all these exploits Vanderbilt showed himself to be tough, courageous, and contemptuous of legal forms yet intent on building a successful business by delivering adequate service at a low price. Once a legislative examiner questioned the Commodore about the propriety of his bare-knuckled competitive tactics, asking, "Did you know that the law provides a remedy for all wrongs, and that railroad corporations have no right to take the redress of their own wrongs into their own hands to the detriment of the public?" With disarming candor Vanderbilt explained, "The law, as I view it, goes too slow for me when I have the remedy in my own hands."

Honed on the wharves that lined South Street, this philosophy was easily transferred to nearby Wall Street. During the 1850s Vanderbilt skillfully used his large fortune to execute a series of brilliant stock market raids and establish a consolidated railroad empire connecting New York City with Albany, the Great Lakes, and Chicago. The heart of this empire was the Hudson and Harlem lines, which ran parallel to the Hudson River between New York City and the Albany area, and the New York Central, which connected Albany with the Great Lakes.

By the 1850s the Harlem was an old and rather pathetic road that followed an unprofitable route northward from New York City to

Albany. Because it had been built at a time when Hudson River steamboats still posed formidable competition, it ran far to the east of the Hudson instead of going along the water's edge. While there was limited competition on this route, there was also paltry traffic; the Harlem was famous on Wall Street for almost never paying a dividend. According to one paper, "of all the railroad shares dealt in, the Harlem probably possesses the least intrinsic value." The road did have one valuable asset, however—namely, its extensive terminal facilities within New York City. Its main terminal was located at Twenty-sixth Street but was connected by horse-drawn cars with terminals at Fourteenth Street and City Hall. Since intracity traffic was its most profitable business, the Harlem sought the right to extend its tracks all the way to the southern tip of Manhattan during the Civil War. Once the petition had been successfully guided through the covetous committees of the Tammany Hall machine, it set off a spectacular rise in the price of Harlem stock. When Vanderbilt—at the time only a major share-holder—was made president of the road, it became clear that he had taken the lead in buying off the city fathers.

The elevated stock price of this fundamentally weak company was an attractive quarry for Vanderbilt's fellow director Daniel Drew, who was by instinct a bear and always most comfortable when he had sold a stock short and was "hammering" its price. After selling short a large block of Harlem shares, Drew drove down its stock by inducing the New York legislature in Albany to grant a competing franchise to another syndicate of investors. Uncle Daniel anticipated large and quick gains from this treachery, but he had not counted on the ample resources of the Vanderbilt group, which was rich enough to purchase the stock of all sellers, whether investors or speculators, and prevent Drew from covering his short position. As the *Tribune* explained, "A corner of the most formidable proportions is impending. The chief owners of the Harlem property are Mr. Cornelius Vanderbilt and his immediate friends, and that portion of the capital stock which they have not already paid for and transferred to their names, they have the cash means in the bank to pay for, whenever the short-sellers—who have contracted for more than the entire capital—are ready to make deliveries." The "Vanderbilt crowd" did indeed trounce the bears, forcing them to purchase stock at prices that were roughly double what they had contracted to sell them for. In the process the Commodore secured a controlling interest in the Harlem.

No sooner had Daniel Drew recovered from this fight than he was at it again, this time bribing the state legislature to deprive the Harlem of its right-of-way in lower Manhattan. But again Drew was defeated by the superior financial muscle of Vanderbilt, losing tens of thousands in the attempt. Two years later the action shifted to the Harlem's main rival, the Hudson River Line, which ran along the river's edge from New York City to Albany—the route that the Harlem's founders should have selected when they planned their road. After surviving a bruising bear raid in Hudson shares, Vanderbilt emerged with a controlling interest in the line. Now in command of the two roads that connected New York City with Albany, Vanderbilt was in an excellent position to dictate terms to the New York Central, which he took over in 1867. Two years later he took control of the Lake Shore and Michigan Southern, which extended his empire to Chicago.

Vanderbilt's approach to managing his roads was ruthless but constructive. As summarized by his biographer, Wheaton J. Lane, it was to "1, buy your line; 2, stop the stealing that went on under the other man; 3, improve it in every practicable way within a reasonable expenditure; 4, consolidate it with other lines for the sake of efficiency; 5, water its stock; and 6, make it pay a large dividend." Point 5 of Vanderbilt's managerial formula—"water its stock"—bears closer scrutiny, because stock watering was one of the chief abuses of railroad finance. Oddly enough, it rested on a conception of corporate finance that was holy gospel in the nineteenth century but seems illogical today. The nineteenth-century investor assumed that a share normally traded at $100. This was its par value and the price at which it had originally been issued. Behind this share, it was assumed, should stand $100 in tangible assets, which would generate income sufficient to pay a dividend of 5 to 8 percent. In modern parlance, the par value, book value, tangible book value (also known as breakup value), and market price all should be $100. Today, by contrast, a stock may have an official par value of $1 per share, a book value of $10 per share, a tangible book value of $20 per share, and a market price of $15. An unusually profitable railroad could reward its owners in one of two ways: either by paying exceptionally high dividends or by accumulating the undistributed earnings as owner's equity and eventually distributing this wealth to shareholders in the form of new stock. This new issue would be considered legitimate because $100 of tangible assets stood behind each new share.

Watered stock was simply this: new stock issues that were not backed by a surplus of accumulated profits. Under the assumptions of nineteenth-century Wall Street, it was an unvarnished fraud—a piece of paper not backed by real assets. Unscrupulous financiers like Drew and Gould were understandably eager to swap stock backed by no assets for $100 in cash. Since the road could seldom pay dividends on watered stock, such antics would eventually depress the share price, but not before the railroad's insiders could profit from the new influx of funds. This was the next best thing to printing money, the equivalent of a modern corporation that doubles the number of common shares outstanding (a two-for-one stock split) without seeing its stock price drop by half. The concept of watered stock seems illogical today, when securities are usually valued primarily on the basis of their *earning power* rather than the *assets* per share and when stock splits normally bring on a proportionate decline in share price, but within the intellectual framework of nineteenth-century finance it was a serious abuse.

Cornelius Vanderbilt loved watered stock. Upon taking over the Hudson Railroad, he modestly raised its equity capitalization, and after acquiring the New York Central, he increased the number of shares by 80 percent. The merger of these two roads in 1869 offered still another opportunity to dump water on Wall Street. As Wheaton Lane has written, "in the short space of three years, $48,684,200 in watered stock had been added to the capitalization of the two roads"—more than half their total equity capitalization. Vanderbilt defended this deluge by insisting, as would most modern investors, that it is earning power, rather than assets per share, that matters most in determining the value of stock. The Commodore knew how to slash costs in order to raise profits, even going to the length of stripping his locomotives of their brass ornaments. Wasn't he able to earn enough money to pay dividends on these "watered" shares?

> He explained: My idea of a railroad is this. If I take possession of a railroad today I send my men over it to examine it in every particular and all over; they report to me its condition and then it is my business to see that it is kept up, equal in every respect to what it is then, for the next year's report, in respect to the rolling stock and everything else; *if I increase it beyond that, that is a subject which may be credited to the road—to the stockholders if you please. . . .* If you have been running a road and you spend nine or ten millions to run it, if I cannot do it for eight, and do it as well, I am ready to go from the road; this is profit

enough for me; that has been my principle with steamships; I never had
any advantage of anybody in running steamships; but if I could not run
a steamship alongside of any other man and do it as well as he for twenty
per cent less than it cost him I would leave the ship.

Unfortunately the Commodore was the exception that proved the rule.
Very few of the waterlogged shares that were strewn about Wall Street
faithfully paid dividends in the manner of the New York Central,
because few roads were as well managed and had such strong business
franchises. Consequently, watered stock was a leading cause of the
endemic financial frailty that plagued the American railway network.
By the count of one expert, water seeped into the balance sheets of
railroads through no less than seven different leaks. Straight stock
dividends, such as Vanderbilt declared after taking over the New York
Central, were the most flagrant method, but mergers, financial reorganizations, and construction programs also presented fine opportunities for loading down a road with new stocks and bonds. The inside
construction companies described earlier in this chapter were one of
the most reliable springs that spewed forth watered securities. When
such abuses were exploited by the likes of Daniel Drew and Jay Gould,
the results could be grotesque indeed. In their famous battle with
Cornelius Vanderbilt for control of the Erie the share capital of the
road increased from $17 million to $78 million in fewer than five years.
Such chicanery infuriated the public at large—not, to be sure, from any
tender regard for the Wall Street operators who traded these suspect
shares but rather from a conviction that railroads charged excessive
rates in order to pay dividends and interest on their swollen capital.

One can argue that America's railway system would never have been
built if the financiers who took great risks and made great exertions to
put the deals together had not been able to earn huge speculative
profits in return. The trouble was that many financiers could make a
killing whether or not the road was a long-term economic success;
indeed, they often had incentives to disrupt the operations of roads that
were quite successful. Unfortunately this is still true (although to a
much lesser extent) today. It is perfectly possible, for example, for a
Wall Street firm to earn a big fee for designing and executing a merger
that is a long-run failure. It is perfectly possible for a financier to issue
paper not backed by underlying asset value or earning power and take
control of a company. Can Carl Icahn emulate Commodore Vanderbilt and run the "steamship" TWA alongside other airlines for 20

percent less, or will the junk bonds issued to finance the purchase assume the characteristics of watered stock? Although Wall Street is a critically valuable source of fresh, objective ideas for using capital more effectively, the basic strategic decisions concerning the future of a company are best left to the executives who run it—not to bankers, consultants, accountants, and lawyers. That is, after all, what the executives are paid to do.

V

Andrew Carnegie's Private War

Although railroads constituted the most important industry of nine-teenth-century America, they were in many ways atypical because they consumed unusually large quantities of capital and included many giant companies that spanned the continent. The typical industrial enter-prise in nineteenth-century America was a family partnership or closely held corporation that had little to do with the stock market. (In fact, so few industrial issues were traded on the New York Stock Exchange that the Dow Jones industrial average was not even invented until 1896.) The history of the steel industry reveals the advantages and disadvantages of this arrangement. Ironmakers did not need vast amounts of capital to commence operations and therefore did not have to distribute large blocks of securities in New York, London, and Washington. Instead, three or four capitalists could pool their talent and money in a partnership, set up a furnace or forge, and, if the business was profitable, expand it simply by reinvesting earnings.

WORKMEN AND CAPITALISTS: ADVANTAGES OF THE PARTNERSHIP

One advantage of the partnership was that iron and steel companies were controlled by industry insiders who had a long-term commitment to making steel. Very often some of the partners were capitalists who had plenty of financial expertise and general business experience, while other partners were workmen who had been making iron and steel all their lives. Such firms possessed, in an informal and ad hoc way, some of the advantages of the modern venture capital firms, which likewise create partnerships between technologically sophisticated entrepreneurs and financially savvy businessmen. The partnership had motivational advantages as well. Dozens of talented junior employees worked intensely for years in the hopes of being given a lucrative partnership in a fast-growing company such as Carnegie Steel. And because they paid no huge salaries to key employees and required that partners reinvest in the company their share of the firm's earnings, the partnership also conserved the funds of these capital-hungry growth companies.

But there was a sometimes fatal drawback to the partnership. They were uneasy coalitions between egotistical superachievers and were often unstable. As key partners got older, they were tempted to sell their interest in the company to an outside company willing to pay a price far above its book value. This problem is illustrated by modern-day Wall Street partnerships. A secret of success for such fine firms as Salomon Brothers, Goldman, Sachs, and Lehman Brothers was that young employees worked very hard in order to be "made partner." But several Wall Street firms, notably Lehman Brothers Kuhn Loeb, sold out at inopportune times because certain partners wanted to "cash out." Much the same problem dogged Carnegie Steel. After financing and overseeing the creation of one of the finest companies in the history of industrial America, Andrew Carnegie decided in 1901 to sell his company to J. P. Morgan, a man of immense financial acumen who had little knowledge of steel. Despite his ignorance of the industry, Morgan combined Carnegie Steel with a large but uneven collection of other companies to create U.S. Steel. This mammoth new company was dominated by cautious lawyers and financiers representing Morgan rather than hard-driving steel executives from Carnegie Steel, and consequently it was flaccid and sluggish. U.S. Steel was more concerned with the threat posed by Washington trustbusters than that of competing steelmakers. Mediocre from inception, U.S. Steel set standards for the American steel industry that foreign competitors have had little trouble beating.

No one appreciated the tremendous differences in the financial structure of the railroad and steel industries more acutely than the steelmakers themselves, for they had an intense love-hate relationship with the railroads: love, because the railroads gobbled up vast quantities of iron and steel when the stock market was hot and railroads were expanding; hate, because these building booms were always cut short by a financial panic and protracted depression that curtailed railroad expansion and iron production for several years. In the dark days of the

1840s, 1870s, and 1890s, iron men sneered at the the railroad barons for their speculative sins, admonishing them to produce an honest product for a change, instead of manufacturing securities to vend in lower Manhattan. In a typical comment *Iron Age* observed: "Before the late Commodore Vanderbilt turned his attention to this subject, railways were looked upon here in the East as a means for affording opportunities for stock jobbing rather than profits from operation." When the steel companies finally began to issue securities on Wall Street during the 1890s, *Iron Age* fretted that "a good many people utterly ignorant of the [steel] industry have become partners in enterprises, either as temporary holders of stock or as investors in steel securities. They can be worked upon and influenced greatly by newspaper reports and brokers' tattle."

One man who understood perfectly the difference between real production and mere speculation was the great steelmaker Andrew Carnegie, himself a master of the devious art of financiering before he focused his attention on steel. Carnegie believed that businessmen who plunged into a multiplicity of speculative schemes, instead of concentrating on one solid business, were sure to meet grief sooner or later. The best policy was "to put all good eggs in one basket and then watch that basket." Securities speculation was to be avoided at all cost; like liquor or opium, it clouded the brain. A businessman's mind "must be kept calm and free," Carnegie urged, "if he is to decide wisely the problems which are continually coming before him. Nothing tells in the long run like good judgment, and no sound judgment can remain with the man whose mind is disturbed by the mercurial changes of the Stock Exchange. It places him under an influence akin to intoxication. What is not, he sees, and what he sees, is not. He cannot judge of relative values or get the true perspective of things. The molehill seems to him a mountain and the mountain a molehill, and he jumps at conclusions which he should arrive at by reason." Having seen more than one successful ironmaster sucked into the Wall Street maelstrom and separated from his capital, Carnegie shrewdly observed that people rarely went broke in the business they really understood; it was the alluring sidelines—the western gold mines and can't-miss railroad schemes—that chewed up fortunes.

With Napoleonic aggressiveness, Carnegie applied these dicta to build the finest steel company in the world. With his American competitors struggling to keep pace the United States developed a superbly efficient steel industry in the last four decades of the nineteenth century. By avoiding the speculative excesses that beset the railroads, American capital markets had served the steel industry and the nation well. It is therefore a bitter irony that this achievement was squandered in the final step of the steel industry's rise to maturity, its consolidation phase, when Andrew Carnegie sold his superb company to J. P. Morgan, a financial colossus who cared little about the operating efficiency of the U.S. steel industry.

Like blind chefs who stumble around the kitchen identifying ingredients by touch and smell alone, nineteenth-century ironmakers had to work with mysterious materials that they understood poorly. The problem was an ignorance of chemistry. So novel was this field in the 1870s that when Andrew Carnegie hired a chemist and dispatched him to the hills of Pennsylvania, the scientist was "suspected of illicit intercourse with the Powers of Evil when he undertook to tell by his suspicious-looking apparatus what a stone contained." The typical ironmaster was a technological innocent, "a veritable quack doctor who applied whatever remedies occurred to him for the troubles of his patient [the blast furnace]." Wandering in a scientific wilderness, ironmasters had to improve technology through a tedious process of trial and error. With the partial exception of Henry Bessemer, whose process took many years to perfect, no geniuses comparable to Thomas Edison or Alexander Graham Bell burst forth from the laboratory with dramatic discoveries that transformed the industry overnight. Only through a continuous process of incremental improvement did iron manufacturers cheapen and accelerate the process of converting iron ore into pig iron, wrought iron, and steel.

Although they became higher and hotter during the nineteenth century, blast furnaces were always the first step in the production process. Iron ore and fuel were dumped into the top of the blast furnace, which, with the help of mechanical bellows, converted the ore into pig iron. This crude metal, also known as cast iron, is full of impurities that make it highly brittle and therefore detestable to blacksmiths, engine makers, and other artisans. Since pig iron could be used only for objects needing little tensile strength (such as pots and pans), much of it was reheated and purged of impurities in order to produce wrought iron. During the early nineteenth century this refining procedure was accomplished by pounding molten pig iron with a gigantic hammer powered by a waterwheel. But by the 1840s wrought iron was produced by stirring and kneading the pig iron in a puddling furnace and then squeezing out the impurities in a rolling mill.

Until the Civil War wrought iron and pig iron formed the metallic skeleton for America's Industrial Revolution. Steel was an expensive specialty metal, mostly imported from Europe, that was used only for knives, axes, scythes, drills, and other tools. Not until the the 1860s and 1870s did American manufacturers successfully adapt the Bessemer method of making steel in large quantities by blowing cold air into molten pig iron in order to drive out the impurities and then reintroducing a controlled amount of carbon to increase the metal's strength. By 1880 at least ten large mills were producing steel by the Bessemer process, leaving the age of iron behind.

As the iron and steel industry matured, its epicenter gradually moved westward. Before the Civil War eastern Pennsylvania was the primary locus of production. Here were situated good beds of iron ore and deposits of hard, clean coal known as anthracite that could be used in blast furnaces, puddling furnaces, and rolling mills. Because timber was still abundant west of the Appalachians while anthracite was unavailable, western ironmakers continued to use a fuel of medieval vintage: charcoal made by slowly burning piles of wood. After the Civil War, however, Pittsburgh ironmasters rapidly moved to the technological van. They perfected methods of producing a fuel known as coke by roasting the region's abundant soft coal in thousands of ovens that looked like miniature igloos. The coke was used to smelt low-phosphorus iron ore—suitable for making Bessemer steel—which was shipped across the Great Lakes from Michigan and Minnesota. Thus midwestern iron ore and Pennsylvania coke sustained the great iron and steel industry of the Ohio Valley. As the market for steel expanded in the Far West and coal was discovered in northern Illinois, Chicago also became a major center of production in the 1880s and 1890s.

To win the iron wars of nineteenth-century America, a company needed plenty of money and plenty of talent. Money was required not only to build a factory but also to keep it intact during the depressions that periodically rocked the industry. And technical talent of a very high order was needed to keep pace with the technological change that was constantly driving prices lower. Recognizing these strategic imperatives, successful entrepreneurs usually created partnerships or closely held corporations and shared ownership with prominent workmen. This was a simple but potent arrangement that maximized the value of every dollar invested. The capitalists were typically successful businessmen conversant with railroads, the key market for iron and steel. They could afford to construct ironworks without floating securities or borrowing large sums from banks because they did not have to build an entire plant—blast furnace, puddling furnaces, rolling mills, and finishing mills—all at once. Usually they first built a rolling mill that turned out rails and iron plates and then integrated backward by adding their own blast furnaces and eventually their own mines.

To run these mills, they attracted the best talent they could find—workmen who had grown up in the iron business and were forever dreaming up ways to run the mills faster and cheaper. More often than not, this meant immigrants from Germany, England, and Wales, for Europe was technologically ahead of the United States until late in the century. Thus the accomplished German ironmaster John Fritz was a founder of Bethlehem Steel, as were the Welshmen John and David Jones for the Cleveland Rolling Mills. Bernard Laugh, a prominent foreign-born inventor of iron-rolling machinery, was a founder of Jones & Laughlin, and a number of foreign workmen became partners of Carnegie Steel. For these immigrant mechanics, long hours at the mill evidently left little time for mastering the English language. At a testimonial dinner to celebrate a successful year, one German iron wizard summed up the challenge that lay before his partners: "What we haf to do, shentlemens, is to get brices up and costs down and efery man *stand on his own bottom.*"

The advantages of these partnerships between capitalists and workmen were many. They lodged control of the company in the hands of industry insiders, who had a strong commitment to the firm's success. They concentrated in a single firm the talents of both expert workmen and savvy businessmen, while giving the key players an ownership stake and thus a strong incentive to excel. They allowed entrepreneurs to start small—on a single rolling mill or nail factory—and learn by doing, rather than initially risk millions on a mammoth project fraught with unanticipated hazards. In short, the iron firms embodied many of the virtues of the modern American venture capital firm. Patient, high-value capital was supplied by experienced businessmen to technologists of awesome skill and energy.

This arrangement was not peculiar to ironmaking; indeed, it was ubiquitous in early American manufacturing. And nowhere was it more so than in America's first bona fide high-tech industry, textile manufacturing, which owed its extraordinary success to partnerships between British immigrant manufacturers and brilliant New England merchants. One cornerstone of the Industrial Revolution—the eighteenth-century equivalent of the microchip—was various machines developed in England to mechanize the spinning of yarn. The technology was a bonanza because it vastly increased labor productivity in a key industry, and the British government made Herculean efforts to keep it in England. Blueprints, models, and plans of the new machines were forbidden to leave the country, and so were the highly skilled artisans who understood the technology. One such artisan was a precocious lad named Samuel Slater, who had been apprenticed for seven years to a leading figure in the textile revolution. Shrewd beyond his years, Slater realized that his expertise at cotton spinning was worth more in America, where it was still a mystery, than in England. So in 1789, at the age of nineteen, Slater memorized the technology by heart, disguised himself as a farm laborer, and took passage for New York. Within a few weeks of his arrival Slater had contacted Moses Brown, founder of Brown University and leader of Rhode Island's greatest mercantile family. For two years Brown had been trying to develop a viable cotton spinning industry in order to revive Rhode Island's distressed economy and secure employment for his fellow Quakers. But all of Brown's efforts had been "defeated by inadequate machines and inadequate mechanics." Slater was just the man he needed, and Brown did not intend to let him slip away by dickering over terms. Come up to Providence, Brown proposed in his plain-style Quaker manner, and construct a workable cotton spinning factory, using my facilities, contacts, and capital, and you will get all the profits for six months, after deducting depreciation charges and the cost of capital. After that, Brown added, we can agree on a long-term arrangement. It was not a bad offer for a nineteen-year-old, and Slater snapped it up. He moved to Providence, set up a profitable spinning mill, and eventually formed a lucrative long-term partnership with the Browns. Imitators quickly appeared, and by 1809 Rhode Island contained twenty-seven spinning mills.

FROM CORPORATION TO PARTNERSHIP AT TREDEGAR

Though few were so successful as the Brown-Slater combination, partnerships between capitalists and workmen were common in the iron industry. The experience of the Tredegar Ironworks in Richmond, Virginia, is a case in point; Tredegar's success stands out with special brilliance in the short and dreary history of industrial enterprise in the Slave South. What makes Tredegar's history instructive is that it was founded as a corporation but did not prosper until it became a partnership dominated by an entrepreneur who was fully committed to making steel—rather than a board of directors comprised of industry outsiders. Unlike most northern ironworks, Tredegar began life as a corporation that resembled the early railroads. Emboldened by the easy money of the inflationary 1830s, a group of Virginia businessmen secured a charter from the state legislature authorizing the creation of a corporation with a capital of $175,000 to $300,000. Perhaps the scarcity of capital in a state dominated by land-poor planters explains why the founders resorted to the corporate plan. Whatever the reason, their timing could not have been worse. Tredegar began operations a few months before Andrew Jackson's war on the Bank of the United States threw the nation into a deflationary paroxysm that crippled the iron industry. After bleeding red ink for several years, the directors turned management of Tredegar over to a man with the brains and guts needed to revive it.

The son of a strict Scotch-Irish Presbyterian, Joseph Anderson grew up in Virginia's Shenandoah Valley in a condition of respectable poverty. According to Anderson's biographer, Charles B. Dew, he was "a dark-haired youth of erect carriage, almost six feet tall, with broad, slightly sloping shoulders. Intense dark eyes dominated his full face, and he possessed prominent cheekbones, a strong jaw, and a wide forehead." For Anderson, as for so many other ambitious southerners before the Civil War, the most direct path to success was military service, so he secured appointment to West Point. As he traveled to the academy in the spring of 1832, Anderson was gripped by an ill-defined ambition "to penetrate the unexplored vista that lies before me." After his four years in the booming Empire State Anderson's "unexplored vista" took on the golden hue of cold cash; the Virginian was struck by how "the immense profits of the New York Canals are enriching the state" and concluded that the straitened life of the army officer was not for him. As a classmate observed, Anderson possessed an "ambition sufficiently grasping to ensure a due portion of the world's gifts and honors." Or as Anderson himself put it, "Those who are not born to fortunes should take every step with a view to its practical benefit." With this point in mind, Anderson acquired training as a civil engineer while still a cadet.

Upon returning to Virginia in 1837, Anderson supervised the construction of various canal and railroad projects sponsored by the state and then joined the business-oriented Whig party. These activities brought him into contact with the businessmen who had founded Tredegar. In 1841, at the depth of the depression, Anderson became commercial agent for Tredegar, a post which paid him a commission of 5 percent on sales of iron and 2.5 percent on collection of debts. Anderson immediately used his military connections to line up orders for shot, shell, cannon, and chain cable, and he was not above using the home state loyalty of fellow Virginians to tap federal largess. When he learned that all four vessels in a new line of iron steamers were to be constructed by northern companies, Anderson paid a visit to President John Tyler at the White House. "I remonstrated with Mr. Tyler against it and still hope to get him to order one to be built here. . . . The President wants only a little persuasion to order one to be built here, and if he does not the north will have the sale and greatly the advantage over us as they will have all the experience when the next parcel are put under contract."

Anderson's skill as a salesman and manager rapidly put Tredegar in the black, but the ambitious engineer chafed under the interference of his board of directors. Desiring full control of the works, he rented them for five years in 1843, taking pleasure in the knowledge that "I will now have no restraint (fear of unkind thoughts or remarks of ignorant & censurous people) in doing justice to the Iron in guns, having to consult only my own judgment and no Board of directors." And when the lease expired in 1848, he purchased the plant for $125,-000, which was to be paid to the stockholders in five annual installments. This deal exposed Anderson to very big risks. He intended to finance the purchase out of the cash flow of the works but was stymied by the erratic profitability of the iron industry, caused in part by competition from cheap British rails. Only by borrowing from Richmond bankers and improvising a series of partnerships was he able to meet his payments. One of the most important partnerships was with John Tanner, a superb manager who was superintendent of the rolling mills. In the manner of Moses Brown, Anderson also used the lure of ownership to attract first-class mechanics. In 1852 he recruited two Boston tradesmen to run a locomotive shop, and in 1854 he formed a partnership with a skilled machinist and two relatives to build a foundry and machine shop.

As iron prices rose during the 1850s, the pieces of Anderson's business plan finally fell into place. He paid off his debts and bought out his minor partners, and in 1859 he formed a partnership consisting of two close relatives, mill superintendent Tanner, and himself. It had taken Anderson fully eighteen years to effect the transition from an unwieldy corporation impeded by an ineffectual board of directors to a tight, well-capitalized partnership in which the managers were owners. A major reason for this lengthy delay—one not found in the telephone, automobile, and computer industries discussed in later chapters of this book—was the highly cyclical nature of the iron industry.

PETER COOPER'S FAMILY FIRM

A good way to combine the deep pocket and experience of a veteran capitalist with the vigor and drive of a young man was through a family partnership. This was an age-old method of business finance stretching back to the Rothschilds, Medicis, and Fuggers, and it still made sense in the iron industry of nineteenth-century America. Joseph Anderson had relied on family members to scrape together the capital needed to buy Tredegar, and in the Philadelphia area two intertwined Quaker families started iron businesses before the Civil War that were still making money in the 1970s. But the most remarkable antebellum iron family was the Cooper-Hewitt clan, whose Trenton Iron Company was a technological leader until the 1870s.

The senior partner in the Trenton Iron Company was a quirky mechanical genius named Peter Cooper. In the tradition of Benjamin Franklin and Thomas Edison, Cooper had the ability to fix his attention on a machine and quickly think of a dozen ways to improve it. "I was always fussing and contriving," Cooper recalled late in life, "and was never satisfied unless I was doing something difficult—something that had never been done before." While he was still a young child, his mother set him to cleaning clothes by soaking them in a tub and pounding them with a long-handled mallet. The task was tedious and tiring, so Cooper designed a crude washing machine that used concentrically rotating barrels to agitate the clothes. Somewhat later in his childhood he pulled apart a set of shoes to analyze their construction. Cooper quickly figured out the basics of shoemaking; obtained last, leather, and awls; and kept his brothers and sisters in shoes for a number of years. And when he had his own children and grew weary of coming home from work every night to rock his baby's cradle, Cooper dreamed up a way to mechanize the task: "I soon concluded that I could find an easier way of having the cradle rocked. I went to my shop and got up a pendulous cradle that not only kept going, but by an attachment, I gave it a mechanical instrument that would sing the child to sleep. It had a still further advantage, for by placing a cloth on the frame, its swinging motion would keep the flies off the little one." When a Yankee peddler saw the contraption, he seized the chance to acquire the patent, saying, "I'll give you my horse and wagon and all there is in it."

A man like Cooper, who invented as easily and naturally as other men breathed, had little trouble making his way in the world. Although he had been apprenticed to a New York coachmaker, he entered the workshop of a mechanic who made machines for shearing the nap from cloth. After saving his wages for three years, Cooper purchased the patent from his boss, improved the machine in a number of ways, and set up a prosperous business. Unfortunately a massive influx of British dry goods after the War of 1812 depressed the American textile industry and injured Cooper's shear-making concern. So the versatile artisan became a grocer, a trade in which he prospered moderately for more than a decade.

Finally, in 1827, Cooper made the move that was to make him rich. He began making glue. Instead of setting up his own plant, he shrewdly purchased for a modest sum a glue factory that was well equipped but poorly managed. Cooper was "determined to make the best glue that could be produced, and found out every method and Ingredient to that end." Rather like ironmaking, glue manufacturing in the age of Jackson was a hit-or-miss affair that involved boiling down hooves, bones, sinews, and skins. The consistency of the final product varied according to the specific ingredients used, so glues tended to be highly uneven in quality. Though totally ignorant of organic chemistry, Cooper per fected a method for standardizing production that turned out glues of many different grades for the varied needs of New York's artisans. Then he diversified into gelatin and isinglass, a thickening agent used in jellies, jams, and other foods. Thanks to Cooper's inventive prowess, his glue factory was enormously profitable in the 1830s and 1840s; it was the "cash cow" that bankrolled the Trenton Iron Company.

While Peter Cooper's glue factory provided the funds for the Trenton ironworks, Abram S. Hewitt furnished the managerial talent. In his own way, Hewitt was no less a prodigy than Cooper. An intense, nervous, hard-driving man, he had known poverty in his childhood, for his father was an earnest and industrious loser who wandered through life, faring poorly in a number of trades. Hewitt attended Columbia

College on a scholarship while working at an assortment of jobs to pay his living expenses, and he won top scholastic honors all four years. He was a ferocious worker and an omnivorous scholar, displaying particular talent in mathematics, classics, and law. One of Hewitt's classmates at Columbia was Peter Cooper's son Edward, and in March 1844 the pair took a trip to England, which Hewitt found to be "the most wonderful country you can possibly conceive of. . . . [I]t is like one continuous town, so populous is it." He was less enthusiastic about the trip home, which ended in a shipwreck.

Upon returning from Europe at the end of 1844, Edward Cooper and Abram Hewitt teamed up with the elder Cooper to establish an ironworks in Trenton, New Jersey, on the western border of the state. Peter Cooper was already operating a small rolling mill in New York City, but he knew that it had to be moved westward, closer to raw materials, if it was to survive. Trenton was a logical site for a number of reasons. Its population of 9,000 provided an adequate labor supply, it was connected by railroad and canal to the Philadelphia and New York markets, excellent iron ore could be obtained from abandoned mines in northern New Jersey, and anthracite (hard coal) was produced across the Delaware River in Pennsylvania's Lehigh and Schuylkill valleys. So in the spring of 1845 Edward Cooper and Abram Hewitt moved to Trenton and set up bar and wire mills as well as puddling furnaces to provide them with wrought iron. Soon a rolling mill for making rails was added. At first the company purchased pig iron from other firms, but before long it integrated backward by acquiring its own mines in New Jersey and building a pair of gigantic blast furnaces that stood fifty-five feet high. The largest furnaces in the country, they smelted a particularly excellent ore that Hewitt discovered at an abandoned eighteenth-century ironworks, and they were the most profitable part of the entire operation. Trenton was one of only seven ironworks in the country that was fully integrated, controlling the entire flow of iron from mine to blast furnace to puddling furnace to finishing mills. It was constantly expanded and upgraded and could accurately be called "without a rival for completeness, substantiality and good work."

In marked contrast with the Tredegar Works, the founding of the Trenton Iron Company was propitiously timed. By 1846 the long national depression that began in 1837 was giving way to a new prosperity based on railroad construction. Thousands of tons of iron were needed for rails, wheels, locomotives, and telegraph wires, yet ironmaking capacity was limited. It was estimated that world ironmaking capacity amounted to only 8,000 miles of rails a year in the early fifties, and the United States alone was annually adding 4,000 miles of track to its system while replacing 2,000 miles more. As one of the nation's most modern mills Trenton had a splendid market opportunity. Initial growth was explosive. Early in 1846 the Camden and Amboy Railroad gave the works an order for $180,000 worth of rails, and within a year the work force was 500 strong.

But it was far from clear that Hewitt, whose commercial experience did not extend much beyond tutoring his Columbia classmates, would be able to manage this growth successfully. As Peter Cooper remarked, "I don't know, that you can get books far enough out of your head to let even a little business in, but if you'd like to try, here's a chance." Hewitt seized the chance with a firm and confident grasp. He was determined to build an estate and put the indignities of poverty behind him. A consummate workaholic, he was everywhere at once in the forties and fifties—landing rail contracts in New York and Boston; visiting mines in the Jersey hills; studying technical journals in his Trenton home; inspecting wire and rails produced at the mill. Although Edward Cooper superintended the mills, Hewitt was clearly captain of the ship. He was imbued with something of a kamikaze spirit and proudly filled his correspondence with lamentations about fatigue, illness, and eyestrain. After struggling through the panic of 1857, he was "able to come to the office for one hour at a time, but any attempt to think results in a nervous headache which it takes twenty-four hours to allay." Things were just as bad during the Civil War. "My health has been in a very precarious condition for months," he wrote in 1862, and the next year he wrote that "it seems as if my eye were required everywhere, and I am so nearly exhausted in body and mind that I feel more like lying down in the ditch than anything else." Holidays provided no respite: "Our merry Christmas was spent all day at the store, at hard work and no dinner. We trust you were better off."

A consuming feeling of financial vulnerability inspired this incessant labor. Iron manufacturing was a "commodity business." Patents, trademarks, or franchises were seldom worth much for long; price and quality were all that mattered. When prices were high, as they were in the early 1850s, the business could be stupendously profitable. Hewitt calculated that pig iron that cost $15 per ton to make was selling for $35 to $40. But such prosperity was always precarious. An expansion of domestic ironmaking capacity, an influx of British imports, a major technological change, or a financial panic could be depended upon to bring prices back to earth—or even plunge them below the cost of production. At such times a manufacturer had two choices: Cut costs, or shift production to a more profitable line of goods. The Trenton Iron Company used both methods with success. When the panic of 1857 hit, Hewitt ordered that costs be reduced to "the lowest point consistent with running the furnace at all. . . . It is a matter of life & death." And his exceptional technical skill enabled the company to shift production swiftly to novel, high-margin products. When British rails flooded the market in the late 1840s, for example, Hewitt began making wire for telegraph systems and bridge construction. One of his key customers was the Prussian genius John Roebling, later the beginning builder of the Brooklyn Bridge and at the time a fellow resident of Trenton. In the mid-fifties the Trenton company pioneered the use of wrought iron beams in constructing large office buildings—a popular innovation that protected structures from the spectacular fires that periodically swept through American cities. And during the Civil War Hewitt traveled to England and discovered the secret for making a superior grade of gunmetal, which he sold to the Union Army.

What most clearly distinguished the management style of the Trenton Iron Company was its unrelenting focus. In contrast with many railroad men, who were forever caught up in a multiplicity of deals and schemes, Hewitt and Cooper hunkered down at their Trenton mill, their attention fixed on the fundamentals of ironmaking. Cost and quality were their obsessions. Hewitt was "willing to do any amount of labor or feel any amount of anxiety that may be necessary to attain a successful issue in this great enterprise." He asserted: "No pains or expenses have been spared to make the mill perfect in its arrangements" and rode herd over his work force to make certain that efficiency was maximized. For him, operating costs were the true test of success or failure. A summary of operations made in 1853 stressed the fact that "We have reduced the cost of making rails from $80 to $40 per ton; of wire rods from $120 to $60. In doing this, the whole time and ability of Mr. Cooper and myself have been consumed for eight years."

A key factor permitting such a single-minded focus on production fundamentals was the relative simplicity of Trenton's financial affairs. Unlike so many railroads, there were no complicated bond issues to think about, no mergers, "bear raids," or government subsidies to divert attention from the task of running a profitable business. And Trenton's financial affairs were far simpler than Tredegar's because the enterprise was well capitalized from the start, was founded in a time of prosperity, and was a closely held family concern. Initially the company was owned by Peter Cooper, for neither of his young associates had significant wealth. But the splendid early progress of the company led Cooper to put the business on a more solid financial footing in 1847 by pushing through the New Jersey legislature an act of incorporation. At first the corporation issued stock worth only $300,000, of which Cooper, Sr., was allotted $151,000 and Cooper, Jr., and Hewitt $149,000. The latter pair borrowed $50,000 from a bank to finance their interest in the firm, and they received an extremely generous joint salary of $25,000 for running the operations. It seems probable that their share of the company was paid for out of this salary and from their share of future profits. Peter Cooper may also have lent them funds to finance their purchase of a portion of the works. Undoubtedly the partnership positions enjoyed by the younger, more energetic members of the firm were a key to its success, for it greatly encouraged the unstinting exertions that kept the firm on top. One suspects that modern American corporations would fare better if they cast aside bureaucratic ladders of advancement and compensated younger employees who made critical contributions to the firms. Such policies, which have long been used successfully in such industries as securities brokerage and advertising, unlock the acquisitive zeal of young and ambitious employees—a priceless resource for any company.

The arrangements of 1847 set the essential financial contours of the Trenton Iron Company for the next two decades. Expansion was financed primarily from profits, for the company was highly successful until the panic of 1857. By 1853 its estimated value was $625,000, and in the fiscal year 1855–56 it earned $173,000 on a net worth of $1 million. Although he was the majority shareholder and therefore controlled the company's affairs, Peter Cooper was more than willing to share the success of the company with his son Edward and with Abram Hewitt, who became his son-in-law in about 1850. Hewitt quickly became a rich man. By 1853—only eight years after entering the firm —he was worth $175,000. The company did issue some bonds to finance operations, and stock was sold to a number of outsiders; but control always rested with the three founders. Thus it was truly a family company, and since the key family members were on the best of terms, there was very little friction between the owners.

The Trenton Iron Company prospered until the end of the Civil War, but then fundamental technological changes gave western iron and steelmakers a decisive advantage over their eastern rivals. To remain competitive, the company would have had to pick up stakes and move to western Pennsylvania or Ohio. But Peter Cooper was now a rich old philanthropist who derived more pleasure from managing Cooper Union, an idealistic New York lyceum the mission of which was to "improve and elevate the working classes of the city," than from further expanding his fortune. As for Abram Hewitt, he remained in the iron and steel business but rechanneled his monumental ability into the fields of politics and municipal reform, becoming a congressman and mayor of New York.

ANDREW CARNEGIE'S PRIVATE WAR

In the hands of a business genius like Andrew Carnegie the traditional partnership between capitalists and workmen could become an unbeatable institution. Carnegie's biography has an unreal storybook quality that never wears off, no matter how many times it is told. But it is a story that any investor or businessperson can contemplate with profit, and a splendid short biography by Harold Livesay has greatly increased our understanding of Carnegie the businessman. He was born into a working-class family in the Scottish town of Dunfermline fifteen miles north of Edinburgh. During his childhood the Industrial Revolution made handloom weavers—including Carnegie's father—obsolete, and to escape poverty, the family emigrated to America in 1848. Carnegie's father never recovered from the trauma of structural unemployment and transatlantic migration, and young Andy became exceedingly close to his strong-willed mother, Margaret. The two were inseparable even after Carnegie had reached maturity; they often traveled around Europe together, and Carnegie freely admitted that "we could be happy anywhere as long as we were together." Rather less enthusiastic about this maternal attachment was Carnegie's fiancée, who detested her prospective mother-in-law and had to endure an extended and tempestuous courtship that did not end until Margaret finally died.

Unlike his father, Carnegie easily adjusted to the new world. At the age of thirteen he went to work in a spinning mill but soon moved on to a telegraph office in Pittsburgh. This was a fortunate choice of employment. Telegraph offices were efficient incubators of businessmen—Thomas Edison and Richard Warren Sears (founder of Sears, Roebuck) also launched their careers in them—for the simple reason that they were the nerve centers of the nineteenth-century economy. Prominent businessmen were constantly rushing into the offices to send important messages, and they appreciated attentive service from smart young men. By providing such service, Carnegie caught the eye of Thomas Scott, superintendent of the western division of the Pennsylvania Railroad. Carnegie was hired as a telegraph operator but rapidly moved up the corporate ladder. Smart, aggressive, and cocky, garrulous and ingratiating when he needed to be, Carnegie quickly mastered the intricacies of the railroad's operations. By working tirelessly to keep the trains running smoothly, he made himself invaluable and received a quick succession of promotions. At the age of twenty-four he was made superintendent of the western division, and six years later he was offered the job of superintendent of the railroad but turned it down because he wanted to strike out on his own.

One of the largest and best-managed railroads in the country, the Pennsylvania made a splendid business school. For one thing, it gave Carnegie an intimate understanding of the key markets for iron, including rails, bridges, boilers, engines, and almost everything else having to do with railroads. He also learned how to think big—in terms of an intricate transportation system that stretched from Jersey City to Chicago rather than in terms of just one or two mills. Moreover, Tom Scott impressed upon his young associate the importance of achieving economies of scale by constantly expanding the volume of business and thereby reducing the per unit cost. Scott's prescription for high profits was "big trains, loaded full, and run fast." But to fill the trains, one had to quote a lower price than the competition, and that was impossible to do without knowing exactly what the costs actually were. Such knowledge was by no means commonplace in nineteenth-century America; most businessmen balanced their books only once a year and then primarily to determine their profits and current financial positions. During the fiscal year they had little idea of either the overall magnitude or individual components of their costs. Thus J. Edgar Thomson, president of the Pennsylvania Railroad, was fomenting a managerial revolution when he instituted systematic cost accounting that provided detailed information about costs and how they could be reduced. As superintendent of the Pennsylvania, Carnegie mastered these tools; later he applied them to the iron and steel business.

As a rising star in the Pennsylvania, Carnegie naturally made the acquaintance of Pittsburgh's leading capitalists, and it was not long before they were cutting him into lucrative business deals. For the son of a handloom weaver the world of loans, profits, dividends, and capital gains was a veritable wonderland; he found it hard to believe that a man's income need not be limited by the hours in the day. In his autobiography Carnegie vividly recalled his initiation to capitalism, his first dividend check: "I opened the envelope. All it contained was a check for ten dollars. I shall remember that check as long as I live. It gave me the first penny of revenue on capital—something that I had not worked for with the sweat of my brow. 'Eureka! I cried. 'Here's the goose that lays the golden eggs!' "

It was not long before Carnegie owned a whole flock of geese laying dozens of golden eggs. The economy of western Pennsylvania was booming in the 1850s and 1860s, and no one was better situated to profit than Pennsylvania Railroad insiders, who, leaving nothing to chance, placed large orders with the companies that they founded. So in combination with Scott, Thomson, and other executives Carnegie made a series of extraordinarily profitable investments. The amount of $600 invested in Adams Express yielded an annual income of $1,440. An investment of $217.50 in the Woodruff Sleeping Car Company was soon generating annual dividends of more than $5,000. And more than $1 million was eventually collected from an $11,000 plunge into the Pennsylvania oil rush of the 1850s. These deals made Carnegie a rich man, worth $400,000 in 1868, and they rounded out his business skills as well. He learned how to size up an investment situation, gauging the potential of a new market and a novel technology. He learned how to grapple with the bulls and bears of Wall Street and mastered the art of peddling bonds to the great investment houses of Europe. He made the acquaintance of nearly every major railroad leader in the country and was even asked by Jay Gould, "the Mephistopheles of Wall Street," to participate in a scheme to take over the Pennsylvania from Scott.

Carnegie's ventures naturally introduced him to Pittsburgh's biggest industry, ironmaking. In 1862 he took an interest in the Keystone Bridge Company, which built river-spanning iron bridges for many railroads, including, of course, the Pennsylvania. It was a company of which he was particularly proud because its product was so visible and so useful. "Almost every concern that had undertaken to erect iron bridges in America had failed. Many of the structures themselves had fallen and some of the worst railway disasters in America had been caused in that way . . . but nothing has ever happened to a Keystone bridge." Since Keystone needed wrought iron of the highest quality,

Carnegie bought into the Union Iron Works, which was managed by the inspired German ironmaster Andrew Kloman—"a great mechanic," Carnegie recalled, "who had discovered, what was then unknown in Pittsburgh, that whatever was worth doing with machinery was worth doing well." The Union works turned out a variety of plates and girders for bridges, engines, buildings, and other structures. In 1872 Carnegie and his partners once again decided to "integrate backward" by constructing the Lucy Furnace, a mammoth blast furnace that stood seventy-five feet high. Incorporating a variety of technical innovations designed by Kloman, the Lucy was soon locked in a celebrated battle with a neighboring furnace, the Isabella. Under the insistent prodding and nursing of Carnegie's partners, the Lucy broke record after record in the 1870s and 1880s: 500 tons of pig iron per week, 700 tons per week, 1,000 tons per week, and on up to nearly 2,000 tons per week. The iron trade looked on with wonderment, asking, "What will these Titans do next?" The Lucy rounded out an integrated iron empire that extended from pig iron production to iron milling to bridge construction. And by investing in the companies that owned the bridges built by Keystone, while also earning a commission for selling that company's bonds in Europe, Carnegie squeezed profits from a single bridge in five different ways.

Carnegie's multiple triumphs as executive, investor, and financier left him rich, famous, and dissatisfied with the direction his life was taking. He wanted to be more than a shrewd scavenger of business deals. He wanted to be a builder, a producer. And he knew enough about railroads and iron to realize that the thing to produce was steel. Not iron but steel. Since the perfection of the Bessemer process American railroads had begun to use steel rails because they were more durable than wrought iron and could carry more weight. Moreover, a torrid railroad building boom was under way in the early 1870s, and the nation had only begun the mammoth task of lacing the American West with track. Here was a promising growth market that would not soon peter out.

So Carnegie gathered his financial resources, formed a partnership with six other capitalists, and began to construct a steel rolling mill that converted pig iron into steel and then rolled it into rails, girders, and other products. In honor of the Pennsylvania Railroad's first president, who was the first American to install steel rails, the mill was named the J. Edgar Thomson Steel Mills. Once construction was well under way, disaster struck. The bankruptcy of Jay Cooke in 1873 plunged American railroads into a depression and deprived Carnegie of not only a booming railroad market but also a goodly portion of his firm's capital. As credit contracted throughout the country, debts could not be collected, and several of Carnegie's partners became overextended. Most wrenching of all for Carnegie was the plight of his patron Tom Scott, who was in the midst of building a big Texas railroad with short-term loans when the panic struck. In order to obtain a British loan that would tide him over, Scott needed Carnegie's endorsement of the note. As the man behind Carnegie's climb to success Scott had a claim on Carnegie's sympathy that could not have been stronger. But the icy clarity of Carnegie's business judgment won out. "It was one of the most trying moments of my whole life," Carnegie admitted. "Yet I was not tempted for a moment to entertain the idea of involving myself. . . . I told Mr. Scott that I had done my best to prevent him from beginning to construct a great railway before he had secured the necessary capital . . . [and] I had insisted that thousands of miles of railways lines could not be constructed by means of temporary loans. . . . [N]othing in the world would ever induce me to be guilty of endorsing the paper of that construction company or of any other concern than our own firm." Since several other partners had similar problems and had to drop out of Carnegie's partnership, its capital shrank. In order to finish work on the Edgar Thomson, Carnegie had to travel to London and borrow $400,000 from Junius Morgan, a prominent Anglo-American banker and the father of J. P. Morgan. Forever after the panic of 1873 Carnegie was thrown into a rage by the merest hint that one of his partners was engaged in speculation. "I would no more have thought of buying stocks than flying," one of his partners later remarked. Not only did speculation endanger the capital base of a partnership, but Carnegie, as mentioned earlier, considered speculation and good business judgment incompatible.

A natural corollary of Carnegie's contempt for speculation was a loathing of the corporations the shares of which were traded on Wall Street. While business historians invariably hail the corporate form of organization as the greatest invention since double-entry bookkeeping, Carnegie viewed it with contempt. In his mind corporations were no match for well-run partnerships. "It is with firms as with nations; 'scattered possessions' are not in it with solid, compact, concentrated forces." For one thing, corporations were clumsy. In his autobiography Carnegie triumphantly described his shrewd purchase of an iron mine and then observed: "And here lies the great advantage of a partnership over a corporation. The president of the latter would have had to consult a board of directors and wait several weeks and perhaps months for their decision. By that time the mine would probably have become the property of others." Years of intimacy with the vices of American railroads taught Carnegie to distrust the loss of personal control that the corporation involved. "It has been with me a cardinal doctrine that I could manage my own capital better than any other person, much better than any board of directors. The losses men encounter during a business life which seriously embarrass them are rarely in their own business, but in enterprises of which the investor is not the master." Moreover, corporations had a difficult time attracting the best people as managers because "a man must necessarily occupy a narrow field who is at the beck and call of others. Even if he becomes president of a great corporation he is hardly his own master, unless he holds control of the stock. The ablest presidents are hampered by boards of directors and shareholders, who can know but little of the enterprise." Just as Carnegie was focusing his financial resources on steelmaking, so he wanted to finance his business in such a way as to concentrate power in his hands.

Unlike Abram Hewitt of Trenton or Joseph Anderson of Tredegar, Carnegie was not a technician who devoted his days and nights to perfecting operations at the plant. Professing ignorance of technical details, he left them to his partners and spent much of his time far away from Pittsburgh, traveling around the world, holding court at his over-size castle in Scotland (it was so big that he preferred to stay in a modest cottage nearby), or soaking up culture in the drawing rooms of New York and London. To be sure, Carnegie did serve as the company's chief salesman; his gregarious personality and extensive railroad contacts made him the best in the iron trade. But he relied on an endless stream of trenchant correspondence to sting, prod, scare, and cajole his partners into molding the company to his specifications.

A few major principles patterned his design. Above all else, he was obsessed with costs. "Watch the costs," he liked to say, "and the profits will take care of themselves." His logic was compelling: "Give me your cost sheets. It is more interesting to know how cheaply and how well you have done this than how much money you have made, because the one is a temporary result, due possibly to special conditions of trade, but the other means a permanency that will go on with the works as long as they last." Always the independent fighter, Carnegie wanted to be the low-cost producer so that he would not have to cooperate with competitors; he much preferred to dictate to them. It was the custom in the late nineteenth century for the major steelmakers to set prices above their market level and then try to keep them there by assigning a specific share of the market to each company. So long as each manufacturer did not sell more steel than he was allotted, competition would not drive down the price to market levels. Such collusion disgusted Carnegie because it limited the size of his sales. By being the low-cost producer, he could threaten to undersell his competitors unless his market share was expanded. As he remarked to one manufacturer, "I can make steel cheaper than any of you and undersell you. The market is mine when I want to take it." Low-cost production also permitted Carnegie to achieve economies of scale, just as he had done on the Pennsylvania Railroad. "Cut the prices; scoop the market; run the mills full," he instructed his partners. He meant that a manufacturer who had low costs, and could therefore quote low prices, could be assured of booking plenty of orders and running at full capacity. And the high-volume production would in turn reduce unit costs.

Apart from high-volume production, the keys to driving costs lower were tight cost controls, superb managers, and aggressive investment in new plant and equipment. Borrowing another page from the Pennsylvania Railroad's book, Carnegie installed cost accounting in all his mills. A platoon of clerks kept track of every brick, every ton of coke, every load of ore, producing data that suggested many ways to reduce costs. The cost sheets also provided a systematic basis for measuring the relative efficiency of every man. Not surprisingly, many workers hated the system. "There goes that —— bookkeeper," said one. "If I use a dozen bricks more than I did last month, he knows it and comes around to ask why!" Top managers were held to an equally high standard. Once a manager sent Carnegie a telegram announcing that he had set a production record. Carnegie's laconic response was: "Congratulations. Why not do it every week?"

Though he cut costs to the bone and beyond, Carnegie was never parsimonious about rewarding the people who really determined costs, the top people at his mills. He strongly believed that "There is no labor so cheap as the dearest in the mechanical field," and he willingly rewarded his most able men with partnerships. Carnegie had an unerring nose for talent, in part because he knew the railroad market so well. He was initially drawn to Andrew Kloman's modest forge because he knew that Kloman produced the sturdiest train axles in Pittsburgh. Kloman's technical virtuosity reduced Carnegie to raptures: "How much this German created! He was the first man to introduce the cold saws that cut cold iron the exact lengths. He invented upsetting machines to make bridge links, and also built the first 'universal' mill in America. All these were erected at our works." Another superstar of the Carnegie works was "Captain" Bill Jones, a short Welshman who managed the J. Edgar Thomson Steel Mills for many years. Jones was a natural leader and had a volcanic personality. He summarily fired employees who displeased him and was constantly quarreling with Carnegie and tendering his resignation. At times he kept a sheaf of resignation letters in his pocket which saved him the trouble of drafting them one by one. They were never accepted because Jones, like Kloman, was a mechanical genius who invented many cost-saving improvements in the Carnegie mills. The most famous of these was the Jones mixer, a gigantic container that received molten iron as it flowed out of the blast furnace and held it in a liquid state until it was transferred to the Bessemer converter. The invention eliminated the fuel and inventory costs associated with reheating pig iron before it was turned into steel.

Carnegie was always on the lookout for "young geniuses" in the ranks who could be given major responsibility and eventually partnership in the company. To this policy Carnegie ascribed much of his success. It worked as follows: A thirty-year-old superintendent might receive a 0.5 percent interest in the firm, and all the profits generated by that interest would be devoted to purchasing the share until it was paid off. Thereafter he would receive dividends on the share, which typically amounted to less than 25 percent of profits, while the balance of the profits were reinvested in the company. Young partners could not advantageously sell off their shares and move to competing firms because they would be required to sell their shares back to the firm at an artificially low book value. Carnegie greatly preferred this partnership system to the payment of large salaries. High salaries involved a major current expense, they did not permanently bind valuable employees to the firm, and they encouraged high living by bright young employees, rather than the moderate life-style that Carnegie advocated. And the system did work splendidly. In addition to producing many of the company's most valuable employees, it was a source of delight to Carnegie, whose autobiography is littered with happy tales of workmen who leaped the chasm from mechanic to millionaire. To Carnegie it was tantamount to being knighted.

But Carnegie's partnership had a serious defect as well. Although he was happy to do comparatively small financial favors to the workmen who made him rich, he instinctively distrusted the few capitalists who were as tough and shrewd as he. Such a man was Henry Clay Frick, a self-made millionaire who sold his coke company to Carnegie Steel and became the number two man in the company. Carnegie and Frick quarreled tempestuously for years, and when Carnegie tried to force Frick to sell his share of the firm back to Carnegie at its artificially low book value, Frick took Carnegie to court and won, in the process divulging to the world many of the firm's financial secrets. If Frick had been a mere employee, he could simply have been fired. But it was not so simple when he was a part owner of Carnegie Steel. Here lay a major weakness of the partnership.

Carnegie was never afraid to spend lavishly on new equipment that would reduce his operating costs. In the 1880s he ripped out the expensive Bessemer converters at the Homestead works and replaced them with more efficient open hearths, and he became famous for the "hard driving" of blast furnaces, a process that accelerated the rate of depreciation and necessitated frequent replacement of equipment. This policy made sense to Carnegie because in an environment of continuous technological change new equipment was always more efficient than the equipment it replaced. The cost of production, not the longevity of his plant, was his chief concern. On one occasion a mill manager was touring a mill with Frick, then Carnegie's senior partner, and casually remarked that he could save ten cents per ton on steel by rearranging the flow of material at the rail finishing mill. Although the change would cost $150,000, Frick told him to do it. But even this policy of aggressive investment could not keep older mills such as the J. Edgar Thomson fully cost-competitive with mills that were built several years later. Here Carnegie benefited from the errors and financial weakness of competitors. Because he took the long view, ran a business that was consistently profitable, paid out a small proportion of his profits in dividends, and had a superb credit rating, Carnegie was able to buy the more modern plants of his competitors when they ran into difficulties. In 1883 he purchased the Homestead works, which was suffering from labor problems and a shortage of working capital, and in 1890 Frick bought the Duquesne works, "at the time the most modern steel mill in the world." Carnegie's success highlights the fact that in a fast-growing, fast-changing industry the companies that come out on top will be the ones with the financial strength needed to innovate continuously. Strong finances allow firms to do what Carnegie did—pick up bargains during industry downturns, when many other companies cannot bid for properties because they are strapped for cash. As the early history of Bell Telephone shows, companies that pay high dividends may please some shareholders in the short term, but they run the danger of being overtaken by competitors. Not until growth has slowed and the technology has stabilized are high dividends justified.

The wisdom of Carnegie's all-out attack on operating expenses was demonstrated in the depressed decade of the 1890s. Most of Carnegie's competitors operated far below full capacity and experienced losses or marginal profitability. Carnegie's strategy was to "take all the orders going and run full. Our competitors believed that we meant what we said and this no doubt operated to clear the field. One after another the others dropped out. . . . We averaged $4 a ton profit on all our product in the worst of times." These depression time profits provided the wherewithal to continue investments in plant and equipment that drove production costs still lower. Consequently, when prosperity finally returned and steel prices rose, the company's earnings were phenomenal. Carnegie Steel's profit picture is best related in numbers rather than words:

1888	$2,000,000
1889	$3,540,000
1890	$5,350,000
1891	$4,300,000
1892	$4,000,000
1893	$3,000,000
1894	$4,000,000
1895	$5,000,000
1896	$6,000,000
1897	$7,000,000
1898	$11,000,000
1899	$21,000,000
1900	$40,000,000

J. P. MORGAN'S KISS OF DEATH

The prodigious profits of 1898, 1899, and 1900 fortified Carnegie for his last and greatest battle, his joust with the steel trusts. In 1898 and 1899 the steel industry was swept by a wave of mergers, most of them engineered by J. P. Morgan (who created National Tube, American

Bridge, and Federal Steel) or the Moore Brothers of Chicago (American Steel and Wire, American Steel Hoop, American Steel Barrel, American Sheet Steel, American Tin Plate, National Steel). These trusts were merely collections of companies that were in the same business and were owned by the same stockholders. Many of their mills were old and decrepit, and they were not integrated into cohesive, dynamic enterprises. And like many of the railroads discussed in the last chapter, the trusts were vastly overcapitalized, weighted down with watered stocks and bonds. In order to induce independent companies to join up, the investment bankers who orchestrated the mergers handed out securities the value of which greatly exceeded the actual value of the properties they purchased. For example, a wire mill worth $2 million might be brought into American Steel and Wire by issuing to the mill's owners $2 million in stock and another $2 million in bonds. Once the trust was in operation, it had to generate enough profits from this $2 million plant to pay not only dividends on the $2 million of stock but also interest on the $2 million of bonds. The financial burden could be heavy indeed. Federal Steel had $200 million in securities outstanding; but the book value of its properties was only $56 million, and their fair market value was roughly $87 million. Depending on how it was counted, between $144 million and $113 million of Federal's capitalization was "water." Of course, not a little of this "water" fattened the bankers who put the deal together.

This was precisely the sort of financial legerdemain that had always disgusted Carnegie. He derisively observed, "I think Federal the greatest concern the world ever saw for manufacturing stock certificates. . . . But they will fail sadly in steel." Some of Carnegie's partners recommended that he cooperate with the trusts, but he would have none of it. He preferred victory to cooperation. "I never believe in combinations. They are only for weak people. They give a little temporary strength to these weak persons, but they are not good for the strong and healthy."

Only two of the trusts, Federal Steel and National Steel, were involved in the same business as Carnegie Steel, the production of crude steel. Much of this crude steel was sold to other steel firms that produced nails, wire, hoops, etc. As their names implied, American Steel and Wire, National Tube, and the other trusts were involved in this downstream business of producing finished goods. Since one of their major suppliers was Carnegie Steel, they posed a major threat to Carnegie: If they decided to integrate backward into basic steel production

—a move that would reduce their costs—Carnegie would lose most of his domestic market.

In 1900 this danger became a reality; American Steel and Wire, National Tube, and American Hoop canceled their contracts with Carnegie Steel. Carnegie's lieutenants wired the news to their boss at Skibo Castle in Scotland. The decisive battle of Carnegie's thirty-year war for steel supremacy was at hand. "A struggle is inevitable," he proclaimed, "and it is a question of survival of the fittest. . . . I would make no dividends upon common stock, save all surplus and spend it for a hoop and cotton tie mills, for wire and nail mills, for tube mills, for lines of boats upon the lakes." Prodigious supplies of capital and operating talent gave Carnegie the upper hand in this fight with the flaccid and scattered trusts. His right-hand man, Charles Schwab, immediately developed a plan to build a modern tube mill at Conneaut on the shores of Lake Erie. It was a $12 million dagger pointed directly at J. P. Morgan's National Tube Company.

Carnegie had Morgan by the throat. The great financier had made his reputation by getting major businessmen to cooperate rather than compete, thereby stabilizing major industries and protecting investors. A large, gruff man with a bulbous red nose and an intimidating glare that reminded one acquaintance of a freight train bearing down on him, Morgan was usually able to bully recalcitrant industrialists into seeing things his way. But now he was overextended, his far-flung steel trusts an easy target for the more cost-efficient Carnegie Steel. Morgan had no alternative but to meet Carnegie's price; in February 1901 he bought out the Scotsman for $480 million. Carnegie Steel became the centerpiece of U.S. Steel, the greatest industrial unit the world had yet seen. No fewer than 8 different corporations, containing 142 separate companies, were merged in the giant combine. It possessed "213 steel mills and transportation companies, including 78 blast furnaces; 41 iron ore mines and a fleet of 112 ore barges; as well as 57,000 acres of coal and coke properties; [and] nearly 1000 miles of railroad tracks." The steel trust accounted for 44 percent of the country's steel ingot capacity, and its share of many key lines of finished goods greatly exceeded 50 percent.

Unfortunately the size of Morgan's newest creation was not matched by its strength. Its far-flung possessions were of highly uneven quality, ranging from the most modern plants in the country to antiques of Civil War vintage. Moreover, it was "waterlogged"; its outstanding stocks and bonds had a total face value of $1,389,144,392 or nearly twice the value of its tangible assets. There was some danger that when steel prices declined in the next economic downturn, the company would have difficulty paying dividends. While the monopoly position of U.S. Steel seemed to mitigate this financial weakness, the company's political vulnerability prevented it from raising prices at will. An affront to the Sherman Antitrust Act, U.S. Steel remained in existence at the pleasure of the attorney general.

Despite these handicaps, the steel trust might have become an efficient and competitive enterprise if it had fallen into the hands of first-class executives who truly understood the industry. As we will see in later chapters, this did occur to two other mammoth organizations associated with the House of Morgan, General Motors and AT&T. But U.S. Steel was controlled in its early years by financiers who kept one eye on Wall Street and one eye on Washington, casting an occasional fleeting glance to Pittsburgh. For them, the firm's survival was first and foremost a political problem; the details of making steel were a secondary concern. With the industry's dominant company hanging back, afraid to innovate aggressively, the steel industry inevitably stagnated. Hence the long-term loser in the great steel merger was the American economy.

Things might have turned out differently if the company had been molded by its first chief, Charles Schwab. The president of Carnegie Steel at the time of the merger, Schwab was cut from the same cloth as Andrew Kloman and Captain Bill Jones. He began his steel career as a manual laborer at the J. Edgar Thomson works and became a protégé of Captain Jones, the superintendent of the works. When Jones was killed in an explosion, Schwab, though only twenty-seven years old, took his place as superintendent. Later he successfully took over management of the Homestead works, after a bloody strike had threatened to hamper productivity. He was a flamboyant and tireless manager of unusual technical ability, brilliant at motivating men and slashing costs. But as soon as Schwab moved out of the familiar orbit of Carnegie Steel, it became apparent that political adroitness was not one of his strengths.

As president of U.S. Steel, Schwab reported to two different committees of the board of directors, the Finance Committee and the Executive Committee. Both were dominated by Morgan's representatives. These pillars of the financial establishment had little use for upstart robber barons like Carnegie and Schwab; they desperately wanted U.S. Steel to show the world a low and respectable profile that would make an elusive target for Washington trustbusters. Schwab had different plans. Enriched by the recent merger and liberated from Carnegie's overbearing supervision, he finally began to live well. He bought a city block at the corner of Seventy-second Street and Riverside Drive in New York City and built a gargantuan mansion, complete with bowling alley, gymnasium, swimming pool, 116-foot lookout tower, a huge organ, and ninety bedrooms. Costing more than $5 million to build and furnish, it used ten tons of coal a day. For entertainment Schwab did not share the Morgan partners' predilection for rustic hunting lodges in the the Adirondacks of New York or the Sea Islands of Georgia. He preferred to drive through Europe in big roadsters and frequent the gaming tables at Monte Carlo. All eyes were on the dynamic "Crown Prince of Steel" as he rolled into Monte Carlo in the winter of 1901, the more so because a famous aristocrat was leaving town after having lost a fortune while testing a scheme for beating the roulette wheel. Elaborately embroidered by the American press, Schwab's exploits at Monte Carlo scandalized respectable opinion throughout the nation. The editors of one newspaper wanted to know, "What guarantee can the holders of the stock of the great corporation of which Mr. Schwab is president have that their holdings are safe? None at all. Here is a moral delinquency that is openly scandalous."

There were other embarrassments, including Schwab's rumored $1 million salary and some unguarded remarks about the limited utility of a college education. Nor did Schwab see eye to eye with his colleagues on matters of business policy. Instead of conserving cash in order to pay dividends on U.S. Steel's huge supply of outstanding common and preferred stock, he wanted to expand and improve the company, just as he had at Carnegie Steel. Schwab later explained, "The members of our committee had not been educated to know the manufacturing business as I knew it . . . and it was with the greatest difficulty that I could get them to buy what I considered most valuable and essential to the company." Eventually he was censured for acting contrary to the board's wishes, and after getting caught up in a minor financial scandal, Schwab resigned from the presidency of U.S. Steel. As if to prove that he deserved better, Schwab took over a small company called Bethlehem Steel and, in the space of a decade, turned it into the nation's second-largest steel producer.

Schwab's replacement at U.S. Steel was a circumspect Chicago lawyer named Elbert Gary who had helped J. P. Morgan put together Federal Steel. Mergers and respectability were Gary's specialties. He knew little about the practical business of running steel mills but presented just the sort of honest and conservative image that the steel trust seemed to need. Indeed, he reminded many businessmen of a Sunday school teacher. By going slowly and showing due respect for U.S. Steel's many constituencies—Wall Street, Washington, labor, competing steel producers, and the public at large—he polished the company's reputation as a progressive and public-spirited organization. Gary admirably suited the mood of America at the turn of the century. Weary of the strife and turmoil associated with the robber barons, middle-class reformers bearing the ambiguous but reassuring title of Progressives pushed businessmen to adopt a more stable, civilized, and bureaucratic posture. In their eyes Judge Gary was a model citizen of corporate America. The muckraker Ida Tarbell, whose damning history of Standard Oil had made life miserable for John D. Rockefeller, wrote a laudatory biography of Gary that celebrated his posture of responsible moderation. He established public confidence in the steel trust by "considering public opinion; by being particularly cordial to stockholders; by no longer damning the government any more than the public, but trying to meet it half way, working with, not against; . . . by putting an end to the old method of competition; by considering, not bludgeoning, labor." The practical effect of this corporate virtue was that, under Gary, administered pricing replaced the vigorous competition of the nineteenth century. U.S. Steel set a "price umbrella" which allowed its competitors a fair profit, and over time these smaller companies increased their market share at Big Steel's expense.

A company that did not need to compete also did not need to innovate; throughout the twentieth century U.S. Steel led the industry's drift toward technical mediocrity. A 1936 report by a team of industrial engineers listed a whole raft of money-saving technologies that the company was slow to adopt, including continuous strip mills; the heat-treating process for the production of steel sheets; the production of stainless steels, cold rolled sheets, and other cold rolled steel products; and the use of low-cost water transportation and waste gases from furnaces. In the year of the report's release the editors of *Fortune* concluded that U.S. Steel's managers were more intent on maintaining their existing physical plant than in spending money to improve it. "And so the chief energies of the men who guided the corporation were directed to preventing deterioration in the investment value of the enormous properties confided to their care. To achieve this, they consistently tried to freeze the steel industry at present, or better yet, past levels." In short, the competitive strategy of U.S. Steel was the precise opposite of Andrew Carnegie's. After intense competition between privately financed firms had forged the finest steel industry in the world, an unholy alliance of Wall Street and Washington encouraged the industry to drift and stagnate.

The history of the steel industry holds important lessons for maintaining America's competitive edge in the twenty-first century. Growth industries should be controlled not by financiers like J. P. Morgan but rather by hard-driving industrialists like Andrew Carnegie who operate in a highly competitive environment and invest heavily in plant and equipment to lower costs. A major reason why foreigners made such major inroads in American markets during the 1970s and early 1980s was that many industries had become oligopolistic and noncompetitive. Firms did not really compete on the basis of price and therefore did not feel compelled to work hard and invest aggressively in order to lower costs. Financial factors contributed to this trend. The weak dollar of the late 1970s shielded U.S. firms from foreign competition, and unfavorable tax laws led to poor corporate cash flow and anemic investment in new plant and equipment. Meanwhile, many foreign firms operated in an intensely competitive environment and were obsessed with getting costs down. In Japan, for example, such industries as automobiles and semiconductors are crowded with competitors and extremely cutthroat—just like the American steel industry in the nineteenth century.

That is the bad news. The good news is that the complacent environment of the 1970s has utterly disappeared. Indeed, it would be only a slight exaggeration to say that the 1980s resemble the 1880s nearly as much as the 1970s. The dramatic decline in the inflation rate—from 13.5 percent in 1980 to 3.4 percent in 1985—once again has forced companies to take cost cutting very seriously. This is particularly true for industrial firms that were hurt by the strong dollar. At the same time the liberalization of corporate tax laws in 1981 has greatly improved the financial position of corporations, giving them the resources needed to invest heavily in plant and equipment. So in a real sense the American economy is returning to the economic environment of the nineteenth century, an environment characterized by disinflation, intense foreign competition, industry deregulation, weaker labor unions, widespread corporate cost cutting, and a less intrusive federal government. Many

American industries have shrieked with pain as they were pulled through the disinflationary wringer. Nevertheless, this transition has been fundamentally beneficial because it is forcing the United States to become competitive again.

VI

Monopoly and Mediocrity on Beacon Hill

There is probably no better way to appreciate the utility of the modern venture capital firm than to view an emerging enterprise that tried to survive without one. After inventing the telephone in 1876, Alexander Graham Bell attempted to commercialize the invention with the help of two acquaintances, parents of children he was teaching. Men of relatively limited wealth and narrow business experience, these amateur venture capitalists could not provide the capital, technological assistance, and managerial advice needed to carry out the very difficult task of building a nationwide telephone network. They even attempted to dissuade Bell from developing the telephone in the first place! Largely because of this inexperience, Bell and his friends rapidly lost control of the enterprise to outsiders, much as Steve Jobs lost control of Apple Computer to the board of directors.

The new masters of the emerging American telephone industry were conservative New England financiers, a group of unusually honest businessmen who stood clear of the speculation and fraud that riddled railroad finance. Boston Brahmins all, they were models of caution and probity. Indeed, their leader was William Murray Forbes, the son of the rich China merchant John Murray Forbes, whose unusually sensible and disciplined approach to railroad investment was described earlier. Displaying precisely the sort of investment acumen that his father had shown in buying the Michigan Central in 1846, William Murray Forbes and his associates secured control of the telephone franchise from the original backers of Alexander Graham Bell in 1879. After swiftly laying to rest a threat from the Western Union Corporation, the Bostonians could look forward to fifteen years of patent protection for Bell's revolutionary invention—fifteen years in which to establish a hammerlock on a major new industry. It was as though IBM had had a monopoly on the computer between 1952 and 1966. Indeed, the opportunity to establish a national telephone franchise was even greater than this because telephony is a "natural monopoly." A single company, interconnecting all the households in the country, provides service that is intrinsically superior to that offered by two companies serving half the nation's households simply because the customers of each company will be unable to speak with customers of the other.

Having shrewdly acquired the rights to this extraordinarily valuable business franchise, the Brahmin financiers did something else that was equally remarkable: They lost it. By failing either to expand the business aggressively or to provide good nationwide telephone service, they left themselves vulnerable to competition once patent protection ended in 1894. In the next eight years the "opposition" companies installed almost as many phones as Bell Telephone had done in twenty-five years. By 1903 only 43 percent of the telephone subscribers in the country were in the Bell System. And in order to maintain even this market share, the company had to go heavily into debt; many observers doubted that Bell had the financial resources needed to maintain its traditional dominance of the telephone market. Evidently aware of the financial risk they were facing, the founding directors of the company had sold most of their shares by 1900. Only the transfer of control of the Bell system to J. P. Morgan in 1907 furnished the wherewithal to rebuild the company's monopoly. Indeed, Morgan prevented the fragmentation of the telephone industry on the theory that a nationwide monopoly could provide better service and a more stable stream of dividends to investors. Eighty years later the Justice Department undid Morgan's handiwork.

Why did Bell nearly lose its grip on the American telephone industry? The heart of the matter seems to be that the venture capitalists of the company usurped managerial functions that should have been left to true entrepreneurs. For the Boston Brahmins viewed the telephone merely as a source of dividends—not as an extraordinary invention that could transform the life of every American. Unlike such businessmen as Andrew Carnegie, Henry Ford, or Cornelius Vanderbilt, William Murray Forbes and his associates did not have the mentality of builders gripped by a compulsion to expand their business for its own sake; they evinced no strong desire to install a telephone in every dwelling in the United States. Rather, they behaved like hard-nosed investors who were intent on nurturing a splendidly profitable property, treating their telephone monopoly like a valuable corner lot in downtown Boston or a lucrative Colorado copper mine. They were mainly interested in laying their hands on the cash that the telephone threw off, and the sooner the better. By emphasizing profitability rather than growth, Bell's Brahmin leaders endangered their company's fundamental franchise. Telephony, like railroading, is a voracious consumer of capital; in order to upgrade equipment and introduce service to new territories, the company needed a constant infusion of fresh funds. Instead of providing this financial sustenance by reinvesting profits and borrowing aggressively, the Bostonians paid out very large dividends and borrowed only $2 million in the bond market between 1880 and 1898. External financing was obtained almost exclusively through new stock issues, which were kept to a minimum. Inevitably this financial stringency demoralized managers in the field who lacked the resources needed to provide high-quality telephone service. Poor service was the logical result.

Excessive intrusion by investors deprived American Bell of a creative partnership between financiers who could furnish capital for the enterprise and energetic managers who could aggressively build the business. American Bell's Yankee directors never entrusted operations to someone who could do for their company what Andrew Kloman, Captain Bill Jones, and Charles Schwab did for Carnegie Steel. They did not have to look far to find such a "genius," for he was already on their staff. Even before the Bostonians took control of the National Bell Corporation in 1879, Theodore Vail had begun to make the company a success. By instinct a promoter and manager rather than a tightfisted investor, Vail had excellent strategic instincts and a superb capacity to infuse confidence and cohesiveness into a far-flung organization. Unfortunately the aloof Bostonians did not appreciate Vail's talents, and he left the company in 1887, not to return until J. P. Morgan took control of the company two decades later.

ALEXANDER GRAHAM BELL: THE INVENTOR AS ENTREPRENEUR

Business observers of the 1870s who witnessed the tortured birth of the American Bell Telephone Company would never have supposed that it could become the biggest company on earth. The earliest leaders of the company, starved for capital and lacking experience in founding a high-technology enterprise, negotiated a host of hazards that might have toppled much larger concerns. Perversely enough, it may actually have been inexperience that sustained Bell's founders through their many trials. Like a group of amateur yachtsmen who are driven off course by a squall, they became irrevocably committed to the venture and had no choice but to push on to the conclusion, no matter what the hardships or risks. A century later Bell's founders could undoubtedly have induced a professional venture capital firm to fit out the ship properly and help chart its course. But in the 1870s the entrepreneurs had to go it alone, relying on instinct and luck to make it into a safe harbor.

The voyage was inspired by the ingenious Scot Alexander Graham Bell, who migrated to Canada in 1870 in order to teach the deaf how to communicate by using a method known as visible speech. Developed by Bell's father, visible speech was an intricate set of written symbols that indicated precisely how to enunciate each vowel and consonant. Long and often frustrating hours of showing deaf students how to talk had made Bell a widely respected expert on the articulation and transmission of human speech. A serious, compassionate, professorial sort of man, he was a superb teacher who was deeply moved by the struggles of his pupils. "My feelings and sympathies are every day more and more aroused," he wrote. "It makes my very heart ache to see the difficulties the little children have to contend with." As a scholar Bell was energetic and imaginative but prone to indecision and perfectionism, racked by headaches and wide mood swings. He was financially ambitious but also financially unsophisticated. "I am not a businessman," he freely admitted, "and must confess that financial dealings are distasteful to me and not at all in my line." Bell's professorial air extended to his appearance, which was casual in the extreme. His future wife said of their first meeting, "I did not like him. He was tall and dark, with jet black hair and eyes, but dressed badly and carelessly in an old-fashioned suit of black broadcloth, making his hair look shiny, and altogether, to one accustomed to the dainty neatness of Harvard students, he seemed hardly a gentleman."

Shortly after moving to Boston in 1871, Bell became interested in developing a device known as a harmonic telegraph, or, more descriptively, a multiple telegraph, which would simultaneously transmit several messages over a telegraph wire by using different musical notes. Bell tinkered with this concept in the evenings in his two-room apartment in Boston's South End while supporting himself as a teacher of speech. He held a professorship at Boston University and also offered private lessons, an arrangement that left little time for experimentation on the harmonic telegraph. Bell's research funds were likewise paltry at first; for a laboratory he had to make do with his apartment, and he had no laboratory assistant to help him construct apparatus. Nevertheless, these constraints were more than balanced by the unique advantages that the city of Boston offered to the young inventor. There was the splendid Boston Public Library, where obscure scientific tracts could be obtained; the lecture series on physical science at the Massachusetts Institute of Technology (MIT); and the excellent electrical equipment shop of Charles Williams, Jr., where, amid the whine of lathes and drill presses, aspiring inventors, including Thomas Edison, could work on their ideas. In short, Boston already possessed many of the intellectual and social advantages that would later make it a fertile seedbed of such high-technology concerns as Wang Laboratories (founded by a Harvard physicist) and Digital Equipment (founded by an MIT engineer).

And Boston had something else that every ambitious inventor needs —money. Many of Bell's students came from wealthy families, and the fathers of two of them, Thomas Sanders and Gardiner Hubbard, became intrigued with the commercial possibilities of a harmonic telegraph and agreed to support Bell's work. Their aid was modest, and Bell continued to teach during the day and work on his invention at night. He was determined to stay out of debt and to avoid becoming financially dependent on Hubbard and Sanders. This was just as well, because Bell's backers tried to dissuade him from shifting his research interests from the harmonic telegraph to a far more ambitious field in which he had become interested, the transmission of the human voice over a wire. "I have been sorry to see how little interest you seem to take in telegraph matters," Hubbard wrote. "Your whole course since you returned has been a very great disappointment to me, and a sore trial." He warned Bell: "While you are flying from one thing to another you may accidentally accomplish something but you probably will never perfect anything." Hubbard had an even more powerful lever than money with which to influence the inventor, for Bell was falling in love with his daughter. There was talk of preventing the two from seeing each other until Bell abandoned telephony and returned to telegraphic experiments, but fortunately these threats never came to anything. Bell's experience in this regard was not unlike that of Henry Ford, whose financial backers insisted that a cheap car would never make much money.

Matters moved onto more formal ground in the spring of 1875, when Bell, Sanders, and Hubbard signed an agreement, later dubbed the Bell Patent Association, wherein the trio agreed to share equally in any profits generated by Bell's patents. It was a classic venture capital arrangement in which Bell provided the technical expertise while Sanders and Hubbard provided the capital and the business skill needed to commercialize the telephone. At about the same time that the Bell Patent Association was created Bell transferred his laboratory to the workshop of the Boston electrician Charles Williams, where he received the assistance of James Watson, Jr., a talented young technician on Williams's staff. While Bell continued to support himself as a professor, he and Watson worked feverishly on the telephone throughout 1875, racing to beat the Chicago inventor Elisha Gray to the patent office. The decisive experimental breakthrough occurred in June 1875, but the first patent was not filed in Washington until February 1876, only a few hours before Gray filed a patent caveat. Gardiner Hubbard filed Bell's patent on his own initiative, without Bell's consent, and if he had not so acted, the Bell interests would almost certainly have been defeated in later legal battles with Gray.

After two more months of experimentation Watson and Bell had a workable, if crude, device for transmitting human voice over a wire. With no little trepidation, they prepared to submit their contraption to public scrutiny. After successful appearances before the American Academy of Arts and Sciences—"a distinguished assemblage of grey heads" Bell later called them—and a gathering at MIT, the telephone made its national debut at one of the great celebrations of moral and material progress during the Victorian age, the Centennial Exposition in Philadelphia. Bell's telephone was stuck off in the education exhibit, and amid all the other marvels that were on display no one paid it much attention. But when Emperor Pedro of Brazil, who was interested in acoustics and had already visited one of Bell's classes, picked up the contraption, visitors to the fair took notice. The first to try the device was Sir William Thompson, engineer of the transatlantic cable. Bell went to the far end of the room and began to sing into the microphone and then shouted, "Do you understand what I say?"

An incredulous Thompson replied, "Yes! Do you understand what I say? Where is Mr. Bell? I must see Mr. Bell."

Dom Pedro was the next dignitary to clap his ear to Professor Bell's device, and his reaction was no less enthusiastic. "I hear, I hear!" he exclaimed.

What was good enough for a British lord and a Brazilian emperor was plenty good enough for the American public; the Centennial triumph wrenched the telephone out of the laboratory and into the glare of public attention. Now Bell and Watson moved confidently into the limelight by staging a series of public demonstrations that dramatized the powers of the telephone. Watson, situated several miles away from a lecture hall, would use a telephone and conventional telegraph wires to sing, read, and converse with members of the audience assembled in the hall. Despite his extensive practice in handling the telephone, Watson's booming voice was often faint and indistinct at the other end of the wire, and the results were even worse when the uninitiated attempted to use the device. When a famous opera singer sang pieces from *The Barber of Seville* into the telephone, it sounded "as if someone a mile away was being smothered; then it swelled; then faded almost away, and its end was [as] uncertain as the line between daylight and darkness." Despite such qualified performances, the public was impressed. After one lecture the *Boston Globe* wrote, "The frequent and long continued applause showed that the audience appreciated fully the wonderful uses and experiments made with these machines." Another newspaper called the telephone a "revolutionary advance in the world's progress worthy to rank with the practical completion of the first printing telegraph . . . and with the laying of the first ocean cables."

It was not just publicity that Bell was after in hitting the lecture circuit. After years of privation he was still living on "next to nothing in Boston," still enduring criticism from his father that his financial life was a "muddle." Bell was desperate to put some cash in his pocket and "take me off the hardships of life and leave me free to follow out the ideas which interest me most." Even more to the point, Bell needed some money before he could marry Mabel Hubbard. Her mother considered lecturing an undignified employment for a prospective son-in-law, but the lure of $200 per night outweighed considerations of professional decorum. Although the lectures proved something of a disappointment financially, Bell was able to finance his marriage and take a honeymoon in England by selling British rights to the telephone for $5,000.

AMATEUR VENTURE CAPITALISTS

Bell's marriage ended his direct involvement in the commercialization of telephony; from that time on the task was in the hands of his two backers, Sanders and Hubbard. By turns impulsive and careful, shrewd and guileless, this duo bore a certain resemblance to a comedy team. Sanders was the fretful straight man, always certain that disaster loomed around the next turn in the road; Hubbard, by contrast, was the gregarious free spirit who exuded confidence that the company would prosper, even though he never seemed to have any funds to help pull it through difficult times. The pair quarreled bitterly as they labored to breathe economic life into Professor Bell's invention, but amid the shrieks and sparks thrown off by their fractious partnership a great deal of useful work was accomplished. In the end the two were more nearly complementary than antagonistic.

A prosperous leather manufacturer who lived on the Bay State's North Shore, Thomas Sanders had a solid credit rating, a love of fine horses, and close ties to Boston's upper crust. What he lacked in flair he made up for in tenacity and good sense, and at the local bank he was usually good for a loan of $10,000 or $20,000. Hubbard, on the other hand, was a prominent patent lawyer with a taste for risky investments, a gifted promoter whose contacts were far more extensive than his credit. Active in political and scientific affairs, he served in the U.S. Congress and on a federal postal commission, helped set up public utilities in the city of Boston, and supported the National Geographic Society and the Smithsonian Institution. During the 1860s Hubbard did battle with the powerful Western Union Corporation by attempting to push through Congress an act creating a competing telegraph system. It is a measure of his lobbying skill that this attack on Western Union was very nearly successful. Hubbard's promotional talent was invaluable to the Bell Telephone Company in its early years. It was he who filed the key telephone patent in the spring of 1876, and it was he who secured a place for the telephone at the Philadelphia Centennial Exposition. But financial support was a different matter. Money-losing investments in a coal mine and a land company left him bereft of liquid capital in the 1870s, and he was never able to make good on the promise of financial support that he made when he joined the Bell Patent Association. He confided to a friend in 1877, "My money matters are as you know entirely deranged by the adverse circumstances of the last few years, and with a very large amount of property I am more in need of money than if I owned nothing for I do owe some debts and have large sums to pay for taxes and have no income from property."

These were the venture capitalists who launched what would become the largest company on the face of the earth. A wide variety of hazards—legal, managerial, technical, political—lay in their path, but financial barriers loomed largest. There were four dimensions to their financial problem. In the first place, the telephone business was very capital-intensive; the company needed enough money not only to develop and manufacture telephones but also to string a grid of wires across the American landscape. Thus in its financial requirements the American Bell Telephone Company more nearly resembled the railroads than such make-and-sell enterprises as steel, automobiles, or computers. While the steel industry was also capital-intensive, it was not necessary to build a fully integrated mill all at once; an entrepreneur could begin with a rolling mill and, once profits had started to come in, reinvest the cash flow in mines and blast furnaces in order to integrate backward and forward. But since a pair of telephones was worthless without wires to connect them, the company needed a large amount of capital from the outset.

The general financial conditions prevailing in the 1870s also worked against American Bell. In what can only be called a serious defect of the American financial system, very few industrial stocks were regularly traded on Wall Street in the mid-nineteenth century. Nor was there anything comparable to the modern new-issues market through which speculative stocks could be distributed to intrepid or foolhardy investors. To be sure, such issues did come to market from time to time, but there was no army of brokers regularly touting such stocks to their customers. The speculative action was in the railroad issues and in commodities, particularly gold. Moreover, there was not much speculative action in any market when American Bell was founded because in 1877 the nation was gripped by depression. Commodity prices were stagnant, unemployment was widespread, and thousands of businesses had gone bankrupt since Jay Cooke and Company closed its doors in 1873. The political climate was no less ominous. An agrarian reform movement known as Grangerism was spreading through the Midwest, beating the drum for stricter regulation of the railroads. A massive strike by Pennsylvania railroad workers turned violent, and eighty-five workers were killed in Pittsburgh and Altoona before the state militia restored order. All in all, this was not the sort of climate in which investors were inclined to take a flyer in an interesting high-technology stock.

But even in a buoyant investment climate American Bell would not have been an attractive issue for any but the most daring speculator. In 1877 one had to look very hard indeed to see in the company a young corporate giant that was about to enter upon a period of rapid growth. It much more resembled a sacrificial lamb that was about to be swallowed whole by one of the nation's largest companies, the Western Union Corporation. After first turning down the chance to buy Bell's patent rights for $100,000, Western Union decided that the telephone was more than a toy after all and jumped into telephony with both feet. It purchased the patents of Amos Dolbear and Elisha Gray and also retained Thomas Edison to devise improvements for the system. Western Union simultaneously challenged American Bell's telephone patent in court. The giant telegraph company was one of the most dangerous competitors that American Bell could have faced, for in addition to its ample financial resources, it controlled a nationwide system of wires and offices that could easily be adapted to telephony. In short, it already owned the expensive infrastructure that American Bell would have to build from the ground up if it ever obtained the requisite capital. And in addition to scaring off investors who might otherwise have supported the Bell interests, the court battle with Western Union consumed thousands of dollars in legal fees.

As if all these burdens were not heavy enough, American Bell's management imposed one of its own. Sometime in 1877 Gardiner Hubbard concluded that telephones should be rented rather than sold and that they should be distributed over the country through a franchise system. Agents for American Bell Telephone would receive an exclusive franchise to rent out telephones within a particular city or region. At first Hubbard expected pairs of telephones to be rented to a customer so that he could communicate between two points—between, say, a doctor's house and his office. But after the invention of the telephone exchange in 1878 the franchises became, in effect, local operating companies that provided telephone service within their region. Although the terms of the franchise varied widely, the agent usually received a commission of 40 percent on the first year's rental and 20 percent on each year thereafter. By 1878 the parent company was also taking an equity position in the local subsidiaries. This imaginative organizational approach was inspired by Hubbard's prior association with a company that had manufactured and rented rather than sold shoemaking equipment. Always aware of the danger of infringements on the simply constructed telephone, the patent lawyer Hubbard believed that this arrangement would safeguard Bell Telephone's control of the device, and he was supported in this judgment by the company's corporate counsel.

Though inspired by legal and technical considerations, the decision to rent, not sell, had momentous organizational and financial implications for the young company. Because it gave the company a permanent revenue stream from the telephones placed in customers' hands, it was a brilliant move in the long run. The short-term effects were far more mixed. On the positive side, it allowed a company that had precious little capital or managerial manpower to establish a national presence rapidly by employing local capital and local business talent. As Theodore Vail put it, "We couldn't get capital, so we had to get young men who were interested in the business with small capital and let them take their energy and their ambition and their prospect of profit to take the place of large capital and in that way we built up, in small territories, the business pretty generally." Inquiries poured in from all over the country, many of them from people who were already involved in the electrical equipment industry. One early franchise was E. T. Holmes, who operated a burglar alarm company in Boston; another was C. H. Sewall, active in the telegraph industry in Albany, who wrote: "Our company has no agency for any kind of instrument except a burglar alarm and we do nothing with that. We have a first class line man and a good organization for working up a business like yours."

Unfortunately the rental plan threatened to bankrupt the company before its virtues could become evident, for it gave the company a negative cash flow from operations. Every time that the company placed a telephone in a customer's hands in 1877 and 1878, its financial position deteriorated. The problem was simply that the company had to bear the entire cost of manufacturing each telephone almost immediately but received the revenue from that phone over a period of years. For example, if the direct cost of manufacturing a telephone was $50 and it was rented out for $20 per year, American Bell had to pay out $30 more for the phone in the first year than it received from rent. A well-established company could easily have borrowed from a bank to finance this shortfall because continued revenue from the rented telephone was fairly certain. But with Western Union nipping at its heels there was no guarantee that Bell Telephone would be around to pay its debts. The rental problem was all the more serious because it compounded a cash shortfall that would have existed even under the best conditions. A common characteristic of start-up companies, frequently highlighted by business school professors who take delight in astounding their students in Finance 101, is that the faster a company grows, the more likely it is to run out of cash—unless it receives an infusion of funds from an outside source. The reason is simply that as a company's sales rapidly expand, a larger and larger percentage of its current assets will consist of accounts receivable, which are generated by recent sales, and of inventories, which are needed to generate future sales, while a smaller and smaller percentage of current assets will consist of cash. Consequently, high profits can be accompanied by a drain on cash, a paradox immortalized in this humble verse:

Though my bottom line is black, I am flat upon my back,
My cash flows out and customers pay slow.
The growth of my receivables is almost unbelievable
The result is certain—unremitting woe!
And I hear the banker utter an ominous low mutter, "Watch cash flow."

Unfortunately Bell Telephone had no loyal banker to supplement its cash flow.

The inevitable effect of this cash squeeze was to prevent American Bell from supplying its franchisees with all the telephones that they needed to meet customer demand. Month after month in 1877 and 1878 agents impatiently waited to receive the phones that they had ordered and had already promised to customers. The long delays demoralized the American Bell organization and undermined the company's public credibility. Potential customers would not wait forever to have a phone installed; if Bell could not provide phone service, then customers would do business with its well-heeled competitor, Western Union. American Bell did not manufacture its instruments in house; they were supplied by the Boston manufacturer Charles Williams, whose electrical shop had been the site of some of Alexander Graham Bell's most important experiments. As operations got under way during 1877, orders rapidly flooded into Williams's little shop. Within a couple of months he doubled the rate of production from twenty-five to fifty telephones per day, and before long he had to expand his facilities to keep up with the quickening order flow. Unfortunately Williams (unlike many of the early suppliers of parts to auto manufacturers) was not a wealthy businessman who, by virtue of his personal resources and borrowing power, could afford to finance his fast-growing but cash-poor customers. His resources were limited, and he was dependent on American Bell for liquidity. In January 1878 Sanders wrote Hubbard, "I have advanced Mr. Williams $2500 out of my own pocket . . . and he must have $2500 more next Tuesday. Will you send me a check for that amount, as . . . we shall not have enough to pay Mr. Williams what we shall owe him as his expenses increase daily." But American Bell failed to supply the requisite funds, and Williams, hard pressed by creditors, attempted to hide the real reason for his tardiness in paying debts: "I have studiously endeavored to keep up the credit of the [Bell Telephone] company and when pressed for bills, instead of intimating that I could not get the money of the Telephone Company I have made other excuses, and none of my creditors have had the least idea of the amount due me from the Company."

The cash flow problems continued, and two and a half months later Sanders was complaining that "Williams is tormenting me for money. . . . Pay day has come and his capital will not carry him another inch." As Williams fell behind in orders, complaints in the field mounted. Though more melodramatic than most, the note from a Missouri franchisee sounded a familiar note: "My people tell me that we are losing customers by this delay. Parties ordering soon get tired of waiting and say they will countermand orders, if you have not sent them on receipt of this. Let me beseech you to write or telegraph me something that I can show to the anxious thousands that are waiting. You can have no idea of the pressure I undergo and the questions I have to answer and the stories I have to fabricate. And why is it all thusly? You can, and you must tell me. I beg you to take pity on this suffering community." Faced with these devastating delays, agents vied with each other to get more than their proper quota of instruments, and agents from the hinterland complained bitterly when Massachusetts agents received more than a proportionate share of the instruments.

The burden of dealing with the cash crunch rested squarely on the shoulders of Hubbard and Sanders, and as the noose tightened in 1878, their correspondence became increasingly acrimonious. Hubbard was a natural optimist in financial affairs but cautious on matters of corporate strategy. He feared loss of control of the telephone patent. This concern had influenced his desire to rent rather than sell telephones, and it caused him to oppose bringing in outside investors, who, he feared, would take control of the company. As for the danger that the company would cede control of the telephone to Western Union simply by going bankrupt, Hubbard cheerfully observed that money wasn't everything. "I do not believe the Western Union Telephone Company have an organization that can accomplish very much; money is by no means the most important thing, it wants judgment, push and enterprise." This was all very well for Hubbard to say because it was not his money that would go down the drain if American Bell went bankrupt. His personal financial position was too straitened for him to invest significant sums in the business. It was Sanders who came up with the cash. The leather manufacturer naïvely thought that after he had made a limited cash infusion, the company would attract outside capital and his financial responsibility to it would end. But Hubbard's resistance to this approach, combined with the threat from Western Union, made it difficult to raise capital. So Sanders had to borrow money from his bankers, who viewed the telephone industry with a jaundiced eye. Although they were willing to lend Sanders $20,000 on his own credit, these "conservative gentlemen" did not consider the telephone patent worthwhile security for a loan. As Sanders explained, "I think the bank was not unreasonable. As Bank officers they felt hardly justified in taking any patent as security for money placed in their hands. . . . They do not look on the Telephone paper in its present stage as strengthening my credit. . . . They know absolutely nothing about the Telephone except what I have told them."

During 1878 Sanders was drawn deeper and deeper into American Bell's treacherous business, fretfully doling out the dollars needed to keep Charles Williams's telephone factory in operation. Eventually he transferred the bulk of his resources from the leather business to telephony and invested more than $100,000 in the new company. Meanwhile, Hubbard loitered in Washington, D.C., demonstrating the telephone to everyone in sight and sending gratuitous advice—but no cash—to Sanders in Boston. The replies of Sanders alternated between exasperation and terror. He continued to insist that an infusion of outside capital was needed but dryly observed that "a bird in the hand is worth two in the bush' does not seem to be one of your maxims:— provided the indefinite future is bright, the present seems to be of little account to you. You have a certain blissful disregard of money, an enviable trait to possess, but scarcely a desirable one in a business partner." A month later the tone was more urgent. Sanders wanted to know "How on earth can we make our position better by fighting when we have nothing to fight with? . . . The Western Union has frightened everyone connected with us, directly or indirectly. My business has suffered, that is, my notes have been thrust onto the market at a high rate [of discount] from the feeling that I am largely interested in a shaky concern, and it will require all the money advanced to the Bell Tel. Co. to take care of the business to which it belongs. Absolute bankruptcy of the whole concern must result if we do not procure money from some source."

Money was available, but it bore a heavy price: control of the firm. In a complicated series of transactions that began in the spring of 1878 and ended in the middle of 1879, modest amounts of fresh capital were obtained from a group of Boston investors who were friends of Thomas Sanders. The sums involved were quite trivial. In January 1878, in return for providing $50,000 in fresh capital, the syndicate was granted control of the New England Telephone Company, which had the telephone franchise for the region. Four months later the non-New England business was incorporated as the Bell Telephone Corporation, and an additional $50,000 was raised, half from Sanders and half from outside investors. In stage three of the restructuring, which occurred in March 1879, the New England Telephone Company and the Bell Telephone Corporation were merged to create a new company called the National Bell Telephone Corporation. Voting control of the new concern was placed in the hands of investors who had provided fresh capital for the enterprise. This arrangement froze Hubbard out of managerial power in the new company—he was gone within a few months—and since Sanders was not intent on running the company, managerial authority naturally passed to the new investors.

This corporate reshuffling was meaningless so long as National Bell was about to be consumed by Western Union, but the telephone company was making progress on that front as well. Assistance came from an unlikely source—Jay Gould. The "Mephistopheles of Wall Street" was winding his tentacles around Western Union by establishing a giant telegraph company of his own, called the Atlantic and Pacific Telegraph Company, which strung up 35,000 miles of wire between 1874 and 1877. Once Western Union entered the telephone market, Gould began to battle his adversary in that sector as well by buying into the regional operating companies of the Bell interests. This unwelcome competition cut into Western Union's earnings, unnerving investors and making the company's stock vulnerable to devastating bear raids. With its business challenged and its stock battered, an attempt by Gould to take over Western Union seemed to be in the offing. Recognizing that a two-front war with both Gould and American Bell was more than it could handle, Western Union decided to make peace with the Bell interests while there was still time. This course of action seemed all the more advisable because evidence was mounting that its litigation to invalidate Alexander Graham Bell's telephone patent was likely to fail.

Negotiations dragged on through much of 1879, and in late autumn an understanding between Western Union and American Bell was finally achieved. By an agreement signed in November, Western Union admitted the validity of the Bell patents, withdrew from the telephone market, and sold its telephone properties to National Bell. Western Union was to receive 20 percent of the telephone rental revenues earned by National Bell over the next seventeen years and during this period was to pay 20 percent of the costs incurred by National Bell in developing telephone technology. Although the price of American Bell stock had been creeping upward for months as the company's legal status improved, the settlement made a sensation on Wall Street. Having traded as low as $50 per share in March and around $350 in September, the price soared to more than $1,000 per share on the day after the announcement. Hubbard, Sanders, and Watson could retire from the field, wealthy and vindicated, and leave the future of the telephone to their wellborn successors.

Since Bell, Hubbard, and Sanders resembled thousands of other investment groups that have formed to commercialize an idea, it is instructive to consider what they did right and what they did wrong. Each member of the trio had certain strengths: Bell in technology, Hubbard in promotion and lobbying, and Sanders in finance. To the extent that they *were* successful, it was because each principal specialized in the area he knew best. Bell followed his technical instincts and did not permit Hubbard and Sanders—who, after all, knew almost nothing about telephony—to push him around. This was not so easy to do, for it was "their money" that was financing his experiments, and they were filled with anxiety that it was being squandered. Of course, it would have made no more sense for Sanders and Hubbard to set the direction of Bell's research than it would for someone to give a famous neurosurgeon a check for $100,000 and then tell him where to drill. The flamboyant, well-connected Hubbard did a great job of winning publicity for the telephone and getting the enterprise off the ground through franchising. The problem was that he had too much power.

He made key strategic decisions, such as the decision to rent rather than sell, with wide financial ramifications he did not understand. Sanders, who had a good grasp of finance, should have stepped in and explained to Hubbard that the need for good cash flow made a rental policy untenable for the first few years of the company's existence. This is one of the most common errors made by entrepreneurs: They map out slightly grandiose strategic plans that do not take account of the enormous need for cash that a small, fast-growing business has. It is easy for even a successful business to run out of cash when it is rapidly building inventory, receivables, and plant and equipment.

SUCCESSFUL INVESTORS, MEDIOCRE INDUSTRIALISTS

William Murray Forbes was the top man at the new American Bell. His father, the railroad investor John Murray Forbes, must have been pleased with the results of his no-nonsense, spare-the-luxury approach to child rearing. The younger Forbes was handsome, aristocratic, and decisive, and if he lacked the spark of acquisitive genius that inspired his father, he nevertheless possessed enough force and stature to get a struggling corporation on its feet. Adulthood had not begun auspiciously for the younger Forbes, however. During his college days he was thrown into jail briefly—and out of Harvard permanently—because he bungled a prank and seriously injured the security guard who tried to apprehend him. He more than acquitted himself during the Civil War by compiling a long and distinguished military record, an achievement that was widely admired in the upper echelons of Boston society, where abolitionist and Republican sentiment ran strong. Perhaps it was fitting that at the close of the war the young hero returned to Boston and married the daughter of the city's leading savant, Ralph Waldo Emerson, himself a staunch foe of slavery.

After his marriage in 1865 William Murray Forbes settled into a demanding but rewarding life of rearing a family and working in his father's business. He took particular delight in improving his two estates and building yachts for his six sons, who sailed them around the family compound on Naushon Island, a splendid strip of land, seven miles long, that lies between Martha's Vineyard and the mainland. In business matters Forbes was competent and cautious. He managed a number of investment trusts and traveled around the country, inspecting the family's railroad properties, but there is little evidence that he had a flair for making investments or engineering deals. Flair was not, after all, what was required of a wealthy son of an established family who was entrusted with managing the property of others. Hardheaded prudence was far more important. The conservatism of Forbes comes out clearly in his letters to clients. To one he wrote, "I don't think I care to invest in Pullman stock any funds for the management of which I am responsible. I do not consider that the property rests on as sure and permanent a basis as many others which will pay good interest, though probably not as good. The Pullman business is so extended that it depends more than most properties on very capable management. I judge that Pullman is much engaged in other things, and think there is great liability to competition and that the railroads will run their own cars instead of his as soon as they can." To Mrs. Edward C. Perkins he wrote: "I know it is likely that the purchase of Calumet & Hecla stock at present prices may be a good business operation, but if I should buy into it and it should go wrong I should be directly responsible, because no one can claim that copper stocks are safe and judicious investments for trustees." Although Forbes's investment in the fledgling telephone industry shows that he was not so cautious with his own money, he does seem to have approached his duties at American Bell from the perspective of the investor, rather than the entrepreneur.

The starchy conservatism of William Murray Forbes clashed with the easygoing optimism of his right-hand man at American Bell, General Manager Theodore Vail. Vail's business career is rare in the annals of nineteenth-century American business because he brought to private enterprise special managerial gifts that were developed in the federal government. Such a transfer of talent was unusual at the time simply because the federal bureaucracy was infested with party hacks and was minuscule in any case—so small, in fact, that during the 1880s the great problem vexing Washington policymakers was what to do about the embarrassingly large federal budget *surplus*. An affable, nonchalant, openhanded fellow, Vail had stumbled into the U.S. postal service after working for a time in a telegraph office. It was soon apparent that he had a special talent for making the mails run more smoothly. He was fascinated with the organizational challenge of inducing a slew of competing private railroads to cooperate in handling the mail, and he knew how to work with unruly entrepreneurs and dim-witted political appointees to get things done. He was able to conceptualize the overall workings of the system while mastering the hundreds of individual joints and junctures of which it was composed. Vail's unusual ability was rewarded by appointment to the number two job in the railway mail service in 1874, when he was twenty-eight years of age. His main accomplishments in the position was to establish a "fast mail" that moved a letter from New York to Chicago in just twenty-four hours. Aside from the challenge of the work itself, an attractive feature of the job was its compensation, which amounted to $3,500 per year, including salary and expense account. Vail needed every penny he earned, and then some, because he spent money freely, both to live well and to make investments in offbeat inventions of every description. "His habit of lavish expenditure . . . I never could understand," a friend later recalled. "He seemed to act on the certainty that the money would be forthcoming in due time. And it always was."

Among the inventions that captured Vail's imagination and capital was the telephone, which Gardiner Hubbard was hawking around Washington. Vail borrowed aggressively to buy stock in the new company and urged his friends to do the same, and when he ran into a dispute about his salary as general superintendent of the railway mails —for he had been promoted to the top post in 1876—he decided to accept a pay cut and take command of the leaky ship manned by Hubbard and Sanders. Vail's friends and associates were appalled by his infatuation with telephony. A friend warned him: "One or two years hence there will be more telephone companies in existence than there are sewing machine companies today." A congressman pleaded, "Can't you wait and see if Congress will not fix your salary? Don't rob the public of an invaluable servant just because we tried to cheat and starve you." And an exchange between two well-placed Washingtonians reportedly ran like this:

"Vail resigned his place? What for?"

"Why, he is going into that thing invented by Bell—the telephone that talks over a wire. He has invested some money in it, and is going to make it his business."

"Well, that's too bad. I always liked Vail. Hubbard tried to sell me some of that stock. I'm sorry he got hold of a nice fellow like Vail."

Vail had the vision and dynamism needed to build up American Bell. His biographer, who knew him well, captures his essence as a businessman: "His first idea was to establish, or extend, some important enterprise—some manufacturing or mining industry that would grow and grow and give labor and benefit to the race. He was pre-eminently a builder, a developer. Mere money—through the purchase of stocks in the market, for instance—did not interest him. He never followed a tip on the Street, never in his life speculated to the extent of a single share." He thus had some of the same instincts as Andrew Carnegie, although he was intent on building systems and providing good service rather than on cutting costs and "scooping the market." He lacked the robber baron's instinct to hammer the competition. At American Bell, Vail devoted much of his effort to tightening the loose confederation of local operating companies that had sprung up around the country. These subsidiaries were linked to the parent corporation in Boston in two ways: American Bell owned between 30 and 50 percent of the stock of the companies and also manufactured and rented out the telephones that they provided customers. Thus American Bell was a holding company the revenues of which consisted of rental fees on telephones and the dividends issued by subsidiaries. The danger in this arrangement was that its growth was dictated by the success of the operating companies. Vail's aim was to expand, coordinate, and energize this far-flung network so that it could "take possession of the field in such a way that, patent or no patent, we could control it." To this end he prodded the operating companies to grow as rapidly as possible, here suggesting that a licensee was not doing all it could to provide good service, there fending off interlopers who wanted to set up a telephone company without respecting Bell patents, and somewhere else consolidating two neighboring operating companies to improve their performance. Knowing that good service was the key to success, he wanted the licensees to reinvest most of their profits in their businesses rather than pay large dividends to the parent company. But on this question he was overruled by Forbes.

Vail pushed for two other steps that would allow American Bell to "get possession of the field" before the patents ran out. To expand the company's manufacturing capability, he advocated purchase of both the Boston telephone factory of Charles Williams, Jr., and the Western Electric Company of Chicago. The largest electrical equipment company in the nation, Western Electric was partly owned by the inventor Elisha Gray, and it had supplied Western Union with telephones during its battle with American Bell. Under Bell's ownership it effectively ended the telephone shortage that had plagued operations under Sanders and Hubbard. A second and still more important innovation supported by Vail was establishment of a new subsidiary that would provide long-distance service between the various operating regions, allowing a lawyer in Boston, for instance, to call his broker in New York or his client in Cleveland. American Telephone and Telegraph, as the new long-distance company was called, played a central role in American Bell's competitive strategy. By linking together the individual operating companies it would greatly enhance the value of their service and make them impervious to local competition. If, for example, a rival company opened up in Toledo in 1896, it would not be able to connect its customers with Detroit or St. Louis, as the Bell company could. Unfortunately the idea behind AT&T was sounder than its execution, for as usual Bell's directors were loath to spend the money necessary to expand aggressively. The company was founded in 1885 with Vail in command, but its initial capital was only $100,000. Extension of the system, in the estimation of one historian, was "gradual." By 1893 wires had been strung between the major cities of New England, the East Coast, and the Midwest, but the South and West were still excluded. The pace of progress was evidently too slow for Vail, who severed his ties with the Bell System in 1887 after eight years with the company and seven under Forbes. Despite his obvious talents, Vail had been excluded from the inner circle of the company by the snobbish New Englanders and compelled to expand the company with limited resources. He allowed that "my present position in the company . . . is in some ways embarrassing and unpleasant."

Theodore Vail's Brahmin bosses simply did not share his enthusiasm for building a first-class telephone network as rapidly as possible. Like that of many another hardheaded investor, their main concern was to maximize profits in the short run. Social usefulness did not excite them unless it paid. To make sure that it did, the Yankees worked hard to boost the rate of return on their investment by attacking both the numerator of the fraction (by keeping telephone rates as high as possible) and the denominator (by investing no more capital than was absolutely necessary). And to make sure that they actually laid their hands on the cash thrown off by their splendid monopoly, they paid out the bulk of their profits in dividends rather than reinvest in new plant and equipment. So long as the profits rolled in, the Yankee investors remained remote and aloof, increasingly out of touch with the extremities of the Bell System, caring little whether the people in Indianapolis or Duluth were receiving good service. Theirs was an honest but myopic vision of business strategy, one that got the telephone industry off the ground far more successfully than Hubbard and Sanders could have but then failed to exploit its full potential. In a real sense the difference between William Murray Forbes and Theodore Vail paralleled the difference between Thomas Sanders and Gardiner

Hubbard. To Hubbard and Vail machines and business schemes were an end in themselves while money was a secondary concern; for Sanders and Forbes the reverse was more nearly true.

As noted, a key ingredient in American Bell's high-profit strategy was to charge all the traffic could bear, and then some. Rates varied widely, depending on the type and amount of service received, but usually ranged between $80 and $200 per year for residential service and considerably more for business service. Such rates placed the device out of reach of most working-class and many middle-class families. Although the national price level declined steadily during the 1880s and early 1890s, telephone rates did not budge. Consumers complained bitterly about the high rates; the state of Indiana even imposed price controls on the telephone. But President Forbes insisted that the maintenance of high rates was justified because the amount of capital behind each phone—and the amount of service that it provided—expanded with the network.

Whether justified or not, telephone rates were far higher in the United States than in Europe. A study conducted in 1897 and 1898 found that the cost of service was about $100 per year in Washington but only $20 in Stockholm and as little as $10 in Zurich. To be sure, European rates were usually set by the government and were often too low to provide good service, and despite these low rates, telephone use was far lower in European countries than in the United States. On the other hand, this lower consumption may be traced in part to the lower average incomes of Europeans; in many European cities telephones per capita were much higher than in American cities of comparable size. However that may be, it is clear that American Bell had no trouble reducing rates dramatically—while still earning a healthy profit—once competition hit the U.S. telephone industry in the 1890s. Between 1885 and 1893 the average rate that American Bell charged its subsidiaries for renting a telephone held up at around $11. But the rate fell to $7.78 in 1894, $4.36 in 1895, and less than $3.00 in 1898—a 64 percent drop in five years. Critics considered the rate reduction long overdue and noted that the potential negative impact on the company's finances was substantially offset by the expansion of the company's market. The *Commercial and Financial Chronicle* observed, "Many friends of the Bell system deplore the policy of high rates and uncompromising treatment which the Bell companies in the past have so generally pursued, but even the latter, it would appear, have recognized their mistake and the gain of fifty per cent within a comparatively few months in the number of Bell telephones in use . . . shows that the public will respond to lower rates."

To enhance profitability, Bell's management complemented high rates with anemic investment in new plant and equipment. The telephone business was not only capital-intensive but also subject to swift technological change which sometimes made equipment obsolete as soon as it was installed. In the annual report for 1884 William Murray Forbes complained: "As an instance of the rapid depreciation of property and of the changes likely to occur in electrical inventions, it may be well to say that the telephone system in Boston has been twice rebuilt, and the new multiple switch-boards for the Boston office had hardly been received and had not been put in place, when the invention of an improvement in detail gave such promise of excellent results that the boards were shipped back to Chicago to have the new invention added to them." To control capital expenditures, the company developed the long-line business quite gradually, as we have seen, and it also dragged its feet in eliminating the unnerving static that crackled and snapped like a raging bonfire in the ear of the poor customer. As early as 1881 it was discovered that static could be reduced by using two wires to form a connection, instead of one, but American Bell management was not enthusiastic about this costly solution. As late as 1892 only an eighth of Bell's customers enjoyed the benefit of two-wire circuits. Similarly the company was slow to eliminate the dense thicket of overhead telephone wires that darkened city streets and came crashing down in heavy snowstorms. Public officials demanded that the wires be placed underground, but an effective insulation for underground wires was not devised until the early 1890s. As with the long-distance system, the prodding of Theodore Vail was instrumental in getting Forbes to finance the research needed to solve this problem.

One reason why American Bell was not unduly anxious to win the favor of its customers by making heavy investments is that the fortunes of the company were determined as much in the courtroom as in the marketplace, or so it seemed. The company had broken into the clear in 1879, after all, not because of any technical or marketing victory but rather by virtue of its impending legal victory over Western Union. Over the next decade American Bell was forced to protect this success by waging a debilitating series of legal battles against a succession of bizarre foes. The disappointed inventor Elisha Gray revived his claim against American Bell in 1885, lost again, and died a bitter man. Tufts University Professor Amos Dolbear attacked the Bell patent by dredging up a patent of a German inventor named Johann Philipp Reis. An eccentric Pennsylvania hillbilly with a string of minor inventions to his credit took his claim against the company all the way to the United States Supreme Court. And a group of former Confederate politicians created a company called the Pan Electric Corporation, handed out stock to influential people in Washington, and attempted to push through Congress a law invalidating the Bell patents. The House passed the measure, but it was defeated in the Senate. These and countless other troublesome lawsuits absorbed the energy of Bell's top management, diverting attention from operations in the field. It is no coincidence that two of Forbes's successors, John E. Hudson and Frederick H. Fish, were lawyers and that despite the manifest unpopularity of the Bell monopoly, Hudson attempted to perpetuate Bell's hegemony into the twentieth century not by aggressive investment or canny marketing moves but rather by enforcing a patent on the Berliner transmitter. The mind of management was in the courts, not the marketplace.

The legal preoccupations of top management reinforced a centrifugal dynamic that was rooted in the fundamental structure of the enterprise. American Bell was a holding company; most of the assets listed on its balance sheet were not inventory, receivables, and telephone lines but rather the stock of the regional operating companies. William Murray Forbes believed that by involving local businessmen in these subsidiaries, the corporation's political position would be enhanced, but in the absence of energetic management from headquarters by a man like Vail, the ties between Beacon Hill and the hinterland became ever more tenuous. After Hudson, an icy Brahmin lawyer well known for his mastery of ancient Greek, had assumed the presidency in 1889, the problem became acute. He and his associates held the purse strings but knew little about local conditions. After traveling through the West and talking to the local managers, the Boston banker Thomas Jefferson Coolidge wrote Hudson, "I was very much struck with the different conditions surrounding the business in the West, compared to the East. Our company should be very liberal in its modifications of the contracts and use of instruments to meet the needs of specific communities served by each company. . . . Some local men think they are so unlikely to get the funds they need, that they are discouraged. The amounts in some cases which they consider absolutely necessary for the protection of their territory, they hardly feel like urging strong as, I presume, they have been frequently cut down in the past." Even more telling is Coolidge's observation that "a few hours of contact in the local territory with the local men has given me a better idea of the complications of our business than I could have gotten from years of discussion with the heads of departments in Boston."

High rates, cautious investment, and decentralized management produced predictable results—namely, high profits, slow growth, and poor service. Thanks to an exhaustive study conducted by the Federal Communications Commission (FCC) during the New Deal, the financial performance of the company between 1880 and 1900 can be easily summarized. During the 1880s about 83 percent of the company's assets consisted of the stock of subsidiaries, and since the corporation issued very little long-term debt before 1898, the right side of its balance sheet consisted largely of owner's equity. During this twenty-year period three types of revenue flowed into the company's coffers: fees paid by operating companies for the phones that they rented, dividends paid out by the subsidiaries to the parent, and revenue from the long-distance system. Initially telephone rentals were most important by far, and they remained the largest single source until the onset of competition forced a reduction of rates after 1894. Meanwhile, the subsidiaries, under the prodding of American Bell management, paid out large dividends to the parent corporation once they had begun to prosper; by 1900 the dividends received by the parent company as revenue were 63 percent larger than rental fees. By the turn of the century the long-line department had also grown to significant proportions, but this was a relatively recent phenomenon. Over the period 1880–1900, 24 percent of American Bell's revenue stream was used to pay taxes and expenses, and the balance was net income of American Bell. Almost from the moment it got control of the company the Forbes group paid out the bulk of these profits in dividends, which over two decades amounted to fully 85.5 percent of the profits.

The common stock of American Bell was a wonderful investment, especially for early stockholders who were permitted to purchase newly issued shares at a steep discount to market value. In 1880 the founders and early investors of New England Bell and National Bell received 51,000 shares of stock in American Bell, a stake in the new company that cost them about $10.39 per share but was soon worth more than fifteen times this amount. Over the next two decades the company issued 210,000 shares of stock, 11,450 in connection with a convertible note issue and the balance for cash. The par or nominal face value of this stock was $100 per share, but because they paid fat dividends of

$15 to $18, American Bell shares traded on the open market for more than $200 in the 1890s. Until the practice was prohibited by Massachusetts in 1894, the company allowed current stockholders to purchase new issues of stock at par. Thus a stockholder was entitled to purchase a newly issued share of stock for $100 in 1884 and receive $15 in dividends during the course of the year. The resulting dividend yield of 15 percent compared very favorably indeed with government bonds, which yielded 3.29 percent in 1884. Because part of the earnings was retained in the surplus account rather than paid out as dividends, the dividend on its common stock is only a general indication of its profitability, not a precise measure. But thanks to the work of the FCC, we know that annual net income per share over the entire period 1881–1899 was $18.40 per share. Since the average cost of all the outstanding shares was $109, the earnings yield was 16.9 percent. Clearly American Bell was an excellent investment until competition got in the way.

The price of this remarkable profitability was mediocre growth that ultimately cost the Bostonians control of their company. The company got off to a fast start, with total assets of American Bell more than tripling between 1881 and 1885, but it became bogged down in the brief recession of 1884 and never regained its momentum. Assets grew 50 percent between 1885 and 1890 and just 44 percent between 1890 and 1895. The onset of competition in the mid-nineties jolted the company into a new aggressiveness; assets nearly doubled between 1895 and 1900 and grew fully 150 percent between 1900 and 1905. In order to finance this expansion in the face of heavy competition that squeezed profit margins, the company had to issue large quantities of bonds; long-term debt ballooned from $2 million in 1895 to $78 million in 1905 and to $116,141,000 in 1910. As we will see shortly, this heavy indebtedness seriously impaired the company's liquidity, making it vulnerable to the advances of one of the few men in the country able to muster the capital that the company needed if it wanted to maintain its monopoly: J. P. Morgan.

Thus there is a fine and logical symmetry to the financial history of American Bell: The short-term orientation of the Brahmin investors who organized the company cost them control in the long run. While protected by patents, American Bell issued little debt and paid out the bulk of its large profits in dividends, but in so doing, it failed to develop its franchise fully. In order to maintain market share once competition struck, the Yankees incurred heavy debts and took large risks but still lost control to the New Yorker Morgan.

The real losers in this drama were not the Yankee investors, who made out very well while the good times lasted, but rather their customers, who paid high rates for inferior service. Just how inferior becomes evident from reading the correspondence of Frederick Fish, the man who took over the presidency of American Bell in 1901. Using an executive style that might be called management by rumor, Fish fired off letters to the presidents of operating companies calling attention to reported defects in their service. While professing to know little about local conditions and stressing his unwillingness to interfere directly, he delicately suggested that perhaps something should be done to keep the customer satisfied. To the general manager of the Colorado Telephone Company he wrote, "A prominent physician of Denver says that the service of your Company is not satisfactory. Frequently when he goes to the telephone, according to his story, to respond to a ring, all that he gets is the statement from the girl that somebody wanted him but that she does not know who it was. He also says that he has to wait almost always an unduly long time for a connection. But what seems to annoy him the most is, to be called up and then have the girl say that she does not know who it was that called him." According to Fish, a man in Dover, New Hampshire, heard his phone ring and picked up the receiver but reached an operator who "seemed to know nothing about it." Soon another operator got on the phone, and a long altercation between the two operators transpired before the connection was finally made. And Fish reported to a Bell official in Kansas City: "My friend takes this opportunity to attack with some severity the service of your company in Kansas City. He says that the instruments are old and not on metallic circuit, that you have the old-fashioned magneto switchboard; [and] that although your company has made promises, nothing has been done."

What made these "telephone incidents" so alarming to Fish was that they created an environment in which the competing "independent" telephone companies could thrive. Independent companies sprang up most rapidly in midwestern states such as Michigan, Iowa, Illinois, and Indiana, all sparsely settled states that American Bell neglected because they were less profitable. President Fish quoted a railroad executive in Indiana who said, "So far as this city of Indianapolis is concerned, the probabilities are that if we were to establish a branch exchange at this time, it would be with the Independent Co., which is furnishing better service than the Central Union [the local Bell company], and only today a prominent official of our [railroad]

Company suggested to me that our service would be improved by discarding every Bell phone in Indianapolis." Independent telephony grew rapidly. From virtually a standing start in 1893 it expanded to 4,117 separate systems in 1902, of which 994 were "mutual" or non-profit systems and the other 3,123 "commercial" systems. At the turn of the new century only 57 percent of the nation's phones were in the Bell System. In view of the facts that a single unified system provides more useful service than two separate systems and that independent companies did not offer long-distance service, the rate of their growth was remarkable—a telling indication of public dissatisfaction with the high prices and poor service provided by the Bell companies.

With characteristic aloofness, Bell's top management paid little attention to the "opposition" companies while they were merely an indistinct cloud on the western horizon, barely visible from the vantage point of Beacon Hill. Competition was not even mentioned in a Bell annual report until 1902. But once the independents had begun to crowd into major markets, Bell's management reacted with unaccustomed vigor. Prices were slashed in contested urban markets, including Cleveland, Pittsburgh, Indianapolis, Toledo, and Detroit. Opposition companies were surreptitiously bought up. Bell companies refused to interconnect with competing companies and used their political muscle to prevent the opposition from stringing wires through New York City's subway tunnels. Most important of all, the Bell System finally began to expand aggressively. After barely doubling between 1885 and 1895 the number of Bell phones in service increased more than seven-fold over the next decade.

The company had to borrow heavily in order to finance the expansion; negligible in 1898, the company's long-term debt had ballooned to 47.6 percent of equity by 1905, and still more capital was required. The need for external financing, combined with the increasingly dangerous competitive threat, thrust AT&T into treacherous waters. To the roving sharks of Wall Street, AT&T looked like an increasingly vulnerable whale, still large and succulent but weakened by the relentless attacks of hundreds of small predators. With the backing of Rockefeller money, two of Philadelphia's "traction kings," Peter A. Brown Widener and William L. Elkins, established the Telephone, Telegraph, and Cable Company and announced their intention of setting up service in New York and Boston—the heart of the Bell System. Their first move, however, was to acquire the Erie Telephone and Telegraph Company, a concern that owned controlling interest in a number of Bell operating companies in the Midwest. The financiers boasted rather grandiosely: "This is a most important acquisition, constituting the foundation upon which can be built an extensive system of long distance lines, and insuring the linking together of cities now and thereafter to be occupied . . . into one comprehensive whole." If Widener and Elkins succeeded—and in view of the success of other independents and the extent of their financial resources, there was a good chance that they would—the wholesale dismemberment of the nation's telephone monopoly would be under way.

PREVENTING THE BREAKUP OF AT&T

One man who opposed the fragmentation of the American telephone system was J. P. Morgan, then at the height of his power. Morgan believed that unrestrained competition in major industries was wasteful rather than productive. As we have seen, he had applied this dictum to the steel industry in 1901, with distinctly mixed results, and he was not afraid to do so again. So Morgan, operating behind the scenes but with great effect, seems to have forestalled the attack by Widener and Elkins by persuading fellow Wall Street bankers not to support the Telephone, Telegraph, and Cable Company. As a result, the company was strapped for working capital with which to carry out its plans, which came to little. Morgan's first positive step toward consolidating the communications industry was to engineer a merger of AT&T and one of the nation's leading telegraph concerns, the Postal Telegraph Company, which was controlled by a silver magnate and his son. Although this deal fell through, it did provide Morgan the opportunity to place three of his people on the AT&T board in 1902. These New Yorkers were not welcomed by the Yankee directors who still controlled the company, but their influence nevertheless increased as the company's need for capital grew. AT&T's Boston bankers, Kidder, Peabody & Company and Lee, Higginson & Company, simply did not have the financial might of the Morgan interests and could not deliver all the financing that the fast-growing, capital-hungry company needed.

In 1905 the Morgan directors suggested that Bell engage the House of Morgan to issue $85 million in bonds, with an option to issue $50 million more, the whole convertible into AT&T stock. President Fish bridled at the proposal because the bankers would have working control of the company while they were underwriting the securities. Fish observed that the bankers could "consolidate this company with other companies or make any other arrangement in regard to its future financing that they saw fit." The proud New Englanders, who had never stooped to the aggressive ways of Wall Street and now were paying the price, viewed such a prospect with distaste. They disliked Morgan but needed the capital that only he could deliver.

In the end the Yankees had no choice. In 1906, after a bitter internal struggle, Bell's divided board agreed to issue a large quantity of convertible bonds, to be underwritten by J. P. Morgan and Company and Kuhn Loeb & Company of New York, Kidder, Peabody of Boston, and Baring Brothers of London. Even this powerful syndicate could not distribute the Bell bonds in a financial market rocked by the panic of 1907; the bonds were not sold for two years, and the syndicate broke apart in June 1908. During this period Morgan had effective control of AT&T, and he used it to good effect by bringing back Theodore Vail as head of the firm. It was a masterful stroke. Vail understood what made the Bell System tick and what its Yankee directors were doing wrong. He forthrightly asserted: "The worst of the opposition has come from the lack of facilities afforded by our companies—that is, either no service, or poor service." Upon seizing the helm, he strengthened the company's finances by issuing about 220,000 shares of stock just a few months before the panic of 1907 convulsed the nation. To raise morale in the field, he brought the top managers of the operating companies to New York City and entertained them on yachting trips on the Hudson River and Long Island Sound, finding out about their problems and learning how the organization could be strengthened. With the might of Morgan behind him, Vail rebuilt the company's monopoly in the next several years under the banner "One Policy, One System, Universal Service." He dealt sternly but fairly with the independent companies by purchasing their assets at a reasonable price.

Thus J. P. Morgan did to the telephone industry what he had done to the steel industry six years earlier but with vastly different results. Whereas the birth of U.S. Steel sapped the long-term vitality of the American steel industry, Morgan's takeover of the Bell System revitalized the national telephone network while preventing its fragmentation. There are two main explanations for the difference. For one thing, steelmaking is a "commodity industry"; the success of firms is largely determined by how cheaply they can produce the commodity in question. As we are finding out today, a steel company with production costs that exceed the market price is simply out of luck. It was violent competition between firms, notably the awesome competitive challenge that Andrew Carnegie presented to his foes, that prodded American steelmakers to become ever more efficient during the nineteenth century. The creation of U.S. Steel suddenly replaced this competition with a complacent oligopoly that set the stage for a long slide into mediocrity. Telephony, by contrast, is a service industry that is likely to operate most efficiently when a single well-financed and well-managed company serves each community and when a single company operates an integrated long-distance system on a nationwide basis. Monopoly, in short, makes operational sense, although there remains the great danger that a lack of competition will lead to stagnation. The second difference between Morgan's maneuvers in the steel and telephone industries involves the men whom he hired to run the companies. Whatever his expertise at engineering mergers and winning the heart of Progressive opinion, Judge Elbert Gary knew little and cared less about the intricacies of making steel cheaply; the bumptious Charles Schwab would have done much more to keep the company competitive. Theodore Vail, on the other hand, was one of the founders of America's telephone network, and no one in the country was better equipped to breathe new life into the Bell System.

When we look back at the first two decades of the telephone industry, we find that the real significance of American Bell's early history lies not in the manifest limitations of its Brahmin leaders but rather in the importance of *competition* to the healthy development of new industries. To grow rapidly, a new industry requires a wide range of ideas and large amounts of capital. A single institution, no matter what its resources, is unlikely to provide adequate amounts of either. In the end any management must adopt a single approach to developing its business while ignoring promising alternatives. By charging high prices for telephone service, for example, Bell's management never found out if inexpensive service could be provided without destroying profits—until competition forced the company to reduce rates dramatically in the 1890s. And the most rational path for many monopoly producers is to make only the more lucrative investments while eschewing marginal projects. American Bell adopted this course by restricting long-distance service to the Northeast and Midwest while ignoring the South and Far West. The company would have had a much stronger incentive to provide long-distance service in the South and West if it had known that a competitor would take control of any markets that it passed up.

In short, there is a trade-off between the short-term profits of companies and the long-run development of an industry that will cause it to be poorly served by a monopoly provider. On this point a comparison between William Murray Forbes and his father is instructive. John Murray Forbes was no less keen for profits than his son, but in the crowded railroad market of the 1850s he had no choice but to expand his railroad network to Chicago and beyond or watch a competitor outflank the Michigan Central and threaten its franchise. The temptation to build ahead of demand undoubtedly did depress the profitability of railroads, but the nation benefited. The significance of this lesson for our own day is that such government-sponsored innovations as satellites, lasers, and space travel should be thrown upon the free market as quickly as possible. Only the give-and-take of competition will disclose all their economic potential.

VII

The Mechanic and the Gambler

The automobile industry more closely resembles the classic high-tech industries of the postwar period—semiconductors, microcomputers, minicomputers, etc.—than any yet discussed because both the risks and the rewards were very high. A few thousand dollars were all that was needed to start a company, and if its first product was successful, enormous profits promptly rolled in. The flip side was that the industry was incredibly volatile, with fast-growing companies sprouting up and then shriveling like so many mushrooms. To cope with these conditions, the industry's two leading entrepreneurs followed diametrically opposite strategies. Henry Ford was a lone wolf who founded and ran his own company with limited help from outsiders and absolutely no help from Wall Street. By contrast Billy Durant, founder of General Motors, was at once an industry insider and a Wall Street operator who collected a ragged group of small automotive companies and turned it into a powerful conglomerate. Although Durant's company was ultimately the more successful, one can only conclude from GM's experience that, just as Andrew Carnegie warned, company building and security speculation did not mix well. Periodically entangled in bear raids and margin calls, Durant twice lost control of his company as it veered toward bankruptcy; only his own extraordinary tenacity and the brilliant management of Alfred Sloan and the Du Ponts saved GM from being dragged down by financial intrigue. Clearly the straightforward approach of Henry Ford worked better than the financial razzle-dazzle of Wall Street operator Billy Durant. And this was true even though Durant—unlike the typical financier—was also a talented entrepreneur who really did understand the automobile industry.

The industry's early financial history carries two other messages. As in the case of the computer, members of the financial community were very slow to appreciate the tremendous commercial potential of the automobile because they did not anticipate how rapidly it would decline in price and improve in performance. This is actually typical of revolutionary technologies; the pattern was similar in semiconductors and biotechnology. But even though they underestimated the automobile's potential, financiers were quick to set up auto companies because at the turn of the century this was a classic "glamour industry." Not only was the technology exciting, but it was the plaything of the rich, who had plenty of money to invest. This, too, is a standard pattern that investors must watch out for. Whether it is automobiles in 1900, semiconductors in 1967, or biotechnology in 1980, Wall Street is quick to assemble glamorous high-tech "companies" simply to create securities to sell to investors. Such companies seldom succeed, particularly if they are assembled by brokers rather than by professional venture capitalists.

THE AUTOMOTIVE REVOLUTION

America's automotive revolution, like the French Revolution of 1789, began at the glittering apex of society and worked downward. The leisured nobility of Newport and Oyster Bay were the first to be affected; then the doctors, lawyers, and merchants of the suburban bourgeoisie; and finally the hard-pressed peasantry of Iowa, Kansas, and Arkansas. To be sure, the auto revolution was more gradual than its French counterpart. It took only five years for France to get from the calling of the Estates-General in 1788 to Robespierre's Reign of Terror in 1793; by contrast a full quarter of a century was needed to transform the American automobile from an expensive toy into a near necessity. But perhaps this slower pace was justified by results. There was no Thermidorian reaction to the auto revolution—no turning back once the humble American pedestrian had laid his hands on the wheel of the Model T. As one philosophe observed, the simple truth was that "Everybody wants to go from A to B sitting down." American automakers satisfied this urge about as quickly as any group of industrialists could have; their performance was infinitely better, certainly, than that of the plodding Brahmins who controlled the telephone. The central reason for this superior performance was that no single company monopolized the automobile; from the beginning the industry was a competitive free-for-all, an investor's nightmare and a consumer's delight. But a second important advantage of the auto industry was that its fate was always in the hands of midwestern entrepreneurs who had faith in the revolution they were fomenting. The financiers of Boston and New York, whose view of the automobile's future was consistently rational, skeptical, and wrong, were kept safely on the periphery where they could not do too much damage.

The forerunner of the automobile was the bicycle, a craze that swept America in the 1890s and introduced consumers to the novel idea of traveling the roadways without the aid of a horse. For the first time in American history the public was exposed to lavish advertisements that laid out the specific technical virtues of a particular "make" of vehicle. For a few years the public was impressed, but the bicycle boom soon collapsed simply because it is less tiring to ride a horse or a horse-drawn buggy than to pedal a bicycle. The logical solution to this difficulty was to connect an engine—whether powered by electricity, steam, or gasoline—to a bicycle, and it was only a short additional step to do the same with the bicycle's close cousins the tricycle and quadricycle. This task absorbed the energies of dozens of mechanics in New England and the upper Midwest during the 1890s. By 1900 the quadricycle, now known as the automobile, was a viable mode of transportation for the wealthy and adventurous sportsman. The gasoline engine was still only one power source among many—and not necessarily the most promising. Many experts preferred the quiet electric engine to the gasoline engine simply because "You cannot get people to sit over an explosion." In 1912 the *New York Times* cited a report that $40 million was invested in electric cars and trucks, and the figure was expected to double within a year.

Prior to 1906 or so the car was still an impractical mode of transportation, an experimental vehicle that had to be treated with all the care due a temperamental racehorse. One venturesome buyer wrote in 1901, "Before purchasing the machine I had obtained the impression that it only required from five to eight minutes to start. I found, however, from experience that blowing up the tires, pumping up the airtank, the supplying of water and getting up steam would occupy on the average twenty-five to thirty minutes." If an automobile stalled, it had to be restarted with caution; the story was told of a man who came to the aid of a woman whose car had stalled out, but when he turned the crank to start the car, it kicked back and broke his jaw. The gallant gentleman later died of gangrene. Breakdowns also posed a problem, for there were very few reliable garages on the open road. For that matter, there were almost no decent roads on which to drive. Although the bicycle industry had begun to agitate for road improvement, the good roads movement was still in its infancy. A census taken in 1904 revealed that only about 7 percent of American roads were surfaced (mostly with gravel), and one industry leader concluded that the motorist had to "pick and choose between bad roads and worse." Few motorists welcomed the chance to lie on their backs on muddy roads and adjust valves or examine mufflers; hence a chauffeur was regarded as a virtual necessity. Since mechanically proficient help was in short supply, many automobilists joined clubs and kept their vehicles in a spacious garage in the clubhouse. Here the vehicles could be stored in the winter, serviced by capable mechanics, and cleaned of mud as soon as they returned from an outing.

Despite its technical limitations, the automobile quickly caught on with America's upper class. It was a captivating item of conspicuous consumption at a time when rich Americans, yet unscathed by income taxes and high inflation, were constantly on the lookout for creative ways to waste money. Thus before 1909 or so newspaper readers were more likely to find auto news in the social pages than the business section. Cars were variously used for in-town social calls, Sunday rides in the countryside, and competitive tours and races. A New Yorker reported that wealthy ladies "do not drive their own autos but use them for paying calls, for shopping and for riding on [Fifth] Avenue, and the style of vehicles which they choose are the Victoria and the brougham. The automobile Victoria, with two men in livery on the box, is certainly a very smart appearing vehicle." Serious sportsmen could compete in both speed races, such as the 284-mile Vanderbilt Cup race run on Long Island, or long-distance reliability tours that tested the durability of vehicle and driver alike. The famous Glidden reliability tours attracted much attention between 1905 and 1913, and in 1908 the front page of the *New York Times* regularly carried items on an upcoming race between New York and Paris. In a quixotic marriage of high technology and the great outdoors, motorists also took jaunts through such wild spaces as the Grand Canyon, the Cascade Mountains, and the Texas plains. What made these journeys intriguing, of course, was that the automobile was still so unreliable that no one knew how many participants, if any, would finish the course.

Motorists who possessed the time and means needed to pursue this hobby did not stint on equipment. *Harper's Weekly* observed in 1906 that "there are more than 200 persons in New York who have from five to ten cars apiece. John Jacob Astor alone is credited with thirty-two. The string of vehicles owned by an enthusiast of this class will include two or three touring cars, a pair of racers, a couple of broughams, a runabout, a station-car, and a work car." To keep their auto collections up-to-date, the wealthy flocked to the annual auto shows, the most important of which was held in Madison Square Garden. It was an elegant and genteel affair, resembling a Park Avenue antiques show much more than a bustling trade fair. One observer called the Madison Square Garden show of 1910 a "magnificent spectacle," adding: "Dignity, elegance, and 'class' form the keynote of the exhibition. A rich decorative scheme, appealing to the eye and aesthetic taste, produced at a cost of more than $30,000, has converted the Garden into an amphitheater of beauty."

Unlike such consumer products as radios, calculators, and video games, autos did not rapidly decline in price and win the favor of middle-class consumers. Far from falling, the price of the typical car actually tripled between 1900 and 1908 because automakers were content to concentrate on the upscale market, in which profit margins were high and economies of scale did not have to be achieved. As late as 1905 a newspaper in Michigan, auto capital of the nation, reported: "An automobile went through our town last Saturday. It was the first automobile that has come this way." But as cars improved in quality and Americans became more affluent, the market expanded. Automakers began to trumpet the "metamorphosis of the pleasure car from a frail, undependable, noisy and inefficient experiment to a sturdy, powerful, reliable, quiet and economical pleasure conveyance of everyday applicability." Such boasts gained credibility during the San Francisco earthquake of 1906, when "even experienced chauffeurs were astonished at the small amount of repairs needed by machines of popular makes after not only days, but weeks of the severest strain." Industry boosters pointed out that cars generated far less pollution than horses (which deposited an estimated 240,000 tons of manure on the streets of a large city each year), and they also claimed—far less plausibly—that cars were cheaper to operate and caused less traffic congestion. These arguments had the intended effect, and middle-class buyers began to frequent dealer showrooms. Doctors were among the first professionals to buy cars aggressively, simply because they spent so much time traveling to the homes of patients.

But practical arguments were only part of the story. The truth is that Americans quickly fell in love with the automobile. The infatuation had many dimensions. Some drivers loved the power: "To take control of this materialized energy, to draw the reins over this monster with its steel muscles and fiery heart—there is something in the idea which appeals to an almost universal sense, the love of power. Add the element of danger, and the fascination inherent in motorvehicalism as a sport is not difficult to understand." For others the automobile was endowed with ineffable sex appeal: "The man who owns a motorcar gets for himself, besides the joys of touring, the adulation of the walking crowd, and the daring driver of a racing machine that bounds and rushes and disappears in the perspective in a thunder of explosions is a god to the women." For still other motorists the car was the quintessence of fashion: "Mothers are neglecting their babies and wives are driving husbands to the wall for the sake of the appearance of wealth. So mad has the race for social supremacy become in the East End [of Pittsburgh] that owners of houses are mortgaging them in order to buy as many and as speedy automobiles as their neighbors."

Such excesses were a source of alarm to the levelheaded financiers of the Northeast, who believed that the auto craze threatened the equilibrium of the economy itself. For one thing they fretted that automobile owners were bad credit risks. The *Sun* of Baltimore reported in 1910 that local bankers were "keeping a close watch on the owners of automobiles, with a view to finding out if such luxuries are within the means of those indulging in them." Financiers also feared that the explosive growth of the auto industry was sucking capital out of the productive economy and diverting it to the purchase of an expensive and useless luxury. Asserted the *Bankers Magazine:* "[T]hat the prevailing stagnation in the market for bonds is due very largely to the automobile seems an incontrovertible fact." And quite aside from its financial effect, motoring corrupted society because it was among the most public of vices: While "gluttony, drink, and gambling may be a source of greater waste than the ownership of an automobile, . . . these extravagances are not open to the public eye. The owner of an automobile, however, glories in his extravagance." Despite these worries, bankers took comfort from the belief that the automobile would quickly saturate its market. There was a strict limit, they reasoned, to how much money the consumer would spend on a useless luxury. Operating on this assumption, eastern bankers were loath to finance midwestern auto manufacturers. When Billy Durant, founder of General Motors, remarked that the auto industry would be producing 500,000 cars within a few years, George W. Perkins, a senior partner in J. P. Morgan and Company, exclaimed that such an idea was preposterous and advised Durant to stop mouthing such nonsense if he wanted financial aid.

In 1908, the year that Perkins dispensed this piece of wisdom, 65,000 cars and trucks were produced; eight years later the figure was 1,617,708. In less than a decade a gigantic new industry, the backbone of the American economy in the twentieth century, sprang to life in the upper Midwest. Residents of Detroit and Flint, Akron and Toledo were stunned by the awesome speed of the transformation. A citizen of Flint, birthplace of General Motors, wrote, "One must see for himself; one must get into the atmosphere of the tremendous undertakings; one must himself walk over the literal miles of factories in process of construction before one begins to grasp the immensity of the manufacturing undertaken." Another observer wrote, "The B. F. Goodrich Company, of Cleveland, Ohio, has quadrupled its tire capacity in the past two years. There has never been a time during this period that buildings for its tire department were not in progress, and there has not been a time in five years when the factory has not been running day and night."

BRICKS WITHOUT STRAW: WHY BANKERS WERE SUPERFLUOUS

Although huge quantities of capital were needed to build the auto industry, the task was accomplished with minimal help from Wall Street. Bond issues, investment bankers, takeover raids, margin calls— all these staples of railroad and telephone history were essentially peripheral to the explosive rise of the auto industry. Although bankers and brokers assuredly do make an appearance in the story, they do not figure largely in the central plot. If Wall Street had not existed between 1900 and 1920, the industry would not have been greatly retarded. Indeed, a case can be made for the argument that eastern financiers actually did more harm than good. Wall Street was irrelevant because automobile manufacturing was one of those rare industries in which the talented and resourceful entrepreneur needed very little outside capital in order to build a giant company. One could very nearly make bricks without straw. The manufacturer who designed the right product—a car that was both technically excellent and properly positioned in the marketplace, with respect to style and price—could set up a "factory" with very little capital and watch enormous profits roll in. From that point onward expansion could be financed out of profits. In an early and brilliant analysis of this pattern Edward D. Kennedy wrote, "It took no capital to get into the industry, in the sense that it took capital to get into the copper industry or the steel industry or the railroad industry. And the profits (when there were profits) bore almost no relation to the money invested. It was no question of making a mere 100 per cent on your money. If your company survived the struggle for existence, you might make 100 per cent on your money every year; with a really successful company you could do a good deal better than that." Thus the Ford Motor Company was started with a capital of just $28,000 and within *fifteen months* had produced a profit amounting to *ten times* that sum. Yet one of Ford's competitors said with a sniff, "It is said that the Ford Motor Co. started with $28,000. We started with much less than that."

Five factors explain this extraordinary profitability. Because auto-making essentially involved the assembly of parts purchased from suppliers, a manufacturer did not need to build a large factory before getting cash flow. All he needed to do was to rent a workshop and fit it out with a modest set of tools. The burden of acquiring the array of sophisticated drills, lathes, dies, and foundries needed to make engines and chassis was transferred to suppliers, who already owned this equipment. The financial role of parts suppliers in the start-up of automakers was so critical that they were virtually partners of the manufacturers; often their identity was disclosed in newspaper articles announcing the formation of a new auto company. Since they were eager for new customers, these suppliers did something else that reduced the capital requirements of automaking: They sold parts on very long credits.

Thirdly, while the automaker was able to take a long time to pay his bills, he sold his cars for cash. Indeed, the standard practice was to receive a 20 percent advance payment from the car dealer even before the car was built and to receive the balance in cash when the product was shipped. As a result, the automaker had very little capital tied up in accounts receivable. The combination of immediate cash receipts from dealers and long credit lines from suppliers made it nearly possible for an automaker to buy the parts, assemble and sell the car, and receive payment from the dealer before payment was due to suppliers. *So long as sales did not decline,* the business nearly financed itself.

A fourth key factor enhancing the industry's profitability was that it was not cyclical. Industry sales expanded almost continuously at a compound rate of 24 percent between 1906 and 1923, and consequently automakers did not have to survive lengthy depressions, as railroads and steel companies did. To be sure, short and surprising financial panics in 1907 and 1920 were enough to bankrupt many oversanguine and undercapitalized firms, but the downturns did not last long. A more favorable economic climate in the decades after 1900 partly explains the difference in the markets faced by Andrew Carnegie and Henry Ford, but the key difference was simply that until 1930 the automobile market was expanding continuously as an ever-larger slice of the American public concluded that it ought to own a car. Unlike steel, therefore, the auto industry was not hostage to the capital spending cycle. Finally, the profit margins on these expanding sales were very high—often 20 percent or more. At these margins a company that produced twenty-five cars per day, six days per week, and sold them for $3,000 could earn $4,680,000 per year. A plant capable of generating this output could easily be built for $300,000, and since (for the reasons stated above) little money was tied up in working capital, one could hope for a return on investment of 1,560 percent.

Here was an industry worth getting into. Thousands of adventurous entrepreneurs did, but few survived for long. One contemporary study concluded that between 1900 and 1908, 485 companies entered the industry, but 262 companies had left it by the latter date. Of course, many of the 243 "survivors" failed in the next few years after 1908, and the failure ratio would be higher if all of the fly-by-night operations were included. Many of these short-lived operations were backyard affairs that never got off the ground, and others were grandiose corporations the raison d'être of which was to sell millions of dollars in watered stock, rather than to produce cars. Such companies did not deserve to succeed, and few of them did. But many legitimate companies also fell into a swift decline after a few years of success. The reason for the high death rate among apparently prosperous companies was that the automobile business, like the personal computer business of the early 1980s, was driven by the product cycle. Every year management had to decide what to build for the upcoming season—what technological innovations to introduce, what new features to offer, and at what price. A wrong decision could be fatal. Such companies as Oldsmobile won the favor of car buyers for a year or two with a popular model and then went into decline as consumer preferences changed. Furthermore, companies had to make the right fundamental technological bets; no amount of marketing savvy or production experience could turn a manufacturer of steam or electric vehicles into a long-term success.

In an industry like this, in which capital requirements did not pose a substantial barrier to entry but the risks of failure through bad management decisions were high, financial expertise counted for little. The key to success was to have top managers who knew the industry intimately and could make the right moves with respect to technology and product design. Unfortunately Wall Street and the investing public learned this lesson slowly and at great cost. The birth of the auto industry coincided with the high tide of finance capitalism, a time when J. P. Morgan and his peers were waxing rich off combinations in dozens of industries. Much to the disgust of auto industry insiders, financiers tried to work their will in the auto industry as well. *Motor World* claimed that the auto companies organized during 1900 alone had a total capitalization of $329.5 million. The magazine asserted that "not one tenth of these concerns will ever get any nearer turning out a motor vehicle than the permission to do so which appears in their incorporation papers." In 1908 automaker Benjamin Briscoe excoriated "concerns which did not have a worthy car or any manufacturing ability, but with large stock issues to sell, and by ingenious exploitation would succeed in stirring up the trade and the public, creating the impression that . . . they, through some newly discovered combination of geniuses, were enabled to sell gold dollars for fifty cents in autos." The most prominent of these Wall Street-sponsored gold bricks was the Electric Vehicle Association, which was put together in 1899 by the "traction kings" William C. Whitney and Peter A. Brown Widener. Boasting a capitalization of $200 million, their sprawling, intricately financed company proposed to build a nationwide fleet of taxis powered by one-ton electric batteries. The plan swiftly failed, enriching a few stockbrokers but providing little in the way of transportation services.

The successful auto companies, like their counterparts in the steel industry, steered clear of the hype and hoopla of Wall Street and tended to be partnerships between a workman and a capitalist—between a technically proficient mechanic who could come up with a good car and a local businessman who could contribute capital, marketing savvy, and general management talent. Most of the mechanics migrated to automobiles from closely allied fields, such as bicycles, carriages, engine making, and auto parts, and therefore had a feel for the automobile business even before they entered it. Bicycle makers had experience in designing metal vehicles and were familiar with the buying habits of the consumers who purchased autos. The rare talents of such gasoline engine makers as Ransom Olds and Henry Leland gave them an invaluable head start in developing efficient and reliable cars. Carriage makers like William Durant and Charles Nash knew how to organize the production and distribution of vehicles efficiently. Henry Ford, the Dodge brothers, and Benjamin Briscoe had been in the industry for many years, either as parts makers or unsuccessful auto-makers, before they struck it rich.

Like Andrew Kloman of Carnegie Steel or Theodore Vail of American Bell, these pioneers had the industry in their blood and possessed great faith in its future. Smart venture capitalists knew that to succeed, a company had to be built around one of these able mechanics. The Boston investment banker James J. Storrow had this to say about his selection of Charles Nash to run his new auto company after he and Nash had left General Motors:

> Charlie Nash had been a good wagon manufacturer, and then a fine Buick factory man. I picked him to be head of General Motors. In five years, he turned a wreck into a concern having $25,000,000 in the bank. [Here Storrow exaggerated greatly.] When Durant took control of General Motors away from us, I wired Nash to come here, and I said: "Charlie, you did a fine job of G.M.; if you could do that once, you can do it again; look around for another wreck; I'll back you." He picked the Jeffery outfit, which we bought for less than $5,000,000. Nash made a hundred million dollars out of it for us in seven years. There was nothing to the Jeffery outfit. Nash was everything. He could do the same with a railroad.

Instead of being spread across the United States, automotive superstars like Charles Nash were concentrated in Michigan and Ohio, where they constantly taught each other, worked together, and competed with rivals at the track. A sort of unofficial "university" for these automakers—an analogue to the University of Pennsylvania in computing or Charles Williams's workshop in telephony—was the Olds Motor Works, a technological pioneer from which no fewer than 150 auto-makers of consequence are said to have graduated.

THE EDUCATION OF HENRY FORD

No one illustrates the precedence of man over money in the emerging auto industry better than Henry Ford, for when he founded his revolutionary company in 1903, Ford was long on talent and hard-won experience but woefully short of funds. He resembled a poor but wizened old miner who has barely enough cash to buy a pick and a mule but who, when he trudges off into the hills to stake his claim, knows exactly where to dig and quickly hits pay dirt. And what pay dirt! One of the most fabulously lucrative franchises in the history of American manufacturing.

The man who spearheaded the premier growth industry of the early twentieth century was himself a product of the nineteenth century. A gaunt, lanky, and unprepossessing man, Ford was born during the Civil War and grew up on a Michigan farm in decent, if modest, circumstances. His childhood differed little from that of many another nineteenth-century American farmboy. He weeded gardens, plowed fields, chopped wood, and walked to school. Wholesome and invigorating they may have been, but these laborious routines of rural life were not much to Ford's liking. Indeed, a primary legacy of Ford's youth was an abiding distaste for the fatiguing labor of farming and a fascination with any tool—including a cheap and versatile vehicle—that would lighten the farmer's load. "I have followed many a weary mile behind a plow and I know all the drudgery of it," he wrote in his memoirs. "What a waste it is for a human being to spend hours and days behind a slowly moving team of horses when in the same time a tractor could do six times as much work!" As a youth Ford was forever tinkering with waterwheels, turbines, furnaces, and other machines, and at the age of sixteen he left the farm to get a job in Detroit. There he rapidly sharpened his mechanical ability by working in various machine shops, but after getting married in 1888, he settled on a small farm belonging to his father. Ford made a good living by operating a sawmill on the place and harvesting its fine stand of timber, but when the timber ran out, so did his interest in the countryside. He returned to Detroit in 1891, this time for good. Ford landed a $45-per-month job as night engineer at the Edison Illuminating Company, and notwithstanding a certain awkward shyness, he quickly advanced up the corporate ladder, eventually becoming chief engineer at a wage of $100 per month. He could have climbed still farther at the company if the automobile had not sidetracked him.

For even as he worked for Detroit Edison, Henry Ford was experimenting with gasoline engines and quadricycles. While housing his family in modest quarters, he poured nearly all his spare cash and spare time into research. He did his work wherever he could—in his wife's kitchen; in a shed behind the house; in a spare room at the plant. Although somewhat eccentric, Ford was no reclusive genius; he had, on the contrary, a real talent for forming productive relationships with other automotive pioneers. Designing automobiles was engrossing and exciting work, and as he approached the completion of his first car in the summer of 1896, Ford's exertions became intense. "We often wondered when Henry Ford slept," a friend later recalled, "because he was putting in long hours [at the Edison plant] and when he went home at night he was always experimenting or reading." On the night of June 4, Ford finally finished his first car—and found that it was too wide to fit through the garage door! Taking ax to wall, Ford promptly liberated his invention and took a short spin around the block, unnoticed by his sleeping neighbors.

Another car followed, and in 1899 Ford joined in the founding of the Detroit Automobile Company, a small but ambitious concern that started life with just $15,000 in paid-in capital. In contrast with the pioneers of the telephone industry, the challenge before this firm and its rivals lay not so much in the realm of fundamental theoretical breakthroughs as in the area of practical design and production problems. The central task was to develop a vehicle that was pleasing to the eye and equipped with the most sophisticated technical systems —engines, brakes, carburetor, muffler, etc. that were available. Many of these parts were produced by outside suppliers, but they were assembled into finished vehicles in the company's own "factory." Because hundreds of different parts were involved, the assembly operation was tedious and time-consuming, as this description of a small part of the process shows: "In assembling front and rear springs we assembled spring bolts and shackles to spring brackets on frame. Grease cups were assembled to spring bolts and shackle bolts on all springs. Rear axle was assembled to rear springs with U bolts and dowel pins and tightened down. Brake bands were assembled to rear axle wheel housing. Front axle was assembled to front springs with U bolts and tightened down." And so on. Needless to say, there was plenty of room for error and delay. Some suppliers made faulty parts, and it was impossible to anticipate all the technical snags that might arise once the car was tested on the open road. "To show the trials of the automobile builder," remarked one of Ford's associates, "let me say that we lost a week simply because we found that the steering rod apparatus would bind in a certain way, on account of a little screw and a small catch. One of the screws was about one-sixteenth of an inch too long; and as there were a lot of other screws in the plate, it took us a long time to locate the trouble." Such production problems were evidently too great for the Detroit Automobile Company to overcome; the company was slow to get its first vehicle out of the shop, and the sum total of its output was only about twenty-five cars. But from Henry Ford's viewpoint the company was less a failure than a learning experience; he was to turn it to good account soon enough.

With the demise of the Detroit Automobile Company Henry Ford turned his attention to racing. "I never thought anything of racing," he later claimed, "but the public refused to consider the automobile in any light other than a fast toy." By designing a speedy car and winning some major races, Ford could hone his automotive talents and gain valuable publicity at the same time. Furthermore, he needed the money; he had already quit his job with Edison and moved his family in with his father in order to economize. The racer that Ford and his helpers designed was light, trim, and compact, but some observers doubted that at six horsepower it was powerful enough to win the $1,000 first prize at an upcoming meet. As the big day approached, the *Detroit Press* did its best to pump up the struggling entrepreneur into a hometown hero, a stalwart challenger of Alexander Winton, one of the leading racers in the country. The *Detroit News* reported that Ford's machine "was tried out on the boulevard recently, and without great effort covered a half mile in 38 seconds. This record compares favorably with the work done by Winton, Murray and Hamilton, although his car has much less horse power than theirs." Detroiters were not disappointed in Ford's performance, for he beat his rival easily after Winton's car developed engine trouble. After the victory the local businessmen who had financed Ford's race car decided they had a winner in their midst and cut Ford into their new automobile company, which they dubbed the Henry Ford Automobile Company. The company was misnamed, for Ford's stake in the new concern was so small that he insisted on having the right to continue to build and drive race cars. When his partners balked at this demand, Ford became disgruntled, and the company dissolved.

By this time, some historians suggest, Henry Ford was beginning to look like a loser, a middle-aged tinkerer with neither capital nor steady job, whose business experience amounted to little more than participation in two business failures. Against this background the success of the Ford Motor Company looks like a miraculous delivery from ruin. Such an interpretation seems questionable, however, for in fact, few entrepreneurs in the country were in a better position than Henry Ford to make a success of the automobile industry, which was just beginning to achieve meaningful sales volume in 1903. Success on the track had made Ford a well-known figure among auto aficionados, and he possessed a thorough grasp of automotive technology in both the laboratory and the commercial factory. Moreover, he had formed valuable alliances with other talented technicians, notably C. Harold Wills, who made a major contribution to all of Ford's early cars. Ford was also acquainted with the snags in the production process that could derail a promising company, and he had seen a company fall apart because of quarreling among the partners. Though still a failure on paper, then, Ford had advanced far up the learning curve, and his expertise was probably worth more to a fledgling auto firm than all the capital that Wall Street could muster.

Still, Ford needed money to set up his third company, and he obtained it in small but adequate amounts through a personal acquaintance, Alexander Malcomson, a shrewd, if overly ambitious, Detroit coal dealer. Malcomson had built up a coal dealership that boasted a fleet of more than 100 wagons serving both commercial and residential customers, but he seems to have been addicted to expansion. By the summer of 1902, when he began to finance the Ford Motor Company, Malcomson was so deeply in debt to his bankers that he kept his risky new commitment to Ford a secret, but this did not stop him from acquiring four new coal dealerships during the next winter. Ford's new enterprise got off the ground modestly with a fairly informal agreement, similar to the Bell Patent Association, wherein Malcomson agreed to contribute $500 for research and development immediately and further amounts as the need arose. These payments tided over the concern until it was incorporated on June 16, 1903, and christened the Ford Motor Company. The firm was capitalized at $100,000, divided into 1,000 shares. Ford and Malcomson were given 255 shares each for the plans, work, and capital already contributed to the enterprise, and the remaining 490 shares were distributed among ten other investors. Of these ten, six were associates of Malcomson's, two were truly outside investors, and two were the company's key parts suppliers, the Dodge brothers. At the time of incorporation only $28,000 of cash was paid into the company's treasury, but in addition to this sum, Malcomson and Ford had already made a significant investment in the firm.

This slender capital would never have been enough to launch Ford Motor Company without the sponsorship of the Dodge brothers, one of the leading machine shops of the upper Midwest. Like so many other pioneers in the auto industry, John and Horace Dodge had manufactured bicycles before getting involved with cars, and in 1903 they elected to work with Ford Motor in preference to one of the leading auto manufacturers in the industry, the Olds Motor Works. Since they were virtually betting their company on the success of Ford's operation, the brothers obviously had great confidence in Ford's automotive talents, despite his previous lack of financial success. But confidence in Ford did not blot out their caution; in their agreement with Ford Motor Company the Dodges spelled out their rights and obligations very precisely. They agreed to deliver 650 engines and chassis to Ford's Detroit factory at a steady rate of 10 per day beginning on July 1, 1903, and they were to receive payments from Ford and Malcomson of $5,000 on March 15, 1903, $5,000 more on April 15, and another $5,000 when deliveries to the Ford plant began. These payments, however, offset only a small part of the up-front cost and overall business risk borne by the Dodge brothers. In a wonderfully informative letter John W. Anderson, one of Ford's partners, reported that "to comply with this contract, which was made last October [1902], Dodge Brothers had to decline all outside orders and devote the entire resources of their plant to the turning out of these automobiles. They were paid only $10,000 on account [this refers to the first two $5,000 payments], and had to take all the rest of the risk themselves. They had to borrow $40,000, place orders for castings all over the country, pay their men from last October (they have a large force), and do everything necessary to manufacture all the machines before they could hope to get a cent back." The Dodge brothers were willing to make this major commitment to Henry Ford's nascent company not only because they stood to earn millions from parts sales if Ford prospered but also because they were given a 10 percent stake in the new company.

If the Dodge brothers carried out their end of the deal and Henry

Ford and his associates designed a car that sold well, the profit potential of the company was tremendous. Ford Motor's prospects were shrewdly dissected by Anderson, who had an insider's view of the company because he had not only invested in Ford Motor Company but also drew up its contracts. Anderson was impressed by the small capital outlay that Ford's operations would require, the simplicity of the production process, and the high potential profit margins. As he saw it, all the company needed to do was to build a modest shop costing $3,000 or $4,000, hire about a dozen workmen each at $1.25 per day, and set them to work bolting together the basic parts of the vehicles —the chassis supplied by the Dodge brothers, the bodies and cushions made by the C. R. Wilson Carriage Company, the wheels made by a firm in Lansing, and the tires made by the Hartford Rubber Company. "Now this is all there is to the whole proposition. . . ." Anderson boasted that "there is absolutely no money to speak of tied up in a big factory. There is the $75 a month rent for three years, and a few machines necessary in the assemblying factory. All the rest is done outside and supplied as ordered, and this, of course, is a big saving in capital outlay to start with." With the cost of parts amounting to about $384 per car, labor costs running at about $20 per car, and overhead amounting to $150 at most, Anderson figured that the cost of producing a car without a back seat amounted to $554. Allowing for unforeseen expenses of $46 per car, he calculated a maximum cost for the standard model of $600 per car. Since this model was to be sold for $750, the profit margin would be a very generous 20 percent, and margins would be even higher—23.5 percent—for the deluxe model, which had a back seat.

Moreover, Ford Motor needed very little working capital to get through its first few months of life because customers sent cash with their orders. As with any start-up situation there was, in effect, a race between cash expenses that drew down the cash account and cash receipts that increased it. Many young firms go bankrupt despite excellent profit potential simply because they run out of cash before turning the corner into profitability. (As noted, this disaster nearly befell American Bell, in part because the company rented phones instead of selling them outright.) Given its skimpy initial capital, Ford Motor clearly ran the risk of running out of money, and indeed, its cash balance did fall as low as $223.65 on July 11. If at this point the company had begun to sell cars to customers but had given them four months to pay their bill, its books would have shown a large profit, but the increase in its assets would have consisted of accounts receivable rather than cash. Since a company cannot pay its bills with accounts receivable, it would have had to obtain cash by either borrowing from a bank or selling its receivables to a factor at a discount to their market value. Fortunately Ford did not need to think about such contingencies because the orders that poured into the firm were accompanied by checks, which swiftly replenished its bank account. By August 20, 1903, just two months after the date of incorporation, Ford Motor's cash position stood at $23,060.67—a sum that amounted to fully 82 percent of its initial capital.

From the beginning, financial results were splendid. The company earned $37,000 in its first three months of operations and $99,000 in the first nine and a half months. At the end of 1904 Ford Motor moved into new and much larger quarters, and during the year ending September 30, 1905, it earned $290,000—not bad for a company that started life with $28,000 in the bank. Clearly the venture capital process had worked splendidly in the case of the Ford Motor Company, and it is instructive to consider why. The timing of the company's founding was certainly propitious, and the overall financial characteristics of the industry were very favorable. But it was the effective configuration of *people* that enabled the company to make the most of the opportunity. The nub of the thing was that Henry Ford, an accomplished mechanic, had joined forces with Alexander Malcomson, an experienced entrepreneur whose wide network of contacts permitted the company to get out of the starting gate quickly. Most of the capital was supplied by Malcomson and his friends, the legal work was done by Malcomson's attorneys, the company's first plant was built by one of Malcomson's associates, and the business affairs of Ford Motor were managed by Malcomson's partner, James Couzens. It is very doubtful that Ford could have succeeded so splendidly without access to this ready-made entrepreneurial infrastructure. The contribution of Couzens was particularly critical. Many fast-growing firms fly apart under the pressure of rapid growth because their managers cannot keep control of the thousands of important decisions that have to be made week after week. Critical mistakes are likely to be made, and as the money rolls in, there is a strong temptation for management to become lax, undisciplined. Couzens was just the man to make sure that this did not happen because he was tough, capable, and ambitious—a real "manhandler," according to one Ford worker. He had general oversight of all of Ford Motor's business affairs, including finance and marketing, and he played a particularly critical role in creating a nationwide network of dependable dealers to sell and service Ford cars. By shouldering these responsibilities successfully, Couzens allowed Henry Ford to focus his energy on developing new vehicles and managing operations on the shop floor.

Thus the Ford Motor Company exhibits a familiar pattern, which we encountered in the steel industry and will see again in the modern venture capital industry: an effective partnership between a creative entrepreneur who understands the technical side of a new industry and a venture capitalist who brings to the enterprise not only money but smart money—money that is supplemented by the contacts and business skill needed to get the company up and running quickly. The *simplicity* of the deal was what made it work so well. As the history of the telephone industry graphically shows, however, there lies in this partnership arrangement a serious danger, which might be labeled "the dictatorship of capital." The danger is simply that the venture capitalist will overstep his proper bounds. After contributing to the successful launching of the company, he may insist on making strategic decisions that ought to be left to the entrepreneur, who has far more expertise in the new industry. The Ford Motor Company almost fell victim to the dictatorship of capital when it confronted a critical decision that capsized some other promising firms—namely, whether to emphasize production of small cars or large. Always keen to make an automobile that the common man, particularly the farmer, could afford, Henry Ford was already talking about producing a $400 car in 1904. The way to do this, he realized, was "to make one automobile like another automobile, to make them all alike, to make them come through the factory just alike; just as one pin is like another pin when it comes from a pin factory, or one match is like another match when it comes from a match factory." Unfortunately Alexander Malcomson had other ideas; like most automakers of the day, he favored large cars that not only sold for higher prices but also carried wider profit margins.

Moreover, Malcomson wanted to increase his own personal managerial authority in the company, for by now it was plain that the auto industry had a bigger future than coal. Hence he pressed for production of an expensive car called the Model K and insisted that he take over James Couzens's place as general manager at Ford Motor. There is little doubt that if Malcomson had prevailed, he would have ruined the Ford Motor Company, for even the company's brief flirtation with luxury cars in 1906 was enough to cut profits. In a nearly parallel situation at the Olds Motor Works the financier behind the company insisted on making a large car, whereupon Ransom Olds quit the company to start a new company. Both the original and the new Olds concerns fared poorly. Fortunately Malcomson did not have enough power to cause this kind of damage because both Ford and Couzens were arrayed against him. After bitter fighting and a major corporate shake-up Malcomson sold his share of the company for $175,000 and went off to start his own auto company, while Henry Ford increased his ownership share at Ford Motor to 58.5 percent.

With Malcomson out of the way, the company broke into the clear and swiftly grabbed a huge share of the burgeoning automobile market. In 1907 Ford Motor brought out a small car called the Model N that sold for $600. Unit sales shot up from 1,599 cars in 1906 to 8,759 cars in 1907, and profits rose to $1,125,000, or more than 300 percent above the results of the best previous year. The following year the company came out with its famous Model T, a light but durable car that originally sold for $825 and was full of technological innovations, including a three-point suspension of the motor, a novel electrical system, a vanadium steel body, and a planetary transmission that made it possible to go directly from forward into reverse. The car was an instant success that pushed up the company's sales to 19,051 cars in 1910, 342,115 cars in 1915, and an extraordinary 845,000 cars in 1921. Ford achieved these huge sales gains by making nothing but Model Ts, carefully standardizing production, and achieving enormous economies of scale that steadily drove down the unit cost. This focus on a single product was a courageous and unorthodox business strategy that none but an experienced automotive pioneer like Henry Ford would be likely to make.

Two aspects of Ford's spectacular performance bear special emphasis. For one thing, the Ford Motor Company—not General Motors— was the dominant force in the automobile industry until the 1920s. Between 1913 and 1921 Ford's share of the national market, in units, ranged between 39 and 56 percent and averaged about 43 percent; General Motors, on the other hand, never garnered more than a fifth of the market and had roughly 14 percent on average. Between 1911 and 1921 Ford made $2.20 for every $1 earned by General Motors. In short, Ford's simple and straightforward partnership approach to venture financing was far more successful than the freewheeling conglomerating style practiced by GM. It was not until the mid-1920s, when GM was restructured under the superb management of Alfred

Sloan while the Ford Motor Company began to stagnate under the unsteady hand of an aging Henry Ford, that the table was turned. Secondly, Ford Motor's rapid rise to greatness was accompanied by breathtaking profitability. Between 1908 and 1914 Ford's return on equity (ROE) was 139 percent, while GM's was only 36 percent between 1909 and 1914. Profitability at both companies declined as they grew in size; Ford's ROE was 41 percent between 1915 and 1921, while GM's was 28 percent. Needless to say, this was still a very good showing in comparison with such capital-intensive companies as American Bell, the ROE of which was only 7 percent. The tremendous profitability of the Ford Motor Company allowed Henry Ford to continue to finance expansion strictly out of profits, with nary a thought to Wall Street.

What can we learn from the success of Henry Ford and his company? Probably the most important lesson is that the investor in high-technology industries—even more than the typical investor—has to bet on the person who runs the company: not the technology, not the overall market, but the individual. The competitive environment of high-tech industries is changing so rapidly in so many ways that it is fraught with risk. In order to succeed, entrepreneurs need the instincts of a fighter pilot—a sixth sense about where the technology and the market are headed and an ability to get there first. The people most likely to have that instinct are the industry's technological pioneers who have made important technical contributions of their own. In addition to Ford, this was true of Ken Olsen of Digital Equipment, An Wang of Wang Labs, the founders of the Eckert-Mauchly Corporation; and Robert Noyce and Gordon Moore of the Intel Corporation. Of course, technical expertise is neither a guarantee of success nor an absolute precondition for it. But it certainly does improve the odds immensely.

THE TRAGIC FLAW OF BILLY DURANT

Henry Ford resembled a disciplined hunter who doggedly stalks his prey for weeks and picks it off with a single shot through the heart after missing on two earlier tries. By contrast his counterpart at General Motors, Billy Durant, was a trigger-happy maniac who ran through the woods with machine gun in hand, spraying bullets at everything that moved—including, on occasion, his own feet. Durant bagged many more trophies than Ford and created America's number two automobile company (destined to take over first place after he had resigned), but he also suffered humiliating financial reverses and died a comparatively poor man. His brilliantly erratic career illustrates the dangers of building a giant enterprise by pyramiding mergers rather than by simply reinvesting profits, in the manner of Henry Ford.

During his lifetime William C. Durant founded the Durant-Dort Carriage Company, one of the leading carriage manufacturers in the United States; turned the Buick Motor Company into the nation's largest auto manufacturer; founded General Motors and lost control of it after only two years; created the highly successful Chevrolet Corporation; created a large auto parts conglomerate called United Motors; regained control of General Motors and then lost it a second time; and became one of the leading speculators on Wall Street during the Roaring Twenties. All in all, an eventful career. It was the life of a man who cannot be neatly categorized, for Billy Durant, like Andrew Carnegie, was a genius whose dazzling talents bridged the gap between entrepreneur and financier. Like Carnegie, he was a superb builder of companies who delighted in taking the best workmen he could find and then adding his own unparalleled skills as a promoter, marketer, and salesman. Also like Carnegie, Durant was a gifted financier who detested the Wall Street establishment and loved to beat the bankers at their own game. Unfortunately Durant differed from Carnegie in one fatal respect: He was, to quote an admiring colleague, "one hell of a gambler." Never was he happier than when sitting in front of a bank of telephones, calling brokers and investors all over the country, orchestrating a financial coup that would be splashed across the front page of the *New York Times*. The greater the danger, the better Durant liked it. "You know W.C. is never happy unless he is hanging to a window sill by his finger tips," an associate wrote.

Durant was a small, modest, carefully groomed man with a perpetual faint smile on his face. He was perfectly calm and polite in the midst of transacting multimillion-dollar deals and not averse to playing a game of checkers with the elevator operator while automobile tycoons cooled their heels in the waiting room. Durant began his automotive career as a turnaround artist. In 1904 he was called back to his hometown of Flint, Michigan, in order to breathe life into a moribund company called Buick that designed excellent automobiles but never managed to ship them out the door in quantity. At the time the forty-two-year-old Durant was dabbling on Wall Street, casting around for a new challenge after making a fortune as a founder of Durant-Dort, the nation's leading carriage manufacturer. Upon taking over Buick in 1904, Durant almost immediately raised its equity capitalization from $75,000 to $500,000. Then he handed out stock to a variety of parties —current shareholders, key employees, Durant-Dort (in order to procure an empty factory), and new investors, who injected fresh cash into the enterprise. During this refinancing operation Durant skillfully held off impatient creditors and played on the civic pride of local bankers, who wished to extend Flint's position as America's "vehicle city" into the automotive age.

As soon as Buick's finances were straightened out, Durant displayed his stupendous selling talent at the New York Automobile Show. Even though Buick had produced fewer than 50 cars during its entire existence, Durant secured orders for 1,108 cars—enough to keep the company busy for well over a year. While Buick's engineers labored to perfect new models and construction workers threw up a new factory on the outskirts of Flint, the company sold all the cars it could make. It produced 725 vehicles in 1905, followed by 1,400 in 1906, 4,641 in 1907, and 8,820 in 1908—more than any other company in the nation, including Ford. Alfred Sloan caught the spirit of the times when he wrote, "Speed! Do what you have been doing, but do it faster. Double your capacity. Quadruple it. Double it again. At times it seemed like madness. Yet people clamored for the cars. There were never enough automobiles to meet the demand. The pressure on production men was desperate." Flint became a boomtown overnight, crowded with new workers who lived in tents and piano crates until housing could be built. The number of factory workers tripled between 1908 and 1910 alone. This spectacular transformation was all the work of Billy Durant, the dapper promoter of boyish charm but Napoleonic will who raced from city to city and town to town, selling cars, planning factories, closing deals, and wheedling money out of bankers. In just three years, his biographer has pointed out, Durant "made the transition from the largest carriage maker to the largest automobile manufacturer."

But this was just the beginning. One night in 1907 Durant received a telephone call from Benjamin Briscoe, a fellow automaker whose Maxwell-Briscoe Company was financed by J. P. Morgan. Briscoe had an idea: He and Durant would create an automotive conglomerate, a collection of companies large enough to dominate the industry just as U.S. Steel dominated the steel industry. Actually the analogy to U.S. Steel was misleading. Briscoe did not intend so much to keep prices at a profitable level by grabbing a mammoth share of the market as to eliminate the technological and consumer market risk that automakers bore when they owned relatively small companies, such as Ford or Buick. Many successful auto companies, Briscoe knew, resembled shooting stars that streaked across the automotive firmament on the strength of one or two hot products and then disappeared into the night as the popularity of those models faded. By the merger of five, ten, or twenty companies into a single enterprise this risk would be greatly reduced. A conglomerate would have real staying power.

Briscoe's proposition was exactly suited to Durant's promotional instincts. The duo plunged into merger negotiations with abandon— and quickly found themselves hip-deep in a syrupy mass of complications and difficulties. Automotive entrepreneurs were headstrong, independent folk; getting a group of them to merge their companies was like convincing a dozen monkeys to stand in a straight line for an hour. At one meeting among Henry Ford, Billy Durant, Benjamin Briscoe, and Ransom Olds, progress was being made when suddenly Ford announced that he would not accept stock in the new enterprise; only $3 million in cold cash would do. Then Olds, whose company was worth much less than Ford's, made the same demand. Olds's position was unreasonable, and the $6 million could not have been raised in any case. The negotiations unraveled. So Briscoe and Durant decided to build a combination by themselves by merging Buick and Maxwell-Briscoe. The negotiations were handled by Briscoe's bankers, the fabled House of Morgan, and Durant quickly learned to detest the hauteur of J. P. Morgan's partners (for he never met the great banker himself). "If you think it is an easy matter to get money from New York capitalists to finance a Motor Car proposition in Michigan you have another guess coming," Durant reported. "Notwithstanding the fact that quoted rates are very low, money is hard to get owing to a somewhat unaccountable feeling of uneasiness and general distrust of the automobile proposition." Durant's observation was accurate enough; but the Morgan partners' suspicions of the speculative promoter were not entirely misplaced, and when details of the impending merger were leaked to the *New York Times,* they peremptorily called off the deal.

By now Durant was gripped by the urge to merge. His plan was simple. By establishing a holding company with a large capitalization and then trading its stock for the stock of many smaller enterprises, Durant intended to become a major force in the industry. As he explained, "I figured if I could acquire a few more companies like the Buick, I would have control of the greatest industry in this country. A great opportunity, no time to lose, I must get busy. I felt confident, because of the hazardous nature of the automobile business, that if money in sufficient quantity could be obtained, a reasonable number of good companies could be induced to sell out or become members of a central organization that would provide engineering and patent protection and minimize the hazards which were constantly developing." In 1908—the same year that the Model T was introduced—Durant created a corporation called General Motors with a capitalization of $12.5 million, and for the next two years he raced around the country, cutting deals with more than two dozen automotive entrepreneurs. It was an extraordinary performance. In addition to buying up one company after another, Durant continued to manage Buick and to take on any other operational details that interested him. He was very proud of the fact that after having bought Oldsmobile, he designed a popular new model that capitalized on the famous Oldsmobile name, and he took special delight in planning new factories, the tangible symbols of his burgeoning automotive empire. Durant's biographer, Lawrence R. Gustin, describes how on one occasion he was meeting with a friend in a hotel room when a building contractor phoned. He told the contractor to come over to the hotel right away; when they sat down to talk, he laid out his plans for a new factory complex: "Now I want you to begin on these buildings. I want this building 150 feet long by 80 wide, and three stories high, concrete and brick just like the others. Then off here at the right a wing 200 feet long, 60 feet wide and three stories high. Over here, two buildings just alike, 400 by 90 feet, three stories high. This street is to be cut through here. See that knoll—you remember it—see that it is leveled down and the street opened. Do you understand? I'll see you in Flint next Friday. Have everything worked out and we'll attend to any details that have to be considered. Good-bye." It was vintage Durant. In his precise and courteous way the little dictator deftly manipulated men and money to hasten the birth of his "baby," General Motors. He was never pushy or bossy. One associate described him as "a very persuasive man, soft-spoken and ingratiating. He was short, conservatively and immaculately dressed, and had an air of being permanently calm—though he was continuously involved in big and complicated financial deals—and he inspired confidence in his character and ability."

As an auto industry insider Durant knew as well as anyone which companies had the best prospects, and he was on a first-name basis with every automotive executive who mattered. On the other hand, Durant had to make most of his acquisitions with General Motors stock, rather than cash, and successful manufacturers were reluctant to accept such suspect currency in return for their fast-growing companies. This financial constraint, when combined with Durant's almost juvenile impulsiveness, made the original General Motors a weird collection of dogs and diamonds. Of his twenty-nine acquisitions the majority were "random gambles" inspired more by a desire to cover the technological waterfront than to buy companies that had superior managers and products. He protested to a friend, "They say I shouldn't have bought Cartercar. . . . Well, how was anyone to know that Cartercar wasn't going to be the thing? It had the friction drive and no other car had it. Maybe friction drive would be the thing. And then there's Elmore, with its two-cycle engine. That's the kind they were using on motorboats; maybe two-cycles were going to be the thing for automobiles. I was for getting every car in sight, playing safe all along the line." Although such reasoning had a certain plausibility it could not explain away Durant's most spectacular blunder: paying more than $7 million in securities and $112,759 in cash for the Heany Lamp Company, a worthless concern that held a fraudulent headlight patent. Durant paid more for this company than for Buick and Oldsmobile combined. By 1927 the GM stock exchanged for Heany had paid $50 million in dividends and possessed a market value of $320 million.

But not all the properties that Durant stuffed in his shopping basket were damaged goods. General Motors' first "acquisition" was, of course, Buick, a splendidly profitable company, and Durant shrewdly backed a promising young French manufacturer of spark plugs named Albert Champion. The purchase of a small automaker called Oakland eventually paid off handsomely, and the Oldsmobile name was also worth something, though not the elevated price that Durant paid for it. By shelling out $4.5 million in cash (obtained partly from Buick earnings), Durant also acquired Cadillac, an investment that looked expensive when it was made but paid for itself in just fourteen months. If Durant had had more cash, he might likewise have purchased the Ford Motor Company for $8 million and the Briscoe-Maxwell Company for $2 million, for both Ford and Briscoe said that they were willing to sell out at the right price.

Billy Durant's edifice, Alfred Sloan later pointed out, was founded on three strategic principles: a "variety of cars for a variety of tastes and fortunes," diversification among many technological alternatives, and an integration of parts manufacturers and auto assemblers. But while applying these principles, GM's architect had to confront the usual problem of the conglomerator: squaring strategic theory with operational reality. It was all very well to celebrate the virtues of synergy, diversification, and holding a large market share (more than 20 percent by 1910), but in the short run these abstractions would not pay the company's bills and permit it to stay in business. If GM's corporate stable had been well stocked with highly profitable thoroughbreds of the caliber of Cadillac and Buick, this would not have been a difficult task, but it harbored a crowd of crippled beasts that were ready for the glue factory. These companies absorbed funds for both working capital and fixed investment but contributed little to the bottom line. Consequently GM's sales grew by 70 percent between 1909 and 1910, but profits advanced by a mere 12 percent. And because GM's divisions operated under independent managements while Durant hunted for new acquisitions, Durant could not even keep track of its overall financial position, let alone coordinate the policies of the different divisions in order to achieve synergies. The dearth of internal controls was all the more dangerous because the optimistic Durant was hell-bent for expansion; during 1910 alone he invested about $8 million in plant expansion and increased inventories from $8.5 million to $40 million. Now, 1910 was an excellent year for the automobile industry—but not that excellent.

The combination of overexpansion, temporary weakness in Buick sales in the summer of 1910, and the acquisition of Cadillac with cash rather than stock created a liquidity squeeze at General Motors. Suddenly Durant had to lay aside his ambitious expansion plans (for he had not yet reached the end of his shopping list) and hit the road in search of loans. Indefatigable as always, he spent seven months knocking on every door in sight, trying country banks and leading Wall Street houses, insurance companies and wealthy individuals. But all to no avail. Financiers considered General Motors completely out of control, the very epitome of the auto industry's speculative excesses. For his part Durant—who was never overburdened with dispassionate objectivity when discussing Wall Street—blamed GM's liquidity crunch on the nasty rumors being spread by bankers rather than any weakness within the company itself.

Once Durant was on the ropes, the bankers moved in with arrogance and competence. A syndicate headed by Lee, Higginson and Company of Boston and J. W. Seligman and Company of New York floated a $15 million bond issue of five-year, first-mortgage bonds carrying an interest rate of 6 percent. Their fee for extending this financial lifeline was steep. They insisted on wresting managerial control of the company from Durant during the life of the loan, and in addition to a commission of $2.5 million on the bond issue, they demanded a bonus of $6 million in GM preferred and common stock. This pound and a half of flesh was justified, the bankers argued, because it was risky to lend $15 million to a struggling company. Durant countered that their financial risks were minimal because Buick's sales were still very strong, and the swift recovery of the company suggests that he was right.

The real significance of the General Motors rescue lies not in the greed of the bankers or the indignation of Billy Durant but rather in the spectacle of conservative financiers laying their hands on one of the great growth companies of the twentieth century. The episode bore a strong resemblance to the bankers' takeover of American Bell in 1877, and for a very good reason: The key figure in the bankers' syndicate, James J. Storrow, operated in the conservative tradition of the Boston investors who had controlled American Bell simply because his father had been the corporate counsel for the telephone company. Storrow's performance was solid but uninspired. He unceremoniously cleaned house at General Motors, tossing out the worthless properties and concentrating production in Buick, Cadillac, Oakland, and Oldsmobile. He wisely put two superior automakers, Charles Nash and Walter Chrysler, in key positions, and he rapidly rebuilt the company's liquidity. A strong balance sheet and steadily rising earnings were more than enough to please a banker like Storrow; he was not interested in taking the risks needed to take full advantage of the auto industry's explosive growth. One GM vice-president complained, "The bankers were too skeptical about the future of the automobile industry. They were chiefly interested in trying to realize savings, so they closed down some plants, concentrating on others. They didn't take advantage of the opportunities." With sales of Ford's Model T racing ahead, General Motors' market share declined from 21 percent in 1910 to just 8.5 percent in 1915. There is no doubt that if Storrow and other financiers had remained in control of General Motors, it never would have become the industry leader that it was destined to become.

As if to prove that GM's new leaders were asleep on the job, Billy Durant plunged into building a new company called Chevrolet. Durant's gutsy performance in developing the company was reminiscent of his work at Buick. Relying partly on the resources of Durant-Dort, he purchased an automobile factory and set out to develop a popular car. After casting around in the dark for more than two years, his team hit upon a money-making formula—two cars, called the Baby Grand and the Royal Mail, that were priced at well under $1,000. For the next three years Chevrolet sold every car it could produce, and by 1917 its share of the total car market was 14 percent. For Durant the success of Chevrolet was significant not because it rebuilt his fortune or made him an automotive titan once again. Durant did not think that way. His main concern was to use Chevrolet as a platform for regaining control of his "baby," General Motors. The mechanics of this extraordinary piece of financial intrigue are too complicated to be detailed here. Suffice it to say that Durant had hung on to a substantial number of GM shares even after losing managerial control of the company, and many of his friends in Flint were likewise major GM shareholders. These associates were understandably loyal to Durant, who had made them rich, and they disliked the stingy eastern bankers who refused to pay dividends on GM common. Durant expanded this base of support by encouraging Du Pont family interests to purchase GM stock, and the Du Pont connection in turn won the backing of a secondary New York banker named Louis G. Kaufman, who helped finance Chevrolet. With the support of these parties Durant purchased GM shares aggressively during 1915, bidding up the market price from $82 to $588. Not inclined to tangle with a madman who was willing to pay any price to buy back the company, Storrow and his associates ceded control to Durant in the spring of 1916 after a tense and bitter proxy war.

The Du Pont connection became increasingly important to GM during the years that followed. Pierre du Pont and John J. Raskob were responsible for converting E. I. du Pont de Nemours & Company from a staid family concern into a dynamic corporation that racked up large profits by producing explosives during World War I. The pair was a study in contrasts. Du Pont was a reticent patrician who had a self-effacing manner but great executive ability; Raskob, his right-hand man in matters of finance, was a voluble social climber of short stature but big ideas who bore a more than passing resemblance to Billy Durant. Perhaps it is not surprising, then, that sometime in 1914 Raskob took a liking to Durant's "baby." Raskob decided that GM's common stock was an excellent investment because it had strong earnings and good growth prospects yet was trading at a depressed price because it paid no dividend. In the tradition of investors everywhere, Raskob bought some shares and then told his bullish story to anyone who would listen, including his boss. Concluding that Raskob was right, Du Pont made a major investment in the enterprise. Du Pont became one of GM's four "neutral" directors during the proxy fight with the bankers in 1915. Durant valued Du Pont's deep pockets and high prestige on Wall Street and encouraged him and Raskob to remain on the board after he had regained full control of General Motors in the spring of 1916.

During the next four years Du Pont committed ever more capital to GM, but these investments were not simply the product of a coldly rational decision to diversify that one reads about in textbooks. They were necessitated in part by two financial crises that hit General Motors broadside as the corporation expanded rapidly between 1916 and 1920. The first crisis occurred in the fall of 1917, when Du Pont and Raskob learned that Durant had suffered major trading losses while attempting to support the price of GM stock (which plummeted when the United States entered World War I). After a payment of $1 million to Durant as a retroactive "salary" had failed to preserve his credit, Raskob convinced the Du Pont board of directors to buy $25 million worth of GM stock. This marked the first investment by the Du Pont *corporation* in General Motors.

Although auto production was held in check during 1918, it expanded very rapidly during the inflationary postwar boom of 1919 and early 1920. GM's leaders optimistically geared up for the automobile shortage that was universally expected to prevail in 1920. The company seemed to expand in all directions at once. GM acquired a 60 percent interest in the Fisher Body Corporation; bought out Durant's positions in Chevrolet and United Motors (an auto parts company); entered the tractor business and the refrigerator business; purchased a number of small automotive companies; built a huge new office building in Detroit and a new laboratory building; established the General Motors Acceptance Corporation; and expanded its plant and equipment. Because these investments greatly exceeded GM's cash flow, they had to be financed by issuing securities to the public and selling more GM stock to Du Pont. Thus the company's finances were stretched very tight indeed when, in response to a tightening of credit by the Federal Reserve Board, auto sales began to sag in the summer of 1920. GM's top executives resembled a group of sun-drenched boaters who are relaxing in a canoe, idly drifting with the current of a river that is about to take them over a waterfall. Luckily for them, $64 million had been raised for expansion in the spring of 1920, just as the boom was ending; these funds were used as working capital during the financial crisis. Nevertheless, the company came dangerously close to bankruptcy and might not have pulled through had it not had the backing of one the nation's richest families, the Du Ponts, and its most powerful bank, J. P. Morgan and Company. Alfred Sloan described the company's plight: "The automobile market had nearly vanished and with it our income. . . . We were loaded with high-priced inventory and commitments at the old inflated price level. We were short of cash. We had a confused product line. There was a lack of control and of any means of control in operations and finance, and a lack of adequate information about anything. In short, there was just about as much crisis, inside and outside, as you could wish for if you liked that sort of thing." Before getting out of the jam, General Motors had written off $100 million in losses.

The crisis was powerfully compounded by a new stock market crisis involving Durant. Unbeknownst to his associates, Durant had been defending his "baby" against the "gamblers of the street," and as the depression of 1920 deepened, his losses mounted to overwhelming proportions. Having made most of these purchases on margin, he had accumulated a debt of $30 million to a dozen brokers and faced the necessity of selling huge blocks of stock in a depressed market. Such a move would have driven down the price still further and threatened the credit of the corporation itself. To avert such a crisis, Du Pont and Raskob huddled with bankers from J. P. Morgan and Company, who raised $27 million and bought out Durant's position, which was added to Du Pont's General Motors investment.

Fortunately for GM and its competitors the depression of 1920–21 was as brief as it was sharp. With the recovery of consumer demand in the late spring of 1921 the corporation's sales rebounded, and its structure was realigned under the expert direction of Alfred Sloan. Durant was out, but his "baby" survived. Nevertheless, the crisis is significant because it illuminates a mode of venture financing that has become increasingly important as the American economy has matured: a major investment by a large, cash-rich company in a high-growth industry with which it is unfamiliar.

As later chapters will show, this approach is full of pitfalls, and some of them are evident here. The essential problem was a lack of focus. Du Pont and Raskob knew little about the auto industry, and the chemical industry absorbed much of their attention. Thus, when they plunged into the financing of a complex, fast-growing, high-risk business like General Motors, they were taking real risks. Four problems contributed to the crisis of 1920. In the first place, they did not really understand Billy Durant's peculiar mental makeup and were almost completely ignorant of his wild stock market speculations. They never really came to grips with his intuitive and careless way of making key decisions. (Durant's managerial style was as bizarre as ever; he interrupted important conferences in order to take calls from his brokers and thought nothing of conducting major conferences from a portable barber chair while he received a clip.) Secondly, Raskob, who had never lived through earlier inventory crises in the automobile industry, must take much of the blame for the gross overexpansion of 1918 and 1919. No one can be faulted for failing to predict the future, but the fact is that in 1919 Durant, smelling trouble ahead, urgently warned Raskob that he was taking great risks. In one memo he wrote: "I feel that I should call your attention to the enormous expenditures and capital commitments which are being authorized by the finance Committee against Prospective Earnings—a method of financing which I do not think is either safe or sound and which, in the event of industrial disturbance or paralysis, might seriously impair our position. Frankly, I am very much worried. . . ." Thirdly, the partial melding of two companies created a chaotic and undisciplined organizational structure. No single body had an overview of the flow of cash into and out of the corporation. Because spending decisions were made by the separate divisions rather than by headquarters, spending was not quickly curtailed when sales began to slow. New investments were made on a horse-trading basis, with the various factions from Du Pont, GM, and various subsidiaries saying in effect, "I'll support your new project if you will support mine." This was an easy way to keep the peace until the money ran out. Finally, the abundance of capital in Du Pont's coffers reduced the financial discipline within GM; new projects did not have to be financed either from operating cash flows or from sales of securities to outside investors. In order to fund a new automotive project, Raskob, acting as a top executive of General Motors, needed to do nothing more than sell some more GM shares to himself, acting as the chief financial officer of Du Pont.

The depression of 1920 was a surprise to almost everyone, but GM's losses were much heavier than those of Ford. GM's clumsy handling of the crisis illustrates the danger of financing new industries in a way that divides managerial responsibility among several groups, including investors who know little about the industry. Able industrialists like Du Pont and Raskob undoubtedly managed GM better than Wall Street bankers or government bureaucrats would have done, but their diverse responsibilities and limited automotive experience contributed to the crisis. And this was not, of course, the first time that General Motors had experienced such problems. The rule of the financiers between 1910 and 1915 had been instrumental in causing GM to fall far behind Ford in the first place. Only the brilliant management of Alfred Sloan and the blunders of Henry Ford turned the tables during the 1920s. As we will see, the danger of forming alliances between big corporations and smaller high-tech companies is a pressing issue in the biotechnology industry today.

The chaotic history of Billy Durant's company also graphically demonstrates that Andrew Carnegie was right: Effective entrepreneurship and ambitious stock market speculation do not mix well. Not only is each activity a full-time job, but they are actually incompatible because their rhythms and time horizons are completely different. Aggressive stock market traders live minute to minute and week to week; for them a year is an eternity. By contrast a company has to be built up logically and patiently over a period of years; an entrepreneur whose eyes are fixed on the ticker tape is sure to lose this perspective.

VIII

David and Goliath
in Silicon Valley

All the infant industries thus far discussed in this book were financed primarily by individual investors, professional financiers, or the entrepreneurs themselves. With the partial exception of the Du Pont-General Motors connection, none was financed by large corporations. By contrast major corporations played a central role in financing the computer industry almost from its inception. As often as not, corporations performed this role quite poorly. It is vital to understand precisely why this was so because the continued vitality of the American economy partly hinges on the ability of corporations in mature industries such as chemicals and automobiles to invest effectively in the industries of the future. This is all the more true because recent tax reforms and economic trends during the 1980s have tremendously increased the amount of money that corporations have to invest in new industries. As the economic competitiveness of the United States waned in the 1970s, investors and policymakers became alarmed about the shortage of capital in corporate America. This problem was solved in surprisingly short order by the Reagan administration's initial tax reforms, which greatly increased the speed with which corporations could depreciate assets, effectively reducing their taxable incomes and their tax bills. At the same time that this reform was increasing corporate cash flow, low inflation of capital goods, such as computers, trucks, and machine tools, meant that the free cash flow of corporations—the amount of money they had left over after making necessary investments in their basic businesses—has also increased greatly. This has been particularly true of capital-intensive basic industries, such as chemicals, oil, autos, utilities, and electrical equipment, which benefited the most from the Reagan reforms because they have large assets to depreciate.

In view of the poor growth prospects of these capital-intensive basic industries, a critical question facing the American economy is whether or not they can successfully redeploy their free cash flows from old industries into new—from petrochemicals to biotechnology or from refining oil to making microcomputers. Rather surprisingly this issue has been largely ignored. Buckets of ink have been spilled by pundits and politicians discussing the wisdom of a governmental industrial policy to finance new industries, even though the realities of the federal deficit mean that such a program would be relatively small. Meanwhile, corporate cash flow has risen by $128 billion (a whopping 55 percent), and almost no one has asked whether this capital is smart money or dumb money—money that is being intelligently channeled into the industries of the future, plowed back into dying industries, or squandered in misguided mergers. This chapter and the next will show why, when it comes to financing new industries, the capital of big U.S. companies has a low IQ; Chapter X will discuss what can be done about the problem.

WANDERING IN A VENTURE CAPITAL DESERT

Like Benjamin Franklin or John Stuart Mill, John Von Neumann possessed such dazzling genius as to make the mental mortals around him quiver with incredulity. At the age of six he routinely exchanged jokes with his father in classical Greek, and in addition to being among the world's greatest mathematicians and physicists, Von Neumann was an accomplished historian. His memory was virtually perfect. He thought nothing of standing in a cocktail party recounting long and complicated mathematical proofs that he had worked out a week earlier, and he delighted partygoers with extraordinarily tortuous and intricate anecdotes. A colleague, Herman H. Goldstine, described him: "On one occasion I tested his ability by asking him to tell me how *The Tale of Two Cities* started. Whereupon, without any pause, he immediately began to recite the first chapter and continued until asked to stop after about ten or fifteen minutes." Appropriately enough, this human computer had a major hand in creating one of the world's first electronic computers, the Electronic Numerical Integrator and Computer, or ENIAC, developed at the University of Pennsylvania during World War II. But Von Neumann was only one of a cluster of titanic intellects who were brought together by the war to develop in Philadelphia the "analytical engine" that was destined to transform the world economy.

The story of ENIAC bears scrutiny because it exemplifies a powerful creative triad that has successfully sustained industrial innovation in the United States since World War II. This triad consists of the federal government, which funds pioneering research; scientists in the great universities who carry out the research; and private businesses that commercialize the new technology and create great industries. Spearheading American enterprise in the fields of computers, semiconductors, aerospace, biotechnology, and nuclear energy, this potent combination has done much to keep the American economy a step ahead of Japan. But the triad was not perfected all at once. As the history of the computer industry vividly shows, it was not until the 1960s that a financial mechanism was developed for *systematically* transplanting the triumphs of academic science into the rocky soil of the competitive marketplace. Until the perfection of the venture capital firm in the 1960s it was frequently difficult for promising young technology companies to obtain the requisite start-up capital. And the few companies that did get off the ground were in danger of acquisition by large corporations with stultifying bureaucracies that smothered entrepreneurial initiative, turning technological gold mines into silicon scrap heaps.

The problem that inspired the creation of ENIAC was nothing more exalted than how to aim a cannon. A joint project of the U.S. Army Ordnance Department and the Moore School of Electrical Engineering at the University of Pennsylvania tackled the task of calculating tables showing the angle at which a cannon had to be fired, given the target's location, the weight of the shells, the heat of the fuse, prevailing air currents, and other factors. To calculate just one trajectory required about 750 multiplications, and there were between 2,000 and 4,000 trajectories in a single table. With the best electromechanical calculators available, it took a month to calculate one table. The war would be over before the calculations could be completed.

Fortunately for the army a few American scientists had already ventured into equally dense computational jungles and had begun to look for faster ways to "crunch numbers." In the 1930s John W. Mauchly, a physicist at a small college outside Philadelphia, became engrossed in research on atmospheric electricity and came to the conclusion that the work would take forever if the calculations were done manually. He gave some thought to developing an electronic calculator to handle the problem, and in 1941 he visited John Vincent Atanasoff, a physicist at Iowa State who had done much creative research on electronic computing. After joining the ballistics project at the Moore School, Mauchly concluded that if ever there was a time to develop an electronic computer, it was before—not after—those thousands of trajectories had to be computed. So he and his colleagues undertook to design an electronic computer, in preference to the safer but slower electromechanical method. It was a gutsy decision. Not only did the logical architecture of the machine still have to be worked out, but exceedingly tedious technical problems had to be resolved because the machine was an electronic monstrosity composed of 18,000 vacuum tubes, 70,000 resistors, 10,000 capacitors, and 6,000 switches. But the army's pockets were deep, and Mauchly was fortunate to have exceedingly able colleagues, including John Von Neumann, who devised the logical structure of ENIAC; the talented mathematician Herman Goldstine, who talked the army into funding the project; and a well-to-do young Philadelphian named J. Presper Eckert, who directed the actual construction of the machine. Wiry and self-assured, Eckert exuded demonic energy as he set about making sure that all the thousands of parts of this electronic labyrinth, covering 15,000 square feet and weighing thirty tons, functioned properly. Goldstine later wrote that Eckert's "standards were the highest, his energies almost limitless, his ingenuity remarkable, and his intelligence extraordinary. From start to finish it was he who gave the project its integrity and ensured its success. . . . It was Eckert's omnipresence that drove everything forward at whatever cost to humans including himself." As in every high-technology project, from building steel mills in Pittsburgh in 1870 to designing microprocessors in Palo Alto in 1985, it was the zeal and talent of this team, rather than the size of its budget, that made it so effective. Money mattered, but only if spent by the right people. Fifty ordinary scientists were worth less than one genius like Von Neumann. This basic reality would continue to shape competitive currents in the computer industry for the next four decades.

ENIAC was finished in 1945, just as the war was ending, and the precipitate decline in military spending threatened to slow the development of electronic computing in the United States. Officials at the Moore School, too dim-witted to perceive the significance of computers, gave the ENIAC staff short shrift, deeming them financial liabilities rather than institutional assets. Some members of the team followed Von Neumann to the Institute for Advanced Study in Princeton, where a second-generation machine, EDVAC, was developed. But Eckert and Mauchly took a different route; they set up the world's first computer company. In 1946 the duo formed a partnership called Electronic Control Corporation, which was soon converted into the Eckert-Mauchly Computer Corporation in order to take advantage of their spreading fame as inventors of the "electronic brain." It took no little courage to think about manufacturing computers commercially in 1946. Conventional wisdom held that the computer was an outsize piece of electronic exotica, not unlike an atom smasher, that might be useful to a few university researchers but was of little practical value to a corporation. But as so often happens in new industries, the people who intimately understood the revolutionary technology—be it Theodore Vail in telephony or Henry Ford in automobiles—had a better understanding of market potential than did outsiders because they realized that costs could be lowered and the market expanded. Eckert and Mauchly resolved to produce a refined and shrunken version of ENIAC, to be called UNIVAC, and sell it to government agencies and large corporations.

The young company's first soundings in the marketplace were highly encouraging, for potential buyers were eager to inspect the plans for UNIVAC. Writing to his brother in January 1948, John Mauchly reported that the company had already completed a research contract for the Bureau of the Census and was about to land a contract to build a UNIVAC for it. The firm also had a contract to deliver special equipment to Northrop Aircraft, and many other organizations—Prudential Insurance, Rose's Department Stores, A. C. Nielsen and Company, several large banks, even a college in Calcutta—had shown an interest in UNIVAC. These potential customers were divided into two categories: scientific organizations that had a few gigantic equations to solve and bureaucratic customers who had to perform simple operations on a large number of cases. To design condensers, for example, the Sprague Electric Company had "a staff of twelve mathematicians operating desk computers in order to arrive at the proper solutions. Their equations involve six unknowns, and each of them varies when one of the others is changed." On the other hand, "the Metropolitan Insurance Company has a large problem involving a total file of 18,000,000 policies with 2,000,000 changes per week. There are about 20 digits of information for each policy. It appears that this is a natural application for the UNIVAC."

In order to meet the expected flood of orders from this diverse array of customers, the company moved into larger quarters and greatly expanded its staff. But to do this, Eckert and Mauchly needed capital, and here the two scientists were clearly out of their depth. In a highly revealing memo outlining the financial situation of the firm, Mauchly warned his associates that they were in danger of confining themselves in a logical echo chamber. The company, he wrote, was "losing a hell of a lot of valuable time by reason of the fact that we are slow in making some necessary decisions" regarding financing. Sale of stock was being delayed because Eckert-Mauchly executives felt that "our position [to sell stock] will be improved when we have more machine orders." But again, "except for A. C. Nielsen, our machine orders seem to be dependent upon having adequate financing." One reason for this costly dithering was a simple lack of financial expertise. Mauchly observed: "We cannot sell machines without first setting a price on them, and the same goes for our stock. We have been groping around for some way to set a price on our stock. I feel that the main reason why we have not as yet advanced very far in our effort to raise capital is that we have been unwilling to stick our necks out and put a definite price on our stock. In every deal, someone has to make the first offer."

What Eckert-Mauchly needed was a good investment banker who had plenty of experience in pricing new issues of stock and would move decisively to raise the necessary funds. But the two scientists found themselves in much the same position as Gardiner Hubbard and Thomas Sanders of American Bell in 1876. It was nearly impossible to make a public offering of stock in 1946 because the triple trauma of the Great Depression, World War II, and the postwar inflation of 1946–48 had shaken investors, turning the canyons of Wall Street into a depressingly tranquil place. Moreover, the United States contained few venture capitalists who were systematically investing in risky high-technology start-up situations. The one exception, of which Eckert and Mauchly were fully aware, was a Boston firm called American Research and Development, or ARD. Directed by Professor Georges Doriot of the Harvard Business School, ARD (as Mauchly told his brother) had "$5,000,000 in capital which is supposed to be invested in new technical enterprises, with no more than 10% of their total capital going into any one enterprise."

Failing to obtain the backing of ARD or some other sophisticated venture capitalist, Eckert-Mauchly had to settle for the support of a small Philadelphia firm called American Totalizator, a maker of racetrack tote boards. In terms of both money and talent American Totalizator's resources were decidedly limited—especially after its CEO was killed in a plane crash in 1949. This mischance might have been overcome if Eckert-Mauchly had been able to generate a positive cash flow by quickly moving into a production mode and shipping product out the door, as the early automobile companies did. But a mainframe computer was a costly investment that would transform the operations of the organization that purchased it; potential customers were understandably cautious about leaping into the electronic age—especially when the vendor was an undercapitalized operation like Eckert-Mauchly. Eckert-Mauchly's cash needs increased still more when it experienced cost overruns and delays in perfecting UNIVAC, and by the middle of 1949 money was running short. Dependent on research contracts from Northrop, Prudential, and Nielsen and on the capital supplied by American Totalizator, Eckert-Mauchly struggled to finish the UNIVAC ordered by the Census Bureau.

With cost overruns continuing and American Totalizator refusing to supply additional funds, Eckert and Mauchly were forced to sell out in the spring of 1950 to a leading producer of office equipment, Remington Rand. The first UNIVAC was shipped in the summer of 1951 to the Census Bureau, where it was a great success, and more machines, priced at a cool $1.1 million apiece, soon followed. For five years UNIVAC was both the best computer in the world and the best known. Without a doubt Remington Rand had a wonderful opportunity to seize a major share of the market for computers and continue to dominate the industry. Yet between 1951 and 1967 the company managed *to lose a quarter of a billion dollars* by making and selling computers. What went wrong? In a word, plenty. Unlike its major competitor, IBM, Remington Rand did not specialize in large and sophisticated business machines; it was a corporate mosaic dealing in typewriters, calculating machines, tabulators, and razors. This lack of focus increased in 1955, when Remington Rand merged with the Sperry Corporation, a maker of hydraulic equipment and electronic defense gear. A company that made everything from typewriters to gyroscopes to razors was poorly positioned to dominate the complex market for computers. Sperry Rand's top executives were not expert in the process of making and selling large business machines, and the efforts of its salesmen were spread over a broad range of products. Computers were just one product among many, and not necessarily the most important. As Katharine Davis Fishman, the leading historian of

the computer industry, has written, "a Remington Rand branch manager in a big city like Chicago made $65,000 to $80,000 a year in
commissions and sat like a ward boss with a big cigar, distributing
patronage plums—the best territory, the most sympathetic quota—to
his favorite aides. Naturally, he spurned promotion and had no enthusiasm for computers; one could do much better selling the machinery one
knew to the customers one knew." Compounding these marketing
problems was organizational chaos in the technical end of the business.
Members of the Eckert-Mauchly contingent constantly tangled with
another group of World War II computer whiz kids from Engineering
Research Associates (ERA), a second small company that James Rand
had shrewdly purchased. Like a pair of vicious tigers, the Eckert-
Mauchly and ERA contingents both had the potential to excel in the
computer industry, but when thrown in the same cage, they chewed
each other to pieces. Eventually the bulk of the ERA staff defected to
set up their own company (of which more later). Thus was Remington
Rand's brilliant move into the computer industry undermined by the
environmental hazards of a huge corporation: organizational chaos, low
morale, ineffectual marketing, a diffuse business strategy. This was only
the first of many instances in which the special challenges of the
computer industry would turn a giant into a Goliath.

Like the early history of Bell Telephone, the trials of Eckert-
Mauchly graphically show the utility of the venture capital firm. A
professional venture capitalist could have provided not only a reliable
source of funds but also the benefit of his experience. He would have
cautioned, for example, that delays were to be expected in developing
for the commercial market an utterly new product such as the computer. He might also have advised Eckert and Mauchly to target their
market more precisely, instead of calling on a wide variety of institutions. With the benefit of such assistance Eckert-Mauchly would have
remained independent instead of being swallowed up by Remington
Rand, and given its big technical lead over IBM, it might well have
been able to grab a major piece of the mainframe market. As we will
see, that is just what other small but highly innovative computer companies were able to do when they did receive the backing of venture
capitalists.

THOMAS AND TOM WATSON: KEEPING CORPORATE
CAPITAL SMART

Remington Rand's chief competitor in the computer business, International Business Machines, was the creation of a a streetwise salesman named Thomas Watson, who over the course of three decades had turned a puny conglomerate into the country's largest and most profitable maker of office equipment. Thanks to an excellent recent book by Robert Sobel, we know much about Watson and his company. Watson began his business career as a salesman in upstate New York, peddling everything from securities to pianos to beef, but he did not perfect his métier until he joined National Cash Register in 1895. NCR was run by a puritanical autocrat named John Patterson who keenly understood a fact that eluded most manufacturers of the period: The proper aim of a manufacturing company was to *sell* a product, not just make it. Salesmen, Patterson believed, were the heart of any successful business —not mere parasites whose commissions decimated profit margins. Inspired by this insight, Patterson became America's greatest sales manager. He demanded great things of his salesmen and paid them huge salaries in return, and he used all sorts of special incentives—sales bonuses, sales clubs, sales conventions, sales newspapers—to spur them on to ever-greater production goals. The biggest producers earned more than $30,000 a year, a huge sum at the time.

No one at NCR responded to these incentives more avidly than Thomas Watson, who in a candid moment once observed, "They say money isn't everything. It isn't everything, but [it] is a great big something when you are trying to get started in the world and haven't anything. I speak feelingly." Watson rapidly advanced in the organization as his sales production grew, but life at the top of NCR was a most precarious perch, not unlike sitting on top of an active volcano. For one thing, not all of Watson's assignments were legitimate; he was convicted and nearly imprisoned for a year for using predatory tactics to shut down small companies that were selling reconditioned cash registers. Ordinarily an employee who risked a year in jail to serve his employer would be due a raise or at least some praise. But John Patterson was afflicted by corporate claustrophobia. When successful, aggressive executives crept too close to the throne, he felt the urge to fire them; the industry was littered with NCR castoffs. And so it was with Thomas Watson. Out of a job in 1914, Watson took control of a rickety conglomerate called Computing-Tabulating-Recording Corporation, which manufactured scales, punch card time clocks, and Hollerith machines (accounting machines run with punched cards that were used by large organizations such as railroads and government agencies).

Watson changed CTR's name to International Business Machines in 1924, and as if to prove that this grandiose appellation was not a misnomer, he expanded its revenues from $4.2 million in 1914 to $119 million in 1945. Shrewdly and patiently, Watson made the most of a good business. Like a crafty Mississippi riverboat pilot, he instinctively kept IBM moving on a dominant current of American life: the bureaucratization of society. As corporations grew ever larger during World War I and the Roaring Twenties, paperwork multiplied, and so did the need for accounting machines. And when depression struck in the 1930s, Franklin Roosevelt's numerous bureaucratic brood—the NRA, CCC, TVA, AAA—needed dozens of IBM machines, as did the War Department during World War II. One reason why IBM captured a large share of this expanding market was that it *rented machines rather than sold them*. It was easier to persuade a customer to rent a machine than to lay out the capital needed to make an outright purchase, and IBM salesmen made certain that every deal with a new customer marked the beginning of a long and lucrative relationship, with the client adding more and more pieces of IBM equipment as its data-processing needs expanded. The business was all the more stable and profitable because IBM supplied not only the machines themselves but the millions of cards that ran through them. Unlike AT&T in its infancy, IBM was not injured by the slower cash flow associated with renting rather than selling equipment because it was a well-established corporation that could borrow funds when necessary.

A major reason for the company's success was that under the tutelage of master salesman Thomas Watson IBM salesmen became the best in the industry, famous for their clean-cut appearances, earnest professionalism, and aggressive resourcefulness. The only reason why a salesman ever lost an account, Watson once said, was "neglect." IBM salesmen became particularly expert in pleasing the data-processing managers in large bureaucracies because the company (unlike most of its competitors) focused on the market for large business equipment instead of diversifying broadly. Like Andrew Carnegie, Watson placed most of his eggs in one basket—and then watched that basket.

IBM emerged from World War II fit and ferocious, seemingly well prepared to prosper in the ever-expanding data-processing market. But appearances were deceiving. This giant was a potential Goliath, in danger of being struck down by the sheer weight of the new electronic computers that were about to take over the office equipment industry. Thomas Watson, Sr., was getting old by 1945, thinking less about changing the company than about conserving what he had built. And since Watson was nearly as autocratic as his mentor from NCR, John Patterson, virtually no one in the company could persuade him of the importance of the computer revolution. "He was good. He was fine," one IBM executive later recalled, "but he couldn't tolerate different points of view." For that matter, most of Watson's colleagues at IBM (particularly the salesmen who had so much influence in the company) had little interest in computers. Thousands of pieces of electrome-chanical IBM equipment had been installed in customers' offices, where they were generating millions of dollars in rental fees every week. To replace them with electronic gear would be costly, disruptive, and dangerous. Why bother?

The one man who had the political power to overcome bureaucratic inertia and save IBM from the Goliath syndrome was Watson's son, Thomas Watson, Jr. Perhaps it is not too much to say that a turning point in IBM history was the day in 1940 when Tom Watson enlisted in the Army Air Corps. By that time he had been working at IBM for three years, but he had less the appearance of a budding captain of industry than of a handsome and convivial man-about-town, more adept at hosting parties and flying his personal airplane than at selling card sorters. Wartime service flying transport planes in Europe sobered Tom Watson's outlook, however, and sharpened his interest in radar and other electronic gadgets. In the late forties IBM was far from a technological innocent in the field of computing. The company had supported development at Harvard of an electromechanical computer called the Mark I, which was completed in 1945, and within the bowels of the IBM organization an engineer named Ralph Palmer was working on electronic approaches to data processing. But top management did not appreciate the significance of ENIAC or the threat posed by Eckert-Mauchly. Watson Sr.'s response to ENIAC was to make yet another electromechanical card sorter, and a strategic study of data storage mechanisms by a group of IBM salesmen concluded that stor-ing data on tape rather than cards was impracticable because it would take much longer to wind halfway through a roll of tape than to get to the middle of a deck of cards. The younger Watson was not so

complacent. Though no engineer himself, he sensed that the technological climate was changing ominously. Thanks to his influence, funding for Palmer's electronic research was continued, and an electronic
calculator developed by IBM engineers was placed in volume production. Moreover, Tom Watson saw to it that a large proportion of new
hirees in the Research Department had Ph.D.'s in electronics.

IBM's first entry into the computer field revealed just how far behind
Eckert-Mauchly the company had fallen. When the Korean War
began in the summer of 1950, Tom Watson got the idea of swooping
down on Washington and finding a bureaucrat who was willing to
finance development of an electronic computer. From the standpoint
of corporate politics this "defense calculator" was shrewdly conceived;
as one of Watson's aides observed, "We were not intruding on the
major product planning effort of IBM that was at that time electro-
mechanically oriented and had a wide cadre of support within IBM.
The majority opinion was that the IBM future was best served this way
rather than the electronic way." Watson's lieutenants walked the corri-
dors of the Pentagon, knocking on doors almost at random, asking the
generals what type of machine they needed. At length they came to
a realization that Eckert and Mauchly had understood as far back as
1946 that it was possible to design a *single* computer that would meet
the needs of various types of customer. They calculated that the cost
of building it would be covered by renting it for $5,200 per month, so
they pegged the rental rate at $8,000 and sent the salesmen out into
the field to get orders. Then the IBM engineers set to work, building
the company's first computer. It was an unnerving experience. Recalled
James L. Birkenstock, Tom Watson's chief aide: "It was about a year
after IBM embarked on this program that we came to realize how little
we really knew about the cost and the intricacies of building a production electronic computer. Perhaps a year later IBM reached a point
where if we continued as planned, the program would be a financial
disaster for the IBM Company." The salesmen were sent back into the
field to explain why the rental fee had to be raised from $8,000 to
$15,000, a piece of news that diminished the order list for the defense
calculator, to say nothing of IBM's credibility.

In comparison to Eckert-Mauchly's UNIVAC I, IBM's defense
calculator (renamed the 701) was a crude and inflexible affair, but it
was all the company had to throw in the breach when Remington Rand
delivered its first UNIVAC to the Census Bureau in June 1951. Remington's revolutionary new product was all the more disturbing for IBM

because the bureau was a major customer and UNIVAC displaced some pieces of IBM equipment. Now the skirmish became a war. It was fought on two fronts. On the marketing front IBM salesmen, ever wily and resourceful, did everything possible to discredit UNIVAC. What would they do if the newfangled gadget broke down? they asked customers. Instead of plunging into a purchase of a UNIVAC, perhaps it would be more prudent to create a committee to study the concept. At the same time IBM salesmen pushed the 701 and a follow-up machine for the nonscientific market called the 702, and they eventually bested their opponents at Remington Rand because instead of mouthing technical gibberish, they emphasized how much money a client would save if he bought one. All in all, it was a virtuoso performance by IBM's salesmen, and a major reason for its success was that IBM, unlike Remington Rand, was firmly focused on the market for large office equipment. Not only were IBM salesmen generally superior to Remington's, but they were particularly expert at exploiting the neuroses of data-processing managers in governments and large corporations.

While salesmen fought a holding action in the field, the generals at headquarters frantically devised new weapons to use against Remington Rand and any other company that might enter the field. It was Tom Watson, Jr., who cut through the bureaucratic sludge and put the company on an entrepreneurial footing. He began by convincing his father, who was chairman of the company until 1955, that the era of electromechanical business machines was ending. To serve the office market, he ordered development of the 702, to supplement the 701, which had been sold to such companies as aerospace companies and government labs. Ralph Palmer's work was used as a springboard for designing the 702, but the initial version of the machine was so inferior to the UNIVAC that it had to be redesigned and rebuilt in a hurry. Recalled T. Vincent Learson, project manager for the 702, "In ninety days I had a new machine announced. The boys worked around the clock. I had engineering people on the manufacturing line. I said no testing and got away with it. The new machine chewed up the market."

In those tense days of the mid-fifties IBM ran scared, constantly looking over its shoulder at General Electric, RCA, PhilcoFord, and other companies that had much more electronics expertise than IBM as well as more capital. Tom Watson and his aides knew that this was no time to play it safe. They borrowed millions of dollars from the Prudential Insurance Company to build up their research capability in electronics, and they took shrewd technological risks as well. Birken-stock recalled: "Tom Watson Jr. made a number of key decisions in the emergence of electronic computing in IBM. One [was] the decision to abandon electrostatic (Williams tube) storage and switch to mag-netic core storage. At the time that he made that decision, magnetic core storage was not economically feasible. Cores were costing us about thirty-five to forty-five cents per core. He foresaw [that] the economy of scale resulting from a hundred percent switch to magnetic core storage would enable IBM to produce a memory system that was economically feasible. It was a bold decision." Another shrewd gamble of Watson's was to have IBM shift its electronic products from vacuum tube technology to solid-state transistors. One time Watson called a meeting of his top staff people and said (according to Birkenstock), " 'You doubting Thomases say that transistor electronics isn't here.' And with that he placed a stack of radios on the table named IDEA. It was the first transistorized radio produced in the United States. The radio used [Texas Instruments] transistors, and was produced by this company IDEA. He said, referring to the transistor, 'They're here for them, and they're here for us in computers.' " Watson, in short, made the most of his ignorance. Though he ran a giant corporation, he thought like an entrepreneur rather than an engineer or a bureaucrat. As Birkenstock has said, "All of this resulted from a bold entre-preneurial decision by Tom Watson, Jr. It simply would not have happened if the entrepreneur had not been involved in the engineering cycle. The engineers would have waited and waited and perfected and perfected until they thought the normal events of technological devel-opment had produced a transistor that was economically feasible or a magnetic core that was economically practical."

By the end of 1956—just three years after shipping its first computer —IBM had turned the competitive corner and controlled more than 70 percent of the market. Actually the significance of this achievement was far from obvious at the time, for the computer revolution, like the automobile revolution before it, constantly surprised contemporaries by burrowing deeper and deeper into the fabric of American society. The computer made its public debut in November 1952, when a robot brain (UNIVAC I) was used to predict the outcome of the presidential election on the strength of early returns. Not until 1954, however, did a corporation take delivery of a computer that was to be used for purely business, as opposed to scientific, applications, and even then many analysts—less astute than Eckert and Mauchly had been—believed that only about 100 corporations were big enough to need one. Yet new applications for the robot brains—tracking inventory, doing payrolls, regulating factory operations, handling billing—kept emerging, and fashion-conscious executives were eager to install one of the technological marvels in their company, if only to show that their company was riding the tide of technological change in the progressive fifties. By 1958 more than 1,200 organizations, counting both companies and government agencies, were using about 1,700 computers. More often than not the first reaction of the new users was frustration and disappointment, for few executives were prepared for the excruciatingly painstaking task of writing the software that would program the computer to perform its appointed function. When General Electric bought a computer in 1957 to do the payroll for its huge Louisville appliance factory, it was expected to do the work in two hours but instead took twenty hours. "Developing such a program involves far more meticulous work than we realized at the beginning," GE's president admitted. One serious problem in the mid-fifties was the paucity of experienced programmers; the secret nightmare that haunted every data-processing manager was that he would convince his boss to lay out $30,000 per month to rent a computer and then watch it sit idle for many months while the necessary software was developed. Leaving nothing to chance, a Los Angeles insurance company did four years of advance planning before computerizing its information system covering 350,000 policies.

In these circumstances the computer vendor that most successfully calmed the fears of customers while they crossed the Rubicon into the computer age would be way ahead of the competition. IBM had long excelled at such hand holding and spent huge sums developing software for customers, offering seminars that explained the diverse uses of computers—doing whatever was necessary to make sure that the users actually found the machines valuable. Because computers, like the electromechanical equipment of prewar days, were rented rather than sold, IBM continued to have close long-term relationships with its clients. More than ever before IBM was a *service* company as well as a manufacturer, and because most of its top managers had come up through the sales side of the business, they were very sensitive to the needs of customers. IBM also enjoyed significant financial advantages over its competitors in the battle to please large corporate customers. It was extraordinarily expensive to make and service computers, not only because the hardware was costly to develop but even more because the manufacturer had to employ thousands of programmers, technicians, and salesmen to develop customized software for a customer and then help him iron out the problems that were sure to arise when the computer was installed. All major manufacturers had to bear these huge service costs, whether they had more than 70 percent of the market (as IBM did) or less than 5 percent (as nearly all its competitors did). But these costs were spread over far more machines for IBM than for its competitors, making it much easier for IBM to turn a profit.

IBM's mastery of the industry was also enhanced by the fact that machines were rented rather than sold. If it costs Computer Company X $1 million to design and produce a computer and it is rented to a customer for $200,000 per year, and if Company X depreciates the computer on a straight-line basis over four years, then it will experience a loss of $50,000 during the first four years ($250,000 − $200,000 = $50,000). In the fifth year the company will finally show a $200,000 profit because the computer has been fully depreciated but is still generating a $200,000 rental fee. But what if, at the beginning of the fifth year, the customer wants a new and faster computer like the one IBM has just developed? Computer Company X has the choice of supplying that new computer or losing a customer. Because it dominated the market, IBM controlled the product cycle of the entire industry and hence was able to do essentially this, manipulating the product cycle to its own advantage. In view of its long experience in data processing and the competitive advantages that it derived from having a dominant share of the market, perhaps it is not surprising that IBM vanquished almost all its rivals.

During the late fifties the computer industry became increasingly crowded as more and more corporate giants decided to grab a piece of this rapidly expanding market. Minneapolis Honeywell, Bendix, RCA, General Electric—one by one they staked major investments on the industry until by 1962 Business Week counted no fewer than fourteen companies battling for profits from computers. They were among the richest, best managed, most technologically sophisticated corporations in the United States, yet IBM held its own against them and eventually forced many of its competitors out of the industry. One reason for this success is that the company, as if to heed the warning of a famous Princeton historian that "nothing fails like success," constantly set new challenges for itself, running hard and scared instead of resting on past accomplishments.

Nothing illustrates this entrepreneurial, not to say reckless, instinct more clearly than the introduction of the 360 line of computers. By 1961 IBM was beginning to gag on its own success. Top management was becoming concerned about the disorderly proliferation of hardware designed and manufactured by different divisions of IBM, for it was straining the company's capacity to develop software and peripheral equipment (printers, disk drives, and the like) for all the different sorts of computers. Given this dilemma, most companies that dominated their industry would have adopted a cautious approach. But under the leadership of the volcanic taskmaster T. Vincent Learson, IBM decided instead to take a $5 billion gamble on revamping its entire product line. The corporation decided to develop a new series of machines, dubbed the 360 line, that would use integrated circuits rather than transistors; would serve the needs of both businesses and laboratories; would be compatible with the same peripheral equipment; and—most important of all—would use the same software. The advantages of such a move were manifest. A customer could buy a smaller machine in the 360 line, obtain the requisite software and peripheral equipment, and then, when he outgrew that computer, easily move up to a bigger 360 machine without changing software or peripheral equipment.

But to many IBMers the advantages were outweighed by the huge risks. The company would be prematurely obsoleting some very popular computers, it would be forced to enter the business of producing semiconductors, factory capacity would have to be vastly expanded, and the company's army of programmers would have to perform major miracles on the software front. This is how Learson summarized initial reaction to the proposal: "[T]hey thought it was too grandiose. The report said we'd have to spend $125 million on programming the system at a time when we were spending only about $10 million a year for programming. Everybody said you just couldn't spend that amount. The job just looked too big to the marketing people, the financial people, and the engineers. Everyone recognized it was a gigantic task that would mean all our resources were tied up in one project and we knew that for a long time we wouldn't be getting anything out of it."

For a harrowing period in the mid-sixties it looked as if the skeptics were right. The System 360 created acute friction within the organization and forced the corporate treasury to raise large amounts of cash in the money markets at unfavorable rates. Control Data and Honeywell came out with impressive competing products while the project was still in development. Moreover, software development was distressingly slow and expensive; because computer programs are such complex and tightly integrated logical constructs, they cannot easily be split up into manageable pieces that are developed by different individuals. Tom Watson once observed, "We are investing nearly as much in System 360 programming as we are in the entire development of System 360 hardware. A few months ago the bill for 1966 was going to be $40 million. I asked Vin Learson last night before I left what he thought it would be for 1966 and he said $50 million. Twenty-four hours later I met Watts Humphrey, who is in charge of programming production, in the hall here and I said, 'Is this figure about right? Can I use it?' He said it's going to be $60 million. You can see that if I keep asking questions we won't pay a dividend this year." But in the end the System 360 was a great success and paid very substantial dividends for the company. The scheme was excessively reckless, to be sure, and management resolved never to undertake another "You bet your company" project. But it was just the sort of bold move that prevents an industry leader from growing flabby, and it exemplified the corporate spirit that permitted IBM to prosper where virtually all its large competitors faltered. More than a decade later, when the microcomputer revolution threatened the company's position in the market, IBM again demonstrated its capacity to use unorthodox methods to stay on top.

HOW DAVID DEFEATED GOLIATH...REPEATEDLY

To be sure, it was not impossible to compete successfully with IBM. All one needed was a little money and a couple of geniuses—a business genius to develop strategy and run the company and a technical genius to design the product. Such were the key assets of the Control Data Corporation when it was founded in 1957. The builder of the company was William Norris, a tough and laconic engineer who, after growing up on a Nebraska farm during the hardscrabble thirties, did a stint in the X-ray division of Westinghouse and then worked on cryptography and electronic calculators for the navy during World War II. Wishing to avoid the breakup of the top secret unit at the end of the war, the admiral in charge of the project encouraged its continuation as a private company called Engineering Research Associates (ERA). A New York financier who was looking for a way to keep his Minneapolis glider plant busy in peacetime agreed to contribute the plant and advance funds to ERA in return for half the equity and the assurance of future navy contracts. The paths of Eckert-Mauchly and ERA, already developing along similar lines, crossed in 1950, when they both were acquired by Remington Rand. As we have seen, James Rand's strategic intuition was far better than his managerial touch. The engineers from ERA and Eckert-Mauchly quarreled often, and Remington Rand quickly lost its lead in computers to IBM, even though it had the better product. Eventually Norris was given control of Sperry Rand's UNIVAC division, but he was disgusted to find that all key decisions had to be cleared with top management in New York, where personnel turnover was high and computer expertise depressingly low. "We sat there with a tremendous technological and sales lead and watched IBM pass us as if we were standing still. When Remington Rand started breaking up the Univac Division part by part, I left."

But Norris did not leave alone. He took fifty other UNIVAC engineers with him and founded the Control Data Corporation in 1957. No slave to tradition, Norris raised $600,000 in start-up capital by selling stock directly to the public, without the help of an investment banker. He set up shop in an old paper warehouse in downtown Minneapolis and soon began to develop CDC's first major product, a large solid-state computer called the 1604 which was designed to solve complex scientific problems. Its intended market was a small group of highly sophisticated users, such as the Atomic Energy Commission and the Department of Defense, that were not well served by the business-oriented number-crunching machines sold by IBM. The company was a nearly instant success. In the late fifties and early sixties the 1604 and its successors swept the market for powerful scientific computers; CDC became the wunderkind of the computer industry and the heart throb of Wall Street. Just five years after being founded, it earned $1.5 million on revenues of $41 million, making it the third-largest company in the industry and the only one besides IBM that was turning a profit. While the corporate behemoths gradually dropped out of the race during the 1960s and early 1970s, Control Data continued to prosper, earning $47 million in 1976.

The company's secret weapon was a reclusive genius named Seymour Cray, whose ruling passion was building the world's biggest computers. Detesting the administrative distractions and organizational formalities that attended corporate life, he insisted on working ninety-five miles from company headquarters, in a secluded laboratory in Chippewa Falls, Wisconsin, where the major distractions were crows, woodpeckers, and an occasional deer. Working late into the night, often flat on his back with soldering gun in hand, Cray virtually constituted a one-man laboratory that not even IBM could match. When CDC announced a powerful new computer in 1964, Tom Watson wrote a sarcastic memo to IBM's research chiefs, pointing out that the Control Data laboratory contained "only 34 people including the janitor. Of these, 14 are engineers and 4 are programmers, and only one person has a Ph.D., a relatively junior programmer. . . . Contrasting this modest effort with our own vast development activities, I fail to understand why we have lost our industry leadership position by letting someone else offer the world's most powerful computer." The explanation, quite simply, was Seymour Cray.

But Cray could not have frightened IBM without the shrewd support of William Norris. The core of Norris's brilliance lay in what he decided *not* to do: compete directly with IBM on its own turf. As he once explained to a reporter, "IBM has a hammerlock on the business data processing market and we'd be fools if we thought we could get it away from them. You may have better equipment, but you can't get a hearing. Most purchasing men won't take a chance on shifting from IBM. It means their jobs if they're wrong." Therefore, Norris concentrated on selling large scientific computers, a product line that had three advantages for a small company like CDC. In the early years supercomputers were normally sold, rather than leased, and this arrangement accelerated the flow of cash into CDC's coffers—always a critical consideration for a start-up company. Because the market consisted of a few dozen universities and government laboratories, CDC did not have to field a huge phalanx of salesmen. The personal contacts of its highly experienced staff laid the groundwork for many sales. Moreover, sophisticated customers were willing to write their own specialized software, saving CDC a major expense that IBM's other competitors had to shoulder.

With Cray up at Chippewa Falls developing superior products, Norris focused on the market for scientific computers with courage and skill. He was a hard taskmaster and an obsessive planner, always pushing to stay ahead of the ubiquitous nemesis, IBM. Unlike many corporate executives, Norris was not afraid to take risks, for he believed that "a well-thought-out, bold course is least risky. In computers it's those who play it safe who are in danger." Since CDC's franchise lay in building the biggest computers in the land, a "bold course" meant pushing the product cycle as fast as possible, never allowing the Armonk monster to catch up. There were some tight moments, as when

CDC encountered delays in perfecting the 6600 machine while IBM's sly salesmen slowed orders for it by spreading the word (which turned out to be false) that IBM would soon be offering an even better machine. The first 6600s to be installed had unexpected flaws, and top management spent much of 1964 and 1965 flying around the globe, placating customers. Moreover, CDC had to pay steep fines to customers when it was unable to deliver some machines on time. For a while profits plummeted, and so did the net worth of CDC managers who owned large blocks of stock. But eventually the kinks were ironed out of the 6600, and it was a big money-maker. Partly to offset the risk of the product cycle, Norris diversified into peripheral equipment and eventually into commercial finance and time-sharing—renting computer time to small users.

Why did Control Data succeed in computers while so many large corporations failed? Having suffered at the hands of Remington Rand's top brass before founding his own company, Bill Norris minced no words in providing the answer. He derided top executives of multidivisional companies as absentee managers: "Control Data and IBM are the only two companies in the computer field making money because they're the only two just in that business. In computers the decisions are pretty big and must be made promptly. In big multidivisional companies like RCA, Sperry Rand, Honeywell or GE, top management is engrossed in many things and is not knowledgeable about the problems in the computer division." Such people, Norris argued, did not have the self-confidence to take the risks needed to thrive in computers because they did not have the thorough knowledge in which self-confidence is grounded: "To run a computer company, it's necessary to have top executives who understand computers. People are afraid of what they don't understand, and losing money makes a man doubly afraid. Top management in the conglomerates doesn't understand computers, and when the division is losing money, they won't take risks. They won't make the necessary budget allocations because they don't understand." But a total knowledge of computers did not merely steel a person to take the necessary risks; it also educated him to take the *right* risks. It was no coincidence that Norris was smart enough to avoid direct competition with IBM while the executives in the large companies did not. By the time he started Control Data, he was one of the most experienced men in the industry. He had a feel for computers just as Andrew Carnegie had a feel for steel, and Henry Ford for automobiles. Norris knew how to identify the right markets, how to retain key employees like Cray, how to develop a corporate strategy that fit this weird new business. Consequently, when Norris invested in a new business, he was using smart money rather than dumb money. When it came to making profits by selling computers, his $600,000 was worth more than GE's $250 million.

The experience of Eckert-Mauchly, Remington Rand, IBM, and Control Data epitomizes the financial dynamics of the computer industry from its inception to the present day. To succeed in this subtle and peripatetic business, where not only the technology changes constantly but so does the relationship between product and customer, money is not enough. It has to be smart money, money wielded by entrepreneurs and executives who have computers in their blood. More often than not this means engineers with a flair for business, the sort of people who took apart TV sets when they were thirteen, turned their college dormitory rooms into miniature computer centers, and made pioneering technological advances while they were graduate students. Such people have a special sense of the technology and the market—a superior dexterity that allows them to identify opportunities ahead of the crowd. Eckert and Mauchly had this gift; at a time when others viewed the computer as a sort of electronic elephant they perceived its many practical applications because they understood the technology better than anyone else—understood that the mammoth ENIAC could be shrunk down to the manageable UNIVAC. Eckert-Mauchly was a fairly well-run company, and if the supply of venture capital had been adequate in the late forties, it could have delivered its first machine to the Census Bureau, picked up more orders, and stayed in business. Instead, the company was snatched up by a conglomerate and smothered in a bureaucratic blanket, where it failed to turn a profit for sixteen years. Whether because of superior entrepreneurship, the stronger computer market of the late fifties, or other factors, William Norris was able to avoid this fate. After seeing his first company, ERA, mauled by Remington Rand, Norris started a new company with $600,000 and swiftly turned it into a major success.

Eckert, Mauchly, and Norris in effect grew up in a new culture that was alien to older businessmen. The great achievement of IBM in the 1950s, which is easy to underestimate precisely because it was so spectacularly successful, was to make a transition from the old culture to the new. Partly because of the fortunate shifting of leadership from the elder Watson to the younger, IBM recognized the threat posed by computers and reacted in time, pushing aside the electromechanical past in favor of the electronic future. But it is clear that a fundamental reason for IBM's success during the fifties was that it understood the market for large data-processing equipment better than its competitors *because that was its only market.* As we will see, this pattern continued to characterize the computer industry for the next two decades.

It is an old story, really—reminiscent of the mediocre performance of American Bell under the Boston Brahmins or the failure of most Wall Street operators to build successful auto companies. In fast-moving high-tech industries, the spoils go to the nimble specialist. Amateurs and interlopers had best stand clear. It follows that a successful system for financing new industries will allow these savvy specialists to get the capital they need in order to build a powerful company without getting ambushed by the likes of Remington Rand. In this respect the performance of the U.S. capital markets since World War II has been distinctly mixed. On the one hand, we have invented one of the most important financial institutions since the joint-stock bank: the venture capital firm. Such firms ensure that a promising small company making, let us say, micro-xonics gets the capital it needs to get off the ground, instead of suffering the fate that befell Eckert-Mauchly. But what happens to this micro-xonics company when it prospers and grows to, say, $400 million in revenues? All too many mid-size high-tech firms are acquired by corporate behemoths characterized by slow growth, plenty of cash, and very persuasive investment bankers. This acquiring firm is far from sinister. It is likely to be run by bright and competent managers who, however, know nothing about micro-xonics, have ten other divisions to worry about, and are accustomed to letting major decisions wait until the budget review at the end of the quarter. Bored and frustrated, the best employees of the target company jump ship and establish their own micro-xonics firm, precisely as William Norris and his associates did in 1957. Meanwhile, the acquiring firm is left with an unprofitable shell. In short, the micro-xonics firm was nurtured by the smart money of the venture capital firm but then poisoned by the dumb money of a giant corporation. This pattern is ubiquitous and alarming, for immense amounts of capital are stashed in the vaults of the Fortune 500. In July 1984, for example, General Motors, a prominent beneficiary of the Reagan tax reforms, had $9 billion in cash in its till—four times the total amount of venture capital raised in the United States in 1983, a record year. Over the next two years GM spent some of the money to acquire two major high-technology companies, Electronic Data Systems and Hughes Aircraft.

If this corporate cash continues to be dumb money, the United States can forget about remaining internationally competitive.

When it came to computers, the corporate cash of RCA was not dumb. It was idiotic—as the fine accounts by *Fortune* reporter Allan T. Demaree and computer historian Katharine Davis Fishman show. The RCA story highlights a major but inadequately appreciated cause of the mixed performance of corporate America since 1965: the conglomerate. A conglomerate is simply a corporation made up of a large number of divisions, each in a completely different business—car rentals, aerospace, bread baking, retailing, etc. Such a company can succeed, the logic of the conglomerator runs, because top management really doesn't need to understand the specifics of each of these industries. Rather like a portfolio manager who runs a mutual fund, all it needs is a basic understanding of the business, together with good general management skills and a big corporate bureaucracy to keep in touch with the far-flung empire. Unfortunately conglomerates rarely work well, particularly when they try to compete in fast-changing high-technology industries.

Long a major factor in the electronics industry, RCA prospered in the early sixties because it dominated the market for color television, a field that RCA founder General David Sarnoff had pioneered. In the late sixties the general passed the leadership baton to his son Robert, a polished and cultured man, prominent in Manhattan social circles, who had spent the bulk of his career in RCA's television network, NBC. Upon taking full command of the corporation in 1968, Robert Sarnoff discovered that his father had given him a very difficult job. Because the elder Sarnoff had kept color television prices high while underinvesting in new plant and equipment, RCA earned good profits in the short run but made itself vulnerable to foreign competition, notably from Japan. RCA was destined to lose its share of the color television market for years to come. With this crown jewel losing its luster, RCA needed a fresh business plan if it was to maintain its traditional growth rate. Sarnoff's new strategy had two prongs. On the one hand, he shifted the company's emphasis from technology to marketing because he believed that major technological advances in consumer electronics were unlikely over the next few years. He recruited a top Ford Motor executive to serve as marketing vice-president, and he built up a large staff at RCA's Rockefeller Center headquarters to identify promising areas for expansion. At the same time RCA, with the help of investment bankers Lazard Frères and

Company, acquired four consumer-oriented companies: a carpet manufacturer, a real estate company, a maker of TV dinners, and Hertz Rent-a-Car. Much to the credit of RCA and its banker, these acquisitions were quite successful.

The second prong of RCA's new business strategy was to make a major push into computers. The company resolved to seize 10 percent of the U.S. market and become the number two manufacturer within a few years. RCA was no stranger to computers—it had been making them since 1953—but it had lost money in the business for a decade, and in 1968 its market share was a pathetic 3 percent. But by beefing up marketing and investing heavily in the data-processing division, RCA intended to make a great leap forward, turning itself into "a major multinational enterprise doing business principally in computer-based information systems." Computers, in effect, were to replace television as the leading growth division of RCA; Sarnoff, Jr., would replicate the triumph of Sarnoff, Sr., but in a different medium. It was a bold strategy, to say the least. Why would a company that was ostensibly moving *away* from technology in favor of marketing make a major commitment to the high-tech, high-stakes computer field? Why did RCA think that it would be notably more successful in challenging IBM in the next five years than it had been in the past fifteen? Given its recent spate of acquisitions, did RCA have the capital needed to succeed in computers? Might not management attention be spread too thin? The fact is that many of these questions were not squarely addressed by Sarnoff and his board of directors, in part because they believed that marketing savvy—not technological superiority or financial strength—was the key to winning in the computer market. One suspects that a major reason for this misconception was that neither Sarnoff nor any board member had firsthand experience at making and selling computers.

RCA's leaders were following a national trend in downplaying the importance of specific industry experience, for these were the go-go years on Wall Street—the era of the mutual fund mania, the high-flying conglomerates, the flimsy little "growth" stocks selling at eighty times' earnings. Fast-moving conglomerators astounded analysts with their slick financial legerdemain. By exchanging the high-priced common stock of their companies for the cheaper stock of less glamorous corporations, conglomerators simultaneously delivered a fat profit to the shareholders of the acquired companies and raised the earnings per share (and hence the stock prices) of their own enterprises. In the process such companies as LTV, ITT, Gulf + Western, and City Investing placed under one roof—or, at least, one board of directors—operations as diverse as (in ITT's case) baking bread, selling insurance, renting cars, and operating telephone systems. Prevailing Wall Street wisdom held that a good businessman could take ostensibly unrelated businesses and generate "synergies" that made the whole corporation more valuable than the sum of its parts. The precise mechanics of this managerial magic were never fully explained, but so long as the stock prices of conglomerates were soaring that did not much matter—least of all to the investment bankers, block traders, security analysts, and fund managers who made millions in the conglomerate game. Industrial ignorance, these promoters argued, was not necessarily a vice; conglomerates actually strengthened the American economy by replacing stodgy managers who had mastered the operations of a particular industry with fast-moving, farsighted "entrepreneurial" businessmen who were not overburdened with detailed knowledge. Summarizing this viewpoint in 1968, *Business Week* wrote, "The business schools are creating a generation of managers who believe that effective management techniques transcend industrial categories. . . . [Diversification] liberates management's thinking about expansion: Uncommitted to any individual industry, management can swing capital quickly into any business field that looks profitable enough." This was precisely what RCA's board was doing when, after moving into the rug, car rental, convenience food, and real estate fields, it made a major bet on computers.

The man hired to make RCA the nation's number two computer maker was L. Edwin Donegan, a charismatic midwesterner who had cut his teeth at IBM. Donegan was hired in 1968 to be sales manager of the computer division, where revenues had been missing targets by a wide margin. By vastly expanding the sales force and pushing salesmen hard, he got results. The computer division's new strategy was derived from a study conducted by Arthur D. Little, Inc., a leading consulting firm. ADL's central conclusion was that IBM would soon be announcing its new 370 line of computers, and RCA would have to come out with a competing line within a year of that announcement. Lacking the time, capital, and talent needed to duplicate IBM's mammoth development effort, Donegan decided simply to revamp RCA's *existing* Spectra line of computers. He would lower their prices, change their exterior casings, expand the computer memory, give them a new name, and sell them to customers. Would this really be enough to compete with IBM's technical innovations? Donegan certainly thought so—in part because he agreed with his colleagues that market-ing, not technology, was the key to success in computers. Unfortunately customers thought otherwise. When IBM's System 370 was an-nounced, it turned out to be decisively superior, on a price-performance basis, to RCA's reconditioned Spectras. Since RCA and IBM machines were compatible in terms of software, customers could easily trade in their RCA Spectras for IBM 370s, and businesses were particularly eager to get good hardware values in 1970 because the economy was in a recession.

Poor sales were only the worst of Donegan's problems. RCA's com-puter division encountered great difficulty in developing software that was compatible with both IBM hardware and older RCA machines. Donegan's free-spending ways greatly inflated the division's costs, and there was no little friction between old hands on the staff and the horde of IBMers whom he recruited. Worse still, the sloppy and optimistic accounting rules that RCA used to book revenues when leasing com-puters partially masked the division's poor performance. Donegan later admitted, "I hadn't seen what was happening. The group financial staff hadn't seen it. The corporate financial staff hadn't seen it. The outside accountants who were in our skivvies hadn't seen it. The trouble was they were all used to seeing a cash sales business [rather than a leasing business]."

In December 1970 work began on a business plan for the upcoming year, which was to be presented to the RCA board in January. Donegan pressured his staff to make revenue projections showing the computer division breaking even in 1971, but a few recalcitrant staff members objected that such estimates would be wildly misleading. Finally Done-gan called Sarnoff to say that the plan would be six weeks late; in fact, it was not presented until June. Meanwhile, the pace of events began to accelerate. Board members bombarded Sarnoff and his top aides with pointed queries about the progress of the computer division. Rumors that RCA's computer business would be sold at a gigantic loss to Xerox circulated on Wall Street. To bolster the company's credibil-ity, Sarnoff appointed a new president who would have direct oversight of the computer division. And to rally the troops in the valley of adversity, a two-day meeting filled with inspirational addresses was held. But there was little to cheer about—certainly not from the revised business plan, which conservatively anticipated a $37 million loss in the coming year. As the summer of 1971 wore on, memos flew back and forth at corporate headquarters, pointing out that as much as $1 billion in fresh capital would be needed before RCA could turn a profit in computers. And it was far from clear that a continuation of the frontal assault on IBM would eventually be successful. Who could be sure that another billion dollars would be enough to wrest market share from the Armonk monster? The only prudent course, Sarnoff and the board finally concluded, was to take a $490 million write-off of the computer division, a move that eliminated no less than a quarter of RCA's net worth. Presumably this was not the outcome that Robert Sarnoff had in mind when he originally set out to do with computers what his father had achieved with color TV. But Sarnoff nevertheless discovered a comforting parallel: "A hell of a lot of people disagreed with my father going ahead with color. It took a certain amount of courage and guts and he stayed with it. There is a kind of a parallel in a way. It took courage to get out of computers."

Not just bastions of mediocrity like RCA were victims of the Goliath syndrome; so were several of the finest corporations in the land, including such thoroughbreds as Xerox and General Electric. Xerox made the monumental error of paying $918 million in stock for a flashy little company the expansion of which was peaking and which did not even make the business computers that Xerox needed to compete in the "office of the future." Xerox abandoned the mainframe business just five years after entering it. As for GE, it had a fine opportunity to enter the computer field very early in the game, long before IBM had built up an insurmountable lead. In 1955 General Electric accepted a $50 million electronic data-processing job from the Bank of America, but after fulfilling the contract at a loss, GE decided to stay out of the industry. The decision was all the more surprising because in the 1950s GE used more computers in its own plants and laboratories than any other company. To be sure, top management frequently toyed with the idea of making computers—"it is a business that we decided not to get into three or four times," an executive later admitted—and eventually GE changed its mind and took the plunge, bringing to bear all its financial and technical might and more than a little arrogance. Observed one executive in 1963: "When you look around, who else is there? This is a blue-chip, $2 billion a year business that takes a lot of money and a lot of technical and marketing ability: it fits GE in every respect. We are prepared to spend whatever is necessary to insure success in this business." The company never found out how much capital was needed to "insure success," but by 1970 it learned that it was well over $250 million—the amount of money GE lost before selling its computer division to Honeywell.

GE's failure astounded many observers. "I was a computer salesman for IBM in 1956 when GE got its first big contract," remarked one. "The people at IBM, which was then less than a $1-billion company, were quaking in their boots." A member of Tom Watson's inner circle, groping to explain GE's poor showing, adverted to the familiar theme of *managerial focus* that William Norris also used to explain the Goliath syndrome: "GE thought that they could run computers like they ran every other division of their company. GE had the muscle, the financial muscle, and certainly the technical muscle. They just didn't understand the computer industry well enough and weren't committed enough to put marketing resources behind their computer business, and didn't have the management viewpoint of staying with it long enough to be successful in it." Or as John F. Welch, GE's present CEO, put it, "You would need somebody who knew and felt that business in his fingertips" in order to succeed.

Such people were available in the 1950s, but they were more readily found in universities and small start-up companies than on the organizational chart of a large corporation. A talented graduate student who grew up with computers could develop billion-dollar insights that no consulting firm or corporate task force was likely to think of. In the early 1950s, for example, a young researcher at the Massachusetts Institute of Technology named Kenneth Olsen worked on two giant computers sponsored by the Defense Department, the Whirlwind and SAGE projects. Because they were meant to provide data in combat situations, these machines could not operate in the conventional manner, with the user entering a batch of data and some computational problems into the computer and then coming back the next day to get the results. By the time a radar control operator had his answer, a Soviet bomber could have flattened Manhattan and returned to Vladivostok! What the Department of Defense needed was a truly flexible machine with which the user could *interact* on a minute-to-minute or "real time" basis. For example, if a radar operator spotted an object on the screen, he could type data concerning speed, position, head winds, trajectory, and a few other variables into the computer and almost immediately get an estimate of the location of its probable target. Though these interactive computers were developed for the military, one did not have to wear a uniform to appreciate the virtue of their flexibility. Olsen discovered that MIT students (in contrast with their use of the IBM computer on the floor below) took to the SAGE computer as ducks to water: "If you walked in there at three o'clock in the morning, the kids were doing what they do today with personal computers. They were all involved. These computers were so captivating that a number of times the administration thought of getting rid of them because people stopped washing, stopped eating, stopped their social life and, of course, stopped studying."

From this observation grew a multibillion-dollar company. Although Olsen did not have an acutely acquisitive personality, the cloistered life of academia began to pall after a while; he felt "there was one thing missing in research. Nobody cared." Moreover, Olsen had spent many months at an IBM facility in Poughkeepsie where SAGE was being built. There he found the art of management to his liking but was appalled by the waste and inefficiency that was tolerated in large corporations. Olsen thought that he could do better. So in 1957 he and a friend named Harlan Anderson decided to start an electronic equipment business. They drafted a business plan and took it to American Research and Development, Boston's leading venture capital firm. ARD continued the long tradition of Yankee financiers, stretching back to the exploits of Moses Brown and John Murray Forbes, of making intelligent long-term investments instead of being buffeted by the speculative passions raging on Wall Street. In 1946, as the financial difficulties of Eckert-Mauchly plainly show, the stock market was nearly moribund; Wall Street was providing little venture capital to small companies that were trying to commercialize the technical advances made during World War II. As we saw in Chapter II, three astute Bostonians—the president of MIT, the president of the Federal Reserve Bank of Boston, and the head of a leading investment firm—established ARD as one of the first venture capital firms in the United States that was not funded by a superrich family. Its mission was to provide long-term equity capital to high-tech start-up companies, and its guiding genius was a Frenchman named Georges Doriot who taught at the Harvard Business School. Calling himself a "doctor of childhood diseases," Doriot patiently nursed along the young companies he funded, giving them courage when times were difficult and seldom badgering them to achieve high profits as quickly as possible. He provided not only capital but plenty of practical advice, moral support, business contacts, and whatever else was needed to make a company successful.

After reviewing the proposal of Olsen and Anderson, the vice-presidents at ADR advised the young entrepreneurs to make three changes before presenting it to ADR's board of directors: "First was, don't use the word computer because *Fortune* magazine said no one had made any money in computers, and no one was about to. . . . Second, they suggested that five percent profit wasn't enough. You see, when we looked through Moody's it seemed that all the good companies made five percent. . . . So we promised ten percent. . . . Lastly, they suggested, promise fast results because most of the board is over eighty. So we promised to make a profit in a year, which we did." With the $70,000 that they received from ARD, Olsen and Anderson rented 90,000 square feet on the second floor of an old woolen mill in Maynard, Massachusetts. They called their company the Digital Equipment Corporation, and its first product was not computers but rather circuit modules that were used to assemble computers. For furnishings the duo made do with old lawn furniture and a rolltop desk. The circuits were developed in Olsen's basement and etched in aquarium tanks bought at a local pet shop. According to Olsen, "We frequently spilled the etch solution onto the furniture store below—I think we bought the same set of furniture several times." Unlike many high-tech entrepreneurs, Olsen and Anderson were not in a crazed rush to make their first million; they did not even hire a salesman for nine months. After making circuit modules for several years, they branched out into making relatively small and cheap interactive computers that were dubbed minicomputers, as distinct from the mainframes that were IBM's forte. In the early days most of Digital Equipment's minicomputers were purchased by engineers who needed small, durable computers that could be used for laboratory work without paying homage to the chieftains in the central data-processing room. These engineers knew a good piece of equipment when they saw it. Unlike the data-processing managers of big bureaucracies who dealt with IBM, they did not require large amounts of customized software, management advice, and supportive hand holding. They just wanted a good sturdy machine that they could interact with directly in the lab.

Thus Digital Equipment, like Control Data, steered clear of IBM's main product, the large business machine. But whereas Control Data went *over* IBM by making supercomputers that only a few huge laboratories could afford, Digital Equipment went *under* IBM by offering a piece of hardware that was both cheaper and more flexible than a mainframe. DEC's early minicomputers were too expensive to command a large market, but the introduction in 1965 of the PDP-8, which sold for $18,000, put the company on the path to rapid growth. As the cost of integrated circuits declined, the price and performance of minicomputers greatly improved, and demand exploded; by the late 1960s the versatile machines were ubiquitous in laboratories, factories, offices, and military installations. A major class of customer was the systems house, which bought minicomputers and peripheral equipment in large quantities; developed the software needed to solve a certain class of problem; and designed customized data-processing systems for a particular type of user, such as hospitals, banks, supermarkets, or catalog retailers. For systems houses the price and performance of minicomputers were all that mattered; they did not crave the feeling of security that came from dealing with IBM.

As the dominant factor in this booming market, DEC grew at a phenomenal pace, and by 1985 it was the second-largest computer maker in the United States with revenues of $6.7 billion. Like Andrew Carnegie, Henry Ford, and many other entrepreneurs, Olsen followed his gut instincts in building his company—and in the process flouted conventional dogma again and again. After going public in 1966, DEC was one of the hottest growth stocks of the go-go years, sporting a stratospheric price/earnings ratio. Yet when securities analysts came calling at corporate headquarters in Maynard, asking what DEC's projected growth for the next five years was going to be, Olsen insisted that growth was not a goal. As he saw it, DEC's business was to make superior computers; if the company did that, the growth would come naturally. Partly for this reason, Olsen refused to borrow heavily in order to speed Digital Equipment's growth and increase its return on equity. Even though this philosophy was the basis of DEC's enduring success, it was impossible to explain to most Wall Street analysts— rather like explaining to the Marlboro Man why smoking can be hazardous to your health. One securities analyst recalls "trekking up to textile-mill country outside of Boston where Digital made its home. Digital's management wasn't exactly a group of flamboyant promoters. In fact, they were colorless. The president, Ken Olsen, discussed canoeing with me, and bragged about his inefficient plant space that cost $2 a square foot to lease." After a while, Olsen recalled, "We gave up and just mouthed the words because they wouldn't understand."

Olsen's orientation toward the integrity of the product, as opposed to financial results, showed up in other ways as well. Instead of hiring salesmen and paying them on commission, he hired engineers and paid them straight salary: "It's demeaning to pay for something you imply a man won't do any other way. We hire qualified technical people. They haven't that tremendous drive for a sale, but there's more stability." In this spirit Olsen attempted to pattern his company after his alma mater: "There was an attitude and environment at MIT that we wanted to duplicate. It's hard to describe, but MIT was and, I think to a large degree, is a very generous, a very trusting, and a very challenging environment. That environment was one of the things we wanted to capture and bring to our own company." This determined effort to encourage engineering creativity, combined with the personal influence of Olsen himself and the policy of keeping engineers in small clusters, made DEC a congenial environment where truly talented researchers would be content and productive. Since the success of a high-technology company partly hinges on the effectiveness of its researchers, this phenomenon is a critical factor separating the Davids from the Goliaths. No matter how much money they have, giant multidivisional companies like RCA have a hard time attracting and retaining the crème de la crème of the engineering schools. Not surprisingly, such people gravitate toward well-focused, technically superior companies like DEC, where they will work for a pioneering engineer who built his own company—not for a salesman like RCA's Ed Donegan who is trying to "make the numbers" in order to please a far-off and poorly informed board of directors.

For anyone concerned about the future success of the U.S. economy, the spectacular success of Digital Equipment is worth contemplating because many of America's high-tech companies developed along similar lines. In the fields of computers and electronic instrumentation Control Data, Scientific Data Systems, Wang Laboratories, Data General, and Hewlett-Packard, fit this pattern as do Intel, National Semiconductor, and Advanced Micro Devices among the semiconductor manufacturers. All of these firms were Davids who successfully battled often awkward and ineffectual corporate Goliaths. A study by a consulting firm of the development of the semiconductor industry concludes, for example: "The history of [large] firms like RCA, PhilcoFord, GE, Westinghouse, and Sylvania points to the possibility that these firms were too tightly controlled and thus inflexible." The inflexibility of the big, rich corporations allowed the small firms to prosper, and the reasons for this success were surprisingly similar. To begin with, there was the Von Neumann factor—the presence of a technical wizard who single-handedly neutralized the tremendous amount of capital that a giant corporation can throw into its research and development effort.

For Control Data it was the reclusive Seymour Cray; for Digital Equipment it was Ken Olsen; for Intel it was Gordon Moore and Robert Noyce; for Wang Laboratories it was An Wang, who designed the magnetic pulsing device that was the basis of computer memory for twenty years. Secondly, each of these Davids had a strong manager who both ran the company on a day-to-day basis and made major strategic decisions as the need arose. Sometimes (as in the case of Digital Equipment or Wang Labs) this manager was also the company's technical wizard; in other cases it was a different individual. Either way, the critical element for success was that this top manager understood the technology and the market intimately and therefore could "guess right" when the company came to a fork in the road, with one fork leading to continued growth and the other to stagnation. During the early 1970s, for example, Wang Labs' key product was desktop calculators, but Dr. Wang realized that this market would soon be dominated by such companies as Texas Instruments that could make calculators cheaply because they produced their own semiconductors. So Wang Labs quickly moved from calculators to word processors, a field in which it rapidly developed a dominant position. Such a shrewd move was likely to be made only if the man at the helm understood the technology and markets perfectly and had the authority to act. A committee of corporate bureaucrats—especially if they did not specialize in electronics—was almost sure to make the wrong decision, if it made any decision at all. One of the chief competitors of Wang Labs in the mid-seventies, for example, was the biggest industrial company on earth, Exxon, which lost $600 million in office equipment before bailing out. The sources of Exxon's failure were straightforward and all too familiar: "Every move had to be reviewed and approved by oil men who just didn't understand the industry." Since smart engineers enjoy working for the likes of Dr. Wang and Ken Olsen, such companies tend to attract the best and the brightest and then encourage them to be imaginative. One engineer recalled how, upon reporting to work at Wang Labs, he met with the doctor: "The first words out of his mouth were, 'Take risks. I want you to feel free to try things. Even if they fail. If you do the same thing the second time, I'll figure you had a new twist. If you do it a third time, I'll fire you.' And he got up and left the room."

Without exception these companies started small and grew rapidly by selling stock, borrowing from banks and the bond market, and reinvesting earnings. Most of the companies that date back to the

1940s and 1950s were financed informally at first, often beginning in basements or garages. By contrast the younger concerns typically received their initial grubstakes from venture capital firms. Since they were in fast-growing noncyclical markets and sold rather than rented their products, profits mounted quickly once they had hit their stride. Reinvested profits might provide most of their early capital, but after they were well known, they could wait for the next bull market and sell stock to the general public at a very high price. All in all, these high-tech companies resembled the young auto companies far more than the railroads, steelmakers, and telephone concerns, for their capital requirements were not excessive and they accumulated profits very rapidly. Consequently they were not beholden to financiers or government bureaucrats—no doubt a source of long-term strength. The one group of financiers who were vital to the welfare of these supergrowth companies were the venture capitalists, the financial launching pads of high-tech America.

IX

The Industry
Without a Profit

The David and Goliath pattern of the computer industry, in which small and agile start-ups tended to outperform large corporations, raises important and disturbing questions about another vital high-technology industry: biotechnology. In stark contrast with computers or automobiles, small biotech companies cannot set up factories, quickly turn a profit, and then expand by reinvesting profits, selling stock, and borrowing. For reasons to be detailed shortly, they must wait many years and spend tens of millions of dollars before turning a substantial profit. Consequently many fine companies will be unable to survive this capital drought and will be forced to sell out to a large corporation—typically a chemical or pharmaceutical company—instead of becoming fast-growing independent companies comparable to Ford Motor or Digital Equipment. This raises the specter that these small companies will be smothered by the dumb money of big corporations, just as Eckert-Mauchly was. After all, they will be controlled by large, bureaucratic corporations the chief executives of which know little about biotechnology; even if all parties are as constructive as possible, the clash of corporate cultures and the confusion inherent in attempting to fuse two organizations may have disastrous results.

But although there are questions about its long-term development, the history of biotechnology powerfully demonstrates the remarkable ability of America's universities to invent, and America's venture capital system to finance, an entire new industry. The achievement is all the more impressive because substantial profits lie far in the future and belies the popular notion that U.S. investors are too impatient to take the long view. America's leadership in this sphere of industrial innovation is exceedingly important because within fifteen years biotechnology will transform a wide variety of fields, perhaps even more profoundly than the computer did. Doctors will be able to administer to cancer patients chemotherapy and radiation therapy with tracer bullets that hit only the malignant cells rather than the entire body. Chemical spills will be cleaned up with bacteria that gobble up the material. The Corn Belt will be moved north, and hogs will be grown to twice their present size.

THE SCIENCE

It is in the medical field that biotechnology will make its most useful and lucrative advances over the next decade. Insulin, for example, was until recently a mystery drug—mysterious enough, at any rate, so that it could be produced only by grinding up the spleens of human cadavers and extracting the hormone in a laborious and expensive process. And factor VIII, the blood-clotting agent that hemophiliacs lack, must be distilled from hundreds of pints of blood, making it so expensive that some patients must spend $10,000 annually for treatment. Not understanding the chemical mechanism by which the body produces these exceedingly complex organic molecules, scientists could not duplicate the process in the laboratory. Biotechnology has changed all that by transforming our understanding of how the cell works. The truth is that biotechnology is finally pulling biology up to the level of precision achieved by physics, chemistry, and mathematics centuries ago. During the seventeenth century, when Isaac Newton invented calculus and discovered the laws of motion, biological knowledge was so rudimentary that William Harvey scored a breakthrough by proving, contrary to Aristotle, that blood circulated from the arteries to the heart to the veins. During the next century a major issue preoccupying biologists was whether maggots and mice could be "spontaneously generated," as if by magic, by an open barrel of grain. Such biological ignorance found its most devastating expression within the confines of the doctor's office. In 1793, for example, a yellow fever epidemic struck Philadelphia, then the medical capital of North America. After extensive cogitation and discussion the city's distinguished medical fraternity responded to the calamity (which eventually killed a tenth of the population) by prescribing a painful battery of bleedings, enemas, and emetics that undoubtedly finished off many a patient who might have pulled through the fever itself. To save themselves from the double menace of the disease and the doctors, Philadelphians resorted to such measures as firing cannons at regular intervals, wearing pieces of garlic around their necks, lighting smoky fires in the streets, and filling rooms with dirt to a depth of six inches. Biological ignorance rested on the extraordinarily minute and complex nature of natural systems; scientists simply did not possess the tools needed to observe biological phenomena at the basic levels of the cell and the molecule. Not until 1867, when physics and chemistry had already given the world the telegraph, the railroad, the oceangoing steamship, and Bessemer steel, did Louis Pasteur discover the germ theory of disease. And not until 1953 did researchers discover DNA, the chemical that directs the workings of the cell and serves as the hereditary blueprint of all life. With that scientists began the long march toward synthetically creating the body's own antidisease mechanisms to restore health and prolong life. This was two millennia after Hippocrates proclaimed, "The physician's chief function is to make conditions propitious for the natural forces in the body to reach harmony and, therefore, health." Over the next three decades biology was revolutionized as researchers gradually came to understand how DNA directs the activity of cells. Biology finally caught up with physics and chemistry.

The United States has long been the world leader in biochemistry, thanks to generous funding of university research by the National Institutes of Health (NIH). During the 1950s and 1960s no one anticipated that experimental work on DNA would spawn a major new industry; the mission that sustained government funding amid the financial hazards of the Vietnam War, the War on Poverty, the inflation of the 1970s, and the Reagan budget cuts was the search for a cancer cure. Since cancer is the uncontrolled growth of cells, its treatment requires an understanding of how DNA regulates cellular reproduction and related functions. At the heart of the matter is a process known as protein synthesis. Cells, essential building blocks for all tissues, can be thought of as protein factories; the difference between a skin cell and a brain cell is largely a matter of what proteins they produce. What, then, is a protein? Essentially it is a chain of amino acids that is configured in a specific three-dimensional pattern. There are twenty-three different amino acids, which are simply different organic molecules. What sets one protein apart from another is the specific order of the amino acids in the chain. Now, since the nature of the proteins produced by a cell largely determines how the cell functions, and since the order of the amino acids determines the identity and characteristics of individual proteins, it stands to reason that the chemical that determines the order of the amino acids in the proteins produced by the cell will control the functioning of the cell itself. That chemical is DNA, the blueprint for the proteins produced by the cell. Various segments of the DNA molecule contain the blueprint for different proteins, and each of these segments is known as a gene.

Drawn schematically, DNA looks like a twisted ladder. The crossbars of the ladder are composed of not one but two pieces of wood that are flimsily nailed together in the middle of the step. Because the crossbars are loosely joined, the ladder can pull apart, rather like a zipper. The pieces of wood in the crossbar, which are known as nucleotides, come in four varieties, and the order of these nucleotides in the DNA molecule determines the order of amino acids in a protein. Protein synthesis is simply the process whereby the DNA molecule "unzips" and the order of the nucleotides in the DNA ladder is, through a series of chemical reactions, expressed in the order of amino acids in the protein. Since an individual protein contains hundreds of amino acids and a cell produces thousands of different proteins, DNA molecules are extremely long.

The outstanding characteristic of protein synthesis is its specificity. There is nothing random about the process. Every chemical reaction fits together with perfect precision. Once scientists understood those chemical reactions, they learned how to manipulate them and could turn the "protein factory" known as a cell into a little workbench for the industrial biologist. Instead of having to harvest insulin from a cadaver, scientists could open up a human spleen cell, snip out the gene (i.c., a DNA segment) that contains the blueprint for insulin, put it in a different and simpler cell, and induce this cell to produce insulin in large and extremely pure quantities. So, too, with a great many other valuable enzymes and hormones, including interferon (of which more below), the human growth hormone (which encourages growth in dwarfs), and the plasminogen activator (which dissolves blood clots). By slightly altering the DNA blueprint, biologists can systematically make changes in proteins as they search for a better compound instead of more or less randomly searching for improved medicines. Recombinant DNA or gene splicing, as this technology is known, is an extraordinary scientific breakthrough with currently unfathomable ramifications and uses—on a par with the computer or the steam engine. Just as Eckert and Mauchly quickly understood the widespread applications of the computer in aerospace, insurance, utilities, and department stores, so, too, have biochemists recognized the relevance of their work to pharmacology, chemistry, agriculture, and pollution control.

INSIDERS AND OUTSIDERS: THE DANGERS OF PROFIT PROCRASTINATION

The critical experiments in recombinant DNA technology were made in the early 1970s by scientists working, for the most part, in such major American universities as Harvard, Stanford, U.C.-Berkeley, and MIT. In the ensuing decade a substantial biotechnology industry, involving an investment of well over $1 billion and the creation of about 200 companies, has grown up in the United States to explore and commercialize most of the potential applications of the new technology. What makes this process remarkable is that even after four to ten years of operation, *very few of these companies have shown a meaningful profit* on invested capital. Until recently many of them, in fact, were not even shipping a major product. This is, of course, the exact opposite of the usual pattern in high-technology start-ups; most venture capital-backed companies are founded to commercialize one or two key products that are already under development. If these products succeed, profits will pour in, generating the capital for further growth while producing a good return to shareholders. Two factors prevented biotechnology from following this path. For one thing, the science was too undeveloped to quickly produce a brisk product flow; it is a long, long way from a handful of pathbreaking experiments in the lab to building a factory that can actually turn out a protein in large quantities. And even after a product has been developed, a company has to clear the Food and Drug Administration, which looms up before a small company the way Mount Everest overshadows a solitary mountain climber. It costs tens of millions of dollars and as much as five years of exhaustive work to carry out the clinical trials needed to satisfy the watchdogs at the FDA. Consequently even the best biotechnology start-ups have failed to produce fast profits. Genentech, the premier company, has been in existence for nine years, but its 1985 earnings amounted to only $6.4 million. We call this phenomenon profit procrastination—a financial characteristic that sets biotechnology apart from virtually all other high-technology industries.

The profit procrastination of biotechnology sharply reduces its attractiveness as an investment because a dollar earned *five years from now* is worth much less than a dollar earned *today*. If one reinvested the dollar earned *today* at 10 percent interest, compounded annually, it would be worth $1.61 after five years. Financial analysts normally express this relationship the other way around, by figuring out how much money one would need *today* to have $1 *five years from now*, assuming a 10 percent annual return. (The answer, known as the present value of a future payment, is sixty-two cents.) And of course, even this smaller sum is not a sure thing because much can go wrong in five years. In view of the costs to investors of profit procrastination, the ability of America's venture capital system to raise hundreds of millions of dollars for biotechnology speaks very well of its versatility and willingness to take the long view, contrary to the oft-repeated charge that America's private investors are too shortsighted to build new industries in competition with the Japanese.

Biotechnology's profit procrastination raises another danger as well —namely, the possibility that the smart money of the venture capitalists could be diluted by the dumb money of large corporations that are committed to the status quo. Over the course of American history, as we have seen, new industries have grown most explosively when they were controlled not by financiers, politicians, or entrenched corporate bureaucracies but rather by the entrepreneurs themselves. The railroads, the telephone, U.S. Steel, and the second-tier mainframe computer companies all suffered from association with businessmen and financiers who were outsiders to the young industries and did not really understand and respect their revolutionary potential. Even General Motors, despite its ultimate dominance of the auto market, was seriously endangered by entangling alliances with State Street and Wall Street. By contrast Carnegie Steel, Ford Motor, and most other auto companies, and the minicomputer makers all prospered because power was lodged with the entrepreneurs. The basis of this entreprenurial autonomy was fundamentally financial; funded primarily by reinvested profits, industrial expansion did not depend heavily on outside capital. In stark contrast, *profit procrastination has forced most biotech companies to form intricate and unwieldy alliances with giant corporations that are their natural competitors.* Thus, despite the tremendous technical promise of the biotech industry, it is far from clear that many small biotech companies will be able, in the manner of Carnegie Steel or Digital Equipment, to take their place among the Fortune 500. The industry may well suffer as a result, for large chemical and pharmaceutical companies are run by people who know little about biotechnology and have made massive investments in more traditional technologies that they will be disinclined to render obsolete swiftly.

The industry is dauntingly complex because it is comprised of dozens of companies with nearly identical names—Genentech, Genex, Genetic Systems, Genetics Institute, Amgen, Biogen, Cytogen, DNAX, Enzo Biochem—that cannot even be differentiated on the basis of operating results because in many cases they have none. Their product lines are a weird array of wonder drugs sporting such labels as alpha interferon, gamma interferon, interleukin-2, and cytotoxic glycoprotein immunoagents. Even security analysts know little about these products, which are sequestered in corporate and government labs. The key to unraveling this biochemical labyrinth is to recognize that the industry is broadly divisible into insiders, who are long on biochemical expertise but short on capital and general industrial know-how, and outsiders, who are in precisely the opposite predicament. These groups simultaneously need and fear each other; the financial history of biotechnology is basically the story of their cautious and complicated linkage.

The industry insiders are university-based scientists who have for decades been carrying on NIH-funded research at America's great research universities. Unlike a Henry Ford or an Alexander Graham Bell, they have academic rather than commercial perspectives. For them science is an obsession, and life an exhausting succession of days and nights in the lab punctuated by engrossing sessions of "talking science" with fellow researchers. For such people money is not the measure of things but rather professional recognition as reflected in papers published and prizes won. The best of these scientists do not lack for professional options and are hardly more interested in joining a large corporation than would be a member of the Soviet Politburo. It is not so much the suspicion of corporate capitalism—though certainly that is part of the problem—as an abiding distaste for what they perceive as the arid intellectual climate and stultifying hierarchy of the large company: "You are just a number in the parking lot, and so is your science." Location alone would dissuade most professors from joining corporations, which are not located in university towns such as Cambridge and Palo Alto. And since almost no biochemistry was practiced in corporate labs in the late 1970s, any biochemist who joined one would become intellectually isolated, out of touch with fast-breaking research developments that are often initiated by graduate students and postdoctoral fellows. This problem is compounded by the refusal of most large corporations to let their scientists publish or discuss research results, for a scientist cannot glean from colleagues the latest scientific scuttlebutt unless he has something to divulge in return.

While unimpressed by large companies, top university scientists were not averse to becoming associated with small entrepreneurial high-technology companies, comparable to Apple Computer or Intel, that operated on the frontiers of knowledge and were managed by scientists. Nor were they averse to becoming millionaires overnight. Thus, when venture capitalists came knocking in the late 1970s, leading biochemists were more than willing to listen to proposals about founding biotechnology companies. It was an attractive proposition with no downside risk. In return for lending their prestige and professional guidance to the new enterprises, the biologists received meaningful ownership stakes without risking their own capital or even abandoning the university. Thus Genentech was founded by venture capitalist Robert A. Swanson and scientist Herbert Boyer; the capital was principally supplied by venture capitalists and public investors, but blocks of stocks have been sold to several corporations. Biogen, a sort of international consortium of scientific superstars, was founded by Ray Schaefer, head of the venture capital subsidiary of Inco Ltd., the big Canadian nickel company, with the help of T. A. Associates, the Boston venture firm, which rustled up additional capital. (Significantly enough, Biogen's founders could raise little capital in Europe, even though most of its scientific board was European.) In this first round of financing the venture capitalists, as usual, played an essential catalytic role. They were in touch with new technical developments within the universities and had plenty of experience in recruiting scientific talent. At the same time they had capital to invest in the new enterprise, ties to other venture capitalists and corporations that would be willing to participate, and contacts with potential managers for the new companies. A major contribution of a good capitalist is to have a sixth sense in spotting personnel that can make the company a winner. Robert Johnston attributes the success of Cytogen in large part to research director Tom McKern, who, in addition to being one of the top ten scientists in his field, "turned out to be a very good manager in terms of building a research team and having a good intuition about what projects to focus on and what is going to be really significant. He really focused the company on this linker technology as opposed to actually manufacturing antibodies. It turns out they have carved out a very neat niche."

Not the least of the venture capitalists' contribution was their feel for how to squeeze capital out of Wall Street. The key to the vault was labeled "interferon." An obscure protein naturally produced by the human body in minute amounts, interferon was so difficult for researchers to obtain that it had eluded close study from scientists since its discovery in 1957. Nevertheless, investors, intoxicated by the new-issues boom of 1980 and intrigued by interferon's reputed efficacy against cancer and the common cold, gobbled up the initial public offerings (IPOs) of many biotechnology stocks in 1980 and 1981. Issued at $35 per share on October 14, 1980, Genentech's stock soared as high as $89 on the first day of trading. "Wall Street was obsessed with the issue of who would clone interferon first," recalls one securities analyst, even though its potential was unknown and it was unlikely to generate real profits for seven or eight years. And biotech infatuation was no six-month phenomenon; despite the absence of notable technical breakthroughs, a second cascade of biotechnology issues was willingly absorbed by investors in the high-tech boom of 1983. Notwithstanding the high risks involved, these biotech stocks were not inexpensive. According to a survey of twenty companies by *Forbes*, stock market investors (as opposed to the scientists, entrepreneurs, and venture capitalists who were also owners) paid in an average of 65 percent of the company's capital while receiving only 24 percent of the stock.

The biotech fever sweeping lower Manhattan gave dozens of companies the capital needed to explore the major potential applications of the new science, but it also demonstrated that for the entrepreneur easy money is tainted money. Some financiers fabricated low-quality companies to grab quick promotional profits, and the huge cash hoards of some companies spared them the necessity of formulating practical, disciplined, well-focused business plans. Recalls venture capitalist Robert Johnston, who founded two specialized biotech concerns: "There were a fair number of venture capitalists who looked around and said, 'Gee, if it is that easy to make money in that business, I want one, too.' And so they funded companies without a great deal of understanding of the technology or the strategy that never should have gotten any money. The quality of the people, both in a management sense and in a technical sense, didn't deserve it relative to other investments they [the venture capitalists] were looking at. But they said, 'If I fund it, I can take it public a year later and I'm off to the races.' " As for the major companies, "Almost every one took on projects where if money had been tighter they would not have taken it on. Often it was not a wise decision. The best example is Cetus, where they have cut back and are now focusing in on the pharmaceutical side of the business. You know if you want to be a pharmaceutical company and you have a hundred million dollars, that isn't a lot of money to be a pharmaceutical company. So you've got to focus. That is the essence of a small company. Management has to figure out what to focus on. Management has to have a gut feeling about the significance of different technologies —where to place your bets."

There were several reasons why some of the big companies such as Biogen and Cetus were slow to focus on a few key products. The potential applications of the technology, like the menu of a good New York deli, are so broad and diverse that it was tough to make a choice, and the companies had so much money that selectivity hardly seemed necessary. Early in 1984 even a security analyst, who is paid to fret about such things as cash flow and debt/equity ratios, commented: "There is plenty of money around. Some companies don't have to have a product out for five years." Moreover, the risks inherent in developing individual drugs made it only prudent to build a diversified portfolio of products. But there was also a more delicate and difficult barrier to disciplined specialization: the whims and desires of the companies' most valuable assets, their scientists. Top academic researchers were attracted to the leading independent companies by a somewhat naïve hope that they were joining scientific utopias. In 1980, for example, a scientist bragged that Biogen "is the only company in the world where scientists have their hands on the company's jugular vein." A top priority of these scientists was plenty of freedom to follow their research wherever it might lead, just as they had in universities. For some scientists a new-ventures department with a $6 million budget was "the most attractive part of Cetus. It helped bring in scientists who wanted to work in industry but didn't want to give up the academic milieu altogether." But as the company's cash hoard has been used up, this and similar programs have been cut back, causing some scientists to leave the companies and return to academia. "I'm a pure scientist at heart," affirmed the recently departed head of Biogen's European operation, "and in the past two years I found myself getting more and more involved in business." Biogen has suffered from its diffuse and unwieldy management structure, which includes both a large board of directors and a powerful board of scientists who are affiliated with a variety of universities in Europe and the United States. For a time the CEO was Walter Gilbert, a Nobel prizewinning Harvard biologist, but eventually he quit and was replaced by a seasoned executive in the pharmaceutical industry.

The second key factor that has blunted the focus of small biotech companies is their financial dependence on the giant pharmaceutical and chemical manufacturers. As the biotechnology revolution unfolded in universities and start-up companies during the late 1970s, big corporations found themselves in the alarming position of being outside spectators in the technical transformation of their own industries. Recalls Hugh D'Andrade, executive vice-president at drugmaker Schering-Plough: "There was an explosion of breakthroughs and a very rapid appreciation of their commercial importance. We didn't have, and almost nobody had, these kinds of people working in our laboratories. That occurred, coincidentally, with an explosion of interest in entrepreneurship. So that, when we looked around to see who could do biotechnology [for Schering-Plough], the people were all going out to set up their own companies—not coming to work for pharmaceutical companies." D'Andrade goes on. "There wasn't the time for the industry to say, 'Look, this is going on in universities and it might be interesting to us and let's hire some people who are now being trained . . . and then ten years from now, when this all becomes important, we will know what to do and will have people to do it.'" If the small biotech firms had had the financial characteristics of the early auto and minicomputer manufacturers, they could have used their proprietary knowledge to crash into established markets and grab a major share. Companies like Schering-Plough could have been frozen out of phase one of the biotech revolution.

But profit procrastination gave the corporate giants plenty of financial leverage over the start-ups. The biotech insiders in the small start-up firms needed the capital of the big firms just as much as big corporations needed the technology of the small firms. Schering-Plough, for example, invested in two small companies to gain a window on biotechnology. On the one hand, it bought into Biogen, which, according to D'Andrade, "came to Schering and said, 'Hey, how would you like to have an opportunity to have a call on this person in Edinburgh, and that person in Zurich, and this person in Geneva, and that person in Heidelberg, and this person in Berlin, all world-class scientists?' It was a terrific idea, and we signed up. Monsanto was interested. Inco signed up." Biotechnology was especially critical to the corporate strategy of Schering-Plough because the patent on its most important drug was about to expire, slowing profit growth dramatically. To help fill the gap, Schering made a major bet on alpha interferon. Biogen scientists did the research and development, while Schering concentrated on the arduous job of conducting the clinical trials needed to clear the FDA. But Schering's Biogen connection was ultimately disappointing, and not just because alpha interferon did not live up to expectations. D'Andrade admits, in effect, that Biogen was not such a "terrific idea" after all: "The strengths of Biogen—having all these international scientists all over the globe—are also its weakness, because that creates sort of a mishmashed confused system. . . . It doesn't have the organization and the clarity we would like to have. We have to start doing a better job at Biogen of imposing some of the disciplines of business on the talents of academia." The organizational diffuseness at Biogen was compounded by the fact that several other corporations besides Schering sit on Biogen's board. And the strains in the Schering-Biogen relationship go beyond Biogen's ethereal corporate structure, for the two companies are actually competitors as well as partners. Even as they cooperate in the development of alpha interferon, they are independently developing a separate version of the drug gamma interferon. "It is unusual for an investor to compete with its minority-owned subsidiary," D'Andrade observed. "There is a potential conflict between Biogen itself, and Schering. . . . We will deal with that conflict on an ad hoc basis."

Here lies the crux of the biotech paradox: Many small start-up firms like Biogen are partly financed by large firms that are their natural adversaries over the long term. There is nothing to prevent the big firms that have invested in Biogen and are represented on its board of directors from advocating company policies that are in their best interests but not in Biogen's. And what is true of Biogen—one of the biggest start-ups in the industry—is doubly true of smaller firms with less staying power that have been swallowed up entirely. Schering's other biotech connection, for example, is a wholly owned subsidiary called DNAX, a group of Stanford biochemists that Schering snapped up when it needed an infusion of capital. Schering's DNAX relationship has worked better than the one with Biogen because it is somewhat more simple: DNAX scientists are concentrated in Palo Alto instead of being spread around the globe, and there are no conflicts of interest because Schering owns the whole company. Still, there are complications. DNAX contains two groups of scientists: on the one hand, a scientific advisory board composed of eminent Stanford faculty members and, on the other hand, the actual scientific staff members, who work for DNAX full-time. Ideally the staff members will do the exacting gruntwork in the laboratory that is needed to commercialize the breakthroughs achieved by Stanford's famous scientists. (This work is not to be confused with the clinical trials for FDA approval, which would be done by Schering scientists.) Melding the world of academe and corporate America requires more than a little managerial tact. Observes D'Andrade of the Stanford scientists: "You have to massage them—and I don't mean that in a negative way, like they're children or animals—but they have to be respected, they have to have the opportunity for input, they have to be told what you're doing and why you're not doing what they think you ought to be doing. They don't expect—not *all* of them expect to have their way all the time—but they expect to be treated like adults, not like ivory tower idiots."

Schering-Plough's intricate alliances with DNAX and Biogen illustrate the dangers in biotech financing. Thanks to profit procrastination and the involvement of big corporations, the industry lacks the sharp and simple organizational clarity of a Ford Motor or a Carnegie Steel, where a few industrial revolutionaries, unencumbered by technological tradition or the interference of outside financial backers, concentrated on building a new industry. Instead of relying on reinvested profits and loans, the industry has depended on a dizzying succession of financial expedients: venture capital in the late seventies, the IPOs of 1980–81, the sale of shares to large corporations, the public offerings of 1983, joint ventures and contract research with corporations, research and development limited partnerships, and finally—if the cash began to run out—merger with a larger firm. Today the typical biotech start-up is partly owned by two to four large companies with which it is also pursuing joint ventures. Even if the large and small companies have identical interests—and they do not—such a convoluted array of financial expedients will blur a company's focus. The Stanford professors on DNAX's scientific board, for example, have dozens of outside commitments, ranging from university politics to landing their next government research grant. And Schering-Plough itself is run by people who are experts in organic chemistry rather than biochemistry, making strategic errors—such as the premature gamble on interferon—far more likely. Furthermore, the relationship can easily go awry if one or two people who set up the deal decide to change jobs. Then there is the simple fact that most large corporations lack the creative intensity, the lunging desire for financial success, that characterizes a good start-up firm. It is no coincidence that the leading biotechnology company,

Genentech, is run by a successful venture capitalist, possesses a relatively simple structure, and has managed to attract excellent young scientists who work full-time for the company. Staff members work hard because they are motivated by both equity participation and the chance to publish their results and receive full recognition from academic scientists. "If you visit a big pharmaceutical company at five-thirty, the parking lot will be empty, but if you visit Genentech at midnight, there will still be cars in the lot," notes one analyst. A top biochemist asserts: "Some of the companies have turned out remarkably good science. Genentech is probably, I think, the best example." It likely will be only the second company since World War II to become a major pharmaceutical company.

BOB SWANSON: THE VENTURE CAPITALIST
AS ENTREPRENEUR

Genentech had its origins deep within the venture capital community. Robert Swanson, Genentech's cofounder and CEO, was a partner at the venture firm of Kleiner, Perkins when he and Herbert Boyer created the company. Swanson had a chemistry degree and an M.B.A. from MIT. He began his venture capital training with Citibank in 1970 during the period when all the banks were creating small business investment corporations to take advantage of low-cost government-guaranteed lending programs for small businesses. He joined Kleiner, Perkins in early 1975, moving over from Citibank's West Coast venture office. "I had developed a fascination with the occurrences in the biotechnology field beginning with the fruit fly experiments in 1972," says Swanson. "This made me sort of an odd duck in the semiconductor-based West Coast venture community. With my background, though, biochemistry made more sense to me than all those electrons spinning around." Swanson believed developments were moving quickly and could see no reason why a company shouldn't be formed to capitalize on this new technology. "I went back to all the scientific papers I had read, pulled off the last name on the papers—that was always the senior scientist—and began making cold calls. Everybody said I was too early—it would take ten years to turn out the first microorganism from a human hormone or maybe twenty years to have a commercial product—everybody except Herb Boyer."

Herb Boyer was a professor of biochemistry at the University of

California at San Francisco and coholder of the Boyer-Cohen patents, which many claim are the basis for the whole biotech industry. A brilliant molecular biologist from the University of Pittsburgh, Boyer moved to California in 1967. He was a participant and a leader in the political protests of the day. He emerged from the period with a full professorship, an iconoclastic approach to the world, a passion for new ideas, and an ability to attract and excite others with his views. A hyperactive human being with strange work habits, he was intent on getting the new technology out of the laboratory and into the real world, where it could do some good. Boyer told Swanson he was intrigued with his ideas but was very busy; maybe they could get together for ten minutes late that Friday afternoon in January 1976. The ten minutes became a long beery evening and resulted in an agreement between Boyer and Swanson to create a partnership to investigate the commercial feasibility of recombinant DNA technology. The name of the venture was to be Genentech, short for genetic engineering technology—an appellation that came out of Boyer's head sometime after the fourth beer of the night.

Swanson went back to Kleiner, Perkins with his idea and proposed that the partnership continue to pay him while he and Boyer developed the business plan. "We kicked him out," Gene Kleiner says. "When you start a new company, you've got to be dedicated to the idea. We wanted to see how serious Bob was. It easily cost us twenty million dollars. We could have owned more of the company for less money if we had gone along with him." Dipping into his savings, Swanson worked with Boyer to develop a business plan and test the hypothesis that commercial products could be developed faster than anyone else expected. In May 1976 Swanson and Boyer made a formal presentation to the Kleiner, Perkins partnership. Genentech proposed to begin working with the California university system on the development of specific human pharmaceutical products. The California system provided for outside funding of proprietary projects using university personnel in return for royalties on any commercial developments. For Genentech this was a perfect arrangement because all the research was already being conducted in the university labs. The company would also begin doing contract research with the intent of generating cash while waiting for product development and ultimate regulatory approval. At the end of the meeting Kleiner, Perkins committed itself to a $100,000 investment for 25 percent of the company, thus valuing the total company at $400,000. Nine months later, with the first management and research teams in place, venture capitalists led by Kleiner & Perkins put in another $850,000, valuing the company at $3.4 million.

Seven months later, in the fall of 1977, the company announced the successful bacterial production of the human brain hormone somatostatin—the *first* useful product made by genetic engineering. "We shrank ten years into seven months," Swanson recalls. "I knew we could do it! We surprised everyone, including the venture capitalists who had wanted an opportunity to invest more money in the company at a low price." The vc's did put more money in—$950,000 for 8.6 percent, valuing the whole company at $11 million. The company began work on the production of human insulin and, once again, a year later announced success. Instead of developing human insulin independently, Genentech immediately licensed the product and technology to Eli Lilly to raise additional cash. Swanson had sound business reasons for following this apparently timid approach: "Lilly had eighty percent of the insulin market already. Even though our technology produced a much less costly product, there was no way they would give up market share without a fight. They also had the resources to see the product through to FDA approval. We had other exciting things going and didn't need the fight but did need the money." In 1984 Genentech followed the same approach with Factor VIII, the blood-clotting protein for hemophiliacs. Factor VIII produced by recombinant DNA technology provides a much purer product than the current source— human blood. Thus the risk of AIDS or hepatitis transmission is eliminated. Genentech has licensed the product to Bayer, a major supplier of factor VIII extracted from blood.

The first product to be marketed and manufactured by Genentech itself was Protropin growth hormone, which was first produced in 1979. On the strength of this breakthrough Genentech raised $10 million from Lubrizol, its first corporate investor, which placed the value of the total company at close to $70 million. Protropin, which counteracts dwarfism and other growth hormone deficiencies, did not receive FDA approval until October 1985, a full six years after initial production. It is now being administered to 4,000 children who had been receiving human pituitary-derived hormone until it was taken off the market in early 1985 because it was found to be related to a deadly virus. While less costly than its human derived counterpart, Protopin is still not cheap; $8,000 a year is the expected treatment cost. It is, however, pure and available. "We are confident that no child who needs it will go without treatment," Swanson states emphatically.

Other drugs that are making their way from Genentech's laboratories to the market include:

> *Activase t-PA*, a tissue type plasminogen activator, which dissolves blood clots in heart attacks. A study by the National Institutes of Health in March 1985 comparing t-PA with an existing thrombolytic, Streptokinase, was cut short because the early trials showed conclusively that t-PA was twice as effective and continuation of the study was deemed unethical. The drug has been called the Pac-Man of the circulatory system because it appears to dissolve clots almost instantaneously, thus significantly increasing the survival rate of heart attack victims.
>
> *Gamma interferon*, a drug for treating cancers and viral infections. While not a "magic bullet" that destroys specific cancers, it has been active in a number of leukemias, solid tumors, and viral infections. It also appears to produce a synergistic effect in combination with other anti-cancer agents including TNF—another Genentech development.
>
> *TNF, tumor necrosis factor*, which appears to be a magic bullet that destroys some malignant tumor cells without measurably affecting healthy cells. As Swanson says, "While gamma interferon inhibits growth of tumor cells and stimulates the immune system, TNF is more like the hit man of the immune system." It appears to kill the tumor cells by disrupting the membranes.

Genentech is working on pure vaccines for hepatitis, herpes, and AIDS, and it has engineered a microorganism that can reduce the number of manufacturing steps to make vitamin C from five to one. The company has also identified growth factors that are key to the formation of bone and cartilage and has isolated a hormone called inhibin which regulates the reproductive functions for both sexes. Not all these projects will end up as Genentech products. In fact, a key to growing a successful company will be to make disciplined choices about which products fit into a coherent and financeable strategy. At this stage in its growth the company has chosen not to fight head-on with the well-entrenched competition. Taking a leaf out of IBM's book, it will pay close attention to marketing by sticking with products that fill unique therapeutic needs and that are prescribed by specialists rather than general practitioners. "We can't serve every one of the four hundred forty thousand doctors practicing in this country," Swanson says. "Where we create broad-market products we will license the technology or sign marketing agreements as we did with insulin. We can develop a sales force to serve the sixty-six hundred cardiologists, the fifteen hundred oncologists, and the thousand pediatric endocrinologists. We can attract the best salesmen from the big competitors. We offer a pipeline of new exciting products." And, characteristic of the venture-supported companies, "we provide the salesman with a chance for equity participation." Will this approach work or will Genentech ultimately be swallowed up by one of the behemoths of the pharmaceutical industry or worse: by an unrelated company looking for high-growth diversification? Venture capitalist Gene Kleiner says, "Genentech has the best chance of making it on its own. They determined early a business strategy which included producing and marketing their own products. The others have realized that need too late. Bob Swanson started with a profit discipline which increased focus and avoided waste. Bob was also able to hire the best people and get out of their way at the right time in the company's development. This is where most entrepreneurs fail. If anyone can succeed, Bob will. He certainly deserves it."

Genentech's bright prospects have not gone unnoticed by investors. After selling about 12 percent of the company to the public in 1980 for $36 million, the stock has recently traded high enough to put a total value on the company of more than $2 billion! For a company with only $70 million in sales and $6.4 million in profits in 1985 it has a long way to go to justify the expectations reflected in today's price. Not surprisingly, Swanson considers the optimism justified. "Only five million dollars of our 1985 revenues were from sales of one of our own products —Protropin. I think we can do over a billion dollars of product sales sometime in the early 1990s, and the profit margins should be quite good. We do have a long way to go, though." As for Swanson personally, his holdings in Genentech are worth more than $120 million. "I want to see that billion dollars in revenue before I think about something different," he says. "It is true that once you arrive, you lose a little bit of the edge; . . . to me, arrival is the other side of a billion. . . ." Although his competitors in this new industry are a couple of laps behind him, the lack of immediate profits raises the specter of failure or absorption. But the promise of the science itself has been fully confirmed, and security analysts believe there is a four out of five chance that by 1990 five or six companies will be producing good financial returns, comparable to those of the early minicomputer companies.

We have focused on the pharmaceutical players in this game. The whole biotech industry may be broadly divided into three types of firm the financial profiles and corporate strategies of which differ radically: therapeutic companies like Genentech that produce drugs, diagnostic companies like Centocor selling products that identify diseases, and specialty companies oriented toward such diverse areas as chemical, agriculture, and pollution control. By far the most glamorous—the companies that are taking major long-term risks in an effort to slam financial home runs—are the therapeutic companies. A patent on a successful drug is a financial gold mine, enabling a corporation to charge a hefty price for a product that will be prescribed by doctors throughout the world. The fortunes of even a large pharmaceutical firm can be transformed by the discovery of one good drug, such as Smith-Kline Beckman's ulcer medicine Tagamet. The complexity of the problem, though, is highlighted by the fact that Tagamet has a molecular weight—the sum of the weight of all the elements in a single molecule —of 252. t-PA, Genentech's anticlotting drug, has a molecular weight of 60,000! The essence of biotech's financial sex appeal is the prospect that companies can produce and manipulate these complex molecules in order to produce drugs systematically, instead of using the conventional hunt-and-peck method. The big three therapeutic firms— Genentech, Biogen, and Cetus—have each focused on three or four key drugs. But with the high potential reward goes proportionately high risks, from both the scientific uncertainties and the years of clinical trials needed to clear the FDA.

For diagnostic companies, by contrast, the risks and the rewards are lower. Instead of developing drugs, they are producing diagnostic kits —such as tests for pregnancy or for herpes—that in many cases compete head-on with products already on the market. The technology is simpler, the regulatory delays are smaller, and a diagnostic company can ship product much more rapidly than a therapeutic company; but financial home runs are unlikely.

As for the specialty biotech companies, they face the special problem of serving markets that, in many cases, are intrinsically less lucrative than medicine. Whatever the merits of its product, a company developing a hardier variety of wheat or a way to recover oil from old wells may not make much money while oil and grain prices are low. It does not pay to make a better mouse trap if no one is currently catching mice. And as usual the small size of most start-ups makes any corporate strategy intrinsically riskier. For example, the Genex Corporation, which uses enzyme technology to produce specialty chemicals more efficiently, invested $30 million in a plant to produce aspartic acid, nearly all of which was sold to G. D. Searle & Company for use in its artificial sweetener aspartame—until Searle severed the relationship. In the wake of that disaster Genex has slashed its payroll by more than two-thirds.

As the biotechnology industry has taken shape over the past eight years, Wall Street has looked on with great interest and no little naïveté, creating opportunities for the shrewd investor. Biotech stocks are volatile in price not only because their market capitalizations are usually small but also because they have no earnings record or dividends. Their intrinsic value is derived from the future promise of their technology. Despite the best efforts of securities analysts, no one can forecast very accurately the scientific pitfalls that lie in the path to profitability. So when investors are high on high technology (during new-issue booms, for instance) and inclined to view technical uncertainties in a rosy light, the stocks rise in price. Other favorable developments, such as the acquisition of two biotech companies in 1985, can also lift the prices of these volatile stocks. But when the high-tech sector of the market is depressed and industry developments are discouraging, biotech stock prices may decline substantially. Moreover, any industry with dozens of small companies and a development period of five to six years will inevitably experience a number of bankruptcies and pass through periods with more than their share of disappointing news. This is the time to buy the stocks—when the news is bad and investors are bored with biotech. Then promising companies can be purchased at discounts of 20 or even 40 percent. As for deciding which stocks to buy, quality is the key. These companies are running a marathon in which a multitude of losers will drop in the gutter while a few firms reach the finish line and make big money. Very few individual investors are qualified to sort out the probable winners and losers.

Unlike the industries already discussed, in which, with hindsight, we can see all the brilliant moves and horrendous mistakes, biotechnology is still in its infancy. Investments today are the closest an investor can come to venture capital in the public marketplace. Genentech could well be the winner here—the Ford Motor of the biotech industry—but who really knows? The one saving grace about investing in this industry is that the level of knowledge in the professional investment community is not very far above that of a well-informed individual. What we do know is that developments here will change our lives as profoundly as the telephone, the automobile or the computer. With that in mind—and contrary to our preferred approach—one should invest in biotech the way Billy Durant approached the early auto industry: by purchasing a diversified basket of issues that should eventually contain some of the superwinners. In this case the chase could be as exciting as the victory.

X

Lessons of History for Wall Street, Main Street, and Pennsylvania Avenue

Even though each industry discussed in this book differs markedly from the other five, a careful analysis of how they were initially financed produces an illuminating composite sketch of the best way to finance a new industry in the United States today. The outline of this portrait becomes clear after seven key features have been drawn in:

1. *Rapidly growing high-tech industries are no place for interlopers and amateurs.* The most successful companies are typically run by entrepreneurs who have an intimate firsthand knowledge of a revolutionary technology and the markets it serves. They have a visceral feel for the industry, appreciate its revolutionary character, and are committed to its long-term prosperity. Far from being flaky prima donnas who can barely manage a lemonade stand, many of these pioneering industrialists have the capacity to turn a small start-up into a billion-dollar enterprise. Examples include Cornelius Vanderbilt, Andrew Carnegie, John D. Rockefeller, Henry Ford, William Durant, Thomas Watson, Kenneth Olsen, An Wang, William Norris, and—one suspects—Robert Swanson of Genentech.

2. Since they usually lack extensive business experience or formal financial training, *these industrialists can benefit tremendously from the assistance of venture capitalists who offer not just money but smart money.* Smart money is imbued with hands-on experience in getting a start-up enterprise off the ground. During the nineteenth century it was supplied, in an informal and often unsatisfactory way, by wealthy businessmen; since World War II its best source has been venture capital firms.

3. But financial advice is not to be confused with managerial

meddling or financial control. *Once outside financiers sink their hooks into a revolutionary enterprise, they very often warp its development to meet their own private ends, thereby damaging the industry's long-term progress.* So it was with the Wall Street gunslingers who exploited railroads; the investment bankers who created the mediocre conglomerate known as U.S. Steel; the Boston Brahmins who milked American Bell for dividends until service became so bad that they had to sell out; the many financiers who dabbled in automaking with little success; and the battery of blue-chip corporations that lost fortunes in the computer business even as entrepreneurs were waxing rich from minis and micros. Thanks to profit procrastination, which is forcing small biotech companies into the arms of major corporations, biotechnology is in danger of falling prey to the Goliath syndrome.

4. From the securities boom touched off by Alexander Hamilton's Report on Government Finance in 1790 to the high-tech bubble of 1983, America's *new industries have been financed most expeditiously in short and spectacular speculative spasms* that invariably chasten all but the nimblest investors. Consequently industrial innovation slows dramatically when depression, inflation, war, or misguided tax reforms depress stock prices for extended periods of time (e.g., 1837–44, 1873–78, 1929–49, 1973–78). This is a key reason why the stock market is more important to economic development than many economists appreciate.

5. *Competition is the creative lifeblood of new industries.* Any constraining financial arrangement, such as domination of the telephone industry by Brahmin financiers or (potentially) control of the space industry by NASA, is virtually guaranteed to impede its development and damage its quality.

6. *The critical intellectual underpinning of industrial innovation is high-powered basic research,* often of the most abstruse and apparently uncommercial kind. Who would have thought that Alexander Graham Bell's experience in teaching mute children would have paved the way for inventing the telephone, or that a mammoth network of vacuum tubes designed to make artillery calculations during World War II would become the most revolutionary invention of the late twentieth century, or that basic cancer research would create a dynamic new industry long before it found a cure for cancer? These developments cannot be foreseen and receive limited

financial support from corporations; they must be encouraged by liberal funding of the *best* scientists in the country.

7. Great growth companies—and here Carnegie Steel and Digital Equipment are preeminent examples—do not bend to the erratic gusts of opinion that blow through Wall Street. Run by hard-driving executives who are *obsessed with serving customers, minimizing costs, and maintaining a technological edge* over the competition, they plan and invest for the long term.

From these seven principles emerges a true-to-life sketch of how industrial innovation is successfully financed in the United States. A smart engineer undertakes pathbreaking federally funded research in a major university or large corporation, starts a company with the expert assistance of a venture capital firm, and later takes the company public at a munificent price in the midst of a new-issues boom. Because expansion is funded primarily by reinvesting profits, *the company remains independent.* It does not merge with a giant corporation, become entangled with the federal bureaucracy, prematurely distribute profits to the coupon clippers of Wall Street, or warp its long-term strategy to please investors by smoothing out dips in its earnings and stock price. Nor does success stunt the growth rate of this hypothetical firm; even as revenues blossom from $2 million to $2 billion, *the company remains tightly focused* on the tasks of developing new products, expanding into new markets, providing superior customer service, and minimizing costs. Instead of playing not to lose, the company plays to win. It is willing to take risks in order to keep growing, just as IBM did with its System 360 gamble or Carnegic Steel did by purchasing new mills in the middle of depressions. Finally, management knows that the guts of any enterprise are people, and winners do not come cheap; employees are paid well for superior performance while top management owns a major stake in the company.

THE TWO STAGES OF FINANCING NEW INDUSTRIES

If the United States is to remain the leader of the world economy, many more new industries must be intelligently developed along these lines. In this chapter we outline specific steps that should be taken to ensure that this occurs. Although we have had to range widely over a number of areas, our central conclusions can be summarized briefly. The good news is that *America's system for creating high-tech start-up companies works very well today, giving us a valuable edge over foreign competitors. Because this system is not broken, it should not be fixed.* A formal industrial policy would, for example, almost certainly do more harm than good. But because the venture capital system is informal, uninstitutionalized, and dependent on a healthy stock market, it can easily be damaged by misguided economic policies, just as it was in the 1970s. Care must be taken to ensure that this does not happen again.

The bad news is that *the* second *stage of America's industry creation process, in which a successful start-up company with $100 million in revenues grows into a powerful corporation with $2 billion in revenues,* does *need to be improved substantially.* It is not too much to say that the United States is in danger of becoming a sort of high-technology nursery for the rest of the world that conducts pathbreaking basic research and creates the companies that commercialize the new technology only to see foreign companies move into these new industries and create multibillion-dollar corporations. A comprehensive remedy to this problem would have to touch on a host of economic and social issues, including education, immigration, patent laws, trade policy, funding basic research, fiscal policy, and America's excessive litigiousness. Here we will restrict ourselves to one central aspect of the problem: capital formation. To avoid becoming a high-technology greenhouse for the rest of the world, the United States must invest aggressively and effectively in its high-growth industries in order to make them low-cost producers that can dominate world markets. This goal has both a quantitative and a qualitative dimension. Not only must capital be available in abundance, but it must be smart money. Thus there are two issues:

Capital creation—generating a sufficiently high savings rate for the entire U.S. economy. Here the central issues are the federal tax code and the budget.

Effective capital transfer—successfully shifting funds from low-growth parts of the U.S. economy to high-quality growth companies that will employ the funds effectively. This goal concerns not only tax and budget matters but also trade policy, corporate restructuring, and the recommendation of some analysts that we adopt a national industrial policy.

AMERICA'S VENTURE CAPITAL SYSTEM:
A UNIQUE COMPETITIVE WEAPON

To appreciate fully the value of America's venture capital system, one should view it from an international perspective. Venture capitalism gives the U.S. economy a creative, hard-edged, forward-looking dynamism that few nations can match because it is firmly rooted in the distinctive virtues and vices of the American people. No other country possesses the economic conditions, institutional arrangements, and national personality quirks that have allowed venture capitalism to flourish in the United States. In this regard America's most important advantage is a willingness to take risks, a propensity as old as the nation itself. Many of the original thirteen colonies were founded, after all, by joint-stock companies bankrolled by optimistic English investors. Pennsylvania was an elaborate real estate development project that made William Penn's descendants far too wealthy to remain upstanding Quakers (they joined the Church of England), and the explosive growth of seventeenth-century Virginia rested on a sordid scramble for the brown gold known as tobacco. Up until World War I the United States continued to be peopled by ambitious immigrants eager to take their chances in the New World in order to raise the quality of their lives or at least their standard of living. Far from all being downtrodden fodder for sweatshops and steel mills, many immigrants—John Jacob Astor, Andrew Carnegie, Alexander Graham Bell, and An Wang come immediately to mind—became leading entrepreneurs. Foreigners have consistently supplied a major share of America's business talent, as have their upwardly mobile descendants. And the immigrant experience was echoed in succeeding generations by the pioneer experience, for as the eastern states became ever more crowded, Americans packed their bags and headed west. Consequently nineteenth-century Americans were a rambunctious, roving, polyglot people whose frenetic acquisitiveness consistently blighted their manners and morals. The unbecoming materialism of Americans—their tolerance for risk and wrenching change—has not much abated, in part because enterprising immigrants continue to stream across the nation's borders. Thus the country is not lacking the aggressive investors and pushy entrepreneurs who make the venture capital process work.

Thanks in part to America's heavy military responsibilities, its entrepreneurs operate on the forefront of technology. This, too, is nothing new. A chronic labor shortage has traditionally pushed U.S. businesses to automate, a tradition typified by Benjamin Franklin, Peter Cooper, Thomas Edison, Alexander Graham Bell, and Henry Ford. But a turning point was reached during World War II. Since the development of the atomic bomb and the computer in the 1940s American technology has consistently benefited from fruitful cooperation between the Pentagon, academia, and corporate America. More recently this pattern has been duplicated in the areas of space exploration and biological research. Radar, semiconductors, lasers, minicomputers, nuclear energy, artificial intelligence, genetic engineering—it is hard to think of a major innovation that was not inspired or accelerated by this three-way cooperation. Star Wars will undoubtedly add some new technologies to the list; for that reason European corporations are eager to participate.

It is not just the billions of dollars thrown around by the federal government that explains the success of America's research triumvirate. American universities deserve much of the credit. Their openness and creativity, their comparative freedom from hierarchy and bureaucracy attract first-class minds from around the world. Since World War II the United States has won 114 Nobel Prizes in science, compared with 39 for Germany, 15 for Great Britain, and 6 for France. Apart from the pernicious tenure system, which invites professors to rest on their laurels after the age of forty, American universities operate on a strict merit system. The research labs of MIT, Stanford, Harvard, and other great universities are packed with ferociously ambitious young scientists who are scrambling to make breakthroughs that will win promotions or renewals of their government research grants. These researchers are nearly as entrepreneurial as venture capitalists or investment bankers, but their quarry is more fame than fortune. In defense-related fields university researchers frequently cooperate with their counterparts in government and corporate laboratories, and as the history of biotechnology demonstrates, they have shown no aversion to founding corporations on their own. Although adequate funding is very important, the key to the universities' contribution is that they have the *best people;* twenty mediocre minds are worth less than one genius. This explains why the billions of dollars spent in government-funded labs produce far less payoff than comparable expenditures in universities.

A third reason for the success of U.S. venture capitalism is the financiers themselves, as we have already noted. Suffice it to say here that it has taken more than three decades of hard experience for the American venture capital community to attain the level of sophistication and maturity it possesses today. A little-noticed advantage enjoyed by these financiers is America's large and sophisticated market for new high-tech products because reinvested profits are ultimately the most important source of financing for most companies. Wall Street, nevertheless, is important, too. Americans take their stock exchanges for granted, but the reality is that no other country has such a large, liquid, versatile, and relatively honest market for corporate equities. Measured in terms of market value, the U.S. stock market accounts for more than half of the world stock markets, and the U.S., Japanese, and British markets together account for no less than 85 percent. Partly because so many companies are government-owned, such major industrial powers as France and Germany have very small stock markets; Germany's, for example, is 5 percent as big as America's while the French equity market is 3 percent as large. And what is true of *overall* stock markets is doubly true of the market for *small and untested* stocks. Although such countries as Great Britain are attempting to develop, with some success, an analogue to America's over-the-counter market, no foreign market has a comparable capacity to absorb new issues.

The collective impact of these various factors is clarified by casting a steadier gaze across the Atlantic, where the process of creating new industries has atrophied, with disastrous implications for job creation. Over the past decade the United States gained 20 million new jobs while the number of jobs in Europe *declined* slightly. Behind this anemic employment growth is the simple fact that European businessmen are generally more conservative than Americans. "The whole continent is risk averse," one observer told a *Wall Street Journal* reporter. Another businessman agrees: "We have, perhaps, a less dynamic character in Europe." Though wealth is respected in Europe, it is not socially acceptable to make a fortune and flaunt it; the halls of corporations do not ring with tales of former engineers who went out on their own and struck it rich. As a result the few businessmen who do found start-ups often feel lonely and demoralized. "In America, you can fail and start again," complains a German entrepreneur. "But here, when one fails, he is branded a flop for the rest of his life. It's always in his record. When you try to do something again, people are afraid to do business with you. We must learn to live with flops." This conservatism extends to Europe's formal and hierarchical universities, where well-established professors wield the power and control the budgets, often stunting the efforts of their younger and more imaginative colleagues. One need only think of Eckert and Mauchly at the University of Pennsylvania, of Ken Olsen at MIT, or of Alexander Graham Bell in his makeshift Boston laboratory to appreciate the dangers of curbing the creative urges of young scientists. After working in the United States, a German physicist marveled at how "Americans have no respect for their elders. They are disorderly, slightly crazy, adventurous and driven for success. But these qualities are so essential for science, and the Nobel Prizes are just one small reflection of that." By contrast European campuses lack the zany, irreverent, competitive climate in which younger researchers can thrive. Missing, too, is the productive interface between universities, corporations, and government agencies.

Another unhelpful expression of European conservatism is government efforts to shore up declining industries. Advocates of a national industrial policy for the United States promise that it would replace the erratic meanderings of the free market with the cold-blooded rationality of government experts. Unfortunately the rationality of government officials tends to be focused on professional self-preservation rather than national economic renewal. For politicians that means getting reelected. And when fundamental economic change is shrinking some industries and expanding others, there is no better way to stay in office than to use public money to prop up failing industries. British coal mines, French steel mills, Italian petrochemical plants, Dutch dairy farms—governments have pumped tens of billions of dollars into such money-losing ventures in order to spare workers (and politicians) the inconvenience of looking for new jobs.

What this has to do with high technology is simply this: One cannot spend the same dollar twice. Capital that is pumped into obsolete coal mines cannot be spent on biotechnology. As one European observer has put it, "Governments have to decide whether they will sacrifice smokestack industries to put money into productive areas such as technology. The brains are there; the capacity is there; it's just political limitation." This "political limitation" is familiar enough to American taxpayers, burdened as they are by massive agricultural subsidies and a military base in every congressional district. Nevertheless, the burden of government—more precisely, the crowding out of the private economy by public spending—is far heavier in Europe than in the United States, even though defense spending is proportionally lower. In 1984 total government spending equaled 34.3 percent of GNP in the United

States as compared with 42.1 percent for six other major economic powers and 46.0 percent for ten smaller countries. At 27 percent Japan's government expenditures are exceptionally low as a share of GNP, which is a key to its prosperity.

Europeans have compounded the error of subsidizing basic industries by directly subsidizing emerging industries as well. In the mid-1970s European nations attempted to shake IBM's hold of the European mainframe market with a joint project that failed miserably. More recently a major project of the Common Market dubbed ESPRIT (European Strategic Program for Research in Information Technology) was launched as a final effort to keep Europe in the global computer race. The scale of the project—$1.5 billion spent over five years—seems modest for this purpose, and like its predecessors, it is getting entangled in bureaucratic wrangling. Indeed, the Common Market has even encountered difficulty in carrying out its original mission: creating a common market. Europe remains so riven by barriers to trade that the products of start-up firms cannot easily reach a large, technically uniform market. Even the design of electrical sockets varies from one country to another. Little wonder that when businessmen are asked how government can hasten Europe's technological progress, the answers run to "Create an environment for free competition," "Be an innovative, intelligent customer," and "Stay out." Such sentiments, it should be emphasized, concur with the record of industrial innovation in the United States—railroads, telephones, U.S. Steel, and mainframe computers particularly come to mind—which suggests that the process can be severely retarded by the excessive interference of financiers or bureaucrats who have no direct stake in the long-run success of the new industry.

The contrast between Europe and the United States reminds us that American proficiency in founding new industries is a valuable and unusual skill that is not to be taken for granted. Indeed, the capacity of the U.S. economy to shift with little effort into dynamic new industries that create millions of new jobs is a national treasure of the first order, on a par with the nation's military strength, its constitutional stability, its tradition of civil liberty. And like those other assets, it is a tradition that has been developed over many decades, going forward from the building of the early textile mills along the eastern seaboard to the steel mills of western Pennsylvania, the booming auto industry of Michigan, and the laboratories of Silicon Valley and South San Francisco. As we have argued, the modern venture capital industry is essentially an improved mechanism for financing industrial innovation, a function that was previously executed on a more informal basis by individual businessmen.

One country that has developed its own distinctive approach to financing new industries is Japan. Although many observers have suggested that the United States should attempt to duplicate the Japanese approach, such a strategy appears neither necessary nor feasible to us. Accomplished cultural borrowers though they are, the Japanese have pursued a course of economic development that is unlike anything found in Europe or North America precisely because it is grounded in the special strengths and circumstances of Japan, including the following:

1. National homogeneity and a willingness to sacrifice for the welfare of the group, be it the family, the nation, or the corporation.

2. A very high savings rate, inspired by a Spartan social welfare system, prosavings tax system, and a postal savings network that encourages saving in small amounts.

3. A deeply engrained national awareness of the importance of a positive trade balance in manufactures, which is needed to pay for raw material imports into a crowded island nation.

4. Heavy borrowing by corporations and a willingness of companies to earn only enough profit to service debt (while building market share) rather than constantly to produce a competitive return on owners' capital.

5. Effective targeting of key growth industries, which owes much, first, to the power of the central bank to direct capital flows to Japan's highly leveraged corporations and, secondly, to the political autonomy of the Ministry of Trade and Industry (MITI), which makes strategic economic decisions without undue influence from interest groups.

6. A highly competitive national market that is difficult for foreigners to penetrate, thanks to cultural barriers, a fragmented retailing system, and the existence of corporate "families" or *keiretsu.*

7. A concentration of Japan's economic resources and national energy on economic rather than politico-military power.

A penetrating study by Harvard Business School researchers has shown how the Japanese have used these policies to contravene one of the most cherished "laws" of economic theory: the principle of comparative advantage. First discovered by David Ricardo in the early nineteenth century, this "law" holds that total world income will be maximized if a labor-abundant, resource-poor island economy like Japan's exports relatively simple, labor-intensive, low-value-added goods (such as textiles and shoes) while importing more complex goods (such as automobiles and machinery) that require heavy inputs of capital and natural resources. Ricardo illustrated this principle with the example of underdeveloped Portugal exporting wine to England and receiving in return cloth and other manufactured goods. After World War II Japan *did* at first concentrate on exporting textiles and other relatively simple goods, but its leaders declined to remain in an economically subordinate position for the next fifty years.

By systematically targeting more sophisticated industries, the Japanese government has moved the economy farther and farther up the value-added chain, from textiles to shipbuilding to automobiles to semiconductors and currently to robotics and computers. Biotechnology and industrial ceramics are next on the list. These targeted industries receive protection from import competition, special research assistance, and financial subsidies that allow them to break into foreign markets and build up productive capacity even as they run heavy losses. This system is characterized by historian Chalmers Johnson as a "developmental state," in which the government takes an active role in directing the evolution of a free economy, in contrast with the "regulatory states" of Europe and North America, where governments *react* to corporations. Japan's developmental state has succeeded spectacularly because it builds on the aforementioned national characteristics of the Japanese people rather than adhering to the abstractions of economic theory.

There are those who would have the United States duplicate the policies that have worked so well in Japan. But this approach would inevitably lead America down the discredited European path of public subsidies for failing industries, subsidies that buy votes without creating jobs. For it is the large, mature, labor-intensive industries, such as steel, autos, and textiles—not budding industries like robotics or biotechnology—that employ the most voters and Washington lobbyists. "The present is organized to the teeth. The future is yet unborn," notes one critic of industrial policy. Certainly there is no reason to suppose that what works in the distinctive political and social climate of Japan would work in the United States. Indeed, if one were to invent a country that was the precise opposite of Japan, it would look very much like the

United States. Where Japan is ethnically homogeneous, the United States is a nation of immigrants. Where Japan is a small island country nearly bereft of resources, the United States spans a bountiful continent. Where Japan has a high personal savings rate, the United States has an extremely low one. Where the Japanese people strive for cooperation and consensus, Americans are contentious and individualistic. Where Japan's national bureaucracy is an autonomous and highly skilled governmental elite that has the power to set industrial policy, the U.S. government is beholden to Congress, which is in turn beholden to dozens of organized interest groups. Where Japan plays a circumscribed role on the international stage, the United States is a major world power. For all these reasons, policies that work in Japan would not succeed in the United States, any more than the leg of a giraffe would be of much service if transplanted to a hippopotamus.

PERFECTING PHASE ONE OF THE VENTURE CAPITAL PROCESS

In view of the unique effectiveness of the U.S. venture capital system, it is vital that it be protected and nurtured. This is all the more important because it is extremely fragile, both politically and economically. Consider this contrast. When in 1969 the U.S. Justice Department decided that IBM had been too successful and should be cut up into several smaller companies, Big Blue struck back. The company virtually acquired Cravath, Swaine & Moore, one of the biggest and most formidable law firms on Wall Street, and launched a protracted legal war that nearly buried the hapless government lawyers in a warehouse of documents for thirteen years. *United States* v. *IBM* was so rarefied, boring, and disconnected from the normal work of a corporate lawyer that Cravath had to pay extra-extravagant salaries in order to seduce the top graduates of the Harvard and Yale law schools into working on the case, at no small risk to their sanity and professional development. Luckily IBM prevailed; the company was too powerful to be dismembered by the machinations of misguided trustbusters. For the U.S. economy this outcome was very fortunate because a dismembered IBM would have been a much weaker foe for the big Japanese firms that are making an assault on the mainframe industry.

Things would be different if the venture capital industry found itself in a similar jam. The industry's political power is very limited because it is not a rich and well-organized institution but merely a congeries of small partnerships investing a few billion dollars a year in industries that do not yet exist. Many participants, such as brokerage houses, banks, and insurance companies, have primary allegiances elsewhere and would not strongly support the venture industry in a political show-down. As the grim experience of the 1970s demonstrates, when the federal government raises capital gains taxes or permits inflation to soar and stock prices to plummet, the supply of venture capital may shrink dramatically and force American entrepreneurs to beg for capital in Europe and Japan. When this happens, the immediate victims are, first, a handful of comparatively wealthy financiers, who can silently slip into greener financial pastures, and, secondly, potential entrepreneurs, who fail to secure financing for their ideas and elect to stick with their present corporate jobs. This is an anomalous economic event—the silent disaster. It is not the sort of thing that grabs headlines, no matter how grave the fundamental damage to the U.S. economy may be. When film editors splice together footage for the nightly news, the computer company that did not get funded is no match for farm country bankruptcy auctions or Rust Belt factory closings.

The vulnerability of the venture capital industry is particularly dis-quieting because within the next decade the industry could well suffer shocks not unlike those of the early 1970s. Recent political develop-ments certainly are not reassuring. Notwithstanding the probusiness cast of the Reagan administration and the clearly beneficial effects of slashing the capital gains tax rate in 1978, the Treasury Department in 1984 recommended raising the capital gains rate from a maximum of 20 percent to 35 percent, indexed for inflation. The president ini-tially scotched this idea but the tax reform plan that did pass is nearly as bad, raising the top capital gains rate to 33 percent. Since the 1820s U.S. history has been characterized by political mood swings lasting ten to twenty years. Currently the nation is in a conservative mood, but elimination of the capital gains "loophole" may be a harbinger of the swing the other way. Tax policy aside, it is possible that within a decade a severe bear market will once again threaten to constrict the flow of venture capital.

To insulate the industry from such shocks we recommend the four reforms specified below. Made in the spirit of "if it ain't broke, don't fix it," they would help ensure the availability of venture capital in bad times as well as good without altering its basic structure.

1. Reduce the maximum capital gains tax on financial assets from 28 to 10 percent, a move that would still leave the rate well above Japan's capital gains rate of zero. Because lower tax *rates* lead to more active trading, a reduction would actually cut revenues from the capital gains tax by a much smaller amount. It is hoped that a reversal of the increased rate in the 1986 act will be one of the first modifications put through Congress once changes to the act are politically possible.

2. Aggressively encourage investment by individuals in financial assets through such measures as *expanding* individual retirement accounts (IRAs) as opposed to contracting them, as was done in the 1986 act (see below).

3. Permit corporate and government pension funds in the United States to invest somewhat more heavily in venture capital start-ups. Recently investing more than $65 billion a year, these funds are so vast that a minor policy shift would greatly expand the flow of capital to small companies while also improving the performance of the funds themselves.

4. Expand the already generous federal support of basic research in universities and in related efforts such as the space program.

FROM START-UP TO MULTINATIONAL: IMPROVING PHASE TWO OF THE VENTURE CAPITAL PROCESS

It is *after* small American high-tech companies have left the launching pad of the venture capital industry that they typically run into trouble. Currently U.S. semiconductor companies are falling behind their well-financed Japanese competitors, foreign microcomputer companies are establishing a strong presence in the U.S. market, and the Japanese are making major strides in biotechnology. *America's central economic challenge today is to ensure that the new industries launched by venture capitalists advance to a prosperous maturity in the United States rather than overseas.* At the heart of this challenge is the problem of capital formation which, as noted, has both a quantitative and a qualitative dimension. The United States must first *generate enough investment capital to keep its high-growth industries competitive and then make sure that this capital is smart money that is effectively channeled into the best companies.* The historical record strongly suggests that the best way to do this is to keep the process of financing new industries simple. As we have seen repeatedly, smart money is typically capital advanced by private investors to an entrepreneur who controls a fast-growing firm, free of excessive interference from Wall Street, Washington, or large corporations. With this in mind, we make the following recommendations:

1. The United States should encourage capital formation by passing a constitutional amendment requiring a balanced federal budget and altering the personal tax code so as to encourage saving and discouraging borrowing.

2. The United States should avoid industrial policies that would increase government interference in the allocation of capital. Whether or not they work in Japan, experience shows that they would work no better in the United States than in Europe.

3. Since the most important source of capital for successful high-tech companies is *expanding profits,* America's trade policy should be revamped to protect America's high-tech, export-oriented winners rather than its low-tech, import-vulnerable losers.

4. The United States should stick with the 1986 reforms in the corporate tax code, which are designed to tax all industries at roughly the same rate instead of providing huge subsidies to capital-intensive industries.

5. Corporate restructuring should be encouraged because it is streamlining diversified corporations and transferring capital from large, mature companies back to shareholders, who can invest it in dynamic independent companies.

6. However, another aspect of corporate restructuring—the wave of big corporate mergers—is far more problematical. In the past such mergers have often worked poorly. A major challenge for U.S. managers is to improve the effectiveness of mergers. The federal government can encourage this by continuing to permit mergers within a single industry.

EXPANDING THE POOL OF CAPITAL

New industries need capital to flourish. To create a high-tech company and then thrust it into a hostile financial environment of high interest rates and depressed stock prices is rather like raising a delicate orchid and then planting it in the snow. We are not likely to regain competitiveness so long as gross fixed capital rises 28 percent in Japan, 21 percent in Germany, 20 percent in France and Canada, 18 percent in Italy, and 17 percent in the United States—even in a year (1983) when the relative economic growth was unusually good. Among major European countries only Great Britain, ominously enough, has a lower rate than the United States. For the United States to regain competitiveness, Lester Thurow estimates, the savings rate must be raised by an amount equal to 25 percent of GNP. What makes this task vital is that living standards cannot rise unless productivity rises, and to raise his or her output per hour, a worker normally must use more and better machinery, whether it is a better drill press or a new word processor. To purchase this machinery, corporations must either invest their own savings or borrow the savings of others. When the supply of savings is low, the cost of borrowing the money—the interest rate—will be higher, and corporations will be able to identify fewer profitable investment opportunities.

Thus it is no coincidence that most of America's foreign competitors have higher savings rates and also faster productivity growth. Between 1973 and 1984 productivity advanced 7.3 percent annually in Japan, 4.6 percent in France, 3.7 percent in Italy, 3.3 percent in Germany, and just 2.0 percent in the United States. To be sure, part of this differential is caused by the much greater ability of the U.S. economy to create new jobs. In Europe an overgenerous welfare system, onerous unemployment insurance levies on employers, and restrictions on layoffs have dissuaded unemployed workers from taking new jobs and discouraged companies from creating them. When European companies expand, they tend to add new machines rather than to hire more workers. The result is chronically high unemployment. The United States, by contrast, has been supremely successful at finding work for the millions of new workers who entered the workplace in the past decade. But with the baby boom cresting and the influx of women into the labor force slowing, future GNP growth in the United States cannot depend on continued rapid expansion of the work force. Productivity growth must be greatly accelerated to build economic growth, and that requires capital.

To understand America's savings problem, it is important to appreciate how Reaganomics and the recent decline of inflation have affected the three components of savings: personal saving, corporate saving, and government dissaving. Many analysts look back wistfully at the modest federal budget deficits of the late 1970s and wish that we could return to that fiscal policy by raising taxes. In fact, this move would tend to choke off economic growth. As most observers at the time recognized, the United States in the late 1970s did not have a stable and economically sensible fiscal policy. Even though he was underspending on defense, Uncle Sam was an inflation junkie who silently sapped the private economy until Federal Reserve Chairman Paul Volcker and President Ronald Reagan made him go cold turkey.

Uncle Sam supported his habit in several ways. For one thing inflation pushed individuals into higher and higher tax brackets, making them liable to higher tax rates even as their real incomes were stable or declining. Secondly, inflation created fictitious capital gains that were taxed as though they were real gains; merely to stay even with inflation during the 1970s an investor needed to see a growth stock that paid no dividend rise 112 percent. Yet if a stock did in fact rise this much (few did), as much as half the "gain" could go to paying taxes. Thirdly, inflation silently raised corporate taxes through the phenomenon of underdepreciation, which works like this: If in 1975 a company built for $1 million a plant which, for tax purposes, was depreciated over five years, it was able to deduct from taxable income $200,000 per year. But if capital goods inflation was running at 12 percent, then at the end of the five-year depreciation period the plant had to be replaced with a new one costing not $1 million but $1,762,000. Through underdepreciation the government was taxing $762,000 in income that should have been set aside for building the new plant. These inflation-induced windfall profits were a godsend to anyone who lived off federal revenue; federal taxes' share of GNP rose from 18 percent in 1965 to 20.4 percent in 1979, even as congressmen periodically enacted "tax cuts." The discretionary income of the federal government was also raised by the fact that investors, slow to recognize that inflation tends to accelerate, were willing to finance the budget deficit at negative real interest rates. On the spending side of the equation, most of Uncle Sam's new revenue was directed to transfer payments and social programs; defense spending as a share of total spending fell from 40.3 percent in 1965 to 21.8 percent in 1979. And despite rising revenues and weak defense spending, the federal budget was almost never balanced—even in the later stages of the business cycle, when Keynesian theory holds that the budget should be in surplus.

By the late 1970s many Americans recognized the dangers inherent in this configuration of policies. In the wake of the Iranian hostage crisis and the Soviet invasion of Afghanistan the need for greater defense spending became clear. Policymakers also concluded that underdepreciation of corporate assets was undermining industrial America because firms could not afford to modernize their factories as rapidly as their foreign competitors. And some economists lamented that the individual savings rate of about 6 percent, though still in line with the postwar average, was too low. Finally supply-siders plausibly argued that marginal tax rates had moved too high, to a point where they discouraged work, saving, and investment and drove taxable income into the underground economy.

These shifting sentiments set the stage for the revolution of 1981, which was led by two radical incendiaries of very different mien, Paul Volcker and Ronald Reagan. By causing the back-to-back recessions of 1980 and 1981–82, Chairman Volcker killed off inflation and greatly expanded the federal debt load because the federal deficit soared as revenues declined and transfer payments rose. Meanwhile, President Reagan's sweeping tax reform of 1981 cut individual tax rates (though implementation of this reform was delayed by two years), ended bracket creep by indexing tax brackets to inflation, and ended underdepreciation of corporate earnings by adding to the tax code more generous depreciation provisions known as accelerated depreciation. Supply-siders expected the reduction in marginal tax rates to encourage more personal savings, but toward the same end they also expanded individual retirement accounts. While federal revenue was being cut by lower inflation and lower tax rates, the president implemented a huge defense buildup. Watching cynically on the sidelines were shell-shocked investors, who, finally wise to the danger of inflation, demanded double-digit bond yields on the recently enlarged national debt. Thus there were no fewer than seven factors tending to create a higher deficit: the recession, lower inflation and the consequent slowing of revenue growth, the ending of bracket creep, implementation of accelerated depreciation, the supply-side cut in personal tax rates, higher real interest rates, and the defense buildup.

The effect of the Reagan-Volcker revolution on the savings rate can be summarized as follows:

	Percent of Gross National Product	
	1980	1985, First Half
Total government dissaving	−1.2	−3.6
Personal saving	4.2	3.4
Business saving	12.4	14.4
Total	15.4	14.2

Thus in the savings department the Reagan administration is currently batting .333: Corporate savings have risen, but individual and government savings have sagged. How can the average be improved? Since accelerated depreciation has worked so well at generating corporate savings, which has indeed sparked an investment boom, it should not be changed further. On the other hand, Reagan's attempts to increase the personal savings rate have failed miserably. Despite IRAs, lower marginal tax rates, and record high real interest rates, Americans are saving less than ever before. The 1983–85 average savings rate is 5.6 percent, compared with 7.3 percent in the 1970s. No one knows why the savings rate has sunk, but as usual, explanations abound. Some point to demographic factors; baby boomers who are forming households typically save less than middle-aged people planning for retirement. Other economists believe that the rise in consumer confidence associated with low inflation has increased the public's willingness to spend rather than save. Still others say that high interest rates retard saving because most people save to buy something, and when high rates facilitate this saving process, consumers actually set aside less.

Whatever the cause of the decline in the savings rate, it is clear by now that a reduction of ambient tax rates will not raise it. What is needed is radical and carefully focused tax reforms that will end the great and long-standing bias of the federal tax code toward spending and against saving. To understand this bias, consider two citizens, Mr. Spender and Mr. Saver, both single professionals making $50,000 per year. A devotee of the good life, Mr. Spender borrows heavily to finance his heavy personal consumption, and his interest expense amounts to $14,000 per year. As for Mr. Saver, he is a nice guy but a bit of a miser who faithfully sets aside $400 per month, which has accumulated to a fund of $120,000. This capital now generates $12,000 per year in interest income. Now let's look at their tax liabilities. Mr. Spender deducts from his gross income $14,000 per year in interest expense, giving him a taxable income of $36,000, while Mr. Saver adds to his gross income $12,000, giving him a taxable income of $62,000 per year. Even if they had identical tax brackets of 30 percent, *Mr. Saver will pay taxes that are 58 percent higher than Mr. Spender's—even though their gross incomes are identical.* And since Mr. Saver is in a higher tax bracket, his relative tax bite is even *higher* than this.

The 1986 tax reform does surprisingly little to change this shocking result. Although interest on consumer debt, such as credit cards, is no longer tax deductible, interest on loans secured by home equity still is. IRAs and 401K plans are cut back considerably, and the exclusion for long-term capital gains is eliminated. Furthermore, the bill encourages consumption—and discourages saving—by reducing the tax burden of individuals $24 billion per year while raising corporate taxes by a similar amount. To eliminate the federal tax code's antisavings bias, the following changes should be made:

> End completely the tax deductibility of consumer interest and mortgage interest payments on second homes.
>
> Limit deductibility of mortgage interest to mortgages totaling $200,000 for primary residences, and end it completely for second homes.
>
> Expand IRAs by permitting investment of up to $50,000 annually in new savings, which could be withdrawn at any time. To close a loophole in the current system—the fact that funds can be transferred from existing savings accounts to the IRA—only new savings should be eligible for the IRA.

These proposals are straightforward, equitable, and acceptable to both conservatives and liberals (they closely resemble the recommendations of Lester Thurow), and unlike across-the-board tax cuts, they would quickly reverse the bias against saving that now exists in the tax code. These methods have worked in Europe and Japan; it is disappointing that the tax reform plans of 1985 and 1986 did not seriously address America's savings problem by taking more decisive steps to discourage consumption and increase saving. In fact, the elimination of IRA deductibility and the reduced scope of 401K plans have discouraged saving still futher.

What about the federal deficit? The solution naturally hinges on the diagnosis. We have already shown that (although President Reagan's supply side tax cut was not self-financing and his defense buildup probably excessive) the main cause of Uncle Sam's financial crisis was that Messrs. Volcker and Reagan kicked away his inflationary crutch. Although the federal budget nearly balanced in the late 1970s, *federal spending was actually out of control, because the budgets relied on many trends that were undesirable and ultimately unsustainable:* bracket creep, taxation of fictitious capital gains, underdepreciation of corporate earnings, inadequate defense spending, and negative real interest rates. It was great while it lasted, but Washington could not indefinitely wax rich off the inflationary virus that was subverting the living standards of the average working American who paid taxes and did not receive a federal pension. (Remember that between 1970 and 1980 real after-tax earnings for nonagricultural workers declined more than 10 percent even though real disposable incomes for all Americans—including federal pensioners—rose nearly 20 percent.) When this inflationary dividend ceased, personal income tax rates were cut, and defense spending was increased, Washington found itself in a financial bind, and the deficit soared to 5.5 percent of GNP.

The central political issue of the 1980s is whether and how this deficit will be closed. We believe that if the budget is balanced by taxes' simply being raised, the United States will quickly return to the fiscal environment of the 1970s, when the federal government took a bigger share of national income every year and slowly weakened the private economy that ultimately sustains all government spending. The concept of balancing the budget with higher taxes has been discredited. For three decades fiscal conservatives have been warning that the federal deficit was inflationary and should be closed with one last tax increase. Over that period the federal budget deficit has been balanced exactly twice while federal spending has grown from 14.3 percent of GNP in 1949 to 24 percent in 1985. There is no reason to suppose that things have finally changed—that if taxes were raised to balance the budget in 1986, the deficit would be closed once and for all. On the contrary, congressional recalcitrance in cutting back domestic programs suggests that Congress will continue to spend every penny it can lay its hands on, plus a little more. Like a dim-witted donkey, the American taxpayer will trudge up the revenue hill in order to grab the carrot of a balanced budget that is dangled in front of him or her, just out of reach.

Many investors would like to see the budget balanced with a tax increase, on the theory that it would lower federal borrowing in the credit markets, reduce crowding out of private borrowers, lower interest rates, and thereby raise stock and bond prices. They may be right in the short term but are dead wrong in the long term. Crowding out is a slippery concept, because it can occur in the entire economy as well as the capital markets. A dollar that is taxed away from a corporation or individual investor and spent on a federal pension cannot be invested in a factory. In this way government spending crowds out private investment that would ultimately expand the tax base. As we have seen, a dramatic rise in corporate savings between 1980 and 1985 nearly offset the increase in the government deficit. If corporate taxes were raised to reduce the budget deficit, federal borrowing would temporarily decline, alleviating crowding out of private borrowers in the credit markets, and interest rates would probably decline. But although corporate borrowers would be better off in the short term, corporate America as a whole would obviously be worse off as its tax bill increased. Low interest rates are nice if you have to borrow, but it is obviously much nicer not to need to borrow in the first place because your taxes are low. And as noted, this tax increase actually would not reduce crowding out in the credit markets over the long term because Congress consistently spends more than it taxes.

What is needed, clearly, is a fresh approach that prevents the federal government from continuing to crowd out the private economy by claiming an ever higher share of GNP. If such steps are not taken, rising government spending will choke off economic growth in the United States much as it has in Europe. Therefore, we would favor a *constitutional amendment* requiring the federal government, except in periods of declared war, to have a balanced budget and forbidding it to raise taxes without explicit, separately legislated tax hikes. The aim of the amendment would be to hold federal spending and taxation at about 19 percent of GNP. It has already been accepted by thirty-two states; after one more state passes it, the amendment will make the rounds for ratification. While many people consider a balanced budget amendment radical, we find this viewpoint hard to understand. After all, every other individual and institution in the country, from the most profligate state legislature to the most financially sound corporation, must operate on a balanced budget. Why not the federal government? Moreover, Congress itself recognized the necessity of a balanced budget amendment by passing Gramm-Rudman-Hollings. If this piece of legislation were clearly a workable and constitutional agent of fiscal discipline that would remain in effect over the long term, a balanced budget amendment would be unnecessary. Unfortunately this is not the case.

The amendment would solve the fundamental problem plaguing the federal government: The self-interest of each legislator is at variance with the collective interest of the nation as a whole. Congressmen spend freely in order to remain in the good graces of special-interest groups that can make or break their political careers. Then they send the bill to the American people as a whole, in the form of higher taxes or a larger budget deficit. The system works precisely like an expense account in which each executive spends as much as he wants in order to do a good job and merit a raise and then passes the bill to corporate headquarters. While every executive does his best to succeed, the corporation as a whole quickly goes bankrupt. Let us emphasize that it is the system—not specific individuals—that is at fault. Senators and representatives who wish to stay in power have no choice but to play the game precisely as their competitors do. What is needed is to change the rules of the game to ensure that legislators' individual actions will benefit the country as a whole. The result would be a much more rigorous and sensible use of the vast resources allocated by the federal government.

WHY AN INDUSTRIAL POLICY WOULD FAIL

To put America back in the fast lane, some analysts would have government experts become the strategic planners of the U.S. economy. Their role would be to determine the most promising course of economic development and shift capital in that direction. In troubled industries like steel and autos, government leaders would sit down with representatives of management and labor to hammer out plans for industrial rejuvenation. Government would provide funds and ease up on regulatory rules in return for pledges from corporations and unions to restore their international competitiveness. In the high-tech sectors, on the other hand, industrial policy advocates would directly invest in industries that are not now well served by the private capital markets. MIT's Thurow, for example, proposes creation of a public investment bank with an initial capitalization of $5 billion—hardly very much, he suggests, in a $990 billion budget. This institution would fund projects that have external benefits not recognized by private financiers, as well as large projects that venture capitalists normally do not fund, and it would be discontinued after ten years if it did not work well.

Thurow's proposal has a familiar ring by now. Catching sight of a currently glamorous segment of the private economy that is not working perfectly, Uncle Sam sidles up to a decidedly haggard John Q. Taxpayer, drapes a friendly arm over his shoulder, and whispers, "Your venture capital industry is good, but I can make it great." Then he moves still closer, deftly dropping a hand into the taxpayer's back pocket. "All I need is some spare change, maybe four or five billion dollars. There is no risk to you because if my scheme doesn't work, I won't ask for any more money—unless perchance that first five billion has created a political constituency that would prefer to see the checks keep coming." To update Everett Dirksen, $5 billion here, $5 billion there, and pretty soon you're talking real money. In fact, $5 billion exceeds all the new commitments of funds to the venture capital industry in 1984, one of the industry's biggest years. If $5 billion is really a trivial sum, Professor Thurow should be able to find it by cutting some small bit of waste out of the current federal budget, which already consumes nearly a quarter of America's GNP.

And one has to wonder how wisely Uncle Sam would spend this $5 billion increase in his allowance. Political considerations strongly influence the spending of federal funds, and in the political arena the industries of the future are no match for the industries of the present, represented as they are by an army of lawyers, consultants, press agents, and lobbyists. Furthermore, federal funds are like kites: There are always strings attached, and long after the kites are aloft, the bureaucracy continues to jerk them around, often for political reasons. Then there is the cultural mismatch. Whereas the investments of private venture capital firms are smart money and investments by corporations in new industries are all too often dumb money, investments made by the federal government would almost certainly be "moronic" money. To be successful, start-up firms must learn to turn a profit, something that normally involves keeping costs low. As the recent performance of the Pentagon suggests, this is not one of Uncle Sam's strong points. And excessive federal largess is only part of the problem. There is a whole range of services—financial advice, executive recruiting, market research, and strategic planning—that venture capitalists routinely give their companies and that government officials are not qualified to deliver. This explains why many defense-related firms that sprang up along Boston's Route 128 during the 1960s went bankrupt when federal funding ran out; the bureaucratic byways of the Department of Defense (DOD) are a poor training ground for the real world of commerce. For similar reasons British efforts to subsidize high-tech start-ups have failed.

What of the scheme, particularly favored by Harvard instructor Robert Reich, to implement systematic strategic plans for individual industries based on negotiations between management, government, and labor? According to Reich, this approach would allow government to get more for its money; in return for granting tariffs, subsidies, and other favors, it should demand wage reductions from the unions and much-needed management reforms from executives. Thus would government experts play a greater role in plotting America's industrial future. Fortunately we can look to history to evaluate this scheme, for the United States has had plenty of experience with industrial policies. The results are not encouraging. From 1953 to 1979 the centerpiece of the federal government's battle against inflation was a more or less formal incomes policy, in which the government pressured managements and unions in basic industries like steel, autos, and chemicals not to grant wage increases that exceeded productivity gains. Only one group was left out of the periodic negotiations: the American consumer. Perhaps that helps explain why the inflation rate rose from under 2 percent in the 1950s to 13.5 percent in 1980. When Paul Volcker used stringent monetary policy to kill off inflation between 1980 and 1982, he prevented companies from raising wages and prices with impunity. One union after another made generous give-backs and the wage-price spiral was magically broken. Government-supported "negotiations" were no match for the marketplace in imposing discipline on politically powerful constituencies. A case in point is the long-languishing railroad industry, in which the federal government plays a major role in labor negotiations, featherbedding is rampant, and workers earn an average of $41,000 per year—just about the highest wage in industrial America.

Industrial policy worked no better when it was used to solve the energy crisis of the 1970s. As usual, part of the problem was wildly inaccurate economic projections. Richard Nixon's 1974 "Project Independence Report" offered the considered opinion that "World oil prices [then at $11 per barrel] are highly uncertain and might fall somewhat lower. . . . Major OPEC cutbacks would be required to sustain $11 world oil prices." Within six years the price of oil was $35 per barrel. The report was equaly off target in its prediction that by 1985 "nuclear power is expected to grow from 4.5% to 30% of total electric power generation." If President Nixon was too sanguine, President Carter was far too pessimistic. His 1977 National Energy Plan warned: "The United States could face repeated jolts as energy supplies become increasingly unreliable and actual shortages occur more frequently. . . . In some cases the American people could experience mere inconvenience, in others, real suffering as economic activity ground to a halt." In view of this dire outlook, one might have expected the federal government quickly to decontrol oil and natural gas prices in order to discourage consumption and encourage production. Instead, the burgeoning federal energy bureaucracy preferred to develop an extraordinarily complex and ultimately unworkable set of price controls and subsidies that was discredited by the gasoline shortages stemming from the Iranian revolution of 1979.

The sight of long lines at gas stations and factories idled for lack of natural gas finally convinced Congress that the situation was indeed as dire as President Carter believed. Hence the Synthetic Fuels Corporation was created in 1980 with immediate spending power of $20 billion —just as U.S. energy consumption began to slow dramatically. In 1983 and 1984, as a growing oil glut was driving down prices from $35 to $28 per barrel, there began to rise out of the Colorado desert shale oil projects that produced oil at a cost of $67 per barrel. These projects became more and more embarrassing to Congress as the federal budget tightened and evidence of serious mismanagement in the corporation mounted. One chairman resigned under charges of influence peddling. The corporation created a staff of 200 people to select and bankroll a handful of projects. Recognizing that synfuels were economically unfeasible, several major oil companies walked away from projects even after construction was under way. The *Wall Street Journal* reported in the summer of 1984 that the corporation "has been crippled by months of political bickering, allegations of financial scandal, an exodus of senior officials, and general industry apathy." An erstwhile congressional supporter called it "the biggest program of waste and abuse I've ever seen." Since the corporation was discredited in the midst of an energy glut and an unprecedented federal budget crisis, the synfuels corporation was a logical target for David Stockman's budgetary meat cleaver. But thanks to the support of coal state legislators, it retained control of immense amounts of capital; in the fall of 1984 it still had authority to spend $12 billion, equal to about three good years of new investment by the entire venture capital industry.

Yet another harrowing example of a federal industrial policy is agriculture. Although many people associate federal waste with grasping defense contractors and crafty welfare mothers, the plainspoken farmers of the Republican heartland have not done badly either. The Rural Electrification Administration, created in 1935 to bring electricity to rural America, sells electricity to 30 million people at about 10 percent below cost, while the Tennessee Valley Authority, another child of the New Deal, offers a 40 percent discount to 2.7 million people. The Farmers Home Administration, holding a loan portfolio of more than $50 billion, writes mortgages at far below market rates. And the liberal lending policies of the Farm Credit Administration, after encouraging the reckless land boom of the 1970s, is now asking Congress for a costly bailout. Subsidies extend beyond electricity, housing, and land to the crops themselves; about $4 billion per year was spent in the 1970s to support commodity prices. But prices were pegged too high for the disinflationary 1980s, and American farmers—still the most efficient in the world—have been priced out of international markets while the cost of subsidies quintupled to $20 billion in 1984. The farm bill passed in 1985 has an annual cost of $35 billion, and all are agreed that this stupendous expenditure will do little to solve the farm crisis. The chief beneficiaries will be relatively wealthy farmers, rather than the mid-size commercial farmers who are most prone to bankruptcy. For a Farm Belt congressman trying to make it through the next election, this might be a "rational" industrial policy; for the country at large—and for the farmers themselves—it is a disaster. Knud Grosen, president of the Montana Grain Growers Association, says, "We've been cutting back production, and countries like Argentina and Canada have been increasing their production to fill the gap. We're going to have to slug it out with our foreign competitors to recapture that lost business."

The dreary examples of inflation, energy, and agriculture policy all suggest that the federal government will spend billions of dollars to avoid tough political decisions—even if it injures the very people it is trying to help. Clearly industrial policies would seriously distort the allocation of resources in the United States, just as it has in Europe. For one thing, they are based on purportedly scientific long-term economic forecasts that are usually dead wrong. Emanating as they do from the chaotic logrolling on Capitol Hill, the major programs based on these false projections are very slow to be made, are often out of date by the time they are implemented, yet are nearly indestructible once they have begun to fertilize the countryside with federal dollars. Although government planners may talk in terms of decades, the real time horizon in official Washington is just four years, which is the joint average term of representatives (two years), presidents (four years), and senators (six years). Politicians looking forward to the next election seldom make the hard-nosed decisions needed to allocate capital efficiently.

In view of their slim chances of success, it is fortunate that the policies advocated by Messrs. Thurow and Reich were never needed in the first place. The venture capital system that Professor Thurow would reform with a $5 billion boost in the federal deficit already works very well. And over the past three years, in one industry after another, unions and managements—fighting for survival now that the crutches of inflation and an undervalued dollar had disappeared—made precisely those difficult decisions that Dr. Reich thought could be implemented only under government pressure. The process has been painful and costly. Marginal businesses have been eliminated, heavy investments in modern plant and equipment have been made, wage increases have been pared back, inefficient work rules have been slashed, and thousands of redundant white-collar workers have been laid off. In addition to increasing industrial efficiency, these reforms have, through such financial stratagems as share buy-backs, mergers, and unit trusts, returned capital to shareholders who could invest it more profitably. If management and labor had been able to wangle some favors from the federal government in return for undertaking these reforms, would they have been hastened or delayed? To ask that question is to answer it.

AN EXPORT-ORIENTED TRADE POLICY: FOUNTAIN OF SMART MONEY

Although formal industrial policies would fail, the United States cannot simply rely on the "magic of the marketplace" to meet the Japanese challenge. After all, federal, state, and local government spend nearly a third of GNP and manage such critical functions as trade policy, defense spending, education, support of advanced research, antitrust policy, and foreign affairs. In every one of these areas government should strive to increase economic efficiency in general and the competitiveness of America's most promising growth industries in particular. Platitudinous though it may sound, this policy has not been followed by the Reagan administration. In 1984 the president formed a Commission on Industrial Competitiveness, chaired by Hewlett-Packard CEO John A. Young, which made a host of intelligent recommendations on how the government could help restore industrial competitiveness. Instead of moving to implement at least some of the proposals, the report was officially ignored. One wonders how many U.S. industries must succumb to foreign competition before the subject merits official alarm.

No area better illustrates the need for such a conscious policy than current U.S. trade policy, which props up uncompetitive, labor-intensive industries, such as textiles, apparel, shoes, and steel, while until very recently ignoring the interests of such industries as telecommunications equipment and semiconductors. From the standpoint of capital formation, this policy increases the profits (hence the capital) of uncompetitive industries while reducing the profits and capital of many high-technology industries that sell to foreign markets. In effect, it channels capital away from industries that can use it most effectively. Apart from considerations of capital formation, this policy should be completely reversed for four good reasons. The policy is costly to the U.S. consumer, and the jobs "saved" in this way are among the poorest-paying in the country; the earnings of the average apparel worker are below the poverty level for a family of four. Moreover, if these low-paying jobs moved overseas, the incomes of important U.S. customers, such as Brazil, Mexico, and Taiwan, would rise, increasing their capacity to purchase our exports. Perhaps most important, protection of failing industries tends to undermine our strongest export-oriented industries. Such commodities as steel are highly important inputs for goods exported by the United States, particularly capital goods of all kinds. When quotas or tariffs raise the price of steel in the United States above the worldwide price, American companies that use steel are placed at a significant disadvantage to their foreign competitors in world markets. If Caterpillar must pay 20 percent more for the steel that goes into tractors than does Komatsu, it is sure to lose market share to the Japanese company in the Brazilian and Australian markets. The long-run result is that Caterpillar has to move factories overseas to remain competitive. Thus, by protecting low-paying jobs, protectionism can reduce the number of high-paying jobs in the U.S. economy.

While protection of America's low-tech industries is being reduced, the U.S. government should much more aggressively help America's high-technology industries make sales around the world, particularly in Japan. It is unwise to alienate our trading partners in the third world by protecting nonstrategic American industries such as textiles (which was widely deemed to be "sick" as long ago as the 1920s), even as we permit the Japanese to lock our telecommunications equipment and semiconductors out of their large, sophisticated, fast-growing market. A more forceful and rational approach, looking to the future rather than the past, is needed. Such a change would in fact merely represent a return to the policies of the nineteenth century, when high-tech infant industries such as textiles and steel were granted some relief from the withering competition of British imports. Such a policy would be justified, for it is well established that Japan is highly protectionist. A lengthy study by the Harvard Business School showed that in contrast with that of Korea, Taiwan, or Hong King, "Japan's pattern is hard to distinguish from a closed market." In all but three categories of manufactured goods Japan's imports equaled only 2 percent of exports. The Japanese exclude many U.S. products that are highly competitive, including cigarettes, citrus, beef, financial services, and telecommunications equipment, the aggregate value of which is somewhere between $5 and $17 billion.

In responding to this commercial discrimination, the Reagan administration has been much less aggressive than it should be. When the Japanese proposed a telecommunications trade policy that in effect gave their producers the right to inspect the detailed technical specifications of U.S. products before they could be sold in Japan, the administration was willing to agree. Only an uproar in Congress led to a more forceful policy. This pattern obviously has to end. The solution is not still another round of negotiations and delay; that approach has already failed so often that the Japanese authorities are properly scornful of U.S. resolve on commercial issues. Instead, the United States should simply hand Japan two lists: a list of high-technology products in which the United States is competitive, stating the amount of each product that we expect Japan to import in the next twelve months, and a list of products—including office equipment, consumer electronics, and automobiles—that the United States will stop importing from Japan if it does not comply with the request. This approach is radical but reasonable. Rimmer de Vries, the highly respected international economist at Morgan Guaranty Trust Company, has proposed a considerably more draconian measure to encourage the Japanese to recognize their growing obligation to be consumers as well as producers in the international marketplace.

RAISING THE IQ OF CORPORATE CASH: THE VIRTUES
OF TAX REFORM AND CORPORATE RESTRUCTURING

Despite the continuing concern caused by the budget deadlock, corporate America as a whole actually benefited greatly from the earlier Reagan tax reforms because implementation of accelerated depreciation increased corporate cash flow dramatically. In effect the burden of high real interest rates was shifted from corporations to the federal government. But a serious difficulty with this trend was that capital flowed disproportionately to capital-intensive industries, which paid little or no taxes because of the investment tax credit and accelerated depreciation, while many service and high-technology companies had tax rates of more than 30 percent. Thus the tax code was perversely discriminating against the industries of the future and in favor of heavy industry. A major virtue of the 1986 Tax Reform Act was to eliminate this distortion. By ending the investment tax credit, reducing the benefits from accelerated depreciation, and lowering the statutory corporate tax rate from 46 to 33 percent, the Tax Reform Act lowered the tax bills of many of America's most profitable industries. This change automatically increased the IQ of America's investment capital because these industries will have more retained earnings to invest in research, plant, and equipment.

A second trend that is raising the IQ of America's investment capital is corporate restructuring. This phenomenon is difficult even for Wall Street professionals to understand fully because it is intrinsically complex and occurs by fits and starts, first in one industry and then in another. Its main components are:

1. Consolidation of industries, both those in good financial health, (media, food, financial services) and those under financial pressure (oil, airlines).

2. Leveraged buyouts of entire companies, in which a group of investors borrow heavily in order to buy a company. The loan is secured by the assets and/or cash flow of the acquired property.

3. Liquidating or streamlining of conglomerates by the sale of divisions.

4. Attempted hostile takeovers of such firms as Revlon and Union Carbide that are oriented toward dismembering the target.

5. Major acquisitions, many designed to raise the acquirer's technological sophistication or alter its business mix.

6. Heavy use of debt and share repurchases to return capital to shareholders, raise earnings per share, and discourage hostile tender offers.

The scale of this activity has been enormous. In both 1984 and 1985 owners' equity in U.S. corporations was reduced by mergers and share buy-backs at the rate of $68 billion per year, shrinking the total equity base of corporate America by about 4 percent annually. Not all aspects of the trend are favorable. As mentioned in our discussion of railroads, there is little reason to suppose that corporate raiders and other independent financiers can play a positive hands-on role in financing high-growth industries. Big mergers are likewise problematical.

Nevertheless, the net economic effect of restructuring is beneficial. To understand why, consider the dilemma of Smokestack, Inc., a major producer of chemicals and papers that also (as a result of a diversification program started in 1975) owns a semiconductor company, a chain of sportswear stores, a major New York publishing house, and a Coca-Cola bottling company. Since the chemical engineers who run the company know little about these subsidiary businesses, results have been uninspiring. They take up a third of top management's time, contribute a quarter of total revenue, but generate only 10 percent of profits. Business in the chemical and paper divisions was only so-so in 1985 and 1986, but thanks to the accelerated depreciation in President Reagan's 1981 tax reforms, Smokestack's cash flow has been very strong. Even after carrying out a major capital spending program to cut costs and remain competitive with foreign imports, the company had $1.2 billion in cash at the end of 1986 and a debt/equity ratio of only 25 percent. The central strategic question facing top management is: What does the company do with that cash? From the standpoint of public policy the question is whether or not this management is able to spend this money intelligently. If not, it should be returned to shareholders, who can invest the capital themselves, perhaps in a mid-size growth company managed by its founder.

Faced with this dilemma ten years ago, of course, Smokestack, Inc. would have followed the advice of its consultants and spent the $1.2 billion to acquire some high-growth consumer products or technology company that would smooth out the highly cyclical earnings pattern of the basic business, raise the rate of earnings growth, give the company a more glamorous image on Wall Street, and thus raise its P/E ratio. In the 1960s and 1970s corporate managements were strongly disposed to follow this advice. It gave them a sense of achievement and power to see the company grow in size and rise through the ranks of the Fortune 500—even if the profitability, as measured by return on capital, was mediocre. Unfortunately Smokestack's top management already tried the diversification strategy once, and it didn't work well. The consultants forgot to mention that a diversification program will succeed only if the new businesses are managed effectively, and they weren't. (Little wonder: The product cycles in the paper industry are measured in decades; those of sportswear fashions in years; and those of books and semiconductors in months.) Furthermore, diversification lowered the company's P/E ratio instead of raising it because no single analyst on Wall Street understands the chemical, paper, semiconductor, bottling, and fashion businesses.

So the question remains: What to do with the $1.2 billion in spare cash? One fact that weighs heavily in this decision is that I. Will Grabum, the ferocious Oklahoma-based corporate raider, has just notified the Securities and Exchange Commission that he owns 6 percent of Smokestack's stock. Moreover, trading volume in the stock has doubled over the past week, suggesting that the company has been put "in play" by Wall Street's arbitrageurs. Meeting in emergency session with a phalanx of investment bankers and lawyers, Smokestack's managers and directors respond to the crisis by formulating the following restructuring plan, in the hopes that it will placate institutional investors and dissuade them from selling their shares to Grabum:

1. Smokestack will borrow $1 billion from commercial banks.

2. Smokestack will sell the bottling, retailing, book, and semiconductor businesses, which, notwithstanding years of mismanagement, should net $1 billion. The first three will be sold to employees in leveraged buyouts; the fourth, to a major technology company.

3. The company will combine the funds so raised with the $1.2 billion of cash in the till and use the $3.2 billion to buy back a third of its shares outstanding.

4. Smokestack will further streamline operations by closing down two unprofitable plants, selling off some timberland, and firing 1,000 white-collar employees.

These moves will have a variety of financial and economic effects, most of them positive. On the negative side, the increase in debt and reduction in equity will greatly increase Smokestack's debt/equity ratio, from 25 to 50 percent. Although this will increase the earnings volatility of a company that is already quite cyclical, it does not much bother investors in a period of declining interest rates. Secondly, the company will be better managed because operations have been streamlined and officers will no longer have to spend so much time on the diversified divisions, which they did not understand in the first place. Thirdly, the company will be more closely followed on Wall Street by chemical and paper analysts. Fourthly, the company's earnings per share will rise dramatically because the stock repurchase program will shrink the number of shares outstanding by more than enough to offset the reduction in total earnings from: (1) the loss of the four divisions, (2) the increased interest costs on the higher debt load, and (3) loss of the interest income generated by the $1.2 billion in cash. In other words, the EPS increases because the denominator (shares outstanding) is reduced *more* than the numerator (total earnings).

This brings us to the effect of Smokestack's restructuring program that motivated management to do it in the first place: Its stock price rises because it has a slightly higher price/earnings ratio (thanks to improved management and more attention from analysts) on substantially higher earnings. Naturally the stock price rise pleases investors, persuading them not to sell out to Grabum, who would merely have restructured the company as Smokestack's management has just proposed to do. So Smokestack's managers and directors get to keep their jobs and see the value of their own Smokestack shares increase substantially.

From the standpoint of overall economic efficiency, Smokestack's strategic program is likewise positive for three reasons. The chemical and paper businesses will now receive the managerial attention they deserve, and costs have been lowered significantly via layoffs and plant closings. Secondly, the diversified businesses that have been spun off will be more entrepreneurial and efficient because they will not be saddled with 5 percent in corporate overhead, are now managed by people who really understand the business, and have a faster decision-making process. Thirdly, the $1.2 billion that Smokestack returned to shareholders by repurchasing stock can be invested by them in independent companies that are much more likely to excel than is a division of a conglomerate. This recycling of capital greatly increases its IQ. With the threat of takeovers giving shareholders much more clout in the boardroom, managements are more eager to make decisions that will maximize profits. Not only do they work harder to cut costs, but they are also returning capital to shareholders if they cannot reinvest it profitably. In the process, billions of dollars are being spent more wisely. The oil industry provides the best example. Under pressure from T. Boone Pickens, big oil companies reduced their massive exploration budgets and paid out the saved capital through dividend boosts and share buy-backs. Tens of billions of dollars that would have been spent drilling for oil in the Arctic Ocean were returned to shareholders, who could invest the money in biotechnology, office equipment, telecommunications, etc. At the time critics excoriated Big Oil and Wall Street for making "short-term decisions" that would impair America's energy future. But shareholders had made a rational assessment that drilling for oil was not the best use of corporate cash compared to its other potential uses in other parts of the U.S. economy. In light of the subsequent plunge in oil prices, this judgment appears to have been correct.

Although Wall Street is good at allocating capital efficiently, it has a poor understanding of the subtler organizational factors that contribute to profitability. A case in point: the recent wave of megamergers. Many cash-rich companies in mature industries, such as chemicals and automaking, have been investing some of their cash in high-technology companies the growth rates of which far exceed that of the acquiring firm. General Motors purchased Electronic Data Systems and Hughes Aircraft; Rockwell bought Allen-Bradley, a leading industrial automation company. It is far from certain that investment capital so deployed will prove over the long run to be smart money. As we have seen again and again in this book—in the creation of U.S. Steel by J. P. Morgan; in the tortured efforts of RCA, GE, Xerox, Exxon, and Remington Rand to enter the computer business; in the traumatic (though ultimately successful) alliance of Du Pont and General Motors; in the early history of biotechnology—mergers have been a poor way to finance new industries in the United States. Indeed, this observation applies to all mergers, which tend to fail for these reasons:

1. The acquirer usually pays a stiff price for the target, especially if there is a bidding war.

2. If the acquirer is intent on raising his own stock price quickly, he is likely to buy a company in Wall Street's glamour group. Not only will the target be expensive, but its fundamentals are likely to be peaking. In the late 1970s, when Wall Street was certain that inflation would continue to accelerate indefinitely, the fashionable acquisition was an "inflation hedge"—an oil or mining company. Virtually without exception these acquisitions were disasters. Nevertheless, by the mid-1980s exactly the opposite fashion ruled, and "disinflation plays"—packaged goods and media companies—were being bought up at high prices.

3. The acquirer often knows less about his quarry than he thinks. After the new owner gets the keys to the castle and peers into the

closets, sundry skeletons—overvalued inventory, inefficient computer systems, decrepit factories—may be discovered.

4. If it is a conglomerate merger, the acquirer will be operating in an industry he knows little about.

5. Most mergers, even if they are officially friendly, have a winner and a loser. The winner is always easy to spot; it is the company the top executives of which get to keep their jobs. But there is a corollary that the winners usually forget: The best executive talent on the losing side is likely to disappear and join the competition. For companies in such people-intensive industries as financial services, high technology, advertising, health care, and publishing, this talent hemorrhage can be disastrous. Particularly likely to disappear are top executives, such as the partners in a brokerage firm and the founders of high-technology firms, who owned a significant stake in the target firm and made a killing by selling out.

6. Serious operational snafus are likely as computer systems, distribution systems, airline routes, etc. are merged.

7. Frequently there is a clash of corporate cultures, especially when a large firm buys a small one.

These problems do not mean that mergers must inevitably fail, and there are some good reasons for hoping that the megamergers of the past three years, including GE/RCA, GM/EDS, Allied/Signal, Capital Cities/ABC, Reynolds/Nabisco, will be more successful than their predecessors of the 1960s and 1970s. For one thing, owing to relaxed antitrust rules, these mergers (unlike those of the 1960s) tend to be *within the same industry or in a related industry,* rather than conglomerate mergers. This significantly raises the probability of success. Not only are managements buying businesses that they understand, but economies of scale are more easily developed when both companies operate in the same market. A second virtue of recent mergers is that the financial stability associated with great size can give high-technology companies the resources to compete with big foreign rivals. U.S. semiconductor firms, which are of medium size, have had great difficulty competing with Japanese firms, which could afford to price their product very aggressively because they were divisions of large conglomerates. Nevertheless, it is far from clear that recent mergers will work better than their predecessors. The keys to success are first to make intelligent, carefully researched investment decisions that are not warped by current Wall Street fashion and then to respect the employees of the acquired firm. And Washington can make a major contribution by continuing a lax antitrust policy that allows companies to merge with other firms in the same or allied industries instead of forcing them to jump into unrelated industries that they do not understand.

XI

The Individual Investor
and the Great Growth Industries

After dissecting the numerous evils that are undermining America's worldwide economic stature, many analysts earnestly call for a greater degree of cooperation at all levels of American life—between management and labor, business and government, Wall Street and corporations, Sun Belt and Frost Belt. While comity and goodwill are all to the good and devoutly to be wished, we would take a slightly different tack. To keep the United States a leader in the world economy, we would like to suggest Americans should become more greedy. The right kind of greed, of course—the enlightened greed that builds up an economy through industrious labor, heavy saving, and savvy investment. The kind of greed that an Andrew Carnegie or a Henry Ford or a Thomas Watson displayed on his way to the top. For in the end the success of every economy hinges on the spirit of enterprise of the people who constitute it. As the example of Great Britain starkly shows, no amount of capital, labor, natural resources, or diplomatic clout will confer economic success and rising living standards on a citizenry that is not keenly focused on material achievement. There is no substitute for hustle.

When it comes to investing, Americans are hustlers. The financial markets of the United States are the largest and most creative in the world; in no other country does such a large share of the public actively participate in the security markets. This is a critical reason for the success of America's venture capital industry and helps explain the country's overall economic vitality. For America's low savings rate is partly offset by the sophistication of its financial markets, which put capital to work with maximum efficiency. Individual investors play a critical role in this process because they are able to invest in the especially profitable nooks and crannies of the American economy that big pension funds, mutual funds, and bank trust departments, by virtue of their large size, are unable to touch. And the individual investor can do very well for himself while he is doing some good for the larger economy. Indeed, for the individual investor who manages his investments shrewdly the payoff can be immense. A portfolio that generates after-tax returns of 20 percent per year—difficult to achieve, but far from impossible—would turn $10,000 into $61,917 in ten years and $154,070 in fifteen years.

THE LIQUIDITY TRAP

Although it looks easy, successful investing is actually very difficult. And one of the main reasons why it is so difficult is precisely that it looks so easy. After all, there is no physical effort involved. Just pick up the phone, call your broker, exchange a few words, and suddenly that block of stock you inherited from your grandfather is turned into cash. A major financial transaction, perhaps involving tens of thousands of dollars, can be carried out in less time than it takes to find a parking space at the supermarket on a Saturday morning. Although it is one of the glories of the modern American economy, the efficiency of the securities markets, paradoxically enough, is a trap for most investors. It might be called, with apologies to John Maynard Keynes, the liquidity trap. Stocks and bonds are so liquid—so easy to buy and to sell— that genuinely thorough, prudent, and sensible investment for the purpose of long-term capital gains is surprisingly rare. Short-term speculation, driven by impulse rather than analysis, is the norm. Mediocre long-term performance is the inevitable result.

Investors can employ several different approaches to avoid the liquidity trap and compile superior long-term investment results, including:

Disciplined speculation in companies that are merging with other companies (aka risk arbitrage)

Buying the depressed securities of bankrupt companies that are in Chapter 11 proceedings

Investing in turnaround situations—unprofitable companies the stocks of which are shunned but the fortunes of which are likely to improve in a couple of years

Investing in undervalued companies throughout the world

Buying cyclical stocks, the profits of which rise and fall substantially as the U.S. economy expands and contracts

Investing in growth stocks that chalk up higher earnings year after year

Pure value investing—buying the stocks of successful companies that are selling below their intrinsic economic value, based on their earning power and net worth

Although a few investment geniuses have mastered more than one of these styles, most savvy professionals stick to a single approach. Individual investors should do likewise. Try to build up a solid fund of experience and knowledge—about the market and about your own strengths and weaknesses as an investor—that will give you a competitive edge in the financial jungle. For an investor should never forget that he is directly competing against every other investor who is stalking through the same market, searching for superior value. Whenever you get on the phone to make a trade, remember that someone is *selling* what you are *buying*. Does he or she know a vital fact that you don't know? The seller might be a top security analyst who has studied the industry for twenty years and knows the company's management intimately. For that matter, he might *himself* be a member of top management. Whoever he is, he is betting that your decision to purchase the security is wrong. The only way to beat the competition is to invest on the basis of superior knowledge, not superior knowledge about investments in general—though that is very helpful, of course—but about the specific security that you are trading.

To win this battle, the individual investor should pick his battleground carefully. Some are more treacherous than others. International investing is not a favorable battleground—unless you have a thorough knowledge of economic conditions in Europe and Asia, eight or ten local brokers to feed you good ideas faithfully, and some grounding in exotic foreign accounting methods. The merger arbitrage game is glamorous and fast-paced, guaranteed to perk up cocktail party chatter that is sagging under a surfeit of golf scores and office gossip. But you aren't likely to win here unless you can pick up tips at the "21" Club bar or the locker room of the New York Athletic Club. Despite the SEC's best efforts, this is very much an insider's game. As for cyclical investing, foreign competition and the gyrations of the dollar have taken most of the fun out of betting on cyclical recoveries in smokestack

America, and in any case it hinges on a superior feel for economic trends and close, continuous scrutiny of the data churned out by the number mills on the Potomac. And prospecting in the junkyard of bankrupt companies and turnaround situations is best left to CPAs and security analysts who know the managements, understand subtle accounting issues, and have time to read reams and reams of soporific legal documents.

That leaves pure value investing and growth stock investing. *We recommend that individual investors use a combination of the two, which might be called value-growth investing. What it involves is simply this: purchasing superior companies with long-term records of continuous earnings growth that are well managed and highly profitable and that are well positioned with respect to the major trends in the national economy.* After these select companies have been identified, they should be *purchased at the right price.* This is a game the individual investor can win, for three important reasons:

1.   Competition is somewhat limited because many of these companies are too small to be of interest to giant institutional investors.

2.   Value-growth investors should buy for relatively long periods —a minimum of two years—whereas many institutions and individual investors have a time horizon of six months or a year.

3.   Success does not hinge on technical knowledge of the financial markets or on close day-to-day scrutiny of price action. Any intelligent and assiduous observer can spot the long-term economic trends that will shape the future of corporate America.

The cornerstone of value-growth investing is superior knowledge of superior companies. Many investors know a lot about their stocks, but they know too much about the wrong things and not enough about the important things. Think back to earlier chapters in this book. Our breakneck tour of America's great growth industries encountered dozens of superb companies that made thousands of investors rich. It is fruitful to ask what would have been the key things to notice in order to spot these great companies before they became cornerstones of the American economy. One would probably mention Andrew Carnegie's superior knowledge of the railroad market for steel products, his salesmanship and financial acumen, his obsession with cutting costs, his knack for promoting and motivating "young geniuses" in the mill. One would emphasize the tremendous amount of automotive experience and knowledge that Henry Ford had accumulated by the time he set up his third company in 1903 and also the fact that automaking was a spectacularly profitable (though highly risky) growth industry. An investor in IBM in the early 1950s would have noted that veteran salesman Thomas Watson had given IBM a superior grasp of the market for business machines, which had allowed the firm to regain its position after missing the technological shift to electronic computers. These are a few of the factors that made for success in these great companies; stock market investors should consider similar factors when shopping for superior companies in the 1980s. Many of the critical variables involve the personal qualities of the management, and this is hardly surprising because a stockholder in effect hands over his cash to management in the expectation that it will make the capital grow. The other key variable, of course, is the intrinsic profitability and growth potential of the industry.

There is one thing we have *not* much mentioned because it has nothing to do with whether the company is good or bad. Yet it is, paradoxically enough, something that almost every investor, professional or amateur, checks first when he settles into his seat on the bus or commuter train, opens up the *Wall Street Journal,* and begins the journey to work. We refer, of course, to the stock price. Now, stock quotations are indeed important to investors because they are the price tags of corporate merchandise. But they are nothing more than that and should not be confused with the fundamentals of the company itself. For stocks, as for suits and automobiles, the intrinsic quality of the merchandise is not changed one whit if the price goes up or down. While this fact might seem too obvious to mention, the stock price is often treated by investors as though it were the soul of the company. Many investors, for example, buy companies because their stock has price momentum—meaning that their main virtue is that they are considerably more expensive today than they were a month ago. In fact, stocks and perfume may be the only merchandise that grow in popularity as they become more overpriced.

Nor is obsession with stock price merely a foible of overwrought speculators. Professors of finance have turned stock price into a fundamental trait of a company by developing the concept of beta. Quite simply, a stock has a beta of 1.2 if it normally rises 120 percent when the overall stock market rises 100 percent. Thus a high-beta stock is a volatile stock. This is fine so far as it goes; it is worth knowing the beta of a stock that you own. But then the professors go a step farther by using beta to compute the *riskiness* of a stock and insisting that the total return earned by purchasing a stock should be adjusted for risk as measured by the stock's beta. This implies that a superb company of moderate size, such as the Dow Jones Corporation (beta: 1.41) is *riskier* than a large, heavily indebted company in a mature industry, such as Phillips Petroleum (beta: 0.90). Dow Jones may be a *more volatile stock*, but it is actually a far *less risky investment* because it is a fine company in a growth industry. It is only riskier for stockholders who will get scared and sell out when the stock market drops, since Dow Jones is likely to drop more than Phillips Petroleum in a down market. Over the long term, however, it is likely to perform much better because *the key long-term determinant of stock price is earnings growth.* This distinction is vital, for many investors mistakenly avoid good smaller companies on the theory that they have higher betas and thus are riskier. Instead, they stick with blue-chip stocks that may have low betas and well-known names but also mediocre managements and uninspiring futures. Investors who follow this line of reasoning would have avoided the high-beta General Motors Corporation in 1910 in favor of a solid, respected, well-known, low-beta blue chip like Amalgamated Buggywhip.

Illogical though it is, stock price fixation is easily explained. Investors are preoccupied with stock prices rather than company fundamentals because *information on stock price is far more accessible.* If you read the paper every day, you can stay abreast of which stock groups are "in favor" on Wall Street and currently "have momentum." If you were thinking of buying the XYZ Corporation but decided against it, and then it shoots up 20 percent, you know you have "missed a move." If the broad market averages move up, you will be told which stocks are the "leaders" and which are the "laggards," and you will encounter learned speculations about where the large institutional investors are likely to move next in the unceasing process of "group rotation" out of some industries and into others. If you are steeped in the lore of technical analysis, you can graph stock prices and spot "head and shoulder" patterns, "double bottoms," and "upside breakouts." While it is important to be aware of the dynamics of market psychology, all this stock market lore can easily induce an investor to plunge thousands of dollars into the market without knowing anything about the company he owns. Fixation on the ebb and flow of stock prices holds the great danger of distracting you from the main essential of good investing: finding out about the companies themselves and why their profits will or will not rise in coming years.

Knowledge is paramount. Remember John Murray Forbes' insistence on investing only in railroads the managements of which he knew well and trusted implicitly, and Andrew Carnegie's warning that "Nothing tells in the long run like good judgment, and no sound judgment can remain with the man whose mind is disturbed by the mercurial changes of the Stock Exchange. . . . He cannot judge of relative values or get the true perspective of things."

Apropos here is a comparison made by John Train, the distinguished author and investment adviser. If you went to an unfamiliar community to buy a house, you would not begin your search by phoning five or six real estate brokers to find out which streets were most popular right now and which houses were most likely to "go up" in price over the next six months. You would probably select one or two pleasant and prosperous neighborhoods with good long-term prospects and then shop for a house that offered the most for the money. You would inspect every room, make sure the plumbing worked and the roof was solid, check the soundness of the foundation and the age of the furnace and a dozen other things. Is the house on a quiet street? Are the grounds attractive? Are the local schools good? Since a mistaken answer to any these mundane questions would cause you endless annoyance and expense, you would make sure you got the answers. By purchasing a good house in a good neighborhood at the right price, you will make a good investment.

Buyers of companies should do much the same thing. It's not easy to do, however, because a company, unlike a house, cannot be entered and inspected room by room. In a curious way, a company listed on the New York Stock Exchange is a rather ethereal piece of property. On the one hand, it is a cluster of tangible and intangible properties spread across the country or across the globe, making and selling an array of products that the investor may never have used. (How many investors have actually seen crude oil?) On the other hand, the company is a set of financial statements, bound in a more or less overoptimistic annual report, which are importantly affected by the choice of abstruse accounting conventions. Moreover, the investor must gauge not only the present state of the company but its future as well. To understand the operations of a company and its future prospects, you have to study reports of brokerage houses, read newspaper and magazine articles, scan statistics in *Value Line* and the *Standard & Poor's Guide*, analyze future economic trends, and, when possible, use a company's products and services. It takes a lot of time—time busy executives and professionals just don't have. Moreover, curling up with the latest edition of *Value Line* is not everyone's idea of high entertainment. It is far more fun to check stock prices and exchange market chitchat with your friends. And if you make a mistake while shopping for a company, well, it's only money. You can take the loss and write it off at tax time. Investment mistakes are costly but far less hassle than replacing a furnace or fixing a leak in the roof. Of course, when you take this attitude you have followed many another investor into the stock market's liquidity trap.

THE MARKINGS OF THE GREAT GROWTH COMPANY

But enough cynicism. Let's assume that you really are going to make a serious hunt for a good company. What should you look for? We think a good company:

1. Will be in a *growing industry*, free of intense competition from the Far East, heavy government regulation, or tough union pressure.

2. Will be *exceptionally profitable*, in part because it has a strong business franchise that competitors cannot easily invade.

3. Will be of modest size and in the *high growth phase* of its development but not so small that the risks of bankruptcy in a recession or short-run adversity are very high.

4. Is recognized as one of the *best companies in the industry* because its plans for the future are clear and ambitious and it is in the van of technological innovation. Industry leaders are also usually *low-cost producers.*

5. Has *superior top managers* who have plenty of hands-on experience and a real feel for the business. Confident of their business judgment, they are not afraid to flout conventional wisdom. Moreover, they are major shareholders who have an incentive to maximize shareholder wealth.

6. Is *well focused* on a few promising markets instead of being broadly diversified.

Few companies will display all these characteristics, but many will have four or five of the six because they are closely correlated with one another. Let's look at them in greater detail.

Growth Industry A "growth industry" by definition has profits that are growing faster than the national economy as a whole, which is currently about 7 percent as measured by *nominal* GNP. Right off the bat, this criterion eliminates at least half of all the companies in the S&P 500, including such broad areas as machine tools, heavy equipment, autos and auto parts, energy, chemicals, containers, department stores, railroads, and utilities. This list has been dramatically changed by the fall of inflation since 1980; many corporate winners of the 1970s are losers in the 1980s. To get a firm analytical grip on which industry groups would prosper in a period of low inflation, the forty-seven industry analysts of a well-known investment banking firm conducted an exhaustive six-month study of the earnings growth outlook for forty-four major industry groups. It reached four key conclusions:

1. Companies possessing *strong consumer franchises* can achieve relatively high earnings growth in a period of low inflation. Brand identification gives a company like Coca-Cola or Kellogg the power to raise its prices without losing many customers. And consumers are particularly likely to accept slight price increases because their own real discretionary income rises in a period of low inflation as the cost of basic necessities like heating oil and meat remains stable. And while it can charge somewhat more for its own products, the cost of raw material inputs—sugar for Coca-Cola, grains for Kellogg—goes down. Therefore, profit margins expand.

2. Because of the acute foreign competition facing corporate America, companies will tend to prosper if they sell goods and services that help their customers use capital, labor, material, and managers more efficiently. In other words, *productivity is their product*. Industries that can benefit from this trend include computers, securities brokers, business information producers, and telecommunications companies.

3. *Service vendors are safer than manufacturers* because their pricing power is better protected from foreign competition. Over the last five years the inflation rate for services has been much higher than the inflation for commodities and manufactures. One reason for this pattern has been the strong dollar, which made imports very competitive; a second factor has been the low labor costs and high productivity of many Asian manufacturers. Among the most promising service sectors are financial services, the media, miscellaneous

business services, advertising, restaurants, business forms, and specialty retailing.

4. *Vendors of proprietary knowledge,* whether in the area of science, marketing, securities trading, health care, or whatever, have a valuable competitive edge. Since the cost of capital and labor is higher in the United States than in many other countries, corporations must rely on advanced knowledge to retain a competitive edge. That means *good people,* well managed and hard working, with strong financial incentives to excel and innovate. Needless to say, the company with the best people is the company with the best reputation within the industry.

Profitable Companies Growth and profitability are not the same thing. If revenues (i.e., sales) rise but profit margins decline—perhaps because of rising overhead or high R&D expenses—profits may be disappointing and the stock may languish. In fact, rapid growth may itself reduce profitability because it requires heavy spending on advertising, research and development, training of new employees, building new stores, etc. Moreover, it is vital to remember that some industries are simply much more profitable than others. We saw how the capital-intensiveness and hypercompetitiveness of the railroad industry made it a bad investment in the nineteenth century; the telephone industry was not much better once competition had begun in the 1890s. During the twentieth century the airline industry has displayed erratic profitability because expansion involves costly investment in new aircraft (which raises interest expense), fare wars periodically break out, and profit margins were hurt by rising energy costs during the 1970s.

To maintain healthy profit margins, a company needs to have some control over both the prices it charges and its own costs. Therefore, monopolies or oligopolies—whether it is Coke and Pepsi's domination of the cola market, or IBM's control of its user base, or a radio station's monopoly of the local country and western audience—is a major plus for a company. These companies have strong business franchises; ace investor Warren Buffett likes to say that a few select companies have businesses that are surrounded with moats full of crocodiles and sharks that ward off competitors. Think of the enormous resources required, for example, to invade American Express's franchise in the upscale credit card market. Some of these profitable companies are relatively dull, but they give their shareholders few unpleasant earnings surprises. Among them are:

Business forms companies
Local broadcasting and newspaper companies
Tobacco companies
Defense contractors
Specialized service companies
Check printers
Greeting card companies

A good way to keep track of the changing profitability of corporate America is to read the industry scoreboards and surveys of American business that appear from time to time in *Business Week*. Pay attention both to profit margins and to return on equity; these measures tend to be overlooked by investors, who pay too much attention to anticipated earnings growth. Profitability tells you whether management is using assets effectively and whether the company has some control over its financial destiny. The great problem of most high-technology companies, for example, is that they have weak or nonexistent business franchises. Their earnings may explode if they are first to the market with a new product but often collapse when a competitor comes out with a better product or prices collapse as other companies enter the market.

High-Growth Phase Companies, like people, tend to grow tired as they get older. Since successful companies are often built by talented entrepreneurs, growth may wane if the founder retires. And even if the founder remains effective, key employees who were full of fire in their twenties and thirties may start to slacken when they get into their forties and fifties. Another subtle danger is a burgeoning bureaucracy that may choke off employee initiative and, like a subtle narcotic, slow down corporate reaction time. Before a product can get to market in a big company, it must clear the hurdles posed by the Strategic Planning Department, the Engineering Department, the Marketing Department, the Finance Department, and the Department of the CEO. Smaller companies can move quicker and grab a major share of the market first. Furthermore, corporate bureaucracies have a big stake in the status quo and may avoid innovations that would invalidate long-held assumptions or challenge major power centers. As we have seen, these are key reasons for the success of small high-tech start-ups; the energy level is higher, and corporate reflexes are sharper. These all are subtle dangers, not easily monitored by outsiders. But a shrewd observer can try to determine whether top management is guarding against them, perhaps by decentralizing the organization to maintain the entrepreneurial fire. Prior to acquiring ABC, Capital Cities Communications, one of the best-managed companies in the United States, was a collection of highly profitable, relatively autonomous media businesses. The 3M corporation bolsters the creativity of its engineers by keeping research units small.

Growth has other dangers as well. From a purely numerical standpoint it is much, much more difficult for a company to achieve 20 percent profit growth when its revenues are $1.8 billion than it was a decade earlier, when they were only $300 million. For the company to keep up the 20 percent growth when it has already hit $1.8 billion in revenues, the annual increase in revenues—$360 million—exceeds the company's total revenues a decade earlier. When it reaches this size, the easy growth is over, and a company may have to tangle with other good strong competitors instead of just squeezing out the underfinanced mom-and-pop concerns. A current example is small-town discount retailers. During the 1970s and early 1980s this relatively obscure industry group contained a number of superb growth stocks, including Walmart, Dollar General, Family Dollar, and Ames Department Stores. A major success factor: They faced limited competition because stores were situated in small agricultural and manufacturing towns where they were the only retailers selling a broad array of products at reasonable prices. Not *too* reasonable, however. Limited competition made for healthy profit margins. But now these chains have grown so big that more than one store may serve the same small town; they are also opening stores in larger towns already served by department stores. A common managerial response to this problem of industry maturation is to move into a more promising industry. But diversification is dangerous, as we will see.

Of course, a growth company will face stiffening competition far less rapidly if it serves a growing market. If a market is growing 20 percent per year, a company can grow at that rate without increasing its market share at all. It is not that simple, however, because a market that is growing 20 percent per year is a young industry undergoing rapid and profound structural change—in a word, consolidation. When an industry is consolidating—as the auto industry did from its inception until 1929 or as the personal computer industry has been doing since its birth —a company must grow *much faster* than its competitors to stay in the race. Firms that fail to increase market share eventually drop out because they are not big enough to finance the research and development and the huge marketing teams needed to stay competitive.

In order to buy growth companies the futures of which are as promising as their pasts, one should concentrate on smaller companies, with revenues in the range of $100 million to $800 million. Just as one would expect, statistical studies have turned up the "small company effect"; on average small companies tend to produce better stock market results than big companies. In addition to producing faster profit growth than large companies, good small companies are more likely to be acquired because they offer good value and are easily digestible by the corporate behemoths. Small companies have a bad reputation among many individual investors, who think of them as speculative stocks that are liable to collapse in a bear market, a recession, or an industry shakeout. The challenge facing investors is to separate the wheat from the chaff—the genuine small growth company from the glamorous shooting star that burns out in a few years.

To make the distinctions, we have three suggestions. To begin with, avoid very small companies, with revenues of under $50 million; companies that have crossed this threshold have some financial staying power in an economic downturn. Still more important, one must differentiate between genuine growth companies and fad stocks. A genuine growth stock has a business—such as discount drugstores or discount department stores or pharmaceuticals—the primary market of which offers plenty of room for growth and the management of which clearly has the ability to exploit this opportunity. By contrast a fad stock—a Mexican restaurant, for example, or a toymaker with a couple of hot products—is at the mercy of consumer tastes even though it has achieved spectacular profit growth over the past few years. Thirdly, a buyer of small stocks, even more than other investors, has to learn to live with market volatility. The stock prices of perfectly good companies with rising earnings and promising prospects may drop quite dramatically in a bear market. Many fine over-the-counter issues declined by a quarter or a third in the comparatively mild bear market of the first half of 1984. Such market dips are an opportunity for you to "average down" by purchasing more of a high-grade growth stock while it is particularly cheap—not as a time to doubt your own judgment and sell out. It is helpful to remember that the market for small stocks is like the market for thinly traded real estate. Even if the property is perfectly good, there may be days when investors are apathetic and simply not interested in bidding much for the company. This is a reflection on the market, not the investment.

In a superb article on John Maynard Keynes, private investor, *Forbes* magazine quotes the famous economist (who also invested on behalf of his Cambridge college): "Some bursars will buy without a tremor unquoted and unmarketable investments in real estate which, if they had a selling quotation for immediate cash available at each Audit [as one does for listed stocks], would turn their hair gray. The fact that you do not know how much its ready money quotation fluctuates does not, as is commonly supposed, make an investment a safe one. . . . It is true, unfortunately, that *the modern organization of the capital market requires for the holder of quoted equities [i.e., stocks] much more nerve, patience, and fortitude than from the holder of wealth in other forms* [our italics]." Instead of panicking when the stock price of a flourishing company declines in a bear market, investors should view the price drop as an opportunity and buy more of the stock, once the selling wave has crested. But to take this step, investors must have enough confidence in their judgment to believe that they are right and the investors who are selling off the stock are wrong—that the stock's price decline really is a buying opportunity, not a sign that the fundamentals of the company have suddenly changed in a negative way. At these critical junctures there is no substitute for knowledge. Now is the time when you wish you had inspected the stock you bought as carefully as you would a house you were going to live in. You can buy a good stock on a tip or a rumor, but you will hold that good stock, through good times and bad, only if you know a great deal about it. This is a key reason why overdiversification is dangerous; amateur investors who own more than ten stocks cannot know their holdings very well. Keynes again: "You won't believe me, I know, but it is out of these big units of the small number of securities about which one feels absolutely happy that all one's profits are made."

Industry Leaders   Every industry has its class acts—companies that are generally recognized to be the best in the business. In aerospace it is Boeing; in computers it is IBM and Digital Equipment; in retailing it is The Limited and Walmart. These companies are not to be confused with "glamour stocks" that are currently in favor on Wall Street and therefore likely to be overpriced. Rather, they are the companies with the best reputations among customers, suppliers, and—probably most important—potential employees. A distinguishing characteristic of these companies is well-defined strategies and a penchant for disciplined innovation. Management takes the long view and invests in the future to stay competitive, even if this hurts profits and stock price in the near term. Citicorp is a case in point. In the mid-1970s the company began to invest heavily in technology to integrate its operations globally and make them highly price-competitive. It also made a major investment in consumer banking. When interest rates soared above legally defined usury ceilings in the late seventies, profits were disappointing for a while, and Wall Street was unhappy. But it was a wise long-run decision, and now, when opportunities to lend to the energy industry, real estate developers, and less developed countries are limited, the company is in a far stronger position than most other money center banks. Management was willing to take some risks in order to give the company strategic direction and in the process made it a dynamic enterprise that would attract talented employees and grab a market share over the long term.

Superior Management   As the Citicorp example illustrates, a hallmark of superior companies is that management has the self-confidence to be unconventional. Andrew Carnegie's purchase of steel mills in the middle of depressions looked dangerous to competitors, and the Model T seemed a bizarre product to an industry still geared to the middle- and upper-class markets. Charles Lazarus, founder of Toys R Us, had the brilliant idea of *not* paying high shopping mall rents but rather of building big freestanding stores near major shopping malls and offering a huge selection of toys. On the way to the shopping mall a Saturday shopper could stop by the Toys R Us store, confident that it would have what he needed. A sophisticated computerized tracking system at Toys R Us keeps abreast of what goods are moving fastest, so that the company can reorder early. In an incisive research report on The Limited, PaineWebber analyst Margo F. McGlade ticks off the novel approaches that Leslie Wexner has used to make The Limited the most successful apparel retailer in the nation:

> The Limited is not an ordinary retailer or even an ordinary growth retailer. It has helped pioneer the realignment of retailing into centrally managed, discreet and specialized profit centers that offer added value to the consumer. The difference between the way Limited is run and the way Sears is run is the difference between a free market and a centrally planned economy. Limited is operated as if it were a group of competing

companies. Each division makes the decisions that will bring maximum profitability to itself, and top management's purpose is to facilitate this process, thereby maximizing the entire company's profitability.

Not surprisingly, many of these supermanagers are also the company's founders. The same skills and energy that allowed them to break into the industry in the first place also help them expand the company successfully. Their own large stakes in the enterprise give them particularly strong motivation to work hard.

Strategic Focus   Before vanquishing the flimsy steel conglomerate that J. P. Morgan put together, Andrew Carnegie asserted: "It is with firms as with nations; 'scattered possessions' are not in it with solid, compact, concentrated force." Corporate America spent much of the 1960s and 1970s relearning this lesson. During the 1960s, as we have seen, a new type of company came upon the corporate scene—the conglomerate comprised of a group of unrelated businesses ranging to everything from meat-packing to moviemaking to motels. The rationale for conglomerates was threefold. For one thing, a cyclical company could reduce the volatility of its earnings by expanding into a different business with a different earnings pattern. Reduced earnings volatility would, in turn, raise the stock price—the aim of management. Secondly, managements claimed to spot synergies between different lines of business that would make the whole worth more than the sum of its parts. This had some plausibility when American Express purchased Shearson Loeb Rhodes, but almost none when ITT, the basic business of which was foreign telephone systems, purchased Sheraton Hotels, Hertz Rent-a-Car, Hartford Insurance, and Continental Bakeries. A third rationale for conglomerates—for which the top business schools must take much of the blame—was that the modern manager really did not need to know much about the details of a business to manage it well. All he needed was a knowledge of modern management skills, including the nebulous systems approach that Robert McNamara installed at the Pentagon in the early 1960s.

Unfortunately the systems approach worked no better on the corporate battlefield than it worked in Vietnam. Systematic studies suggest that at least half of all acquisitions are financial failures, and most of the classic conglomerates of the late sixties are now being dismantled. After cheering conglomeratization in the late sixties, Wall Street today applauds its opposite: the widespread restructuring of corporate America that was discussed in the previous chapter. It now appears that none of the rationales for conglomerates were valid. There is no reason for a company to acquire extraneous enterprises in order to reduce earnings volatility; investors can diversify for themselves simply by purchasing companies in a variety of industries. As for synergies, they are usually illusory. Even if there *are* theoretical synergies between different enterprises, they are extraordinarily difficult to achieve in the real world because companies are located in different places and possess different corporate cultures. Thirdly, the highly touted modern management approach usually boiled down to a headquarters staff in New York or Chicago, unencumbered with much firsthand knowledge of the businesses in the corporate portfolio, managing these divisions "by the numbers." This typically meant compensating executives on the basis of their division's *current* profitability. This being the case, operating executives maximized their incomes by neglecting investments that would enhance competitiveness in the long term but depress return on investment in the short term. As RCA's misadventures in the computer business show, mistakes in the field were often compounded by errors at headquarters. Acquisitions were planned and major strategic decisions were made by executives with no hands-on operational experience, no feel for the market or the technology. Managements frequently overpay in acquisitions because they have to buy companies in a hurry, at a large premium to the market price and without having full details of operations. And acquisitions are often made at the top of the market, when the strategic rationale behind the acquisition is widely accepted on Wall Street and thus likely to boost the stock price in the short term. For all these reasons, *beware of companies that plan to grow through acquisition—expecially acquisitions in new, unfamiliar businesses.* It is safer to own a company that has plenty of room to grow within a business it has already mastered.

STALKING THE GREAT GROWTH COMPANIES

After identifying attractive growth companies, one has to buy them at an attractive price. Without going into all the technicalities of determining the fair value of a stock, we would simply emphasize that it is safest to buy companies that are cheap in relation to their past price /earnings ratio, the price/earnings ratios of other companies in the industry, and the stock market in general. Of course, a company becomes cheap for a reason: Either it is facing some fundamental problem or it is simply out of favor on Wall Street because a different class of stocks is performing better. If you conclude, after close investigation, that the market is wrong—that a superior growth company is selling cheaply for a reason that is invalid—call your broker and buy it in quantity. But leave yourself enough cash to buy more if the stock becomes cheaper still.

To have the stomach for such independent thinking and action, one needs a streak of contrarianism, which may be defined as a conviction that the conventional investment wisdom is either (1) dead wrong or (2) correct but is worthless as a guide to action because investors have already acted on it and bid up prices accordingly. Keynes, for example, asserted: "My central principle of investment is to go contrary to general opinion, on the ground that, if everyone is agreed about its merits, the investment is inevitably too dear and therefore unattractive." Master investor John Templeton follows the principle that you cannot make a lot of money in the stock market if you buy what everyone else is buying. Crowded bazaars offer few bargains. While few would argue with this proposition in theory, many ignore it in practice and pile into the popular corners of the market, where prices are being marked up daily. Two main factors explain this anomaly. Many people crave the positive reinforcement of buying the same stocks that interest other investors; they mistakenly sense a safety in numbers and believe that they are reducing their risks. Moreover, many people are greedy and prefer to buy stocks that will go up *soon* because they are currently moving up. This tendency has been reinforced by the pressure on pension fund managers to beat the stock market every quarter; managers cannot afford to buy good values that will be "dead money" over the next six months. In fact, however, this short-term orientation is nothing new. Keynes observed: "Very few American investors buy any stock for the sake of something which is going to happen more than six months hence, even though its probability is exceedingly high; and it is out of taking advantage of this psychological peculiarity of theirs that most money is made." Keynes reasoned: "It is a mistake to sell a £1 note for 15 shillings in the hope of buying it back for 12 shillings 6d., and a mistake to refuse to buy a £1 note for 15 shillings on the ground that it cannot really be a £1 note (for there is abundant experience that a £1 note can be bought for 15 shillings at a time when they are expected by many people to fall to 12 shillings 6d)." By using this perspective, one can purchase high-quality companies fitting the aforementioned criteria when they are unusually cheap.

We have outlined a very tough set of criteria for the companies that will be in your portfolio. Only the superstars of corporate America will make it past the gate, and then only at the right price. This is as it should be. After all, your long-term financial success is at stake. A natural by-product of tough selection criteria is a limited portfolio, which should number between six and ten issues. One often hears about the virtues of diversification, and there is something to it. It is dangerous to own fewer than six stocks, and those six should be in different industries. But the shibboleth of diversification may become an excuse for failing to make sound, disciplined decisions. When faced with the choice of buying Company A or Company B, one may buy a little of each with the happy thought "It's better to be diversified!" Or you may use the same excuse to take a flyer in a stock you don't understand. Pretty soon your portfolio becomes a grab bag of companies about which you know little. And because no one company represents a very large investment, you have little incentive to keep on top of each stock. It is a vicious circle: An undisciplined investment approach may lead to a large portfolio, and a large portfolio in turn provides little incentive to be a disciplined investor. Keyncs asserted: "Out of the ordinary mixed bag of investments nobody ever makes anything. . . . I am quite incapable of having adequate knowledge of more than a very limited range of investments. Time and opportunity do not allow more." Warren Buffett likes to say that investors should know the companies they own well enough to feel like a partner of management. This is unlikely if you own more than a dozen stocks.

The Tides of the Stock Market   One of the major virtues of intclligent growth stock investing is that you do not need a bull market to make money. But a bull market makes the task a lot easier, so it is wise to have a sense of the long-term trends in stock market history and know where you stand in the cycle. In the spring of 1984 the PaineWebber Research Department conducted a short historical analysis of the U.S. stock market which clearly suggested that stock market performance during the 1980s should be relatively strong. It computed, for each decade from the 1870s through the 1970s, just two numbers: the average level of the S&P 500 for the decade—a standard measure of stock market performance—and the average level of real per capita GNP for the decade—a standard measure of economic growth. Then it calculated the percent change over the previous decade. From these twenty numbers emerged a clear pattern. In a decade of strong market performance stock prices typically *lurched ahead* of the economy; during 1900–10, for example, S&P 500 prices were up 50 percent over the preceding decade while real per capita GNP was up just 29 percent. But in the succeeding decade the market tended to *lag behind* the economy. Between 1910 and 1920 real per capita GNP was up 16 percent while average S&P 500 prices were up only 4 percent because investors were frightened by the economic upheaval associated with World War I—even though the war was immensely beneficial to the economic stature of the United States.

This lag-and-lurch pattern is characteristic of the past century of stock market history. Because stocks represent a claim on a major segment of the productive capacity of the American economy, their prices have tended to rise as the economy itself has grown. Between the 1870s and 1981 real per capita GNP rose 694 percent while the S&P 500 index rose 2,914 percent, or more than four times as much. Nevertheless, in the 1890s, 1910s, and 1940s the average level of the S&P 500 index increased over the average for the preceding decade *by a much smaller percentage than did real per capita GNP.* In the three succeeding decades—1900–09, 1920–29, and 1950–59—*equity prices increased sharply.* One of the best examples of the lag-and-lurch pattern is the 1940s and 1950s. During the forties average real GNP per capita increased by 61 percent over the depressed level of the 1930s, and investors reacted with a long and loud yawn. NYSE volume during the forties amounted to only about half the Big Board volume of the 1920s and 1930s. Investors were worried about a return of depression after World War II ended and also by rapid worldwide inflation during the late 1940s. Stocks did not interest them, no matter how cheap they were or how strong their recent profit growth had been. But once Wall Street became convinced that a new depression was not lurking beyond the next peak in the business cycle, capital poured into equities, lifting the S&P 500 by 212 percent between 1950 and 1959 even though economic growth during the decade was far from spectacular.

The 1970s and 1980s resemble these earlier lag-and-lurch episodes because during the 1970s inflation and related dangers once again heightened the risk of investing in equities. Although the United States was at peace through most of the decade, investors dodged many hazards normally associated with a wartime economy, including large budget deficits, high inflation, high interest rates, government price controls, shortages of imported commodities, and two recessions. Although the nation's economy grew about as rapidly as it had during the 1950s, this array of dangers prevented investors from looking into the distant future and sighting an ever-increasing stream of earnings and dividends. Such rosy visions were usually obscured by the dark clouds of inflation and recession. *Consequently the market lagged behind the economy in the seventies,* with prices rising only 22 percent while average per capita GNP rose 28 percent. If the past is any guide and lurch follows lag, the 1980s should be a decade of strong stock market performance. There is, of course, no guarantee that this will occur; stocks languished during both the 1930s and 1940s because a severe depression was followed by a world war. However, a lurch is likely if the country solves the key problem that has been holding down stock prices. In the 1970s that factor was inflation; with inflation now under control the stage is set for a substantial rise in stock prices not unlike that of the 1950s.

To take advantage of these long-term swings, one should remember that bull markets *climb a wall of worry* and then—if we may mix metaphors—*fall off a cliff of complacency.* After a prolonged period of poor performance the market's climb is slow and unsteady at first and Wall Street confronts the paradox of profits without pleasure. During the late 1940s many investors remained on the sidelines and refused to believe that the problems that had been depressing stock prices were finally being corrected. As stock prices tripled during the 1950s, for example, investors viewed the bull move with trepidation, believing that a replay of the 1929 market crash was imminent. New York Stock Exchange trading volume merely matched that of the mid-1920s, when the U.S. economy was less than half as large. When in January 1955 the Dow industrials began to explore the uncharted territory above 400, the Senate Committee on Banking and Currency thought it prudent to hold hearings on the dangers of Wall Street speculation. During the hearings Harvard Professor John Kenneth Galbraith unsettled the market by drawing parallels between the 1920s and 1950s, prompting such newspaper headlines as EGG-HEAD SCRAMBLES MARKET. By the time that equities were finally perceived to be "safe," in the late 1950s, a good part of the bull move was already completed. It is this very skepticism—which recently has revolved around the federal budget deficit—that creates investment opportunity. While there is no guarantee that old problems will be solved, the very awareness of their existence and the dangers they pose raises the probability that politicians will really do something about them. During the 1950s, for example, economic policy pursued a cautious path between the widely appreciated dangers of a depression on the one hand and inflation on the other.

After a decade or so of rising stock prices and generally good economic performance, a ruddy glow of optimism spreads over Wall Street and the country at large. Since rising stock prices now seem to be the natural order of things, caution dissipates and stock market action becomes more speculative as it becomes more popular. Thus in August 1929 the *Ladies' Home Journal* published an interview with John J. Raskob, a leader of the Du Pont interests and a major Wall Street operator, entitled "Everybody Ought to Be Rich." It is at this point, when market conditions look most favorable and the national economy has nary a cloud in the sky, that stocks are likely to fall off a cliff of complacency. For one thing, stocks are no longer a bargain; their P/E ratios are so high that they reflect a conviction that good economic news will last forever. In fact, of course, investors' crystal balls are as cloudy as ever; no one can be sure that good times will continue. If the probabilities of good, bad, and indifferent economic performance are each 33 percent, and stocks are priced to reflect an expectation of good performance, the odds are clearly against you. You have a 67 percent chance of a disappointment, a 33 percent chance of an acceptable but unspectacular return, and no chance of a really pleasant surprise.

Furthermore—and this is a subtler point—the probability of poor economic performance in the coming decade is *actually higher* after stocks have experienced an extended bull run. Since Wall Street opinion reflects the larger national mood, the complacency of investors infects Washington as well. Feeling that the major problems have been solved, policymakers take chances undreamed of a decade earlier. Thus management of the economy becomes sloppy even as the high valuations of stocks leave no room for nasty surprises. During the 1920s Republican administrations, behaving as though businessmen could do no wrong, failed to take prompt steps to curb stock market speculation. Similarly in the mid-1960s economists convinced themselves that through the wonders of econometrics they could use fiscal and monetary policy to fine-tune the economy and virtually abolish the business cycle. In May 1966 *Wall Street Journal* columnist George Shea pointed out: "A special feature of most business forecasts these days is that they project continuous growth as far ahead as they dare to look. Quite often the authors cautiously say they believe that business-cycle downs as well as ups are still possible, but their estimates for the future, quarter-year by quarter-year, show nothing but rising figures. Of course this is not surprising after a little more than five years of practically uninterrupted boom. . . . Anyone who during that period attempted to spot a downturn in general business failed miserably, and almost no one dares try that any more." In this complacent environment it was easy for the Johnson administration to launch simultaneously the war on poverty and the war in Vietnam without bothering to raise taxes. High inflation, leading to the stock market collapse of 1973–74, was the inevitable result. Shea's skeptical comments bear scrutiny because they remind us that most long-term forecasts are merely extrapolations of the recent past. Even after conditions have clearly shifted away from the past trend, most investors are slow to believe it. Instead of *predicting* a turning point, therefore, one need only recognize the new reality (for example, high inflation by the early seventies, low inflation by the early 1980s) ahead of the crowd.

Just like its predecessors, the present bull market has climbed a wall of worry. While stock prices were doubling between 1982 and 1986, many investors were fretting fearfully about the serious and apparently unprecedented problems that besieged the U.S. economy: the huge federal budget deficit, the overvalued dollar, the enormous trade deficit, the debt problem of the less developed countries, the buildup of consumer debt, etc., etc. But as in the past, this sense of alarm was itself a bullish signal, for only when politicians are truly frightened by a problem will they take steps to solve it. A splendid example is the federal deficit; consternation on the Potomac finally led to constructive action, which should make the 1980s a lurch decade in the annals of stock market history, in the wake of the lag decade of the 1970s. This is a very favorable environment in which to use the insights on financing growth industries that are discussed in this book by making long-term investments in a few great growth companies. It will not be easy. Holding on to the great companies is the hard part. There will be times when the strategy does not seem to work, when it seems simpler and more profitable just to "play the market" by buying what everyone else is buying. But only a disciplined long-term approach, similar to that which you would use to buy a house to live in, will give you the results you are looking for. It is a satisfying avocation, as well as a remunerative one, because you will be helping the U.S. economy to stay on top by financing the Ford Motors, Genentechs, IBMs, and Digital Equipments of the twenty-first century.

Bibliography

CHAPTER II. SMART MONEY: THE ROLE OF THE
VENTURE CAPITALIST

This chapter is based on our own experience in the financial community, conversations with other venture capitalists, government publica-
tions, a few books, and many articles. While the names and some
details have been changed, the story of FastComp is based on the
experiences of a real company. Particularly important are the following:
Gene Bylinsky, *The Innovation Millionares: How They Succeed* (New
York: 1967); Everett M. Rogers and Judith K. Larsen, *Silicon Valley
Fever: Growth of High-Technology Culture* (New York: 1982); Dirk
Hanson, *The New Alchemists: Silicon Valley and the Microelectronics
Revolution* (Boston: 1982). Valuable articles include: John Thackray,
"Venture Capital's Great Identity Crisis," *Institutional Investor* (July
1974); John Merwin, "Have You Got What It Takes?" *Forbes* (August
3, 1981); John W. Dizard, "Do We Have Too Many Venture Capital-
ists?" *Fortune* (October 4, 1982); "America Rushes to High Tech for
Growth," *Business Week (March 28, 1983).* "The New Entre-
preneurs," *Business Week* (April 18, 1983); Robert Reinhold, "Silicon
Valley, in Its Maturity, Fights Crowding and Rivals," *New York Times*
(April 21, 1984.)

CHAPTER III. FROM SMART MONEY TO DUMB:
HOW BULL MARKETS SEDUCE VENTURE CAPITALISTS

Irwin Ross, "What's New About This Boom," *Fortune* (May 30,
1983); "Product Development: The New Entrepreneurs," *Business*

Week (April 18, 1983); John Brooks, *The Go-Go Years* (New York: 1973); "The Breakdown of U.S. Innovation," *Business Week* (February 16, 1976); Susie Gharib Nazem, "The Folks Who Brought You Apple," *Fortune* (January 12, 1981); Gary Slutsker, "Venture Capital's Heavy Hitters," *Venture* (July 1981); Bro Uttal, "Gene Amdahl Takes Aim at I.B.M.," *Fortune* (September 1977); the regular *Forbes* column written by Thomas P. Murphy between 1981 and 1984; Martin T. Sosnoff, "Apple Fever," *Forbes* (January 3, 1981); Diane Harris, "New Issues Stampede," *Financial World* (April 30, 1983); Hilary Rosenberg, "The Anatomy of a Hot Stock," *Financial World* (May 31, 1983); Richard Phalon, "A Cautionary Tale," *Forbes* (June 22, 1981); Jon Levine, "The Rising Tide of Venture Capital Failures," *Venture* (April 1983); Kevin Farrell, "Going Public, 1982," *Venture* (April 1982); Myron Magnet, "Diasonics' Winning Ways to Look Inside You," *Fortune* (May 16, 1983); Marilyn Chase, "Venture Capitalists Rush in to Back Emerging High-Technology Firms," *Wall Street Journal* (March 18, 1981); David Lindorff, "New Issues Boom," *Venture* (December 1980); Kevin Farrell, "100 Who Made Millions in 1981," *Venture* (April 1982); Gary Slutsker, "It's Go-Go Time Again for Computer Startups," *Venture* (March 1981); Patricia A. Bellew, "As Computer Firms Take Their Plunges, Ross Dove Flies High," *Wall Street Journal* (December 17, 1984); "Cashing in Big," *Time* (January 23, 1984); Lawren J. Tell, "Bleeding Edge of Technology," *Barron's* (April 23, 1984). On venture capital's crisis of the mid-1970s, see Bro Uttal, "Gene Amdahl Takes Aim at I.B.M.," *Fortune* (September 1977); "The Breakdown of U.S. Innovation," *Business Week* (February 16, 1976); William M. Bulkeley and Lindley B. Richert, "Venture Capital Is Plentiful Once More, Partly Due to Change in Capital-Gains Tax," *Wall Street Journal* (June 15, 1979). Assorted articles in the magazine *Venture Capital*, edited by Stanley Pratt, are also valuable. Federal government reports of value are: "Role of the Venture Capital Industry in the American Economy," *Hearings Before the Subcommittee on International Trade and Finance of the Joint Economic Committee of the U.S. Congress* (September 30, 1982); "Government-Industry Cooperation Can Enhance the Venture Capital Process," U.S. General Accounting Office Report to Senator Lloyd Bentsen, Joint Economic Committee (August 12, 1982); "Role of Technology in Promoting Industrial Competitiveness," *Hearings Before the Committee on Science, Technology and Space of U.S. Senate* (June 21 and 23, 1983).

CHAPTER IV. THE RAILROADS: WALL STREET'S MISTRESS

The literature on the history of the railroads is vast, but much of it consists of long narratives that ensnare the reader in a dense web of mergers, reorganizations, routes, and bear raids. A good place to begin is with contemporary discussions of the "railroad problem," notably William Z. Ripley, *Railroads: Finance and Organization* (New York: 1915) and Frederick A. Cleveland and Fred Wilbur Powell, *Railroad Finance* (New York: 1912). Also valuable is Alfred D. Chandler, Jr., *Henry Varnum Poor: Business Editor, Analyst, and Reformer* (Cambridge, Mass.: 1956), which describes the rise of an organized market for railroad securities in the 1850s. Albert Fishlow, *American Railroads and the Transformation of the Ante-bellum Economy* (Cambridge, Mass.: 1965) is a useful economic analysis but makes an unconvincing case that the midwestern railroads were good investments. Three fine general studies are Thomas C. Cochran, *Railroad Leaders, 1845–1890: The Business Mind in Action* (New York: 1965); George Rogers Taylor's classic work *The Transportation Revolution, 1815–1860* (New York: 1951), and Carter Goodrich, *Government Promotion of American Canals and Railroads, 1800–1890* (New York: 1960). Three good studies of nineteenth-century railroad financiers are Dolores Greenberg, *Financiers and Railroads, 1869–1889: A Study of Morton, Bliss & Company* (Newark, Del.: 1980); Henrietta M. Larson, *Jay Cooke, Private Banker* (Cambridge, Mass.: 1936); and Vincent P. Carosso, *More Than a Century of Investment Banking: The Kidder, Peabody & Co. Story* (New York: 1979). On Massachusetts railroad activity, see Stephen Salsbury, *The State, the Investor, and the Railroad: The Boston & Albany, 1825–1867* (Cambridge, Mass.: 1967); Arthur M. Johnson and Barry E. Supple, *Boston Capitalists and Western Railroads: A Study in the Nineteenth-Century Railroad Investment Process* (Cambridge, Mass.: 1867); Henry Greenleaf Pearson, *An American Railroad Builder: John Murray Forbes* (Boston: 1911); and Edward Chase Kirkland, *Charles Francis Adams, Jr., 1835–1915: The Patrician at Bay* (Cambridge, Mass.: 1965). On New York railroad financiers, see Wheaton J. Lane, *Commodore Vanderbilt: An Epic of the Steam Age* (New York: 1942), Julius Grodinsky, *Jay Gould: His Business Career, 1867–1872* (Philadelphia: 1957); Irene D. Neu, *Erastus Corning: Merchant and Financier, 1794–1872* (Ithaca, N.Y.: 1960); and Henry Clews, *Fifty Years in Wall Street* (New York: 1908). On British investment in American railroads, see Muriel Emmie Hidy, *George Peabody:*

Merchant and Financier, 1829–1845 ([Ph.D. dissertation, Radcliffe College, 1939] New York: 1978); and Dorothy R. Adler, *British Investment in American Railways, 1834–1898* (Charlottesville, Va.: 1970). Studies of particular roads and groups of roads are legion. See especially Oscar Lewis, *The Big Four: The Story of Huntington, Stanford, Hopkins, and Crocker, and of the Building of the Central Pacific* (New York: 1946); Paul Wallace Gates, *The Illinois Central Railroad and Its Colonization Work* (Cambridge, Mass.: 1934); Robert William Fogel, *The Union Pacific Railroad: A Case in Premature Enterprise* (Baltimore: 1960); James McCabe, *Moguls and Iron Men: The Story of the First Transcontinental Railroad* (New York: 1964). Also valuable is the trade press, particularly the *American Railroad Journal,* which was edited by Henry Varnum Poor during the 1850s.

CHAPTER V. ANDREW CARNEGIE'S PRIVATE WAR

This chapter relied heavily on Charles B. Dew, *Ironmaker to the Confederacy: Joseph R. Anderson and the Tredegar Iron Works* (New Haven: 1966); Allan Nevins, *Abram S. Hewitt, with Some Account of Peter Cooper* (New York: 1935); Robert Hessen, *Steel Titan: The Life of Charles Schwab* (New York: 1975); and particularly Harold C. Livesey's short but splendid *Andrew Carnegie and the Rise of Big Business* (Boston: 1975). See also Joseph Frazier Wall's *Andrew Carnegie* (New York: 1970) and Carnegie's own *Autobiography,* which vividly conveys the spirit of the man even if the author's memory was highly selective. Two popular histories of value are James Howard Bridge, *The Inside History of the Carnegie Steel Company, A Romance of Millions* (New York: 1903) and Herbert N. Casson, *The Romance of Steel: The Story of a Thousand Millionaires* (New York: 1907). On the development of the steel industry, see Peter Temin, *Iron and Steel in Nineteenth-Century America: An Economic Inquiry* (Cambridge, Mass.: 1964); William T. Hogan, S.J., *Economic History of the Iron and Steel Industry in the United States* (Lexington, Mass.: 1971), Gertrude G. Schroeder, *The Growth of Major Steel Companies, 1900–1950,* Johns Hopkins University Studies in Historical and Political Science (Baltimore: 1953); and Donald F. Barnett and Louis Schorsch, *Steel: Upheaval in a Basic Industry* (Cambridge, Mass.: 1983). Ida M. Tarbell, *The Life of Elbert H. Gary: A Story of Steel* (1925; New York: 1969) reveals the Progressives' view of the steel trust under Gary. Two fine works on labor history are John A. Fitch, *The Steel Workers* (New York: 1911) and David Brody, *Steel Workers in America: The Nonunion Era* (New York: 1970). Nineteenth-century issues of *Iron Age,* the industry's major trade journal, are worthwhile and available on microfilm.

CHAPTER VI. MONOPOLY AND MEDIOCRITY ON BEACON HILL

John Brooks, *Telephone: The First Hundred Years* (New York: 1975) is the best general introduction to the early history of AT&T; Horace Coon, *American Tel & Tel: The Story of a Great Monopoly* (New York: 1939) is also worthwhile. Albert Bigelow Paine, *In One Man's Life, Being Chapters from the Personal & Business Career of Theodore N. Vail* (New York: 1921) is an old but excellent book that can be profitably supplemented by Chapter VI of Robert Sobel, *The Entrepreneurs: Explorations Within the American Business Tradition* (New York: 1974). Robert V. Bruce, *Bell: Alexander Graham Bell and the Conquest of Solitude* (Boston: 1973) is the standard biography but too long by half. Arthur S. Pier, *Forbes: Telephone Pioneer* (New York: 1953) is of limited value, and J. Warren Stehman, *The Financial History of the American Telephone and Telegraph Company* (Boston: 1925) is also disappointing. For financial data on the company, the place to go is Federal Communications Commission, *Investigation of the Telephone Industry in the United States* (Washington, D.C.: 1939). Rosario Joseph Tosiello, "The Birth and Early Years of the Bell Telephone System, 1876–1880" (Ph.D. dissertation, Boston University, 1971) is a valuable work that provides much information available nowhere else, while N. R. Danielian, *A.T.&T.: The Story of Industrial Conquest* (New York: 1939) is an amusing and sometimes useful piece of New Deal muckraking. The staff of the archives of A.T.&T. was unfailingly helpful, and the records themselves are of considerable interest, as are the T. Jefferson Coolidge Papers in the manuscript room of the Baker Library, Harvard Business School.

CHAPTER VII. THE MECHANIC AND THE GAMBLER

The literature on the auto industry is large and excellent. The best overview, which vividly describes the profitability of the industry, is E.

D. Kennedy, *The Automobile Industry: The Coming of Age of Capitalism's Favorite Child* (New York: 1941), Lawrence H. Seltzer, *A Financial History of the American Automobile Industry* (Boston: 1928) is also valuable. John B. Rae, *American Automobile Manufacturers: The First Forty Years* (Philadelphia: 1959) describes early entrepreneurship in the industry from a technical viewpoint. Two books by James J. Flink —*America Adopts the Automobile, 1895–1910* (Cambridge, Mass.: 1970) and *The Car Culture* (Cambridge, Mass.: 1975)—cover the automobile's social history. Alfred D. Chandler, Jr., *Giant Enterprise: Ford, General Motors, and the Automobile Industry* (New York: 1964) is a very useful collection of well-selected documents. The standard biography of Henry Ford, which depicts the early development of the industry, is Allan Nevins and Frank Ernest Hill, *Ford: The Times, the Man, the Company*, 3 vols. (New York: 1954–62), but the authors' somewhat uncritical interpretation of Ford should be balanced by Chapter 7 of Jonathan R. T. Hughes, *The Vital Few: American Economic Progress and Its Protagonists* (Boston: 1966) and Anne Jardim, *The First Henry Ford: A Study in Personality and Business Leadership* (Cambridge, Mass.: 1970). One of the most valuable works on General Motors is Alfred P. Sloan, Jr., *My Years with General Motors* (Garden City, N.Y.: 1963). Alfred D. Chandler, Jr., and Stephen Salsbury, *Pierre S. Du Pont and the Making of the Modern Corporation* (New York: 1971) covers the Du Pont connection in detail. Bernard A. Weisberger, *The Dream Maker: William C. Durant, Founder of General Motors* (Boston: 1979) is the standard biography, but Lawrence R. Gustin, *Billy Durant, Creator of General Motors* (Grand Rapids, Mich.: 1973) better conveys the spirit of the man and the times. Among the many trade publications on the auto industry *Horseless Age* captures the world of the early, wealthy automobilists but is disappointing on business matters, for which see *Motor* and *Automotive Industries: The Automobile*.

CHAPTER VIII. DAVID AND GOLIATH IN SILICON VALLEY

The single most useful book on the computer industry is Katharine Davis Fishman, *The Computer Establishment* (New York: 1981). Also invaluable are Robert Sobel, *I.B.M.: Colossus in Transition* (New York: 1981) and, on the origins of the computer industry, Herman H. Goldstine, *The Computer from Pascal to Von Neumann* (Princeton: 1972).

See also Richard B. Cole, "Brain Trouble: Electronic Computers Can Create Problems as Well as Solve Them," *Wall Street Journal* (November 11, 1955). Our discussion of the rise and fall of Eckert-Mauchly is based on the original records of the firm, now housed at the Eleutherian Mills Historical Library, Greenville, Delaware. On IBM's conversion to electronics, see, in addition to Sobel and Fishman, the transcript of a highly informative interview with James L. Birkenstock (August 12, 1980, Babbage Institute), University of Minnesota, as well as two fine articles by T. A. Wise, "I.B.M.'s $5,000,000,000 Gamble," *Fortune* (September 1966) and "The Rocky Road to the Marketplace," *Fortune* (October 1966). Also useful is "Can IBM Keep Up the Pace?," *Business Week* (February 2, 1963). Bro Uttal, "I.B.M.'s Battle to Look Superhuman Again," *Fortune* (May 19, 1980). On Control Data, see "Small, Smart, Sharp," *Business Week* (May 25, 1963); T. A. Wise, "Control Data's Magnificent Fumble," *Fortune* (April 1966); Gregory H. Wierzynski, "Control Data's Newest Cliffhanger," *Fortune* (February 1968); "Control Data: Big Success, Big Gamble" *Forbes* (June 1, 1964). "When a Whiz Kid Grows Up," *Business Week* (July 30, 1966). On the early use of computers by corporations, see the articles in *Business Week* (April 19, 1952; November 1, 1952; Sept. 15, 1956; June 21, 1958), and the *Wall Street Journal* of November 11, 1955. On the later development of the industry, see Gilbert Burck, "The Computer Industry's Great Expectations," *Fortune* (August 1968); "The $5-Billion World Market for Computers," *Business Week* (February 19, 1966); Fred J. Borch, "A New Team Rewires GE for the Future," *Business Week* (March 30, 1968); "Hot Race for Far-Off Profits," *Business Week* (March 31, 1962); Howard Banks, "General Electric—Going with the Winners," *Forbes* (March 26, 1984). On the misadventures of RCA in computers, see Chapter VIII of Fishman, *The Computer Establishment* and Allan T. Demaree, "RCA After the Bath," *Fortune* (September 1972). On Digital Equipment, see a booklet by Kenneth H. Olsen, *Digital Equipment Corporation: The First Twenty-five Years* (New York: 1983). On Scientific Data Systems, see "Only No. 7, So It Tries Harder," *Business Week* (March 20, 1965). The entire chapter benefited from the work of PaineWebber's security analysts covering the technology sector, particularly Jonathan Fram and Stephen K. Smith.

CHAPTER IX. THE INDUSTRY WITHOUT A PROFIT

In addition to interviews with a number of entrepreneurs, venture capitalists, and scientists active in biotechnology, we benefited greatly from the research reports written by PaineWebber analysts David H. McCallum, Nina M. Siegler, and Linda I. Miller. The views of a diverse group of Wall Street analysts are detailed in the roundtable discussions of biotechnology appearing in *The Wall Street Transcript*. Also useful are packets of information assembled by various companies to enlighten securities analysts and investors. There are not many books on biotechnology; two worth reading are Edward J. Sylvester and Lynn C. Klotz, *The Gene Age: Genetic Engineering and the Next Industrial Revolution* (New York: 1983) and Office of Technology Assessment, *Commercial Biotechnology: An International Analysis* (Washington, D.C.: Government Printing Office, OTA-BA-218, January 1984). Albert Toney and Thomas Tilling, *High Tech: How to Find and Profit from Today's New Super Stocks* (New York: 1983) contains useful insights. Valuable articles include "Academic Research and Big Business: A Delicate Balance," *New York Times Magazine* (September 11, 1983); Jim Mintz, "Biotechnology: The Biological Revolution Will Change How We Think About Life Itself," *Venture* (February 1984); Bob Tamarkin, "The Growth Industry," *Forbes* (March 2, 1981); Vivian Lee et al., "New Trends in Financing Biotechnology," *Biotechnology* (September 1983); Jerry E. Bishop, "New Technique to Produce Proteins May Alter Biotechnology Industry," *Wall Street Journal* (November 10, 1983); Jerry E. Bishop and Michael Waldholz, "New Genetically Engineered Vaccines Aim at Blocking Infectious Diseases in Millions," *Wall Street Journal* (October 25, 1983); "Biotechnology's New Strain of R&D Cash," *Business Week* (April 18, 1983); Vartanig G. Vartan, "A Way to Play Biotechnology," *New York Times* (May 6, 1983); Arthur Klausner and Tazewell Wilson, "Gene Detection Technology Opens Doors for Many Industries," *Biotechnology* (August 1983); Anise C. Wallace, "Magic Financing via R&D Partnerships," *High Technology* (July 1983); Arthur Klausner, "Activating the Body's Blood Clot Dissolvers: Biotech's New Role," *Biotechnology* (June 1983); Richard L. Hudson, "Denmark's Novo Hits Trouble in Fast-Moving Biotechnology Industry, but Vows to Recoup," *Wall Street Journal* (December 19, 1984); Gene Bylinsky, "DNA Can Build Companies, Too," *Fortune* (June 16, 1980); Tabitha M. Powledge, "Biogen in Transition: From Research Specialist to Manufacturer,"

Biotechnology (July 1983); "Biotech Comes of Age," *Business Week* (January 23, 1984); and Jerry E. Bishop, "Biotech Firms Race to Market a Protein Hemophiliacs Need" *Wall Street Journal* (July 25, 1985). Michael Waldholz, "Ballyhoo Has Faded, but Interferon Still Has Boosters at High Levels," *Wall Street Journal* (September 30, 1983); Marilyn Chase, "Newest Cancer Drug Gets Favorable Results in Early Tests in Japan," *Wall Street Journal* (June 19, 1985); Katharine Bouton, "Academic Research and Big Business: A Delicate Balance," *New York Times Magazine* (September 11, 1983). Fast-breaking information is available in such newsletters as *Biotechnology News, Genetic Technology News, McGraw-Hill Biotechnology News-watch;* and *Genetic Engineering Letter.*

CHAPTER X. LESSONS OF HISTORY FOR WALL STREET, MAIN STREET, AND PENNSYLVANIA AVENUE

Much of the research for this chapter was done in connection with PaineWebber research reports on investment strategy, and we benefited greatly from discussions with other analysts in the firm. Books related to industrial policy include Robert B. Reich, *The Next American Frontier* (New York: 1983), which is disappointing; Michael L. Wachter and Susan M. Wachter, eds., *Toward a New U.S. Industrial Policy?* (Philadelphia: 1981); Lester C. Thurow, *The Zero-Sum Society* (New York: 1980) and *The Zero-Sum Solution* (New York: 1985); Peter F. Drucker, *Innovation and Entrepreneurship, Practice and Principles,* (New York: 1985); J. Peter Grace, *Burning Money: The Waste of Your Tax Dollars* (New York: 1984); Felix G. Rohatyn, *The Twenty-Year Century: Essays on Economics and Public Finance* (New York: 1983); Robert Z. Lawrence, *Can America Compete?* (Washington, D.C.: 1984); Christopher Freeman, *The Economics of Industrial Innovation* (Cambridge, Mass.: 1982); and Bruce R. Scott and George C. Lodge, eds., *U.S. Competitiveness in the World Economy* (Boston: 1985). See also "Promoting Economic Growth and Competitiveness," unpublished report of the Industrial Policy Study Group, January 1984. Worthwhile articles include Peter F. Drucker, "Why America's Got So Many Jobs," *Wall Street Journal* (January 24, 1984); and James Cook, "The Molting of America," *Forbes* (November 22, 1982), which is excellent. Our discussion of the great restructuring is based on a PaineWebber research report, "Back to the Future: America's Second

Great Restructuring," February 18, 1986, produced by the entire Equity Research Department. On this subject see also Kenneth M. Davidson, *Mega-Mergers: Corporate America's Billion-Dollar Takeovers* (Cambridge, Mass.: 1985) and "Impact of Corporate Takeovers," *Hearings before the Subcommittee On Securities of the Committee on Banking, Housing, and Urban Affairs, U.S. Senate* (April 3, 4, and June 6, 12, 1985). Very useful on the conglomerate movement of the 1960s is *The Conglomerate Commotion* (New York: 1970), a collection of *Fortune* magazine articles.

On Japan, see William H. Davidson, *The Amazing Race: Winning the Technorivalry with Japan* (New York: 1984); Chalmers Johnson, *MITI and the Japanese Miracle: The Growth of Industrial Policy, 1925–1975* (Stanford, Calif.: 1982); G. C. Allen, *Japan's Economic Expansion* (London: 1964); Robert Guillain, *The Japanese Challenge* (Philadelphia: 1970). See also Edward Boyer, "How Japan Manages Declining Industries," *Fortune* (January 10, 1983); and "Chip Wars: the Japanese Threat," *Business Week* (May 23, 1983).

On Europe, see particularly Richard L. Hudson, "West European Firms Seek Role in 'Star Wars,' Mindful of Widening Technology Gap with U.S.," *Wall Street Journal* (May 23, 1985); George Anders, "European Executives Consider U.S. Prime Area for Expansion Abroad, Journal Poll Shows," *Wall Street Journal* (December 5, 1984); articles by John Huey, Beth Kerlin, and George Anders on the theme "Executives Assess Europe's Technology Decline," *Wall Street Journal* (February 1, 1984); Beth Kerlin and George Anders, "Europe Looks Abroad for High Technology It Lags in Developing," *Wall Street Journal* (October 5, 1983); Diane L. Coutu, "European Nations Fret over Mounting Losses of Scientists to the U.S.," *Wall Street Journal* (October 21, 1983); Maile Hulihan, "French Venture-Capital Industry Lags Despite New Policies by the Government," *Wall Street Journal* (November 30, 1983); Isabel Bass, "Venture Capital Goes Continental," *Institutional Investor* (July 1983); Roger Thurow, "New Vigor Is Infusing Small-Business Sector of German Economy," *Wall Street Journal* (August 28, 1984); Barry Newman, "In Britain, the Jobless Tend to Stay Jobless as Hirers Shun Them," *Wall Street Journal* (May 30, 1984); Robert Ball, "Europe's Durable Unemployment Woes," *Fortune* (January 11, 1982); Lawrence Minard, "Can Europe Catch Up?," *Forbes* (July 4, 1983).

On energy policy, see Andy Pazstor, "Without Big Changes, Synfuels Corp. Seems Likely to Perish," *Wall Street Journal* (August 9,

1984); Doug Bandow, "Sinfuels, No Win Fuels," *New York Times* (September 1, 1983); George Paly, "Recall the Attempts at a Mini-Industrial Policy," *Wall Street Journal* (March 16, 1984); John S. Herrington, "The Synfuels Energy Dinosaur," *Wall Street Journal* (August 15, 1984). On agriculture, see Doug Bandow, "Subsidizing Rural America," *Wall Street Journal* (May 9, 1984).

CHAPTER XI. THE INDIVIDUAL INVESTOR AND THE
GREAT GROWTH INDUSTRIES

This chapter partly relies on work originally done in connection with PaineWebber research reports, notably an August 21, 1985, piece entitled "A New 'Nifty Fifty'—Here We Grow Again: PaineWebber's Industry Growth Projections, 1985–1990," to which the entire Equity Research Department contributed, and "Climbing the Wall of Worry," November 1, 1985, by Thomas M. Doerflinger and Edward M. Kerchner. Also available is Robert Sobel, *Inside Wall Street* (New York: 1959). A few classics on the subject of personal investing that are well worth reading are John Train, *The Money Masters* (New York: 1980); David Dreman, *The New Contrarian Investment Strategy* (New York: 1983); Benjamin Graham, *The Intelligent Investor*, 4th ed., (New York: 1973); and George Clairmont and Kiril Sokoloff, *Street Smart Investing* (New York: 1983). James Grant, *Bernard M. Baruch: The Adventures of a Wall Street Legend* (New York: 1983) is also worthwhile. The best investment newsletter for value growth investors is Charles Allmon's *Growth Stock Outlook*.

Index

Thomas M. Doerflinger is a securities analyst in the Research Department of PaineWebber Incorporated, where he specializes in investment strategy. The holder of a B.A. from Princeton and a Ph.D. from Harvard, he is the author of seven scholarly articles and *A Vigorous Spirit of Enterprise: Merchants and Economic Development in Revolutionary Philadelphia.* Mr. Doerflinger has also served as a fellow and visiting editor of publications at the Institute of Early American History and Culture in Williamsburg, Virginia.

Jack L. Rivkin is a former president of the venture capital division of PaineWebber Capital, Inc. He has previously held positions as a securities analyst, director of research, and president of PaineWebber's institutional brokerage and asset management business, as well as chief financial officer and chairman of the executive group of PaineWebber, Inc. In 1987, Rivkin joined Shearson Lehman Brothers as executive vice-president and director of research. Mr. Rivkin received his B.S. from the Colorado School of Mines and his M.B.A. from Harvard.